SOLOMON'S SECRET ARTS

SOLOMON'S SECRET ARTS

The OCCULT IN THE AGE *of* ENLIGHTENMENT

Paul Kléber Monod

YALE UNIVERSITY PRESS
NEW HAVEN AND LONDON

For information about this and other Yale University Press publications, please contact:
U.S. Office: sales.press@yale.edu   www.yalebooks.com
Europe Office: sales@yaleup.co.uk   www.yalebooks.co.uk

Set in Minion Pro by IDSUK (DataConnection) Ltd
Printed in Great Britain by TJ International Ltd, Padstow, Cornwall

Library of Congress Cataloging-in-Publication Data
Monod, Paul Kléber.
Solomon's Secret Arts: The Occult in the Age of Enlightenment/Paul Kleber Monod.
pages cm
ISBN 978-0-300-12358-6 (hardback)
1. Magic. 2. Science—History—Miscellanea. 3. Alchemy. 4. Occult sciences.
5. Enlightenment. I. Title.
BF1611.M65 2013
130.9—dc23

2012043028

A catalogue record for this book is available from the British Library.

10 9 8 7 6 5 4 3 2 1

To Jan and Evan, as always.

Contents

Illustrations

Acknowledgments

This book has taken longer to realize than any alchemical recipe known to me. The journey, however, has been fascinating. It has included a visiting fellowship at Harris Manchester College, Oxford University, in 2001–2, as well as research fellowships at the Getty Research Institute in 2004 and the Huntington Library in 2008. During a leave year in 2007–8, research on this project was supported by a fellowship from the National Endowment for the Humanities. The most consistent support came from Middlebury College, largely through the A. Barton Hepburn Professorship. Parts of this book have been presented in seminar talks at the University of California at Los Angeles, the Newbury Library, Warwick University, the University of Glasgow and McGill University, as well as conference talks at the Università del Salento in Lecce, the British Institute, the University of Strathclyde, the Eberhard Karls Universität Tübingen and the Karl Franzens Universität Graz. The organizers of those seminars and conferences deserve gratitude for inviting me to speak on often half-baked ideas.

I must also thank a host of individuals who assisted me along the way with advice, information, suggestions and comments. They include David Armando, Robin Briggs, Bob Bucholz, Louisa Burnham, R.J. Evans, Antoine Faivre, Joscelyn Godwin, Anthony Grafton, Wouter Hanegraaff, Ronald Hutton, Sarah Hutton, Colin Kidd, Jim Larrabee, Diarmaid MacCulloch, Scott Mandelbrote, Alex Marr, Mark Morrisson, Victor Nuovo, Kapil Raj, Peter Reill, Isabel Rivers, Teofilo Ruiz, Bill Sherman, Marsha Keith Schuchard, Susan Sommers, Bob Tittler, John Walsh, David Womersley and David Wykes. The staff at all the institutions listed in the bibliography deserve praise, in particular those at the Getty Research Library, the Clark Library, Dr Williams's Library, the Library of Freemasonry, Swedenborg House and Chetham's Library. I must especially thank the duke of Northumberland for permission to use the archive at

Alnwick Castle, and the estate office at Alnwick for assisting me in working there.

My greatest debt, as always, is to my wife, Jan Albers, who has lived cheerfully with this rather offbeat project for the past eleven years. Our son, Evan, wonders why I am not able to perform conjuring tricks, because he does not realize that he is the best magic his mother and I could produce. My own mother has provided constant reminders of how receptive West Country Methodists were to the supernatural, while my late father bequeathed to me a French-Swiss scepticism that occasionally surfaces in this book. In carrying out research, I have depended on the unflagging hospitality of Colin and Lucy Kidd at Glasgow, my ever-welcoming cousin Margaret Monod and her wonderful partner, Joyce Chester, in Sussex and my dear uncle Dennis Donovan, who kept me up to date with happenings in his village of West Lydford, Somerset, where John Cannon lived.

This book is not a gateway to occult knowledge, but it should help to explain why that knowledge has been of such vital interest to past generations of Britons. What distinguishes the British version of the occult is its openness to both learned and popular ideas, making its history intellectually messy yet constantly surprising. If this book brings some surprises, a few insights and some pleasure, then perhaps its flaws, which are entirely my own responsibility, may be forgiven. As for the Philosopher's Stone, readers, seek that out for yourselves.

Weybridge, Vermont, June 2012

Introduction

What Was the Occult?

LIKE POVERTY, death and taxes, the occult seems always to have been with us. From the mysterious cave painters of Lascaux to today's online astrologers and televised psychic readers, human beings throughout history have sought ways of tapping into hidden powers, to gain knowledge and influence through what is now commonly referred to as "the unexplained." Contemporary British culture is hardly immune to a fascination with the occult—witness the immense popular success of the Harry Potter novels, replete with witches, wizards and alchemists, or the stupendous magical confrontations of the *Lord of the Rings* film trilogy, or any number of "sword and sorcery" computer games. More serious manifestations of occult belief, from Spiritualism to Wicca to Druids to the Hermetic Order of the Golden Dawn, have proliferated in Britain over the past century. Although the United States (where the Golden Dawn has been incorporated since 1988) is now the intellectual hub and chief recruiting ground for occult organizations, a large number of them have British origins or maintain affiliates in the United Kingdom. "Occultism" is often associated with the New Age religious philosophies of California, but many of its roots are thoroughly British.[1]

The lines that connect occult ways of thinking, however, are intricate, ramified and frequently imaginary. Most modern devotees of occult organizations lay claim to some body of ancient wisdom on which their beliefs are purportedly based. For them, the appeal of such wisdom is direct and unmediated by time—it speaks to them just as clearly as it did to the ancients. Adherents of such beliefs are rarely open to the suggestion that they may have changed, that they have to be understood in a historical context, or that they might actually have been invented at some point, for some now-forgotten purpose. The believer is more likely to regard with wonder what he or she sees as the vast chronological and cultural scope of the occult. Scholars have sometimes adopted the same perspective. This has encouraged a few of them—notably, the psychologist Carl Jung—to conclude that the occult is a universal category, better explored through the structures of human personality than through any time-bound discipline like history.[2] The occult, for Jung and his followers, represented a fundamental state of mind, a yearning or need to express the "collective unconscious" of the psyche, which surpassed temporal boundaries and approached the eternal. To his critics, Jung's approach represents an abdication of intellectual inquiry, constituting not an explanation but an obfuscation, yet another form of "occultism."

However we judge Jung, his theories confront us with a serious question that any scholar who is not a devotee must ask: how universal or unchanging is the phenomenon known as the occult? A sceptical observer who follows astrological predictions or peruses the web pages of various occult organizations will soon wonder how much they have to do with "ancient wisdom" of any identifiable variety. The further one travels from cosmically vague concepts, and the more one hones in on specific examples of occult thinking, the greater the role of cultural and historical factors appears to be. Under this scrutiny, the agelessness of the occult turns out to be an illusion—or, in many cases, a mystification, because its adherents have made such efforts to disguise its recent origins. It seems doubtful that much in the commercialized occultism of today can be traced back beyond the late nineteenth century. Examined closely, the promotional activities of contemporary psychics and astrologers do not bear much resemblance to the ritual practices of Egyptian or Babylonian priests.[3] Even the foundations of serious occult thinking owe more to modern anxieties, and to modern marketing techniques, than to the builders of pyramids or ziggurats. To borrow the terminology of Eric Hobsbawm, the occult as we know it today seems largely to be an "invented tradition."[4] Its direct evocation of the past, its venerable heritage and alleged roots in "the wisdom of the ages," have as often as not been misappropriated, distorted, embellished or even fabricated, whether out of enthusiasm, ignorance or just plain chicanery.

This is not to say that the modern occult tradition is deliberately spurious, that it was wholly manufactured at some particular point in time, or that it was created (magically, perhaps?) out of nothing. Even traditions that are constantly reinvented may be honest in sticking to their established goals. They may also have legitimate antecedents, whose influence is hard to trace. As will be suggested here, there is indeed a lineage of occult thinking that goes back to the early centuries of Christianity. While it may have been reinterpreted several times since 1400, and substantially rewritten since 1875, it provides a series of points of reference that are more or less fixed. The occult tradition might be regarded as an old ritual garment, worked and reworked at regular intervals, with new patterns and colours added, until almost nothing original is left in it, apart from the overall shape and a few stray threads. With every repair, the garment has taken on an altered appearance, suited to the demands of contemporary society, although it has been presented to the public as if it were the miraculous product of an eternal and unchanging heritage. In this respect, of course, the occult is not very different from most organized religious traditions—except that it has not usually been very organized, and its beliefs, however broad their philosophical reach, have not always possessed the theological or ethical dimensions of a religion.

It might be objected at this point that we have begun to discuss the historical features of a phenomenon that remains undefined, and may not be coherent at all. What exactly are we looking for in tracing the history of "the occult" in a pre-modern age? How can we hope to put to use such a vague and mutable concept, so deeply imbued with modern implications, in making sense of the ideas of Britons who lived before television and the Internet—even before general literacy and mass communication? We might begin by asking how the term was used at different times in the English language. In Samuel Johnson's 1755 *Dictionary*, "occult" is not listed as a noun; instead, it appears as an adjective meaning "secret; hidden; unknown; undiscoverable."[5] Before the late eighteenth century, the idea of "*the* occult" would not have made much sense to speakers of English. In dealing with earlier periods, we are imposing a modern expression on a diverse body of material that was identified by contemporaries in various ways: as occult philosophy, occult science or the occult arts. Evidently, we have to separate the early-modern occult from contemporary, organized "occultism," which is largely a product of the period since 1875—although we also have to explain how the former began to point towards the latter. At the same time, our use of "the occult" has to be distinguished from the assumption that there is a real Philosopher's Stone, the substance that turns base metals into gold—in other words, that an occult realm of knowledge *objectively* exists, beyond the personal views and experiences of those who seek it. While this is certainly possible, it cannot be proven historically, one way or the other. For better or worse, the author of this book does not believe in it. For the purposes of our argument, the occult existed purely in the minds and actions of its adherents.

In writings of the late seventeenth and the eighteenth century, most uses of the adjective "occult" were in broad accordance with Samuel Johnson's definition, which is to say that they referred to things that were "hidden." This led to expressions like "occult motion," "occult [political] influences," or, in medical literature, "occult wounds."[6] Hence, when the philosopher Lord Kames, in a work published in 1774, wrote of "occult crimes, hid from every mortal eye," he did not mean to imply that such crimes were committed by spirits.[7] Evidently, what was occult need not have been supernatural. In fact, the term was often used to designate purely natural phenomena that were not immediately intelligible, but might become so through further investigation. As the physician and antiquarian Walter Charleton put it in 1654, "what difference is there, whether we say, that such a thing is Occult; or that we know nothing of it?"[8] He was confident that all natural things, visible and invisible, could be explained through mechanical causes.

Behind Charleton's question lay a simmering intellectual debate. Charleton was objecting to the philosophy of Aristotle, long dominant in western Europe, which posited that natural qualities must be "manifest," or open to the senses, in order to be understood. Occult qualities had no place in traditional Aristotelian science, because they could not be seen, felt, heard, smelled or tasted and were therefore imperceptible. By the late seventeenth century, however, this view was under attack from writers like Charleton, who believed that nature was often affected by insensible or occult forces: magnetic attraction or repulsion, movement at a distance, gravity. Such occult qualities, which were hidden but not supernatural, might be explored through "*magia naturalis*" or natural magic. The latter had famously been described by the Italian scientist Giambattista della Porta as "nothing else but the survey of the whole course of Nature." Della Porta was scrupulous in separating natural magic from the "infamous, and unhappie" kind, that had to do with "foul spirits . . . Inchantments, and wicked Curiosity": that is, with anything supernatural or otherworldly. Natural magic, by contrast, was simply "the dutiful hand-maid" of nature in revealing the secrets of occult things.[9] In short, it was an experimental science devoted to the unveiling of hidden natural properties.

The distinction within occult qualities between natural and supernatural, however, could be slippery. A treatise on miracles published in 1683, for example, explained that "*Moses*'s rod had many great, many occult, yet Natural Qualities, very hard indeed to explain or conceive, and very admirable though not miraculous."[10] The author accepted that true miracles violated natural laws, and were therefore extremely rare. This led him to argue, somewhat tortuously, that while God *could* ignore the laws of nature when he chose to do so, in cases where he opted to observe them, his actions might be called hidden or occult, but were not, strictly speaking, supernatural. A less scrupulous mind, of course, might perceive an instrument like Moses' rod, which summoned up winds and rain, as both occult *and* supernatural. In any case, the debate over where to draw the boundary between nature and the supernatural remained contentious and unresolved. It was nonetheless highly important to orthodox religious writers, who believed that only God—not angels or spirits or even the Devil—could transgress the limits of nature.[11]

The distinction between natural and supernatural was not always strictly held by those who were fascinated by occult sciences and philosophy, including alchemy, astrology and ritual magic. They might place themselves within a tradition of occult thinking that sought to explain nature in terms of spiritual or even supernatural forces over which human beings exercised some control. The element of human intervention in the supernatural was crucial: it distinguished occult enthusiasts from those who accepted the existence of spirits, but believed any traffic with them was unlawful or demonic. In the following argument, the occult will be understood as a type of thinking, expressed either in writing or in action, that allowed the boundary between the natural and the supernatural to be crossed by the actions of human beings.

The historian of science John Henry has written of a "fragmentation" of occult thinking in the seventeenth century, between those who favoured natural explanations and those who sought after supernatural wisdom.[12] The fracture line between the two, however, tends to be less precise or obvious than we might wish it to be. Even the apparently level-headed Della Porta was prone to quote ancient writers who promoted contact with spirits. Many of those who pursued experimental science in the late seventeenth century, including highly respected figures, were tempted towards the supernatural wonders that lay beyond, which from a strictly orthodox perspective were forbidden. In their own view, they were approaching an angelic or spiritual realm of freedom and power, but as far as their critics were concerned, they were wandering blindly into a pandemonium of superstition, heterodoxy and witchcraft: in short, into demonic magic.

Popular Magic

How mixed up was occult thinking with magic, other than the natural variety? In addressing the question, many modern scholars have heeded the shrill warnings of seventeenth-century critics, and have sought to keep the two apart. Cultural historians of early-modern Britain have given a great deal of attention to the question of magical practices, but they have tended to treat the occult as if it were a separate issue, to be left mainly to scholars of science, philosophy and religion.[13] The publication in 1971 of Keith Thomas's magisterial *Religion and the Decline of Magic* provided this segregated approach with a powerful foundation.[14] Thomas was mainly concerned with the *practical* uses of magic, which he interpreted as behavioural responses to the predicament of not having more effective means of dealing with everyday problems. These encompassed all sorts of "superstitious" practices. Thomas did not see magic as a coherent belief system, or as having much to do with contemporary philosophical thought. Its aspirations were not supernatural; rather, they were functional and worldly. Magic rested on customary usage and was chiefly characterized by a more or less irrational belief in the effects of certain actions, perhaps even including prayer. In other words, what made something magic was its *outcome* rather than the way by which it might work. How a philtre caused someone to fall in love was irrelevant to its users, so long as it led to the desired results. Who cared about the specific words inscribed on a charm so long as they did the job of ridding the house of rats?[15] Such practices constituted magic because no fully rational person could accept them as efficacious.

Thomas's interpretation of magic, anchored in modern social science, was extremely helpful in explaining why people resorted to such methods, but it was not especially conducive to the unravelling of magical ways of thinking. Apart from astrology, on which subject he made some brilliant remarks, Thomas was not particularly interested in the more learned aspects of his theme.[16] Instead, he presented an exhaustive and highly perceptive examination of popular magical practices and beliefs. This left him at a disadvantage, however, when he came to the end of his immense work, and to the trickiest aspect of his argument: answering the question of when and why magic declined. His painstaking treatment of witchcraft accusations, which occupied a significant portion of the book, suggested that they mirrored the fate of magic as a whole. Witch prosecutions clearly waned in England after 1660, disappearing entirely after 1717. Thomas implied that the resort to magical solutions of all kinds declined after the mid-seventeenth century, due to greater social stability as well as the emergence of new (and presumably more successful) means of addressing everyday problems, such as fire insurance. Although his conclusions about the decline of magic were extremely cautious, Thomas left the impression that a threshold had been passed by 1700, the point at which magic seemed to have been found wanting in many, if not most, English minds.

Keith Thomas's influence on the study of magic in England has been enormous. Gradually, however, scholars have begun to stray from the imposing pathways set down by *Religion and the Decline of Magic*. Many of them have been students of the history of witchcraft. James Sharpe and others have pointed out that cultural factors, including gender, family relations and local rivalries, played at least as great a role in witch accusations as did the socio-economic explanation favoured by Thomas.[17] Ian Bostridge and Owen Davies have argued for the persistence of witch beliefs, far beyond the formal ending of trials for witchcraft or the repeal of existing witchcraft legislation in 1736.

Davies has also published a remarkable series of works on the survival of popular magic through village cunning-folk or traditional healers as well as through *grimoires* or ritual magic books. It is now evident that, in England as in other parts of Europe, ordinary people did not cast off their adherence to magic, no matter what their social betters might have thought, so that the question of when magic declined has become a much more complicated one.[18] The continuing popular appeal of astrological predictions has been traced down to the eighteenth century and beyond by Bernard Capp and Patrick Curry, while the importance of astrology in human and veterinary medicine down to 1700 has been emphasized by Louise Hill Curth.[19] Alan Macfarlane, whose work on witchcraft preceded and inspired that of Thomas, has suggested recently that the gradual decline of magical beliefs in England may be related less to the impact of urbanization, medicine or science than to the slow growth of "civility," or of human control over private space.[20] While it is unlikely that any of these scholars would claim that they have overturned the basic premise of Thomas's thesis that magic began to lose its appeal to segments of the public at some point in the mid-seventeenth century, they have certainly qualified it.

Scotland was outside the scope of Thomas's research and never quite fit his approach. Witch prosecutions there were more numerous and the results bloodier. Scottish judges, who exercised wider authority than their English counterparts, have been assigned a greater portion of the blame for the witch craze. Because they were learned men, whose attitudes may have been shaped by what they read, the impact of occult thinking on witch trials was from the start given more attention in Scotland than was the case in England. Major witch trials dragged on later in the northern kingdom, with the last outbreak in 1697–1700, but their disappearance has not been seen by historians as representing any sort of turning point in popular attitudes towards magic.[21] The assumption of cultural conservatism or even "backwardness," especially in the Highlands, meant that few scholars were willing to argue in favour of an overall decline in Scottish magical beliefs, similar to that which had supposedly happened in England. As we now know from the researches of Lizanne Henderson and Edward Cowan, rural Scots were convinced of the existence of the fairy folk, or Sithian, throughout the eighteenth century, and their acceptance of witchcraft certainly did not end with the repeal of previous witch legislation in 1736.[22]

The English situation may have been closer to that of Scotland than has usually been thought, with popular confidence in the reality of witches and fairy folk surviving for long periods of time (my own grandmother, born in Somerset in 1889, was a strong believer in fairies). What can no longer be sustained is the hypothesis that magical beliefs had less appeal to ordinary labouring folk in

England after the mid-seventeenth century than in the preceding hundred years. While Thomas may be correct in assuming a decline in belief among educated people, it was not a uniform or straightforward process, and was far from complete even by 1800. How such a limited decline might have affected magical practices is unclear, since these did not require the active participation of educated members of the community and could be sustained in a private setting, leaving few traces in the archives. Arguably, the actual downfall of popular magical beliefs in Britain may not have come until the early twentieth century, through an increasingly universal system of education.

Revisionist assertions such as these are no longer particularly original or controversial, especially in relation to witchcraft. To assume that magic survived into the modern period has become a new orthodoxy, although its broader cultural implications have not been fully considered. As it relates to the eighteenth century, however, the argument for the survival of magic has to be qualified. Something in the magical cultures of England and Scotland did change after 1688, although the transformation was not one whose effects were found at every social level. The occult never again attained the intellectual impact or coherence it had enjoyed in the mid-seventeenth century. The argument that follows in the rest of this book will take an approach that emphasizes change as well as continuity. It is based on the occult writings favoured by the literate rather than on the magical behaviour of ordinary, and mostly illiterate, people. In short, it is a study of texts and how they were used, rather than of inherited customs or beliefs, which are difficult to isolate without using the testimony of educated observers.

How did these texts relate to magical practices? A basic assumption adopted here is that popular magic shared with occult thinking a desire to make use of spiritual or supernatural power. The wise woman or traditional healer, the alchemist, the astrologer and the ritual magus were engaged in similar endeavours, whose significance was as much intellectual as practical: that is, they wanted to exceed the boundaries of nature as they knew it, and to take charge of hidden forces that might be seen as diabolic or angelic, Satanic or divine. The village magician may not have given much thought to the philosophical significance of his philtres and potions, but he was nonetheless traversing the same territory as the learned astrological physician. Whether their methods were active or contemplative, efficacious or inefficacious, makes no real difference; nor does our modern view of them as rational or irrational, learned or half-crazed. What does matter is their relationship to what they perceived as the wonderful, the inexplicable or the supernatural. The herbal remedies of a cunning man may not have been magical at all, unless they claimed some power that went beyond that of nature. Similarly, alchemy was not always infused with the same level of occult thinking, although its practitioners so frequently summoned angelic forces in pursuing their "great work" that it has to be wondered whether they were ever able to make a distinction between natural and supernatural results.[23]

If magic, like the occult, is associated with human use of the supernatural, it might encompass aspects of formal religion, such as miracles, prophecy or even prayer. The practitioners of magic, in Britain as elsewhere, seldom saw any contradiction between their pursuits and religion; indeed, many of them perceived magical activity as a form of religious devotion. Others, however, saw a very deep contradiction. In the minds of the defenders of Christian orthodoxy, magic was always demonic. No truly pious practice, in their opinion, could aspire to any measure of *control* over supernatural forces; a Christian could merely *petition* God to intervene in nature through miracles, which only the deity was able to perform. As William Fleetwood put it in 1701, "no Power less than that of God, can unsettle that establish'd Course of Nature, which no Power less than his could settle and establish."[24] The weighty impact of this view on the history of occult thinking will be measured in later chapters.

Magic has been described by Richard Kieckhefer as "a kind of crossroads . . . a point of intersection" where religion met science, popular culture met learned culture, and fiction met reality.[25] For our purposes, the metaphor is felicitous, because popular magic and occult thinking often travelled through the same points. This does not mean that they were identical, or that one simply depended on the other. Popular magic had its own vitality, its own methods and its own history; it was neither a "debased" form of the occult nor a misreading of learned interpretations of the supernatural. On the other hand, occult philosophers were not simply trying to elevate popular practices by endowing them with the aura of intellectual legitimacy. Few of them had any time or patience for "vulgar" customs; rather, they prided themselves on being the proponents of a distinct type of higher knowledge that dated back to the beginning of time, a *prisca sapientia* that had been known to Adam, Moses and King Solomon. The last of these Biblical figures was regarded as the master of all forms of secret knowledge, which he was thought to have enshrined in the features of his Temple (hence the use of his name in the title of this work). Once we begin to explore such ways of thinking, the history of magic as a set of practices or behaviours no longer explains much about the occult, and we have to find a different means of entrance into a narrow and very crowded sanctuary.

The Esoteric

If popular magic has dominated the field in British historical scholarship, the occult as a theoretical construct has been a pre-eminent concern outside

Britain. A leading figure in this field of investigation has been the French religious scholar Antoine Faivre. In a dazzling variety of works, he has defined the occult as a category within what he has called esoteric religion.[26] According to Faivre and others who adhere to his approach, the occult is neither a response to a lack of effective solutions to worldly problems, nor a set of practices distinguished by a desire to gain control over nature. Rather, it is part of a coherent tradition of knowledge, expressed in a body of writings that flourished for centuries on the fringes of the three major monotheistic religions: Judaism, Christianity and Islam. The basic premise of occult knowledge is that a search for hidden causes in nature may lead towards something higher than nature: absolute wisdom, supernatural power or the divine.

Faivre's esoteric approach might be accused of giving too much unity and direction to writings that are often characterized by highly individualistic, sometimes conflicting and occasionally chaotic points of view. This deprives certain occult writers—William Blake comes immediately to mind—of what may be their most salient feature: their inventiveness or even quirkiness. In addition, students of esoteric religion are open to the criticism that they have regarded the texts they study as comprising a discrete and largely self-referential intellectual tradition, hermetically sealed so as to ward off the taint of other forms of thought, not to mention social trends and popular practices. This has led, on the one hand, to some dubious claims of connections between writers whose similarities may be less significant than their differences and, on the other hand, to a lack of interest in what may be classified as "non-esoteric" influences. Finally, scholars of esoteric religion have a tendency to interpret whatever they are studying with the greatest seriousness, so that hucksters or charlatans turn into philosophers, and minor references in obscure esoteric works take on labyrinthine significances that would have bewildered their original authors.

In spite of these shortcomings, the esoteric approach has helped to restore the philosophical and theological importance of writings that have too often been dismissed as irrelevant. By relating these works primarily to religious questions, it has placed them, correctly, within a sphere of inquiry that was dominant in western European thought until the nineteenth century. Because occult writers quoted frequently from one another and drew freely on one another's ideas, the suggestion that they perceived themselves as working within an intellectual tradition is certainly not misguided, although it is easily overstated. Even if that tradition was indebted to invention as much as to inheritance, it represented received wisdom to those who tried to make sense out of it. Occult thinking, in short, was a hybrid plant with very deep roots. It had an extensive, albeit episodic, intellectual history, which has to be reviewed here briefly, as a background to the argument that follows.

Many of the chief sources of occult thinking in Europe appeared in Egypt during the early Christian centuries, a period of remarkable religious syncretism. This was the age of the Gnostics, who sought divine wisdom through philosophy, of the Alexandrian alchemist Zosimus of Panopolis and, above all, of "Hermes Trismegistus," the mythical author of the diverse Greek and Latin works later collected under the title of *Corpus Hermeticum*. While the *Corpus Hermeticum* was set down on papyrus long after the building of the pyramids by writers familiar with Christianity and Gnostic thought, its various components were to some extent informed by memories of the learning of Pharaonic Egypt. Until the mid-seventeenth century and beyond, the *Corpus Hermeticum* was read more or less uncritically as a pure distillation of ancient Egyptian teachings on everything from hieroglyphs to alchemy. Another ancient school of thought, emphasizing the dominance of spirit over matter, was introduced in the third century CE by Greek and Near Eastern philosophers: Plotinus, his student Porphyry and Porphyry's Syrian follower Iamblichus. Because they sought to revive a version of the Platonic theory of forms (which they called spirits), they were known as Neoplatonists. Plotinus saw the Divine Mind or *Nous* as an emanation of the indivisible One; in turn, the World Spirit and all individual spirits emanated from the *Nous*. Iamblichus was particularly interested in magic, which he linked with the preservation of polytheism. During the early Middle Ages, these Egyptian and Neoplatonic texts were preserved, reinterpreted and augmented, not by Christian but by Arab scholars, many of whom made original contributions to occult thinking. Meanwhile, a Jewish form of *gnosis*, or divine wisdom, was elaborated in the writings known as the Kabbala, gathered together and transcribed in the thirteenth century.

Medieval Arabs, Jews and Byzantines passed this grab-bag of heterodox thinking on to Western Christians, some of whom embraced it as a source of ultimate knowledge. Gradually, it was pieced together by European thinkers into a single tradition of occult philosophy. This began in the late Middle Ages in the secret treatises of Western Christian alchemists and ritual magicians, but it continued in the public writings of humanist scholars. The most celebrated humanist contributions to occult philosophy were made by the Florentines Marsilio Ficino and Giovanni Pico della Mirandola, as well as by the German humanist Heinrich Cornelius Agrippa. Ficino revived the Neoplatonic theory of spirit, which he saw as existing throughout all of creation in the form of an organic "World Soul." His younger colleague Pico, in spite of misgivings about the uses of magic, was fascinated by astrology and by the possibility of uniting all religions through occult philosophy. Although he too was inspired by Neoplatonism, Agrippa was more open in his embrace of practical and even popular magic, so much so that his name became notorious in connection with it. Agrippa seems later to have recanted his interest in the workings of the occult, although the reasons for his recantation, and even its significance, are open to question.

To the works of these humanist philosophers may be added the medical-alchemical treatises of the Swiss-born doctor Paracelsus (Theophrastus Philippus Aureolus Bombastus von Hohenheim), who developed a complex anti-Aristotelian theory of the body and pioneered the use of chemical treatments for disease. The most important English contributions to occult philosophy in the age of humanism were the astrological and magical works of the extraordinarily talented John Dee, and the breathtaking theories of his compatriot Robert Fludd. Seeking to bind together the microcosmic and macrocosmic worlds in a single overarching explanation, Fludd delved into topics as diverse as music, memory, perception and the circulation of the blood, publishing his findings in massive and expensively illustrated volumes.[27] The writings of these humanists, mixing heterodoxy and strokes of paganism with mysticism and the rudiments of experimental science, remained on the edge of intellectual respectability, yet they helped to stimulate a liberation of thought and imagination that spread across Renaissance Europe. As Paracelsus put it, "Thoughts are free and are subject to no rule. On them rests the freedom of man."[28]

Those who were suspicious of occult philosophy equated it with demonic magic. This implied that it was heretical, diabolical or unlawful, but could also suggest that it was "ignorant," improvised or imaginary rather than rooted in learned sources. It therefore bore the mark of popular "superstition" as well as devil worship.[29] In Western Christian lands, the occult never escaped this damaging, double-edged association with magic, which prevented it from becoming fully acceptable. Some writers, like Della Porta, Agrippa and Dee, were bold enough to appropriate the term magic for their own uses, but others studiously avoided it. By the mid-eighteenth century, almost no learned person in Britain was willing to label his or her own occult interests as magic, whether natural or supernatural, and the term became almost entirely associated with popular beliefs. By 1800, in spite of a striking revival of occult thinking, magic was widely linked in commercial discourse with conjuring, which was disdained as an unabashed form of trickery. Thus, magic and occult thinking would have different historical trajectories.

Yet the tangled linkages between the two do not allow either to be studied in isolation. While the subsequent chapters of this study concentrate on written sources rather than practices, magical behaviour will constantly impinge on the argument. The occult always retained a practical as well as an intellectual aspect. Writers on occult subjects might refer to popular magic favourably, although this depended on how secure they felt in endorsing what many rejected as "superstition." The astrological healer Nicholas Culpeper, for example, was fascinated by the potions, salves and curatives employed by village cunning men or wise women. Conversely, other famous astrologers who marketed their art with such great success in the late seventeenth century were careful to deny that they were mere "empirics," dispensing practical solutions without regard to the theoretical basis of what they were selling. A history of the occult cannot restrict itself to the intellectual tradition of esoteric knowledge; it also has to chronicle the many points of contact, and of friction, between occult learning and traditional customs or beliefs.

The chapters of this book are synthetic in bringing together a variety of sources and approaches, but they are not meant to be encyclopaedic. Many minor writers are not discussed; others are dealt with only in passing. Issues that may be of great concern to individual readers may not be raised at all, or be explored in any detail. Witchcraft, for example, will not be discussed as much in the following chapters as some would like. Its importance to this argument is peripheral. Many writers saw witchcraft as evidence of the existence of malign or diabolical spirits. Because the activities of witches existed mainly in the minds of their supposed victims and judges, however, they do not fit comfortably into a history that examines the intersection of occult thinking and practice. No English or Scottish writer in the early-modern period, with the sole exception of William Blake, identified himself or herself as an admirer of the Devil. Witchcraft was seldom tied to the occult except by those who disliked both, and some occult writers had no belief in its reality at all. As a result, the fate of witches, important as it is to any understanding of social, cultural and gender relations in early-modern Britain, does not cast as much light on our theme as might be assumed.

While the main sources for this study are contemporary printed works, they can only be understood by taking other materials (letters, manuscripts, diaries) into account. But even the latter provide only partial and fragmented answers to the question of how contemporaries interpreted what they saw on the page. Reading is never a straightforward process, and we cannot hope to recover in any immediate sense the variable ways in which seventeenth- and eighteenth-century texts were read—least of all, texts that aspired to mystery and arcane knowledge. Moreover, by annotating and copying printed texts, readers made them into new works bearing their own imprints, so that in a sense texts were multiplied into further texts. Historians can accurately reconstruct the printing history of books, the strategies by which they were marketed, the visual and rhetorical ploys by which they established authority, the references they contain and the responses to them registered by individual readers. In summarizing and analysing the arguments of these texts, however, we are adding our own notations, informed by our own insights, including what we *think* might have been the reactions of contemporary readers. Of course, we cannot avoid this process of approximation and guesswork, or we are left with no more than the shell of a text, without much sense of its elusive content.[30]

Our responses to occult writings may be very different from those of seventeenth- or eighteenth-century readers, but we still need to work out what they signified at the time, often in the absence of clear guides. Alchemical writers were notorious for using a cryptic jargon in their works, so that only the "illuminated" reader would understand them. Uninitiated enthusiasts hoped to untangle that jargon, but it is questionable whether any really could, because its allusions pointed in so many different directions at once. In the same way, historians will never be able to unweave fully the intricate networks of allusion that make up the writings of Thomas Vaughan, William Stukeley or William Blake. This should not discourage us from trying to come as close as we can to what a contemporary reader might have made of them, or from attempting to reconstruct the patterns of thinking that informed their works, even if we can get no closer to these goals than a tentative gloss.

We should also remain aware that many of these texts were consciously written for *use*, not simply for edification: that is, they were designed to be employed in some form of practice. How they were used is often very difficult to reconstruct. At times, the text demanded a rigorous adherence to every word, but this was possible only through some sort of translation of symbols or jargon. At other times, texts were more user-friendly, providing explanations and allowing themselves to be considered selectively. Of course, unless we can follow the strategies of the author, we cannot really know to what purposes they were to be put. Still, that there was a constant connection in occult writings between the written word and practical activity of some sort cannot be overlooked.

The occult strove to unlock ultimate truths. They will not be discovered in these pages, where every interpretation is only a partial truth. Plenty of writers and publishers in the early-modern period used the promise of "secrets revealed" as a lure to attract customers for their books. The purpose of this investigation is more modest: to devise a general framework within which the history of occult thinking can be understood in the century and a half after the English Civil War period. It has to take account of a changing cultural context, including religious transformations, the impact of a commercialized press, the rise of new types of sociability and the emergence of partisan politics. Each of these factors had a profound impact on the occult. Alchemy, astrology and ritual magic were tied from the first to religious heterodoxy and sectarianism, an association that lasted throughout the eighteenth century. Occult writers took full advantage of the commercial possibilities of publishing, especially in the hotly competitive cultural atmosphere of the 1780s. Occult secrets became selling points for clubs and associations that have been seen as models of early-modern sociability. Finally, the decline of occult thinking in the early eighteenth century was in part due to political struggles, just as its revival after 1780 can be attributed to a shift in the general cultural situation. We will not proceed very far in placing our subject in a historical context, however, before we encounter what seem to be two formidable obstacles to the survival of any type of occult thinking: namely, the scientific revolution and the Enlightenment.

Science, Enlightenment and the Occult

The concept of a scientific revolution was only retroactively applied. Derived from the ideals of human progress that dominated nineteenth-century scholarship, it was characterized by the concept of revolution, necessary for any sudden, fundamental break with the past. A radical change in ways of thinking, it was proposed, separated medieval from modern thought about nature. The features of this scientific revolution were eloquently expressed in a famous work by Herbert Butterfield, published in 1949. His formulation has been enormously influential ever since.[31] Its chief English protagonists were experimentalists like Robert Boyle and theorists like Sir Isaac Newton, who sought to understand the natural universe in rational and mathematical terms. They set European natural philosophers, or scientists, on a new track that distinguished them not just from their forebears, but from observers of nature in every other part of the world. Above all, their ideas *worked*, and to them we owe everything in modern technology, from microscopes to smartphones, as well as every aspect of our modern scientific mindset.

In recent decades, the concept of a scientific revolution has been assailed from a number of angles: for emphasizing change rather than continuity in science, for not taking enough account of the cultural context in which knowledge was pursued, for ignoring the contributions to science of occult ways of thinking, and for assuming a steady advance in verifiable scientific explanations.[32] Few scholars would argue that science progressed in a linear fashion through revolutionary leaps, or by simple binary oppositions between right and wrong. The emphasis on slowly changing paradigms leaves plenty of room for contradictions and anomalies, for religious beliefs and spiritual objectives, as well as for eccentric or imaginative thinking. It also allows for the importance of social status, connections and intellectual credentials in establishing the respectability or trustworthiness of a natural philosopher.[33] The role of figures like Ficino, Pico, Agrippa, Paracelsus, Dee and Fludd in fostering new interpretations of nature has been newly stressed by those who argue that science did not emerge as the antithesis of occult philosophy.

This last line of argument can of course be taken too far, and it has been. In the 1960s, the relationship of the occult to the prevailing conception of a scientific revolution became tangled up with a hypothesis attributed, somewhat unfairly, to Frances Yates. A leading scholar of occult philosophy in the Renaissance period, Yates was one of the earliest proponents of its influence on science. More particularly, she connected the formation of the Royal Society, the flag-bearing institution of scientific revolution in England, with the Hermetic and alchemical sensibilities of the mysterious secret society known as the Rosicrucian Brotherhood. Although this was more a suggestion than a full-fledged theory, it set off a long-running debate. Decades of research have shown that, while numerous scholars and publicists throughout Europe wrote under the Rosicrucian label and claimed an association with Rosicrucian ideas, the notion of an organized international "Brotherhood," widely accepted at the time, was a misconception that stemmed from a well-intentioned hoax by a group of enthusiastic German academics.[34] On the other hand, the alchemical and occult interests of several leading members of the Royal Society and pillars of the English scientific revolution, including Boyle and Newton, are now so well substantiated as to be undeniable.[35]

The precise relationship between scientific discovery and occult thinking remains complex but, as the first three chapters of this book will demonstrate, the two were not at war with one another. Natural science did not advance by brushing aside the occult, or by disproving magic. On the contrary, when occult claims were submitted to scientific scrutiny, few definite conclusions were drawn, and no concerted process of outright debunking took place. For their part, the devotees of occult thinking eagerly embraced scientific terminology and new scientific findings. In the eighteenth century, to be sure, the formal dialogue between natural science and the occult gradually died out, but this was due not so much to scientific advancements as to the imposition of a rigorous distinction between questions that could be answered by natural explanations and those that could not. Scientists ceased to write about occult qualities in nature, and natural magic in Della Porta's sense of the term either became experimental science or faded away.

As a result, in the decades after 1688, occult thinking was set adrift from natural philosophy and experimental science. Chapter Four examines that difficult transition, after which the occult began to take on different characteristics. Some influential thinkers in the first half of the eighteenth century, as will be shown in Chapter Five, tried privately to reconcile aspects of occult thinking with a Newtonian world-view. While firmly rejecting anything that smacked of popular magic, they continued to draw inspiration from astrology, alchemy and the interpretation of supernatural signs, but they did not want the general public to know about it and usually consigned their speculations to private writings, such as journals and diaries. In the end, their efforts to keep up the exchange between natural philosophy and the occult cannot be judged successful. Increasingly, as Chapter Six will show, the occult appealed to figures on the margins of intellectual respectability, who sought to counter mechanistic explanations of the universe by espousing various spiritual or supernatural theories that drew on one aspect or another of occult philosophy. Many of them were also attracted to mysticism, but it was their approach to nature, not their desire for union with God, that made their thinking occult. They differed from the experimental scientists who appear in the initial chapters of this book, but not entirely. While their attitudes to natural science were certainly out of step with those of the learned establishment, they aimed at addressing similar questions through spiritual rather than material suppositions. Their efforts would have a particular significance for the development of theories of the mind.

The occult lost much of its intellectual coherence after 1715, at least until the 1780s. We have to dig into the personal records of relatively obscure individuals in order to find its scattered traces. The withdrawal of the occult into private life, in an age that was dominated by an increasingly frenetic and dynamic commercial press, denoted a definite failure, but it also opened up certain opportunities. The booming public sphere of the eighteenth century was balanced by a quieter private sphere of contemplation and close friendships, usually exclusively male, in which ideas could be worked out and discussed between like-minded individuals. The cultivation of this private sphere was one of the purposes of Freemasonry, a sociable organization that rested on vows of secrecy, mysterious rituals and an elaborate mythology of origins.[36] Freemasonry provided a set of principles concerning male sociability and moral behaviour, bolstered by a highly imaginative collection of myths and legends. The principles of Freemasonry could be interpreted in a variety of ways: as a key to the mysteries of Scripture, as a rational system of ethics, as an explanation of the workings of nature or as a symbolic representation of occult philosophy. These were not contradictory or mutually exclusive readings, and all of them flourished within Masonic lodges.

In the rest of Europe, Freemasonry is associated by historians with the spread of the Enlightenment, which has often been seen as the antithesis of the occult. No better summary of this intellectual movement can be provided than that of Immanuel Kant, for whom enlightenment meant thinking for oneself, "daring to know," rather than simply accepting received wisdom or "superstition."[37] Of course, the assumption of Kant and most other contemporary philosophers was that enlightened thinking would tend towards rationality, and would be more or less the same for all rational human beings. Unfortunately for those who have sought to characterize the historical Enlightenment in such linear terms, thinking for oneself might mean a ferocious individuality and a high degree of what contemporaries described as irrationality. It helped to bring about, as the last three chapters of this book will demonstrate, not the extinction, but the dramatic and tempestuous revival of the occult. Once again, occult thinking was reinvented, this time in a self-professedly enlightened form, but with all of the peculiarities that it had developed in the years after 1715. Just as the formal Enlightenment produced radical critics like Jean-Jacques Rousseau who used its own language of "thinking for oneself" to hold it to account, so too did the occult revival give birth to dissenters like William Blake, who perceived it as insufficiently removed from the ways of the establishment.

These observations would not be surprising to historians of the Enlightenment in continental Europe. The enlightened connection to occult philosophies and practices, encompassing everything from Swedenborgianism and Mesmerism to various strains of occult Freemasonry, has long been recognized by French and German scholars as an integral feature of the cultural life of the last decades of the eighteenth century.[38] The British Enlightenments, on the other hand, have seldom been viewed in such a way. The Enlightenment in Scotland is identified with the scepticism of David Hume, the "progressive" historicism of William Robertson and the "common-sense" philosophy of Thomas Reid.[39] Its English counterpart has been seen as a fundamental cultural shift towards reason, secularism and transparency—"the creation of the modern world," in the late Roy Porter's breathless assessment.[40] The suggestion that alchemists, astrologers, ritual magicians, magnetic healers and occult Freemasons could have had something to do with this triumphant procession towards modernity is not one that has occurred to many British historians. Yet, as the final chapters of this book will argue, such was the case. Outside the institutions of learning, the informal connections between occult thinking and science may actually have *grown* in the eighteenth century, as a once-rarefied field of knowledge opened up to enthusiastic amateurs as well as to the commercialized publicity surrounding processes like electricity and magnetism.[41]

The winding, muddy and often submerged paths of occult thinking in the eighteenth century may not be as familiar to British historians as its more visible public byways in the late seventeenth century, but they were well travelled nonetheless. Adherents of the occult kept up a lively interaction with conventional intellectual trends, reconfiguring Hermeticism and Neoplatonism to suit the age of steam engines and revolutionary politics. As in the past, they eagerly absorbed heterodox religious ideas and maintained a keen interest in popular magic. Far from seeking to undermine the Enlightenment, they wanted to be a part of it, which should cause us to question just how far the boundaries of "thinking for oneself" might extend. Yet occult thinkers continued to lack respectability and remained vulnerable to attacks by those in authority, as well as to the vagaries of public opinion. The reaction to the French Revolution in the 1790s proved devastating to them, because they were now associated with dangerous political ideas. But the attempt to stamp them out was not successful, and they survived long beyond the end point of this book. When the guardians of the temple of British intellectual orthodoxy, founded on the cultural values of the educated Anglican elite, reluctantly began to make room for other points of view in the course of the nineteenth century, the denizens of occult philosophy were still swarming in the shadows, perhaps more numerous than ever. They emerged into the daylight after 1875, calling themselves Theosophists, Spiritualists, Hermeticists, Rosicrucians, Druids, Wiccans, Knights of the Golden Dawn, all lending their voices to the cacophonous yet vibrant disharmony of British public culture.

PART ONE
AURORA, 1650–1688

CHAPTER ONE

The Alchemical Heyday

WHEN WAS alchemy at its peak in England and Scotland? Ask somebody that question today, and the answer is likely to be "the Middle Ages" or perhaps "the Tudor period." The term "alchemy," after all, conjures up the image of damp monastic walls harbouring a sage in a long robe, with unkempt hair and a preoccupied look, who stares intently at mysterious crucibles and bubbling retorts. He is a seeker after the mad goal of making gold, half-scientist and half-mystic, immortalized (and frequently lampooned) by artists and writers throughout the early-modern period, from Pieter Bruegel the Elder to Ben Jonson. If the imaginary alchemist bears a resemblance to any historical personage, it might be to John Dee, the Elizabethan magus, with his scholar's cap, wizened features and long white beard, a subject of continuing fascination from his own time to ours.[1]

Measured in terms of the printed word, however, the high point of alchemy in Great Britain was actually in the last half of the seventeenth century. The vast majority of printed alchemical works in English, perhaps as many as two-thirds of them, appeared between 1650 and 1700.[2] Manuscript sources of alchemy are more difficult to date or count up effectively, as we cannot always be certain when they were written or copied. Nevertheless, the biggest collection by far of alchemical manuscripts ever held in English hands was assembled by Elias Ashmole, a fervent alchemical adept, between 1648 and 1692. At his death, he left 620 volumes of manuscript materials to Oxford University, including hundreds of alchemical works. The contents of his collection stretch back to the Middle Ages, but Ashmole's fervent collecting belongs to the same period as the majority of printed books.[3] Our imagined alchemist, then, should really be wearing a cravat, long coat and breeches. His surroundings should be a panelled room or even the garden of a college at Oxford or Cambridge. Bewigged and clean-shaven, he should look more like Isaac Newton than John Dee. As this chapter will show, however, late seventeenth-century alchemists came in a variety of disguises, and they did not all share the same attitudes. To understand alchemy, therefore, it is not enough to bring a "typical" figure back to life: we have to imagine the lives, complex and vibrant, of the members of a diverse intellectual community, before asking what exactly made their work occult.

The Community of Alchemists

Although *chrysopoeia* or *spagyria*, the alchemical art of making gold from base metals, was heating up throughout Great Britain in the second half of the seventeenth century, the great wen of London was its principal furnace. There, crowded into the tiny alleys of Little Britain, a neighbourhood behind St Paul's Cathedral that stretched down to Fleet Street, lived the booksellers—William Cooper, Matthew Smelt, Andrew Sowle, Thomas Salusbury and others—from whose shops alchemical treatises could be purchased. Nobody could hope for success in the alchemical art without reading many of them. London was a magnet for anyone who wanted to make money out of the occult sciences, no matter where they were born. The astrologer-alchemist-magician John Heydon, a West Countryman by birth, settled in the capital, first as a lawyer, then as an "Astromagus," as he termed himself. London also drew the celebrated George Starkey, who was born in Bermuda, educated at Harvard College and became famous in England under his pseudonym of "Eirenaeus Philalethes." Both writers spent time in the English capital's notorious prisons.[4] Others were drawn to London for more philanthropic reasons. From Charing Cross, where Parliament pulled down the Eleanor cross, the medieval monument that gave it its name, in 1647 and replaced it with a fish shop, the German immigrant Samuel Hartlib managed his "Office of Address," an international web of communication for those interested in scientific knowledge, including alchemy. Hartlib promoted the careers of Starkey and many other alchemical adepts, including a fellow German, Frederick Clodius, who eventually married Hartlib's daughter.[5] A later Dutch immigrant, the mysterious W. Yworth, William Yarworth or Willem Ijvaert, set up a "New Spagyrical Academy" in the London suburb of Shadwell, near the bustling Thames dockyards.[6]

Oxford and Cambridge were more genteel hotbeds of alchemy. The university towns provided a protective environment for the secretive experiments of Robert Boyle and Isaac Newton, but they also sheltered many lesser figures with Hermetic passions—men like Ezekiel Foxcroft, a Fellow of King's College who lovingly translated a Rosicrucian work, *The Hermetic Romance*, in 1690.[7] Flashes of evidence provide glimpses of how *chrysopeia* fired the imaginations of adepts in other provincial English towns. A wonderful story spread in 1651 of how a stranger named Mervin had made gold from lead at the shop of a Bath goldsmith.[8] Why he chose to do this in Bath is anybody's guess. George Starkey moved for a time to Bristol, "to asist [sic] the work of Refining there and to pr[actise] physick."[9] Apparently, the work of refining at Bristol preceded his arrival, but nothing more is known about the local alchemists whom he assisted. Meanwhile, Starkey's former roommate at Harvard College, the clergyman and alchemist John Allin, migrated to the tiny, declining port of Rye in Sussex, where he served as vicar from 1654 to 1662. There, Allin found himself among a little group of adepts, including the amateur astrologer Samuel Jeake, who received from the generous minister the gift of a book describing "the true use of the Elixir Magnus." Reverend Allin apparently introduced Starkey to some of his Rye friends, with whom the great alchemist shared secrets concerning the great process.[10] At nearby Dover a few years later, the former mayor John Matson corresponded enthusiastically with Robert Boyle, sending him alchemical recipes and complaining that his experiments could proceed no further without "The Comeing of a lampe furnace from paris."[11]

No matter how isolated their home towns may have seemed, these provincial enthusiasts read alchemical publications just as avidly as did their metropolitan counterparts. John Beale, one of Hartlib's correspondents, kept up with the latest alchemical debates while residing in rural Herefordshire. John Webster, a former Anglican clergyman who became a radical sectarian and an ardent alchemist, collected together a remarkable library of books, including over a hundred volumes on occult philosophy, at his home in Clitheroe, Lancashire. Webster was the editor of a beautifully produced English translation of *The Last Will and Testament of Basil Valentine*, which appeared in 1670.[12] Decades later, John Yardley, a glover turned silversmith of Worcester, claimed to have developed his own spagyric process out of reading "all the Chymical authors I could procure."[13] Presumably, he procured them in Worcester.

Wales may have been poorer than England, but it was certainly not backward in generating alchemists. Bassett Jones of Glamorganshire studied at Jesus College, Cambridge, became a medical doctor and in 1648 published a book on the Philosopher's Stone. According to his friend Samuel Hartlib, copies became so scarce due to high demand that within a few years not even Jones himself could find one.[14] Another graduate of Jesus College was Thomas Vaughan, the Welsh-speaking rector of Llansanffraid, a remote parish in rural Brecon. He was twin brother of the poet Henry Vaughan, known as "the Silurist" or South Welshman. John Heydon mocked Thomas Vaughan for his "Welch Philosophie," but did not hesitate to plagiarize him.[15] A royalist, Vaughan withdrew to London during the Civil War period, where he wrote a series of important magical-alchemical works in English under the pen name

"Eugenius Philalethes." This brought him to the attention of the Hartlib circle. More interested in alchemical philosophy than in ministering to his parish, he declined to return to his duties in Brecon after the Restoration.[16]

The kingdom of Scotland was no less noted for producing devotees of the art. Thomas Vaughan's later alchemical experiments depended on the financial support of Sir Robert Moray, Charles II's deputy lieutenant for Scotland. According to his friend John Aubrey, Moray was "a good Chymist and assisted his Majestie in his Chymicall operations."[17] In the 1650s, Moray wrote frequently to his Scottish friend the earl of Kincardine on alchemical matters, and confided in him the occult meaning of his "mason mark," a pentacle or five-pointed star.[18] Scotland was also the reputed homeland of the mythic Alexander Seton, thought in the early seventeenth century to be identical with "Elias Artista," the wandering "Cosmopolite" who possessed the secret of the Stone. With its many medical schools and university courses in "Chymistry," Scotland harboured a number of active alchemical communities. One of Samuel Hartlib's alchemical correspondents in the late 1640s was William Hamilton, who had taught at the University of Glasgow before moving to London.[19] The high regard in which the Hermetic art was held among medical practitioners in Scotland can be judged from the earl of Cromarty's gift of his grandfather's collection of alchemical manuscripts (including a "Ripley Scroll," a set of beautifully illustrated verses supposedly written by George Ripley, medieval canon of Bridlington) to the Edinburgh College of Physicians in 1707. The earl bragged that his grandsire was "a great student in natural philosophy, even to a considerable advancement in the Hermeticke schoole," which must have impressed the learned doctors of Edinburgh.[20]

Physicians were prominent among alchemical adepts everywhere in Britain. They included men of considerable influence and renown, like Dr Edmund Dickinson, physician in ordinary to Charles II; Dr Albert Otto Faber of Lübeck, the king's personal physician; and John Twysden, brother of an eminent Parliamentarian.[21] Works of alchemy were advertised and sold by medical booksellers like Dorman Newman.[22] So popular was alchemy among doctors that William Salmon, MD, did not feel it necessary to apologize for devoting the vast majority of pages in a general treatise on medicine to the pursuit of making gold.[23] His readers may have included the anonymous doctor living near London who left a manuscript, dating from the late 1680s, that intersperses various accounts of medical treatments with recipes for finding the Philosopher's Stone.[24] Alchemy, which held out the promise of an elixir of life and a cure for all diseases, offered obvious benefits to physicians, especially those who were forward enough to espouse the controversial "iatrochemistry" of the German doctor Paracelsus, based on medicines made from metals.[25]

In 1665, an attempt was made to obtain a royal patent for a Society of Chymical Physicians, in opposition to the existing College of Physicians, which was accused of resisting the new medicines. Thirty-five chemical adepts signed a petition in favour of the Society, including Marchamont Needham, a prominent Parliamentary publicist and physician.[26] The project failed, probably due to resistance from outraged members of the College of Physicians. In spite of this setback, the opinions of sceptical observers regarding chemical remedies tended to be cautious rather than hostile. The theologian Meric Casaubon, who despised ritual magic and was suspicious of the philosophical claims of alchemy, nonetheless praised its contributions to medicine, confessing that, while a student at Oxford, he had been cured of a near-fatal disease by "some Chymical composition" given to him by an unconventional doctor. If there was a "new medical regime" in the late seventeenth century, one that united medical practice with scientific theory and experiment, then alchemy was without doubt a factor in its rise.[27]

It was not only doctors who developed a taste for alchemy. Lawyers like Elias Ashmole and clergymen like Thomas Vaughan and John Beale made equally eager adepts. Men of lesser social status occasionally pop up as assistants in alchemical laboratories. Yworth, for example, was aided by John Baker, a periwig-maker who had a shop in the Strand.[28] The most noted alchemists, however, tended to be men of the learned professions or skilled craftsmen. These occupations were closed to women, and there were no women among the prominent alchemical writers of this period. Women could read alchemical works, of course, and in one copy of Ashmole's *Way to Bliss* appears the commanding inscription, "Mary Marston Her Book Steal not this."[29] Women could also practise alchemy. Hartlib claimed that the mother of his friend Thomas Henshaw was a "great chymist." He further referred to one "Mistress Ogleby," who owned manuscripts by George Ripley, as "a rare chymical gentlewoman."[30] Thomas Vaughan's wife assisted him in his chemical operations.

Leaving aside the occasional female adept, the alchemists were, by and large, men of the professional "middling sort," living in towns rather than the countryside. They might call themselves "gentlemen," and many were related to gentry families. They were literate and used to the idea of protecting the "secrets" of their professions from outsiders. They needed money to buy equipment and supply their experiments, but few of them could be called wealthy. In a culture that was dominated by the landowning classes, it is noteworthy that relatively few serious adepts were substantial landowners or peers. There were exceptions, of course, especially in Scotland where spagyric knowledge seems to have been handed down in aristocratic families like those of Balcarres or Cromarty. Several "chymical gentlemen" in England set up furnaces on their estates, among them Sir Cheney Culpeper of Kent, one of Hartlib's correspondents. Robert Boyle was the wealthy son of the fabulously rich earl of Cork (together with his many brothers and sisters, Boyle can still be seen praying in effigy on his parents' magnificent funeral monument in St Patrick's Cathedral in Dublin). Another aristocratic seeker of the Stone was Henry Carey, earl of Dover, who entered into "secret transactions" with George Starkey in 1654.[31] Goodwin Wharton, son of the puritan Lord Wharton, wasted a fortune in the early 1680s funding an alchemist named Broune. His partner in this venture was the former republican and compulsive conspirator Major John Wildman. After Broune's laboratory burned down, Wharton and Wildman turned to other ventures, including communicating with angels and finding fairy treasure.[32] Most alchemists, however, were from humbler origins than Wharton and lacked his financial means. If they sought gold, it was in part as a means to social mobility.

Elias Ashmole may not have been typical in his dazzling success at climbing the social ladder, but he was a model of advancement to other alchemists. The son of a saddler of Lichfield, he used his mother's gentry relatives to promote his status. He became a lawyer, amassing property and prestige through carefully planned marriage alliances. By attaching himself to the royalist cause early in the Civil War, Ashmole gained a lucrative position with the excise. Litigious and grasping, he fought his in-laws for control of family estates, and compelled Hester, the widow of John Tradescant the younger, to recognize his right to her husband's collection of curiosities, which later formed the basis of the Ashmolean Museum. After the Restoration, Ashmole's loyalty to the Stuarts was rewarded with the comptrollership of the excise, along with the post of Windsor Herald, which involved the validation of family titles and coats of arms. Ashmole grew rich from the fruits of two quite different offices: the excise, which looked forward to the bureaucratic state; and the heraldship, redolent of a hierarchical, aristocratic past.[33] The combination of dynamism and conservatism that drove Ashmole's career was not unusual among professional men in the late seventeenth century. Another self-made man, Samuel Pepys, praised Ashmole as "a very ingenious Gentleman" after their first meeting in 1660, when the two of them sang together in the study of William Lilly, the astrologer. Ashmole later assured Pepys "that frogs and other insects do often fall from the skye ready-formed," a wonderful piece of biological misinformation that was widely believed at the time.[34]

We cannot be certain whether a greater number of individuals who thought like Elias Ashmole existed in Britain between 1650 and 1688 than in earlier or later periods. We do know, however, that more material on alchemy was published in those decades than previously or afterwards—a statement that applies not just to Britain, but to Europe as a whole. Equally important, these books and pamphlets appeared in vernacular languages, not in Latin, which made them available to a wider reading public. In his old age, Arthur Dee, son of the famous magus John Dee, was shocked by this. He complained to Elias Ashmole, who translated one of his own alchemical works from Latin into English, that since scholars already derided alchemy, "how then can th^{t} any way be aduanced by the vulgar [multitude]"?[35] It may not have been advanced socially by "middling" men, but its appeal had certainly broadened. What explains this success?

The first and most important cause may have been the breakdown of the Anglican Church during the Civil War and Interregnum period from 1642 to 1660. As a result, a pool of underground religious ideas was carried to the surface that would previously have been condemned as heterodox or blasphemous. Alchemical writing was frequently accompanied by religious speculation, which might have led to prosecution in an earlier period. A second, connected cause was the loosening of censorship. At the start of the Civil War, Parliament deprived episcopal authorities of their powers to inspect and license works of the press. The privilege of licensing books was now to be shared between the Company of Stationers and various appointed officials. Political and religious divisions among the licensers, however, rendered censorship largely ineffective.[36]

The impact of these two factors changed again after 1660, when the Church of England was restored along with the monarchy, and licensing of the press became much stricter.[37] At the Restoration, however, continuing divisions within Anglicanism prevented the Church from maintaining a united front against speculative religion. In addition, a number of prominent alchemists in England—for example, Ashmole and Moray—had been royalists during the Civil War period. They could argue that their alchemical work was not motivated by radical religious views and was consistent with support for the king. Charles II clearly sympathized with them, as he set up his own chemical laboratory at Whitehall Palace, directly beneath his closet, as early as 1669. Although little is known about the king's involvement with alchemy, it has been suggested that his experiments eventually led to chronic mercury poisoning, which caused his death by kidney failure in 1685.[38] As for renewed censorship by the Stationers' Company, which regained its monopoly on licensing in 1660, it tended to focus on political sedition rather than on unusual philosophical views.

It seems fair, then, to call the period 1650–88 an alchemical heyday. This did not mean that alchemy was accepted by everyone, or that its practitioners necessarily felt they were in the ascendant. On the contrary, most were convinced that alchemy was losing ground to an ill-founded scepticism. Ashmole himself lamented, in the preface to his translation of Arthur Dee's work that alchemy was being traduced "as *false* and *deceitful*." Employing an argument based on his own reason and experience, Ashmole begged the sceptics, "these (otherwise well accomplisht) *Men*," to "but consider how many occult, specifick, incomprehensible, and inexplicable qualities there lies dormant and observed in *Nature*."[39] The self-styled "Astromagus," George Thor, who prided himself on his fluency in Greek, was more dismissive of "those who look upon this Sacred Science (as the wise *Democritus* calls it) as on . . . Aristophan's *Cuccou Town in the Clouds*." Such critics "were such as are shut up, by a wonderfull, and necessary providence of God, under the vast, heavie cloud of the vulgar, from which they are never like to escape."[40] To deny the truth of alchemy, according to Thor, was to reveal oneself as unlearned, uneducated, unprofessional—exactly what the critics thought about those who practised alchemy. Yet scepticism was evidently widespread, even in the mid-seventeenth century. The philosopher's Stone was called "a chaste whore" by the learned John Wilkins in his 1648 treatise *Mathematical Magic*, "because it allures many and admits none."[41] Of course, such views may have arisen from disillusionment and a failure to produce results rather than from a perception that the search for gold was inherently a waste of time.

Virtually every alchemical writer called *spagyria* a science. Does this mean that they saw the "great work" as falling into the same category as Boyle's experiments on gases or Robert Hooke's microscopic discoveries? Was it natural, transparent, perhaps even "mechanical" in the sense of having no need of a divine operator? Or did the alchemists acknowledge something supernatural in the spagyric process? These are crucial questions. To answer them, we will have to examine the writings of some of the alchemists themselves, focusing on theoretical rather than practical works.[42] We will consider figures who commanded considerable individual attention in their own time, like Elias Ashmole and Thomas Vaughan. Both exploited the popularity of alchemy, but each had to come to terms with the problematic associations of occult philosophy, which dipped into enthusiasm, unorthodoxy and even ritual magic. To understand the commercial and cultural framework of alchemy, the last section of this chapter deals with a relative nobody, a London bookseller who never achieved fame, but nonetheless made an enormous contribution to the public image of the spagyric art in the late seventeenth century: William Cooper, publisher, of the Sign of the Pelican in Little Britain.

The Respectable Magus: Elias Ashmole

Examine late seventeenth-century alchemy as a theoretical philosophy, rather than as a set of practical operations, and it will not be long before magic makes an appearance, directly or indirectly. Elias Ashmole and Thomas Vaughan were not intimidated by the term, which so alienated, frustrated and disgusted other educated minds of the time, not to mention historians of science today. And Ashmole and Vaughan were not alone, as a surprising number of their contemporaries shared their audacity. Indeed, for any aficionado of alchemy who was residing in England or Scotland, and who yearned to know more about supernatural magic, the unbridled 1650s and even the more staid 1660s and 1670s constituted a heady time. The forbidden subject had never been discussed more fully and openly, or in a greater variety of publications.

Any alchemist who was building up a collection of works on learned magic in the mid-seventeenth century might have started with a little book by a man who was certainly not orthodox. In fact, he was imprisoned so long for his offensive religious views that King James I opined his name should be "Never-Out." The victim of this miserable pun was the sometime clergyman John Everard, "a perpetual heretic," according to Christopher Hill, who was said to follow an egalitarian and utopian sect of the sixteenth century, the Family of Love. Everard dreamed of spreading his Neoplatonic philosophy "to the lowest of men . . . tinkers, cobblers, weavers, and poor beggarly fellows that come running."[43] Was he trying to address "the lowest of men" when he translated the works of Hermes Trismegistus into plain English? In late 1649, just before his death, Everard appeared as the translator, allegedly from Arabic, of an edition of *The Divine Pymander*, the first fourteen books of the *Corpus Hermeticum*, along with assorted Hermetic excerpts. In reality, Everard's translation was neither from Arabic nor Greek, but from Francesco Patrizzi's Latin version of 1593. The preface to this little volume was written by John French, physician to the Parliamentary army. One of its publishers was Thomas Brewster, later official printer to the Council of State under Cromwell.[44] Clearly, in spite of Everard's notorious past, his work had friends in high places under the Republic. It may not have reached "poor beggarly fellows," but, remarkably, it remained the standard English translation of the *Corpus Hermeticum* for 350 years.

The second classic that any alchemist would have wanted in his or her collection of magical texts was the 1651 translation by John French of Agrippa's *Three Books of Occult Philosophy*. The original, published in 1531, had long been available to readers of Latin, but this was the first complete English translation. It was preceded by an effusive poetic encomium to Agrippa, who is described as "Natures *Apostle*, and her Choice *High Priest*, Her *Mysticall*, and bright *Evangelist*." This verse was written by a certain "Eugenius Philalethes," the pen name of Thomas Vaughan. The book's dedication was to Dr Robert Child, whose life epitomizes the extraordinary range of careers and biographies of alchemists of the 1650s. Child, a correspondent of Samuel Hartlib, had managed the Massachusetts ironworks of his friend and fellow alchemist John Winthrop the younger. Child fled New England in 1647 after his Presbyterianism landed him in trouble with the religious Independents who dominated the colony, and eventually settled in Ireland. The translator of Agrippa's *Three Books* praised Child for "being converted from vulgar, and irrational incredulities to the rational embracing of the sublime, Hermeticall and Theomagicall truths."[45] To read Agrippa's massive compendium of magic, apparently, was to enter the bosom of reason.

Agrippa's first book provides a definition of magic that is worth citing, because its influence spread throughout the occult thinking of the time:

> Magick is a faculty of wonderfull vertue, full of most high mysteries, containing the most profound Contemplation of most secret things, together with the nature, power, quality, substance and virtues thereof, as also the knowledge of whole nature, and it doth instruct us concerning the differing, and agreement of things amongst themselves, whence it produceth its wonderfull effects, by uniting the virtues of all things through the application of them one to the other, and to their inferior sutable subjects, joining and knitting them together thoroughly by the powers and virtues of the superior Bodies. This is the most perfect, and chief Science, that sacred, and sublime kind of Phylosophy, and lastly the most absolute perfection of all most excellent Philosophy.[46]

If we leave out the "high mysteries," which are not in any case made very specific, this definition resembles della Porta's "natural magic." It too dealt with "secret things," or at least hidden ones, through their power, quality, substance and virtues, with the aim of understanding the whole of nature. The word "Science" as used in Agrippa's last sentence would have carried more resonance in 1651 than it did when the author was alive, because by then it would have evoked the experimental methods espoused by Francis Bacon, and encouraged more recently by Samuel Hartlib.

When he suggested that magic was "the most absolute perfection of all most excellent Philosophy," however, Agrippa implied that it gave insight into divine as well as natural things. This was a highly questionable position for orthodox Protestants, who recognized the divine only as it appeared in Scripture. Anything beyond that was suspect, because it might be inspired by the Devil. As D.P. Walker has pointed out, Agrippa was deliberately imprecise in distinguishing his ideas of magic from diabolism or devil worship.[47] His second and third books rashly proceeded far beyond natural magic, into the realms of celestial magic (numerology, geometric figures) and ceremonial magic (the ritual evocation of angels or demons). This terrain was particularly dangerous in the sixteenth and seventeenth centuries, when diabolism was officially anathematized throughout Europe, leading to the execution of some sixty thousand alleged witches. In England, active witch-hunting revived in the late 1640s, with the encouragement of Parliament.[48] Although its targets were elderly women, usually indigent or dependent on charity, rather than educated men, the possibility of running foul of the laws against witchcraft remained a real one for the devotees of Agrippa.

How could one reconcile Agrippa's problematic understanding of magic with intellectual respectability and Protestant religious orthodoxy? Some writers, like the botanist Robert Turner, were not much bothered by the question. In 1657, Turner translated and edited the first printed version of the *Ars Notoria* (the "Notory Arts of Solomon," also known as the "Little Key of Solomon"), which was in fact a manual for summoning up spirits or angels, often condemned as a source for black magic. The *Ars Notoria* was the third book that every alchemical devotee of learned magic in the 1650s would have wanted to own, and probably the most subversive from an orthodox Protestant perspective. Turner was no obscure autodidact: he had studied at Cambridge, and was renowned for his translations of Paracelsus, as well as for a compendium of herbal remedies that included astrological notations. Nor was Turner simply a reviser of tired old magical formulae. Updating the fusty medieval prayers and rituals of the *Ars Notoria*, he included in his work "A certain Magnetick Experiment," allowing "every Man or Woman" to convey thoughts telepathically to another person "by the virtue of the Loadstone," that is, by magnetism.[49] Apparently, Turner had no difficulty in uniting ritual magic with "*magia naturalis*." He was also responsible for translating Agrippa's alleged *Fourth Book*, dealing with geomancy or divination by mathematical charts. Published in 1655, the edition proved popular enough to merit a reissue nine years later.[50]

By contrast with the radical Everard, the headstrong Agrippa or the mercurial Turner, Elias Ashmole was preoccupied not with publicizing magic, but with giving it intellectual respectability. If he never fully succeeded, at least he was able to cover his own occult thinking with an orthodox veneer. Ashmole was the editor of what must have been the most desirable addition to any collection of works on alchemy and magic in the 1650s, the magnificent *Theatrum Chemicum Britannicum*. This lengthy, beautifully produced, copiously illustrated anthology of alchemical works in verse by English authors—Thomas Norton, George Ripley, Geoffrey Chaucer, Thomas Charnock, Edward Kelly, John Dee—was first published in 1652. Because it celebrated only *English* seekers after the Stone, *Theatrum Chemicum* can be read as a call to national unity at a time of political crisis. "Our *English Philosophers* Generally, (like *Prophets*) *have received little honour . . . in their owne Countrey*," wrote Ashmole, who intended to give it to them. English alchemists were ranked with those of ancient Israel, Greece, Rome and Arabia, implying a providential destiny for the nation as well as for those who shared in the great secret of the universe.[51] Since Ashmole was a royalist, the longed-for rediscovery of the Stone may have been linked in his mind with the return of the Stuarts. Yet he avoided any mention of politics in the pages of *Theatrum Chemicum*, and nothing in his famous book would have been offensive to supporters of the Commonwealth. He strove to be accommodating towards those who held power, whoever they might be. Similarly, he tried to blunt any potential criticism from those who might object on religious grounds to the pursuit of alchemy.

In short, Ashmole was no Agrippa. Cautious and calculating, he preferred to edit rather than to author texts. Although his alchemical publications belong to the turbulent, sectarian 1650s, Ashmole remained, at least outwardly, a pillar of old-fashioned Anglicanism and respect for authority. Apart from a few brief passages in the "Prolegomenon" to *Theatrum Chemicum*, he never articulated a fully developed occult philosophy in print, although he was certainly familiar with the main Hermetic, Neoplatonic and Paracelsian authors, and had tried his hand at ritual magic. His own beliefs reflected an amalgamation of popular and learned sources that dealt with magic, including many texts of dubious origin or authorship, but he strove to present them as non-controversial, which involved him in some oddly twisted argumentation.

Ashmole's practical knowledge of alchemy was largely derived from his friend William Backhouse of Swallowfield, Berkshire, who "adopted" him as a "Son," that is, as an alchemical pupil, in June 1651, just as the "Prolegomenon" was being written. On his deathbed two years later, according to Ashmole, Backhouse "told me in Silables the true Matter of the Philosophers Stone: which he bequeathed to me as a Legacy."[52] What "the true Matter" was, Ashmole did not reveal. Interestingly, Backhouse had also befriended Robert Turner, editor of the *Ars Notoria*, who dedicated a translation of Paracelsus to him, calling him a "worthy *Mecaenas*."[53] Unlike Turner's, however, Ashmole's published works never delved very deeply into the occult thought that originated in other European nations. Instead, they focused on English adepts, envisioning a national school of alchemy of which Ashmole was, in many respects, the inventor as well as the intellectual heir. He presented alchemy as "a Way to Bliss," a road to personal fulfilment rather than to universal enlightenment. It was a narrow path open only to the educated few, not a broad way to which the many might aspire. This helped to separate Ashmole's work from the unorthodox writings of utopians or sectarians like John Everard, whose learning he nonetheless grudgingly admired.[54] Ashmole was writing for the benefit of an elite, not for "poor beggarly fellows."

No matter how respectable he may have wanted to appear, Ashmole was strongly attracted to magic, which continually peeps out from beneath the opaque surfaces of his prose. The "Prolegomenon" to *Theatrum Chemicum* is haunted by a barely disguised desire for the supernatural power that the alchemist might attain. In these remarkable pages, which represent his sole, brief public foray into theory, Ashmole freely borrowed from a strange, visionary sixteenth-century manuscript in his collection entitled "Epitome of the Treasure of Health."[55] Like its anonymous author, Ashmole imagined not one but four Philosopher's Stones, the Natural as well as the "*Vegitable, Magicall,* and *Angelicall,*" of which only the first could be reproduced by modern efforts, informed by the chemical knowledge that the Greek poet Orpheus brought out of Egypt. Ashmole was evidently most fascinated, however, by the last Stone, which "affords the *Apparition* of *Angells*, and gives a power of conversing with them, by *Dreams* or *Revelations*." Unfortunately, it had been known only to Moses, Solomon and Hermes Trismegistus.[56] In his musings on the Angelical Stone, Ashmole revealed an aspect of *spagyria* that was seldom discussed by alchemical writers: namely, its efficacy as a conduit to the world of spirits. While he lamented that such a marvel was now humanly unattainable, he may not genuinely have believed that to be the case, especially in light of the discussion that he presented in the endnotes to *Theatrum Chemicum*.

Those remarkable notes, which discuss magic in some detail, veer back and forth between the natural and the supernatural, the respectable and the radical. The definition of magic that Ashmole initially proposes is lifted, almost verbatim, from Agrippa's quasi-scientific formulation. "*Magick*," Ashmole writes, "*is the Connexion of natural Agents and Patients, answerable each to other, wrought by a wise Man to the bringing forth of such effects as are wonderfull to those that know not their causes*." Does this mean that magic consists simply of natural effects, or does "wonderfull" imply, as it did for Agrippa, something supernatural? Ashmole does not immediately elucidate. Instead, he turns his back on the darker side of Agrippa, by reassuring "the most *Pious*" that "here is no *Incantations*, no *Words*, no *Circles*, no *Charmes*, no other Fragments of invented *Fopperies*." In short, no demonic magic is to be found in true alchemy, only "*Nature* (with whom true *Magicians* only deale)." The statement does not accord very well with Ashmole's own private practices. In fact, he was addicted to the use of astrological charms, talismans and sigils. He even used them to drive rats and moles from his house.[57] In his 1650 preface to an alchemical tract by Arthur Dee, Ashmole had maintained that charms and spells "have their several powers, if judiciously and warily disposed and handled."[58] Two years later, in *Theatrum Chemicum*, he was more circumspect in addressing the detestation of magic by "the most *Pious*," perhaps because he saw them as holding authority within the Commonwealth.

In the end, however, Ashmole could not confine his investigations to nature. He eventually admits that natural magic, or "the bare application of *Actives* to *Passives*," cannot penetrate "those *Hidden Secrets*, which *God* would have conceal'd." Yet it is precisely those secrets that the alchemist wants to reveal. He aims beyond the sub-celestial or natural region, to approach the celestial and even the super-celestial. According to Ashmole, this allows the "great work" of alchemy to become truly virtuous: "the Production of things is Naturall, but the bringing forth of the vertue is not Naturall: because the things are Create, but the Vertues Increate." What exactly did Ashmole mean here by the unusual adjective "Increate"? Perhaps virtues, because they are of divine origin, can only be brought forth by a magic higher than nature: that is, by something that is *not* created, meaning God. As he approaches the "Increate," the magician or alchemist transcends nature and, "wrought up to his *highest degree of Perfection*, he shall see things not fit to be written; for (may I aver it with awfull Reverence) *Angelicall wisdome* is to be obteyned by it." Ashmole has returned, by a roundabout route, to the forbidden concept of an Angelical Stone that grants divine revelations. Far from being unattainable, it now appears within the grasp of the adept, who has reached the limits of nature. He will stand with Moses, Solomon and Hermes Trismegistus as the possessor of an ultimate supernatural wisdom and power. With a reticence befitting an adept, Ashmole writes no more about it.[59]

The tortured shifts in argument that can be detected in Ashmole's *Theatrum Chemicum* give an appearance of inconsistency. This is understandable: in an age of political and religious upheaval, Ashmole was trying to shape a national heritage out of a body of material that was rife with dangerous invention, not to mention enthusiasm verging on heresy. Craving both divine knowledge and worldly respectability, he wanted to gesture towards the supernatural aims of alchemy while simultaneously associating it with the natural philosophy that had become a fixture of English intellectual life. Extraordinarily, he seems to have succeeded, to the extent that his book enhanced rather than damaged his own reputation among the scholars who dominated public learning after the Restoration. Ashmole's role as a founding Fellow of the Royal Society was sufficient evidence of that. By then, he had given up alchemical publications, and the promised second volume of *Theatrum Chemicum* never appeared, although he told the bookseller William Cooper that he had finished it in the late 1650s.[60] Instead, the canny lawyer devoted himself to antiquarianism, heraldry and the formation of a museum of curiosities at Oxford. To be sure, alchemy and magic were never far from his thoughts, as his vast manuscript collection attests.

Ashmole's publications illustrate the difficulty of dividing late seventeenth-century alchemists into two different camps: "practical chemists" and "mystics" or "magi" who drew on occult philosophy.[61] Ashmole was always fascinated by practical chemical recipes that might lead him towards "the Natural Stone," but at the same time his view of alchemy was unquestionably rooted in the supernatural. He registered little awareness of a tension between magic and experimentalism or natural science. On the other hand, he was acutely sensitive to potential friction between alchemy and the tenets of orthodox religion, which he tried to minimize. As for religious mysticism, it held no attraction for him. He probably identified mystical views, like those of Everard, with the radical sectarianism that had brought down the monarchy. Ashmole may not have been typical, but other alchemists were clearly entranced by the supernatural foundations of their art. Isaac Newton owned a copy of the "Epitome of the Treasure of Health," while Robert Boyle apparently dreamt, like Ashmole, of an Angelical Stone that would allow him to talk with superior beings.[62] Perhaps more tellingly, no practical alchemist saw fit to answer Ashmole's magical notions in print. They circulated widely on account of the fame of *Theatrum Chemicum*, but we may search in vain for an outright refutation of them by any alchemical writer.

Magic did not inspire every alchemist equally. It rarely figures in George Starkey's famous works, most of which were written under the pseudonym "Eirenaeus Philalethes" and published posthumously. To be sure, "Philalethes" expressed himself in the oblique and allusive jargon of alchemy, which could be interpreted as concealing an occult philosophy as well as setting out a way to make gold. He also endorsed the processes of George Ripley, a favourite of Elias Ashmole. Ripley had written of "the Magical *Chalybs*" and the "Magical Solution of *Sol*," terms that do not seem to have bothered "Philalethes" any more than they did Ashmole. In a meditation inspired by his reading of Ripley, "Philalethes" is reassured by a female figure of nature that "what you admire in this strange Metamorphosis of me, know that it is by a Magical Vertue, which is alone given to me from GOD," rather than arrived at by "Diabolic arts."[63] This suggests that divine magic lies at the heart of alchemy, and that "Philalethes" was sensitive, as Ashmole was, to the accusation of diabolism. Still, it would be rash to claim "Philalethes" as an occult writer. During his lifetime, George Starkey was best known for giving practical alchemical advice aimed largely at medical practitioners. Eager to advertise his expertise with a view to finding patronage, he was more interested in challenging the medical establishment than in discussing occult philosophy.[64] The contrast with Ashmole was as much professional as intellectual.

Ashmole himself was hardly an innovative occult thinker. His awkward, derivative and somewhat rudimentary evocation of alchemical magic did not really amount to a coherent philosophy. It provides a stark contrast with the far more original and provocative views of Thomas Vaughan who, in spite of being a priest of the Church of England, did not hesitate to publish the most effusive occult speculations. Unlike Ashmole, Vaughan was fiercely attacked, because he was not guarded enough in what he wrote about religion. He provides a clear example of what Ashmole feared so much: that an imaginative approach to the magical foundations of alchemy would attract vigorous condemnation from the outraged defenders of religious orthodoxy.

Thomas Vaughan, Theomagus

Ashmole identified a higher magic that dealt with divine things, but he did not dwell on its theological implications. He could not have done so without compromising his image of strict Anglican orthodoxy. This was where the most inventive magical writer of the 1650s, "Eugenius Philalethes," added something of his own, which he called "Theomagia" or theological magic. "Eugenius Philalethes" was the pen name of Thomas Vaughan, the Welsh clergyman, royalist soldier, medical practitioner and alchemist. He invented it seven years before George Starkey began to call himself "Eirenaeus Philalethes," so there is no question of who was imitating whom. Any serious collector of alchemical tracts in the 1650s would have eagerly awaited the appearance of Vaughan's publications, starting with *Anthroposophia Theomagica* (probably written in 1648, published in 1650), followed by *Anima Magica Abscondita* and *Magia Adamica* (both also 1650), *Lumen de Lumine* (1651), *Aula Lucis* (written in 1651, published under the pseudonym "S.N." in 1652) and finally *Euphrates* (1655), not to mention his two comical replies to a scurrilous attack on his philosophy by Henry More, *The Man-Mouse Taken in a Trap, and Tortur'd to Death* (1650), and *The Second Wash, or The Moore Scour'd Once More* (1651).[65] Although he had ceased to write before the Restoration, Vaughan's works continued to be both praised and attacked throughout the late seventeenth century.

Vaughan was a virtual one-man alchemical-magical industry in the early 1650s, and it is not surprising that Samuel Hartlib wanted to harness his protean energy. From reading *Magia Adamica*, Hartlib became convinced that Vaughan knew the formula of the "*Menstruum Universale*" or universal medicine. The German polymath had been alerted to the work of "this ingenious young man" by his friend Robert Child. It turned out that Child, Vaughan and another former royalist officer, Thomas Henshaw, had formed, probably at Oxford, an alchemical club modelled on the "College" or "Christian Learned Society" described by the German Rosicrucian writer J.V. Andreæ. It was to his fellow club members, those "truly reborn Brothers of the Rosy Cross," that Vaughan dedicated his first published work.[66]

The little club is of some importance, because it represents the only group of self-styled seventeenth-century English Rosicrucians about which anything is known. Although the Rosicrucian Brotherhood had started out as a high-minded prank dreamed up by Andreæ and some friends, intellectuals throughout Europe took it very seriously, and the joke took on a life of its own.[67] A supposed haven of fraternal tolerance, the mythical Brotherhood represented a kind of collective wish fulfilment for educated minds struggling through troubled times. They pictured the secretive Rosicrucians as possessors of universal or "Pansophic" knowledge, the same lofty intellectual target that Samuel Hartlib's circle aspired to hit. Some enthusiastic Rosicrucian publicists, like the German writer who called himself "Theophilus Schweighardt," happily included magic in their fanciful visions of "Pansophia."[68] Vaughan was clearly a true believer, as he wrote an admiring preface to a 1653 edition of the *Fame and Confession* by "Christian Rosenkreuz," the fictional founder of the Brotherhood. Like most would-be Rosicrucians, however, Vaughan ignored Rosenkreuz's inconvenient dislike of practical alchemy. The Welsh clergyman was also careful to deny his membership in the Brotherhood (a disclaimer that was required of all true Brothers), although he admitted, rather archly, that he knew their "Doctrine."[69]

Vaughan's club lends a touch of credibility to the much-disputed theory concerning Rosicrucian influence on the Royal Society. Thomas Henshaw, the swashbuckling Cavalier to whom Vaughan dedicated *Magia Adamica*, calling him "my best of Friends," became a founding member of the Society. So did Vaughan's protector Sir Robert Moray, who was called by Anthony Wood "a great patron of the Rosie-Crucians." Nevertheless, Vaughan himself was never a Fellow, and none of the other founders can be connected with Rosicrucianism (which was in any case a highly amorphous phenomenon). At most, it can be said that the Royal Society attracted some members, like Henshaw and Moray, who shared a Rosicrucian disposition.[70]

For his part, Thomas Vaughan had no doubt that Rosicrucianism was favourable to magic, a word that appears in the titles of his first three books. He did not define the term in his first treatise, which is the most obscure and rambling of his works, and may have been intended for a select audience. In *Magia Adamica*, however, he starts out with this statement: "That I should professe *Magic* in this Discourse, and Justifie the Professors of it withall, is *Impietie* with Many, but *Religion* with Mee." Ashmole would have been horrified. Vaughan makes magic into a personal religion, in opposition to that of the "Many," meaning the godly Protestants then in control of the state. He continues: "It is a *Conscience* I have learnt from *Authors* greater than my Self, and *Scriptures* greater than both." These "*Scriptures*" are the works of other magical writers like Agrippa, as well as portions of the Bible on which magical interpretations could be placed. Vaughan then comes to the point: "*Magic* is nothing else but the *Wisdom* of the *Creator* revealed and planted in the *Creature*."[71] More succinctly than his master Agrippa, Vaughan sums up here both the natural and the supernatural character of magical knowledge. For him, magic is not based on Aristotelian observation of manifest qualities; rather, it is divine wisdom, relating both to nature itself and to the supernatural purposes of creation. It is "revealed and planted" by God, meaning that science or experimentation can only uncover, by divine grace, the secrets that were once known to Adam and that are hinted at in Scripture.

This definition was more theologically sophisticated than Agrippa's or Ashmole's. Vaughan's magical writings, in fact, are far more concerned with divine things than are theirs, and are generally free of the bits and pieces of popular lore that litter the works of many previous magical writers. We cannot be certain where Vaughan derived his theological conceptions from, but one of his sources may have been the German Lutheran shoemaker and "Theosophist" Jacob Boehme. As will be seen, Boehme's writings were a constant inspiration to occult thinkers for the next 150 years and more. A marginal reference in *Magia Adamica* cites a translation of Boehme that had recently been issued by Vaughan's publisher, Humphrey Blunden.[72] Vaughan also used the Behmenist term "Theosophy" in the preface to *Anthroposophia Theomagica*. There, in a diatribe against accepted views of nature, Vaughan opposes the "*vomit of Aristotle*" to "the Ancient, reall *Theosophie* of the *Hebrewes* and *Egyptians*." The *Oxford English Dictionary* refers to this passage as the first use of "Theosophy" in English. Actually, an English translation of Boehme's "Theosophicall Letter" had been published a year earlier by Giles Calvert, Samuel Hartlib's publisher and the bookseller for whom Thomas Vaughan wrote his preface to the *Fame and Confession*.[73] Vaughan may well have borrowed the word "Theosophie" from Boehme, as he did the notion of a threefold division of creation into elementary, celestial and spiritual principles, and the assumption of an "*Angelicall*, or *rationall spirit*," inherent in man but hidden since the Fall of Adam.[74] Like Boehme, Vaughan saw human beings as perfectible through a process of redemption that is best described as an alchemical quest.

Vaughan, however, was not a strict Behmenist. He did not use "Theosophy" in the same way as the pious shoemaker, who would never have applied it to pagan Egyptians. Vaughan's sense of the term, in fact, is closer to the writings of the magical-alchemical writer Heinrich Khunrath, who was much admired by Samuel Hartlib. Khunrath used "Theosophy" to mean the highest type of sacred knowledge, above "physical" and "hyperphysical" magic.[75] Moreover, although many of Vaughan's scriptural references are the same as Boehme's, the two writers did not always interpret them in the same way. For example, both were fascinated by the account in Genesis 1:1 of how "the Spirit of God moved upon the face of the waters." Both related "the Spirit" or "breath" of God to the Holy Spirit, and interpreted "the waters" as the primitive chaos referred to by Hermes Trismegistus. For Boehme, however, this primal act of creation gave rise to the "divine Wisdom" or "Sophia," a kind of female counterpart to God, who arose from the primitive chaos. Vaughan does not mention Sophia. Instead, he implies that the Spirit moving on the waters is an allegorical foreshadowing of the alchemical separation of the supreme matter from the chaos of the world, an interpretation that may have been derived from Robert Fludd.[76] The difference between Boehme and Vaughan, in fact, is fundamental. Boehme used alchemy, with some misgivings, as a key to Scripture. Vaughan, by contrast, saw Scripture as a key to alchemy.

Vaughan adapted from Agrippa, Khunrath and other German writers an alchemical interpretation of the Kabbala. Its source was not the Kabbala itself, which was inaccessible to almost all Christian readers, but the Kabbalistic researches of the early sixteenth-century humanist Johannes Reuchlin. Vaughan confidently asserted "that the learning of the *Jewes*, I mean their *Cabala*, was *Chimicall*, and ended in true *Physicall performance*." At the same time, Vaughan was careful to acknowledge the mysticism of the Kabbalist writers: that is, their desire to make contact with God. This was summed up for him in the image of Jacob's ladder, "the greatest *Mysterie* in the *Cabala*." Jacob's vision of a ladder ascending to heaven, with angels climbing up and down it, meant that any man, with the help of spirits, might ascend to the divine. Vaughan identified this process with a kind of trance, "the *Death* of the *Kiss*, of which I must not speake one Syllable."[77] His reluctance to write more on the subject was, to some extent, a marketing ploy, meant to suggest that he possessed deeper wisdom than he was willing to impart; but he clearly believed in what he wrote. He was eager to embrace the truth of mystical experience, whether Kabbalist or Behmenist, although the spiritual message of mysticism was never as interesting to him as was its contribution to the "true *Physicall performance*" of alchemy.

The religious unorthodoxy of Vaughan's writings was more obvious to his contemporaries than it is to us today. He was brought up in an Anglican Church that was increasingly polarized between alternative visions of salvation: the Calvinist, based on the utter dependence of a degraded humanity on the freely bestowed grace of God; and the Arminian, by which good works were the necessary signs of grace.[78] Vaughan essentially turned his back on both, in favour of a religion based neither on Scripture nor on good works, but on a theory of nature. In this respect, he resembled some of the religious radicals of the time, like the Digger Gerrard Winstanley or the early Quakers, who perceived salvation as inherent in humanity and therefore available to all. This resemblance explains why his antagonist Henry More labelled "Theomagy" as a form of religious enthusiasm.[79] Unlike other religious radicals, however, Vaughan did not look inwards for redemption; rather, he sought the "seed" of human divinity in the basic structure of the universe.

Vaughan's first published treatise begins by posing the central Christian question of the consequences of the Fall of Man, but it represents the Fall as a matter of physical inheritance that can somehow be remedied by discovering the meaning of nature:

> When I found out this *Trueth*, That *Man in his Originall was a Branch planted in God* and that there was a continual Influxe from the *Stock* to the *Sion* [i.e. Scion], I was much troubl'd at his *Corruptions* . . . But when I was told he had tasted of an other *Tree*, my admiration was quickly off, it being my chiefe care to *reduce* him to his *first Simplicitie*, and separate his *Mixtures* of *Good* and Evill . . . In this Perplexity I studied severall *Arts*, and rambl'd over all those *Inventions* which the folly of man call'd *Sciences*; But these Indeavours sorting not to my *purpose*, I quitted this *Booke-businesse*, and thought it a better course to study *Nature* then *Opinion*.[80]

Thus, Vaughan begins his search for the divine "seed" from which a corrupt humanity and a degraded world have sprung. Out of that "seed" he hopes to regenerate both an "Angelicall" humanity and the Philosopher's Stone. Vaughan borrowed the "seminal" theory from the influential Polish alchemist Michael Sendivogius.[81] By interpreting it as the divine seed in Adam, however, Vaughan opens redemption to everyone, which puts him at odds with the Calvinist restriction of salvation to "the elect." On the other hand, the "seminal" theory does not leave much room for the sacraments and ceremonies of the Church, which would have been crucial for an Arminian. By contrast, the poetry of Vaughan's twin brother, Henry, Hermetically tinged but not fully soaked in the occult, manifests a greater concern about preserving traditional religious practices.[82]

Thomas Vaughan's alchemical theology can be interpreted as a way to escape from the destructive religious debates of his day, which had brought down the Church and the king. Should we also interpret his position as scientific, because it was based on a theory of nature? His philosophical vision was always fixed on alchemical results. He may in fact have felt increasing pressure from his fellow Rosicrucians to come up with specific alchemical recipes to back up his theories. Vaughan's later treatises (especially *Lumen de Lumine*, *Aula Lucis* and *Euphrates*) were much more explicit than his earlier ones in casting light (a frequently used image) on the fiery path to the Philosopher's Stone. While his alchemical concepts were rarely experimental, he clearly practised alchemy as well as theorizing about it. He was sued in 1661 by a man named Edward Bolnest who claimed to have loaned him £250 on the understanding "that he could in three monthes tyme at the furthest gett obtayne or make the Philosophers stone." Vaughan's works are also peppered with curious scientific arguments, such as his rejection of the concept of atoms. The emphasis on the central role of fire in *Euphrates* owes less to Agrippa or the Kabbala than it does to the experimental alchemy of the Flemish chemist J.B. van Helmont.[83]

One reader, to be sure, did not see anything scientific in Vaughan. "The Fundamentals of Science," the Cambridge philosopher Henry More wrote, "should be certain, plain, reall and perspicuous to reason; not muddy and imaginary as all your discourse is." More's formulation of science was taken straight out of the rationalist philosophy of René Descartes. He was evidently scandalized by Vaughan's characterization of the great Frenchman's views as "Whymzies."[84] In a spirited response to More, the "Theomagus" thundered back with renewed hostility to Descartes, in spite of their shared dislike of Aristotelianism. The Frenchman, Vaughan implied, was no better than an atomist or materialist.[85] Not surprisingly, More returned to the fray with a "Second Lash" against "Eugenius Philalethes," in which he upheld Cartesian philosophy as "indeed a fine neat subtill Thing." He scorned Vaughan's ignorance of the sciences, from human biology to astronomy: "Thou art so Magical, thou knowst none of these sober and usefull mysteries of Nature." More went further in asserting that the Bible was not a scientific text ("Scripture speaks according to the outward appearance of things to sense"), the same view that had landed Galileo in trouble with the Papal Inquisition two decades previously. These Cartesian opinions, however, were mitigated by two further, somewhat paradoxical attitudes: first, More's insistent defence of Aristotle as a natural philosopher; second, his underlying Neoplatonism, which revealed itself in frequent citations of Plotinus and Ficino.[86]

The More-Vaughan debate was not a straightforward confrontation between science and magic; rather, as More himself recognized, it was a battle between truth based on conventional philosophies and truth based on personal revelation. More connected the fantastical views of his adversary with the rise of religious sectarianism. He labelled Vaughan a doctrinal "Independent" and lamented that "innumerable swarms of Sects rise in all the world. For Falsehood and Imagination is infinite; but Truth is one."[87] Five years later, eschewing *ad hominem* assaults, More penned a final riposte to the "Theomagus" and issued a general condemnation of "this distemper of *Fantastrie* and *Enthusiasme.*" He meant religious enthusiasm, a source of dread among orthodox Protestants in an era when Fifth Monarchists, Baptists and Quakers seemed to be popping up everywhere. More noted acidly that "it is the enormous strength of imagination . . . that thus peremptorily engages a man to believe a lie."[88]

More was right about the source of his opponents' certainty. Ultimately, Thomas Vaughan's writings are meant to be *revelations* of nature, not scientific or philosophical *observations*. They are obsessive and urgent rather than systematic or contemplative. They assault the reader with a bewildering stream of references and connections, rather than empirical proofs. Vaughan's theories cannot be verified against an objective, outside world, because they encompass the whole universe in a web of inferences. Their logical completeness or self-referentiality is what makes them "true." Gradually, we realize that Vaughan's imagination is operating on the world like the mind of God, giving it structure and meaning. The seed of creation turns out to be the creativity of the author. Vaughan maintains this astonishing intellectual conceit with a furious energy that makes him the most entertaining, as well as the most brilliant, of magical writers of the 1650s.

In spite of Henry More's furious repudiations, Vaughan was a serious philosopher as well as an active alchemist. Along with Ashmole, Robert Turner, George Starkey, William Salmon, George Thor and others, he kept the intellectual discussion of alchemy alive in the late seventeenth century. It was not so much a dialogue as a group conversation, an "Office of Address" to use Samuel Hartlib's term, in which everybody expressed an opinion and the end of the exercise was never reached. For the most part, no matter what their philosophy or method, members of the alchemical community addressed each other without accusations or recriminations, which was unusual in an age of bitter controversy. Some opinions were more inclined to magic than others, but nothing was explicitly ruled out or denied, just as nothing was given the full sanction of authority. Alchemy was not a source of fixed truths, but a dynamic, evolving, inspiring dialogue—not a modern science, with strict rules of verifiability, but not a formless, pre-modern fantasy either. It was an art, whose beauty and usefulness depended on the skill of the artist as much as on the precise combination of materials.

The public face of that art was determined by printers and booksellers as much as by writers. Perhaps the most important alchemical bookseller of the late seventeenth century was William Cooper, who was also a practising alchemist. The main promoter of the works of "Eirenaeus Philalethes," Cooper had a hand in almost every aspect of contemporary alchemy. His publications illustrate how seemingly contradictory approaches—supernatural magic and empirical science—could blend together in the "great work."

William Cooper Reveal'd

If William Cooper is known today for anything, it is for being the first British book auctioneer. A Dutch invention, the public auction can be associated with commercial innovation and an increasing degree of social fluidity. Anyone could attend an auction (Cooper gave away free copies of his catalogues), and anyone with ready cash could bid on an item. Auction sales were not predictable, so they violated assumptions about a fixed social order in which objects conferring prestige were passed down from one genteel owner to the next. Cooper, in short, was an innovator, and he knew where to find an audience. Some of his auctions were held at Jonathan's Coffee-House in Exchange Alley opposite the Royal Exchange in the city of London, a hub of financial capitalism and the favourite haunt of speculators. Of course, the association of auctions with social levelling should not be carried too far. Cooper printed the title pages of his auction catalogues in Latin (even referring to himself as "*Guilelmus Cooper bibliopolam*"), and he hoped that they would "not be unacceptable to Schollers." However unconventional his spelling, he was clearly aiming his sales at an educated public, not at ordinary people. Nevertheless, he remained an enterprising businessman who was not constrained by the usual conventions.[89]

Cooper's independence and boldness stand out in the introduction to *Collectanea Chymica*, a compendium of ten alchemical treatises that he published in 1684. Unlike most publicists of his day, he refused to pay court to a patron or protector, taking it upon himself to defend alchemy from its critics:

> We seek no Mecaenas to flatter with a Dedication, nor crave we any shelter from great Personages, for we know that our Philosophy is the Worlds Contempt, and its Professors their scorn and derision, therefore we neither crave their Pardon nor fear their Frowns, but shall assert this truth only, that Arts have no Enemies but such as are Ignorant thereof, for which reason we fear no Jack-straws Insurrection though levelled against our learning, for true Wisdom is justified of her Children.[90]

In the charged political atmosphere of 1684, when the waning authority of Charles II had barely been re-established after the Exclusion Crisis, the reference to an insurrection by Jack Straws or social revolutionaries would have struck a responsive chord in the minds of many anxious readers. Cooper feared no such instability, because he possessed true wisdom.

He may have obtained it from the alchemical books that he published between 1669 and his death twenty years later. They included several new works by "Eirenaeus Philalethes" (Starkey): *Secrets Reveal'd* (Cooper's first known publication, issued in 1669), *An Exposition upon Sir George Ripley's Epistle to King Edward IV* (two editions appeared in 1677), *Ripley Reviv'd* (issued in 1679 in four parts, including the aforementioned *Epistle*, that were sold either together or separately), and *The Secret of the Immortal Liquor Called Alkahest* (included in Cooper's *Collectanea Chymica*, 1684). Before Starkey's premature death in 1665, only two works had appeared under his Philalethan pseudonym (*The Marrow of Alchemy* in 1654 and a pirated 1655 version of *Ripley's Epistle* that differs from Cooper's), while a third treatise, *Introitus Apertus*, appeared in a Latin version at Amsterdam in 1667. Cooper's editions resuscitated "Philalethes," going so far as to claim that he was still alive. They also pressed the bookseller's rights to the alchemist's inheritance by asserting that the texts were based on original manuscripts, although *Secrets Reveal'd* was probably a translation from Latin. Adepts accepted the authenticity of these claims, and eagerly bought up Cooper's volumes. Isaac Newton, for example, owned and carefully annotated a copy of *Secrets Reveal'd*. It would not be far-fetched to assert that it was Cooper, rather than Starkey, who really established the reputation of "Eirenaeus Philalethes" as the greatest alchemist of the age.[91]

Unfortunately, Cooper was as secretive about himself as Starkey was about his supposed "friend" Philalethes. Cooper was born at Leicester in 1639, served his apprenticeship in London from 1655 to 1663, and was married in 1669 to Mary Cleere, who took over his business after his death in 1689. These few bare facts are almost all that we know about the man. Other details often cited in connection with his life relate to the mysterious "W.C., Esq.," who edited *Secrets Reveal'd* and later wrote a *Philosophicall Epitaph* that was published by Cooper; but in spite of what scholars have long believed, this shadowy individual was not Cooper (who signed himself "W.C.B.," and had no right to call himself "Esquire"), but William Chamberlayne, a minor royalist poet, physician and mayor of Shaftesbury in Dorset.[92] While Cooper undoubtedly relished the confusion created by their initials, he never claimed that he had written or edited any work that appeared under the name "W.C., Esq." It was Chamberlayne, not Cooper, who ran foul of the authorities under the English Republic, and who referred to the year 1652 as "a Living Grave," implying that he had been imprisoned. Likewise, it was Chamberlayne who thanked his friend Elias Ashmole for "the small intermission of my Long troubles, 1662," and who obtained from him a coat of arms.[93]

Cooper also knew Ashmole, and through examining his publications we can reconstruct some of his other personal ties, including a connection with a group of London Presbyterian divines. Prominent among these was Lazarus Seaman, former vice-chancellor of Cambridge, whose library was sold in Cooper's first auction in 1676. The previous year, Cooper had issued a funeral sermon for Seaman, written by the Reverend William Jenkyn.[94] It was the only sermon he ever published. Jenkyn had been involved in a conspiracy against the government of the Commonwealth in 1651, for which he was imprisoned. Two years after the Restoration, Jenkyn was ejected from his London parish because of his Presbyterian opinions, and became a lecturer at Pinners' Hall, where Dissenting ministers were able to preach under the protection of sympathetic City merchants. Jenkyn was arrested again in 1684, in the Tory revenge that followed the Exclusion Crisis, and died in prison. We can conjecture that Cooper's opinions paralleled those of Jenkyn in some respects, perhaps in many. Cooper can also be linked with a third eminent Presbyterian minister, the Reverend Thomas Manton who, like Jenkyn, had been mixed up in the 1651 conspiracy and ended up as a preacher at Pinners' Hall. Cooper sold Manton's book collection after his death.[95]

William Cooper, then, was probably a Presbyterian in religion. We can imagine him as unhappy with the Commonwealth, whose governors could not agree on a religious settlement, and equally disgruntled with the return of bishops and ceremonies after 1660. Yet he gave no obvious sign of being a political radical. The only known political work that he published, an anonymous 1674 "Defence of the Laws," advocated obedience to established powers in Church and State—while acknowledging that many people were grumbling about both. "Lord chase out all Flashiness of opinion," the author prayerfully concluded, "all Growlingness of Humour: And Restore them to their right senses to render *obedience to thy Word, and submission to the Law*: And they must be Happy, even against their Wills."[96] Perhaps we should picture Cooper as striving to be happy and loyal in late Stuart London, even against his will.

Alchemy may have taken his mind off religious controversy, because it rested on a truth that went beyond doctrinal differences. Judging by the material he chose to publish, Cooper believed that the practice of alchemy was spiritual as well as empirical. This was certainly the view of the other "W.C.," Chamberlayne. Introducing a treatise on the Philosopher's Stone by the German physician Friedrich Helvetius, Chamberlayne advised his readers to "magnifie the great Creator, who hath not only given us this pretious Stone for our health and wealth, but withal a most glorious white Stone, clothed in Scarlet, *viz.* his Son Christ Jesus."[97] The analogy between the Stone and the body of Christ was evidently important to Cooper as well. His bookshop was marked by the sign of the pelican, a bird that was said to bleed itself to death in order to feed its young. The pelican was frequently used as a symbol of the Stone, transferring its gold-making tincture or "blood" to its "children," the base metals. According to an even older piece of Christian symbolism, the pelican represented Christ, sacrificing himself for the world.[98]

For Chamberlayne, and presumably for Cooper too, the aim of alchemy was the same as that of Christianity: the regeneration of human life. The

Philosopher's Stone would achieve this on earth as Christ did in the afterlife. The worldly and divine spheres, however, were mixed up with one another. The alchemist's task was to figure out what brought them together, and what could separate them again. The divine power, according to the 1673 *Philosophicall Epitaph*, imparted life to all creation through the *anima mundi* or "Soul of the World." Here Chamberlayne openly espoused an organic vision of the universe, according to which nature was informed by a living spirit, a manifestation of God: "Nature hath, nor had but one onely Agent (Hidden in the Universe) which is *Anima Mundi*, working by its universal Spirit." We might trace this concept of the *anima mundi* back to the Hermetic tracts, Ficino, Robert Fludd or, most recently, Thomas Vaughan—but Chamberlayne was no pedant, and he gave no exalted lineage for an idea that he accepted as a fact of nature. The *anima mundi* expressed itself particularly through mercury, which could be imagined as a person (Mercury or Hermes) endowed with much the same regenerative properties as Jesus Christ himself. Chamberlayne summed up the excellence of mercury in three "Hieroglyphical Scutcheons," to which he appended some cryptic verses about the "second birth":

> No Man's happy before his Death.
> MerCVry's *BIrth's best after's death,*
> MerCVrI's Life *Was pVrg'D by StrIfe.*
> All's in Mervcury that the wise men seek.[99]

Evidently, finding the secrets of mercury was for him analogous to being reborn in Christ.

The *Philosophicall Epitaph*'s religious-alchemical rhetoric builds up to a sublime crescendo in which the adept is transferred into the divine sphere, just as his art reaches its earthly completion:

> And therefore pray affectionately, That God, in and through Christ's spirit, may enliven thee from dead works, and separate light from thy dark body and Chaos of sin, that so being truly baptized into him and his Righteousness, by an Essential and Living Seed of Faith, thou maiest improve thy Talent, and mount through and above the quaternary defiling world into the Triune power, and at last come to the quintessential, or Super celestial Central circle of Peace, and Heavenly Beatitude.[100]

Alchemy, in other words, was not just a process within nature, a thing of the "quaternary defiling world." It would lead the adept beyond the four elements, into the quintessential or fifth matter, and towards a "Heavenly Beatitude" that sounds like some sort of union with the divine. Ficino had famously written about the quintessence as the medium of communication between the *anima mundi* and the elemental world.[101] This spiritual formulation for the "great work" ultimately has little to do with chemical mixtures.

Chamberlayne's words also point towards the magical. While he did not use the term magic in the *Philosophicall Epitaph*, he did not shy away from it when others chose to employ it. Bound with the *Philosophicall Epitaph* was an anonymous treatise named *Jehior or The Day Dawning; or Morning Light of Wisdom*, to which Chamberlayne wrote an enthusiastic preface. *Jehior*'s author was Paul Felgenhauer, a Bohemian Lutheran teacher and physician who penned apocalyptic propaganda for the Protestant side in the Thirty Years' War, but who later became a pacifist.[102] The title is clearly derived from *Aurora*, an unfinished early work by Jacob Boehme, and the argument is loosely based on Boehme's mystical-alchemical Theosophy, with strong doses of Paracelsus added. The universe, according to Felgenhauer, is ordered by triads. There are three basic principles of God, nature and the elements; three *special* principles of spirit, wind and water; and three *particular* principles of body, soul and spirit. Human beings themselves have a threefold existence: worldly, heavenly and divine: "So is an Elementary body, an Angelical and a Divine, very well to be distinguished on man." The potential divinity of human beings can be put to use on earth, since inside man is "a threefold *Magnet* or Loadstone, whereby he can draw to him all *Spirits* in the world, and can do *wonders*." This is the basis of "*Natural Magick*, which cometh out of *Natural Faith*" and operates within the world to alter nature. Natural magic is not caused by the stars, and it is not equivalent to witchcraft; on the contrary, it was studied by Moses and Daniel and the Prophets, and is perfectly godly. Nevertheless, it can be imitated by sorcerers and witches who are inspired by Lucifer.

Higher than natural magic, Felgenhauer asserts, is "a Prophetical and Apostolical Magical art, which cometh out of Gods Spirit in his Children, in which the word with glory dwelleth." It is equivalent to prophecy, and it employs an inward rather than an outward voice. "Prophetical Magick" is mimicked by the Devil in the use by his agents of crystals and magic rings to communicate with spirits. More exalted still is "a higher *Magick* of God's Children, which worketh over and beyond nature, and that through *faith*, as when *Moses* divided the waters with his Rod; and *Joshua* bade the Sun and Moon to stand still." Interestingly enough, sorcerers can also copy this supernatural sort of magic, and "things are really performed by them," although their inspiration is Satanic rather than godly.[103]

It might be assumed that alchemy is confined to the first type, or natural magic, but Felgenhauer continually suggests that it has a higher, supernatural purpose as well. This becomes manifest in the changes that take place in the human body as it ascends to a god-like state. The transition from the elementary to the angelical to the divine body is represented as a chemical process, based on salt, which has its own elementary, angelical and divine forms (the central role of salt was derived from Paracelsus). All sublunary creatures "have a Coelestial body hid within them inwardly" that is "nothing else but a Christalline, yea new born salt of life." Attaining knowledge of this hidden body is itself an alchemical process. Wisdom, like gold, should be passed through the crucible of fire seven times, before receiving a "new birth" through a baptism with water.[104]

Seventeenth-century Anglican clergymen would have shaken their venerable heads at the author of *Jehior*, judging him to be an unorthodox Christian, perhaps even a member of some eccentric sect. After all, the followers of Jacob Boehme in England tended to be mystical enthusiasts, like Samuel Pordage, or radical sectarians, like William Erbery.[105] Felgenhauer's own works had been burned by Lutheran authorities. His assumption of an innate divinity within human beings would have shocked any Calvinist, who saw the body as wholly corrupt and utterly dependent on the grace of God for salvation. Even a Quaker, who believed that an "inner light" could be found within all, might have been nonplussed to discover that the light was nothing more than a type of salt. More disturbing still, the author of *Jehior* suggests that "the Coelestial body" is discovered through humanly attained knowledge, not by divine revelation. Felgenhauer's version of the "new birth" sounds like a supernatural transformation induced by human efforts. In *Jehior*, the whole structure of the Church of England, or of any Church for that matter, has been replaced by the mind of the adept operating on the universe.

William Chamberlayne evidently saw his own views reflected in *Jehior*. Yet there is no evidence that he was anything other than a communicating Anglican. He must have taken the oaths attached to the Test and Corporation Acts, declaring adherence to the Church of England, in order to serve as mayor of Shaftesbury. He might have replied to accusations of unorthodoxy by pointing out that *Jehior* posed no direct challenge to any doctrine of the established Church. It was a meditation on the divine, not a call to separation or sectarianism. Radical in its implications, undemonstrative in its approach, *Jehior* might have been regarded as eccentric, but not as dangerous to the Restoration settlement in Church and State.

Read in conjunction with the *Philosophicall Epitaph*, however, *Jehior* casts William Chamberlayne—and through him, his publisher, William Cooper—as a high-flying, magical alchemist, whose occult views were far removed from the experimental alchemy of George Starkey. The implied opposition between magus and scientist is misleading. As the first editor of the works of "Eirenaeus Philalethes," Chamberlayne was as much an advocate of empirical or experimental methods as were any of his contemporaries. In fact, most of the alchemical works published by William Cooper were step-by-step descriptions of laboratory processes, written by "Philalethes," Sir Kenelm Digby, Van Helmont or the great "Arab" alchemist (in reality, he was probably a medieval monk) who wrote under the name of Geber. All of these men were experimentalists. They have all been associated with the "scientific revolution," and particularly with the corpuscular theory of matter that provided chemistry with a new intellectual foundation in the late seventeenth century.[106]

Cooper seems to have been just as pleased to publicize their writings as he was to affix his name to the mystical effusions of *Jehior*. In the *Catalogue of Chymical Books* that he first published in 1673, Cooper made no distinction between works that we would today call scientific, like Robert Boyle's *Sceptical Chymist*, and those that declared themselves to be magical, like the writings of John Heydon. Van Helmont's works stand alongside those of Elias Ashmole and "Eugenius Philalethes," as if they comprised a single body of knowledge. Cooper added an appendix to the catalogue in 1675, in which he included a few books that "cannot absolutely be called Chymical, but have a very near affinity thereunto, the knowledge of natural Philosophy being an Introduction to supernatural things." Among them we may be surprised to find, not only four translated works by Jacob Boehme, but also the *Ars Notoria* by Robert Turner, and the *Fourth Book of Occult Philosophy* spuriously ascribed to Agrippa. Judging by the diverse entries in his *Catalogue*, Cooper was not abashed by the magical associations of such publications. They were all part of a chemical philosophy that blended supernatural and natural wisdom. The concluding section of the *Catalogue* indexes chemical articles that had appeared in the *Philosophical Transactions of the Royal Society*, the leading scientific periodical of the day. It may be hard for us to understand how anyone can have treated the *Ars Notoria* as seriously as the *Philosophical Transactions*, or read Boyle's tracts on the hidden properties of air as "an Introduction to supernatural things," but this perhaps proves nothing more than the distance at which we stand from the alchemical mindset behind Cooper's *Catalogue*.[107]

Magic and science, empiricism and the supernatural: within alchemy, these were not in opposition, but constantly played off each other, combining and separating through a language both allusive and elusive, never fully merging but never wholly apart. Today we may regard the product of this alchemical marriage as an intellectual monster, an unnatural union of opposites, but Cooper and Chamberlayne obviously found it enchanting and believed it would bring forth the greatest secrets of nature. They were wrong. Cooper's *Catalogue* was the swansong of the alchemical heyday, not the opening for an even grander second act. If it had been updated a century later, very little that was new could have been added to it. Alchemical theory, along with ritual magic and other occult ways of thinking that were flourishing in late seventeenth century, began to fade away after 1688. This does not mean that alchemical practice disappeared—there is plenty of evidence that it did not—but few people wrote about it. Before the 1690s, few signs can be seen that occult philosophy was about to falter. Its chief opponent, however, was already very apparent: not the natural sciences, but religious orthodoxy. Did the accusation of demonic magic finally bring alchemy down?

Before we come to the question of why alchemy failed, we have to consider astrology, which followed a very different orbit. Astrology remained enormously popular in the late seventeenth century, although it was already beginning to lose some of its intellectual bearings. Astrologers governed over a highly commercialized occult science, which they had removed from the restricted sphere of intellectual speculation and allowed to circulate in the open marketplace. The fate of astrology has to be addressed before we can determine why Elias Ashmole, Thomas Vaughan and William Cooper would have no successors in the early eighteenth century.

CHAPTER TWO

The Silver Age of the Astrologers

If the late seventeenth century was the golden age of the alchemists, it was the silver age of the astrologers. Arguably, the intellectual peak of English astrology came earlier, perhaps between 1603, when Sir Christopher Heydon published his influential *Defence of Judiciall Astrologie*, and the 1650s.[1] During the Civil Wars and Interregnum period when predictions and prophecies made a powerful political impact, the careers of numerous famous astrologers reached their height, among them John Booker, Nicholas Culpeper, William Lilly, Richard Saunders, John Tanner, George Wharton and Vincent Wing.[2] Astrological almanacs circulated in impressive numbers—Lilly's *Merlinus Anglicus* reportedly sold thirty thousand copies in 1649. The spread of almanacs made astrologers into household names and obliged them to adopt a more public face. To show the respectability and collegiality of their profession, the astrologers of London organized an annual feast between 1647 and 1658.[3] What better sign that the readers of the stars, no matter how humble their origins (many of them had in fact been skilled artisans before turning to the study of the heavens), formed a learned society, no less distinguished than that of doctors?

The analogy with physicians is not random; at its height, astrology was closely bound up with medicine.[4] In the late sixteenth century, an irregular practitioner of healing like the astrologer Simon Forman could still land himself in trouble with qualified doctors (he was finally licensed to practise by Cambridge University in 1603), but by the early seventeenth century, such medical luminaries as Richard Forster, president of the College of Physicians, or Richard Napier, who specialized in mental disorders, freely consulted the stars in effecting cures.[5] Regularly studied at the English and Scottish universities, astrology was accepted by many educated people as a subject that could be seriously debated, and whose methods could be changed by new information. Joshua Childrey, a clergyman who ended up as archdeacon of

Salisbury after the Restoration, published a brief pamphlet in 1652 that endorsed the Copernican or heliocentric system and condemned the "old Astrology" as "pur-blind."[6] Within little more than a decade, several professional readers of the stars had abandoned the Ptolemaic or geocentric model, and were using heliocentric ephemerides, or tables of planetary movements, such as those calculated by Childrey, Vincent Wing and Thomas Streete. Henry Coley wrote in 1687 that "this *Hypothesis* of *Copernicus*, is now generally approv'd of by all, or most of the most learned *Mathematicians* [i.e. astrologers and astronomers] of all Nations."[7] Nothing better illustrates the intellectual vitality of astrology than this rapid alteration, among many important practitioners, of its most basic principles.

The popularity and acceptability of astrology did not change suddenly in 1660. Every year, thousands of clients were advised and hundreds of thousands of almanacs were sold. Lilly, Booker, Saunders, Tanner, Wharton and Wing lived on into the reign of Charles II, and were succeeded by younger professional astrologers like William Andrews, Henry Coley, John Gadbury, George Parker and John Partridge.[8] Censorship became more rigorous after the Restoration, and the political views of astrologers occasionally landed them in trouble, as in earlier periods, but the abandonment of overt prognostications about the government probably did not make a great difference to the astrological profession, because so many of the younger practitioners were royalists. William Lilly, who was closely associated with the former republican regime, was exceptional in his experience of censorship, imprisonment and repeated legal difficulties. A political lightning rod, he had in fact suffered much the same treatment at the hands of the republican government.[9]

Meanwhile, simple "how-to" books for astrological beginners proliferated, among them the physician Joseph Blagrave's *Introduction to Astrology*, which appeared in 1682, dedicated to his patient Elias Ashmole.[10] Lilly, Coley, Gadbury and Partridge wrote similar treatises on the basic principles of drawing up and reading charts. On the other hand, expensive and erudite studies of astrology were still being published, like John Goad's magnificent *Astro-Meteorologica*, a collection of astrological aphorisms that appeared in 1686. A few months after Goad's death in October 1689, a Latin version of his book appeared under the slightly altered title *Astro-meteorologia Sana*. It included a long preface studded with classical quotations, many of them in Greek, alongside references to the mathematician Isaac Barrow and the chemist Robert Boyle.[11] Even if astrological prophecies, or "*Vulgar Prognosticks*" as Goad called them, had fallen into disrepute for political reasons since the restoration of the monarchy, it remained possible for him to claim that "*Natural* Astrology . . . conduceth to the advance of *Religion*."[12] Of course, there were opponents of the art, including the future astronomer royal John Flamsteed, who fumed in an unpublished manuscript of the early 1670s that "Astrology finds no ground to sustaine it in nature," and complained of its "equal vanity and falsehood." The astrologers had answers for them. "None ever yet condemn'd *Astrology* that thoroughly understood it," counselled John Gadbury, adding that "the Noblest and Most useful *Sciences*, or *Mysteries*, are liable to Fraud and Deceipt . . . and yet in themselves are not the worse or less serviceable to Mankind."[13]

Ultimately, however, not even the learned Goad, the only astrologer for whom Flamsteed had any respect, could wholly mask the religious and intellectual problems that plagued astrology, and were to steer its uncertain future. Was it compatible with Christian theology, particularly with doctrines like the omniscience of God and the responsibility of individual human beings for their own behaviour? Did it have a scientific foundation, or was it just an elaborate form of self-deception? Finally—and this was a question that astrologers tended to ask themselves—was it a purely practical art, without much theory, mystery or magic to it? Did it have anything original to contribute to occult philosophy or was it simply designed to satisfy the "superstitious Vulgar," as Flamsteed claimed?[14] The second section of this chapter will discuss how the community of professional astrologers tackled such questions, and how their responses changed over time. The final sections concentrate on two figures who characterize contrasting approaches to astrology: the ambitious plagiarist John Heydon, self-styled "Astromagus," and the earnest, pious amateur Samuel Jeake of Rye.

Before we deal with astrology as a subject for learned discussion, however, we have to understand it as a thriving and expanding business. The steady commercialization of astrology would have profound consequences for its development as an intellectual discipline—or, perhaps more accurately, for its failure to develop as an intellectual discipline. While it would be misleading to argue that astrology was ruined by financial success, its focus was increasingly fixed on competition between popular astrologers rather than on serious study. Commercialization also contributed to a lessening of astrology's scholarly acceptability and the fraying of its connections with formal learning. As a result, the silver age would not last.

The Business of Astrology

Astrologers made money in two ways: first, as consultants to individuals who wanted to have a particular question answered, a specific problem solved, or the meaning of the present or the future revealed; and second, as the authors of books, pamphlets and almanacs. For most professional astrologers, the profits of the art lay in consultancy. This usually involved "judicial" rather than "natural" astrology: that is, giving answers to precise questions about individuals, rather than foretelling the weather or the general course of events. Judicial astrology in turn was divided into three main branches: genethliacal, horary and electional. The first involved the casting of a geniture or nativity, a birth chart with the client's name and birth date written on a diamond-shaped space in the middle, while the stars and planets that influenced the exact time of birth were inscribed on twelve triangles that surrounded the edges. A nativity could be interpreted in order to explain the present circumstances of the client, to predict what might happen in the future or to diagnose disease. Horary astrology answered specific questions posed by the client through a mapping of the heavens at precisely the moment at which the question was asked. Because the responses depended on vague "spiritual forces," horary queries were particularly suspect to those who identified astrology with black magic or derided it as superstitious nonsense. Electional astrology worked backwards, in a sense, by setting up a propitious hypothetical chart for the initiation of an action, like marriage or travel or a business deal, then determining the time that best fitted such a configuration.[15]

An astrologer might follow up a consultancy by offering to sell the client a medicinal cure, like Nicholas Culpeper's *Aurum Potabile* (edible gold), "a rare Cordiall, and Universall Medicine," which his widow, Alice, after his death in 1654, called "the TRUE LEGACY, which he left me."[16] Culpeper was known for his herbal remedies, but other astrologers associated themselves with the new metallic or iatrochemical medicines. In the late 1680s, Lancelot Coelson marketed his *Elixir Proprietaris* as "the great Antidote of the ancient Philosophers, *Van Helmont, Paracelsus*, and *Crollius*." He sold it for a shilling a bottle.[17] Astrologers also provided their clients with sigils, charms or talismans inscribed with zodiacal and planetary signs. They were supposed to confer good fortune or ward off evil by concentrating the beneficial aura of particular celestial bodies. The trade in sigils, however, was controversial, as it bore the taint of diabolic magic. One of the few published references to the use of a sigil in this period concerns a 1664 case of demonic possession, in which the astrologer Richard Saunders was consulted.[18] No astrologer openly discussed the sale of sigils, although it was undoubtedly a widespread practice. Elias Ashmole cast his own sigils, and by the late 1670s was making them for a friend. William Lilly was impressed that Ashmole, "though a Gentleman and so educated . . . can ingraue, and cast medals or Sigills or any other the like curiositys."[19] Of course, Lilly must have made and sold many of them himself among his astonishingly large crowd of clients.

Lilly owed his considerable fortune to consultations. His voluminous consultancy records for 1644–66, along with those of John Booker for 1656–65, have survived among Ashmole's collection of manuscripts. While Lilly's casebooks are not complete—only horary figures are contained in them—they reveal that he saw more than two thousand clients a year. Unfortunately, Booker's meticulous records of horary figures and nativities were kept in indecipherable shorthand, but Keith Thomas counted about a thousand cases a year, reaching an astonishing total of 16,500 for the whole period. As Lilly apparently charged the average client half a crown, and those of high rank far more, he was making a very good living (at least £500 *per annum*) out of horary consultations alone. Unfortunately, he did not identify his clients in the surviving casebooks of the 1650s and 1660s, so nothing much can be said about their social backgrounds. Booker at least recorded the names of his customers, showing that men and women were about equally represented.[20] The horary questions posed to Lilly usually concerned missing people and things, or decisions that had to be taken by the client. Women tended to ask about future marriage prospects (one who faced a choice between "a black haird man" and "a fair haird man" was told "fair will wynn") or difficulties with their boyfriends. One customer wanted to know whether he would "obtain the Philosophers stones."[21] More typically, Lilly gave advice on medical ailments, marital complaints, sea voyages and various states of mind. Much of what he told his customers was based on common sense and experience rather than any supernatural insight.

Judging by the rapidity with which Lilly dealt with clients, horary astrology was a fast and relatively easy process. By contrast, calculating genitures or nativities often required considerable work, and they were probably the most expensive figures drawn up by astrologers. The nativities of famous people were often used as advertising, in order to demonstrate the effectiveness of the astrologer's art to less exalted clients. Richard Edlyn, for example, drew up genitures for Charles II, his brothers James, duke of York, and Henry, duke of Gloucester, who died shortly after the Restoration. Other famous men whose nativities were calculated by Edlyn included the French scholar and astronomer Nicolas-Claude Fabri de Peiresc ("Peireskius" in Edlyn's spelling), the anti-Trinitarian theologian Faustus Socinus and the Anglican martyr Archbishop Laud. He noted on the nativity of William of Orange (later King William III of Great Britain): "There was born in November 1650 A child who will subvert the Laws of that Countrey; saith Mr Lilly in one off his Almanackes." This was the sort of prediction that might really impress a potential client, as it evidently did the antiquarian William Stukeley, the owner of this manuscript in the eighteenth century. Edlyn was also willing to draw up a nativity for an inanimate object, "His Maj.^{ties} Great ship the Royall Charles 1st [*sic*—in fact, it was the

Charles II] Lansht [i.e. launched] March 1667." The subject of this figure was a replacement for the *Royal Charles*, the enormous vessel that had carried the king to England in 1660 and was captured by the Dutch in the Medway in June 1667.[22] Plotting the ship's geniture must have been designed as a confidence-boosting exercise after the demoralizing loss of its predecessor.

Clients visited astrologers, Keith Thomas suggests, because "they hoped to lessen their own anxiety." Lacking more effective means of resolving issues or addressing problems, they consulted those who claimed to be able to read certainty in the stars. Thomas also points out, however, that astrology provided "a coherent and comprehensive system of thought," as well as "that greater freedom which comes from self-knowledge."[23] These aspects of astrology's appeal were important. Because we do not really know how clients reacted to astrological advice, it is hard to say whether or not their anxiety was substantially lessened by it, but at least they were given solutions and explanations that rested on an impressive body of learning and on a fairly strict methodology. As a way of reading the universe, and of interpreting one's life or situation within that universe, astrology made as much sense to seventeenth-century minds as any other natural system. Of course, its plausibility rested on the internal logic and consistency of its operations. A corpus of learned professionals, trained in seminaries of astrological learning and employed mainly by the elite, might have kept up the coherence of such a system for a long time, as was the case in China or India, but astrologers in England and Scotland received little systematic training in their art, and were motivated as much by commercial as by intellectual factors. They had to cater to a broad audience that wanted to be awed and entertained as well as comforted. To maintain the intellectual plausibility of astrology in such a competitive universe required careful calculation indeed.

By the 1650s, the ruling planet in the astrological universe was the almanac. These little books, full of information both useful and arcane, vastly increased the public profile of astrology, and expanded its commercial possibilities.[24] To be sure, few astrologers made much money from writing them. The main profits from the sale of almanacs went to the Stationers' Company, which since 1603 had possessed a monopoly on printing them. Cyprian Blagden estimated that the normal payment for authors was £2, although the Company records for 1664 show that Vincent Wing was given £7, Richard Saunders £10 and John Booker £12, while William Lilly, quite exceptionally, received £48. Reportedly, by an arrangement of 1658, Lilly was to have £60 if sales of his almanac reached twenty thousand copies. These sums paid to Lilly were equivalent to the income of a skilled labourer. They added up to only a small proportion, however, of the yearly value of almanacs delivered to the Company's treasurer, which averaged around £2,500.[25] Blagden demonstrated that the Company was clearing up to £1,500 per annum in profit from almanacs by the late seventeenth century.[26] The Stationers were aware how important almanacs were to them financially, which explains why they made Obadiah Blagrave, publisher of astrological and occult works, their treasurer in the mid-1680s.

While the financial proceeds to the Company were certainly healthy, they do not express the full impact of almanacs, which involved a large number of printers and publishers. Each year, between twenty and thirty different almanacs were printed as books, others as individual sheets, at London, Cambridge and Oxford. The Stationers jealously guarded their monopoly, and pursued any interlopers who pirated editions. Scotland was beyond the Company's purview, however, and legitimate independent almanacs appeared there throughout the seventeenth century. The simply titled *Almanack, or New Prognostication*, printed by John Forbes at Aberdeen, was selling as many as fifty thousand copies annually in the late 1670s. Not surprisingly, Forbes soon faced competition from the printers of Edinburgh.[27] In 1683, *Edinburgh's True Almanack*, compiled by the mathematician James Paterson, began to appear in the Scottish capital. Within a year, Paterson had to obtain legal protection from the Scottish Privy Council against the making of unlicensed copies of his work.[28]

How many English book almanacs were printed by the Stationers' Company in the late seventeenth century? The quantity was staggering: never fewer than 280,000 copies, and at times more than 400,000. It is important to keep in mind, however, that the number of copies sold did not equal the number of readers. Some people bought multiple almanacs, while a few possessed expensive bound volumes consisting of a dozen almanacs or more. Unlike pamphlets or newspapers, almanacs were designed for a single user, not for being shared by several readers or read aloud to an audience. As a result, the total number of printed copies was certainly greater than the number of purchasers or users. We have no way of knowing the exact ratio of copies to purchasers, but as the vast majority of people probably bought only one almanac, a multiplier of 1.5 might provide a rough estimate. We could guess, therefore, at 190,000 to 300,000 English purchasers of legally printed book almanacs every year (plus an incalculable number of purchasers of pirated, illegal or imported almanacs), which would place these little volumes among the biggest sellers of any books printed in the seventeenth century.[29]

The peak of almanac production came during the Exclusion Crisis of 1679–81, when public anxiety over a possible Catholic overthrow of the government ran high among zealous Protestants, known as Whigs. Their opponents, called Tories, suspected Whigs and Dissenting Protestants of planning to establish a republic. Tories rallied to King Charles and his Catholic brother,

James, and upheld the Church of England against its critics.[30] Henry Coley predicted for 1680 that there would be "great reason to fear a general Dissatisfaction and Uneasiness amongst the People in general; also much Treachery and secret Plotting and Heart-burning one against another."[31] It seems incredible that anybody needed the stars to tell them that, but at least it alerted the public to continuing instability. Coley was staunchly loyal to the king, and might be considered a Tory, along with Saunders, Andrews and several other prominent almanac writers. *Poor Robin's Almanac*, of which 20,000–25,000 copies were printed every year during the Exclusion Crisis, was vehemently abusive towards Protestant Dissenters. In fact, jeering attacks on "Rumpers" and "Saints" constituted its only line of jest. The almanac written by John Gadbury, who was imprisoned for complicity in the alleged Catholic conspiracy known as the "Meal Tub Plot," and twice burned in effigy by Whig demonstrators, also sold briskly during the Crisis, when 18,000–20,000 copies were printed every year.[32]

The Whig side was represented by John Partridge, who made his debut as an almanac writer in 1678, by the old republican John Tanner and by the *Protestant Almanack*. The number of printed copies of Partridge's almanac, which displayed its Whig leanings mainly through a ferocious dislike of "Popery"—"*Rome*, Prepare thy self to entertain showers of Judgements," etc—rose steadily from 4,000 in 1680 to an astonishing 23,000 in 1686.[33] Tanner, who praised the Whigs as "true Patriots to their King and Country," saw the production of his almanac increase from 12,000 to 15,000 copies during the Exclusion Crisis, while the virulently anti-Catholic *Protestant Almanack* peaked at 8,000 copies in 1683, before disappearing in the first year of James II's reign.[34] The Stationers' Company evidently did its best to respond to the shifting demands of a politicized public, although it is worth adding that most almanacs remained neutral during this turbulent period. If they encouraged commercial competition, the Stationers were also sensitive to pressure from the licensers of the press. In 1685, the archbishop of Canterbury compelled the Company to enforce a total ban on political predictions, which lasted throughout the short reign of the Catholic King James II.[35]

From an occult point of view as from a political one, all almanacs were not created equal. It would be a mistake to assume that up to 300,000 people in England (plus perhaps thirty to forty thousand in Scotland) bought them in search of an annual dose of magical discourse. Most were far more mundane in their content. Almanacs of this period generally contained similar features: lists of upcoming eclipses, moveable feasts of the Church of England, country fairs, a tidal table, a table showing the phases of the moon, a table showing the zodiacal houses, a chronology and a calendar. Many also included an illustration showing the dominion of the planets over different parts of the human body.

While medical information, such as the most auspicious times for purging or letting blood, was common, its astrological derivation was rarely a subject for comment. The calendar was usually accompanied by predictions, made from natural astrology and pertaining to the weather or important national events. Well-known astrologers like Lilly, Booker, Coley, Gadbury, Partridge, Saunders and Andrews personalized their almanacs with remarks addressed to the reader, which might contain discussions of astrological principles. The Scottish compilers of almanacs put mathematical problems into their remarks, and serious students of the heavens, like John Wing, provided descriptions of planetary movements. The satirical almanacs, like *Poor Robin* and *Yea and Nay*, were full of jokes and stories. Not surprisingly, the Cambridge almanacs, designed for a rural public, offered advice on husbandry and gardening.

In short, the information provided by the almanacs of the late seventeenth century was overwhelmingly practical. Although much of it had an occult basis, it gave readers little understanding of the meaning and methods of astrology. Only occasionally did the celebrated prognosticators of the period deign to explicate the foundations of their art within the pages of an almanac. When they did, however, their attitudes could be revealing. Set alongside more substantial printed works on astrology, these rare comments in almanacs provide considerable insight into the changing nature of astrology towards the end of the century.

What Made Astrology Occult?

Astrology might be called occult by definition. As Henry Coley's almanac put it in 1679, "the Principles and Notions of this Art are so sublime and difficult to be found out by the most Sagacious Researchers of Humane Understanding, that they seem to require some supernatural Declaration."[36] What could be more occult than the idea that unexplained influences emanating from the stars had a role in determining human destiny? Some astrological writers, however, longed to give a natural explanation of those influences. "Planetary *Aspects*," advised John Goad, "are no *vain Terms* of a Bawbling Art, but are Mysterious *Schematisms* of a secret Force and Power towards the Alteration of the *Sublunar* World, especially the Air."[37] Others had no desire to tarnish their art by an association with occult philosophy, or with any type of theoretical explanation, and instead represented it as purely experiential knowledge, gathered through careful observation. John Partridge opined in his *Prodromus* that "*Astrology*, like *Physick*, is but a Bundle of Experience; which the Industrious Observators have heaped up, as a Portion and Legacy to after Ages."[38] Unlike alchemists, who rarely feuded with one another, astrologers regularly launched into bitter debates over such principles. No clear winner emerged before the 1690s, so inquisitive readers were left with the open question: was astrology supernatural, natural or simply empirical?

Members of the older generation of astrologers would have had no difficulty in answering that question. For them, astrology was magic as Agrippa had defined it: that is, it reached supernatural results through natural means. They were not always eager to say so publicly, however, because it made their profession vulnerable to accusations of diabolism or conjuring. William Lilly's massive instructional guide *Christian Astrology*, which appeared in 1647 and went into a second edition in 1659, claimed to "lay down the whole naturall grounds of the Art, in a fit Method that thereby I may undeceive those, who misled by some Pedling Divines . . . conceived Astrology to be based upon Diabolical Principles: a most scandalous untruth."[39] Yet Lilly had nothing further to say about the "naturall grounds of the Art" in the 650 pages of his book. His pupil and successor Henry Coley called astrology "a part or member of Natural Philosophy, which teacheth by the Motions, Configurations, and Influences of the Signes, Stars, and Coelestial Planets, to Prognosticate, or Predict of the Natural effects and Mutations to come in the Elements, and these inferiour Elementary Bodies."[40] This sounded very empirical, although the causal link between heavenly signs and their worldly consequences remained wholly mysterious.

That the connection between the stars and elementary bodies might be magical rather than physical was made more explicit in Lilly's memoirs, written at the request of Elias Ashmole and not published until 1715. Lilly returned again and again to the theme of magic, and especially to communication with spirits. As a servant in the early 1630s, he had become fascinated by the astrological sigils kept in a bag by his master's wife, including one that had been cast by Simon Forman. He later learned astrology from one Evans, "an excellent wise Man, and studied the Black Art," meaning ritual magic. In a revealing passage, Lilly admits that Evans "had some Arts above, and beyond Astrology, for he was well versed in the Nature of Spirits, and had many times used the circular Way of Invocating"—that is, invoking spirits by standing in a circle. Lilly himself later used a copy of the *Ars Notoria* to perform ritual magic, "but of this no more." He also recalled invoking angels in the early 1630s in the company of Dr Richard Napier. In 1654, however, he was charged at the Middlesex sessions court with using diabolic magic in giving a judgment on a theft, and testified "that I never had or ever did, use any Charms, Sorceries, or Inchantments."[41] We may doubt the veracity of this statement. For his own part, Lilly passed no further comment upon it.

That court case may have made Lilly more cautious about revealing publicly his interest in magic, but it did not make him more reticent in relaying such matters to his friend Ashmole. The last part of his memoirs presents a gallery of ritual magicians and seers, with anecdotes about their lives: John a Windsor, a scrivener known to have invoked spirits; the celebrated John Dee and his sidekick, Edward Kelly; Sarah Skelhorn, "Speculatrix" to a physician in Gray's Inn Lane, who "had a perfect Sight, and indeed the best Eyes for that purpose I ever yet did see," and who claimed to be followed by angels, "until she was weary of them"; Ellen Evans, daughter of Lilly's tutor; one Gladwell of Suffolk, "who formerly had Sight and Conference with Uriel and Raphael, but lost them both by Carelessness"; and Gilbert Wakering, who bequeathed to Lilly his beryl or crystal, the size of an orange and inscribed with the names of angels.[42] The presence of two women among these crystal-gazers is interesting, as so few women are known to have become astrologers in the late seventeenth century.[43] Lilly's confessions must have delighted Ashmole, and perhaps he was catering somewhat to his friend's fixations. Still, the old astrologer seems genuinely to have regarded conversations with angels as a "higher" form of supernatural prognostication, similar to reading the stars, although more direct and effective, because it did not involve complicated calculations or the possibility of human error. In 1680, Lilly even wrote an astrological history of the world, presumably for Ashmole, that fixed the name of an angel to each chronological epoch.[44]

The comparison of the stars with angels was not unique to Lilly, of course. Agrippa argued that angels and stars performed the same duties for God, and that each planet and zodiacal sign had an angel attached to it:

> Now whatsoever God doth by Angels, as by ministers, the same doth he by heavens, Stars, but as it were by instruments, that after this manner all things might work together to serve him, that as every part of Heaven, and every Star doth discern every corner or place of the Earth, and time, species and Individuall: so it is fit that the Angelical vertue of that part and Star should be applyed to them, *viz.* place, time, and species.[45]

Similarly, Robert Fludd had argued that "the Angels give life and vigour, first unto the stars, then unto the winds," which in turn affect the earth.[46] The celebrated physician and essayist Sir Thomas Browne wrote in his *Religio Medici* (1643) that "many mysteries ascribed to our owne inventions, have beene the courteous revelations of Spirites," especially "prodigies and ominous prognosticks."[47] Ultimately, such notions may have derived from the Neoplatonic *anima mundi* or Soul of the World, which breathed spirit into all animate and inanimate things.

Whether their source was Agrippa, Fludd, Marsilius Ficino or popular tradition, English astrologers were clearly familiar with the idea that angels guided the stars. According to George Wharton, the world was "Living, Animate, Intellectual . . . Where we term it *Intellectual*, we mean the *Angelical Intellects*, which are properly *Perfect* and *Indivisible* (according to Place,) in their Government of the *Spheres*." The expression of Intellect was the Soul of the World, which acted through Spirit on the "*Astral Soul*" of Man, which was "infused from the *Heavens* and *Stars*, at the time of Generation."[48] On a less exalted plane, John Booker, writing a dedication to Elias Ashmole in the final almanac he ever produced, which happened to appear in the aftermath of the Great Fire of London, considered "the late notable Coelestial Phenomenons, which it hath pleased God to shew us . . . as Messengers, and Ambassadors to inform us of his divine will of Judgment or Mercy."[49] Nobody would have had to explain to Ashmole that the biblical messengers of God were angels. Any astrologer who had made sigils would have understood the reference. The manufacture of these mysterious talismans involved an invocation of the names of angels as well as "suffumigation;" both practices derived from ritual magic.[50]

If astrology was understood as a type of angelic magic, then it should have been useful in undoing demonic magic. Indeed, for older astrologers, the occult foundations of their art were nowhere better revealed than through its ability to expose witchcraft. Lilly, for example, argued in *Christian Astrology* that horary charts could reveal a bewitchment, and he further proposed "Naturall *Remedies* for WITCH-CRAFT" that could be used to cure the victim.[51] A considerable portion of Joseph Blagrave's *Astrological Practice of Physick*, first published in 1671, with further editions in 1672 and 1689, was devoted to the discovery and cure of diseases caused by witchcraft or sorcery. An admirer of Agrippa and friend of Ashmole, Blagrave asserted of astrology that God "hath given so much knowledge thereby (next unto the Angels) that he is able to reveale and make known in a great measure his Heavenly Will thereby unto his People."[52] He proposed a particular astrological method for determining the possibility of witchcraft. From observing patients who were bewitched or demonically possessed, Blagrave had discovered that "at the time of any strong fit, or when they are more than usually tormented, that then the ascendant together with its Lord doth exactly personate the sick; and at that very time, the Lord of the twelfth house doth one way or other afflict, either the ascendant, or its Lord."[53] In other words, victims of witchcraft were afflicted through the malign influence of a planet, and the remedy was usually a herb or plant sympathetic to that planet. Blagrave was convinced that "Witchcraft or Sorcery can no way be discovered, nor yet cured, but by the way of *Astrology*, except a Miracle be wrought."[54]

In Blagrave's imagination, witchcraft amounted to the inversion of astrology, a perversion of his own art. Its malevolent power was derived from the stars, just like the benign power of astrological healing. If this was a widespread conception, it might help to explain the appeal of astrology, which linked learned and popular culture in a way that alchemy was never able to imitate. In educated minds, astrology drew on the power of angelic magic; in the minds of the less educated, it stood for the opposite of the demonic magic that was thought to hide in every corner. The most widely read astrological almanacs, like John Booker's, were quick to associate misfortune with witchcraft and sorcery, suggesting that only astrology could discover such wickedness. "[I]t is to be feared," wrote Booker in 1664, "much Sorcery and Witchcraft may be used, and many Venifices [*sic*] practiced, that I trust in God they may be discovered in due time, and have their reward."[55] This was a subtle form of self-advertisement. A reader troubled by suspected witchcraft knew exactly whom to consult in order to discover it.

By the time Booker was writing, however, an alternative approach to the supernatural basis of astrology was already being championed by the young reformer John Gadbury. Better educated than most astrologers of the older generation, he had nonetheless enjoyed their support in rising to the heights of astrological fame. Gadbury was a protégé of George Wharton, and edited the works of that venerable figure, whose royalist politics he shared. It was Gadbury who first published Wharton's Neoplatonist treatise on the Spirit of the World, and he praised the writings of his mentor, including his tracts on chiromancy or palm reading, as "little less than a compleat *Encyclopedia*, or Summary of all Sciences."[56] Gadbury became celebrated as a foe to "conjuring" and a bitter critic of other astrologers, whose slipshod methods he deplored. Rightly or wrongly, he excoriated most of his competitors, including William Lilly, as religious Dissenters. Although he was accused of flirting with esoteric religious groups himself during the Civil War and Interregnum period, after 1660 Gadbury loudly declared his devotion to the Church of England and his undying hostility to religious sectarians, whom he now associated with fanaticism and fraud. "Dreams, Whimsies, Enthusiastical Nonsense and Blasphemies, under pretence of Divine Inspiration, will no longer befool this (of late twenty years) cheated Kingdome," he wrote in 1663, adding: "The Imposture is discovered."[57] In an age of restored monarchy and religious uniformity, astrology should abandon the occult "fooleries" of Lilly and embrace a rational method.

The impostures denounced by Gadbury in his almanac included many cases of bewitchment and possession, which he judged without exception to be phony or due to natural causes. In 1679, he went into great detail concerning a woman in London who claimed to be tormented by evil spirits, including that of her late husband, which had supposedly impregnated her. By reading her nativity, Gadbury judged her to be "flagitiously hypocritical." The story prefaced a diatribe against those astrologers "who, (with great impudence, and greater fraud) have pretended to discover and cure witchcraft by the Stars ... Astrology teacheth no such thing. The influences of the Stars are purely natural, and directed by natural Beams, or Aspects Geometrical: and do incline, but compel or constrain none. Therefore can they neither cause, nor cure witchcraft."[58] While he did not deny that witchcraft was possible, as was evident in Scripture, Gadbury apparently never met a witch or bewitched person whom he did not believe was mad, deluded or faking their symptoms. Of course, he reached these conclusions by charting their nativities. Apparently, astrology could still reveal that someone was *not* a witch. It could also precisely diagnose diseases. Gadbury did not doubt that the "true Astrological Physician ... can justly distinguish of these differences [in diseases] by consulting the proper Significators of the Nerves, and Humors peccant, in the Decumbiture, Crisis, or Garniture of the Patient concern'd; and by considering their Position in Aiery, Watery, Erthy or Fiery Signs or Constellations."[59]

While he certainly wanted to disentangle astrology from its relationship with witchcraft, Gadbury was not in general a debunker of occult thinking. In fact, he was drawn towards those who sought to construct occult philosophies, like his friend Sir George Wharton. As will be seen, he endorsed the writings of the "Astromagus" John Heydon in the 1660s. As late as 1684, he recalled the pamphlet war between the "Theomagus" Thomas Vaughan and Henry More, noting that "Eugenius Philalethes [Vaughan] was treated in an exceeding base and scurrilous Manner by Dr. M. And therefore his severe censure of the Dr. was justly merited, as not only injuring him, but the Truth itself."[60] Gadbury's aim was thus not to reject the occult basis of astrology, but to separate it from "vulgar" or "superstitious" elements like ritual magic or witchcraft, which he represented as offshoots of religious enthusiasm. The problem with this high-minded approach was that it cut astrology off from one of its sustaining roots—popular belief in the everyday presence of angelic or demonic forces. For all his lofty Neoplatonic or humanist rhetoric, Agrippa had not hesitated to draw on popular belief; nor had Wharton or Ashmole or Vaughan. Gadbury was blazing a new trail for English astrology, but he was not enough of a sustained thinker to mark it out in a philosophical sense. Moreover, as a working astrologer of humble background, he lacked the authority necessary to impress the educated public.

John Goad was admirably equipped to make up for those failings. A fellow of St John's College, Oxford, and headmaster of Merchant Taylors' School in London, Goad was not a professional astrologer, and he never edited an almanac. Widely read and thoughtful, he deplored equally "the unlucky Principle of *Mechanism* among the Learned, and of *Nature* (in the Brutish

Notion) amongst the Vulgar."[61] He recognized Cartesian rationalism as the chief enemy of natural philosophy, and argued instead in favour of a celestial causality that united spirit and matter. Its agent was light, the subject of a recent, bitter dispute within the Royal Society between Robert Hooke and Isaac Newton. Goad agreed with Newton in supposing that light was a body, rather than a "pulse" or motion propagated by a body. In a test of Newton's theory, Robert Moray had observed light from the planet Venus, and had published his findings in the Royal Society's *Philosophical Transactions* for 1672.[62] Goad must have known of this experiment, carried out by another prominent exponent of occult philosophy. Goad's own theory was derived from the Neoplatonic assumption that light transmitted spirit. He noted that if anything "may be entitled to what Philosophers call the *Spirit* of the *World*, This is it, the smallest and most active *Body* in the World; in *Motion* confest to be *Instantaneous*, in subtlety incredible, and absolutely incomprehensible."[63] The energy of heavenly light, according to Goad, acted on the earthly air in order to produce changes in the weather, to cause diseases and to influence human behaviour.

Goad was well versed in every aspect of seventeenth-century natural philosophy. A traditionalist, he rejected the heliocentrism of Galileo and Johannes Kepler, in favour of Tycho Brahe's concept of the planets circling the sun, which in turn circled the earth. He answered Pierre Gassendi's objections to astrology—"*If it rain to day, it doth not rain again the same day 12 Month*"—by pointing out that the planetary aspects did not follow a yearly cycle. He was familiar with the debate between Robert Boyle and Thomas Hobbes concerning the elasticity of air, although he referred to it in a peculiar way. He denied Hobbes's contention that frost was due to wind, "of which he is excellently admonished by the Noble Mr. Boyle," and ascribed it to planetary aspects instead. This led him into a rather twisted argument about whether planetary light, which presumably conveyed warmth, could in fact be "a Friend to Cold," although the "Faculty" of cold was not contained in it. From there, Goad proceeded to consider the phenomenon of armies in the air, portents of war that had often been perceived in the troubled 1640s. In opposition to Descartes, who had attributed them to superstition, Goad defended their existence. "A Supe[r]natural Power cloathed in Nature," he wrote, "may be Legible, as Visible."[64]

Goad's insistence on the legibility of the supernatural led him to admit that "there may be something in *Cabala, Gematry*, something in the mysterious Force of *Numbers*, in *Critical* Days, *Climacteric* Years, The Doctrine of *Magnetisms, Sympathies*, and *Natural* Magic, *Transmutations* of Metals, Doctrine of *Moles* in the Body, Doctrine of *Signatures* of *Planets, Dreams, Chiromancy, Genethliacal* Skill," etc. However, he was adamant in rejecting anything that smacked of hidden qualities or might be associated with demonic powers. "Let not the Reader think in the least we will add *Geomancy, Steganography* [hidden messages], *occult Philosophy*, or any thing whose grounds hide from Mortal search, or have a Sulphurous flavour of the *unclean Spirit*."[65] His inclusion of occult philosophy in this list was an obvious swipe at Agrippa. Unlike Blagrave or Lilly, Goad did not believe that the language of the stars conveyed angelic authority. The power of astrology lay in its proper interpretation, not in its magical potential. By suggesting that the supernatural was, like nature, a book to be read correctly, Goad was surprisingly modern in his sensibilities. Applied rigorously, however, his principles would rule out horary astrology, or asking direct questions of the stars—the bread-and-butter of professional astrologers. Would the latter accept the views of a man who sought to deprive them of their most lucrative source of business?

In the event, Goad's views never had much chance to make an impact. They were fatally undermined by his religion. Goad was dismissed in 1685 as headmaster of Merchant Taylors' School on a charge of having converted to "Popery." It was not a false accusation: he publicly announced his adherence to Roman Catholicism in the year that *Astro-Meteorologica* appeared. Goad prefaced the book with a fulsome dedication to King James II (not surprisingly, it was missing from the 1689 Latin version). Isaac Newton, who was engaged in a furious campaign to prevent Catholics from receiving appointments at Cambridge, would certainly not have appreciated Goad's endorsement of his theory of light, no matter what the great scientist may have thought of astrology. After the Glorious Revolution, which he did not long survive, Goad's scholarship faded into obscurity.

The attempt by Gadbury and Goad to separate astrology from popular and demonic magic, while retaining its supernatural foundations, may have foundered for political and religious reasons, but it was not the only reformist initiative undertaken by the astrological writers of late seventeenth-century England. Josiah Childrey, the Anglican cleric, inventor of improved telescopes and defender of heliocentrism, advocated astrology as a purely empirical study, carried out in accordance with Francis Bacon's methods of scientific inquiry. "The stars have an influence on us, and some small matter touching this influence Astrology knows," Childrey argued, "yet no more, and of no more use, than to assure her that she doth know something of it. But her vanity is, she promiseth more than she is able to perform: and is led much more by fancy & plausibilities, than sound reason."[66] He urged astrologers to compile charts of the stars and compare them to historical events in order to demonstrate the correspondences that would establish their art as a science in the Baconian sense.

No prominent astrologer strictly followed Childrey's advice until the emergence of John Partridge in the late 1670s. Where Childrey was a royalist who had studied at Oxford, Partridge was an outspoken Whig who had trained as a cobbler. Although John Gadbury would become his mortal enemy during the Exclusion Crisis, in 1679 the two men were close enough for Gadbury to contribute a preface to one of Partridge's books. The dedication was to the royalist astrologer—and Gadbury's mentor—Sir George Wharton. Already, however, Partridge was insistent that astrology was a science, resting on strict rules and not on the influence of any occult forces. "ASTROLOGY is a singular, innocent Science," he explained, "Teaching how to judge of all future Events, by the Motion of the Stars only, and not by the help of any kind of Prophetical or Diabolical Inspiration, as some think."[67] In this as in all of his subsequent writings, Partridge provided no explanation whatsoever of why the motion of the stars foretold future events. He was not interested in such questions, which might have led to supernatural conclusions. In this regard, Partridge was a paragon of Baconian science, the astrologer of whom Childrey had dreamed; but he remained a stubborn traditionalist in his methods, sticking to the pre-Copernican universe. Although he was forced into exile during the reign of James II, Partridge was to return after 1688, full of resentment at his enemies. In the subsequent decade, he became the most influential astrologer in the kingdom. The scientific supernaturalism of John Goad's astrology would give way to a severe astrological rationalism that forsook any attempt at theory.

The Astromagus: John Heydon of Hermupolis

If the tendency in astrology after 1660 was to minimize the role of the occult and to pursue instead the scientific and the empirical, we nonetheless have to take into account one great exception: John Heydon, the so-called "Astromagus." In the late 1650s and 1660s, he published a series of hefty tomes that expounded a unique cosmology based on a hodgepodge of alchemy, astrology and magic. His works made a remarkable impact for about a decade, only to become virtually irrelevant in the early 1670s. Heydon exemplifies the occult road that astrology failed to travel in the late seventeenth century, but that was to emerge again in the late eighteenth century in the works of Ebenezer Sibly.

It is often difficult to determine when a writer of the past should be called a charlatan or a con man. In the case of John Heydon, no evidence exists to suggest that he did not believe what he wrote, although his vaunted world-system was based as much on blatant imitation as on inventive fantasies. He had his critics: Elias Ashmole called him "an Ignoramus and a Cheate," while an anonymous adversary dubbed him a "Powder-Monkey, Roguy-Crucian,

Pimp-master-general, Universal Mountebank."[68] What we can deduce with some certainty is that he was a plagiarist and highly inconsistent in his opinions. He wrote less from personal conviction than from a desire to make a name for himself through grandiose assertions and copying the labours of others. Yet amid the intellectual ferment of the 1660s, his strategy worked. Heydon gained a following, which reached into the highest circles of Charles II's court.

He seems to have come from a distinguished gentry family, although his followers made outrageous claims that he was descended from an improbable Roman, Caesar Heydon, and from a nonexistent king of Hungary. If we can believe the less exalted genealogical information found in his works, then he was the grandson of Sir Christopher Heydon, a noted gentleman astrologer of the early seventeenth century, and the son of a lieutenant-general of the ordnance to Charles I. It is unlikely that he commanded troops in the Civil War (he was too young), or that he travelled to Egypt and Persia, as one admirer maintained. He began writing in the mid-1650s, just as he was settling down to the mundane life of an attorney at Clifford's Inn. Like other ambitious young men, he picked up astrology as a lucrative hobby, and married the widow of a leading practitioner of the art, Nicholas Culpeper. From the first, he used the stars unwisely, by meddling in politics. As early as 1658, he announced in print that only a Rosicrucian (presumably like himself) could have predicted Charles I's death, adding ominously, "and now others, are so written."[69] His willingness to forecast the deaths of rulers landed Heydon in prison on two occasions, once under the Protectorate and again under Charles II. The second forecast was made in 1667 for the duke of Buckingham, one of the most conniving politicians at the Restoration court and Heydon's chief patron. Samuel Pepys was informed that Buckingham "hath been endeavouring to have the King's nativity calculated, which was done, and the fellow now in the Tower about it—which itself hath heretofore . . . been held treason, and people died for it."[70] Heydon was not put to death; instead, he found time between bouts of confinement to write bulky tomes on "Rosie-Crucian Physick," alchemical philosophy, magic, numerology and cosmology.[71]

Heydon's name first appeared in print in 1655, as the author of a long, dull visionary poem dedicated to Henry Cromwell, the Protector's younger son.[72] Soon after, he jumped on the Rosicrucian bandwagon. Although he maintained that he was not a member of the Brotherhood (as any true Brother would have been obliged to do), he nonetheless seemed to have access to all of their supposed secrets, in particular their medical remedies. He defined a Rosicrucian as "a partaker of Divine things, and a companion of the holy company of unbodied souls and immortal Angels." Heydon apparently knew two of them, residents of the West Country, Mr Walfoord and Mr T. Williams, both of whom had miraculous powers: "they walk in the Air; they frustrate the Malicious aspect of Witches; they cure all diseases." The second characteristic was important, because a Rosicrucian might otherwise be taken for a witch. The resemblance between Heydon's exalted Brothers of the Rosy Cross and the *benandanti* of Friuli, supernatural witch-fighters who have been investigated by Carlo Ginzburg, is striking, but it is doubtless due to a common store of western European magical lore rather than to any familiarity on Heydon's part with Venetian Inquisitorial records.[73] In any case, Heydon was not overly knowledgeable about the literature of Rosicrucianism. Nevertheless, he billed himself as the only reliable source on the subject, dismissing Thomas Vaughan, who had translated Christian Rosenkreuz's *Testament*, as "swift and rash."[74]

Writers who offer to reveal secrets to the public, but are not able to deliver on the promise, must either then further raise the stakes of the game or risk losing their audience. After the Restoration, Heydon chose the first option. He dedicated a book on Rosicrucian "Axiomata" to James, duke of York, and filled it with geomantic figures, used for summoning angels. This ceremonial activity, usually derived from the *Little Key of Solomon*, had excited aficionados of the occult from John Dee to Elias Ashmole, and was particularly fascinating to an older generation of astrologers, who saw it as an exalted manifestation of their art. According to Heydon, in order to master the "Naturall Magic, in which we believe King *Solomon* excelled," one simply had to cast a *telesme* or sigil engraved with the angel's name and assorted numerological information, and the angel would appear "like a man sitting on a chair, holding a balance in his hand." It was as simple as that. "Angels may be as frequently converst with as Devills by the direction and help of the Figure before," the Astromagus cheerfully announced.[75]

Heydon followed up this exercise with a series of volumes that drew on alchemy, astrology, numerology and ritual magic to compose a complex cosmology. These had grand titles, often including Greek words: *The Harmony of the World* (1662); *The Holy Guide, Leading the Way to Unite Art and Nature* (1662); *Theomagia, or The Temple of Wisdom* (1663); a second edition of *The Wise-Man's Crown*, including new materials (three volumes, 1664–5); and *Elhavareuna or The English Physitians Tutor* (1665). As if all this were not enough, he wrote a staunchly monarchist treatise on government, entitled *The Idea of the Law Charactered from Moses to King Charles*, which he published in the year of the Restoration, as well as a Rosicrucian argument in favour of Christianity, *Psontonphancia* (1664). His works had a number of different publishers, which suggests that he was an author much in demand. Judging by the dedications and endorsements that he proudly attached to his writings, he also had influential friends. These included Prince Rupert, the duke of

Ormonde and the earl of Oxford, not to mention a host of alchemical and occult writers, from George Starkey to Robert Turner.[76] We may wonder whether all of these encomia were genuine, or all of the dedications well received, but Heydon was certainly known to Ormonde and Buckingham, and for a few years in the early 1660s, he was a darling of the reading public.

Heydon's works are mostly compilations of occult knowledge, bits and pieces that do not add up to much of a system, except in his own vibrant imagination. Unlike Thomas Vaughan, he was content to repeat the ideas of others (sometimes in their own words), rather than to reimagine the universe himself. He remained obsessed with the Rosicrucians, who took on increasingly bizarre features in his writings. In *Theomagia*, he describes how "the *Rosie Crucian* Priests shave their heads, and wear no hair upon them . . . they not only refuse to eat most part of pulse, and of flesh meats, Mutton and Pork, for that sheep and swine breed much excrement, but also upon their daies of sanctification and expiatory solemnities, they will not allow any Salt to be eaten with their viands." Heydon was here evoking the image of an Egyptian priesthood dedicated to the myth of the sister and brother "Beata" (Nature) and "Eugenius," who resemble Isis and Osiris.[77] Such passages might seem like pure fancy, but decades later they would be paralleled in the lore of Freemasonry. The conviction that occult secrets ultimately originated with the mysterious Egyptians was hardly original, of course, but Heydon's elaborations may have been picked up by later promoters of secret societies.

In most respects, Heydon was a traditionalist who sought to defend occult practices and concepts that were commonly held, especially by astrologers. For example, he was determined to vindicate the use of magical figures, sigils and *telesmes*. He argued—without offering any evidence—that they originated in the figures of cherubim and seraphim that were employed by the ancient magi of Persia.[78] The Rosicucrians, naturally enough, employed "Telesmaticall Images" for all their magical purposes: "by them the dead are raised to life, by them they alter [,] change and amend bodies, cure the deseased prolong Life . . . by these Arts they know all things and resolve all manner of questions present or to come."[79] As for alchemy, Heydon provided much heat and little light. Although he constantly hinted that the Rosicrucians had knowledge of the Philosopher's Stone, because they had access to universal medicines, he gave no indication of how they had arrived at it, which probably reflected his own ignorance of alchemical practice. He even condemned "the ungodly and accursed Gold-making, which has gotten so much the upper hand."[80] In fact, Heydon could barely raise the subject of alchemy without falling back on sigils or figures.

Like Lilly and other astrologers, Heydon believed that the planets were guided by angels, but he was willing to admit the point openly, and he suggested that angelic influences could be controlled by human beings. Thus, astrology and ritual magic might be combined. Heydon gave these angelic influences the remarkable name of "Genii," which he must have derived from occult literature, possibly Agrippa. To know the name of the Genius that presided over one's own destiny was to gain great power. This required drawing up a nativity and projecting a larger figure from it, based on the shape of a pentacle. As Heydon explained, somewhat obscurely, "to find the name of my *Genius*, I look in the places of the fire *Hylegiaus*, and making projection always from the beginning of *Aries*, & the Letters being found out, and being joined together according to the degree ascending, make the name of my genius *Malhitiriel*, who *had upon Earth familiarity with Elias*."[81] The human body also had Genii—not just one, but three of them, whose names could be discovered through a combination of astrology, geomancy and "Cabala" that was unique to Heydon.

Although he shared and voiced many of their own preoccupations, other astrologers were as hostile to the "Astromagus" as he was to them. Elias Ashmole was infuriated when Heydon published a poorly edited version of an alchemical poem, *The Way to Bliss*, that Ashmole himself was preparing for print.[82] In turn, Heydon attacked Ashmole's friend William Lilly as "*a Labouror or Ditchers Son, by education a Taylor*" and "*a Lying Sycophanticall Knave*."[83] Churlishly, he lumped his wife's late husband, Nicholas Culpeper, in with Thomas Vaughan and "other *Pretenders*" who were "*too young and childish*" to penetrate Rosicrucian mysteries.[84] Heydon turned against John Gadbury in 1664, writing of him to William Lilly, whose good opinion he sought to gain, as "[t]he scorpean that studies Mischiefe."[85] He also cited a grandiose list of writers and thinkers who "will testifie for me," including Moses, Enoch, Hermes Trismegistus, Francis Bacon, Robert Fludd (whose theory of the relationship of planets to music he pilfered), Marsilius Ficino, Henry More, René Descartes and Thomas Hobbes. It would be hard to imagine a writer who was further removed intellectually from the last three than Heydon.[86] He presented no evidence of having read any of them. How familiar he was with Paracelsus is unclear, but he did not hesitate to lampoon the German doctor's "new, odd, cross, and unheard names," or to condemn his iatrochemical remedies. He actually accused the medical writer George Thomson, a friend of the alchemist George Starkey, of plagiarizing him in a pamphlet that recommended chemical medicines to counter the 1665 London plague. The charge was patently false, but in defending Galenic medicine and the anti-Paracelsian position of the Royal College of Physicians, Heydon revealed himself to be a medical as well as an astrological traditionalist.[87]

The novelty of the "Heydonian Philosophy" consisted in its revelation of secrets about which other astrologers were guarded or silent. He continually hinted that further Rosicrucian mysteries remained to be broadcast. The creation of earth and water, he confided to his readers in 1665, "is a very great secret, neither is it lawfull to publish it expressly, & as the Nature of the thing requires, but in the *Magicall work* it is to be seen, and I have been an eye *witnesse* of it my self."[88] By that date he had reached the height of his success. His printed portraits show that he was a lavish dresser with plenty of money to spend on expensive clothes. He addressed readers from "our Virgin Pallace in Hermupolis," which sounds grand, whatever it might have meant. Around 1670, however, Heydon disappeared. No record of his death has come to light; perhaps he just dissolved into the ether. Although a few of his writings appear on William Cooper's lists of chemical publications in the early 1670s, they were hardly mentioned after that. The "Astromagus" vanished without trace.

For all his pomposity, self-promotion and pretensions to learning, John Heydon was important. His brief success shows that astrology was not inevitably bound on a path of accommodation with contemporary science. It might have pursued a different course, towards cultivating an audience among those who wanted to unveil the secrets of nature without engaging in the bothersome experimental rigour of Boyle or Newton. Heydon was not an enemy to experimental science: he simply offered a quicker and easier method of achieving the same ends. He fearlessly put into print all the magical ideas that other astrologers were hesitant to publicize. While he added his own strange Rosicrucian spin on many of them, this can only have enhanced his appeal to those who were impressed by the idea of a society that already held the secrets of the universe—unlike the Royal Society, whose progress towards ultimate revelation was slow and painful.

The alternative astrology represented by the "Astromagus" depended heavily on the protection of patrons at court such as like the duke of Buckingham. While he was a successful writer, Heydon could easily have run foul of the religious authorities. In fact, he was allegedly attacked in a sermon at St Paul's in May 1664, delivered before the lord mayor, in which a preacher "aspersed me with Atheism."[89] But for the protection afforded him by his social superiors, he might have been a prime target for clerical criticism on account of the occult extravagances of his thinking. The possibility of a confrontation was averted by his disappearance from public view in 1670, at the height of his fame. Whatever its cause, it preserved his reputation for later readers, who sometimes held a surprising admiration for "Heydonian philosophy." A marginal comment from around 1817, found in a copy of *Theomagia* in the British Library, expressed wonderment at how "the learned John heydon after having brought this science to great perfection hath been much abusd there in, but w[h]o Ever will Examin the science Candidly will find it upon the Baises of truth and honesty."[90] Apparently, 150 years of scientific revolution had made little impression on this reader.

The Amateur: Samuel Jeake of Rye

The field of astrology was dominated by professionals concentrated in the English capital. The exceptions included the Scottish almanac-makers and the Wing family, who lived at North Luffenham and later Pickworth in Rutland. The anonymous compilers of the Cambridge almanacs probably resided in East Anglia, where the relatively flat terrain made it easier to observe the stars. Sir George Wharton worked at Oxford in the 1640s, and later lived at Enfield in Middlesex. Because of the importance of electional astrology to overseas merchants and sea captains, who had to choose propitious dates to set sail on voyages, it is likely that professional astrologers could also be found in seaports like Bristol and Plymouth.

Unlike alchemy, however, astrology was not a widespread amateur pursuit or hobby. The reasons for this are not hard to grasp. To calculate the actual movements of stars and planets demanded a high level of mathematical expertise. To draw up and interpret charts based on published information was easier—one could use a variety of ephemerides as well as the instructions on chart-making found in Lilly's *Christian Astrology*—but it remained a difficult, time-consuming and potentially rather dull exercise. As a result, few amateurs attempted it, and those who did often had professional reasons for doing so. They included doctors like Joseph Blagrave, who specialized in astrological diagnoses, and sea captains like Jeremy Roche. The latter was an officer of the Royal Navy who drew up elections for the ships on which he sailed, inserting them in journals of his voyages from 1665 to 1692. A devotee of John Gadbury, Roche helpfully appended to his first journal a section on drawing up elections. With surprising candour, he admitted that he could not "absolutely affirm" their veracity, since "I can produce not many experiments to prove it." Nevertheless, he sought to demonstrate that "all actions, designs and affairs" relating to his naval adventures were "attended or followed with successes suitable to such influences as the configuration of the Heavens and aspects of the Stars and Planets did then dispense."[91] He obviously wanted others to read his observations, which were beautifully illustrated with charts and charming drawings.

Among those who practised astrology purely for their own edification or pleasure during the Restoration period, two figures are very well known: Elias Ashmole and Samuel Jeake the younger. The publication of Ashmole's autobiographical writings and of Jeake's diary, however, may have obscured how exceptional these two men were as serious astrological hobbyists. While they were certainly not unique, their remarkable devotion to the astral art set them apart, as did their burning desire to make their hobby both credible and respectable. They had certain traits in common. Both were men of the middling sort whose origins lay in provincial towns: Lichfield in Staffordshire and Rye in Sussex, respectively. Neither was born into the intellectual establishment, although Ashmole gradually worked his way into it. Proximity to the booksellers of the capital was important to both of them, as they depended on printed sources of astrological knowledge. Both felt personally oppressed by the political tumults and religious upheavals of their times; both sought to understand what was happening to them and their country through the stars. The restless ambition of the Oxford lawyer was matched in many ways by the indefatigable enterprise of the Rye merchant.

In other important ways, however, they were very different. Ashmole was a royalist and Anglican whose cultivation of status and respectability masked a passion to uncover the secrets of ritual magic. Like his hero William Lilly, he was obsessed with horary predictions. Jeake was a republican and Nonconformist who had no yearning for social success. He seems never to have drawn up horary charts, restricting himself to natural astrology, genitures and elections. If Ashmole looked back to the golden age of astrology in the first half of the seventeenth century, Jeake wanted to rethink the art. Sharing the scientific views of Whig astrologers like John Partridge, he tested astrology by controlled experiments, but remained an entrenched opponent of the Copernican system. The most important difference between Ashmole and Jeake, however, may have been in their relationship to their fathers. Ashmole's was a saddler by trade, who, according to his son, "through ill Husbandry, became a great Enimy to himselfe, and poor Family."[92] His son acknowledged no debt to him. Jeake's father, by contrast, was an admired patriarch and the chief influence on his life. To some extent, astrology was a way for the younger Jeake to justify the opinions of his beloved sire, a man who embodied the radical sectarianism of the Commonwealth period.

Samuel Jeake the elder was a Rye lawyer, accomplished mathematician, historian of the Cinque Ports and ardent puritan. He also served as town clerk of Rye until the Restoration, when he resigned rather than serve under the new monarch. He then became the leader of a congregation of religious Dissenters.[93] Following the advice of one of his own sermons, that "the Saints must remove their stations from the Tents of ungodly men," Jeake senior had no further involvement in town government for the next thirty years, until his death in 1690.[94] His religion was an eclectic mixture, combining anti-Catholicism with the fierce independence of an Anabaptist and an emphasis on personal revelation that verged on Quakerism. A voracious reader, the elder Jeake aquired and catalogued a remarkable library of more than two thousand volumes later inherited by his son. It included four works by Paracelsus, ten volumes of Nicholas Culpeper's astrological and medical writings, Elias Ashmole's edition of *Collectanea Chymica*, Robert Fludd's *Mosaic Philosophy*, four volumes by John Gadbury, two tracts by Christopher Heydon and three by William Lilly, among many others that dealt with alchemical or astrological subjects.[95] The collection was largely purchased through London booksellers, among them Obadiah Blagrave, the leading publisher of expensive astrological treatises.[96]

Evidently, Jeake the elder was well versed in the occult philosophies of the period, although his voluminous correspondence provides few direct clues as to how he reconciled them with his religious views. The younger Jeake was educated by his father to pursue both a public business career and a life of private study. From an early age, he was heavily influenced by the supernatural. He remembered hearing about a "Prodigy," a vision of Jesus Christ becoming king, in 1663, at the age of eleven. Although he was not sure whether it was true or false, it "was the first occasion of my Conversion, & serious thoughts about my future condition."[97] By the age of fourteen, he had read a number of books on medicine and natural history, as well as Agrippa's *De Occulta Philosophia*.[98] This last work does not appear in his father's library catalogue, but it has to be assumed that Jeake senior knew and approved of his teenage son's exposure to this notorious text. What effect it had on the young man is difficult to say. He did not mention it in the list of books that he had read by the age of fifteen, and his understanding of astrology does not seem to have been influenced by Agrippa's obsession with the role of spirits. Still, the younger Jeake remained a believer in the everyday power of supernatural forces that were not strictly biblical. For example, he recorded in his diary an incident that took place in June 1671, when two bed-staffs seemed to shift position during the night due to "the ridiculous and trifling actions of some of the meanest rank among the Infernal Spirits."[99]

Soon after his first reading of Agrippa, Jeake's father began to instruct him in the study of the heavens. The "astrological diary" that the younger Jeake drew up later in life notes the following for 25 June 1667: "About noon I began to learn Astrology."[100] In the summer of 1670, he drew up more than 150 nativities. Most of them were for his friends and neighbours in Rye, although some bore the names of the children of royalty, among then the duke of Monmouth.[101] These were exercises to make him more proficient in the astrological art. At the same time, Jeake junior was engaged in writing a treatise on astrology entitled *Diaposon: The Harmony of the Signes of Heaven*. Its frontispiece was a "Hieroglyphick" depicting his own descent from the symbols of Jupiter and Venus, which he associated with his father and mother. It also included his own nativity and the horoscope for the moment of his conception, an odd subject for a teenager to contemplate.[102] Evidently, astrology provided the younger Jeake with a language by which to define and express his personal identity, especially his devotion to his father. His past, present and future were, in a sense, contained in a bundle of astral signs, which his god-like father had taught him how to read.

The politics of Rye in the late 1670s and early 1680s placed the Jeakes at the centre of a bitter and furious factional confrontation. The national struggle between Whigs and Tories was played out in the small town as a battle between radical Dissenters and moderates for control of the corporation. The Jeakes were the spiritual leaders of the radical party, although they were careful not to present themselves as its political standard-bearers.[103] In the end, the radicals lost, and loyal adherents of the Church of England began to harass, fine and imprison Dissenters. The elder Jeake was obliged to leave Rye for London late in 1682, where he remained until the summer of 1687. His son later recalled a dream that he had had around November 1678, at the beginning of these events, in which his future troubles may have been foretold. He had seen a pale sun surrounded by "horsemen & their horses, all in Confusion; tramping upon one another; some riding, some overthrown." Around them were the twelve signs of the zodiac, "all perfect only that of Pisces defective." In interpreting this dream, Jeake emphasized its personal connotations, giving himself a central position: "I was signified by the Sun because he was Lord of the ascendant in my Nativity." The paleness of the sun "portended that I should never be in any Place of Honor or Authority over others." The horsemen were his enemies, seeking to destroy him, while the defective sign of Pisces was his father, who "should receive some prejudice & be partly separated from me; but not totally, nor for ever."[104]

Jeake's reading of this dream in personal rather than political terms was not due to concern over possible repercussions, as he was writing in the 1690s, after his enemies had been overthrown in the Glorious Revolution. Rather, it reflects his constant tendency to relate astrology to his inner self—a self that was highly restrained, rather depressive and apparently lacking in emotional outlets. He was by his own account prone to bouts of "excessive Melancholy," which made him "pass some whole nights without sleep."[105] His conversations with himself through astrology were ways of coming to terms with his emotions as well as the events of his life. His father was always an important part of these conversations; his mother played a very minor role. As for the younger Jeake's wife, Elizabeth Hartshorne, whom he married in 1680 when she was just thirteen years old, she barely figured at all in his astrological musings.

As he matured, Jeake may have begun to harbour feelings of competitiveness with his father. Above all, he wanted to vindicate the art of astrology in terms that his father would not have recognized: namely, as an experimental science. Following his father's return to Rye, Jeake began an ambitious attempt to achieve this goal. For a full year, from 5 July 1687 to 5 July 1688, he kept daily notes on every significant occurrence in his life, from King James II's alteration of corporations to allow "the putting in of Whigs & dissenters," to attacks of melancholy "by reason of the disappointments about wooll," to his being "stung under the left knee with an Humble bee." His stated purpose was to vindicate astrology from the accusation that "her Prognostiques are not deprehended [*sic*] to have equal Certitude with those of other Arts." He therefore set out to examine "a Large Exemplification of such Experimental impressions, as being formed by their genuine Astral causes." In his role as "Experimenter," he was to "deveste himselfe entirely of all his prejudices & prepossessions; either in specificating the Effects of Directions, or in imagining great Successes in his proper Themes." He must renounce both "Tradition" and "a passionate & inordinate self Love; whereby all things are drawn violently to signify such preconceptions as the mind had fancied to it self." After all, a self-interested mind, "failing of her desired effect, becomes fill'd at last with a continued Scepticism, if not a total renunciation of the credit of every Aphorism."[106]

The denial of self-interest is particularly interesting, since the main object of Jeake's astrology was to know himself better. His treatise begins, somewhat paradoxically, with a list of facts about himself entitled "The Native's Condition at the Revolution." It includes an admission that his "Complexion" was "Choleric Melancholy." His friends, who presumably comprised the readers of the treatise, were "few, but firme," while his enemies included "The Magistrates of the Place, Customehouse officers, & Debauchees." He mentions his father and his mother-in-law, his wife, one child and two servants as the members of his family, but nothing more is said about them. Once we have met the man, we are introduced to his method. Jeake explains that, in calculating the daily directions of ascendant planets, he will employ the theories of the French astrologer Jean-Baptiste Morin, as laid out in *Astrologia Gallica* (1661).[107] In short, this was not to be his father's astrology. On the contrary, his treatise would propound to its readers a new, experimental philosophy, worthy of the name science and equal to any in certitude.

It took Jeake almost four years to write up his data. In the interval, King James II had fallen from power, an event that could have been foreseen, according to Jeake, by a change in the revolution or yearly position of the sun.[108] This observation, made in hindsight, confirms that Jeake was not about to use his grand experiment to disprove astrology. On the contrary, his aim was to vindicate the art, and of course he succeeded. His account of the events of the year ended with a set of "Theoremes insurging from the Contemplation of the Preceding Experiments," of which the first was that "Sublunary Causes frequently incline the Effects to deviate from the commensurate time of their Directions." In other words, conditions on earth might retard the influence of the stars. This was an honest admission, but it seriously damaged his hypothesis, since if astral causes were not felt immediately, it was not clear how they could be proven to exist at all. Jeake was not deterred by this finding: he proceeded to enumerate thirteen further "Theoremes," most of them having to do with the significance of specific planets.[109] In short, his experiment had been a resounding success, at least in his own mind.

By 1692, when he finished writing up his experiment, Jeake's father was dead, and he may have needed the consolation of astrology more than ever. As the elder Jeake lay ill, his son carefully recorded daily astral directions. He also wrote down their final conversation: "When I said farewell Dear Father, & kist his dying lips; he answered; Farewell my Dear lamb, The Lord bless thee, & prosper all that thou undertakest."[110] It is the most emotional passage in the diary. Jeake was by then a man of substance, having made a small fortune as a merchant, and would soon begin investing his money in public funds, including Bank of England stocks. To some extent, he was turning his back on the austerity and self-denial of his father's puritanism. At the same time, he was more eager than ever to validate the truth of astrology. The diary, which he transcribed in 1694, recorded the occurrences of his entire life, along with the planets that influenced each day. He did not add any new "Theoremes" or conclusions to the manuscript, but if he had, they would no doubt have upheld the faith in the stars that he had inherited from his beloved father.

This account has stressed the personal aspects of Samuel Jeake the younger's astrology, because they illustrate so emphatically that reading the stars could play a complex psychological role. It was not simply a matter of explaining the unpredictable or alleviating the anxiety caused by misfortune; astrology could also be a way of interpreting oneself. To be sure, the younger Jeake was not a typical astrologer. He deliberately avoided predictions, and he was fascinated by every influence, no matter how slight, that the stars might have on his everyday life. After his childhood, he did not exhibit much interest in occult philosophy, but his acceptance of "Astral Causes" reveals that he perceived the stars to have direct effects on "Sublunar" events. While those effects could be delayed by earthly conditions, they were constant, fixed by the character of the ascendant planet. No matter how much of an experimentalist he may have been, Jeake never questioned the assumption that the heavens guided what happened on earth. He flatly ignored the advice of John Flamsteed, who counselled him in 1698 that "he may Imploy his time much better then in the study of Astrology."[111]

Jeake's purposes in pursuing astrology were markedly different from those of Elias Ashmole, who was obsessed with its more occult aspects and spent many hours drawing up horary predictions. The two men illustrate the variety of social meanings that astrology might hold. Given this complexity, and the strength of astrology as a business in the period from 1650 to 1689, one might have predicted that the silver age of the celestial art would have lasted for many decades longer. In fact, it ended pretty abruptly in the twenty years after the Glorious Revolution. To understand why, we have to take a closer look at how occult ways of thinking were integrated with the broader intellectual world of the late seventeenth century. Was it the professed enemies of astrology or its bickering friends who eventually brought it crashing down from the skies?

CHAPTER THREE

The Occult Contested

> Thus Ralph became infallible,
> As three or four-legg'd Oracle . . .
> For mystick Learning, wondrous able
> In Magic, *Talisman*, and *Cabal*,
> Whose primitive tradition reaches
> As far as *Adam*'s first green breeches . . .
> A deep occult Philosopher
> As learn'd as the *Wild Irish* are,
> Or Sir *Agrippa*, for profound
> And solid Lying much renown'd:
> He *Anthroposophus*, and *Floud*,
> And *Jacob Behmen* understood;
> Knew many an Amulet and Charm,
> That would do neither good nor harm:
> In *Rosy-Crucian* Lore as learned,
> As he that *Verè Adeptus* earned.[1]

Thus, in the person of Ralpho, the semi-educated, gullible squire of Sir Hudibras, Samuel Butler satirized occult philosophy in the first canto of his classic mock epic of the 1660s, *Hudibras*. The poem makes merciless fun of Hermeticists, Rosicrucians, ritual magicians, alchemists, astrologers, almanac-makers, conjurors and those who believe in the black magic of witches. All are associated with vulgar ignorance, credulity, fraud and the fanatical religious sectarianism that precipitated the Civil War. All, in Butler's view, were equally ridiculous and contemptible.

Hudibras reminds us that, even in the golden age of alchemy and the silver age of astrology, occult philosophy might be altogether rejected. To be sure, the poem affirms that mid-seventeenth-century England was teeming with occult practitioners, like Sidrophel the false conjuror, who has a run-in with the hero in the third canto. Yet *Hudibras* also suggests that these alchemists, astrologers and ritual magicians were justified in their continual anxiety about the intellectual acceptability of their interests. "[W]e know that our Philosophy is the Worlds Contempt," moaned William Cooper in the 1684 preface to *Collectanea Chymica*, "and its Professors their scorn and derision."[2] The absurd figure of Ralpho should lead any historian to wonder: how integrated were occult philosophy and science in the intellectual life of the second half of the seventeenth century? Were they part of a cultural mainstream, or were they associated with marginal thinkers and fringe movements? To what extent were they challenged and undermined by scepticism, rationalism and empirical science?

The answers to these questions would once have seemed self-evident. Before the renewal of interest in Paracelsian medicine in the late 1950s, the rehabilitation of spiritual and demonic magic in the 1960s and the rediscovery of Newton's alchemy in the 1970s, few would have questioned that modern science and reason were relentlessly driving occult thinking out of the realm of intellectual respectability.[3] Today, however, most historians have changed their minds about this. They are more likely to respond to questions like those posed above by remarking that supernatural beliefs were deeply rooted in the mentalities of the seventeenth century, so that the credibility extended to occult science and philosophy should not surprise us. After all, people believed in prodigies, prophecies and special providences until well into the eighteenth century; why should they not also have accepted alchemy, astrology and ritual magic?[4]

This is not an entirely satisfactory response to our initial questions, for two main reasons. First, by the mid-seventeenth century, if not earlier, it was possible to doubt and even deny the everyday occurrence of supernatural events. Some people limited their possibility to instances of direct divine intervention in which the laws of nature were clearly overturned; others simply demanded empirical proof that they had happened. Second, belief in human power over supernatural events often collided with religious orthodoxy, a matter of increasing concern to those who governed the Church of England after 1660. The defenders of Anglicanism—like Samuel Butler—did not deny that supernatural happenings might take place, but they regarded with deep suspicion those who claimed to be able to channel, initiate or control them. Such people were at best misguided, at worst diabolists. The defence of orthodoxy after the Civil War period posed a much more formidable challenge to occult thinking than did experimental science.

The answers to our initial questions, then, turn out to be complicated. The occult may have been everywhere in British culture, but nowhere was it uncontested. For some, it was a legitimate source of knowledge, while for others, it was diabolical and taboo. Prophecy that drew on occult sources, the subject of the first section of this chapter, was anathematized by established authorities. The late seventeenth-century debate over witchcraft, on the other hand, was more muddled, because witch beliefs became for orthodox clergymen a mark of resistance against scepticism. Unfortunately, historians have often discussed witchcraft as if it were a defining feature of occult beliefs, when it was actually tangential to them, and was frequently used to taint or disparage them. One could deny witchcraft and believe in occult philosophy. Conversely, it was possible to condemn occult philosophy while arguing passionately for the existence of witches. The second section below tries to sort out such distinctions. Even those who were prepared to grant a measure of truth to the occult, however, might argue that its claims should not be accepted without being tested. This might take the form of an experiment, such as the compilation of a set of observations. The third section deals with attempts by scientific thinkers to test occult claims. The pursuit of hidden knowledge or secrets was another enticing area of learning, which is considered in the final section of this chapter. When revealed in print, secrets lost their allure. They could be preserved through restricting access to them, so that only initiates would know them. This was the driving principle of the secret societies, of which Freemasonry would be the most enduring.

The Prophets

Proof of the claims of occult knowledge might be entirely personal, individual and spiritual. If it could elevate the believer to a higher state of awareness of the divine, of scriptural prophecy or of the meaning of the world, then the occult might be justified by what seemed to be irrefutable evidence. As the Church of England disintegrated in the 1640s and 1650s, prophets proliferated, and it was not uncommon for them to claim certainty about occult matters through divine revelation, rejecting rational, scientific or worldly thinking. Among these prophetic souls was Thomas Totney, a goldsmith of London who renamed himself TheaurauJohn (that is, The-aurora-John) Tany after experiencing a vision that convinced him that he was God's emissary in preparing the world for the Second Coming. Tany's prophetic message, which denied hell and damnation, was supposedly based on revelation alone. "[T]ake notice scholars," he instructed, "I am not book-learned, but I am heart-knowledged by divine inspiration."[5] In reality, like so many other prophets of the time, he drew upon written sources, particularly alchemical texts (not surprising for a goldsmith), astrology, the *Corpus Hermeticum*, Agrippa and Boehme. Calling himself "High Priest of the

Jews," Tany believed it was his mission to gather up the remnants of the Jewish people throughout England—an aspiration that would be revived in the 1790s. Arrested for blasphemy but acquitted of the charge in 1652, he went on a rampage in the lobby of the House of Commons three years later, attacking the doorkeeper with his sword after hearing that Oliver Cromwell was to be offered the crown. Tany probably died in 1659; he left no movement behind him.[6]

A more influential, and better-connected, prophet of the Interregnum was the Reverend John Pordage, who with his wife, Mary, headed a small group of Behmenists in their Berkshire parish. The parish was in the gift of Elias Ashmole, who admired the vicar enough to send him a copy of his *Fasciculus Chemicus* in 1650, and who commended his knowledge of astronomy. Pordage was deprived of his clerical living in 1654 after being accused of blasphemy, scandal, necromancy and communicating with spirits.[7] In forced retirement, he wrote works of mystical theology that were published after his death by his followers. In them, he insisted that mysteries could only be revealed by visions, "when the *Spirit* of the mind is thorowly illustrated, or enlightened by a Raie, or Beam proceeding from the Holy Spirit." He was contemptuous of "the *Rational* [Power], which the confounding *Jesuit* would make the *pure Religionist beleev* to be Mechanism (*the Diana of this inquisitive Age*) and the whole Encylopaede of Arts and sciences but a brisk circulation of the Blood."[8] Evidently, he had in mind Cartesian mechanical philosophy. Although a learned man with an interest in alchemy, Pordage had no patience for the experimental science that was gaining ground after the Restoration. His theology was indebted to Boehme, but his conception of a universe brimming over with innumerable spirits owed a good deal to Neoplatonism as well.

Pordage's son Samuel, who shared his parents' religious views, published an enormous poem in 1661 that offered a mystical explanation of the universe. It concludes with an alchemical quest for the Stone that can command devils, angels and all spirits. In verses more passionate than mellifluous, Samuel Pordage urged his jaded contemporaries to abandon the "natural Magic" of worldly science for the "higher Magic" of the spirit:

> *Magick* is threefold: this *world's* natural,
> *Sacred* the light, *dark*, *diabolical*:
> Great is the *Magic* of this world, but yet
> Greater the dark, the *light* more great than it.
> When this worlds secrets, Man knows from the light,
> He knows the *Magic* of this *world* aright,
> But otherwise he deals preposterous,
> Lets go a Jewel; doth a bauble choose.[9]

Unlike Elias Ashmole, Samuel Pordage was suspicious of astrology, which could lead the unwitting into necromancy, and dismissive of practical alchemy. He further advised "the worldly Wise" to avoid philosophers like Plato or Hermes Trismegistus, along with "*Magii*" like Paracelsus or Agrippa, who proclaimed their own knowledge rather than that of God. Instead, the true magician should follow the path of a spiritual pilgrim, seeking the eternal virgin Sophia, "The Spouse of *Christ*, and all the Saints beside."[10]

The tendency of mystical writers to borrow occult language and concepts while distancing themselves from occult science began with Boehme, and would survive the Pordages. Their writings inspired a female prophet of the next generation, Jane Lead. She came from a minor gentry family and married her cousin, a wealthy London merchant, who left her destitute after his death in 1670. Her close contact with the Pordages gave her spiritual if not material capital, and she edited John Pordage's works after his death in 1681.[11] Her powerful visions were centred on *Magia*, or "the created Power of the Holy Ghost" which would bring forth "fruitful Gifts and high working Powers" from the womb of a hermaphroditic Virgin ("both Male & Female for Angelical Generation") named Sophia or Wisdom.[12] Lead's mystic language was infused with her own imaginative and highly gendered interpretations of spiritual things. To a far greater extent than her mentors, she came to reject reason and science. Her aversion to them may have been due in part to a feeling of exclusion—few women had access to scientific knowledge, and none was a member of the Royal Society—but it also stemmed from an ardent attachment to prophecy, and from an inspired reading of Behmenism. She would be at the centre of a significant religious movement in the 1690s.

At least one Behmenist visionary, however, embraced practical methods and made a fortune from providing medical advice: Thomas Tryon, a prosperous hatter who lived in the London suburb of Hackney. Tryon had experienced visions since the age of six, and as a young man studied astrology—"a Science too rashly decried by some," he later opined, "who consider not the Subordinate Administration of the Almighty, by the Illuminated Powers of the Coelestial Regions, nor discern their Operations in Nature, and Influences on the Animal Life, in the complexions of Men and Things, and in the Generation and Preservation thereof." Tryon did not seek to read fortunes, but "to discern the Complexion and Qualities of Animals, Minerals, and Vegetations" in order to diagnose ailments.[13] It was his acquaintance with Boehme's writings that led him to quit an Anabaptist congregation in the late 1650s and follow his own beliefs, which increasingly centred on vegetarianism. Tryon began producing pamphlets on the subject in the early 1680s, connecting it with a mystical cleansing of the body. His admirers included the playwright Aphra Behn and, much later, Benjamin Franklin. Tryon was also a believer in dreams as a means of communication with the spirit world, which he advertised as part of the "Mystick Philosophy" of Pythagoras.[14] Describing himself as a "Student in Physick," he wrote on a variety of medical subjects, including madness, as well as on overseas plantations, which he heartily endorsed, although he argued for better treatment for slaves.[15]

Tryon was financially successful, but in his theological views he remained an outsider. No matter how much we may now wish to restore the reputations of visionaries and prophets, their open espousal of sectarian and heterodox principles made them a fringe element in British culture. Their insights depended on personal experience and testimony, not on acceptance by an established community of scholars. We will return to them later, but for now our attention will rest with those who struck out in a different direction, like Pordage's former patron, Elias Ashmole. For him, occult thinking rested on the hope that supernatural forces could be understood and employed in a physical endeavour that might be demonstrated publicly to others, especially to sceptics. This does not mean that occult thinking was merely functional or practical, because the *process* of understanding was for many of its adherents tantamount to evidence that it was "working." Moreover, the mere promise of success could keep scholars toiling at their furnaces or staring at the stars for long periods of time. In one way or another, they were trying to test the occult, whether as a process or as a ritual or even as a pathway to visionary experience.

Belief, Doubt, Denial

Those who opposed occult thinking outright denied that it could ever be tested because it was based on error or delusion. The most extreme among these deniers was without doubt Thomas Hobbes, who combined a materialist approach to natural philosophy with a severely rationalist reading of Scripture. In his celebrated work *Leviathan* (1651), he ascribed "the opinion that rude people have of Fayries, Ghosts and Goblins; and of the power of Witches" to an inability to distinguish between sense impressions and dreams. Like all products of the imagination, dreams derived from "*decaying sense*": that is, from weak and often erroneous impressions of reality that were left in the memory. While an omnipotent God certainly had the power to send dreams or apparitions into the material world, Hobbes saw no reason to believe that he did so very often.[16]

Hobbes's scrupulous deity was similarly stinting in his use of miracles. One of the most controversial passages in *Leviathan* defined miracles in a very precise way:

> By *Miracles* are signified the Admirable works of God: & therefore they are also called *Wonders* . . . And there be but two things which make men wonder at any event. The one is, if it be strange, that is to say, such, as the like of it hath never, or very rarely been produced: The other is, if when it is produced, we cannot imagine it to have been done by naturall means, but onely by the immediate hand of God.[17]

Miracles, then, were very rare events, designed to reveal the mission of God's extraordinary ministers, like Moses and Christ. As no devil, angel or spirit could perform a miracle, any wonders ascribed to them "must either be by vertue of some naturall science, or by Incantation, that is, by vertue of words [i.e. deception]."[18] Even the "Arts of Magick" supposedly employed by Moses in his competition with the Egyptian magicians—a favourite story among those who sought to justify the conjuring of spirits—were actually illusions, because they were not performed for the edification of the elect.

Hobbes drove home his attack on the occult in the fourth book of *Leviathan*, where he dedicated a chapter to the refutation of "*Daemonology*," the theory that incorporeal spirits operated in the world. Firmly based on materialist assumptions, this was a response, not just to popular belief in devils and ghosts, but to Neoplatonic philosophy as well. Hobbes sought to disprove—not very convincingly, it should be admitted—that spirits, including angels as well as demons, ever appeared without bodies in Scripture. They were always corporeal, and therefore could not inhabit or possess another person or thing, since two bodies could not occupy the same space at the same time. When Christ was said to have cast out demons, he was actually using God's word "to command Madnesse, or Lunacy (under the appellation of Devils, by which they were then commonly understood), to depart out of a mans body."[19] Belief in spirits without bodies, according to Hobbes, was derived from the relics of "Gentilisme" or pagan religion. Such superstition had no place in true Christian faith.

Thus, Hobbes decried the common "Wonders" that were taken by the public as miracles or signs of divine providence, as well as the bodiless spirits that flitted through the literature of alchemy, astrology and ritual magic. Only bodies, extension and matter existed: all else was fantasy. His strict materialist approach, however, was too radical for most late seventeenth-century thinkers, even those who shared Hobbes's hostility to certain aspects of the occult. Perhaps the only contemporary writer on occult subjects who mirrored Hobbes's philosophical attitude was the Oxford scholar John Wagstaffe, known in his time as a "wit" and a hard drinker. He argued in 1669 that all scriptural references to spirits, magic and witchcraft were mistranslations of the original

Hebrew. The real sources of witch beliefs, in Wagstaffe's opinion, were "Heathen Fables," falsely propagated as Christian doctrine by "Papal Inquisitours." Wagstaffe chose witchcraft as a specific target, but he was aiming at all "superstitious" beliefs, including those of Neoplatonists, who were "addicted unto Fabling and Allegorizing."[20]

As materialists, Hobbes and Wagstaffe were suspected of denying the existence of the soul, and were equated with atheists. Their influence during the Restoration period could not compare with that of another writer on witchcraft, a pillar of Anglican orthodoxy with a highly respected surname, who was famous in his lifetime although he is now largely forgotten: the Reverend Meric Casaubon. In contrast to Hobbes and Wagstaffe, Casaubon argued that spirits were real and could exist in a disembodied form. He regarded communication with them as absolutely unlawful, however, and therefore held occult pursuits to be vain, dangerous and ultimately Satanic. Casaubon's position was, to a large extent, representative of Anglican orthodoxy during the Restoration period.

Meric Casaubon was the son of the renowned classical scholar Isaac Casaubon, who had shown that the Hermetic writings dated from the Christian era and not from ancient Egypt.[21] (Few Hermeticists paid any attention to the findings.) Meric shared his father's suspicious attitude towards occult philosophy, which in his mind appealed mainly to religious enthusiasts and sectarians who were ultimately led astray by the Devil. To demonstrate the point, Casaubon published in 1659 a wordy, rambling preface to an edition of the experiments in ritual magic of the Elizabethan magus John Dee. Casaubon presented the experiences of Dr Dee as certain evidence of the reality of spirits, and therefore as a blow to atheists like Hobbes. He was in no doubt, however, that the spirits contacted by the "Skryer" or medium Edward Kelly were not angelic, as the deluded Dr Dee fondly imagined, but were instead manifestations of the Devil. Casaubon extended this accusation of diabolism to the works of Paracelsus, to mystical alchemy (he called the Philosopher's Stone "a meer cheet"), to Kabbalism and even to the mysterious Book of Enoch, "a very superstitious, foolish, fabulous writing; or to conclude all in one word, Cabalistical, such as the Divel might own very well, and in all probability was the author of."[22]

In a postscript, Casaubon even hinted darkly, without saying so directly, that Elias Ashmole, who had recently published excerpts from Dee's experiments in his *Theatrum Chemicum Britannicum*, was moving down the same dark path as his Elizabethan predecessor. This was a serious charge, which may have influenced Ashmole's decision not to publish the second part of his *magnum opus*. Unfortunately, Casaubon's pious purposes were partially undermined by his printer. Trying to lure the curious and the magically inclined to buy the book, he made Dee's name more prominent than the author's own on the title page, and added a frontispiece that depicted other famous practitioners of magic. Yet nobody could mistake the message of Casaubon's text—contact with spirits was never lawful.

Casaubon followed up the exposure of Dee with a learned tract entitled *Of Credulity and Incredulity*, published in 1668. It contained a crushingly sarcastic commentary on "the wonders of Chymistry: by some so much doted upon (right Mountebanks, and cheaters in this) that they would refer all mysteries and miracles, even of Religion, unto it." Casaubon admitted nonetheless that he had been cured of a near-fatal illness by Dr Thory's pills.[23] Seeking out a middle ground, he admitted the existence of occult qualities in nature, including celestial influences, because the ancients believed in them, but painted spiritual interference in the world as malign. To dissociate himself from Hobbesianism, Casaubon made a point-by-point answer to the "atheist" John Wagstaffe, whom he denounced as wrong about Scripture, wrong about the origins of witch beliefs and utterly wrong about the reality of witchcraft.[24] The last point became crucial to *Of Credulity*'s success. Although the discussion of witches took up only twenty out of more than two hundred pages of dense theological reasoning, it clearly helped to sell copies. When a reprint appeared in 1672, after Casaubon's death, it was retitled *A Treatise Proving Spirits, Witches and Supernatural Operations by Pregnant Instances and Evidences*—a title Casaubon was unlikely to have agreed to, had he still been alive. Evidently, the public was perceived as wanting to read about witches, not about the heavier subjects of credulity and incredulity.

Casaubon's writings incensed one reader, the Lancashire schoolmaster John Webster. He was by no means a Hobbesian; rather, he was a practising alchemist whose views on occult philosophy were not very different from those of Elias Ashmole. Unlike Ashmole, however, Webster had a sectarian past—during the Civil War period, he had attached himself to the mystic William Erbery, an admirer of Jacob Boehme. He had already set off a major controversy regarding English higher education by publishing in 1653 an attack on what he saw as a university system mired in outdated Aristotelian values. To the intellectually impoverished undergraduates of his day, Webster recommended the study of astrology, singling out for praise "my learned, and industrious Countrymen Mr. Ashmole, Mr. William Lilly, Mr. Booker, Mr. Culpepper, and others." He went on to endorse Plato, Paracelsus, J.B. van Helmont and Descartes, a quartet certain to enlighten (or thoroughly bewilder) any young man. A furious reply to Webster's book followed from John Wilkins, warden of Wadham College, Oxford, and the Oxford professor of astronomy Seth Ward. They defended the existing university curriculum from charges of backwardness and dismissed the "gullery" of astrology—although they were also careful to express personal respect for Ashmole.[25]

After the Restoration, Webster switched his politics to royalism and apparently conformed to the Church of England, but he remained an ardent alchemist, with a pronounced magical bent. In his 1671 work *Metallographia*, dedicated to the royalist hero Prince Rupert, he extolled the "natural and lawful Magick" of the Egyptians, while revealing his own preference for "the Mystical part of Chymistry."[26] He even took on the great Isaac Casaubon, explicitly rejecting his critical views on the antiquity of the *Corpus Hermeticum*.[27]

It might seem implausible that John Webster, alchemist, astrologer and magician, would become one of the leading denouncers of witch beliefs. That he did can only be understood as a reaction to those defenders of orthodoxy who, like Meric Casaubon, lumped witchcraft together with occult philosophy under the rubric of diabolism. The enormous book that Webster published in 1677 on what he carefully labelled "Supposed Witchcraft" explains his position pretty clearly, although it has often mystified students of the period who have read it in search of a sceptical critique of magic. Webster begins with the complaint that alchemists and writers on occult subjects, including John Dee, have been falsely suspected of practising witchcraft by "the monster-Headed Multitude."[28] This seems an odd way to attack Meric Casaubon, who had never courted popularity, but it may reflect the harassed feelings of a former sectarian living amid the loud triumphs of the revived Church of England. For Webster, witchcraft was essentially a scurrilous accusation that rubbed off on serious students of the occult.

That accusation was manifestly unfair, in Webster's opinion, because witches, unlike occult philosophers, were not able to do anything supernatural. While he accepted that not all witches were imaginary, he insisted that they could not possibly possess the powers that were ascribed to them. He agreed fully with Casaubon's point that evil spirits, even the Devil himself, existed as incorporeal entities. Demons could do nothing in the physical world, however, without the approval of God; so their followers were deluded, as were those who saw the works of Satan everywhere around them. While Webster accepted that "the force of imagination" might be responsible for strange physical effects, like the altering of fetuses in the womb, he hastened to add that "the Devil acteth nothing in it at all, but the setting of his will upon that mischief."[29] Webster devoted an entire chapter of his work to demonstrating that spirits might "separately exist," apart from bodies and even souls—a point expressly denied by the materialists Hobbes and Wagstaffe. He was also inclined to believe in the efficacy of magical charms.[30] Webster devoted as much attention to these topics as he did to debunking witchcraft, which may explain why his work was not reprinted in the eighteenth century by those who sought to remove witch beliefs from the law.

Webster's book was answered by one final, tremendous blast from the Anglican trumpet: Joseph Glanvill's celebrated *Saducismus Triumphatus*, published in 1681. Glanville was a more conflicted upholder of orthodoxy than Casaubon. A Neoplatonist and promoter of science as well as a clergyman, he had begun to publish stories recounting cases of witchcraft or supernatural events in the mid-1660s, in an attempt to undermine scepticism, or "Sadducism" as he called it. When John Webster cast doubt on some of his evidence, Glanvill responded by editing a bumper collection of tales, all supposedly true, which he did not live to see into print.[31] Many of the stories dealt with cases of supernatural possession or apparitions rather than witchcraft, indicating how these categories were jumbled together in the worried minds of orthodox clergymen. Glanvill's main purpose was to illustrate through extended testimonies that evil spirits could move things, occupy the bodies of human beings and make general mayhem within the physical world. His personal experience of a particular haunting, involving "the drummer of Tedworth," may have bolstered his credibility.[32] The posthumously published compendium was a great success, and went through numerous editions by the early eighteenth century. It seems to have been just what readers wanted: a group of scary, well-documented and easily interpreted stories demonstrating a point everybody except Hobbes and his followers seemed to acknowledge: that supernatural events were commonplace and happened to very ordinary people.

Yet *Saducismus Triumphatus* was not only a story book; it also proffered an argument about invisible forces. It contained a long letter by Glanvill, addressing general objections to the reality of evil spirits: for example, that their actions were absurd or that they had no need to resort to the assistance of poor old women. His characteristic response to such scepticism was to point to human inability to grasp the meaning of supernatural events. In philosophical terms, Glanvill fell back on what he called "the *Platonick Hypothesis, that Spirits are embodied*," or rather that they could occupy and manipulate material substances.[33] Unlike Casaubon, he did not regard all spirits as diabolical, and went so far as to assert "that much of the *Government* of us, and our Affairs, is committed to the *better Spirits*." Human contact with these good spirits, however, "is not needful for the Designs of the *better world*," so their operations remain beyond our understanding or control.[34] This was a rather weak argument, which would never have persuaded a ritual magician to desist from importuning angels. Surprisingly, Glanvill did not answer Webster directly in this letter, perhaps because he shared some of his antagonist's assumptions about the spirit world.

Glanvill's friend the philosopher Henry More was even more careful in his response to Webster, but in the end just as ambivalent about benign spirits. More, whom we have already encountered as the chief opponent of Thomas Vaughan, edited *Saducismus Triumphatus* after Glanvill's death. Having abandoned Cartesianism for Neoplatonism, he openly accepted the reality of spirits, and he did not consider all of them to be evil. In the philosophical essay that he appended to Glanvill's book, More argued against Descartes, the "*Hobbians*" and others who doubted that spirits could exist without physical bodies. If this was so, he asked, what was to be made of thoughts, the soul or even God? Using geometric diagrams that gave his argument a scientific appearance, he demonstrated to his own satisfaction that spirits could join with and act upon matter, just as matter might mysteriously adhere to itself. As More put it, "the *unition* of *Spirit* with *Matter*, is as intelligible as the *unition* of one *part* of *Matter* with *another*."[35] What he did not explain in this essay was whether human contact with immaterial spirits was ever benign and lawful. A letter written by More to Samuel Hartlib in 1652, however, contains the reflection that "if good spiritts enter into any man, any how, I should not easily suspect that man to be a bad man, for I conceive all spiritts have sense and are passible and abhor from coming near unchast impure, and wicked men, as we do to come near a stinking dunghill."[36] On this occasion, More conceded that good spirits could indeed have contact with humans, and only with good humans at that.

This was not what he wrote in the epistolary preface to Glanvill's book, however, where he implied that attempts to converse with spirits would play into the hands of the Evil One. He illustrated the point, appropriately enough, with a story. More recalled an old acquaintance, a country magistrate who confessed to having "used all the Magical Ceremonies of Conjuration he could to raise the Devil or a Spirit, and had a most earnest desire to meet with one, but never could do it." This gentleman ardently believed that once, while a servant was pulling off his boots, he had felt the invisible hand of a spirit on his back. More drily advised him that such a "Goblin" would "be the first that will bid you welcome into the other World."[37] In other words, the spirit was a demon, and the man was bound for hell. The warning might have been addressed to John Webster, but it is offered in a tone of friendly counsel, and it lacks the condescension of Meric Casaubon. More felt a connection to the deluded adherents of occult philosophy. But for his attachment to orthodoxy and order, he might have been one himself.

Did the learned More believe his colleague Glanvill's fantastic tales of phantom drummers, levitating children and ghostly apparitions? In fact, he had recounted similar incidents to his pupil Lady Anne Conway in the 1660s.[38]

More saw them as useful moral lessons, and did not deign to question them. To be sure, others thought that they *should* be questioned. Margaret Cavendish, duchess of Newcastle, herself an accomplished philosopher and advocate of empirical science, corresponded with Glanvill, but dismissed his supernatural tales as "nothing but slights and jugling tricks." She confessed to a belief in "Natural Magick; which is, that the sensitive and rational Matter oft moves in such a way, as is unknown to us," such as when a corpse moved in the presence of its murderer, but she refused to accept that "Spirits wander about in the Air, and have their mansion there; for men may talk as well of impossibilities, as of such Things which are not composed of Natural Matter." She did not object to astrology, because if the light of stars can reach our eyes, "their effects may come to our bodies." The "spiritual rays" cast out by witches, however, she found to be entirely incredible. Although Cavendish had a Hobbesian streak, she did not reject spirits entirely, and she was even willing to accept the reality of fairies. As for witches, she expressed concern that "many a good, old honest woman hath been condemned innocently, and suffered death wrongfully, by the sentence of some foolish and cruel Judges."[39] Critics of witchcraft seldom sympathized with wrongly accused old women. Cavendish may have done so because, unusually for a learned writer, she was a woman herself.

In an intellectual world dominated by educated men, the "Hags" who comprised the main victims in witch trials, and who were still being hanged in the 1660s and 1670s, did not command much attention. The controversy over witchcraft was never really about them. Even Margaret Cavendish was ultimately less concerned with witches than she was with the fundamental philosophical issue, the reality of spirits. Her arguments, like those of Hobbes, Wagstaffe, Casaubon, Webster and Glanvill, were composed for the edification of learned readers; they were not designed to sway the minds of the justices of the peace who presided over witch trials. If English witchcraft accusations slowly came to an end after 1660, it was because judges became reluctant to put their trust in the testimonies of poor, illiterate and often malicious accusers, not because they had suddenly become Hobbesian materialists.[40]

The fading away of witch trials also happened in Restoration Scotland, where no intellectual debate over witchcraft took place, and where "thinking with demons" was strongly upheld by both the established Episcopalian clergy and the displaced Presbyterians.[41] The main Scottish writer on the subject was the Presbyterian George Sinclair, former professor of philosophy at Glasgow University and an experimental scientist who was best known for having written a treatise on hydrostatics. His book *Satan's Invisible World Discovered*, published in 1685, imitated the strategy of *Saducismus Triumphatus* by publishing eyewitness accounts of the works of the Devil in Scotland, to which other stories were added, including several lifted directly from Glanvill. Sinclair's preface poured scorn on Hobbes, Benedict Spinoza ("or rather *Maledictus*") and Descartes, as the founders of modern atheism.[42] He made no attempt to countenance "benign spirits" or to argue from Neoplatonic principles about the existence of incorporeal forms. Sinclair was the Casaubon of the north, and the continuing popularity of his book, down to the nineteenth century, reminds us that, if the defenders of strict religious orthodoxy had been the only voices heard in the British Isles, witches might have continued to hang—or, north of the Tweed, to burn.[43]

We cannot trace the decline of witchcraft to the debate (or, in Scotland, to the lack of debate) of the Restoration period. On the other hand, we *can* draw from these writings the observation that occult philosophy faced formidable, albeit divided, opponents: materialists on the one hand, orthodox Anglicans on the other, with prominent Neoplatonists providing unexpected assistance to the latter. From different philosophical positions, the critics of occult thinking hammered away at alchemy, astrology and ritual magic, which they reviled as superstitious, enthusiastic or diabolic. Facing such strong intellectual and theological opposition, many who were attracted to the occult came to believe they could best defend themselves by adopting an empirical approach. By detached observation and "disinterested" experimentation, the watchwords of the Restoration intellectual establishment, the claims of occult philosophy, occult science and even popular magic could be put to the test, and proven true or false.

The Occult Experimentalists

All practising alchemists were experimentalists, but the individuals who will be considered in this section were known as experimental scientists for reasons that went beyond any specific interest they might have had in the occult. Without exception, they were inclined towards occult science from the start, and were trying to vindicate pre-formed assumptions. This may lead us to take a rather sceptical view of their objectivity, and to agree with the influential critique of seventeenth-century science proposed by Steven Shapin and Simon Shaffer. In studying Robert Boyle's air-pump experiments, Shapin and Shaffer question the "disinterested" basis of experimentalism. They represent "disinterest" as a calculated device, designed to separate the "modest" scientific practitioner, who relied only on empirical data, from the mere "enthusiast," who depended on personal visions or insights.[44] In short, scientific method was a ruse, which merely gave the appearance of separating experimentalists from prophets. To some extent, this section will uphold such an interpretation, by illustrating how experimentalism was repeatedly used to erase the telltale traces of occult philosophy and science.

To characterize the methods of late seventeenth-century science in this way, however, does not do them full justice. For a start, the power of "disinterest" to limit and shape scientific claims was not just a cultural subterfuge; it set down parameters for experimentalism, requiring practitioners to employ a certain type of nonsectarian language, to communicate with a recognized "fellowship" of natural philosophers and to acknowledge the objections that might be raised by those within or even outside that privileged group. While Restoration science was often guided by underlying philosophical motivations that interfered with the patient observation of expanding gases or celestial ellipses, it was equally constrained by the convention of presenting information publicly before various communities: scholars, clerics, educated amateurs, even the occasional foreign observer. Experiments could be repeated by those who did not entirely share the assumptions of their original performers, so different points of view had to be addressed or accommodated. Under such conditions, a "disinterested" scientist was not able to proclaim his adherence to occult philosophy openly, or even to publish experiments that rested on them. It would have ruined his credibility, even among those who shared similar beliefs. "Disinterested" science, in relation to the occult, was a self-denying ordinance with severely restrictive effects.

On the other hand, the free flow of ideas during the 1640s and 1650s, and the relative lack of concern with issues of heterodoxy, had made it possible to merge occult questions with experimental science, to a greater extent than would subsequently be imaginable. An easy-going interchange between the two permeates the voluminous correspondence of Samuel Hartlib, the German polymath. From the standpoint of practical alchemy, Hartlib's circle set an experimental standard that would be imitated for the rest of the century. The records of Hartlib's "Office of Address" are full of alchemical recipes, "Hermetic secrets" and notes on "secret experiments."[45] They were apparently shared among Hartlib's alchemical collaborators, including his son-in-law Frederick Clodius, Robert Child, John Dury and George Starkey. The strict regime of data collection, record-keeping and observation that Starkey adopted in carrying out his alchemical research has been praised by recent commentators.[46] His influence on the thinking of other members of the Hartlib circle was profound. They too stuck to a "disinterested" line of inquiry in tackling alchemical issues.

Hartlib's correspondents did not, however, neglect occult questions, even when they involved the supernatural. Astrology was particularly frustrating for them, because the mysteries of its operations presented difficulties for the experimental method. "Tis very probable," commented the clergyman John Beale in 1657, "That wee oft times call those Influences planetary, which are but the operations or emanations of our owne inhabitable globe, though occasioned by the Light, or other applications of other Orbes." In other words, natural earthly phenomena, like the movement of tides, should not be ascribed to planetary influences, although they might be related to the movement of celestial bodies. This did not mean that Beale wholly rejected astrological influences; rather, as he noted later in the same letter, "I am of this Heresy, That Astrology is a most serious affayre, if it were handled with ancient sanctity, as I conceive & find anciently recorded, That the holy Patriarchs did doe."[47] The problem with astrology was that its sacred and scriptural basis had yet to be rediscovered. We might not consider this to be a strictly scientific issue, but to the extraordinarily multitalented Beale—agricultural reformer, expert on cider-making and all-round source of expertise for Hartlib—it was just another area of natural inquiry, as it would later be for William Stukeley.

In the late 1650s, Beale wrote a series of detailed letters to Hartlib on visions, spirits and apparitions. Unlike Tany, the Pordages or Jane Lead, however, he took a methodical and experimental approach to these occult matters. His means of testing them included personal experience, as he described in a letter of 1657: "But whilst with much humiliation, fasting, & prayer I sought the Lord for his heavenly wisedome & instructions, & closely adherd to the revelations of the holy worde, & weighed all the kinds of wisedome there particularised, recited, or exemplifyed, I found those depths that made mee very much despise all other kinds of humane learneing." Beale was approaching what he believed to be the highest form of knowledge: communication with spirits. Although he saw spirits as either heavenly or demonic, and did not believe, as the Neoplatonists did, that they inhabited all things, Beale was nonetheless convinced that "the Angells have as much to doe with us & for us nowe, as ever they did for our forefathers."[48] Mystical conversation with them, he maintained, could be facilitated by proper preparation. He advised Hartlib that "the Spirite of Man by art & discipline, by preparation of ye body & minde may in dreames & trances, in syncopes, & fits of bodily weakenesses have a deepe insight into things absent, & things to come, & things secrete."[49] What "things secrete" did he see? The letters do not reveal this.

His silence is understandable. Even under the Protectorate, natural philosophers were concerned with the possibility of being accused of practising magic, heterodoxy or diabolism. They might take refuge in a delicate combination of mechanical explanations and vague occult metaphors. This was the case, for example, with Sir Kenelm Digby's weapon salve, the recipe for which appears in a note contained in Hartlib's papers.[50] Digby, a Roman

Catholic naval commander and diplomat as well as an alchemist, had gone into exile during the Civil War period.[51] He raised a furore in 1658 when he published an address that he had delivered at Montpellier, claiming discovery of the much sought-after weapon salve, which "naturally, without any Magic, cures wounds without touching them, yea, without seeing of the Patient."[52] The weapon salve debate had begun in the late sixteenth century and had long fascinated natural philosophers. If a "sympathetic" cure of this sort could be shown to work, then it might validate the thesis that the objects of nature had affinities with one another that were either supernatural or caused by unknown, unseen factors.

Historians of science have praised Digby for suggesting a purely mechanistic rather than spiritual approach to the problem of the weapon salve, but his discovery was more complicated than that.[53] Digby invented a yarn about getting the secret of the salve—actually, a powder of vitriol—from a travelling Carmelite monk, a figure of mystery straight out of an alchemical romance. His theory of how the powder worked was based on a fantastic tale of light carrying atoms out of the wound, "like Cavaliers mounted on winged coursers." Digby's *Discourse* also contained references to other remedies, like one for the removal of warts that involved rubbing hands in the light of the moon.[54] While these were supposedly natural, the parallel with magical cures was evidently a selling point. By dressing up mechanical science with touches of the supernatural, Digby was able to promote his discovery with great success. His lecture went through no fewer than forty editions by the early eighteenth century.

Digby was more of a showman than Robert Boyle, who regarded the occult seriously but took pains to exclude it from his published work. Boyle was the most celebrated English scientist of his time, until the appearance of Newton's *Principia Mathematica*. Through his connection with the Hartlib circle, he was able to learn the methods of experimental alchemy from George Starkey. His alchemical pursuits over the next forty years have been brilliantly reconstructed by Michael Hunter and Lawrence Principe.[55] While his approach to alchemy was essentially empirical, Boyle was fascinated by spirits and never gave up hope of contacting them through the Philosopher's Stone. Apart from one notable lapse, however, Boyle kept his ideas on alchemy and its supernatural ends out of his many publications on purely mechanical science. His concern with respectability and Anglican orthodoxy, especially after the Restoration, made him unwilling to expose himself to charges of enthusiasm or diabolism.

Boyle's earliest writings bear the clearest marks of occult philosophy and mystical religion. His unpublished draft of a "Study of the Booke of Nature," written in 1649, contained numerous citations from John Everard's translation of Hermes Trismegistus, "that great Philosopher, Priest & King, whom some have esteem'd ancenter than Moses."[56] A decade later, Boyle published a religious work, *Seraphic Love*, whose title was derived from "those nobler Spirits of the Caelestial Hierarchie, whose Name . . . expresses them to be of a flaming Nature."[57] In this treatise, the use of "Chymicall Metaphor" along with celestial and magnetic images is reminiscent of Jacob Boehme, whose writings Boyle may have encountered during his trips to Europe. *Seraphic Love* follows Boehme's Theosophy in equating God with a dialectical principle of Love that contains "so strong a Magick, as to Transform the Lover into the Object Lov'd."[58] When, in 1660, Boyle published the results of his famous experiments on the air pump, however, he avoided any reference to spiritual forces and offered strictly mechanical explanations. After Henry More raised objections to these experiments, and proposed the existence of a spiritual "Hylarchic Principle" that might explain them, Boyle responded by reiterating the "purely Corporeal and Mechanical" nature of compression, and vigorously denying the possibility of any such "Incorporeal Creature."[59] According to Boyle, More's spiritual view of nature was no different from that of the Chinese ruler who mistook a watch for a living thing.

Boyle's rejection of spiritual or supernatural explanations for experimental results might be read as a cautious reaction to the re-establishment of Anglican orthodoxy after 1660. The Restoration had changed many acolytes of occult thinking into conformists. John Beale and even John Webster returned, at least outwardly, to the embrace of the Church of England. Boyle's conformism, however, went deeper than a mere defensive reaction. Unlike the Neoplatonists, Boyle had never seen spirits as residing in all of nature; rather, as *Seraphic Love* made clear, good spirits occupied the ranks of angels and provided the models for communication between human beings and the deity. Of course, bad spirits also existed, as Boyle acknowledged in the preface that he appended in 1658 to an account of the noisy interactions of a demon with a French Protestant minister.[60] Because he linked them either with the promise of mystical experience or the threat of diabolism, not with natural phenomena, Boyle was determined not to involve spirits in mechanical explanations.

He reserved his private thoughts on spirits for the observations on alchemy that he kept among his personal papers. Through the 1670s and early 1680s, Boyle carried out alchemical experiments, although most of his correspondence with other alchemists was destroyed by later editors. In a rare surviving work, a dialogue on alchemy written around 1680, Boyle imagined a conversation between friends that turns to the subject of whether "the acquisition of the Philosopher's-stone may be an inlett into another sort of knowledge and a step to the attainment of some intercourse with good spirits." "Arnobius" (who seems to speak for the author) responds to the objections that intercourse with spirits was either impossible or diabolical, by demonstrating, first, that there have been proven conversations between men and demons, and, second, by providing "some instances of Spirits whom wee have more reason to look upon as good than bad that have conversd with men."[61] Boyle knew that his friend Joseph Glanvill was compiling a collection of examples of the first sort, that is, conversations with diabolic spirits, but he may also have been aware of the reluctance of Glanvill (and More) to comment publicly on communication with good spirits.[62] The views of "Arnobius" constituted Boyle's answer to Glanvill's reticence, as well as to More's error in seeing spirits at work everywhere.

The dialogue remained unpublished, however, perhaps because Boyle had been sensitized to the difficulties of making even the most oblique public references to alchemy. In 1676, he published (under a pseudonym, with a Latin translation alongside it) an article in the *Philosophical Transactions* in which he hinted that he had discovered "that which the Chrysopaean Writers mean by their *Philosophick Mercury*," allowing the transmutation of metals into gold. He also let it slip that the president of the Royal Society, viscount Brouncker, had already repeated his experiment. When he read the article, Isaac Newton was concerned enough to write to the journal's editor, Henry Oldenbourg, to register his doubts about the process and complain that such revelations could lead to "immense dammage to the world if there should be any verity in the Hermetick writers." He recommended "high silence" to the "the noble Author."[63] The incident was not repeated. Boyle would thereafter maintain a distinction between public and private experiments. His reputation as a scientist would come to rest on his espousal of a mechanical philosophy rather than his conviction that the possessor of the Philosopher's Stone could hold conversations with angelic spirits.

The foundation of the Royal Society in 1660 encouraged the discreet separation of mechanical and occult experiments that was demanded by Newton and accepted by Boyle. Of course, the Society attracted devotees of the occult, but they did not dominate its proceedings. John Beale became co-editor of the *Philosophical Transactions*, to which he contributed many papers, none of them on an occult subject. The public face of the Royal Society looked coldly on the occult.[64] In his history of the Society, first published in 1667, the Reverend Thomas Sprat scorned those whom he labelled "*Chymists*" or alchemists, as if they were religious sectarians:

> in the Chase of the *Philosopher's Stone*, they are so earnest, that they are scarce capable of any other Thoughts . . . This Secret they prosecute so impetuously, that they believe they see some Footsteps of it, in every Line of *Moses, Solomon*,

> or *Virgil.* The Truth is, they are downright *Enthusiasts* about it. And seeing we cast *Enthusiasme* out of *Divinity* it selfe, we shall hardly sure be persuaded, to admit it into Philosophy.

Nevertheless, some alchemists were moderate enough in their pursuits to be useful. Sprat went on to praise "the Advantages that accrue to Physick, by the industrious Labours of such *Chymists*, as have only the discreet, and sober Flame, and not the wild lightning of the others Brains."[65] We might read into this passage a contrast between the "sober" Robert Boyle and the "wild" Elias Ashmole—both of them prominent Fellows of the Royal Society. Yet the main distinction between the two was their level of discretion: Ashmole put into print ideas that Boyle only speculated about in private. From the first, the public meetings of the Royal Society had avoided discussion of "speculative" subjects like alchemy, which makes Boyle's blunder of 1676 all the more extraordinary.

The alchemists, however, were not the only occult researchers within the Royal Society. Among its founding members was John Aubrey, a prominent experimental scientist and mathematician whose private interests tended towards ritual and popular magic. In 1674, Aubrey copied out a manuscript entitled "Zecorbeni," a version of the fourth book of the *Clavicula Salomonis*, which he intended to include as part of a study of "the Remaines of Gentilisme," the same expression that had been used so disdainfully by Hobbes. Aubrey's approach to this material, however, was the opposite of Hobbesian. In discussing the use of pentagrams, crystal balls and charms, Aubrey included many notes based on communications with friends and acquaintances, indicating that he knew a lot of educated people who shared a predilection for magic and were aware of its uses.[66] He appended to this manuscript a variety of spells and incantations, many of which he had tried out himself, marking them "*probatum est*" ("It is proved").

In exploring such strange magical paths, which ranged from calling up a spirit in a crystal to expelling a witch, Aubrey was scrupulously following the rules of scientific inquiry: collecting and classifying observations, testing each procedure and recording the results. He recognized, of course, that he was dealing with questions that went beyond conventional science. The manner of the experiments was often outlandish—for example, to make a woman confess in her sleep, take "the tongue of a Frogge and lay it upon the womans brest & she shall confesse"—and he knew better than to submit any of them to the *Philosophical Transactions*.[67] Nevertheless, in 1696 he would publish a catalogue of notes on apparitions, visions, crystals and magic under the generic title *Miscellanies*. "The Matter of this Collection is beyond Humane reach," he stated, "we being miserably in the dark, as to the Oeconomy of the Invisible World."[68]

Robert Boyle carried out investigations similar to Aubrey's, although with more detachment. In the 1660s, he became intrigued by Valentine Greatrakes, known as "the Stroker," an Irish healer who claimed to be able to cure various ailments by laying on his hands. As the curing of scrofula by touch was a traditional practice of the English monarchy which had been revived after the Restoration by Charles II, Greatrakes was making a politically sensitive assertion about himself.[69] He was careful to avoid the suggestion of radical or sectarian motives, although some of his supporters were less scrupulous. Greatrakes was not invariably a success: he failed to rid Lady Anne Conway of migraine headaches, and he did not manage to convince the king of his powers when summoned to perform at court. Nevertheless, he impressed Boyle, whose brother happened to be his landlord back in Ireland. Greatrakes addressed his published autobiography to the famous scientist, including in it numerous testimonials signed by Boyle that confirmed the genuineness of the cures of "the stroker." In private correspondence, however, Boyle was cautious about endorsing a miraculous explanation of Greatrakes's "stupendious Performances." He was unsure as to whether he thought them to be supernatural or natural; if the latter, then they might be due to some corpuscular emission of "Effluvia," reminiscent of Digby's weapon salve.[70] Boyle was equally curious about "the Second Sight", a power to predict the future that was enjoyed by certain Highland Scots who believed themselves to be in communication with fairies.[71]

For established men of learning like Aubrey and Boyle, these investigations were not without risk. Ritual magic was condemned by the Church; magical healing was seen by many educated observers as superstition; and second sight was a popular belief, questionable on both religious and empirical grounds. Aubrey chose not to publish his researches until shortly before his death, and then did so in a calculatedly innocuous fashion. Boyle was undecided about why Greatrakes was successful, and he never proceeded very far with his examination of second sight. The methods used by both men were curiously conventional and unimaginative: they simply accumulated written and hearsay evidence, or watched the subject in operation. Aubrey may have "proved" some spells and charms, but we have no idea how he did so. The contemporary conviction that "disinterested" science should involve a direct unveiling of the principles of nature, rather than a controlled testing of hypotheses under artificially created circumstances, meant that nobody dreamed of subjecting magical practices to trial by experiment in the laboratory. Witnessing a phenomenon in nature, and bearing reliable testimony to it, was seen as a better experimental method than re-creating the phenomenon artificially.

Whether controlled experiments might have made a difference to men like Aubrey or Boyle is of course debatable, since observation of the occult tends to verify what one already believes.

What about Isaac Newton, that legendary scientist who wrote of himself as standing on the shoulders of giants, yet who had been so quick to condemn Boyle's Hermetic indiscretions? The mind-boggling scale of Newton's own alchemical obsession has been known to historians of science since the sale of his private papers in the 1930s, but its significance to his scientific thinking remains a matter of considerable debate. No wonder: almost all of the several hundred pages of alchemical manuscripts in Newton's hand consist of copied recipes, notes on experiments and extracts from various publications. Only in a few fragments does Newton offer his own comments on this vast body of material, and these are usually limited to practical considerations. Newton was liberal in his selection of sources: he copied out everything from Arnoldus de Villa Nova and the fictional Basil Valentine to Ashmole's *Theatrum Chemicum Britannicum* and the works of "Eirenaeus Philalethes."[72] While the emphasis in these manuscripts is on practical alchemical experiments, they also include a great deal of occult philosophy, from the *Tabula Smaragdina* to the writings of "Maria the Prophetess," the supposed sister of Moses. In a document drawn up in the early 1680s, Newton listed "the best Authors" and writings as Hermes Trismegistus, the *Turba Philosophorum* (a thirteenth-century dialogue of philosophers), Morien (mythical father of Merlin), Artephius, "Abraham the Jew" and his disciple Nicolas Flammel, Paolo della Scala, Sir George Ripley, Michael Maier, the *Rosarium Philosophorum* (a sixteenth-century collection of aphorisms), Thomas Charnock, Bernard of Trevisan, "Philaletha" (i.e. George Starkey) and Jean d'Espagnet.[73] Most of the writers on this list can be considered philosophical as well as practical alchemists, and while Newton may have read them for guidance on his experiments, he cannot entirely have avoided their speculative remarks.

Yet he said almost nothing about them. Perhaps the closest we can come to a first-hand understanding of what Newton saw in alchemy is in the letter he wrote after reading Boyle's article on philosophic mercury. The results of Boyle's experiment, he suggests, should be judged by "a true Hermetic Philosopher, whose judgmt (if there be any such) would be more to be regarded in this point then that of all the world beside to the contrary, there being other things beside the transmutation of metals (if those pretenders bragg not) wch none but they understand."[74] In other words, a "true Hermetic Philosopher" would know that the Philosopher's Stone could do much more than make base metals into gold. What more, though? Would it offer communication with angels? Eternal life? A key to natural magic? Newton retained his own "high silence" on these, so any precise answer must be speculative. The most thoughtful conjectures on this vexed issue have been offered by Richard Westfall and Betty Jo Teeter Dobbs.[75] Both have argued that Newton's alchemy has to be reconciled with his religious and scientific views, an immensely difficult undertaking. In religion, he maintained a fervent but secret adherence to the Arian heresy, which held Jesus Christ to be of a different substance from God and not co-eternal with the deity. Although divine, Jesus was a created being, made from some exalted form of matter and not part of a unified Trinity. Newton's fascination with the Hermetic concept of Chaos, the original substance from which the universe and everything in it was made, suggests that he may have perceived alchemy as a way to understand both the matter and process of Christ's unique genesis: in other words, to capture the essence of the Redeemer in a beaker.[76]

Whether or not this was linked to Newton's great theories of the universe is an even more intractable problem. Newton's reading of the Polish alchemist Michael Sendivogius may have helped him to conceptualize the idea of gravity. Sendivogius argued that metals were planted as seeds in the centre of the earth and were drawn by cosmic forces towards the surface. Newton, reversing the argument, saw all things as pulled towards the centre. His favourite alchemical experiment involved the "Martian Regulus" of antimony, a combination of iron and stibnite that could be cracked open to reveal a star shape, with lines radiating towards a central point. Did Newton perceive a microcosmic illustration of gravity in the Martian Regulus? Perhaps he did, but if so, he never said so. Instead, in a famous comment made in the third part of the *Principia Mathematica*, he admitted that he had no explanation of the cause of gravity, "and I frame no hypotheses; for whatever is not deduced from the phenomena is called a hypothesis; and hypotheses, whether metaphysical or physical, whether of occult qualities or mechanical, have no place in experimental philosophy." Paradoxically, he immediately went on to hypothesize about "a certain most subtle spirit which lies in and pervades all gross bodies," but of this "electric and elastic spirit" he would say no more.[77] His use of the term "spirit" must have been enormously exciting to anyone who had an attachment to occult beliefs, but he adamantly refused to give them any further satisfaction. Years later, in response to Leibniz's criticism of his theory of gravity, Newton wrote: "Occult qualities have been exploded not because their causes have been unknown to us but because by giving this name to the specific qualities of things, a stop has been put to all enquiry."[78] In other words, occult speculation led nowhere.

Newton's sensitivity to the claim that his work had something to do with occult philosophy seems to have grown over time, perhaps in response to trends that he truly abhorred, like Kabbalism. Whether he feared that his discoveries would be labelled as heterodox, enthusiastic, superstitious or simply wrong is far from clear, but he became much more phobic about the taint of the occult than Boyle ever was. All the same, he spent an enormous amount of time and effort on alchemical work between the 1660s and the early eighteenth century. It might be conjectured that Newton's scientific writings tested *implicit* occult hypotheses about phenomena like gravity or the nature of light through the *explicit* application of purely mechanical or mathematical explanations, but this would deny the veracity of Newton's own words: "*hypotheses non fingo*" ("I feign no hypotheses"). In the end, the mind of the greatest scientist of the late seventeenth century remains a partially closed book. Newton was an extreme case of the ambivalence that affected so many experimental scientists of the period: pulled towards the occult by an ineffable attraction, yet prevented by the contrary pull of respectability and reputation from revealing what he wanted to find there.

Ultimately, the most significant result of the occult experimentalism of the Restoration era was that it *proved* nothing at all. Alchemy, astrology, ritual magic and even popular magic were observed, described and occasionally tested, but never with the intention of finding out whether they were true or false. Rather, the emphasis of "disinterested" science was on how they worked; that is, determining the mechanical or supernatural character of occult phenomena whose existence was more or less assumed. Only the hardest of materialists denied their reality; only the most distracted of prophets warned that they could not be encompassed by human minds. To inquirers like Boyle, Aubrey and Newton, the secret meanings of such phenomena were a matter for speculation or hypothesis, not for experimental science. This did not mean that secrets were of no interest to the scholars of the Restoration; on the contrary, throughout this troubled period, secrets were a veritable obsession.

The Nature of Secrets

The late seventeenth century was an age of fearful secrets. King Charles II guarded his own: about his private religious views, the influence of his mistresses or the 1670 Treaty of Dover that he had made with France. Concerning these things, the public heard only rumours. The sectarians and republicans who conspired against him kept their plots secret, and while they seldom amounted to much, the public was encouraged to feel constant anxiety about the security of the crown. The fear of secret conspiracies extended to Roman Catholics as well: Jesuits were suspected of having lit the fire that incinerated much of London in 1666, and in 1678 the biggest secret of all, the so-called "Popish Plot" to assassinate the king and put his brother James on the throne, was revealed to an astonished public by the informers Titus Oates and his colleague Israel Tonge (an alchemist and acquaintance of John Aubrey).[79]

The opening of secrets was fundamental to the success of the Restoration press—which included newspapers, periodicals, broadsheets, song sheets and pamphlets. The press was responsible for creating, exaggerating, misreading and overpublicizing the hidden operations that supposedly put the kingdom in jeopardy. The press gave a new urgency to the notion that keeping secrets was dangerous and that everything hidden should be subjected to public inspection. Memories of the Civil War and Interregnum alarmed contemporary observers about the potential of secrets to corrode and dissolve the body politic. In such an atmosphere, the hidden meanings of occult philosophy and science were bound to arouse suspicion. It would be better to bring them to light at once.

Practitioners of the occult sciences, of course, did not agree. To be sure, the alchemists of the Restoration period were willing to publish their findings and theories to a far greater extent than their predecessors, but they used so much arcane jargon that their secrets were never fully exposed to view. If they were hesitant to tell all, it was because they held to an older understanding of secrets, one that persisted amid the new atmosphere of political fear. It connected "the secret," not with operations, but with ultimate meanings. The alchemists aimed to uncover, not just the workings, but the significances of nature—precisely what Newton stated he did *not* wish to discuss. This entailed a personal quest that could not easily be related to others.

The alchemists were not alone in trying to protect secrets. Many thirsted for private knowledge of the Bible's hidden mysteries, especially those pertaining to the final coming of Christ. On a more mundane level, apprentices were still trained for years in the "art and mystery" of a craft, the practice of which was forbidden to the uninitiated on pain of legal retribution.[80] In the late seventeenth century, however, these remaining areas of exclusive knowledge were being transformed by social change. The signs of the impending Apocalypse were daily proclaimed in ephemeral publications, from the visionary effusions of self-styled prophets to the broadsheet and newspaper reports that recorded wonderful sights and occurrences. Meanwhile, those who wanted to explore mysterious techniques like glass-making or the workings of machinery no longer had to struggle through long apprenticeships. They could turn to a burgeoning literature, ranging from simple explanatory tracts to erudite works like John Wilkins's *Mathematical Magick* (1648). Secrets were no longer the domain of the scholar or learned acolyte; they could be unravelled by anyone who was able to read and had access to publications. Increasingly, "the secret" was a bookseller's gambit whose moment of inception was very close to the moment of revelation.

The popularization of secrets in the late seventeenth century is exemplified by William Salmon's curious publication *Polygraphice*, five editions of which appeared between 1672 and 1685. Salmon, a medical doctor, vendor of patent medicines and author of an astrological almanac, was an experienced publicist, determined to reach a very wide audience. He consequently provided a remarkable variety of information on subjects that might have enticed any ambitious young man wanting to learn the mysteries of a trade, the secrets of medicine or the processes of alchemy. The fifth edition of his compendium was subtitled "The Arts of Drawing, Engraving, Etching, Limning, Painting, Washing, Varnishing, Gilding, Colouring, Dying, Beautifying and Perfuming." For good measure, Salmon added a section on chiromancy or palm reading, a translation of "The one hundred and twelve Chymical Arcanums of Petrus Johannes Faber," and a collection of alchemical recipes "fitted for Vulgar Use, for curing most diseases incident to Humane Bodies." Salmon flagrantly plagiarized Robert Boyle's research on colours, but he may not have imagined that anyone would notice, as he evidently did not think of his readers as connoisseurs of scientific tracts.[81] The simple, didactic tone of his writing suggests that he was addressing himself to people who wanted straightforward information on practical subjects. Salmon's description of chiromancy lacks any hint of mystery whatsoever. Avoiding "long or abstruse" explanations, he suggests that the lines of the hand can be read like a book, without any ambiguities or doubts. An extended *Cingulum Veneris*, for example, "shows intemperance and lust in both Sexes, a base and bestial Life; a filthy *Sodomite*, who abuses himself with beasts."[82] One can only imagine what a young apprentice would have done with that information.

Chiromancy was supposed to be a Jewish mystical art, a secret cherished by the Kabbalists, but Salmon did not bother to explain its origins. Learned readers might well have been annoyed by his lack of scholarship. They sought after secrets of a more profound sort—decipherments of nature and Scripture, not the rudiments of palmistry. Yet the idea that a single text would unlock these mysteries for them, dispelling any philosophical doubts they might have about spirits and resolving the discrepancies between the natural world and God's word, was intoxicating to many.

In 1677, a book arrived that promised to fulfil those aspirations. Its title was *Kabbala Denudata* or *Kabbala Unveiled*, and it consisted of Latin versions of medieval Jewish mystical works, including the *Zohar*, along with rabbinical commentaries and contemporary articles by well-known scholars. The editor and translator was Christian Knorr von Rosenroth, a German Lutheran alchemist and poet, who had studied the Kabbala with a rabbi in Amsterdam. He was described by a contemporary as "strange, but charming," which is not a bad description of his book, either.[83] The frontispiece to the first volume was indeed strange and charming: it showed a scantily clad woman running between parting waves towards a tall closet with an open door inscribed "PALATIUM ARCANORUM"—"THE PALACE OF SECRETS." The initial two volumes, organized with a bewildering lack of consideration for the reader, contained various contributions by Henry More, Rosenroth and Francis Mercurius van Helmont, a noted alchemist whose father, J.B. van Helmont, had been one of the leading theorists of the art. Because the compilation was intended for an international audience of scholarly readers, the essays were in Latin.[84] The great secrets of Jewish mysticism—God's hidden attributes, the divine character of Adam, the reality of spirits—were now available to every educated person, although not to the apprentices, amateur artists and medical quacks who might have purchased William Salmon's *Polygraphice*.

Kabbala Denudata was not designed for the vulgar public. It is an immensely complex work, and any attempt to sum it up in a few words will be inadequate. In broad terms, however, it can be understood as having three main purposes—three levels of secrets, as it were. The first and most obvious concerned the relationship between Christians and Jews. By drawing out the hitherto hidden parallels between Christianity and Jewish mysticism, Rosenroth and Van Helmont sought to encourage the conversion of the Jews, which was widely thought to be a harbinger of the end of time. As a result, they read the Christian Trinity into the Kabbalist *Sephiroth* or attributes of God, and interpreted Adam Kadmon, the cosmic figure who was central to the writings of the sixteenth-century rabbi Yitzchak Luria, as the Christian Messiah. "And precisely what with you is named Adam Kadmon, with us is called Christ," notes the Christian philosopher conversing with a Jewish Kabbalist in the section titled "*Adumbratio*."[85] Thus, Christianity and its parent religion were happily reunited.

The reunion, however, took place on heterodox terrain. This was the second secret of *Kabbala Denudata*, one not easy for the uninitiated reader to comprehend, then or now. Rabbi Luria had imagined the souls or spirits of all living things to be contained in Adam Kadmon's body, which was composed of the traces of divine light. Through "the breaking of the vessels," from which evil arose, the multiplicity of spirits had been forced out into the material world, but would eventually be reunited with the divine being through a process of restoration (*tikkun*). With his keen nose for heterodoxy, Henry More had quickly picked up on the problems inherent in the conflation of Adam Kadmon with Christ. Even before the publication of *Kabbala Denudata*, he had written to Rosenroth to register his objections. Pitting his own visionary experiences against those of the Jewish mystics, More claimed to have learned of their errors from a strange dream. In this, an eagle flew in at his window and, as More stroked its head, turned into a boy. When questioned, the boy asserted that he believed not in one God but in many. The irate More began to kick the impious boy, at which point he changed into a bee. On waking, More started to suspect that his visitor represented the Kabbala, and realized just how dangerous the secret of Jewish mysticism was. It amounted to pantheism, the doctrine that God was in everything, a heresy represented at that time by the writings of the Dutch-Jewish philosopher Benedict Spinoza.[86]

Today we might interpret More's dream differently. The eagle and boy might remind us of the story of Ganymede, and of a type of erotic desire with which More's mentor Plato would have been familiar. Whether or not More shared such feelings is less important than his evident ambivalence towards the figures in his dream. As with so many occult ideas, he was both drawn to and irritated by them. Of course, he was right to see heterodoxy hidden within *Kabbala Denudata*. It was indeed a dangerous book, no matter how strenuously its editors strove to deny it. Van Helmont vigorously countered the assertion that God's divine spirit was equivalent to the souls of his creatures, but he also conceded that there was not a very big difference between the two.[87] In the end, spirits were made of the same divine essence as God, which meant that the deity must be everywhere, imprisoned in the material world. This had further implications that might shock any conforming Anglican. First, if God was in every spirit, then should they not be as eternal as He was? Since matter decayed, however, this meant that spirits must change bodies in order to persist over time. Second, did it make any sense that God would condemn and punish for all eternity that which was part of Himself? What Van Helmont really wanted to draw out of the Kabbala was not pantheism, but an equally heterodox doctrine to which the Neoplatonist More was far less hostile: namely, the transmigration of souls, which led to the assumption that all souls were to be saved.[88]

Van Helmont recognized "the Revolution of Human Souls" in the Kabbalist myth of the dispersal of spirits from Adam Kadmon's body. He hinted strongly at this in *Kabbala Denudata*, but only revealed his hand fully in a pamphlet published in 1685. In that work, Van Helmont defended the idea that "God is a God of Order, who hath created every living thing . . . to the end that by a never-ceasing Revolution it might be still renewed." The soul moved towards perfection through up to a dozen transmigrations. Van Helmont did not shrink from the corollary, that every soul would eventually be redeemed and there would be no eternal punishment: "For is not every Creature of God Infinite?"[89] Universal salvation was hardly a new idea, but Van Helmont would give it renewed intellectual vigour, to the horror of those who believed in eternal judgment. The prophetess Jane Lead was one of the few who agreed with him, although her key to secrets was personal revelation, not Jewish mysticism.

The third and deepest secret of *Kabbala Denudata* concerned alchemy. The first volume contained a Latin translation of the *Aesch Mezereph* or "Purifying Fire," an allegorical treatise on metals dating from the fifteenth or sixteenth century. It consists of a mixture of alchemical recipes, numerology and arcane pronouncements on biblical verses. Because the editors of *Kabbala Denudata* believed the Kabbala to be ancient, this virtually impenetrable text would take on a great deal of importance for alchemists. In 1714, it became one of the first parts of Rosenroth's collection to be rendered into English.[90] The similarities between the *Aesch Mezereph* and the *Corpus Hermeticum* were duly noted by Rosenroth, who pointed out that that the Kabbala expressed the values of an original, "Oriental" philosophy, "just as is to be seen in Hermes Trismegistus."[91] This was not implausible, since the Kabbalists, who lived in western Europe, may have been influenced by the Hermetic writings, but Rosenroth meant to suggest a basic unity among ancient philosophers of the mysterious "Orient." What he did not know was that ten centuries and the length of the Mediterranean separated the Jewish mystical texts from the works ascribed to Hermes Trismegistus.

Kabbala Denudata made a considerable splash, but it also exemplified a basic problem with the revelation of secrets: namely, they were most convincing to those already disposed to believe them. Through her reading of the collection, as well as her friendship with Van Helmont, Lady Anne Conway was convinced of the doctrine of the transmigration of souls, which became central to her own philosophical writings.[92] On the other hand, while John Locke read *Kabbala Denudata* with care and took copious notes on it, he objected to the ambiguities of the language and gave the title "Doubts about the Oriental Philosophy" to his observations.[93] Isaac Newton, an enemy to Gnostics and Neoplatonists, also read *Kabbala Denudata*, but rejected its portrayal of lesser spirits as sharing in God's substance. His long search for a "religion of Noah" that would counter Jewish mysticism can be viewed as a response to the book.[94] Its ultimate significance for "the sons of Hermes" may also be doubted. It was simply too complex for the average alchemist. Van Helmont himself was not very successful in applying it to the spagyric art. Admittedly, some of the "Chymical Aphorisms" that he published in 1688 have a Kabbalistic ring to them. Alchemy, he wrote, "is a Science whereby the Beginnings, Causes, Properties and Passions of all the Metals, are radically known; that those which are imperfect, incompleat, mixt and corrupt, may be transmuted into true Gold."[95] This statement may have been inspired by the Lurian concept of the restoration of souls to perfect unity with God, but, then again, the language is not very different from that of traditional alchemical texts. As for the *Aesch*

Mezereph, Van Helmont seems to have found its recipes and tables as indecipherable as they appear to readers today.

Its doors finally opened, the palace of Kabbalistic secrets became a home to heterodoxy and the scene of furious controversy. *Kabbala Denudata* did not initiate a new age for the Christian Kabbala; rather, it ended a fruitful period of speculation, which now gave way to criticism and disillusionment. The magical aura of the Kabbala among its Christian admirers began to dissipate once its principles were known. While it continued to intrigue philosophers like Leibniz, it lost much of its conjuring power in popular literature—at least until the late eighteenth century, when its theological principles had again been largely forgotten. In an embarrassing demonstration of its newly contested status, the Kabbala was even satirized. The original French version of this satire by the Abbé de Villars had appeared in 1670, but it was translated and reprinted at London ten years later, evidently in response to *Kabbala Denudata. The Count of Gabalis: or The Extravagant Mysteries of the Cabalists Exposed* was a subtle parody of occult philosophy. A sceptical young man is visited by a German Kabbalist count who advises him to renounce sexual relations with women and confine his lusts to sylphs, nymphs and "Gnomides." He eventually reveals the secret that Plato and other philosophers were the offspring of unions between men and spirits. Although very funny, the book has deceived gullible readers up to the present into thinking that it is intended as a serious work of occult thought—the Internet is littered with their comments. Of course, the subtitle gives the game away.[96]

The anonymous printer of *The Count of Gabalis* exposed another secret on the title page, by designating himself as "Printer to the Cabalistical Society of the Sages, at the Signe of the *Rosy-Crusian*." No such organization had sponsored the appearance of *Kabbala Denudata*, and none arose from its publication. Nevertheless, to understand the nature of secrets in the late seventeenth century, we have to consider the lure of secret societies. Men of learning continued to hope that secrets could be passed down from teacher to pupil, like the arts and mysteries of a skilled craft. A secret society based on initiation into such mysteries might preserve them forever. This atavistic vision of occult philosophy as a kind of underground activity, passed down over generations, was in part a reaction to the "vulgarization" of learning through print culture. It was a socially exclusive and gendered vision: only educated men of acceptable character and learning were allowed to participate in the transmission of wisdom.

The willingness to believe in the existence of such groups had sparked the Rosicrucian episode of the early seventeenth century, the effects of which lingered for generations. It also led Robert Boyle into one of the strangest experiences of his career. In 1677, Boyle met a French alchemist, Georges Pierre des Clozets, who introduced him to an international society known as "the Asterism."[97] Boyle was named to a vacant seat in the organization by the "Patriarch of Antioch," a man whom Pierre called his "great master" and who bore the office of chancellor in this "most powerful and most magnanimous Cabalistic Society of the Sons of Wisdom."[98] Through Pierre, the patriarch asked Boyle to send him various items, including cannons, telescopes, microscopes and chemical apparatus. For his part, Georges Pierre sent Boyle alchemical recipes and reports about the activities of members of the society, including the creation by one of them of a homunculus or miniature human being. Pierre also periodically requested sums of money to cover his expenses. Alas, it was all too good to be true. In September 1678, Boyle learned from a friend of Pierre that he had not been using the money to travel, and instead had been living at Caen with his pregnant girlfriend.[99] "The Asterism" turned out to be an ingenious hoax, so elaborate that Pierre had even gone to the trouble of placing advertisements in Dutch and French newspapers announcing the election of the "Patriarch of Antioch." Boyle was probably not his only victim. Interestingly, only a month after Pierre's fabrications were revealed to him, Boyle received a copy of *Kabbala Denudata*.[100] From "the Asterism," he turned to a book whose secrets were less exclusive but equally mysterious.

Georges Pierre's secret society resembled the Rosicrucians, but its elaborate titles and Near Eastern orbit gave it the aura of a Crusading order of the Middle Ages. In a sense, "the Asterism" was what many learned men in the late seventeenth century would have liked the Brotherhood of Freemasons to be: an organization that spread occult secrets, not by publicity, but through initiation. The early history of the Masons is notoriously difficult to untangle, but they were descended from active lodges or professional meeting places of medieval stonemasons, who possessed elaborate constitutions and "charges" that spun fantastic myths out of biblical stories, for instance, about the building of the Temple of Jerusalem. In 1598–9, the master of works for King James VI of Scotland, William Schaw, issued new statutes for the Scottish lodges that included tests in the art of memory, a method of symbolically reconstructing knowledge that was associated with occult philosophy.[101] From that point on, the humble lodges of stonemasons began to gain a reputation among the learned as privileged and closed spaces where secrets were imparted through strange rituals. The first known non-operative or "speculative" Freemason was none other than Robert Moray, the Scottish alchemist. He was admitted at Edinburgh in 1641, along with Alexander Hamilton, commander of artillery for the Covenanting army then fighting against King Charles I. Moray later enjoyed affixing his "mason mark" to letters, either as a seal or a drawing—it consisted of a pentacle, the five-sided star associated with ritual magic and familiar to readers of the *Clavicula Salomonis*.[102] Elias Ashmole, who joined a lodge at Warrington, Lancashire, in 1646, was the first English Mason to record his initiation.[103] Given the known interests of Moray and Ashmole, there would seem to be little doubt that their attraction to Freemasonry was related to the promise of learning secrets about occult philosophy or science.

The actual secrets of the Freemasons were rooted in their myths and rituals, not in any hidden knowledge of nature that they were able to impart. Nonetheless, the press connected them with occult philosophy from the start. A satirical advertisement or "Divertisement" published in the newspaper *Poor Robin's Intelligencer* for 10 October 1676 makes the point uproariously, adding a political twist to it:

> These are to give notice, that the Modern Green-ribbon'd Caball, together with the Ancient Brother-hood of the Rosy-Cross; the Hermetick Adepti, and the Company of accepted Masons, intend all to Dine together on the 31 of November next, at the Flying-Bull in Wind-Mill-Crown-Street; having already given order for great store of Black-Swan Pies, Poach'd Phoenixes Eggs, Haunches of Unicorns, &c. To be provided on that occasion; All idle people that can spare so much time from the Coffee-house, may repair thither to be spectators of the Solemnity: But are advised to provide themselves Spectacles of Malleable Glass; For otherwise 'tis thought the said Societies will (as hitherto) make their Appearance Invisible.[104]

The Green-Ribbon Club, which met at the King's Head tavern in Chancery Lane, was composed of opposition Members of Parliament, most of whom later became Whigs. The duke of Buckingham, whose interest in alchemy and astrology has already been noted, was a leading member.[105]

By lumping an opposition club together with the Rosicrucians, Hermeticists and Freemasons, the newspaper writer was suggesting not just that they were all secret cabals, but that they shared the same sort of fantastical notions, such as about eating imaginary dishes or becoming invisible. The mention of coffee-house idlers is also worth noting. Sites for business, political discussion and cultural exchanges as well as leisure, coffee-houses were springing up throughout the fashionable parts of London in the 1670s.[106] They often provided newspapers for their clients, so *Poor Robin's Intelligencer* was actually making fun of some of its own readers.

The presence among their Fraternity of Elias Ashmole demonstrates that not all Freemasons were crypto-republicans. In fact, as the English lodges had little or no central organization before 1717, it would be unwise to make *any* broad generalizations about their religious or political dispositions at this time. Most likely, each lodge adopted a political tenor according to the views of its members. In London, the lodges may well have had a general affiliation with the emerging Whig Party. Whether occult philosophy was actually discussed in them is another matter, to which no satisfactory answer can be given, as evidence is entirely lacking. Perhaps the most surprising aspect of the 1676 "Divertisement" is that the author expected readers to recognize all of these groups, including the Freemasons. Like coffee-houses, they were already a part of literate culture in London and the provinces, and they were there to stay.

The hidden wisdom of *Kabbala Denudata* lost its appeal within a few years. The mysteries of Freemasonry, on the other hand, continued to fascinate both initiates and "cowans," or non-Masons, for generations to come. Because they remained private associations, the lodges were not in danger of losing their secrets to the public, so long as members kept their mouths shut. Paradoxically, however, Freemasonry would soon develop a dependence on publicity. While they did not want their rites and practices to be revealed to the world, the attention given to them by the press (and in coffee-house conversations) helped Masons to maintain their profile within English and Scottish society. Freemasonry became a strange mixture of secrecy and publicity, of ritualism and tolerance, of the traditional and the innovative.

To return to our original question: how integrated were occult philosophy and science in the intellectual life of the late seventeenth century? The short answer is that their integration was uneven and their position insecure. On the one hand, we might point to the interest taken in them by so many major scientific and philosophical figure of the late 1600s: Hartlib, Beale, Boyle, Newton, Aubrey, More, Glanvill, Locke. On the other hand, the results of that interest were limited. The dangers of transgressing the limits of "disinterest" or religious orthodoxy kept opinions private and experiments hidden from public scrutiny. In the atmosphere of fear and suspicion after 1660, occult thinking provided the defenders of religious authority with an easy target, which could be attacked even if it could not be suppressed.

The occult made definite contributions to the knowledge of the late seventeenth century, but its influence was usually disguised. Alchemy, astrology and ritual magic never enjoyed the respectability that so many of their practitioners craved. This could be seen as early as the 1680s in the field of medicine. In spite of the widespread use of pills and nostrums that had their origins in Paracelsian theories and alchemical experiments, most doctors continued to rely on older Galenic theories of the humours, and on techniques derived from them, like bleeding.[107] The practical results of alchemy were praised, but its "higher" aims aroused the suspicions of many observers, and it was never established as a formal course of study at any of the universities in the British Isles. The enormous popularity of astrology served to associate it with vulgar forms of learning and, apart from John Goad, no leading intellectual of the period devoted much attention to it. Ritual magic was too close to diabolism to be openly espoused. As for philosophical trends like Neoplatonism, Hermeticism or Kabbalism, they were the subjects of heated debate among scholars, and were likely to be condemned in strong terms whenever they verged on heterodoxy, which they frequently did. Prophets who drew upon occult philosophy were denounced as sectarians, and their messages reached only small audiences.

In spite of its widespread appeal, therefore, the occult was continually relegated to the sidelines of late seventeenth-century thought. Its nemesis remained religious orthodoxy, but it had gained a further adversary in the Hobbesian materialism that denied the possibility of disembodied spirits, and it was increasingly seen as incompatible with natural science. The new dawn that had excited so many occult enthusiasts in the 1650s had soon been overshadowed by opposition and doubt. Even before the Glorious Revolution, therefore, occult thinking was entering a period of eclipse, a retreat from publicity back into the private realm. Only after the pillars of orthodoxy began to shift in the mid-eighteenth century would this period of relative darkness end, and an occult revival begin.

PART TWO
ECLIPSE, 1688–1760

CHAPTER FOUR

A Fading Flame

In 1688, the Catholic King James II fled from his kingdoms, losing his throne to his Protestant son-in-law William of Orange and his daughter Mary in what became known as the Glorious Revolution. Nothing in this political change would have signalled imminent catastrophe to those who were interested in occult philosophy and science. On the contrary, many adherents of the occult were sectarians or heterodox Anglicans. They might be seen as beneficiaries of the revolution, which ushered in a Parliamentary Act of Toleration that encompassed mainstream Protestant groups. Within a decade of 1688, however, occult thinking was suffering from a severe loss of intellectual energy and by 1715, it appears to have been in a state of decline. Why did this happen?

To begin with, we should consider what "decline" actually meant. It translated into fewer works on alchemy, less respect for astrology and the virtual disappearance of ritual magic among the educated. The publication of alchemical books in English had peaked between 1650 and 1675, with ten or more works appearing in some years. While the trade in newly published alchemical texts slowed down over the next quarter-century, up to a half-dozen new publications might become available every year. After 1700, this was reduced to a couple of volumes annually, and by the 1710s many years passed without any new book coming onto the market at all. Of course, educated people also read Latin. Alchemical publications in that language (including those printed outside Britain) similarly declined after 1700, but less dramatically.[1] Because English and Scottish alchemists had access to older works, as well as to foreign publications, we should be cautious in asserting that there was an overall decline in the number of volumes available to readers. On the other hand, British publishers, always on the lookout for commercially lucrative possibilities, clearly perceived the alchemy market as being less strong after 1700 than it had been in the previous half-century. They gradually gave up on an area of publishing that was no longer viewed as profitable.

Astrology was a different case. It suffered a further loss of prestige, but not of popularity. The number of almanacs published in England remained at more or less the same level throughout the period, so there was no drying-up of the public thirst for predictions.[2] Serious studies of astrology, however, became rare. Few bothered to examine whether it worked through natural magic or angelic influence.[3] The field was now dominated by John Partridge, an ardent Whig who had gone into exile during James II's reign and returned at the Glorious Revolution. His empirical approach to the celestial art pleased some privileged customers, but it was eccentric: anti-Copernican, firmly opposed to magic and fixated on the "Hileg" or predictor of death. Partridge's politics led to ferocious attacks on him, which he reciprocated. His bitter rival John Gadbury continued to practise his own reformed (and heliocentric) version of astrology, but his clients were of distinctly lower status. The silver age of English astrology ground to a bitter finish in the competition between these two men.[4]

By the early eighteenth century, a fashionable tone of scepticism about supernatural claims was taking hold among younger intellectuals. It was hotly resisted by orthodox clerics, especially in Scotland, where an Edinburgh University student, Thomas Aikenhead, was hanged for blasphemy in 1697. He had dubbed Scripture "Ezra's fables" and called both Moses and Jesus magicians—a weird conflation of occult lore and irreligion.[5] Meanwhile, party politics raised the level of rhetoric concerning the occult to a very high pitch. The Whigs accused their Tory opponents of "superstition," because some of them argued for the reality of witches or accepted the charms and spells associated with an older type of astrology. In exchange, the Tories accused Whigs who practised alchemy or supported astrology of being "enthusiasts" and "fanatics." Party conflict was a crucial factor in determining the destiny of occult thinking after 1688, but it was only one strand among several that contributed to the decline. The precarious intellectual position of occult philosophy, evident since at least the 1660s, was arguably the underlying reason for its loss of momentum. Never having enjoyed the respectability and authority that it craved, the occult slid into retreat after 1688 because its place in an altered society became even more insecure.

Perhaps the hardest blows to fall on occult learning were the deaths of respected intellectuals: Robert Boyle died in 1691, Elias Ashmole in 1692, Henry Coley in 1695, John Aubrey in 1697, Samuel Jeake the younger in 1699. The alchemical publisher William Cooper barely survived the Glorious Revolution and his last known works date from 1689. Other major figures, like Thomas Vaughan, George Starkey, Robert Moray, John Heydon, William Lilly,

John Webster and William Andrews, did not live to see the Revolution. Sir Isaac Newton, of course, outlived them all, but he turned away from alchemy in the first decade of the eighteenth century. No scholars of similar stature emerged to replace these men, indicating how the occult had failed to establish itself as a recognized field of inquiry. At the same time, it cannot be argued that scientific endeavour benefited. On the contrary, the Royal Society shed much of its own reforming zeal after 1689, becoming more like a gentlemen's club.[6] The publication of Newton's *Opticks* in 1704 effectively marked the end of an era of burning scientific questions.

If it lacked giants, the period after 1689 saw the popularization of science through periodicals like *The Athenian Mercury*, published by John Dunton between 1690 and 1697. In its pages, a group of writers answered questions from the public, often concerning scientific matters. Their views summed up the impact of the new scientific philosophy. *The Athenian Mercury* never discussed alchemy, and was contemptuous of the astrology found in almanacs, "the best of which more often *miss* than *hitt*."[7] It issued a brief, dismissive reply to a pointed inquiry by Samuel Jeake that was designed to cast doubt on the heliocentric theory.[8] Asked whether charms had any real force, the writers replied that "if there's any thing in 'em, *abstracted from Fancy* . . . it must be Diabolical—but they can't do no more than the Devil himself, who can only *represent the Object*, not force the Will to embrace it."[9] Surprisingly, given this assumption that diabolic power was restricted, the journal fully accepted the reality of ghostly apparitions, to which a whole issue was devoted on Halloween 1691.[10] It also endorsed belief in witchcraft, reprinting as evidence testimony from the Salem witch trials. Admittedly, not all readers of *The Athenian Mercury* trembled at the thought of ghosts or witches. One of them wrote that belief in the Devil's works was "against the Essence of God Almighty . . . and scarce any Story of Witchcraft, *&c*, but has been detected to be Artifice, or Natural."[11] His scepticism, however, seems to have been exceptional.

The opinions of *The Athenian Mercury* show that at least one major organ of scientific thought did not reject supernatural occurrences, although it tended to see them as caused by the Devil. The emphasis on diabolism was widely reiterated in the aftermath of the Glorious Revolution: for example, by the influential Presbyterian divine Richard Baxter in a 1691 work entitled *The Certainty of the World of Spirits*. Baxter emulated Glanvill's *Saducismus Triumphatus* by presenting eyewitness examples of witchcraft, apparitions, spirit voices and other interventions of the Devil. He admitted that angels had a role in human affairs, but hastily added: "I will not desire so to alter the stated Government and Order of God, as to expect here visible Communion with Angels."[12] Such views, which were common to Scots Presbyterian, Anglican and Dissenting clerics, served to bind Protestants together at a moment of deep political division. They posed a challenge to those who espoused occult thinking, because they judged spiritual communication as diabolic.

The resurgence of the Devil in religious writings after 1688 did not reverse the downward trend in witch trials, which in England had already dwindled to almost nothing. Yet it surely contributed to the noticeable decline in works that dealt seriously with occult philosophy. Decline, to be sure, did not mean demise. The continuation of a small stream of new writing on alchemy allowed adepts to find fresh works to excite them, even in the post-revolutionary decades. Astrology continued to guide the hopes and fears of many readers, and the desire to talk with spirits was not extinguished. It would be another ninety years, however, before the occult would begin to regain the public profile that it had enjoyed in the late seventeenth century.

Alchemy between Philosophy and Commerce

The Glorious Revolution initially raised the hopes of the alchemists, but the results of the subsequent two decades can hardly have lived up to their expectations—except perhaps in a commercial sense. Alchemy was already changing into a business before 1688, but in the next two decades it would be transformed from a subject of philosophical speculation to a set of practices valued mainly as a basis for proprietary medicines. As a result, it lost much of its intellectual significance and became tied to the fortunes of ambitious businessmen whose commercial empires extended throughout Britain and abroad. At the same time, the remaining alchemists gradually lost touch with a post-revolutionary culture that emphasized competition, moderation and openness.

This development could not have been foretold in 1689, when alchemy still seemed to be riding high. An impressive illustration was the list of 190 subscribers to an edition of the works of the celebrated German alchemist Johann Rudolph Glauber, discoverer of many useful medicinal compounds. The enormous folio volume, translated by Christopher Peake, writing under the personal title "Philo-Chymico-Medicus," was one of the last works published by William Cooper. The subscribers included the lord mayor of London, the Quaker William Penn, the president of the Royal College of Physicians and a large number of doctors and surgeons. The handsome book, prepared before the Glorious Revolution, was dedicated to Edmund Dickinson, a noted alchemist who had been physician in ordinary to Charles II and James II. The preface also praised Dickinson's friend Robert Boyle, "The Honour both of our Age and Country." The two men had led "Chymistry" out of the dark age, when few were "so much as lightly Tincted with the *Hermetick Philosophy*."[13] Yet we may wonder how many of the medical practitioners who subscribed to the book were themselves even "lightly Tincted" with Hermeticism. No doubt many just wanted to be associated with the prestigious names of Glauber, Dickinson and Boyle, or with chemical processes that might lead to profits.

The new regime seemed even better disposed to alchemy than the old. A smashing political triumph for the alchemists came in the immediate wake of William and Mary's accession, when the Act of Henry IV outlawing "multiplying," or the transmutation of base metals into gold, was repealed. As early as 29 April 1689, only two weeks after the new monarchs had been crowned, Robert Boyle wrote to Christopher Kirkby, a merchant and alchemist living in Cornwall, opining "that the act of *Henry* the 4th has been, and, whilst it shall remain in force, will be, a great discouragement to the industry of skilful men, which is very happily improved in this inquisitive age. And therefore, that the repealing of a law, so darkly and ambiguously penned, will much conduct to the public good."[14] Boyle went on to testify before Parliament that he had witnessed transmutation, which must have excited MPs who were increasingly worried by the lack of silver and gold coinage in a nation on the verge of a major war against France. For them, the removal of legal restrictions on alchemy amounted to sound monetary policy.[15] By August 1689, the Whig-dominated Parliament had passed a bill repealing the medieval statute, and King William III had signed it into law (1 W. & M. c. 30). The new Act recognized that "divers Persons have by their Study, Industry and Learning, arrived to great Skill and Perfection in the Art of Melting and Refining of Metals, and otherwise Improving their Ores . . . and Extracting Gold and Silver out of them," which must constitute the most explicit legislative endorsement of alchemy ever given in England. *Spagyria*, however, would now benefit the state, not the individual adept. Any gold or silver made out of copper, tin, iron or lead was to be brought to the Mint in the Tower of London, assayed and used for "the Increase of Moneys."[16]

It is very likely that Isaac Newton, MP for Cambridge University, had a hand in the passage of the bill. Yet nothing is known about his involvement, because he continued in his guarded attitude towards alchemy after the Revolution. Following Boyle's death in 1691, Newton confided to John Locke, a trustee of Boyle's papers, that he had no wish to learn the alchemical secrets of his late friend. In an arrogant tone all too typical of the great scientist, Newton declared that he was not interested in Boyle's recipe for transmutation, based on the "red earth" or dry mercury that was linked to the essence of Adam (whose name, in Hebrew, means "red earth"). "I do not desire to know what he has communicated," he wrote to Locke, "but rather that you would keep the particulars from me . . . because I have no mind to be concerned wth this R_x [recipe] any further then just to know the entrance [the first step]."[17] Newton had not renounced alchemy, of course, and for the first time his efforts enjoyed the assistance of another human being, the young Swiss mathematician Nicolas Fatio de Duillier. They remained secret.

Perhaps encouraged by the Parliamentary Act, Newton's alchemy reached a culmination in 1693, when he wrote in his personal papers a long comment entitled "Praxis" that recorded his discovery of a process by which "you may multiply to infinity."[18] Shortly thereafter, he entered a period of depression and paranoia that some historians have linked to mercury poisoning, although he did not suffer the tremors or loss of teeth that usually accompany that condition. After his recovery, he was appointed as warden of the Mint by the Whig government, from which position he guided the major recoinage effort of 1696. He became master of the Mint in 1700.[19] So far as is known, he never tried to increase the production of English specie by "multiplication."

If Newton was not prepared to give up alchemy after 1688, neither were many others. In the immediate aftermath of the Glorious Revolution, the Hermetic philosophy was still good business for the book trade. In 1690, the printer Henry Faithorne had enough confidence in the sales of a collection of alchemical aphorisms by the mysterious "Baro Urbigerus" to attach to it a splendidly elaborate frontispiece, showing the Tree of Life with Apollo and Diana standing in water beneath it. The picture was explained as "mystically representing all our Subjects and Operations." "Baro" was a philosophical alchemist who longed for the spiritual power that *spagyria* had always offered to its adepts. Claiming that he would reveal "the Secret of Secrets," he described the "Green Dragon" or "Philosophical Gold" as "spiritual and living, having the generative Faculty in it self."[20] Alchemy remained an occult as well as a mechanical art, and it continued to revel in the allusive language of symbols and myths.

Then, abruptly, the spagyric flame began to flicker and die. In the years that followed the aphorisms of "Baro Urbigerus," would-be adepts virtually stopped writing about alchemy. A number of celebrated works on the subject were reprinted, including those of "Eirenaeus Philalethes" and the two Van Helmonts, but very few original alchemical tracts appeared alongside them. Some that might be called "original" were in fact commentaries on earlier works, like the appendices to the 1709 edition of *The Marrow of Alchemy*, or the notes included with the 1714 version of the *Aesch Mezereph.*[21] No intellectual successor to Ashmole or Vaughan or "W.C." or "Baro" came to the fore—with a sole possible exception.

The only alchemical writer of significance who published works in English between 1690 and 1715 was the Dutch immigrant William Yworth, who wrote under the extraordinary pseudonym "Cleidophorus Mystagogus." The name is composed from the Greek κλειδοφορέω, or "to bear keys," and the Latin word for "a guide to mysteries." Yworth was indeed a mysterious character, who had practised as an alchemical physician in his native Rotterdam before emigrating to England around 1691. He began to market medicines and became an expert in wine-making. Yworth's first published alchemical treatise, a guide to equipment and processes that appeared in 1692, included a fine print showing the laboratory at his "New Spagyrical Academy" in Shadwell. He was connected with several prominent Quakers, including the publisher Andrew Sowle, although his own religion is unknown.[22] Yworth later moved to Moorfields in north London, where he published two works under the pseudonym "Mystagogus" in 1702 and 1704. He sent copies of his alchemical writings to Isaac Newton, who took extensive notes on the Dutchman's processes and tried to repeat them in his own experiments. Newton also agreed to pay the penurious alchemist an allowance. By 1710, Yworth had retired to Woodbridge, Suffolk, and his son Theophilus had taken over the "Academy."[23]

Yworth did not have either the social status or the intellectual background of earlier alchemists like Vaughan, Starkey or Boyle. Yet he was no less an occult philosopher than they. He described his point of view as "Theophisical," meaning that he was trying to reconcile alchemy and Scripture. The term may have been intended to contrast with Jacob Boehme's "Theosophy," to which Yworth, like Newton, never showed any affinity. Neither did he accept the theory of Francis Mercurius van Helmont, delineated in *Kabbala Denudata*, that matter was created from nothing, and was therefore infused with God's own substance. Instead, he argued for creation out of original "Chaos," which was separate from God. Despite his coolness towards *Kabbala Denudata*, Yworth claimed to understand the "Cabalistical" knowledge of the ancient Jews, and hinted at membership in a brotherhood of Kabbalists. In his first alchemical pamphlet, "Mystagogus" included an oath taken by an adept "upon the Adopting of a Brother into the Cabalistical Society." He also appended to the work a "Philosophical Epistle" full of references to "that Cabalistical Wisdom, which contains the Secrets of Nature."[24] Yworth's Kabbalism entirely ignored the researches of Rosenroth, which must have pleased Newton, who did not think much of them either.

Even more gratifying for the great scientist, "Mystagogus" associated "the Mercury of the Philosophers" with Christ, calling it "God's Vicegerent." As Mercury was formed out of the original Chaos, it might be assumed that Christ was too, which implied that he was of a different substance from God, and not by nature divine. This was not far removed from Newton's deeply hidden Arian beliefs. Like the Saviour, moreover, mercury "died" and was "reborn" in the alchemical process. In an ecstatic description of this moment of fulfilment, "Mystagogus" envisioned the attainment of the Philosopher's Stone as the prelude to a Second Coming:

> The Gold-making Art, so-call'd, will become common to the men of the new World, when Wisdom shall be esteemed for Wisdom's sake . . . indeed it cannot otherwise be expected untill the fullness of time shall come, that the Golden Calf shall be ground to Powder, and Money shall be esteemed like Dross, and the prop of Antichrist dash'd in pieces. O that we might be all prepared for that long expected, yet now approaching universal Day of Redemption.[25]

In this striking passage, gold-making destroys the value of money and brings about the social equality that is necessary for re-entry into paradise. Heterodoxy comes together with a radical social agenda in shaping the happy future of humanity.

Despite his philosophical agenda, "Mystagogus" was preoccupied with finding ways to make money. His second treatise dealt with the "Universal Dissolvent" or "Liquor Alkahest" that was widely sought as the basis for medicines. It too sprang from Chaos and "the Universal Spirit," but it differed from the "Philosopher's Mercury" in being artificial rather than natural. It was therefore "made unfit for the Act of Generation" and could only destroy rather than create.[26] Towards the end of his treatise, "Mystagogus" pointed to "the want of Subsistance or Money of your own to carry on your Search or Labours" as a great difficulty in pursuing alchemy. The obligation to support his own large family had often prevented him from spending more time on his alchemical quest.[27] Clearly, he was not in the privileged position of Boyle or Newton, who could afford to treat alchemy as a purely intellectual endeavour.

While he aspired to be a philosopher, Yworth was compelled to become a businessman, developing medicines in the laboratory of the "New Spagyric Academy" that he could sell in the booming London market. Many alchemists had adopted the same dual role in the past, either by choice or by necessity, but few of them had been so candid about it. In fact, Yworth was representative of a period when alchemy was shifting its main focus towards the development of patent medicines. This helps explain the abiding interest in the works of "Eirenaeus Philalethes," which were of considerable practical use in developing pills and potions from metals. "Philalethes" himself encouraged this pursuit, concluding his *Marrow of Alchemy* with a short discussion of "the universal medicine."[28] Most alchemists were prepared to settle for more specific remedies. To a great extent, the future of alchemy belonged to the tonic- and pill-makers.

The evidence for this can be found everywhere in the literature of the period, especially in newspapers, which mushroomed after the Licensing Act lapsed in 1695. Advertisements for proprietary medicines in newspapers increased fivefold between 1696 and 1700, and they sprang up in other unlikely places as well.[29] When Anne Conway's philosophical writings were posthumously published by Dorman Newman in 1692, her argument for "the persistence of Souls" or universal salvation shocked readers. What may shock us today is the advertisement that Newman affixed to the inside cover, praising

> [t]he *Elixir Proprietatis* (so highly commended by the Renowned *Paracelsus* and *Helmont*) it resisteth all Putrefaction of the *Blood*, strengtheneth the Digestive Faculty... This Noble *Elixir* is Philosophically prepared by *John Spire, Chymico Medicus*, at four Shillings the Ounce. Who hath, by his Labour and Study in the Chymical Art, attained unto several secret Arcanums (not vulgarly known), particularly a Sovereign Remedy for the *Gout*.

The elixir was available from Newman's printing house in the Poultry or from Spire's houses in Southwark and Twickenham.[30] The fact that Spire *owned* a villa in Twickenham shows how well his elixir was selling. Newman sold a variety of other medicines from his business premises, including Dr Patrick Anderson's Scotch pills, Bateman's Spirit of Scurvy-grass, Daffy's Elixir and Glauber's Spirit of Salt of the World.[31]

All of these medicines had been developed before 1688. The most famous of them was probably Lionel Lockyer's Pill, "Call'd by the Name of *Pillula Radiis Solis Extracta*," or pill extracted from the rays of the sun. The connection of the sun with gold boosted the reputation of this "Universal Medicine," which was supposed to be able to do anything a physician could – more cheaply, of course. The pills were distributed by agents throughout England and Ireland, as well as in Barbados and the North American colonies. Lockyer, who placed a splendid print of himself in his advertising pamphlets, demonstrated how his pills were made before Charles II in 1664. His growing fame led to a violent attack on him in print by George Starkey, who called him both a "Silly, Sawcy Fool" and "a pitiful, creeping, dirty thing." Starkey pointed out that his pills were little more than roasted antimony, and suggested that taking them might cause vomiting as well as other dangerous side effects.[32] A defender of Lockyer shot back at Starkey: "One of your Wives told me, I had better similiz'd you to an Ape than an Ass, he [*sic*] being certainly informed you are deficient in the tail-piece."[33] Verbal boxing matches between the makers of medicines were commonplace, and they certainly generated sales. Lockyer died rich in 1672, and was buried in a magnificent tomb in Southwark Cathedral. The fame of his pills lived an, inspiring many imitators.

The best-chronicled medicine of the era was Daffy's Elixir, developed in the mid-seventeenth century by an ejected clergyman, Thomas Daffy, and popularized by his kinsman the London shoemaker and self-styled "Doctor" Anthony Daffy. His account books for 1674–85 reveal that the latter distributed 4,000 gallons of the liquid medicine throughout the British Isles, western Europe, the English colonies in North America and the Caribbean, and beyond to Tangier and India. The empire was awash with Daffy's Elixir, by virtue of a network of agents that included merchants, booksellers, grocers and coffee-sellers. Charging between 2s. 6d. and 3 shillings per bottle, Daffy's agents sold £8,400 worth of elixir during this eleven-year period. At his death in 1685, he owned a house in London as well as a farm in Essex, and his estate was worth about £2,000, making him a successful small businessman. What happened next shows how patent medicines proliferated after 1688. Daffy wanted to leave the formula for the Elixir to his daughters, Martha and Mary, but his widow, Ellen, quickly remarried, and her scheming new husband successfully claimed the formula as his own, after a long lawsuit. Daffy's daughters continued to sell their own elixir, as did their brother Elias, who had a medical degree from Cambridge. Elias built a thriving London practice, and his widow owned two country estates. Their son Anthony remained the "preparer of Daffy's elixir" until his own death in 1750. He was challenged by numerous imitators, each claiming to sell the genuine product. Between them, they kept Daffy's Elixir in production for another century.[34]

According to two surviving recipes, Daffy's Elixir was composed of various herbs, roots and foodstuffs, including the laxative senna, infused in distilled alcohol. Unlike Lockyer's Pill, it was not a metallic or iatrochemical drug, and its production owed little to alchemy. Nevertheless, to copy the Elixir required knowledge of distilling, which comprised a chapter in every alchemical text. Other proprietary medications made more use of alchemy, like the "*Sympathetical Rings*" that were advertised in the 1709 edition of the *True Light of Alchemy*. A cure for haemorrhoids, the rings were sold by W. Langham of Moorfields, "Licensed Physician," who boasted of his "sedulous Industry, careful Toil, and Study for many Years in the Chymical Art." The rings were "Compounded from the Metallick Issue, and Decocted by the Spagyrick Art, in a proper *Menstruum*, agreeable to their Radical Principles, till the Bodies be Unlockt or Opened . . . freely illuminating and radiating the *Archaeus* [a term of Paracelsian medicine], when stupefied, oppressed, or enraged, causing the Disease soon to depart and vanish away, at the arrival of the *Arcanum*."[35] This was high spagyric parlance, as well as utter nonsense. To market Langham's Sympathetical Rings or Daffy's Elixir—or, for that matter, Newman's Elixir, Lockyer's Pills, Anderson's Scotch pills, Bateman's Spirit of Scurvy-grass, Glauber's Spirit of Salt of the World or any other proprietary medicine—it was advisable to appropriate the mysterious jargon that had been developed over centuries by the alchemists.

One of the little kings of proprietary medicine in the 1690s was William Salmon, "Professor of Physick" and popularizer of alchemy as well as other occult sciences. In the early 1690s, his *London Almanack* turned into an extended advertisement for his many medicines. These included Salmon's Family Pills, his Family Powder, his Elixir and his Lozenges for coughs and colds. He sold a variety of other cures, recipes and pills, and jealously protected his trade names. He attacked John Hollier, a London publisher, who "unworthily and basely assumes my name, Effigies and Seal" on his own Family Pills. Salmon sold his cures at bargain prices: pills were 9 pence per box, powder 6 pence per paper and the Elixir 18 pence per glass.[36] Established doctors were suspicious of his remedies, which cut into their own business, and his writings themselves were mocked as "bless'd Opiats."[37] Salmon was ready to take on all his critics. In the late 1690s, he rallied the apothecaries and other manufacturers of medicines to oppose an attempt by the Royal College of Physicians to establish control over the dispensing of drugs. Salmon excoriated "the Pride, Covetousness and Idleness of the Physicians" who sought "to Monopolize all the Practise of Physick into their own hands."[38] The College's efforts at regulation would continue into the early eighteenth century, but without any discernible impact on the booming, irrepressible trade in proprietary medicines.

William Salmon was a brilliant publicist, but not much of a philosopher. In the alchemical field, expanding commercial potential tended to drive out ideas, particularly the occult philosophy that had been the foundation of alchemical writing in the late seventeenth century. It would be an oversimplification, of course, to suggest that the trade in medicines replaced speculative thinking, but it certainly redirected the focus of alchemical writings. One writer, using the pseudonym "Eyranaeus Philoctetes," urged the public teaching of alchemy for the benefit of medicine. "Who would it *serve*, and what would it *merit*?" "Philoctetes" asked rhetorically, "If the *production* of their *Red Land*, and *Reduction* into Potability were *familiarly* taught, tho the *first water*, and its *Preparation* were *wholly concealed*. Would not the sick be helped, and the happy attainer of the *first water* be made early *serviceable*?"[39] The author was unmoved by the goal that had captivated Newton, of "multiplying" a metal by introducing the "seed" or "sperm" of another metal. Instead, he praised the virtues of

"Virgin Mercury," free of sulphur, which sounds more like a basis for medicines than an entrance to the Philosopher's Stone.

Those alchemists who sought for higher results than pills or tonics may have been losing heart. True adepts like Boyle or "Philalethes" had vanished, and who was to replace them? A pamphlet published by "Philadept" in 1698 proposed to remedy the situation through sweeping social reform. The author set forth a novel plan for a utopia based on communal labour, with the aim of achieving the goals of alchemy. "Philadept" admitted that he had never known a true adept, but remained convinced that "there are many reasons to believe there is such a thing" as the Philosopher's Stone. The promised benefits accruing from the work of adepts—riches, contentment and virtue, health and strength—were considerable, leading "Philadept" to wonder "why they do no more good than we generally see they do."[40] To encourage them to share the results of their experiments, sovereigns should oblige adepts to "live all in common, with regard to the possession of the goods of the Earth and inferior Offices," in the manner of the ancient Spartans. In fact, he recommended a communal way of living for everyone. Once the social problems of the world were solved, adepts would reveal themselves. "It is certain," the author maintained, "if there are Adepts in the World, God will never permit them to communicate themselves to any Nation except that People be reformed and become actually Righteous and Just."[41]

The pamphlet ended with a pathetic appeal for rich patrons to support the work of adepts in the present naughty world. According to "Philadept," "the Honourable Mr. *B.*," evidently Robert Boyle, had offered to do this for "Eirenaeus Philalethes," but Boyle's inability to keep secrets had discouraged the great spagyrist from teaching him the mysteries of "the *White Elixir*."[42] "Philadept" heaped scorn on those wealthy men who might refuse to imitate Mr B. "What? Dost thou not consider the wretched condition the generality of Mankind is in, and how miserably they fare in this evil World, where men wickedly oppress and devoure one another? And wilt thou do nothing to attempt to relieve good part of them from the heavy Burthen they groan under? Hard-hearted Creatures!"[43] "Philadept" seems to have been thinking of his own wretched condition, and his utopian vision degenerates into a self-serving rant.

Two years later, a second pamphlet by the same author extended the theme of social idealism by proposing that adepts should be "declared sacred" and "admitted to the share of Government."[44] The pamphlet also recommended the creation of a unicameral Senate, the institution of public examinations for access to higher education and putting the poor to work: "It is, then, visibly, horribly shameful to have Beggars in a Common-wealth." Cities were to be rebuilt on a regular plan, "unnecessary Trades" abolished and a moral reformation instituted. The last change would particularly affect women, who were to be required to wear handkerchiefs around their necks to prevent "obscenity and immodesty."[45] The underlying misogyny of the lonely male alchemist, clinging with almost monastic dedication to personal purity and resentful of the "frivolity" of women, endured to the end of the golden age, and beyond.

"Philadept" sounds at times like the utopian socialist Robert Owen, but he was actually a voice from the past. His mixture of social reform with moral regeneration is reminiscent of the radical sectarians of the 1650s. The personal patronage that he craved was drying up under a new cultural regime in which writers and artists competed for a public audience. "Philadept" had little sympathy with the expansive and exploitative commercial society that was spreading its influence all around him. He strikes an interesting contrast with Daniel Defoe, a moderate Dissenter who was an enthusiastic exponent of speculative ventures or "Projects," especially those that were concerned with practical innovations or new scientific discoveries. In 1697, Defoe had published an *Essay on Projects*, in which he compared the investment opportunities of his own age to the building of Noah's Ark or even the Tower of Babel (he regarded it as a well-intentioned failure). A project, according to Defoe, was "a vast Undertaking, too big to be manag'd, and therefore likely enough to come to nothing," but which might sometimes bring about both "*Public Good*, and *Private Advantage*."[46] His definition might apply to alchemy as well. "Projection" bore a well-known alchemical meaning, relating to the "multiplication" of metals endorsed by the 1689 Parliamentary Act. In Defoe's pamphlet, investment in projects represents a new and more acceptable alchemy, free from the religiously suspect implications of the old.

No wonder "Philadept" sounded such a glum tone, reaching at times a note of desperation. The old style of alchemical projection was simply going out of fashion, replaced by schemes for enriching oneself that had nothing to do with the attainment of a higher state of being. "Philadept" could have cited as an example of this decline the celebrated writer Richard Steele, author of *The Tatler*, who under the direction of a reputed adept carried out a series of alchemical experiments between 1697 and 1702. By his own admission, Steele was seeking a "Chymical Medicine for Poverty," not enlightenment, but he soon renounced the spagyric art as "a plain Illusion of some evil Spirit."[47] "He wanted to rise faster than he did," scoffed the satirist Delarivier Manley, whose lover John Tilly, governor of the Fleet prison, had helped to finance Steele's expensive efforts. According to Manley, the "secret in nature" that Steele sought "was never yet purchased, if purchased at all, but with great charge and experience."[48] While her mocking tone was quite different from his, Manley's views were not so far removed from those of "Philadept." In his anxiety-filled writings, the despairing alchemist made a last appeal for a total revolution of society. Evidently, the promise of 1689, when Parliament called on every devotee of the art to work for the common good, was far from being realized. Instead, alchemy had become a path to riches for some, a huge disappointment for others.

At this moment of supreme doubt came a renewed literary attack. Alchemy still offered fair game to the satirists of the early eighteenth century. The most subtle of them was Jonathan Swift, who landed some choice blows on the alchemists in *A Tale of a Tub* and *The Battle of the Books*, published together in 1704. He derided Thomas Vaughan's *Anthroposophia Theomagia* as "a Piece of the most unintelligible Fustian, that, perhaps, was ever publish'd in any Language." Paracelsus, like other "great Introducers of new Schemes in Philosophy," was listed among "Persons Crazed, or out of their Wits." Swift proposed that "wise Philosophers hold all Writings to be *fruitful* in the Proportion they are *dark*; And therefore, the *true illuminated* (that is to say, the Darkest of all) have met with . . . numberless Commentators." Next to "*true illuminated*" appears a note: "A Name of the *Rosycrucians*." Swift mischievously counselled the brothers of the Rosy Cross to "pray fervently for sixty three Mornings, with a Lively Faith, and then transpose certain Letters and syllables according to Prescription . . . they will certainly reveal into a full Receit of the *Opus Magnus*." Swift also made merciless fun of the Kabbalists. "I have couched a very profound Mystery in the Number of Os multiply'd by Seven, and divided by Nine," he informed them knowingly.[49]

Alchemists had been mocked before, but Swift's satirical jabs were particularly sharp. Only half-crazed dreamers and poorly educated dupes would accept such "Fustian" as occult philosophy, he said. Swift associated the alchemists with religious enthusiasm and magic, just as Ben Jonson, Samuel Butler and other earlier satirists had, but he went further in implying that reason itself scoffed at such outlandish new ideas, which had no basis in classical learning or worldly experience. Swift was a Tory, but his message was designed to appeal to the whole English elite. If they wanted to leave the strife of the seventeenth century behind them, they must abandon the "crazed" modern systems that had inspired it.

With occult philosophy under such withering attack, it is no wonder that alchemists chose to pursue their art in private, and in conditions of secrecy. One of them was Robert Kellum, whose alchemical papers from 1702 to 1721 survive in the collection of the antiquarian Sir Hans Sloane. Details about Kellum's life are uncertain, but he wrote under a pseudonym, "J.D.," that also appears on a pamphlet of 1724, protesting a Parliamentary Bill that restricted the sale of medicines by apothecaries and "Chymists."[50] Kellum's papers include many medicinal recipes and prescriptions, but he also wrote about various aspects of occult philosophy, including astrology and dreams. One of his female patients dreamed "that Nature like a Woman came to her Naked only in flannel." The visitor then produced a "most poysonnous Creature," with a yellow body and black and blue feathered wings, but no head. Nature informed the woman that if Kellum "knewe of the Use of this Creature, then I [i.e. Kellum] shou'd have or had all things in the World."[51] Here was the eternal dream of the alchemists, of using supernatural power to take control of nature—but with a dangerous twist. The secrets of nature turned out to be poisonous.

Secrets were held to be just as politically dangerous in the decades after the Glorious Revolution as they had been under Charles II. The plots and conspiracies of the post-revolutionary era, however, were those of Jacobites, not of republicans. The supporters of the exiled James II and his son strove incessantly to undermine, subvert and overthrow the regime of William and Mary and their successors.[52] The post-revolutionary regime was understandably averse to secrecy, which threatened its existence. That hostility carried over into the behavioural norms of its supporters. The Whig social commentator Joseph Addison urged readers of his journal, *The Spectator*, to cultivate openness of character as a mark of good breeding and education. He praised "Discretion," but condemned the low, secretive trait of "Cunning," which "makes a Man incapable of bringing about even those Events which he might have done, had he passed only for a plain Man."[53]

Addison, along with his collaborator Richard Steele, helped to shape a post-revolutionary culture of polite manners and moderate religious principles that was compatible with commercial growth. Alchemy, with its veiled heterodoxy and radical social aspirations, was at odds with that culture. As a result, it went into a period of intellectual torpor or decline. Yet it was not discredited or refuted by science. The most direct assault on alchemy during this period was a religious one, made by, of all people, Thomas Tryon, the Behmenist astrologer and advocate of herbal remedies. He stated categorically that "the changing of Forms is forbidden by God's hand," denied that anybody had ever isolated "the Seed of a Metal," and described universal medicines as "altogether impossible, and as much to oppose the unalterable law of God."[54] Tryon had many admirers, but his outright condemnation of alchemy was not typical. The spagyric art was more often quietly laughed at as a waste of time or passed over in silence than countered by argument. It entered the new century in a diminished state, although not a condition of ignominy. It had, after all, stimulated a whole medicinal industry, and parts of it were integrated into university science curricula, within a discipline that was increasingly called "chymistry."[55] The art was not dead and, like the "Philosophical Mercury," it might rise again.

Astrology Falls from the Heavens

Astrology, already highly commercialized, was less at odds with British culture after the Glorious Revolution. Measured by the number of almanacs published between 1689 and 1715, the celestial art does not appear to have declined at all. This ignores their actual content, however, which by the early 1690s was overwhelmingly tame, repetitive and dull. The Stationers' Company continued to hold a monopoly on their production and sale, and was more determined than ever to keep their writers from putting anything controversial in print.[56] Overall, there is little reason to disagree with the assessment of historian Bernard Capp, who wrote that, by 1720, the almanac "lacked the vitality and individuality of many of its Tudor and Stuart forebears."[57] The decline in content began to set in after the Glorious Revolution, when only two almanac writers devoted much attention to the principles of their art: John Partridge and John Gadbury. They were engaged in a bitter conflict with one another over the significance of astrology, which in the end damaged its already shaky intellectual foundations.

The Glorious Revolution was a supreme moment of victory for Partridge, who returned from exile in the Netherlands to launch explosive salvos against his Tory enemies. In a characteristically passionate pamphlet of 1689 entitled *Mene Tekel* (which might be translated as "The Writing is on the Wall"), Partridge vindicated his own prediction for "this wonderful Year" of 1688: namely, that James II would die, which had come to pass in a symbolic sense. He then went on to savage his enemy John Gadbury as a former Ranter, a toady to Oliver Cromwell, a pimp and a convert to Roman Catholicism.[58] Gadbury responded by accusing Partridge of being a republican, of abusing Charles I and Archbishop Laud, and of having "Labour'd hard, Sir, to approve your self another Stephen Colledge [an anti-Catholic activist executed for high treason in 1681], and been guilty of as many Anti-Monarchical *Gim cracks* . . . and have presented the World with as many *Raree-Shows*."[59] The quarrel continued in their almanacs, where Partridge went so far as to accuse Gadbury of hiring assassins to murder a man whom he suspected of sleeping with his wife. For his part, Gadbury refused to answer "the *Ungrateful, Scurrilous*, (not to say horridly Scandalous) *Snarlings* of my Quondam *Pupil* J.P. against me, year after year."[60]

The mud-slinging between Partridge and Gadbury went on fitfully until the latter's death in 1704. Without doubt, it helped to sell almanacs, and so was tolerated by the Stationers' Company. It also produced some of the last serious philosophical discussions of early-modern astrology. After temporarily renouncing further attacks on Partridge, Gadbury attempted in 1693 to present a more intellectual justification for his art, in a supplement that was added to his regular almanac. His theories, he explains, rest on traditional foundations: a hierarchical view of nature, the assumption of sympathetic powers and the view that bodies are vehicles for spirits. "That *Inferiours* are influenc'd by *Superiours*, none are so Sceptical to deny," Gadbury begins. To him, "it is very obvious that the *Sympathies* and *Antipathies* of the *planets* and *Stars* above, with *persons* and *things* below, do certainly produce the true *Sorites* [heaps] of Nature, that hold together (by *Lincks* as it were) all *Mundane Beings*." As the stars are at a great altitude, so too are they "very *Powerful, Excellent* and *Pure*; and may therefore most reasonably be supposed to *Influence, Alter, preserve, Increase* and *Destroy* all these *lesser* and *grosser* Terrene Compositions."

The effects of the stars are felt not within matter or "Atoms" but in movements of the spirit. What could explain emotional states like love, hatred or evenness of temper other than astrology? The heavens could even give a spirit to inanimate objects. "If it [a Body] be Soul-less, then it is moved or changed by something Superiour to it, which serves as a *Soul*, or *Principle* of *Life*, to inform and govern. It is indeed the *Spirit* of *Breath* that is in it, that gives it *Motion, Augmentation, Vision, Gust*, and *Odour*." Bodies are in themselves nothing, except "*Domicils* or Habitations for *Souls* or *Spirits* to dwell in." Because the human body is "a Map, or Epitomy of the Coelestial Clock-work," the changes in its soul follow those in the heavens. Put simply, "the *Stars* alter our Humours; our Humours change our Minds; our Constitutions mutate our Judgments; our Judgments create in us divers *Appetites* and *Desires*." Of course, the influence of the stars is not irresistible—that would deny the reality of sin. All astrologers, according to Gadbury, reject the idea that the stars impose a fatal necessity on human beings.[61] This last point would prove another bone of contention with Partridge.

Gadbury's multi-part essay may be the most extensive explanation of astrology ever offered in an almanac. It owes nothing to corpuscular theory, Newtonian gravity or any recent scientific argument. Not surprisingly, it was strongly denounced by the leading scientific periodical of the day, *The Athenian Mercury*, which attacked it point by point in an effort to discredit "the *Folly* and *Impiety* of such as pretend to *Judicial Astrology*."[62] Intellectually, Gadbury's article resembles the writings of John Goad, whose Catholicism made him unacceptable to post-revolutionary astrologers, and whom Gadbury was brave enough to memorialize in 1694, five years after Goad's death. It also bears strong traces of Neoplatonism, although these may be derived from astrological sources rather than Henry More or the Cambridge Platonists. Gadbury was still a serious practitioner of his art, but in his understanding of it nothing much had changed since the days of Josiah Childrey.

Partridge's almanac, meanwhile, continued to fire off explosive salvos at the pope, Louis XIV and Catholics in general. As a response to Gadbury, however, he issued his own astrological manifesto, *Opus Reformatum*. In this extraordinary work, Partridge denied that "I intend to destroy the Art of Astrology . . . my real Intent and Design is to excite the Lovers of this Contemptible Science, to refine it, and make it more coherent in its Principles, and more certain in its Use and Practice."[63] In other words, he wanted to turn it into "a Branch of Natural Philosophy." He was not at all interested in establishing a philosophical basis for the celestial art. On the contrary, he defined astrology as "a bundle of Experience improved into Rules by continued observations of those Accidents and Effects that did always attend different Directions and Positions: Hence it then follows, That *Like Common Causes must always have Like Effects*, or else Rules of Exception laid down."[64] The problem with this approach, of course, is that it fails to explain the causal link between changes in the heavens and events on earth. Even if a precise parallel between them could be proven by observation, as Partridge believed it could, it would not demonstrate that one was acting on the other.

This did not bother Partridge at all. He rejected theories that proposed rays of light or ethereal forces as conduits for astral power, and he was implacably hostile to any explanation that rested on spirits, which he associated with superstition and conjuring tricks. He decried one "little ruddy-faced *Conjurer*" who always made excuses when he failed to raise spirits, and who foolishly used finger- or toenail parings in his attempts to read the future. Partridge was utterly scornful of astrologers who claimed to be able to make people fall in love or find lost persons ("by force of Magic as they call it") or detect withcraft, calling them "a Crew of Scandalous Cheats."[65] While he could not lump "Catholick John" Gadbury in with them, he nonetheless heaped abuse on his rival's methods, accusing him of conspiring with Goad to turn Protestants into papists.

Partridge had his own peculiarities. A large part of *Opus Reformatum* was reserved for discussion of the Hileg, or "Giver of Life," the point on a nativity that gives celestial indications of death. The main astrological sources for the Hileg relied on Ptolemy's earth-centred conception of the universe. This was another anomaly in Partridge's "scientific" astrology: he rejected the heliocentric Copernican universe. In this respect, the Whig astrologer had learned nothing from the most celebrated Whig scientist, Isaac Newton. Gadbury recognized his opponent's weakness on the point, and in 1695 included in his almanac "A brief Enquiry into the Copernican Astrology," which reproduced material from the writings of "my late Learned Friend" Joshua Childrey.[66] Partridge was provoked into issuing a blistering reply in a 1697 pamphlet entitled *Defectio Geniturarum*. With scathing comments, he systematically picked apart nativities by Gadbury and Henry Coley, illustrating their mistakes and incorrect interpretations. In a flood of patriotic zeal, Partridge also attacked the methods of J.B. Morin, the French astrologer whose *Astrologia Gallica* had inspired Samuel Jeake the younger. Nonetheless, his assessment of contemporary English astrology in *Defectio Geniturarum* was thoroughly grim: "Astrology is now like a dead Carkass, to which every *Crow* or *Rook* resorts and takes a Mouthful, and then flies to the next Tree." It had been ruined by "your *Magick Mongers, Sigil-Merchants, Charm-Broakers*, &c. A Crew of Knaves more fit to be punished than encouraged."[67] Partridge denounced Gadbury's theories as "nothing else but *Pythagorean* Whims, or *Rosicrucian Maggots* and Delusions, set on foot to undermine Truth."[68]

To be sure, Partridge gave some ground on heliocentrism, admitting that it helped in weather predictions. He also conceded that the reason for holding to geocentric aspects in astrology was not because the sun went around the earth, but because the movements of the heavens were *perceived* from the earth. Partridge may not have realized how significant an admission this was, as it suggested that astrology rested on the way movements of the stars were seen, rather than their real movements. Partridge did not dwell on it. Instead, he quickly moved back to his principal fixation: that the Hileg could only be calculated by using the old Ptolemaic methods. John Gadbury replied to this assertion in his almanac for 1698. He labelled Partridge's approach "Placidian," from Placidus de Titus, a sixteenth-century Italian monk and mathematician. The epithet was loaded with implications, as Placidus's writings had been used by the Catholic Church to counter the Copernican theory.[69] Hence, Gadbury was linking his virulently anti-Catholic foe with the scientific teachings of the Church of Rome. Gadbury found Placidus's theory of the Hileg as a specific predictor of the end of life to be "*crazie* and *infirm*." He agreed that astrology needed reform, but not in this way.[70]

Meanwhile, Partridge had widened his attacks to include other astrologers. He answered a challenge from the almanac writer George Parker with a withering reply, calling him both "a *broken Jacobite Cutler*" and a "*Mountebank Conjurer*" who relied on the methods of the German astronomer Johannes Kepler. According to Partridge, Kepler's heliocentric theories were devised "to puzzle and confound" astrologers. He further held Parker to be guilty of relying on the work of the astronomer Edmond Halley and of plagiarizing articles from the *Philosophical Transactions*.[71] Once again, Partridge's fundamental hostility to recent scientific writings is evident. For his part, Parker threw back plenty of invective at "that silly and ill-bred Buffoon John Partridge," although he acknowledged that some of his tables were derived from John Flamsteed.[72]

Partridge made a more telling personal attack in his 1698 almanac, where he accused the almanac writer Henry Coley of selling sigils or charms. He even reproduced one of them: a round charm drawn on pasteboard with a complex diagram and the names of two angels, Sachiel and Raphael, on one side, while on the other side were astrological signs, a five-pointed star and the name of Raphael repeated. It sold for two guineas. Partridge then issued a bitingly sarcastic advertisement:

> Ladies and Gentlemen, you that are desirous of these ingenious deceipts and Delusions, pray repair to *Baldwin's Gardens* [Coley's residence], and there you may be furnish'd. One to keep your Gallants true to you is six Guineas. One to keep you from being yet with Child, four Guineas. One to make you fortunate in Play any one day, half a Crown. According to your Pocket, so your Price.[73]

Partridge recommended that the sellers of charms be prosecuted as "*Notorious Cheats*." Coley, a quiet man who was doubtless guilty of the charge, could only feebly protest against those who tell "*A Thousand Lies* of me."[74]

Partridge continued his criticism of the sellers of magical charms and sigils into the first decade of the eighteenth century. After the deaths of his rivals Gadbury and Coley, the magic-vendors became his main targets, along with Tories, Jacobites and the French. He took delight in the story of a conjuror near Aldgate church who had "a B—h of a Wife himself," but did not hesitate to sell a charm to cure a gentleman's wife of her "*Violence* and *Ill Nature*."[75] At the same time, Partridge began to give ground on spirits. He did not deny the existence of "the Aerial Spirits and Angels, that can see the Clock-work of Nature in its original Motion, and are either sent or permitted sometimes to inform Mankind of their approaching Mischiefs." While spirits were not able to know "the Secrets of Almighty God," they might have "Prescience from the Order of things appointed, or else sent by a higher Power." He admitted that "there is such a thing as a *Second Sight*, and that they do see such dreadful Appearances which prove too true afterward."[76] He was opposed, in short, to the commercialization of magic, not to the existence of supernatural forces. This anti-commercial scruple seems to have extended to medicines as well. Unlike most other almanac writers, Partridge did not include advertisements for proprietary medicines in his publication.

Did John Partridge damage the reputation of astrology? It seems likely that he did, simply because he entered into so many angry confrontations with his brethren, denouncing them as cheats, mountebanks, etc. Partridge was nonetheless a popular writer, and he may have been gaining an audience for his own reformed version of astrology. The evidence of his astrological consultations suggests, surprisingly, that he was extremely well connected in elite social circles. They present an interesting contrast with a surviving casebook of John Gadbury, which covers the 1690s.

The two casebooks record primarily nativities, the most difficult and expensive figures drawn up by astrologers, and they are limited to a few dozen examples. The absence of horary questions (specific queries about a decision or event) in Gadbury's casebook is striking, although it may be misleading; perhaps they were recorded elsewhere. Partridge thought they had nothing to do with true astrology. Compared to earlier periods, the impression remains that both astrologers were providing more detailed services to fewer clients, presumably for a higher price. Although the types of questions posed by their clients were similar, the approaches to astrological practice of these two professionals were very different.

Gadbury's casebook is filled with mundane information about less famous people, including members of his own family. He was nonetheless conscious of status, and was proud to record that Dr Henry Brickhead or Bricket, Doctor of Civil Law, whose nativity was apparently cast after his death in 1696, had been "one of the best Grecians [i.e. scholars of Greek] in England," as well as a poet and philosopher. More typical of his clients was "A Gentile Quaker woman, born in Rotterdam," or "Mrs. Buster, Mrs. Wallis the Clockmakers friend." Gadbury was consulted by numerous female clients, among them a Mrs Edwards of whom he noted "No Children yet in her 37y. of Age . . . Great differences wth her Husband . . . She never had her Mensural Reliefs." Clearly, this was a worried woman, and it can be hoped that astrology allayed some of her anxiety. No personal issue was too weighty or too irrelevant for Gadbury; he drew up elections to determine the best timing for a marriage, and to find the most propitious moment for letting a house.[77] In addressing the physical and psychological problems of his patients, Gadbury might be compared to a modern doctor or therapist, although we cannot be sure what sort of advice he gave.

He seems to have made a speciality of cases involving suspicions of witchcraft. This is shown by the notes attached to the nativity of William Hoare of Great Tew, Oxfordshire, who "is swell'd in's Ankles & stung wth humours running ab^{t}. Him, as wth Bees, Restles, &c. So th^{t} he thinks himselfe bewitch'd."[78] Some years earlier, Gadbury had published in his almanac the story of Elizabeth Holbron, a widow "who pretended to be haunted by an evil Spirit, which none but herself could see." Gadbury visited her at her home near Westminster Abbey and drew up a geniture, showing her to be "Popular," probably meaning gregarious, melancholy and "flagitiously hypocritical." Noting her bad relationship with her late husband, by whose ghost she believed herself to have been impregnated, Gadbury opined "that she might be haunted by the terrors of Conscience, as well as with the Spirit of lying and deceit; whence, what she feign'd her self possessed of at first, turn'd to a disease at last." When her deception was discovered, she moved to the other end of town and died within a month. Gadbury did not deny the reality of witches, but he denounced astrologers "who, (with great impudence, and greater fraud) have pretended to discover and cure witchcraft by the Stars . . . Astrology teacheth no such thing."[79]

John Partridge's casebook is peppered with caustic remarks. Partridge drew up numerous nativities of famous people, including King Frederick Augustus of Poland ("A damn'd Knave") and King Charles XII of Sweden, of whom he commentes "it was this Horrid fellow that supported ffrance and kept up the War." Frederick IV of Denmark is described as "one of the Northern Tyrants," which reflects Partridge's strong Whig opinions.[80] In spite of his partisan affiliations, Partridge's customers were a mixture of Whigs and Tories, and of higher social standing than Gadbury's. Among them, surprisingly enough, were the leading Tory politicians Robert Harley and Henry St John, "Called Bullinbrook." Partridge was cutting in his assessment of Tories, writing of the earl of Salisbury that he had "an ill Nativity his wife and he will differ, and he will prove an odd Man." He added that, in 1707, the earl "went to the University of Oxford in the spring to be poisoned in his principles by that Horrid breed of— [Jacobites]."[81] Without doubt, this casebook was for Partridge's personal use, and was not intended to be seen by clients. It displays a remarkable self-confidence, as well as an insistence on accuracy. Of the duke of Marlborough's nativity, which he derived from another astrologer, Partridge wrote that it had been altered "by a direction not true; for I am sure it was not given to 52 minutes . . . This Can not be this Mans true lines of Birth, because by this he had the Ascendant directed to the body of Saturn just before the victory at Hochsted or Blenheim."[82]

Only ten of the forty-one nativities in this notebook are of women, and several of them are the female children of male clients. This may reflect the expense as well as the exclusiveness of Partridge's consultations. He seems to have appealed mainly to wealthy, well-established men and their families, rather than to young people, women or those of the middling sort. With his sarcastic sense of humour, Partridge may not have been very good at giving the kind of personal advice that seems to have been valued by ordinary clients. Like his rival Gadbury, however, he did a good deal of business interpreting medical ailments. William Aldersey "was taken with a disorder in his head and a kind of Loss of sense & Reason." General Charles Churchill "began to drivel about Christmas, at which time or a little before, A fitt of the palsy in his tongue & one side."[83] Partridge carefully recorded the past illnesses of his clients, which might affect his reading of a nativity or give him clues to future health. In the case of viscount Bolingbroke, bouts of childhood sickness were written down, probably by a secretary who then transferred the information to Partridge. It seems unlikely that the Tory politician visited the Whig astrologer in person. Partridge also drew up the nativities of people who were already dead, apparently in order to determine the astrological circumstances connected with their demise. This may have been in order to prove his theories about the Hileg.

In 1708, Partridge finally met his nemesis in the form of "Isaac Bickerstaff, Esquire," alias Jonathan Swift. This was not the first time Partridge had been attacked by a Tory wit. For twenty years, he had been a target for the satirists Tom Brown and Ned Ward.[84] Swift added a series of twists to the satirical knife-thrust, however, by parodying Partridge's own attitude to astrology. He lamented "the gross Abuse of Astrology in this Kingdom," which had led learned men to contend "that the whole is a Cheat." Bickerstaff ascribed the low state of the celestial art to "a few mean illiterate Traders between us and the Stars; who import a yearly Stock of Nonsense, Lies, Follies and Impertinence." So far, Partridge himself could have written the pamphlet. Abruptly, however, the tone changes, as Bickerstaff wonders at the gullibility of country gentlemen who plan their hunting matches according to the weather predictions of Gadbury (who was long dead) or Partridge. Both were "not only Astrologers, but Conjurors too" (this was a particularly low blow at Partridge, who hated conjurors); they were poor writers; and their vague predictions "will equally suit any Age, or Country in the World."[85]

The remainder of the pamphlet consisted of Bickerstaff's own ludicrously precise predictions. The most outrageous was one the author described as "but a Trifle": namely, that John Partridge "will infallibly die upon the 29th of March next, about eleven at Night, of a raging Fever; Therefore I advise him to consider of it, and settle his Affairs in Time."[86] This was obviously a joke about Partridge's own obsession with the Hileg or predictor of death. The irascible Partridge replied with a pamphlet vilifying his antagonist as a cheat and a "rare Conjurer," who by predicting his death was making a threat on his life.[87]

On 30 March 1708, Swift published a now very rare pamphlet, declaring that the prediction had come true and that Partridge had indeed died on the previous night. Some months later, as he was preparing his almanac for 1709, the abused astrologer saw fit to insert a brief paragraph asserting that he was actually still alive and in good health. He called the satirist, whose identity he did not know, "an *Impudent Lying Fellow*." In response, "Bickerstaff" appealed to "the *learned*

World" against the "ungentlemanly Manner" in which Partridge had treated him—and proposed to demonstrate that the astrologer was, in fact, dead. That he continued to write an almanac was no proof that he was alive, he said, since the names of many dead astrologers still appeared on their former works. In this hilarious riposte, Swift claimed that Partridge "pretends to tell Fortunes, and recover stolen Goods; which all the Parish says he must do by conversing with the Devil, and other evil Spirits."[88] Partridge must have been livid.

How damaging was Swift's scuffle with Partridge to contemporary astrology? Nobody could have been more critical of the celestial art as it was then practised than Partridge himself. Swift's satire implied, however, that educated people should not put their confidence in any predictions that rested on such shaky premises, and were issued from such uneducated sources. His emphasis was on the social vulgarity of astrology. Bickerstaff refrained from reviling Partridge as a Whig or Dissenter. Instead, what disgusted him, not just about Partridge but about all astrologers, was their low birth, poor education, bad writing and general lack of genteel manners. Partridge had noticed this condescending tone, which is why he called his antagonist "Mr. Esquire" and wrote of himself in mock disparagement as "a Poor Cobling *Almanack-maker*." Bickerstaff maintained that he was actually standing up for "the Republick of Letters," meaning men of polite manners, refined knowledge and good taste. The same values informed Richard Steele's weekly magazine *The Tatler*, where the comments of Bickerstaff, the magazine's fictional editor, on Partridge's death became a running joke.[89]

Like alchemy, then, astrology was cast further into the cultural depths after 1700 by men of wit and fashion. Its fall was more noticeable because it enjoyed so much publicity. The wits, however, did not give it the initial shove out of the heavens. The astrologers themselves had done that, by failing to reconcile their art with intellectual change. While John Partridge bears a lot of the blame for astrology's loss of prestige, on account of his constant attacks on the methods of other astrologers and his dogged refusal to assimilate Newtonian science, it would be a mistake to see him simply as a wrecking ball. He genuinely wanted to set astrology on firmer foundations. Unfortunately, these were derived from mid-seventeenth-century models. Like so many alchemists, Partridge was a relic of puritanism, which had sought to wipe out all traces of Popery and superstition. He had little in common with moderate, sophisticated and polite Whigs like Steele or his collaborator Joseph Addison, latitudinarians who rejected extreme views and venerated rational order in Church and State—even if one of them was not beyond a little dabbling in alchemy.

Partridge certainly had a popular audience, as his almanac sold better than any of its competitors. This became obvious in 1709–12, when he entered into the last fight of his career, with the Stationers' Company itself. Claiming control over his own writings, he sold the publication rights for his almanac directly, instead of accepting the Company's annual stipend. As a result, the Stationers brought out their own edition of Partridge's almanac, which appeared for three years without his participation or consent. Partridge protested that this was an unlawful extension of the crown's prerogative over the press, and sued. "Having resisted the tyranny of James II," he wrote, "I could not be so inconsistent with my self, as supinely to submit to the Tyranny of my Fellow-Subjects."[90] In the end, the Company agreed to pay him £100 a year, far more than any other almanac writer had ever received. He died two years later, in 1715, just after the accession of George I. His will includes over £2,000 in legacies, showing that Partridge was a relatively wealthy man.[91] Typically, he had quarrelled with his chief pupil, Francis Moore, after Moore had founded his own almanac in 1706. Moore was not mentioned in the will, but he had learned much from his erstwhile master, including the importance of appealing directly to the less educated.

The audience for astrology still included amateurs, such as Norris Purslow, a clothier of Wapping who may have been a Quaker. He composed an astrological record of his entire life, including "My First Perriwig I ever wore" in 1698, his arrests for debt, his authorship of astrological treatises and his second wife running off with another man in 1723. He knew Partridge and became a member of an "Astrological Club" at Tower Hill in 1703. Purslow's annual account, which runs to the late 1740s, gives no indication of a decline in the appeal of astrology.[92] Another dedicated amateur was Samuel Hieron, who drew up a collection of nativities between about 1690 and 1723. Hieron was the son of an ejected Presbyterian minister of the same name.[93] His origins lay in the West Country, but he lived close to London. Like other astrologers, Hieron enjoyed making nativities of famous people from the past, including Pico and Agrippa, and of current celebrities, but he also made them for his family, friends and neighbours. They included a merchant, a clerk in the customs house and other people of small importance. One of them was a soldier who "was soe addicted to lying that scarce any encouragement whatsoever woulde make him speake truth: he loved lying as an ambitious man doth honour."[94] Many women appear in Hieron's collection, including Mrs M. Brigham, who died in 1710 at the age of sixty-one. She "was a smart ingenious person & the most accurate in astrolgye that I ever did converse [with] . . . her husband had another wife if no more," and she lived with him only a year before they separated.[95] Women never appear in the ranks of professional astrologers in this period, but Mrs Brigham raises the possibility that some of them knew more about the heavens than printed sources would lead us to believe.

The ordinary folk who populate Hieron's notebook also remind us of astrology's continuing popularity in the early eighteenth century. In spite of Isaac Bickerstaff, Esquire, the celestial art was not quite dead and buried.

The Spirits Withdraw

John Partridge's insistence that any attempt to communicate with spirits amounted to imposture was unusual only because it came from a practising astrologer. It was an attitude typical of the post-revolutionary period, when Neoplatonism gave way to empirical philosophies. Talking with spirits, a long-established fixture of ritual magic, or cavorting with creatures like fairies were simply too outlandish for most educated people, although few were prepared to deny the existence of spirits altogether. The outcome of this emerging consensus was that witch accusations finally became unacceptable, although not until the issue had been hashed out in a final partisan debate.

The Neoplatonists were mocked in Swift's *A Tale of a Tub* as seekers after wind. Cunningly, he called them "Learned *Aeolists*," from the ruler of the winds in Greek mythology.[96] Henry More, their chief spokesman, had died in 1687, and his role as the leading English philosopher of the age had passed to John Locke. In his *Essay Concerning Human Understanding*, Locke did not deny the existence of spirits, to whom he attributed motion and active power over matter. He argued, however, that human understanding could have no knowledge of them, beyond what was derived from observing one's own soul: "the mind getting, only by reflecting on its own operations, those simple ideas which it attributes to spirits, it hath or can have no other notion of spirit but by attributing all those operations it finds within itself to a sort of beings, without consideration of matter."[97] If nothing could be learned about spirits through sense impressions, then evidently no ritual magician or Neoplatonic philosopher could communicate directly with them. Indeed, Locke wrote, "what we hope to know of separate spirits in this world, we must, I think, expect only from revelation."[98] This was not so much a refutation of More as a sad admission that nothing about spirits could be learned from his philosophy.

Ritual magicians would not have been affected by such arguments, but the proof of their survival in the post-revolutionary period is limited. A letter of 1703 from Arthur Bedford, minister of Temple Church in Bristol, recounts the story of Thomas Perks of Mangotsfield, a gunsmith's son, twenty years old and "extremely well skilled in Mathematical and Astronomical Studies," including astrology, who had summoned up "little maidens, about a foot and a half high," with the aid of a magical book. Bedford was certain these fairy-folk were demons. Later, Perks stood at a crossway with a "Virgin Parchment" and called up spirits. Unfortunately, "they appeared faster than he desired, and in most dismal shapes, like serpents, lions, bears, &c. hissing and roaring, and attempting to throw spears and balls of fire at him, which did very much affright him." He became ill and never recovered.[99] This tragic tale, which was published in Bristol in 1704, shows that ordinary people were quite capable of using learned sources of ritual magic. Among the educated elite, however, a taste for ritual magic had to be kept deeply hidden. A conjuring manual appears in the collection of George Ballard, numismatist of Magdalen College, Oxford, and a university bedell—did he use it to curse recalcitrant undergraduates? The Nonjuring clergyman Richard Rawlinson owned a rare book of incantations to summon angels for "Friendly Society and Verball Commers." Doubtless the property of a professional magician, it contains the names of several clients.[100]

The most extensive set of magical texts from these years is a manuscript collection ascribed to "Dr. Rudd," purportedly transcribed between 1699 and 1714 by "Peter Smart Master of Arts." The manuscripts formed part of the collection of the Tory politician Edward Harley, 2nd earl of Oxford. They constitute an occult smorgasbord, including various "Rosie Crucian" writings, works on geomancy or conjuring by figures, a treatise on the talismans made by Persian magi and a tract entitled "Of the Miraculous Descensions and Ascensions of Spirits as Verified by a Practical Examination of Principles in the Great World."[101] Several of these are in fact copies of works published in the late seventeenth century, including sections plagiarized from Thomas Vaughan's writings and parts of Casaubon's edition of Dr Dee's experiments with spirits.[102] Incongruously, one of the manuscript volumes contains a transcription of a standard book of grammar and orthography. The only work in the collection that might be original (although this remains questionable) is on evil spirits or "Goetia." Ostensibly part of the *Lemegeton* or *Little Key of Solomon*, it contains "all the names, Orders and Offices of all the Spirits Salomon ever conversed with."[103]

The existence of an actual "Dr. Rudd" seems doubtful. He resembles the magical "Rosy Crucians" invented by John Heydon. As for "Peter Smart M.A.," he cannot be identified with any certainty either. The name was shared by a puritan preacher of the mid-seventeenth century, as well as by the father of the poet Christopher Smart, but whether the ritual magician had any connection with them is unknown. In a note that he later crossed out, Smart claimed to have received one of Dr Dee's manuscripts from John Gadbury in 1686, but this seems unlikely as Gadbury was hostile to ritual magic.[104] If true, it suggests that Smart was an astrologer or medical practitioner. The most likely explanation for these manuscripts is that they were created in order to impress a customer. Because he falsely ascribed works to "Dr. Rudd" that had been published by others, Smart might be regarded as a charlatan, but he was also showing good business sense. As a composite of previous magicians, the learned figure of "Dr. Rudd" proved persuasive enough to cause the earl of Oxford to purchase the Smart manuscripts, and he has continued to convince readers of his otherworldly wisdom down to the present.

Spiritual communication remained alluring to those who held mystical views of religion. Foremost among them were the followers of the visionary Jane Lead. She had been rediscovered in 1692, living in a home for retired gentlewomen, by a physician named Francis Lee, a former fellow of St John's College, Cambridge, who had been deprived of his academic sinecure because he refused to swear oaths to William and Mary. This made him a Nonjuror, although he was not strongly inclined towards the Jacobite political sentiments that usually went along with the title. Lee was a religious seeker, and he found spiritual truth in Lead's prophetic visions. Along with his friend the clergyman Richard Roach, rector of Hackney, Lee organized the Philadelphian Society, whose name was derived from an early Christian church. Alchemists used the term to describe the gold-making utopia of their dreams. The Philadelphian Society held regular meetings in London, at first using Mrs Lead's house as well as that of Mrs Anne Bathurst near Gray's Inn Road, before, as more listeners began to attend, expanding to two further meetings, one of them at Hungerford Market near Charing Cross.[105]

Like the Quakers, the Philadelphians accepted the doctrine of the "inner light" in every human being, and they believed in universal salvation. They were quickly labelled sectarians. Henry Dodwell, an eminent theologian who had also refused the oaths, and who happened to know Lee's brother, wrote to him in 1697, deploring his lapse into "enthusiasm." Dodwell observed that Jane Lead's teachings consisted "of the old Platonick mystical divinity, of all the modern enthusiasts, of JACOB BEHME, of the judicial astrologers, of the magical oracles, of the alchymists, of which too many are in English, but not ordinarily to be met with." Lee denied these allegations, and was particularly concerned to stress his mentor's "estrangedness from whatever savours of the pretended angelical art, the *Ars Paulina*, or the Key of Solomon."[106]

He was not being entirely honest. While there is no reason to believe that Jane Lead was influenced by the *Little Key of Solomon*, there can be no doubt that she had been communicating with spirits. As recorded in her spiritual diary, which was published in the 1690s, these conversations often happened in natural settings, as she was thinking of divine things. Her first vision of the "Virgin Wisdom" came in 1670, when she was visiting the country house of a friend, "often frequenting lonely Walks in a Grove or Woods; contemplating the happy state of the Angelical World; and how desirous I was to have my

Conversation there." All of a sudden, "there came upon me an overshadowing bright Cloud, and in the midst of it the Figure of a Woman, most richly adorned with transparent Gold, her Hair hanging down, and her Face as the terrible Crystal for brightness, but her countenance was sweet and mild."[107] Most of Lead's subsequent insights came from a disembodied voice, but she had no doubt that she was speaking with a spirit. Lee, who edited Lead's journal, appended to it his learned view that spirits were to be discerned by "Internal Sensation" and that "Spiritual Things are spiritually discerned, felt, and received."[108] Yet Lead felt them physically and witnessed them visually in natural settings, reflecting a less erudite, more immediate approach to the spirit world, one shaped by her own experience.

Because she used no magical operations to communicate with spirits, Lead's visions did not amount to ritual magic. Her follower Richard Roach, on the other hand, interacted with spirits in more deliberate ways. As he informed Lead, he began experimenting with visions as an undergraduate at St John's College, Oxford, where

> I had many divine powers in a wonderfull manner lodgd wthin me & become as it were part of me . . . One night I was wth some other persons in a joint endeavor to press into a superior Region, sailing as it were, on a river, as I apprehended it in the Ark of Faith . . . I heard a pretty shrill loud voice crying out—O break through. But we could not.[109]

Later, he did break through. On the anniversary of King Charles II's restoration in 1699, a day celebrated by Jacobites throughout the kingdom, "I had the Spirit of Solomon with me wth his Name at his first Approach given Articulately as I usually have upon the Apulse [*sic*] of any Good Spirit & sometimes also of Bad or Indifferent." On other occasions, he was visited by the spirits of Francis Lee, Jane Lead and Anne Bathurst, all of whom were still alive.[110] Roach kept a spiritual diary, which eventually passed into the hands of his friend Richard Rawlinson. It might reveal much about his use of ceremonial magic and his lively intercourse with spirits were it not written partly in a mysterious shorthand, partly in an undecipherable script. One wonders, for example, what he talked about on the last day of 1706 with "K[ing]. Gabricius & Queen Beia the Centrall magicall K. & Qu."[111]

The king and queen sound like fairies, creatures that often provided access to the spririt world. Roach may have known about the research that had been carried out in Scotland on fairies, because his friend Francis Lee was connected with the Nonjuring Episcopalian mystics of Aberdeen. One of them was James Garden, former professor of theology at the University of Aberdeen. He corresponded with John Aubrey in the 1690s about second sight, which was said to be gained "by converse with those demons, we call Fairies."[112] A more positive description of fairies was offered by the Reverend Robert Kirk, Episcopal minister of Aberfoyle, a parish in the woodland glen known as the Trossachs, north of Glasgow. Kirk's manuscript account, *The Secret Commonwealth*, contains considerable detail on "the Lychnobious people, Their nature, constitutions, actions, apparel, Language, Armour and Religion; with the quality of those Amphibious Seers, that correspond with them."[113] Their bodies, according to Kirk, are "somewhat of the nature of a condens'd cloud, and best seen in twilight." As they move from one subterranean house to another, "[t]heir Chamaeleon-like bodies swim in the air, neer the Earth with bagg and bagadge. And at such revolution of time, Seers or men of the second sight (Females being but seldom so qualified) have verie terrifying encounters with them." They live in tribal societies, with "Aristocratical Rulers and Laws, but no discernible Religion, Love or Devotion towards God the Blessed Maker of all."[114] Although they cause mischief and steal children, the fairies are not really demonic. They are reminiscent of Africans or North American Indians, a primitive, impious and not entirely human folk who proved the value of Christianity and civilization.

Fairies had another characteristic in common with the native peoples of Africa or the Americas: they were a source of wealth. Kirk mentioned "Fayrie hills" full of treasure that had been found in the Highlands. Further to the south, Goodwin Wharton was still searching after 1688 for the gold of the "lowlanders" or fairies living in southeast England. Like his brother, the Whig leader Thomas, Baron Wharton, Goodwin had prospered from the Glorious Revolution, gaining a seat in Parliament and appointment as a Lord of the Admiralty. With the help of the seer Mary Parish, he continued to hunt for the treasure of the lowlanders, which Parish now reported to be buried at the gate of the ruined castle at Southampton. Although the lowlanders threw small purses of gold into Goodwin's coach to keep up his enthusiasm, he was never able to find their trove. Nevertheless, he learned a great deal from Parish about their hierarchical society, ruled by a king and queen, just as in Richard Roach's vision. Apparently, their religion was a version of Catholicism, headed by a sort of fairy pope.[115]

For those who claimed second sight, fairies were alarming. According to Kirk, the novice seer perceived them as "a multitude of Wight's like furious hardy men flocking to him hastily from all quarters." Fear might "strick him breathless and speechless," but the experienced visionary, "defending the Lawfulness of his skill, forbids such horrour." Seeing the future was hardly pleasant. James Garden reported that all his informants told him that second sight was "troublsome, and they would gladly be freed from it; but cannot."[116] The role of the seer was similar to that of the *benandanti* of Friuli, who flew through the air one night a year to fight against witches in an effort to save the crops from their destructive wrath. It was not a pleasant job, but for the good of the community, somebody had to do it.[117]

Some educated men eagerly sought conversation with fairies; others saw them as demons. *The Athenian Mercury* opined that they were "Devils assuming such little *Airy Bodies*," adding that "they were never found, but where people were superstitious and credulous."[118] Alexander Pope, in his celebrated poem *The Rape of the Lock*, gently mocked the fairy folk. Pope claimed that the poem's "*Machinery*" was based on "the *Rosicrucian* Doctrine of Spirits," which he had derived from the Abbé de Montfaucon de Villars's *Count of Gabalis*.[119] As that work was a satire, Pope was clearly snickering at those who took Rosicrucians and fairies seriously. In keeping with their silliness, Pope's fairies are feminized and "[t]o Maids alone and Children are reveal'd." They represent the negative characteristics associated with elite women: vanity, anger, weakness, prudery, coquettishness. Pope's fairies guard "the purity of melting Maids" and are obsessed with hierarchy:

> For Sylphs, yet mindful of their ancient Race,
> Are, as when Women, wondrous fond of Place.

Yet they cannot protect the fair Belinda from the assault on her hair made by the amorous baron.[120] The only recourse these ineffectual spirits have is to raise Belinda's spleen to a fit of anger. Pope's fairies represent feminine vices rather than native or "savage" peoples and, while charming, they are also ridiculous. In an age of real wars and revolutions (including that of 1688, which was often compared to a rape), the little, bickering world of spirits, like that of women, was considered petty and inconsequential by the literary elite.

The Devil Survives

Not everybody laughed at the power of spirits, or made light of their influence. The fear of demons, and of their role in enticing witches, continued to have a wide social compass. Whether or not the impact of witchcraft was shrinking in the decades after the Glorious Revolution is difficult to determine. English witch trials had declined to virtually nothing by 1700, but this had happened before for periods in the sixteenth and seventeenth centuries, so it was not necessarily an indication that the witch craze was over, let alone a sign that popular witch beliefs were disappearing.[121]

In Scotland, the execution of witches continued, with the encouragement of local ministers and presbyteries. The southwestern counties of Dumfries and Galloway saw a spate of accusations between 1690 and 1710. A particularly gruesome case at Paisley in 1697 ended with six witches being strangled and burned; a seventh committed suicide.[122] The fishing village of Pittenweem in Fife became obsessed by witches in 1704, after a blacksmith's apprentice thought he had been bewitched. Accused witches were tortured in the local tollbooth; one of them starved to death in a cell. A woman who escaped was recaptured by an angry mob and taken to the town beach, where she was crushed to death under a door laden with boulders.[123] This incident hardly betokened a lessening of popular fear of witches in Scotland. Meanwhile, Scottish writers railed against the diabolism of all forms of magic. Some, like John Bell, Presbyterian minister of Gladsmuir, chose to stress the covenant witches made with the Devil.[124] In England, despite the decline in prosecutions, fear of witches persisted. A peculiar feature of the period was the appearance of false, but entirely plausible, reports of witch trials. These included a description of two women being convicted at Northampton, then hanged almost to death and burned, a Scottish practice that was not used as a punishment for English witches. The purpose of these fabrications can only have been to encourage English readers to believe in witches, and to treat them as their Scots brethren did.[125]

Scepticism about the power of the Devil may have been gaining ground among some educated minds in England, as was indicated in 1695 by the publication of a translation of Balthasar Bekker's *Die Betooverde Wereld* (*The World Bewitched*). This voluminous study by a Dutch Calvinist clergyman used biblical exegesis to demonstrate that magic was a pagan or popish invention, and that the Devil had no real influence over humanity.[126] In 1705, however, the physician John Beaumont launched a counterblast to such arguments, which he associated with "Young Wits, who are well opinioned of their Parts." Beaumont published his own massive and highly learned treatise on diabolical spirits, or "Genii" as he called them.[127] He was no theologian; in fact, he was a geologist, who had contributed articles on fossils and minerals to the *Philosophical Transactions*. He dedicated his book on witches to a former president of the Royal Society, Lord Carbery. While he accepted that the existence of spirits was conducive to belief in God, Beaumont did not depend on pious exhortations or questionable narratives to prove his point. His approach was very different from that of Joseph Glanvill.

In response to Bekker, Beaumont compiled an enormous number of instances from classical literature, early Christian writers, European folklore, recent history and his own personal experiences, to show that spirits had been perceived by sight, hearing and the other senses. Such an approach was fully consistent with the empirical philosophy propounded by John Locke. Beaumont's carefully chosen examples were presented with plenty of analytical comment. They led him towards what he believed to be a rational and irrefutable conclusion:

> If there are Effects that cannot be produc'd by Bodies, there must necessarily be in the World other Beings than Bodies; and if among these prodigious Effects, there are some that do not carry men to God, and make them fall into Error and Illusion, it's a farther invincible Argument that we must acknowledge other Beings than the Being absolutely perfect and Bodies . . . we must admit created Spirits capable of amusing Men, and seducing them by Deceits.[128]

The conjunction of natural causes with moral effects may jar with a modern reader's sensibilities, but it was hardly an unusual mixture for the period. The annual lectures on science and religion that were set up at London in the 1690s through the will of the late Robert Boyle often conveyed exactly the same point: namely, that the natural universe had an overriding moral purpose.[129] Beaumont, however, saw no place at all for benevolent spirits. The Genii he described were always malign. For him, magic was the domain of demons, and those who thought otherwise were simply deluded.[130]

Beaumont's views were not shared by that arbiter of politeness, *The Spectator*. In a July 1711 essay, Joseph Addison adopted what he presented as a "Neuter" position on the subject of witchcraft—except that neutrality, as Addison was well aware, was not really possible:

> When I hear the Relations that are made from all Parts of the World . . . I cannot forbear thinking that there is such an Intercourse and Commerce with Evil Spirits, as that which we express by the Name of Witchcraft. But when I consider that the ignorant and credulous Parts of the World abound most in these Relations, and that the Persons among us who are supposed to engage in such an Infernal Commerce are People of a weak Understanding and crazed Imagination, and at the same time reflect upon the many Impostures and Delusions of this Nature that have been detected in all Ages, I endeavour to suspend my Belief till I hear more certain Accounts than any which have yet come to my Knowledge . . . I believe in general that there is, and has been such a thing as Witchcraft; but at the same time can give no Credit to any Particular Instance of it.[131]

Addison's "neutrality" was clearly no endorsement of Beaumont's work, or of the three recent editions of *Saducismus Triumphatus*. He ignored their assertion that the existence of witchcraft disproved materialism and atheism, although shortly after the *Spectator* article, Daniel Defoe would forcefully restate that opinion in his weekly *Review*.[132]

Ultimately, according to *The Spectator*, the polite gentleman would be moved by reason and sentiment, rather than religious belief or scepticism, to reject the possibility of witchcraft. The imaginary reader of the *Spectator* essays, of course, was a moderate latitudinarian in religion, not a Dissenter like Defoe. Addison drove the case against witchcraft home, not by religious appeals, but by creating a fictional character, an old woman named Moll White who lived in a hovel, kept a cat and had often been reported to the local magistrates as a witch. "I hear there is scarce a Village in *England* that has not a *Moll White* in it," Addison observed. "When an old Woman begins to doat, and grow chargeable to a Parish, she is generally turned into a Witch . . . This frequently cuts off Charity from the greatest Objects of Compassion." The old woman's pathetic physical and mental condition accounted for the charges made against her, and might even explain her confessing to witchcraft, from being "frighted at her self."[133]

Within a year of Addison's *Spectator* article, the argument over witchcraft had turned ferocious, due to the politically motivated debate over the case of Jane Wenham. She was an elderly, indigent woman living in the tiny village of Walkern in Hertfordshire. Insulted by a local farmer who suspected her of killing cattle and horses by witchcraft, she complained to a local justice of the peace and noted antiquarian, Sir Henry Chauncy, who allowed her to choose an arbitrator to settle the affair. Wenham selected the parish minister, Godfrey Gardiner, who ordered the farmer to pay her a shilling for defaming her character. Wenham unwisely refused this solution, however, and Gardiner subsequently became convinced that his teenage servant, Anne Thorne, who was behaving strangely, had been bewitched by the angry woman. After she confessed, a charge of witchcraft was brought against Wenham at the county assizes in March 1712. She was found guilty, but the judge, Sir John Powell, immediately reprieved her. Powell had merrily poked fun at the accusations in court—when told that Wenham was seen flying, he responded that there was no law against it.[134] The case was rooted in local antagonisms, no doubt worsened by the economic depression that accompanied the War of the Spanish Succession. Twice-married and childless, Jane Wenham was aggressive, impoverished and fitted perfectly the stereotype of the infertile, "malevolent mother" that so frightened the defenders of religion.[135] The situation became serious because it involved local dignitaries, including Chauncy's grandson Francis Bragge junior, who witnessed Anne Thorne's fits. Bragge, a Cambridge graduate who had read *Saducismus Triumphatus* carefully, saw the case as delivering a blow against atheism.

The Wenham affair might never have come to public attention if it had not been for Bragge, who wrote an account of the trial proceedings in order to refute "several Gentlemen who would not believe that there are any Witches since the time of our Saviour *Christ*, who came to destroy the Works of the Devil."[136] Bragge's pamphlet, which went through four editions, was published by the notorious Edmund Curll, known for his promotion of various scurrilous, seditious and salacious works. Curll must have felt that Bragge was on to a winning theme, because he brought out a sequel soon after, adding further details and evidence from an unconnected Irish witch trial of the 1660s.[137] A challenger then appeared, in the form of a Whig newspaper, *The Protestant Post-Boy*. It replied to Bragge's account with a series of articles, partly plagiarized from John Wagstaffe's 1669 work, *The Question of Witchcraft Debated*. Collected in a pamphlet under the unequivocal title *The Impossibility of Witchcraft*, these articles concentrated heavily on the religious argument that God did not allow the Devil to carry out wicked deeds by supernatural means.[138]

Predictably, the pamphlet was answered by Bragge in two further reiterations of the case against Jane Wenham, as well as by a writer using the initials "G.R.," who rehearsed the scriptural basis of witchcraft.[139] The sceptical side was then taken up by "a Physician in *Hertfordshire*," who condemned belief in witches as "Priestcraft," rejected the exorcism of evil spirits as "*Popish* Supersitition" and denied that anybody since Jesus Christ had been able to cure demoniacs by prayer.[140] The only relatively impartial treatment of the subject came from the pen of an anonymous author, later identified as the Reverend Henry Stebbing of St Catharine's College, Cambridge, a Tory divine. As to the existence of witches, he was "very inclinable to believe, there are such Persons in the World," but he rejected the evidence against Wenham as based on prejudice.[141]

The Wenham trial received more attention from the press than any previous case of witchcraft. Its details, however, were not particularly compelling, and the level of notice given to it had more to do with partisan politics than with the debate over diabolic influence. Within Parliament, the Tories were triumphant in 1712, and party backbenchers were pushing hard to limit the activities of religious Dissenters. Jane Wenham herself was accused of attending Dissenting meetings. The Whigs fought back by denouncing "priestcraft" and accusing their opponents of wanting to restore the Stuart Pretender. Wenham's prosecution by an "Ignorant" parish minister who accepted the "*Popish* Superstition" of exorcism was therefore politically combustible stuff.[142]

Publicity, however, worked in favour of the Whigs. A full-scale debate in the London press over a particular instance of *maleficium* or malevolent magic was bound to turn many readers against the idea of witchcraft. Accusations in witch cases were usually constructed out of small-scale, personal tensions that looked petty or absurd when magnified by press coverage. Testimony about diabolic activity tended to be highly subjective, peppered with innuendo and seasoned with long-standing prejudices. None of this came off very well in the rhetorical world of printed discourse, which favoured an appearance of disinterest. In short, publicity tainted the Wenham case from the start, making it seem wrong-headed and even malevolent. Bragge's response was to provide more and more details, which proved a losing gambit. His antagonist John Roberts, printer of *The Protestant Post-Boy* and publisher of most of the anti-Bragge pamphlets, gleefully advertised works on both sides of the case, knowing that publicity was bound to strengthen his arguments, as well as to enrich him.

As it turned out, Wenham would be the last person convicted of witchcraft in England. The last accusations were made in 1717. The laws against *maleficia* or using witchcraft to do harm would remain on the statute books until 1736, but they were a dead letter. While the attitudes of rural folk may not have altered, the disappearance of witchcraft prosecutions reflected a definite shift in English elite attitudes. It was not merely partisan, as it seems to have affected both Whig and Tory judges. Was belief in the existence of good and bad spirits similarly waning among the elite? The subject of spirits, unfortunately, was hardly mentioned at all in the Wenham controversy.

Four years later, however, the last important debate about witchcraft in England closed the door firmly on the notion that there was a difference between the summoning of good and bad spirits. It was set off by Richard Boulton, a physician and medical writer.[143] While Boulton was a Tory, he was not a party hack, and his *Complete History of Magick, Sorcery and Witchcraft*, published in two parts in 1715 and 1716, should not be regarded simply as a High Church reaction to the return of the Whig Party to power under George I. Boulton quoted with approval John Locke's *Essay Concerning Human Understanding*, and he did not mention the Wenham case. The purpose of his *Complete History* was to encourage individual moral reflection, "to put us in Mind of the Delusions of Satan, and the ill Consequences that attend such who serve so bad a Master as the Devil," not to encourage more witch prosecutions.[144]

Satan's delusions, according to Boulton, included magic, both ritual and popular. Two sorts of persons, he maintained, were attracted to magic, "*viz.* learned and unlearned; and [there were] two Methods also of exciting them to this forbidden Curiosity, *viz.* the Devil's School and his Rudiments." The Devil's School began where natural causes ended. Those who sought further knowledge were often "apt to advance too high; and where lawful Arts and Sciences fail of giving them Satisfaction, they are apt to apply themselves to the black and unlawful Science of Magick." Boulton knew a lot about the circles and conjurations found in works like the *Little Key of Solomon*, but he considered them to be "forbidden Fruits" that made practitioners into slaves of the Devil. As for "the Devil's Rudiments" or unlearned magic, it consisted of "such unlawful Charms, which old Women often make use of to produce Effects without natural Causes." The professional contempt of a medical man for the homeopathic cures of village wise women is palpable here. Boulton further condemned judicial astrology, chiromancy or palm reading and fortune-telling, "which are unfit to be practiced amongst Christians."[145] Witchcraft was no worse than magic, except that its practitioners knew they were truckling with the Devil. Witches, according to Boulton, had access to four types of evil spirits. The first were "*Lemures* or *Spectra*, which sometimes appear in the Form of dead Persons"—a mere trick, "since it is not possible the Souls of the Defunct should return." The second were spirits "such as haunt and follow several persons," while the third, "*Incubi* and *Succubi*," enter into human bodies. Finally, there were "*Fayries*," no longer innocent, whose king and queen made court with "those who were Brothers and Sisters of the Art of Witchcraft."[146]

The Whig clergyman Francis Hutchinson's *Historical Essay Concerning Witchcraft* is often regarded as a reply to Boulton, but in fact he had thought of publishing it as early as 1706. He had been dissuaded by the archbishop of Canterbury, who felt it would have a bad effect on the proposed union with Scotland—probably an accurate observation.[147] When it appeared in 1718, Hutchinson's work marked a turning point for mainstream Anglican argument about witchcraft. While he did not deny the existence of spirits, he asserted that it was both unlawful and impossible to contact them: "tho' the sober Belief of good and bad Spirits is an essential Part of every good Christian's Faith, yet imaginary Communications with them, have been the Spring both of the worst corruptions of Religion, and the greatest Perversions of Justice." Books that dealt with witchcraft—he counted twenty-seven of them since 1660—simply promoted superstitious beliefs among the vulgar. "These books and Narratives are in Tradesmen's Shops, and Farmer's Houses, and are read with great Eagerness, and are continually levening the Minds of the Youth, who delight in such Subjects."[148] Hutchinson used narratives, including that of Jane Wenham, to disprove the notion that witches made compacts with the Devil, or could do harm through supernatural powers. Flushed with patriotism, Hutchinson connected "true Judgment" regarding witchcraft with "modern Improvements of natural and experimental Philosophy," in which Great Britain led the world.[149]

It took four years for Boulton to reply with an impassioned vindication of his *Complete History*, which Hutchinson had not explicitly mentioned. Making a point-by-point reply to his presumed foe, Boulton accused the Whig cleric of trying to make "Party-Business of believing what the Scripture declares for Truth," as well as of "excusing and extenuating the Sin of *Witchcraft*."[150] The last part of Boulton's book included a long section on how immaterial substances could affect material ones, a subject on which he again cited John Locke. In fact, he overstated the differences between himself and Hutchinson. Both regarded spirits as real, and condemned attempts to communicate with them. For Hutchinson, the goal of such efforts was impossible, while for Boulton they would inevitably lead to bad results. The main distinction between the two writers was their view of the reality of witchcraft. As no witches were being prosecuted in England at the time, the dispute was not as significant as Boulton implied.

No third voice appeared in the controversy, to propose, with John Webster, that witches might not be real, but benevolent spirits were, and could do good things for humanity. An intellectual pathway that had been open in the Restoration period was now closed. Until the late eighteenth century, nobody would again make a serious argument in print to the effect that the summoning of spirits was both possible and lawful. Witches would no longer hang in England and, after 1727, they would no longer burn in Scotland, but the devotees of occult thinking, whether learned or unlearned, had become intellectual outcasts. They had no more place in Hutchinson's "modern" universe than they had in Boulton's pious cosmology. Yet they persisted in the shadows for the next half-century, and in the end they came back out into the light, in altered form.

CHAPTER FIVE

The Newtonian Magi

ANATHEMATIZED BY the orthodox, deprecated by the polite, the occult was fading by 1715. Yet remarkably, a small number of influential men within the English intellectual elite still longed, if not to resuscitate it, then at least to appropriate it in ways that were compatible with natural philosophy. They were Newtonians, and the period after 1715 was their age of glory. Although the revered scientist lived only until 1727, Sir Isaac's disciples would dominate scientific and philosophical discourse until the 1760s.[1] Whigs to a man, they had lofty aspirations, hoping to reshape the entire British cultural landscape to accord with their master's genius. As Newton was himself reticent and occasionally enigmatic about the wider implications of his work, his followers were relatively free to interpret what it all meant, and they went about it with gusto. They questioned prodigies or wonders, derided popular "superstitions" and scorned magical explanations—or, at least, in some contexts they did.[2]

Perhaps the most enthusiastic of Newton's interpreters was the French Huguenot exile, Anglican clergyman and preparer of experiments for the Royal Society Jean-Théophile Desaguliers. In 1728, Desaguliers published a gushing poetic tribute to his recently deceased mentor, in which he demonstrated to his own satisfaction that the Newtonian system was not just the best explanation of the universe, but "The Best Form of Government." Newton appears in the poem as a "tow'ring Genius" who "shews th'*Almighty Architect*'s unalter'd Laws." These divine laws apply to political as well as celestial affairs:

> By Newton's help, 'tis evidently seen
> Attraction governs all the World's Machine.

The same principle of attraction underlies the "*perfect Model*" of government, one in which mutual love and respect for law keep both the king (i.e. the sun) and his subjects (i.e. the planets) in harmony.[3]

Newton's "*perfect Model*" seemed to leave no room for supernatural explanations. Indeed, the triumph of the Newtonians might be interpreted as a death knell for the occult. Despite his long-lasting addiction to alchemy, Newton had never *publicly* espoused any intellectual position that could be tied to occult thinking. Limiting himself to mathematical proofs and empirical observations, he kept aloof from the hypotheses of Hermetic philosophers and speculations of Behmenists. "Inchanters, Magicians, Sorcerers, Necromancers & Witches," he wrote about ancient magic, "signified deceivers & cheats who . . . pretended to supernatural powers."[4] He reviled both "Popish superstition" and popular gullibility.

Of course, to depict Newton as a foe of the occult meant suppressing the evidence of his private alchemical writings. Accordingly, when his devoted acolyte the antiquarian William Stukeley penned a memoir of Newton in 1752, he glossed over the problem of the master's hidden fixations with a baldly disingenuous claim: "as to chymistry in general, we may very well presume, Sr. Isaac from his long, & constant application to that pyrotechnical amusement, had made very important discoverys, in this branch of philosophy, w[hic]h. had need enough of his masterly skill, to rescue it from Superstition, from vanity, & imposture; from the fond inquiry of alchymy, & transmutation."[5] Stukeley, who had access to Newton's manuscripts, must have known these words to be untrue, but their veracity remained unchallenged for nearly two centuries. The unpublished but frequently cited memoir further characterized Newton's religious views as thoroughly conformist. Stukeley asserted that, while "those of Arrian principles, have taken great pains to inlist Sr. Isaac into th[e]ir party," they did so in vain, because "the ch[urch]. of England intirely claims him as her Son, in faith, & in practise."[6] As a young man, Newton would probably have been deeply disturbed by this statement, but the older Newton might well have nodded his grey head in assent. An office-holder and pillar of respectability, he had no wish to be known as a heretic. Indeed, he had suppressed the publication of two anti-Trinitarian letters that he had written to John Locke.[7]

Despite Stukeley's obfuscations, however, Newton's heirs did not wholly obliterate these embarrassing aspects of his legacy—nor did they actually wish to do so. Like their mentor, they too felt the attraction of occult thinking, but they imitated his reticence and did not publicize their desire for hidden knowledge. Instead, they disguised what was not fully respectable in the garb of observations on antiquity, philosophy, religion and cosmology. Scouring learned accounts in search of hidden connections, they attempted to rewrite occult thinking as a historical artifact that retained meaning and power in the present. Desaguliers himself provides an example. His poem on the Newtonian system linked the harmony of the universe with the Pythagorean "Music of the Spheres," describing the planets as circling the sun "in Mystick Dance."[8] The ancient Greek philosopher Pythagoras, noted for his idea of the transmigration of souls as well as for heliocentrism, had fascinated occult writers from Ficino to Fludd, and his theory of music had drawn Newton's interest.[9] Stukeley would later echo Desaguliers on the "Music of the Spheres" and the "Mystick Dance."[10] Was this meant as a metaphor or as a more literal description of a supernatural process?

The answer was not straightforward. The Newtonians insisted on natural explanations for any phenomenon that could not be classified as a divine sign, but this left a great deal of space for speculation. For them, the mythology of the Egyptians, the cosmologies of the Greeks and the healing powers of pagan priests provided fragmentary evidence of God's plan for the universe. Understanding them or, better still, reconciling them with scriptural revelation could lead to personal insight, which might elevate its possessor to a higher plane. Stukeley called those who held such insight Druids. As he imagined the ancient British holy men to be cousins of the Zoroastrian priesthood of Persia, he did not object to referring to them as "Magi," although he would have insisted that the term had nothing to do with conjuring. At the same time, their divine wisdom was not purely natural, because it illuminated the mind and intentions of God.

While he did not put his more unconventional ideas into print, Stukeley did not keep them to himself either. He spread them to like-minded friends through his membership of a host of clubs and societies. Unlike Sir Isaac, who was notably reclusive, the Newtonian Magi were eminently sociable beings. Leaders of the Royal Society and of the Society of Antiquaries, they flocked to Freemasonry after 1717, when the creation of the Grand Lodge of England conferred a new social status on what had previously been a shadowy, quasi-plebeian movement.[11] Desaguliers served in 1719–20 as Master of the Grand Lodge, and Stukeley was a devoted Brother. As Freemasons, the Newtonians added layers of mythic significance to the rites and history of what initiates called the "Craft." In particular, they were captivated by the notion that Masonry was descended from the mystery cults of ancient Greece and Egypt.

Few outside observers recognized the significance of these endeavours, although one who did was the satirist Jonathan Swift. A biting portrait of the Newtonian Magi appears in the third book of *Gulliver's Travels* (1726). The wandering hero Lemuel Gulliver travels upwards to the floating island of

Laputa, which is kept airborne by the occult power of a "Loadstone" or magnet. Its inhabitants are slant-headed astronomers and mathematicians whose minds "are so taken up with intense Speculations, that they neither can speak, nor attend to the Discourse of others, without being roused by some external Taction [touching] upon the Organs of Speech and Hearing." To Gulliver's amazement, the astronomers of Laputa "have great faith in judicial Astrology, although they are ashamed to own it publickly."[12] Descending back to the surface of the earth, Gulliver visits Balnibarbi, where the king has set up "an Academy of *PROJECTORS*" (the Royal Society) made up of those who have returned from the floating island "full of Volatile Spirits acquired in that Airy Region."[13] Alas, their various schemes have all proven disastrous. In a later chapter, the ghost of the French philosopher and scientist Gassendi is summoned and predicts that "*Attraction*, whereof the present Learned are such zealous Asserters," will soon be exploded.[14] This strange episode takes place on Glubbdubdrib, "the Island of *Sorcerers* or *Magicians*," where the king is served by the spirits of the dead. The classical literary reference is to Aeneas's descent into the underworld, but the contemporary cultural reference is to Freemasonry. Swift throws another barb at Masonry in the final chapter of book three, in which Gulliver enters a kingdom where certain individuals live forever, although they become old, infirm and senile.[15]

The third book of *Gulliver's Travels* is, among other things, a sustained attack on the influence of the Newtonian Magi. It ridicules them as impractical speculators, their minds floating in the air like windy Neoplatonists. It depicts them as heirs to astrology, and suggests that their basic principle, gravitational attraction, is no more than a fantasy. Swift also mocks the Freemasons, with whom Newton's disciples were closely associated, for their fixation with ancient mysteries and their pursuit of immortality.[16] In sum, *Gulliver's Travels* links the Newtonians with occult thinking in ways that they would not have relished, but which may nonetheless be surprisingly accurate.

Newton and the Argonauts

Any discussion of the Newtonian attitude towards the occult has to begin with the great man himself. Master of the Mint from 1699, president of the Royal Society from 1703 and knighted in 1705, Newton had achieved greater rewards from the state than any contemporary scientist.[17] He had abandoned alchemical experiments, but he was increasingly absorbed by questions of prophecy. These were not in themselves occult issues; rather, they were of concern to every Christian. On two particular subjects, however, Newton was drawn back to occult writings, which he reworked according to his own peculiar understanding of God's intentions. These were the biblical Temple of Solomon and the mythical voyage of the Argonauts. Newton's attempts to hunt down the meaning of these phenomena led him towards a reconsideration of the relationship between the natural world and the divine.

The Temple of Solomon was an intellectual playground for those who entertained occult notions. The idea that it provided a kind of encyclopaedia of universal knowledge had a long history.[18] The scriptural reasons for believing this seemed abundant to anyone who was determined to seek them. Like the heavens, the Temple was designed by God; it was the first such structure built in the world, and the only true one; it provided the foundation for sacred architecture and was thought to reflect cosmic verities. The Temple harboured the Ark of the Covenant, the particular abode of God, just as the universe was the Almighty's general residence (or "sensorium," to use Newton's phrase). The measurements of the Temple invited mathematical speculations about the dimensions of the universe and prophecies of future events. The Temple was the place of sacrifice for the ancient Jews, prefiguring Christ's later sacrifice of himself. The prophet Ezekiel's vision of the Temple implied that the building was tied up with the destiny of the world. Added to all this, the builder of the Temple, King Solomon, was thought to have understood every aspect of natural philosophy. As a result, his great work of construction became the focus for an extraordinary variety of interpretations.

The height of occult speculation about the Temple was reached with the publication in 1605 of the Spanish Jesuit J.B. Villalpando's massive study of the building as it was described in Ezekiel's vision. In the measurements of Solomon's Temple, Villalpando perceived the harmony of the heavens and of the musical scale. In its proportions, he envisioned the dimensions of the human body and, more particularly, the body of Christ. In its stylistic features, he recognized the origins of the three classical orders of ancient architecture. In short, it was a microcosm of divine creation, a universal map whose features could be read like the letters of a prophetic text or the night sky. Its interpretation was a kind of astrology, an occult science aimed at entering God's mind.[19] English Protestant commentators were quick to reject Villalpando's work. His transposition of the physical features of the body of Christ onto the layout of the Temple, according to the Reverend Samuel Lee, writing in 1659, was "not a little strained and forced, savouring more of the sharpness and subtlety of human wit, then of the solid wisdom and teachings of the holy Spirit."[20] Puritans like Lee regarded each feature of Solomon's building as a "Type": that is, "an Arbitrary sign, representing future and spiritual matters by divine institution."[21] Individual types might indicate later events, but they did not collectively incorporate the entirety of the divine plan.

Nevertheless, some Protestant writers saw Solomon's Temple as providing a model for the perfection of nature. Utopian versions of the Temple were found in Johann Valentin Andreæ's *Christianopolis* and Francis Bacon's *New Atlantis*. In *Christianopolis* (1619), Andreæ, a German Lutheran theologian and chief author of the early Rosicrucian manifestos, conceived of a city at whose centre lay a perfectly square temple. It contained a college with a chemical laboratory as well as facilities for studying anatomy, natural history, astronomy, mathematics and the "mystic numbers" by which "the Supreme Architect" measured out the harmony of the world.[22] Francis Bacon may have been inspired by *Christianopolis* when he wrote *New Atlantis*, published posthumously in English in 1627. Bacon imagined a secretive college of fellows named "Solomon's House," located on an island in the Pacific with the strangely biblical name of Bensalem. "Solomon's House" was founded by a mythical king, Solamona, and was "dedicated to the Study of the Works and Creatures of God."[23] The image of the utopian Temple was later picked up by the German polymath Samuel Hartlib, who assisted a colleague in writing a scheme for the reformation of English economic life. Like Bacon, they envisioned an ideal society based in an island kingdom, named "Macaria" or the Blessed Isles. Hartlib was also curious about Villalpando's work, although we do not know what he thought of it.[24]

The Temple did not inspire everybody. Neither its occult nor its utopian aspects meant much to the celebrated architect Christopher Wren, in spite of his connections with the Hartlib circle. Believing that little could be known about the structure's appearance, Wren dismissed Villalpando's reconstruction as an "imaginary Scheme," a "fine romantick Piece" that amounted to "mere Fancy."[25] His coolness towards Solomonic architecture persisted even as Wren designed and constructed a modern temple, St Paul's Cathedral. Yet in 1675 he became involved in importing Solomon's Temple into England, in the form of a model brought from Amsterdam by Rabbi Jacob Judah Leon. Leon died before the model could be presented to the Royal Society, but Wren was sufficiently interested to discuss it with the Society's curator of experiments, Robert Hooke.[26] Apparently, he learned little from it. If the pediment façade and triple tiers of columns on Rabbi Leon's model were reflected in the façade and double tiers of columns of St Paul's, Wren never said so. In spite of the plausible claim that he served as Grand Master of London Freemasons between 1685 and 1717, Wren seems to have been unimpressed by the Temple, which came to hold a central place in Masonic lore.[27]

As a strict Anglican, what Wren may have feared in the image of the Temple was heterodoxy. Who knew what the minds of religious enthusiasts could read into it? Newton, on the other hand, was unconstrained by orthodoxy, at least in his private thinking. He chose not to regard the Temple as a natural or utopian scheme, turning back instead towards its most occult expositor, Villalpando. Newton's extended inquiry into the meaning of the Temple, in a manuscript entitled "Treatise or Remarks on Solomon's Temple," may have been written as early as the 1690s or as late as 1725–7, just before his death. The latter date might be preferred for one simple reason: the Temple was much more discussed in the decades after 1714 than it had been in the preceding post-Revolution period. This was due to a number of factors, including the spread of Freemasonry and the frequent comparison of the Hanoverian dynasty to the House of David, which had divine approval but no hereditary right to the throne.[28] In an expanding economy, moreover, the riches of Solomon were an intriguing subject. George Renolds, "Professor of the Mathematicks" at Bristol (probably an astrologer), even published a work in which the value of the king of Israel's treasure was calculated very precisely at £1,217,170,828.9s. 1d.—well in excess of the £400 million valuation of the whole kingdom of Great Britain.[29]

Public fascination with the Temple of Solomon reached its apogee with the exhibition in London of a huge model of the building, designed by Gerhard Schott, proprietor of the Hamburg Opera House. This was 20 feet square by 12 feet high and contained 2,000 chambers, 7,000 pillars and 300 figures. Finished between 1693 and 1698 at a staggering cost, it was sold to an English buyer after Schott's death. The model displayed every well-known detail of the celebrated building, from the "Table of Shew-bread" to the cherubim guarding the Ark of the Covenant. The publicity pamphlet issued in connection with its first London exhibition in 1724–5 boasted that more could be learned from the model "than out of all the Books and Writings of *Vitruvius, Vignola, Scamotzius* [Scammozi], and all other noted architects," because the Temple was "to be built not after the Invention of Man, but after the Pattern which the *Lord* himself had given."[30] Judging by the plans attached to the pamphlet, the model drew heavily on Villalpando's reconstruction. A great success with the public, it was displayed again in 1729–30 at the Royal Exchange, the hub of British finance. Evidently, Solomon was a figure of interest to the moneyed men of the capital.

It would be pleasing to think that Newton wrote his treatise on the Temple while Schott's model was on display in London, but there is no proof of this, and the great man had already been contemplating the subject for many years. His main source was Villalpando, on whose writings he made extensive and careful notes.[31] The Jesuit's argument that the Temple reflected the body of Christ may have reminded Newton of William Yworth's comparison of Christ with the Philosopher's Stone. Like Christ or the Stone, the building was a perfect creation of God. Evidence derived from the historian Josephus and other sources, however, led Newton to disagree with Villalpando's measurement of the "sacred cubit," which he reduced from two and a half Roman feet to just over two.[32] This made Newton's Temple smaller than Villalpando's, although it was no less universal in its implications.

Like Villalpando, Newton focused on the prophetic significance of the Temple as revealed to Ezekiel. The first senteces of Newton's treatise underline the point:

> That the future is represented in the legal constructions [*legalibus constitionibus*: i.e. worldly structures built by divine command] is acknowledged by all . . . Hence it happens that these constructions were more suitable than the natural world as a system of things from which the prophets might choose types, and as the Apocalypse abounds to the maximum extent in this kind of types, so these constitutions and the Apocalypse are as it were twins of the same prophetic things, they explain themselves mutually nor can they be exactly understood separately.[33]

This is a terse yet multilayered statement. First, it suggests that divinely ordered constructions like Noah's Ark or the Tabernacle or the Temple were *superior* to nature as sources of prophetic typology, on account of their perfect design. Second, it ties those constructions, not to the "arbitrary" types proposed by Samuel Lee, but to the unavoidable events of the Apocalypse, to which they are "twins." Knowing the hidden meaning of the "legal constructions," therefore, will elucidate prophecies concerning the end of time. The reasons for Newton's concern with the correct measurement of the sacred cubit thus become more comprehensible. He was seeking the prophetic authority that lay within the divine prescriptions for the Temple, just as an astrologer sought to prognosticate by correctly charting the skies.

Unfortunately, after writing those first provocative sentences, Newton turned immediately to descriptive and mathematical questions concerning the Temple. We learn no more about what the reconfigured building meant. Newton was no more forthcoming in *The Chronology of Ancient Kingdoms Amended*, the controversial work on which he spent the last years of his life, and which was posthumously published in 1728 by his literary executor, John Conduitt. The *Chronology* purportedly aimed at correcting the dates of events in the history of ancient pagan peoples by correlating them with astronomical as well as biblical occurrences. The key to Newton's dating system turned out to be the celestial sphere that guided the mythical Greek hero Jason and his Argonauts on their voyage in search of the Golden Fleece. Devised by the centaur Chiron (Newton does not explicate how his horsey half was physically possible), the sphere placed the cardinal points of the ecliptic, the apparent path of the sun around the earth that forms the centre of the zodiac, in four celestial constellations. Because the precession of the equinoxes had shifted the location of the cardinal points at a fixed rate per year, it was possible, at least in theory, to calculate the date of the sailing of the Argo as 937 BCE, or about forty-three years after the building at Jerusalem of the Temple of Solomon.[34]

The rest of the *Chronology* is a rambling disquisition, with chapters devoted to the Greeks, Egyptians, Assyrians, Babylonians, Medes and Persians. Newton pauses to consider "primitive religion"—the religion of Noah, partly maintained by the Jews, but debased elsewhere into paganism. He deals only with its moral principles, however, not with its theological precepts.[35] A chapter of the *Chronology* is devoted to a description of the Temple of Solomon and to Newton's reading of the vision of Ezekiel. Again, it provides few surprises, only hinting at the possibility of prophetic insights.[36] To a modern reader, the oddest feature of Newton's *Chronology* may be its assumption that the gods of Egyptian and Greek mythology were actual human beings, mostly kings or heroes. It is hard for us to grasp the point that underlies this: namely, that paganism was a *choice*, not an inheritance, for peoples who had decided to set aside true religion in favour of false deities and magical practices. The worst of them were apparently the Babylonians, who "were extremely addicted to Sorcery, Inchantments, Astrology and Divinations."[37] Even paganism, however, might retain some glimmer of truth, and "heathen" societies could excel in the worldly realm of the arts and sciences. The Edomites, conquered by David, were able "to carry to all places their Arts and Sciences, amongst which were their Navigation, Astronomy, and Letters, for in *Idumea* they had Constellations and Letters before the days of *Job*, who mentions them; and there *Moses* learnt to write the Law in a book." Literacy and astronomy were closely related in Newton's mind. Later, the Argonauts set out on a similar "embassy to the nations," carrying navigation as well as knowledge of the heavens.[38]

Newton's *Chronology*, which is hostile to magic and "Sorcery," might not seem like much of an endorsement of occult thinking. Its argument nonetheless points towards a reclaiming of the occult. First, Newton gives intellectual validation to ancient astrology as the precursor to astronomy. While he does not justify the predictive power of astrology, he allows it to be an accurate way of reading time and motion, the foundations of science. As a means of mapping nature, moreover, astrology provided the pagan Greeks with a way to recognize divine intentions. Thus, a natural art allowed for supernatural insight. Second, by focusing his *Chronology* on the story of the Argonauts, Newton evokes one of the most widespread legends of alchemy. As Antoine Faivre has pointed out, it was a commonplace among alchemists that the pursuit of the Golden Fleece was an allegory of the quest for gold. Every detail of Jason's adventures was connected to a stage in the spagyric process, and the Fleece itself was seen as a recipe. Two works that dealt with this theme—Michael Maier's *Arcana Arcanissima* and J.V. Andreæ's *Chemical Wedding of Christian Rosenkreuz*—were cited by Newton in his alchemical notes. Another, *Aurei Velleris* by Guilielmus Mennes, was included in the collection *Theatrum Chemicum*, owned by Newton since 1669. He may also have read Clovis Hesteau de Nuysement's *Traittez du vray sel*, a favourite work among the Hartlib circle.[39] Typically, Newton did not mention the alchemical significance of the voyage of the Argo in his *Chronology*, but by affirming that the ship carried science and the arts to the whole world, he implied that the spagyric quest was the beginning of knowledge and fulfilled a divine purpose.

A third aspect of Newton's rewriting of the occult concerns the ancient mysteries, which were soon to be closely associated with the rituals of Freemasonry. No proof exists of Newton's membership in a lodge, despite the Masonic affiliations of many of his disciples. Admittedly, the Temple plan inserted in the *Chronology* marks the Holy of Holies with a "G," which to the initiated Mason meant "Geometry" as well as God—but Conduitt or the printer may have inserted this. More suggestive is Newton's description of the origins of ancient mysteries. With blithe assurance, he asserts that in 1007 BCE, or eight years after the founding of Solomon's Temple, "*Ceres* a woman of Sicily, in seeking her daughter who was stolen, comes into *Attica*, and there teaches the Greeks to sow corn; for which Benefaction she was Deified after death." The Eleusinian mysteries were initiated in her honour.[40] Here, Newton recounts the myth of Ceres (Demeter) and Proserpine (Persephone), whose rescue from the underworld was a template for the Masonic raising of an initiate from symbolic death. He adds that temple building began in Greece soon after, indicating that the pagan mysteries and the Temple of Solomon were parts of the same divine plan. Newton further asserts that Orpheus, an Argonaut and composer of mystic hymns in praise of the planets, was responsible for the deification of the Egyptian king Bacchus. Both Orpheus and Bacchus were celebrated in mystery cults. Orpheus was beloved by Neoplatonists and astrologers, including Ficino; his music, which charmed wild beasts, is the model for the magic flute of Mozart's Masonic opera.[41]

We should not assume from this evidence that Newton was a Freemason or that in old age he had adopted the Neoplatonism of his Cambridge colleague Henry More. The claim of Freemasonry to be heir to the mystery cults was no secret, and Newton may have been aware of it even if he was not initiated. As with astrology and alchemy, he imposed a strictly historical interpretation on the mystery cults. Yet their ultimate purpose, like that of astrology and alchemy, surpassed nature and reflected intentions of God that were more perfectly embodied in the construction of the Temple. Apparently, the spread of science and the arts would preserve and eventually restore "primitive religion," so that the meaning of the Temple would at last be known. For the octogenarian Newton, obsessed by prophecy, science and the arts were not merely the ornaments of civilized manners or politeness; rather, they revealed universal truths. The *Chronology* was a final attempt to comprehend those truths, and a parting gesture towards a bygone era of anguished religious searching. Throughout his last work, Newton returned to aspects of occult philosophy, not to vindicate them, but to tease the divine plan out of them. His disciples would pick up on that approach, and for the next thirty years would keep both the Temple and the ancient gods at the centre of their intellectual universe.

William Stukeley, Arch-Druid

Newton's complex relationship with occult thinking was shared by his biographer and apologist William Stukeley. Known today for careful measurement of the ancient stone circles of Stonehenge and Avebury, Stukeley has been praised as a pioneering antiquarian and the originator of modern British archaeology. His insistence that the Druids were the builders of these prehistoric structures was, until recently, dismissed by scholars as either an honest mistake or a curious personal aberration of no great importance; it is now understood as a long-standing preoccupation. His private diaries and unpublished papers further testify to Stukeley's passionate attachment to astrology, his peculiar zodiacal approach to classical mythology and his evolving conception of the Neoplatonic *anima mundi* or Soul of the World.[42] As a result, Stukeley has begun to emerge as a far more interesting and complicated intellectual figure than anyone had previously imagined. His borrowings from occult science and philosophy, however, have never been fully discussed—and, without doubt, he would not have wished them to be.

Stukeley's diary is an indispensable key to the development of his thinking. He first kept a diary in 1720–6, when he lived in London and was friendly with Newton. He took it up again in 1730, when he was forty-three years old and had just been ordained as a clergyman of the Church of England. His friends were shocked by Stukeley's decision to enter the clergy. Until then, he had been known as a Cambridge-trained medical doctor who had published a learned study of the diseases of the spleen. His antiquarian pursuits had already led him to publish *Itinerarium Curiosum*, a series of papers on "Remarkable Curiositys in Nature or Art," and to make a survey of Stonehenge, but so far these were peripheral interests. Stukeley was also extremely sociable. He had become a leading figure in the Royal Society, as well as a founder of both the Antiquarian Society and the Society of Roman Knights, dedicated to the study of classical antiquities. Since January 1721, he had been an active Freemason. He joined that brotherhood, as he later explained in an autobiographical memoir, "suspecting it to be the remains of the mysterys of the antients."[43] After his marriage in 1728, however, Stukeley changed the whole direction of his career by taking holy orders and moving to a living at Stamford in his native county of Lincolnshire.

From 1730 until 1765, Stukeley wrote his daily observations into almanacs—not the newfangled type of almanac, full of mathematical puzzles, but the old-fashioned kind, with prognostications, astronomical tables and essays on celestial happenings.[44] The almanacs bought by Stukeley, such as Edmund Weaver's *British Telescope*, accepted the heliocentric order of the universe, which now reigned supreme. Weaver proudly defended the astronomer royal Edmond Halley's astronomical tables against accusations of inaccuracy made by a rival almanac-maker, Tycho Wing.[45] Stukeley was well acquainted with Weaver, who lived not far away, at Freiston near Grantham. After Weaver's death in 1748, Stukeley eulogized him as "a very uncommon genius . . . much esteem'd by Mr. Martin Folkes," president of the Society of Antiquaries.[46] In 1730, Weaver had dropped in on Stukeley, accompanied by none other than his antagonist Tycho Wing, which suggests that their quarrel in print was somewhat artificial. The Wing family, settled in the county of Rutland, had been compiling almanacs since 1641, and the industrious Tycho (named after the Danish astronomer Tycho Brahe) wrote those of Henry Coley, Francis More and Thomas Andrews as well as his own. If he was no admirer of Halley, at least Wing had declared his allegiance to the theories of Sir Isaac Newton.[47]

Stukeley's enthusiasm for astrology emerged from his close relationship with Weaver and Wing. It runs through thirty-five volumes of his diaries. At first, it appears in cryptic comments referring to the deaths of local people at the rising of the moon, or the timing of his wife's monthly periods.[48] Early in 1735, Stukeley purchased an astrological manuscript of the Restoration period, to which he appended his own nativity, calculated by Tycho Wing. He included some revealing notes in his own hand. Stukeley confessed, "I am a stranger to Astrology & therefore cannot pretend to say any thing for or against it," but he had nonetheless observed that the twelve signs of the zodiac governed "the menstrual flux of women." While "no one of sense can think the stars irresistibly domineer over him & his actions . . . yet I see no absurdity in admitting, they may in some degree prefigure the events which generally flow from a combination of many causes & incidents." He concluded that "there possibly may be somewhat in the Art, more than the generality of the learned now allow."[49] Wing had already gained his confidence by forecasting a bad year for

Stukeley, as well as a major inundation in Germany. Impressed, Stukeley wrote, "I cannot but admire at Mr Wyngs prognostic."[50]

Always eager to make a mark in a new field, Stukeley soon began working on his own astrological theory. By February 1737, he had completed "my planetary scheme called Eimarmene or a project of rational Astrology," which he never published. *Heimarmene* is a Greek term that can mean fate or destiny, but for the Neoplatonists it denoted "the justice-dealing activity of god" or the divine response to human acts.[51] Stukeley was apparently trying to reconcile astrology with Christian ideas of providence. More celestial excitement was to follow. About a year later, the diary records a conversation with Wing in which the astrologer imparted to Stukeley an idea that proved highly significant in his subsequent work: "Mr Wyng says the minute & degree of Signs which now by astrologers is called respectively the exaltation of the planets, was the real aphelion point of the planets about 50 years before the deluge in one certain year. wh[ich] he takes to be noble monuments of antiquity, being the result of the observation of some antidiluvian astronomer."[52] A planet is "exalted" when placed in a zodiacal constellation that is considered favourable to it, while the aphelion is the point at which it is farthest from the sun. Wing's clever notion resembled Newton's attempt to fix the date of the Argo from the zodiacal position of the cardinal points of the ecliptic. The zodiac, however, related in Wing's view to a much earlier period, the time *before* the Flood: that is, when the original form of religion was still practised around the world. Stukeley had discussed ancient chronology with Newton before his death. Now he had the means to reconstruct through astrology what had always eluded the great scientist: the *prisca theologia* or original religion itself.[53]

Stukeley became convinced that the symbols used to identify the signs of the zodiac were themselves of antediluvian origin, and related to pristine religious practices. Although his diary presents this insight as a pure "discovery," it was almost certainly derived from a well-known source book of seventeenth-century occult learning: the Jesuit Athanasius Kircher's massive treatise *Oedipus Aegyptiacus* (*The Egyptian Oedipus*). In an amazing display of imaginative reconstruction, Kircher here revealed the mathematical, astrological, alchemical and magical practices of the Egyptians. His main evidence was his own symbolic reading of ancient Egyptian hieroglyphs. Kircher argued that hieroglyphs were invented by the original alchemist, Hermes Trismegistus, to express the true patriarchal religion. The zodiacal signs, according to Kircher, made use of the hieroglyphs of the Egyptian deities, and therefore continued to display elements of the *prisca theologia*, in spite of the debasement of worship in Egypt through idolatry.[54] Stukeley's thinking was similar but, typically, he gave the Jesuit writer no credit.

Stukeley's reconstruction of the zodiac led him to examine the sign for Cancer, which he thought resembled the two pigeons that were Adam's first sacrifice to God. He maintained that the pigeons stood for the *anima mundi* or Soul of the World, a Neoplatonic concept that also runs through *Oedipus Aegyptiacus*. Stukeley's diary entry on this subject included a long reverie about the sacrifices of pigeons at the summer solstice in patriarchal times, the meaning of the feast of Pentecost and the connection between the zodiac and parts of the body, an old trope of astrological medicine. The sacrifice of birds, specifically doves, would recur later in Stukeley's work, notably in *Palæographia Britannica* (1752), where he connects it with Mithraic altars found in Britain.[55] As with Newton's use of the myth of the Golden Fleece, we may wonder whether this attempt to recapture the symbolism of the primordial religion was mixed up with the intellectual residue of alchemy. "The doves of Diana" was a particularly difficult stage in the alchemical process, involving pure silver. Described in *Secrets Reveal'd* by the celebrated "Philalethes," it had caused Newton much difficulty in his experiments of the mid-1690s, and it puzzled would-be adepts as late as 1714.[56] Stukeley had made chemical experiments while at Cambridge, and he remained interested in the topic—his diary for March 1737, for example, records tests made by the Dutch chemist Herman Boerhaave on gold and mercury.[57] He would certainly have understood the alchemical significance of sacrificing doves, but, for him, they did not belong to Diana. He identified the Cancer sign with her brother Apollo.

Astrology became increasingly central to Stukeley's interpretation of the *prisca theologia*. In 1741, he wrote of the signs of the zodiac as "pictures in the original & antediluvian sphere," a position from which he never wavered. Three years later, he presented his patron the duke of Montagu, former grand master of the Grand Lodge, with a pamphlet he had written on Adam's sacrifice of the two pigeons, along with a drawing of the constellation of "Engonasis the serpent" (Engonasis, identified with Hercules, is under attack from Draco, the serpent or dragon). He was still working on the meaning of the zodiac in 1750, when "I found out, that originally, the sign Gemini II was the altar, whereto ENOCH heinochus brought his offering of the kids . . . this is not understood by astronomers."[58] As Enoch spoke with God and was the purported author of a lost book of Scripture, this was a mighty discovery, although, as with all his zodiacal insights, Stukeley presented no evidence whatever of how he had arrived at it. At some point, probably in the 1750s, he came to believe that the zodiacal signs represented both the Twelve Tribes of Israel and the jewels of the breastplate worn by Aaron, the first high priest. In turn, the jewels mirrored the colours of the Shekhinah, the dwelling place of God in the Tabernacle. Because the term Shekhinah was feminine in the original Hebrew, it stood for the female attributes of the godhead, which Stukeley recognized in pagan goddesses like Isis and Diana. Even in the early 1720s, he had believed that the statues of Isis at Ammon and of Diana at Ephesus were the oldest images of gods in the world. By the 1750s, he was certain that these depictions of female divinity were in fact images of the one patriarchal deity, the God of Noah, another idea he may have lifted from Kircher.[59]

To see pagan goddesses as forms of the Hebrew God was doctrinally questionable, and should have been accompanied by a denunciation of "heathen" errors. Stukeley, however, did not spill much ink chastising the pagans, which may indicate an attraction to the heterodox notion, shared by the Neoplatonist Pico, that all religions *remained* essentially one, in spite of their decline from patriarchal purity. If this was what Stukeley really thought, he never spelled it out. The stated intention of his astrological theory was to deliver a mortal blow to the atheism and scepticism that he saw all around him. His anxiety over these issues became especially acute after he moved back to London in 1747.

From then until his death in 1765, Stukeley lived in Bloomsbury as minister of the church of St George the Martyr, a living bestowed upon him by the duke of Montagu. In the last phase of his life, his attachment to astrology waxed stronger, but he began to realize that he would not be successful in promoting it. He frequented the Royal Society, where he was periodically annoyed by the refusal to allow papers on astrology to be read. He supported a proposal, brought by the Jewish naturalist Emanuel Mendes da Costa, that "the Society had not acted judiciously, in rejecting all papers relating to longitude, squaring the circle, perpetual motion, philosophers stone & the like. tho' those matters probably will never be discover'd: yet 'tis notorious, such pursuits have brought forth many useful discoverys in medicine, mechanics, mathematics." Stukeley was furious when the proposal was not adopted, complaining that governance of the Society had fallen into the hands of "a coffee-house junto, & those generally very young members, who never gave any entertainment to us." He feared that the Society was on the wane, along with "learning in general," due to the present spirit of licentiousness and irreligion. Later that year, he presented a book on the history of astronomy to the Society. This led him to write a long critique of Newton's *Chronology*, which he faulted for dating the voyage of the Argo three hundred years too late. He also tried to persuade the Fellows to print a paper he had read to the Royal Society on an ancient eclipse predicted by Thales of Miletus, but "the infidel part of the Council" rejected it.[60]

In 1762, at a meeting of the Society of Antiquaries, of which he was president, Stukeley refuted an author who "fancys" that the zodiac was of Egyptian origin, by "vindicating it to the Patriarchal times."[61] This episode may have prompted him to argue, in an essay on cosmogony published in 1763, that the zodiacal signs were "a part of the most antient manner of writing, not unlikely to be that of ADAM."[62] If this was the case, then Adam, not Hermes Trismegistus, was the inventor of hieroglyphics, and the sacred language of the first man could be seen in the zodiacal symbols found in any common almanac. Stukeley's failure to convince others that he was right can be taken as a final rejection of his astrological theories.

By then, of course, Stukeley had become famous for his depictions of the ancient British guardians of patriarchal religion: the Druids, priests of Celtic Britain in pre-Roman times. He had announced his findings about them in two important published studies of the architecture of Stonehenge (1740) and Avebury (1743).[63] Ascribing these structures to the Druids had both a religious and a patriotic intention. Stukeley portrayed the Druids, not as pagans who practised human sacrifice, but as pillars of patriarchal religion. Furthermore, as he informed the princess of Wales in 1754, "the ch[urch] of England is exactly parallel to it [patriarchal religion], & in every particular," which was why he perceived the Druids as forebears of the modern Anglican clergy.[64] His close personal identification with them even led him to adopt a fictitious ancient British name, "Chyndonax," and to organize his friends into a Druidic society, for which he composed elaborate rites. Stukeley took a fierce national pride in the greatness of the Druids. He told the princess of Wales, in answer to her question as to why he never travelled abroad, "that I lov'd my own country, & that there was curiosity & antiquity enough at home to entertain any genius."[65] The country in which he sought out curiosity and antiquity was England; apparently, he never visited Scotland or Ireland. For him, patriarchal religion survived in no Church other than the Anglican.

Stukeley did not "discover" the Druids. Since the Glorious Revolution, they had frequently been depicted by historians and antiquarians as a powerful clerical caste, similar to the clergymen of the Church of England but with even greater political authority. Writers on Druidism were indebted to the Abbé Pezron's glorification of the Celts as a mighty people whose kings, warriors and sages provided the models for ancient Greek gods and heroes.[66] Drawing on this theory, the Welsh cleric Henry Rowlands, in a 1723 book on the antiquities of Anglesey, exalted the Druids as possessors of "the Patriarchal *Cabala*," in which "the *ante Diluvian* Knowledge in all its Branches was carefully preserv'd." Their "*Cabalistick Traditions*" included the pre-existence and transmigration of souls, doctrines associated with the Greek philosopher Pythagoras. Rowlands had no doubt that Pythagoras had learned these principles from the Druids.[67] Even more extraordinary was their natural philosophy, which Rowlands held to be "Corpuscularian . . . more agreeable with the *Sydonian* [i.e. Phoenician] Philosophy, which was plainly Atomical." Rowlands was referring here to the philosophy of Thales and Pythagoras, both of whom were said to have been of Phoenician ancestry, but the term "Corpuscularian" was derived from Robert Boyle's writings.[68] Evidently, the Druids were not just priestly guardians of the *prisca theologia*; they were far ahead of their time in scientific thought as well.

Rowlands wanted to boost Welsh national pride through lauding the wisdom and "civility" of the Druids, but in theological terms their "*Cabalistick Traditions*" harked back to the heterodoxy of *Kabbala Denudata*. Like Franciscus Mercurius van Helmont, the Druids accepted a doctrine of transmigration that pointed unmistakably towards universal salvation. The thirty-nine Articles of the Anglican Church flatly rejected such a possibility. High Churchman he may have been, but Rowlands did not seem willing to admit that the patriarchal religion might be in error on this point. Transmigration led him to the brink of heterodoxy, even if he was careful not to be seen tumbling into the abyss.

The theologically wayward Rowlands has usually been seen as an arch-traditionalist compared to John Toland, the famous deist and anticlerical writer whose *Account of the Druids* appeared posthumously in 1726. Yet Toland added surprisingly little to the account of Druidism given by his Welsh predecessor. To be sure, he was far less flattering in his depiction of the Druids, for whom he had no more respect than he had for the clergy of his own day. Relying on evidence from his native Ireland, Toland excoriated the Druids as a "Heathen Priesthood" dedicated "to beget Ignorance and an Implicite disposition in the People."[69] Yet he did admire one Druid: Abaris, a native of the Hebrides according to Toland, who reputedly studied sciences alongside Pythagoras. As to who taught whom the doctrine of transmigration, Toland was uncertain, and it did not seem to matter to him.[70]

Strikingly, William Stukeley's book-length studies of the Druidic "temples" of Stonehenge and Avebury (or Abury, as Stukeley called it) do not mention the transmigration of souls at all. *Stonehenge* insists that "the Druids were of Abraham's religion intirely, at least in the earliest times, and worshipp'd the supreme Being in the same manner as he did." *Abury* deals only briefly with Abaris, who is introduced as a student of Pythagoras, not as his teacher. As to who was responsible for thinking up transmigration, Stukeley studiously avoids the issue.[71] No hints of heterodoxy mar his account; on the contrary, he was so determined to prove that the patriarchal religion of the Druids was acceptable to a conventional Anglican of the eighteenth century that he even turned them into Trinitarians. The circle, snake and wings that he observed in the plan of the temple at Avebury supposedly represented the Father, Son and Holy Spirit or *anima mundi*.[72] Just as he had buried Newton's Arianism, so Stukeley also buried the paganism of the Druids.

On the surface, Stukeley's theories about Stonehenge and Avebury may be orthodox, but they reveal a fantastical chain of alchemical as well as astrological allusions. Athanasius Kircher provided him with a wellspring of ideas and, for once, Stukeley acknowledged drawing from it. The all-important winged snake that he discerned at Avebury was by his own account derived from an Egyptian hieroglyph discussed by Kircher: a snake hanging from a circle with wings. The Jesuit writer beheld in this strange configuration a "symbol of the arcane mysteries," by which he meant the mysteries of the essence of God, not simply the Holy Trinity. "By the circle," Kircher wrote, "is signified the pure form of divinity, the eternal and immense God, abstracted from all base matter; by the serpent, the second form of divinity . . . or the Word of God . . . by the wings fixed on the globe, the third form of divinity, the Spirit pervading everything, is aptly expressed." In his chapter on Egyptian astrology, Kircher placed this Trinitarian design, which he calls the *Tetragrammaton* or sacred name of God, at the centre of a graphic depiction of the zodiac.[73] Stukeley could scarcely have missed it.

In the flying snake, we might discern a winged dragon. Kircher was intrigued by dragons, which he discussed in *Mundus Subterraneus* (first published 1664–5), another classic of wonder-inducing speculation. He believed that such creatures existed in the Swiss Alps and were related to the dragons of legend.[74] He would have been well aware of their alchemical significance. Pictures of winged dragons, variously representing the spiritualization of matter, a volatile spirit, sublimated mercury or mercuric acid, appear frequently in alchemical manuscripts, starting with the Ripley Scrolls. By the seventeenth century, they were perhaps the most familiar of all emblems in alchemy. Kircher's winged dragons closely resemble those found in alchemical texts, and their underground existence suggests that he linked them with metals. Moreover, he regarded alchemy as an Egyptian science, invented by Hermes Trismegistus. In *Oedipus Aegyptiacus*, Kircher equated the alchemical signs for metals with what he supposed to be the hieroglyphs of Egyptian gods and goddesses, as well as with those of the planets. He thought the particular hieroglyph of alchemy consisted of the winged circle with serpent motif hovering above a scarab. The mythic voyage of the scarab across the heavens traced not only an astrological journey but an alchemical process.[75]

Stukeley, of course, had seen a winged dragon in the sky, in the form of Draco, the never-setting constellation of the northern sky.[76] Draco had various roles in mythology: as the protector of the golden apples of the Hesperides sought by Hercules and as the guardian of the Golden Fleece. Stukeley was particularly taken with the first of these myths, just as Newton had been with the second. He decided that the dragon's nemesis, Hercules, was none other than the founder of Stonehenge and the first reader of the zodiac. In a 1752 letter, Stukeley argued that Midian, son of the patriarch Abraham, "formed the zodiac for use of Hercules of Tyre in navigation." Hercules went on to build the first patriarchal temple, Beth-el, to the specifications of a celestial vision. Presumably steering by the northern stars, the hero then travelled to Britain, where Stukeley could not "see any absurdity" in the idea that he set up the sacrificial altar at Stonehenge.[77] Thus, the treasure of the astrological-alchemical dragon, the secret of the zodiac, turned out to be the famous British temple itself. Draco the winged dragon guided Hercules to Stonehenge, to be re-created in stone through the serpent-like temple at Avebury.

In discussing the serpentine plan of Avebury, Stukeley referred to the brazen serpent raised by Moses to cure the Israelites of snakebites (the Nehushtan), which was accepted by theologians as a type of Christ. The brazen serpent, as illustrated for example in the famous seventeenth-century emblem book of George Wither, was wrapped around an upright cross, forming a shape similar to the Avebury serpent. Wither, however, also displays the emblem of the Orobouros or snake devouring itself, a symbol of infinitude that may have been in Stukeley's mind.[78] Both emblems were common in alchemy. A flying serpent or dragon bent into an Orobouros was found in many German alchemical works, from the *Book of Lambspringke* (1577) to Michael Maier's *Atalanta Fugiens* (1618).[79] Serpents rudely swallowing a virgin comprise the first "Hieroglyphic Figure" in a famous treatise falsely attributed to the medieval French alchemist Nicholas Flamel. The strange scene was usually shown in the form of an Orobouros gobbling up a young girl. The second of "Flamel's" hieroglyphs was the Nehushtan, "a *Crosse* where a *Serpent* was crucified."[80] Whether Stukeley ever read "Flamel" is unknown, but Newton knew the work well and made transcripts from it.[81]

Stukeley's use of astrological and alchemical allusions helps us to understand his indulgent interpretation of Druidic magic. The text of *Stonehenge* did not mention magic at all, but in *Abury* Stukeley admitted that the Druids were magicians. He defined magic as "nothing else but the science that teaches us to perform wonderful and surprizing things, in the later acceptance of the world." In other words, the Druids used *magia naturalis*, although supernatural magic is not ruled out here. Stukeley further asserted that the term *magus* was equivalent to priest, and derived from *maaghim meditabundi*, or "people of a contemplative, retir'd life."[82] Druidic magic, in short, was more akin to the quiet pursuits of rural vicars than to the spells and charms of village wise women. Stukeley would later write that the Druids were called magi "at first understood in its best sense: but it degenerated into the ill sense of magician."[83] Even "the best sense" of magus meant the possession of a power that verged on the supernatural; this power might have survived into the present, in vulgarized form. On hearing of a Druidic "temple" in Shropshire, where "the mythologic report [local legend] . . . is of a Cow wh[ich] to good women gave as much milk as they desired: but to ill women, none," Stukeley noted that this was "a remain of the notion of magic." At another "temple" in Berkshire, an invisible blacksmith would shoe your horse for a penny. "I have often taken notice of these magic notions affixed to Druid temples," observed Stukeley, without indicating whether or not he believed in them.[84]

Stukeley may have taken such "superstitious" beliefs seriously because he linked them with the hidden forces of nature, especially the *anima mundi* or Soul of the World. In his early writings, he ascribed supernatural effects in nature to what he called "animal spirits," which existed both in the macrocosm of the universe and the microcosm of the human body. He compared these animal spirits to fire, and suggested that people "have been observed as it were encompass'd with a lambent Flame, when the Spirits have broke out in fiery Rays, upon the outward Surface of the body."[85] In passages like these, Stukeley employs a language that would have made sense to seventeenth-century alchemists. Occasionally, he may have borrowed directly from them—for example, in writing that "the earth has really veins & arteries, as well as an animal body," which sounds like a passage from Sendivogius.[86]

In his later works, however, Stukeley abandoned "animal spirits" in favour of a more fashionable source of hidden power: namely, electricity. He was profoundly affected by the earthquake of February 1750, which many felt to be a divine warning to the British people. Searching for an explanation of the event that would satisfy both his religious and scientific beliefs, and convinced that one need not "lose sight of the theological purpose of these amazing alarms whilst we Endeavour to find out the Philosophy of them," he decided that earthquakes were due to "electrical shock." Soon after the London tremors, Stukeley presented a paper to the Royal Society on electricity and earthquakes, which drew on the interest generated by the experiments of Benjamin Franklin of Pennsylvania. Stukeley quickly found all manner of further applications of "electrical motion," first as a cause of sickness, then as "the principle of all generation in animals." By 1755, he was convinced that "sexual communion . . . is really an electrical operation in all respects," and that electricity was "that great soul of the material world."[87] In other words, the *anima mundi* was fulfilled in electrical intercourse.

Stukeley's reading of sex was self-justifying. At the time he made this "discovery," he was romantically involved with a "Druidess" whom he called "Miriam." In pursuing the adulterous affair, he satisfied himself that he had a right to transgress moral boundaries, which were designed for "the vulgar, who have not a proper command on themselves," not for "a philosopher" like himself. The common people, he continued, had to be deceived by the wise man, who "hides his actions from the world." What would be the reaction of the vulgar if they were told "there is no life hereafter[?] I need not tell the consequences of it. or were we to tell them the punish[men]t of hell is not eternal[?]"[88] It is difficult to read this extraordinary private confession without wondering whether Stukeley's orthodoxy was a mere deception.

He was certainly unconcerned with spirituality. Stukeley's sense of the sacred was surprisingly mundane: it was a mystery to be solved, a secret to be unlocked, not a source of eternal awe. This is apparent in his definition of a symbol. As so much of Stukeley's work was devoted to the esoteric significance of symbols, one might expect that he saw in them the marks of divine authority. On the contrary: for him, they were simply the products of social and cultural necessity. "A symbol," he wrote, "is an arbitrary, sensible sign of an intellectual idea. And I believe that the art of writing at first was no other, than that of making symbols, pictures, or marks of things they wanted to express."[89] So much for the sacred writing of Adam. Far from being dictated by God, it was no less arbitrary or intelligible than any other human system of expression. Of course, it required a "philosopher" to interpret the ideas behind symbols. Stukeley's brash self-assurance in reading the universe, which contrasts so markedly with the painful reticence of Newton, was characteristic of eighteenth-century natural philosophy, in which the inquiring mind of the individual stood supreme. The supernatural power of the *anima mundi* flowed through the observer, not through the symbol.

How unique was Stukeley among the Newtonians? He certainly imparted his opinions to close friends, like Martin Ffoulkes or Roger Gale, with whom he mingled in a multitude of clubs and societies. He also shared an outlook with less intimate associates like Sir Hans Sloane, the medical doctor whose vast collection of curiosities became the foundation of the British Museum. Sloane avidly sought out magical rings, healing charms and relics of the Elizabethan magus John Dee, who also interested Stukeley. Among the enormous number of manuscripts purchased by Sloane were almost four hundred volumes of alchemical writings.[90] With Sloane as with Stukeley, however, occult items were mere props in a world of artifacts that was centred on the collector himself, who classified, arranged and displayed them.

The Newtonian who was closest to Stukeley in his varied interests, although certainly not in his religious opinions, was William Whiston. A gifted young scientist, he became Newton's successor as Lucasian professor of mathematics at Cambridge. Whiston gained fame in 1696 through the publication of *A New Theory of the Earth*, in which he postulated the origin of the terrestrial globe in "a confus'd Chaos," formed from "the *Atmosphere of a Comet*."[91] Chaos was beloved by alchemists, who saw it as the *prima materia*, and Whiston obliged them by including marvellous diagrams of the developing cosmos, strikingly similar to those of Robert Fludd. Whiston's *New Theory* was frequently republished, but his academic career was less successful. Deprived of his professorship in 1710 on account of his anti-Trinitarian views, Whiston became a public lecturer and popularizer of science.[92]

To trace his subsequent opinions is a bewildering task, because he frequently altered them. In 1716, he decried "the Folly of Judicial Astrology, and of all such Methods of Divination and Prognostication as the Vulgar Superstitious People are so fond of . . . if any thing be thus foretold, it is by a Power plainly Daemoniacal."[93] He later changed his mind. In October 1737, he met Stukeley at Tycho Wing's observatory in Rutland, where "we had a good deal of talk about Astrology. Mr Whiston says Dr. Halley foretold the month the [Glorious] Revolution happened: nov[r] 1688."[94] Whiston's new-found taste for astrology probably sprang from a passionate attachment to prophecy, which also motivated him to endorse the ancient Sibylline oracles—all of them, not just those that supposedly foretold the birth of Christ—as divinely inspired.[95] On issues concerning the supernatural, Whiston came to his own offbeat conclusions. He suggested in 1717 that "miraculous Operations" were caused not by divine suspension of the laws of nature, but "by the means of Angels, or of some other Spiritual and Invisible Beings," because natural laws were fixed and could not be altered. He accepted that demons existed in the world, but argued that the "*Magical Arts*" of witches and conjurors were "*Diabolical* or *Daemonical Delusions*," whose effects were not real.[96] Nevertheless, he continued to believe in "wonders" that seemed prophetic to him. At the end of his very long life, Whiston became notorious for asserting that the case of Mary Toft, a clothier's wife who falsely claimed that she had given birth to a litter of rabbits, had confirmed a prophecy that "menstruous women will bring forth monsters" in 2 Esdras 5:8.[97]

Like Stukeley, Whiston used diverse strands of occult thinking to support his arguments against vulgar "superstition" or religious scepticism. Unlike Stukeley, however, he did not labour to construct an interpretation of nature or history out of occult symbols; rather, he saw himself as verifying God's own design, even if it meant embracing the supernatural. In this respect, he was more akin to his mentor, Newton. Yet his dependence on public lecturing and the sale of sensational writings made Whiston a creature of the new commercial age, whether he liked it or not. He depended on a public always eager to read about prophecies, angels, demons and monsters. These readers were not much bothered by inconsistencies or lapses from orthodoxy. The reaction of the educated elite was less favourable. The shipwreck of Whiston's academic ambitions demonstrates how heterodox religious beliefs could instantly relegate even a Newtonian to the margins of intellectual respectability. It was not Whiston's views on the Sibylline oracles that made him an outsider: it was his doubts about the Trinity.

Ultimately, the Newtonian Magi were not successful in rehabilitating occult thinking. Newton's *Chronology* was widely criticized. Stukeley failed to make astrology acceptable to the Royal Society, and Whiston ended up as a joke due to Mrs Tofts the rabbit-woman. Nevertheless, their appropriation of the occult shows the inadequacy of setting up an eighteenth-century Newtonian Enlightenment in opposition to the occult "irrationalism" of a former age. The interchange between natural philosophy and occult thinking continued, albeit on a more abstract level. Perhaps the most enduring result of the interchange can be seen in the development of Freemasonry. Whether Whiston was initiated is unknown, but he was willing to tap into the favourite themes of the Masons. He translated the works of the Jewish historian Josephus, including an account of the Temple of Jerusalem, and in 1726 he supervised the construction of a model of Solomon's Temple, on which he gave numerous lectures, opining that the Jews would soon be restored to the Holy Land.[98] As in so many other respects, his views were eccentric, but audiences were drawn to them by a fascination with the Temple that was sustained in large part by Freemasonry. Stukeley, a dedicated Mason, catered to the same spirit when he linked Stonehenge to the Temple of Solomon. "It seems likely," he stated, "that when *Stonehenge* was built, the Druids had some notice from *phoenician* traders, of the nature of *Solomon's* temple."[99] British Freemasons would have been thrilled to learn that the sacred building from which the secrets of the Craft were derived had been rebuilt on their shores. Stukeley's greatest gift to Masonry, however, was to verify its ancestry in the mystery cults of the ancient world.

The Ancient Mysteries

In May 1738, William Stukeley was visited at his home near Stamford by his friend and clerical colleague William Warburton. "I observed to him," noted Stukeley in his diary, "that our modern Free-masonry Ceremonys are derivd from the antient initiations of the Myst[er]ys, or descent into hell."[100] Stukeley was aware, of course, that the clergyman to whom he was speaking was the recent author of a controversial work, *The Divine Legation of Moses*, in which the belief in an afterlife was traced to the ancient mystery cults. He did not record Warburton's reply, but it is hard to imagine Stukeley making such a remark to somebody who would be unreceptive to it. In fact, Warburton's treatment of the mysteries upheld Stukeley's claim, which had become widespread among Freemasons. For some readers, *The Divine Legation* gave a dense, deeply learned reply to the question: what was Masonry about?

Freemasonry was about many things in the early eighteenth century. Within the official Grand Lodge, it was a means of bolstering Hanoverian loyalty and support for the government, through the election of grand masters who were connected to the ruling regime. It was also the forum for a quasi-democratic male sociability that brought members of the aristocracy and gentry together with representatives of the middling sort. It imparted the values of politeness, civility and religious tolerance. It provided a network of patronage by which artists and high-end craftsmen could establish links with potential customers. Finally, it had the allure of a secret society, whose arcane rituals offered a promise of hidden knowledge.[101] The impact of Freemasonry was no doubt profound, but it should not be exaggerated. Although Masons might share certain attitudes, there was no single unifying Masonic project beyond the preservation of the secrets of the Craft.

Masonic secrets were handed down through initiation rites that related to death and rebirth. These ceremonies employed imagery (skulls, ladders, the zodiac, stars, pentacles) that was reminiscent of occult science or even ritual magic. Whether the secrets of Masonry amounted to knowledge of the supernatural, however, was a matter of opinion. Its rites could be regarded as purely symbolic or as opening an entrance to divine wisdom. Three writers whose works have been associated with early Masonry—John Toland, Robert Samber and Martin Clare—took very different approaches to the issue. Toland called for a priesthood of Brothers, dedicated to pantheism and natural magic, while Samber flirted with the supernatural. Clare, like William Stukeley, dredged up aspects of occult philosophy in order to vindicate the tie between Masonry and the ancient mysteries.

Plenty of mystery surrounds the writings of these men. John Toland's relationship to the occult is as difficult to unravel as his personal background (he was reputed to be the illegitimate son of an Irish priest). His fervent admiration for the Italian philosopher Giordano Bruno, burned at the stake for heresy in Rome in 1600, may have originated in a shared opposition to what Toland called "priestcraft," but it extended to Bruno's unorthodox opinions on religion and the universe as well. Egyptian polytheism, according to Bruno, was a pure form of the original religion, notably in its recognition of the divine in natural creatures. This observation alone would have placed Bruno perilously close to the flames of inquisitorial retribution. He believed in the infinitude of space and the existence of innumerable worlds, concepts that flew directly in the face of the Newtonian system.[102] Toland endorsed all of these views, and even defended Bruno's use of the term *Magia*. "It is certain that by *Magia* in his writings nothing else is meant," Toland wrote, unhelpfully, "other than learned and not vulgar, although especially natural, knowledge."[103] Did it also mean supernatural knowledge?

Bruno's theories of the universe were the starting point for *Pantheisticon* (1720). Written in Latin and aimed at a European audience that was as yet unfamiliar with Freemasonry, it introduced a "*New Fellowship*" of "SOCRATIC SOCIETIES" composed of "*Pantheists*." The first part of Toland's work outlined a materialist philosophy of the universe, based on the idea that from "the infinite Whole [*Totius infiniti*] . . . innumerable species of things arise, of which every single individual is no less form than matter, as form is nothing else, than a disposition of certain parts in a body."[104] The number of elements is infinite, and each element is both eternal and indestructible. While the process by which elements are made has no beginning and no end, the "*Hebrew* Cabalists" and certain "gentile Philosophers"—meaning, no doubt, Francis Mercurius van Helmont—are chided for believing that anything can be created out of nothing. Toland displayed more sympathy towards alchemists, who seek to change the elements back to an original substance, although they too are to be disappointed: "Here, Spagyricists, alas! no hope is left of *Chrysopoeia* [i.e. gold-making]."[105]

Toland's pantheism left the spagyricists at a dead end. In a universe of infinite differentiation, with no prime mover and no ultimate resolution, alchemy was unable to reconstruct the orderly, purposeful stages of creation. The pantheist cosmos was certainly not Newtonian; neither can it easily be reconciled with the Masonic emphasis on the harmonious work of the divine Architect. Yet the Socratic Society described in the second part of Toland's work was very similar to Freemasonry: a brotherhood of equals, meeting for sociable and intellectual purposes. They were also priests. In spite of his contempt for "Priest-craft [*Hierotechnen*]," the pantheists are themselves called by Toland "Mystics and Hierophants of Nature." Like the Druids, to whom they are explicitly compared, they are followers of Pythagoras and "seekers of occult things [*quaestoribus occultarum rerum*]."[106]

If Toland had the Freemasons in mind when he wrote of the Socratic Society, he was dreaming: they were not a band of modern pantheists, and they did not worship nature. More likely, he was encouraging the Masons to model themselves on his ideal brotherhood. He was not notably successful, although his writings may have contributed to negative images of Masonry. Toland's was in fact the first attempt to link the Craft to a specific philosophy of the universe. While it was extreme in its materialism and its rejection of revealed religion, it retained a healthy regard for hidden or occult knowledge. Toland was also the first to compare Masons openly to a Druidic priesthood. In this, he foreshadowed a generation of Masonic enthusiasts who would become prominent in the 1720s and 1730s, including Stukeley.

The writings of Robert Samber point in a more supernatural direction. Born into a prominent Protestant family of Lymington in Hampshire, Samber had a Catholic mother, and in his early twenties he entered the English College at Rome to pursue a clerical career. Changing his mind, Samber then scurried back to England, where he became a hack writer and translator. His best-known translations were of the racy novel *Venus in the Cloister*, for which the publisher Edmund Curll was prosecuted for obscenity in 1725, and Charles Perrault's *Tales of Mother Goose*.[107] Samber was extraordinarily well connected in Masonic circles. His 1722 translation of a French treatise on the art and architecture of Rome was dedicated to the earl of Burlington, the celebrated Whig nobleman and foremost instigator of the revival of classical architecture that became known as Palladianism.[108] Burlington was almost certainly a Freemason, although he never served as an officer of the Grand Lodge and may have been a member of the rival York Lodge, based in northern England.[109] Apart from Burlington, Samber attached himself to the duke of Wharton, the headstrong scion of an eminent Whig family who became grand master of the Grand Lodge in 1722–3. A secret Jacobite, Wharton later revealed his political sympathies and fled from England. Among Samber's papers is a letter written to Wharton in 1727, deploring a report that the duke had become a Catholic monk and begging him to throw himself on the mercy of King George II. In his own wayward youth, Samber had almost certainly been a Jacobite, but by the late 1720s he was eager to dissociate himself from the inconvenient cause of the exiled Stuarts.[110]

Samber's most significant Masonic relationship was with a staunch government Whig, the 2nd duke of Montagu, whose lavish patronage was also enjoyed by William Stukeley. In 1721–2, Montagu had become the first nobleman to serve as grand master of the Grand Lodge. Although a notorious practical joker, Montagu was also a man of learning and Fellow of the Royal Society. His London townhouse later became the site of the British Museum. Both the mischievous and the serious sides of Montagu's character would have been entertained by a bizarre French work translated by Samber in 1722, entitled *Long Livers*. The name "Eugenius Philalethes" appears on the title page, a reference of course to the alchemical philosopher Thomas Vaughan, although Samber was generous enough to bestow a Fellowship of the Royal Society on his pseudonymous self. Samber had recently used the same alias in a work recommending home remedies for the plague (including chemical antidotes) that was dedicated to Montagu. *Long Livers* was even more ambitious: it promised to reveal "the rare SECRET of REJUVENESCENCY" discovered by the thirteenth-century Aragonese alchemist Arnaldus de Villa-Nova, as well as to give the recipe for "the UNIVERSAL MEDICINE," a by-product of the Philosopher's Stone.[111]

The verbose dedication of *Long Livers* to the "Fraternity of Free Masons of *Great-Britain* and *Ireland*" makes no secret of appealing to a Masonic audience. Like Toland, "Philalethes" extols the Freemasons as "a royal Priesthood." In praising the wonders of creation, however, and in rejecting atheism, *Long Livers* stands in sharp contrast to *Pantheisticon*. Most of the dedication is a strange, rambling concoction of biblical history, anti-Catholicism and violent prejudices against lawyers, punctuated with thinly disguised Masonic themes. Moses, for example, is described as "a great Astonomer," who, while casting out idolatry, preserved a religion of "pompous Sacrifices, Rites and Ceremonies, magnificent Sacerdotal and Levitical Vestments, and a vast Number of mystical Hieroglyphics." Samber evidently had in mind the rituals, vestments and symbols of the Masonic fraternity. He made a single enticing reference to Rosicrucian lore by citing "the book *M*" (probably *Magia*), which Christian Rosenkreuz had translated from Arabic into Latin, and which contained the secret wisdom of ancient days. The dedication to *Long Livers* was rounded off with an alchemical tour of Solomon's Temple, in which the Holy of Holies becomes "the King of GEMMS," a light emanating out of "that transparent Pyramid of purple Salt more sparkling and radiant than the finest orient Ruby."[112]

Unlike Toland, Samber had few philosophical pretensions. He enhanced the air of mystery that surrounded the Freemasons by suggesting that they possessed hidden knowledge of real value, similar to that of the alchemists and Rosicrucians. He even attempted to rewrite Masonic rituals in accordance with this occult programme. Among Samber's surviving manuscripts are a series of prayers and invocations for initiation ceremonies, which blend the alchemical imagery of *Long Livers* ("celestial Salt more precious and shining than the Orient Ruby") with standard Masonic formulations.[113] Whether they were actually used in any lodge is doubtful, but they were surely devised to impress the author's aristocratic patrons.

Samber's involvement with the occult went further than this. While the dedication to *Long Livers* does not refer to ritual magic, Samber's private papers do not avoid the topic. They contain the manuscripts of two treatises on the raising of spirits. The first, entitled "The Magician," was purportedly an edition of some letters exchanged in 1704 between the Huguenot minister Pierre Jurieu and the Dutch scholar Gijsbert Cuper, concerning a vision of the English royal family seen in a "looking glass" by a Roman necromancer during the reign of

Henry VII. Samber added to the work a long introduction, describing the "Teraphims" or cult images used by the ancient Israelites. He refers to them as "human figures, or perhaps mystical ones, and mixed with the figure or some animals, made under certain constellations, by the influences of which constellations, these figures or statues received the power of speech, when they were consulted about obscure matters."[114] Evidently, he was searching for a biblical justification for ritual magic, but the idea of prophesying images is curiously redolent of the alleged heresy of the medieval Knights Templar, who were accused of worshipping a talking head. A second, unfinished work among Samber's papers, bearing the intriguing title "Psychology," deals with apparitions of spirits. In this, he admitted that some apparitions could be explained by natural causes, but asserted that many were real. Furthermore, he did not shrink from putting his readers in touch with them. One of the last, unwritten chapters of this work was devoted to "The way to conjure Spirits."[115]

Samber cannot be dismissed as a mere hack or crank. He was connected with some of the most influential figures in Freemasonry, including Richard Steele, and he evidently believed they wanted to read about magic.[116] There was apparently a deep fascination with occult lore beneath the placid intellectual façade of the early Masonic movement. Furthermore, his ideas were not without consequences. Within a few years, more cautious writers had picked up one of his main suggestions: namely, that Freemasonry was essentially about "REJUVENESCENCE" or rebirth. For them, however, the discovery pointed in the direction, not of Rosicrucian myths, but of ancient mystery cults.

The first known statement of this theory in Masonic literature is in a very short work entitled "A Defense of Masonry." Apparently, no original copies of the pamphlet survive, but it was reprinted in 1738 as an appendix to the second edition of James Anderson's *Constitutions*. Often attributed to Anderson, it was probably written by Martin Clare, who ran an academy in Soho Square where "YOUTH are Boarded, Educated and qualified either for the University, or the Compting House, or the Publick Offices."[117] His clients were boys of the middling ranks of society, whom he shaped into gentlemen through instruction in French, dancing and fencing. At the same time, Clare did not neglect practical studies, and he wrote a frequently republished guide to trade and business for young men. He served as deputy grand master of the Grand Lodge in 1741, and was a Fellow of the Royal Society. His interest in science led to the publication in 1737 of a work on hydrostatics, based on lectures "privately read to a set of Gentlemen" and dedicated to the earl of Burlington.[118]

The "Defense of Masonry" shares the didactic tone of Clare's other writings, but it displays considerable ingenuity in linking Masonry with every conceivable occult predecessor. To begin with, the pamphlet cites the ancient Egyptians, "who conceal'd the Chief *Mysteries* of their Religion under *Signs* and *Symbols*, call'd HIEROGLYPHICS," and who venerated Harpocrates, the god of silence (his image, with finger on mouth, appears in the decorations of Lord Burlington's house at Chiswick). According to Clare, "Pythagoras, travelling into *Egypt*, became instructed in the *Mysteries* of that Nation; and here he laid the Foundations of all his *Symbolical* Wisdom." The ancient Jewish sect of Essenes are identified, oddly enough, as followers of Pythagoras. The Kabbala, of course, could not escape mention, although it merits little explanation beyond a mention of its emphasis on the ordering of letters and the remark that "DAVID and SOLOMON, they say, were exquisitely skill'd in it." Finally, the Druids make an appearance as prefiguring Masonry through their white clothing, ceremonial feasts and mysterious sciences. "The Conformity between the *Rites* and Principles of *Masonry*," concludes the writer, with evident satisfaction, "... and the many Customs and *Ceremonies* of the *Ancients*, must give Delight to a Person of any Taste and Curiosity."[119]

Taste and curiosity were defining features of the politely educated gentleman, perhaps a graduate of Clare's academy, who prided himself on cultural accomplishments more than on genealogy. Such a man would, of course, be familiar with Virgil's *Aeneid*, specifically with the passage in book six that describes the voyage of Aeneas into Hades. The hero is magically assisted in his journey by a golden bough, just as in an earlier passage from book three he finds the body of the Trojan prince Polydorus with the aid of a shrub. The author of the "Defense" compared both of these episodes to the discovery of the corpse of the Temple architect Hiram Abiff, who was buried under an acacia shrub, according to the legend associated with the Master Mason degree, the third and highest of the traditional degrees of English Freemasonry.[120] Every classically educated person knew that the journey to Hades was a central motif of the mystery cults of ancient Greece, particularly the Eleusinian mysteries, so by linking Freemasonry with the Greek underworld, Clare was entering a rich territory of mythical speculation.[121] The immediate impact of his theories may be reflected at Chiswick House, where an enormous painting of the rape of Proserpine, the story on which the rites of Eleusis were based, can still be admired in the octagonal Upper Tribunal.

This was occult thinking fit for any polite reader: highly suggestive, but not overtly magical. Clare's essay would reach a large Masonic audience throughout the British Isles and beyond, by its inclusion in both Anderson's *Constitutions* and *The Free-Mason's Pocket Companion*. Clare implied that the Freemasons possessed a supernatural wisdom previously known to the Egyptians, the Kabbalists and the initiates of mystery cults, but he gave little hint of what that wisdom might be. What impact his essay had on the far more critical approach of William Warburton is difficult to judge. We cannot even be certain that Warburton was a Freemason. His correspondence with Stukeley reveals nothing about the issue, and the only reference to Masonry in his printed letters is not very serious.[122] Yet the argument of Warburton's *Divine Legation of Moses* not only builds on the suppositions of Clare's "Defense," it uncovers the secret of the ancient mysteries in a way that would have thrilled Stukeley.

The secret was life after death. Warburton maintained that the idea of an afterlife was not found in ancient Judaism, but was instead derived from "the most sacred Part of Pagan Religion." He included in this category the Egyptian rites of Isis and Osiris, as well as the Greek and Roman cults. In this "secret Worship . . . none were admitted but those who had been selected by preparatory Ceremonies, called *Initiations*."[123] The sixth book of *The Aeneid*, Warburton opined, "is nothing else but a Description, and so designed by the Author, of his Hero's Initiation into the Mysteries of one Part of the ELEUSINIAN SPECTACLES."[124] Pythagoras, according to Warburton, used the mystery cults as the basis for his theory of the transmigration of souls. Less admirable was Hermes Trismegistus, a figure tainted with pantheism and "the rankest Spinozism"—unlike the exemplary Druids, who were heirs to the wisdom of the Egyptians concerning the afterlife.[125] Hermes seems to correspond to John Toland, while the Druids, unsurprisingly, resemble Warburton's friend Stukeley.

Warburton, however, was far more hostile to paganism than Stukeley. He took pains to point out that the ancient myths offered "vicious Examples" of the immorality of "licentious Deities." The old trope of occult philosophy, that Moses had learned magic from the Egyptians, was transformed in the second part of *The Divine Legation* into the hypothesis that the great lawgiver had simply recognized the doctrine of eternal rewards and punishments in the hieroglyphic writings of the Egyptian priests. Originally conceived as a means of communication, hieroglyphics had become "a Vehicle of Secrecy," just as the ancient mysteries had "degenerated into MAGIC."[126] Warburton was utterly contemptuous of the superstitious beliefs of the later Egyptians, including judicial astrology. He recognized no vital elements of the *prisca theologia* in Egyptian religion, and he delivered a grudging, back-handed compliment to the theories of Athanasius Kircher, who, "extravagant as he was, had yet some ground for his Reveries." As for Newton's *Chronology*, Warburton considered it to have been misled "by little lying *Greek* Mythologists and Story-tellers."[127]

The Divine Legation removed any element of the supernatural from its account of ritual. This becomes evident in its discussion of the use of types. The typological repetition of elements, according to Warburton, changes an action from mere arbitrariness to having moral significance. In his view, typological stories were modelled on rituals, by which apparently meaningless events were re-created over and over so as to impart a moral message. Writing was related to ritual in combining arbitrary signs with a hidden message. Thus, while types are "rational Modes of Information," they employ methods that are "obscure and mysterious."[128] They are occult without being supernatural. At the same time, Warburton's interpretation of writing excludes the possibility of fully rational interpretation. As soon as anything is written, it takes on a double meaning. In his insistence that social factors shape religious beliefs, Warburton was a man of the Enlightenment, but his sophisticated theory of types looks beyond enlightened reason, towards the cultural criticism of a later age.

The reverend author may have been too far ahead of his time, as well as overly detached and equivocal in his approach to fundamental religious issues. *The Divine Legation* shocked its first readers and left them cold, and it has a similar effect today. Unlike Stukeley's mythic fantasies of Stonehenge, it inspired no imitators. In relation to Freemasonry, which he never explicitly mentioned, Warburton provided a long-winded, confusingly structured justification for an idea summed up in ten pages by Martin Clare's "Defense," that the rituals of the Masons were descended from ancient mystery cults. While he removed that idea from occult speculation, Warburton added a further twist to it, by arguing that pagan rituals had bestowed the concept of life after death on the Jews. Ancient (or Masonic) initiations, therefore, were not just symbolic re-enactments; they were sacred practices that manifested a truth not known to the ancient Hebrews. This bestowed a weighty and universal purpose on Masonic rites.

In the decades after the "Defense" and *The Divine Legation*, the secrets of Freemasonry failed to measure up to such high-flown expectations, whether supernatural or not. Many of the mysteries of the Craft had already been openly revealed in print, by disgruntled Brothers or critics of the lodges. The result was what might be called an inflation of secrets. Competing Masonic groups offered new mysteries and even new degrees that promised higher levels of secret knowledge. The result was division and disillusionment within the ranks of the Brotherhood. Whether the number of lodges or members actually fell in this period is difficult to determine, but, by 1760, the Grand Lodge of England could not claim to control a unified Masonic movement.[129] The high hopes of the 1720s and 1730s had not been fulfilled.

Yet the Masonic writings of Toland, Samber and Clare, along with the theories of Stukeley and Warburton, had defined the parameters of an enduring Masonic discourse. This represented the Craft in exalted terms, as the inheritor of fundamental secrets that were certainly sacred and might be supernatural. Picturing themselves as priests or Druids, alchemists or Pythagoreans, many Masons retained an attachment to the occult mindset that had inspired

Ashmole and Moray in the seventeenth century. It would be wrong to claim that Masonry was an occult movement in any focused intellectual sense, but it exploited a symbolic language that had been dredged out of a vast reservoir of occult beliefs and practices, including Rosicrucianism, Hermeticism, the raising of spirits, alchemy and astrology.

A similar process of appropriation, as this chapter has shown, can be detected among the Newtonians who formed the intellectual establishment of the early Hanoverian period. In searching for ultimate meanings and divine intentions, they were willing to sacrifice natural or rational explanations in favour of what we would call imagination and contemporaries sometimes decried as "Fancy." Accordingly, they turned back towards the occult philosophies of earlier centuries, which they revised to suit their own purposes. The supernatural elements in these philosophies were adapted to scriptural, historical, mythic or even scientific scenarios. In Newton's *Chronology*, Stukeley's zodiacal studies, Whiston's rambling prophecies and the evocation of ancient mysteries by Masonic writers, traces of occult philosophy coexisted with the initial glimmerings of the Enlightenment. This may seem a sad anticlimax to the occult heyday of the late seventeenth century, when alchemy, astrology and magic burned so brightly, but it represents a significant survival, which would have further ramifications within British culture. For some who stood outside the intellectual establishment, however, the legacy of occult thinking remained a coherent system whose appeal had never been reduced, and a force that could be used to subvert rather than to enhance enlightened reason. We have to turn to these marginal figures in order to recognize how strong the attraction of the occult remained, despite the massive gravitational pull of Newtonianism.

CHAPTER SIX

The Occult on the Margins

THE NEWTONIANS who sought to reclaim the occult as support for their own theories were not concerned with its coherence. They borrowed what they needed from alchemy, astrology or Neoplatonism, ignoring the rest. This chapter, by contrast, deals with those who faithfully preserved one aspect or another of occult tradition. Few of them were well connected. For social, political or religious reasons, they existed on the margins of cultural authority. Some of them belonged to the wide and nebulous region that separated formally educated members of the elite from the rest of the English and Scottish population—that is, they had a measure of learning but were not gentlemen, even in the loosest sense of the term. Others were set apart by fundamental beliefs, because they were mystics, Tories, Jacobites or Nonjurors. Less obstructed by the constraints of respectability than the Newtonians, these marginal men and women embraced the fading glow of occult philosophy in ways that were spiritually adventurous. They were often suspicious of "reason," which they associated with the hegemony of Whigs in Church and State, or Newtonianism in natural philosophy. Their espousal of spirituality, sentiment and feeling, however, placed them in harmony with cultural trends of growing significance.

Marginality is a relative concept that may not apply to all aspects of an individual's life. It did not mean insignificance or total lack of influence. The religious sect known as the French Prophets was small, but it made a considerable impression. The Nonjurors John Byrom and William Law or the architect John Wood of Bath cultivated their own circles of admirers. In some cases, marginal thinkers may have been closer to the mainstream of popular culture than their better-established rivals, especially in their views on spirits, ritual magic, alchemy and astrology. We should be cautious, however, about pressing such claims too far. The marginal writers considered in this chapter were often just as disdainful of popular "superstition" as were the Newtonians. In addition, to make a valid comparison between popular beliefs and the ideas of more educated people, even those who may have been outside the intellectual establishment, content and significance have to be taken into account. This is not an easy task, as the following section explains.

Popular Belief under Scrutiny

What did the common people believe?[1] We can convey a sense of what learned observers *thought* they believed, but such accounts were always coloured by strong biases. In addition, some first-hand material from the practitioners of popular magic has survived; we may debate whether or not it was typical. To discover what ordinary people generally thought about the occult, we have to make inferences on the basis of thin evidence. Testimony from members of the lower ranks of society about their own beliefs is seldom available. Nevertheless, the chronicles of John Cannon, considered in the last part of the section, allow a remarkable measure of insight into the mind of one rural connoisseur of occult matters.

Any interpretation of popular culture relating to the occult is bound to be heavily dependent on elite impressions. With monotonous predictability, these tended to condemn the occult beliefs of the common people as "superstition." The Protestant ministers who were largely responsible for defining "superstition" equated it not with blind irrationality, but with the remains of paganism or Roman Catholicism.[2] Never simply descriptive, the term was a fizzing bomb to be hurled at one's enemies in a continuing cultural war. The assault troops in that war were the clerical commentators who compiled collections of material on the customs of the common people. The most famous of such collections was published in 1725 by Henry Bourne, an Anglican curate of Newcastle-upon-Tyne, under the revealing title *Antiquitates Vulgares*, or "Vulgar Antiquities." Bourne expressed his aim as the regulation of customs, and the abolition of "such only as are sinful and wicked." He nonetheless objected to many of the attitudes or beliefs of the common people, because he linked them with pagan cults and "Popery." "As to the opinions they hold," he wrote, "they are almost all superstitious, being generally either the produce of Heathenism, or the Inventions of indolent *Monks*."[3] The opinions that he described, of course, were selected precisely because they illustrated his central point.

Bourne's book is crammed with details concerning rituals like bowing towards altars (a bad thing, in his view, because "Popish"), well dressings (a more or less innocent thing) and twelfth-night ceremonies (very bad indeed, as they led to immorality and vice). Occult beliefs enter his discussion in connection with "superstitions" pertaining to the spirits of the dead. Bourne was convinced that popular beliefs concerning spirits comprised, not just a set of false assumptions based on ignorance, but the remains of antiquated and discredited religious systems. For example, he insisted that to believe ghosts wandered about graveyards at night was to embrace a relic of the "Heathenism" that could be found in the writings of classical authors. While he could not deny that apparitions of blessed saints had frequently been seen at holy places, his explanation was that they were "not the Souls of the Saints themselves, but the good Angels appearing in their Likeness."[4] Spirits really were moving about everywhere, but they were angels, not ghosts.

According to Bourne, the common people amused themselves in the evenings by recounting fanciful stories of apparitions. "Some of them have seen *Fairies*, some *Spirits* in the Shapes of *Cows* and *Dogs* and *Horses*; and some have even seen the *Devil* himself, with a *cloven Foot*. All of which, is either *Hearsay* or a *strong Imagination*." The Devil might indeed be seen abroad in the world, affirmed Bourne, but fairies, hobgoblins and sprites were the detritus of paganism; they "wander'd in the Night of Ignorance and Error," but "did really vanish at the Dawn of Truth and the Light of Knowledge."[5] Truth and knowledge were spread by correct faith, which certainly countenanced the possibility of supernatural events. Bourne himself accepted that the Devil might have a physical presence and inhabit some haunted places. He consequently included in his text a version of the Roman Catholic exorcism ceremony, commenting that prayer would surely work better against the Devil than "such feeble Instruments as *Water* and *Herbs* and *Crucifixes*." As for guardian angels, Bourne fully endorsed the popular belief in them, but opined "that it seems more consonant with Scripture, that we are attended by a Number of Angels, than by a particular *Tutelar Angel*."[6]

In relation to occult matters, Bourne's analysis of popular antiquities reveals more about the author than it does about the common people in and around Newcastle. On the subject of spirits, he adopted neither a rationalist nor a sceptical stance, but rather an orthodox one, mixing a heavy dose of conventional Protestantism with a dash of seventeenth-century Neoplatonism. Ultimately, he sought to replace a "superstitious" interpretation of spirits with a doctrinally acceptable one. We may doubt, of course, whether the beliefs of ordinary Northumbrians in 1725 were actually so close to those of the ancient Britons as Bourne suggested, or whether they adhered to them with the consistent level of credulity that he implied. We can also fault him for ignoring printed sources that might have had an impact on folklore, like the ghost stories that had appeared in popular ballads and chapbooks since the late seventeenth century.[7]

Bourne's attempt to transform popular beliefs into Christian orthodoxy had been undertaken for decades in the Scottish Highlands by clerical observers of second sight. The fairies that had so perplexed Robert Kirk, however, ceased to play a part in these accounts. In 1707, a new collection of cases documenting second sight was posthumously published by the Episcopal dean of the Isles (the Inner Hebrides), the Reverend John Frazer. Having witnessed several instances of visions, Frazer accepted their veracity, but suggested that they might be due either to prior impressions made on the optic nerve or to angels. "Let us therefore Consider," he proposed, "that an evil Angel, being permitted thereunto, can muster in our Brain the Latent intentional Species of external absent Objects, and can present the same to the Fancy in the methods best fitting his purpose."[8] Preoccupied with such explanations, Frazer paid scant attention to the beliefs involved in the cases he described. One old woman of Tiree who had second sight "freely confessed that her Father upon his Death-Bed taught her a Charm composed of Barbarous Words, and some untelligible [*sic*] terms," which would result in the projection of images on the wall.[9] How close this charm may have been to ritual magic is impossible to determine, as Frazer neglected to record its details.

Clerical writers consistently underplayed the actual content of "superstitions" in order to condemn their pagan or "papist" origins. Equally they ignored the role of print culture in shaping beliefs. A more nuanced, albeit condemnatory, approach was provided by the celebrated writer Daniel Defoe in three works published in quick succession in 1726–7: *The Political History of the Devil*, *The History and Reality of Apparitions* and *A System of Magick*. Defoe wrote them because he knew they would sell. By this time, he was bereft of important political patrons and dependent on book sales in order to maintain his family. In his novels and other writings, he had frequently courted a broad audience of the middling sort of people—those whose status lay between the great landed families and the labouring poor. His works did reach their targeted readers, as they generally made money and went into multiple editions. *The Political History of the Devil* was a minor hit in this respect, appearing in five editions by 1754 and being reprinted several more times before the end of the century. No doubt many of its readers were, like the author, religious Dissenters, for whom the Devil held a special fascination. Defoe's later works on apparitions and magic also sold briskly, judging by the number of editions that appeared before 1760.[10]

The Political History of the Devil is often ironic in its treatment, and many scholars have longed to see in it some sceptical purpose. Alas, they long in vain. The main intention of the work is to determine when the Devil is actually operating in the world, and when he is being blamed for things that are really the fault of human beings. Defoe never questions the reality of Satan, who is envisaged as a spirit, not as a physical being. The author affirms that "the *Devil* is really and *bona fide* in a great many of our honest weak-headed friends, when they themselves know nothing of the matter." Underhand and devious, Satan's aim is "that he may get all his Business carried on by the Instrumentality of Fools . . . and that he may have all his Work done in such a Manner as that he may seem to have no Hand in it."[11] In pagan times the Devil worked mainly through omens and auguries, but in the present his minions are witches and magicians, to whom he has given the power "to walk invisible, to fly in the Air, ride upon Broom-sticks, and other Wooden Gear, to interpret Dreams . . . to raise Storms, sell Winds, bring up Spirits, disturb the Dead, and torment the living." These powers turn out to be illusory. Through them, however, the Devil has "engross'd all the Wise-Men of the East," including the famous Magi, as well as magicians and astrologers.[12]

Nothing in Defoe's *Political History of the Devil* is unorthodox from a contemporary Protestant point of view. The work affirms the omnipotence of God and strikes a blow against popular "superstition," such as belief in the Devil's cloven hoof. Occult philosophy is continually ridiculed. The same themes are visited again in *The History and Reality of Apparitions*. Here, too, Defoe debunks many popular tales of ghosts and visions, reducing them to psychological reactions, but insists that some apparitions are real and that they represent good or evil spirits. This subject finally brings Defoe to the edge of unorthodoxy, and the threshold of occult thinking. Not wanting to cross it, he avoids any extended discussion of spirits and instead instructs the reader not to fear them:

> Whether they are good Spirits or bad, Angelick Appearances or Diabolick, they are under superior Limitations: the *Devil* we know is chain'd, he can go no further than the length of his Tether; he has not a Hand to act, or a Foot to walk, or a Mouth to speak, but as he is permitted . . . If then we are sure the Devil is restrained from hurting us, any otherwise than he is directed and limited . . . we may be sure that good Spirits are; for their Nature, their Business, their Desires are all fix'd in a general Beneficence to Mankind.[13]

Having arrived at what might be regarded as the crux of his argument, Defoe refuses to commit himself to *any* particular theory of spirits. After all, as he put it in an earlier discussion of angels, "we are not writing Divinity."[14]

A System of Magick completes Defoe's three-pronged assault on the occult. The title is deliberately misleading: Defoe recognized that many would purchase the book hoping to find in it "a Book of Rules for Instruction in the

Practice." Instead, it contains a history of "the Black Art," from antiquity to the present. In ancient Egypt, Persia and Babylon, according to Defoe, a magician was "a *Mathematician*, a Man of Science . . . a Kind of walking Dictionary to other People." Magicians "studied Nature . . . made Observations from the Motions of the Stars and other Heavenly Bodies . . . and were Masters of *perhaps a little* experimental Philosophy."[15] Over time, however, this admirable system of natural magic degenerated into diabolism, initially among the Egyptians, who were "ridiculously Superstitious" and "soon mixt their Religion and their Magick together, their Philosophy and their Idolatry were made assistant to the general Fraud." Satan, of course, facilitated this change by "subtily insinuating Dreams into the Heads of Princes and Great Men, and then by like Dreams communicating to his Correspondents . . . This was a particular Favour done in Aid of those *Magicians*, who were more than ordinarily in his good Graces." From this devilish distortion of original magic arose what Defoe calls "the Black Art," whose practitioners include "the Diviner and Soothsayer, the judicial Astrologer and Conjurer, the Inchanter and Charmer, the Witch and the Wizard, the Necromancer and Dealer with a Familiar Spirit."[16]

The Devil ultimately proved himself to be a deceiver. The magicians of the present age, though in league with Satan, have no power to perform any supernatural acts. They have become mere tricksters. Defoe gives as his example of a modern magician one Dr Boreman, a cunning-man who lived near Maidstone in Kent. Described as a gentleman by his neighbours, Boreman lived in a house with a servant and enjoyed a considerable reputation for detection of lost items, giving advice to lovers, fighting the influence of witches and performing various other kinds of magic. Boreman denied that he used "unlawful Arts" or that he was in contact with a familiar, a sure sign of a witch.[17] Defoe remained convinced nonetheless that the doctor "must have had some unlawful Conversation with such Spririts or such Beings as I should still call Devils." Boreman had apparently written many books, copies of which Defoe had not managed to obtain. Nonetheless, he compared them to those of "the right famous Enthusiast *Jacob Behemen*," the German Theosopher, who is described as "a Kind of Visionist . . . His Writings are either Magick or Enthusiastick, or both." One of Boreman's manuscripts was even entitled "177 Theosophick Questions."[18] This leaves the reader puzzled: could such a learned cunning-man actually be in league with the Devil?

Defoe heightens our uncertainty in the following pages, by admitting the possibility of good spirits and providing examples of them. He dwells on particular cases of second sight among the inhabitants of the Scottish Highlands.[19] Yet he soon lurches back into an attack on astrological charms and talismans, which leads him to a final, conclusive statement: good spirits may exist, but magicians do not command them. The spirits who answer spells and serve the desires of human beings are of a different order. "How are they thus ready and beneficent," Defoe asks, "if they are thus to be call'd out of their happy Abodes, like *Devils*, with Spells and Conjurations, with Necromancy and Wizardism?" Why would prescient spirits have to be informed by a magician about the circumstances in which they are being asked to assist?[20] Evidently, if Dr Boreman was in contact with spirits, they were demons.

Defoe represented magical practices as widespread in England. Unlike Bourne or Frazer, however, he related those practices, not to folk traditions, but to occult philosophy and science, derived largely from books. He admitted that the distinction between good and bad spirits was commonly accepted among practitioners of magic, although he rejected it personally. Finally, he wrote almost nothing about witchcraft, conceding at one point that it was "quite out of Use, and we have heard very little of it in this Part of the World for many Years."[21] The age of witches, apparently, had given way to the age of cunning-men.

The practitioners of popular magic themselves sided with the novelist rather than with the clerics in affirming the significance of print culture. Two magical healers of the early eighteenth century, Duncan Campbel and Timothy Crowther, left first-hand evidence of their familiarity with occult sources. Campbel (he always spelled his surname in this fashion) was a deaf and mute Scotsman resident in London who claimed to have second sight. He specialized in cases of witchcraft, which he treated according to traditional methods, using charms and sympathetic cures. One of his bewitched clients, the vintner and tobacco merchant Richard Coates, was advised to boil his own urine. Cured of the "Distemper" that distorted his head and limbs, the grateful Coates made a legal affidavit testifying to the effectiveness of Campbel's practices in 1725.[22] Wary of astrology, Campbel nonetheless made extensive use of talismans, which he argued "ought not to be condemned by Persons the most averse to Superstition; and it would be as stupid to deny their Force, as it would be to refuse the Sun the Honour of warming us."[23] Occasionally, Campbel combined popular magic with alchemical treatments. He ascribed his own cure from epilepsy to the intervention of a Genius or "Guardian Angel," who visited him in a dream with a recipe for a "Powder of Sympathy" made with the aid of a loadstone.[24] Campbel enjoyed some high-ranking connections—he claimed that Queen Anne herself was "no Stranger to my Scrawls," and the subscription list to his *Memoirs*, published posthumously in 1732, includes the names of several Scottish lords as well as Tory politicians. The bulk of his clients, however, seem to have been merchants and tradesmen of London, their wives and families.[25]

Campbel's well-to-do clientele and fervent self-promotion were not matched by Timothy Crowther, parish clerk of Craven, near Skipton in North

Yorkshire, who practised as a rural astrologer and cunning-man between 1714 and 1761. One of his last acts, related to a dubious John Wesley shortly before Crowther's death, was to find a missing man: he had a boy stare into a looking glass until the man's murder was magically revealed. Crowther also dealt with cases of bewitchment, affliction by the King's Evil and the recovery of lost goods. His surviving "Charm-book" attests to his knowledge of astrological texts as well as of ritual magic. It includes ceremonial incantations straight out of the *Little Key of Solomon*: "I conjure and constrain, adjure and command the wise and subtle Spirits Abadan, Appolyon, Mephostophilis . . . that yu appear in the Crystall Stone or Berril Glass. Fiat, fiat, fiat."[26]

Campbel and Crowther attest to a continuing exchange between popular magic and occult writings. This was further demonstrated by John Cannon, a Somerset excise officer and schoolteacher who kept a remarkable chronicle of his life down to 1743. As a literate man who read widely and held positions of importance in local affairs, Cannon does not belong to the lowest ranks of English society. Nonetheless, he grew up in a farming family in West Lydford, worked as a farm servant and mingled throughout his life with ordinary people who shared many of his attitudes. Cannon's ideas regarding the occult were indebted to folk traditions, but they were also shaped by reading or hearing about books on prophecy, astrology and ritual magic, the same publications that might have influenced a better-educated person. Cannon's chronicle makes no precise division between elite and plebeian beliefs, or between written and oral culture—in his experience, they were mingled together. He may not offer us a wholly "authentic" voice from the lower ranks, one untainted by elite learning, but he comes as close to a genuine plebeian voice as any source we are likely to find.

Cannon's first reference to the occult comes in an entry for 1688, when his brother was cured of a rupture by a "sympathizing remedy"—being passed naked three times each morning through the split sapling of an ash tree. This was done on the advice of "doctors & others who thought themselves able and experienced in such cases."[27] No doubt they were cunning-men like Timothy Crowther, their knowledge a mixture of tradition and book learning. Fifteen years later, Cannon had an encounter with a ritual magician, John Read, a shepherd and farm servant who "gave himself to know English learning, figuring, poetry, and a smack of Astronomy [i.e. astrology]," and who possessed "occult wit." One Sunday, young Cannon was walking in a field with Read, when

> he thought convenient to shew me a piece of his cunning. For making a circle on the ground with a stick he had in his hand, having ordered me to abide in the center, & having also drawn some figures or characters in the dust &

> use[d] words, the air suddenly changed & grew darkish & became like a mist with a rushing wind, & rumbling like thunder at a distance, that it surprised me, insomuch as I requested him not to proceed any further for I believed it diabolical . . . This I confess was no delight to me . . . On the contrary, I utterly despised anything sounding of magick or occult sciences.

Nevertheless, Cannon knew enough about what Read was doing to call it "occult sciences." The shepherd-magus later moved to Dorset, after carefully burying "two books of the magic art, one of which was entitled Cornelius Agrippa's Occult Philosophy," probably the 1651 English translation with a preface by Thomas Vaughan.[28]

That a farm labourer in rural Somerset was using Agrippa's *Three Books* for conjuring may seem extraordinary, but it aptly illuminates the commerce between popular and educated magic. It is less surprising to discover that Cannon was a believer in omens, portents and prophetic dreams, precisely the beliefs Henry Bourne had condemned as symptomatic of plebeian "superstition." Many of the omens mentioned by Cannon were linked to animals—a hare, breeding rooks, a croaking raven, a perching cormorant—which suggests that their predictive authority may have originated in some long-established, orally transmitted folk belief.[29] He derived other omens, however, from reading contemporary newspapers, thus turning the latest form of written communication into a source for prognostication. One of these newspaper accounts concerned a "sky battle" seen over Edinburgh in 1740, a portent of impending Jacobite rebellion.[30] Cannon was also fascinated by "Merlin's prophecies," found in Geoffrey of Monmouth's *British History*. He transcribed them from Aaron Thompson's 1718 edition, blithely disregarding Thompson's condemnation of them as "Nonsense and unintelligible Jargon." Cannon bound this transcription with copies of the sixteenth-century predictions of Mother Shipton and Robert Nixon.[31] Nixon's prophecies were hugely popular: at least twenty-one editions were printed between 1714 and 1745. Their first editor, the Whig historian John Oldmixon, made them pointedly political, maintaining that they upheld the succession of the Hanoverian dynasty.[32] Whether or not Cannon would have agreed with this interpretation is unclear—his politics tended towards Toryism—but he evidently regarded the cryptic words of "the Cheshire prophet" as meaningful for his own day.

Cannon was also an avid reader of almanacs, as can be surmised from occasional references in his chronicle. He copied out the allegorical poem and "hieroglyphic" from Francis Moore's *Vox Stellarum* for 1740, and took notes on the eclipses forecast in John Partridge's *Merlinus Liberatus* for 1743, including a major lunar eclipse in October.[33] He wrote out a letter by the York mathematician

George Smith that he came across in the *Gentleman's Magazine* for March 1737, relating the lunar occultation or "transit" of the star Aldebaran to the downfall of the Babylonian Empire.[34] Cannon trained himself in astrology by reading instructional books of the late seventeeth century, including John Middleton's *Practical Astrology* (1679), Richard Saunders's *Astrological Judgements* (1677) and an unidentified work by the almanac-maker Daniel Woodward.[35] He was also familiar with more recent writings, such as William Whiston's theory that a comet preceded the biblical Deluge. A serious student of astronomy, Cannon was interested in comets, particularly that of 1680, which had seemed to reverse its direction when it drew near to the sun. In fact, *two* comets had been observed. Cannon cited Newton and Halley on the comet, wondering what might have happened if it had actually hit the sun.[36]

Evidently, John Cannon did not regard Newtonianism as having made the heavens unsuitable for predictions. To be sure, he was slightly self-conscious about his taste for augury, confessing himself "on certain occasions to be somewhat superstitiously given to the art," but he never mentioned any scientific or rational objections to it.[37] Cannon could be dismissive of some who shared his passion for prognostication, like Samuel Downton, "an old sophistical fellow pretending surgery, philosophy, astrology &c."[38] Yet on the whole he did not judge the Somerset folk around him to be particularly backward or ignorant. Cannon might not have been unwilling to see himself as enlightened: after all, he thought for himself, came to his own conclusions, read widely and took advantage of every opportunity to learn about the world. He even expressed a passing interest in Freemasonry, although he never joined a lodge.[39] He would probably have been astonished if anyone had informed him that astrology, augury and occult science had been outmoded and debunked by an enlightened age.

Cannon's outlook, like Campbel's and Crowther's, was in large measure a survival from the seventeenth century, when critical inquiry and occult philosophy were more congenial partners. By the mid-eighteenth century, occult thinking was no longer respectable or fashionable among the learned elite, but Cannon did not move in such august circles. The print culture that he appropriated, through pamphlets, chapbooks, periodicals and newspapers, gave him no reason to question his acceptance of occult beliefs, and even supported the assumption that his attitudes were compatible with modern trends. Cannon personified, with remarkable accuracy, the "enchanted world" that was imagined by Defoe in his works on the occult, and he even shared some of Defoe's opinions of that world: that the Devil was at work in it, that visions and apparitions were potentially beneficial, that magicians served Satan even when they imagined otherwise. This occult outlook may have been under threat at the universities or among the "wits" of the Royal Society, but John Cannon was blissfully unaware of it.

The Witchcraft Act: A Turning Point?

John Cannon lived through the passage of the celebrated Witchcraft Act of 1736. Could he possibly have had nothing to say about it? In fact, he ignored it entirely. Like Daniel Defoe, he did not have much to say about witchcraft itself either. Two incidents mentioned in his chronicle indicate that he accepted its reality, but they do not demonstrate any desire to revive the persecutions of the past. In October 1736, only a few months after the new law went into effect, "a strange & sudden hurricane of wind and rain" swept through Glastonbury. People said it was "conjuring weather," meaning it had been caused by a witch. Indeed, one Margaret Dewdney of Glastonbury, "who was suspected naughty" (that is, of being a witch), had reputedly put a curse on a local farmer for refusing her "a pig's innard." Being unable to make milk or cheese thereafter, the farmer asked Dr Bathurst of Devizes in Wiltshire, presumably a cunning-man, to raise the Devil in order to reveal who had brought this affliction upon him. The Devil duly appeared, occasioning the tremendous storm. When he vanished, the doctor beheld "the representation of 2 women & one man," the true perpetrators of the curse.[40]

This was as much a story of ritual magic as of witchcraft. Under the witchcraft statute passed under James I in 1604, which condemned necromancy, the good doctor was just as guilty of diabolism as Margaret Dewdney or her associates, and just as liable to face capital punishment. The identification of the culprits, however, seems to have brought the case to an end. No attempt was made to punish them. Four years later, Cannon recorded a second case of sorcery, which had a similar outcome. After an argument with a female customer, a saddler named William West of Street felt uneasy and unable to drink. On his way home through Glastonbury, he "was by an invisible hand hurried into the abbey over gates, stiles, rubbish & the ruinated walls." Arriving home, he saw in his room the same customer with whom he had quarrelled. He consulted "a certain woman," probably a village wise woman, who burned his fingernails and a lock of his hair in a piece of paper, "which they pretended a remedy & cure for witchcraft." Apparently, it worked, although West's head was twisted backwards in the course of the cure. Cannon acknowledged that there were many opinions about what had happened, but in his view West was "overlooked, bewitched or the Devil was in him."[41]

In both of these instances, the concern of the victim was to end the effects of witchcraft, not to inflict justice on the witch. This reaction was not conditioned by the recent Witchcraft Act; rather, it reflected the long-term decline of witch prosecutions. The magical methods used to end the enchantment, however, were in both cases just as criminal under the 1604 legislation as witchcraft itself, and they actually remained criminal after 1736. Apparently, rural people had learned by the mid-eighteenth century how to deal with witch cases on their own, without the assistance of magistrates, but their solutions distinguished "good" from "bad" conjuring in ways that were sanctioned neither by the old law nor by the new. The stories in Cannon's chronicle help to explain why the Witchcraft Act did not evoke a greater response from the public: they were already used to sidestepping its provisions.

The Act of 1736 undermined the reality of witchcraft by repealing all previous English and Scottish legislation that criminalized it. Instead, penalties were to be levied "for the more effectual preventing and punishing of any Pretences to such Arts or Powers as are before mentioned, whereby ignorant Persons are frequently deluded and defrauded." Anyone convicted of pretending "to exercise or use any kind of Witchcraft, Sorcery, Inchantment, or Conjuration, or [who] undertake to tell Fortunes, or pretend from his or her Skill or Knowledge in any occult or crafty Science, to discover where or in what manner any Goods or Chattels, supposed to have been stolen or lost, may be found," was to be imprisoned for a year and pilloried at four consecutive market days.[42] If the Act had been strictly enforced, it might have revealed a great deal about popular beliefs, giving historians an insight into the vexed question of how much interplay there was between popular magic and occult thinking or "crafty Science," which for the first time in any English or Scottish witchcraft law is specifically identified as criminal.

Some thought that the new Act should be strictly enforced. A writer in the *London Journal* in April 1738, for example, blasted fortune-tellers as deserving of prosecution: "Whoever consults one of these blind Oracles, whether in Jest or in Earnest, with a Desire of knowing, or without, willfully puts himself out of *God*'s Providence, and by this very Act, becomes an Outlaw with respect to his Creator." Such people are "Dealers in Superstition." Two popular types of fortune-telling are specifically mentioned: namely, "a Tirewoman's shuffling a Pack of Cards, or poking in the Bottom of a Coffee-Cup." The writer duly praised the 1736 Act, which "inflicts very high Pains on these Impostors."[43] Yet only a handful of fortune-tellers are known to have been prosecuted under the Act in the eighteenth century.

Perhaps the Act was never intended to be used in this way. From the first, it had been a political measure, calculated to strengthen Whig Party solidarity rather than to reform existing abuses. When it was passed in 1735, the Whig government of Sir Robert Walpole was floundering. Walpole was forced to accommodate his party's restless backbenchers in order to maintain a majority in the House of Commons. The result was a spate of religious and moral legislation that pleased old-fashioned Whigs and horrified Tories.[44] The Witchcraft Bill was relatively uncontroversial, however, because witch prosecutions had effectively ceased. The only recorded opposition to it in the House came from James Erskine of the Grange, a Scottish Tory (although a Presbyterian in religion) and brother to the earl of Mar, leader of the Scottish Jacobite rebellion of 1715. His "long, canting speech" reportedly "set the House in a titter of laughter." Erskine may have been dull, but he was certainly knowledgeable about the subject, as the library at his house near Prestonpans contained "a large collection of books on dæmonologia, which was Grange's [i.e. Erksine's] particular study."[45]

Erskine spoke for a considerable body of opinion within Scottish Presbyterianism. As late as 1743, the "Seceders" of the Associate Presbytery, who had split from the established Kirk over issues of doctrine and patronage, expressed the view that the Witchcraft Act was "contrary to the express law of God."[46] Without doubt, this opinion was shared by many mainstream Presbyterians as well. They adhered to the established view that witchcraft was the work of the Devil.[47] The polite culture of the Edinburgh elite, however, was already departing from these pious notions. The best-known Scottish witch of this period was a theatrical character, Mausy in Alan Ramsay's comedy of 1727, *The Gentle Shepherd*. Her reputation for witchcraft was as dreadful as any Presbyterian minister could envisage:

> She can o'ercast the night, and cloud the moon,
> And mak the deils obedient to her crune.[48]

In reality, Mausy was merely a clever woman who knew the secrets of the village. She neither worshipped the Devil nor made magical effigies of her enemies. Strict Presbyterians may have been appalled by Ramsay's laxity, but hardly surprised, as the playwright was an Episcopalian, tainted by contact with Jacobite friends and freethinking ideas.

In the Highlands, where Presbyterianism was on the march against its Episcopal and Catholic enemies, the fearsome image of the witch remained real long after 1736. The English military engineer Edward Burt, who served in Scotland around 1730 and published a series of letters on his experiences, recounted the "ridiculous stories and imaginations" attached to a certain hill near Inverness: "the *Fairies* within it are innumerable, and *Witches* find it the most convenient Place for their Frolics and Gambols in the Night-time." It was the witches, not the fairies, who commanded Burt's scornful attention. He complained that while "the Notion of Witches is pretty much worn out among People of any tolerable Sense or Education in *England* . . . here it remains even among some that sit judicially; and Witchcraft and *Charming* (as it is called) make up a considerable Article in the recorded Acts of the General Assembly [of the Kirk]." With disgust, Burt recounted the execution of the last Scottish witch, who had reportedly been burned in a pitch barrel at Dornoch in Sutherland as recently as 1727.[49] When a Presbyterian minister tried to convince Burt of the reality of witchcraft, he retorted with the argument that "the Woman of Endor was only an Impostor, like our Astrologers or Fortune-tellers, and not a *Witch* in the present Acceptation of the Word."[50] Like so many English colonizers around the world, Burt was determined not to surrender his superior rationality to the blind ignorance of the natives.

At least Burt was willing to admit, reluctantly, that popular violence against suspected witches might occur in Hertfordshire as much as in the Highlands. In fact, it was far more likely to be seen in southern England. While several cases of witch-mobbing, or crowd attacks on suspected witches, occurred there between 1736 and 1760, none has been documented in Scotland.[51] In England, the practice of "swimming" a witch was relatively common. It consisted of throwing a tied-up suspect into water to determine whether he or she would innocently sink or float like a witch—rejected by the water as she had rejected her own baptism. Witches were "swum" in 1737 at Oakley, Bedfordshire; in 1748 at Monk's Eleigh, Suffolk; in 1751 at Tring, Hertfordshire; in 1760 at Great Glen and Burton Overy, Leicestershire, as well as at Wilton, Wiltshire. An attempt to "swim" two women at Leighton Buzzard, Bedfordshire, in 1751 was foiled by the intervention of some gentlemen.[52] This brutal procedure, peculiar to southern England, had begun almost a century before 1736. It was not a response to the Parliamentary Act.

The long history of "swimming" in his parish was lamented by the Reverend Joseph Juxon, rector of Twyford, Leicestershire, in a sermon given shortly after the passage of the Witchcraft Act. Juxon argued that, while the ancient witches were idolaters who deserved death, "modern Notions of Witchcraft . . . have no other Foundation than Ignorance or Superstition."[53] In spite of Reverend Juxon, a good portion of the English rural populace held to "modern Notions of Witchcraft," which had more to do with fear of malevolent old people than with horror at diabolism. The relative complacency of John Cannon's Somerset neighbours seems admirable by comparison with the incidents of "swimming," although West Countrymen might also perhaps have been pushed to vengeance against a "naughty" person under the right circumstances. In rural Scotland, the lack of violence against witches may indicate that the machinations of the Devil were still receiving attention from clerical authorities. The Pittenweem case of 1705 showed what could happen when a Scottish crowd became convinced that the magistrates and the clergy were not doing their duty against the instruments of Satan.

The reaction of the English press to the 1736 Witchcraft Act was muted, to say the least. The only published opposition to it came in the guise of a reprint of a 1679 pamphlet by the infamous Titus Oates, which aimed at conflating witchcraft with Roman Catholicism. The anonymous preface to the work vindicated the existence of good and evil spirits, rehearsed the biblical passages demonstrating the reality of witchcraft and argued that "*Endorian Witches*" were still active. The author granted nonetheless that previous legislation against conjuring was too severe, as it would "punish with *Death* a *poor Hocus-Pocus Vagrant*."[54] In response, John Wagstaffe's *Discourse on Witchcraft* was republished, with a preface accusing the opponents of the Act of being "Heathens . . . as their Opinion implies a Plurality of Gods, by attributing omnipotent Effects to more than one."[55] Apart from these works and a few brief mentions in newspapers, the usually cacophonous English press was silent.

Over the ensuing decades, a number of Anglican clergymen, many of them in the West Country, would register their disapproval of the Act in journals or private conversations, but none of them launched a public attack on it.[56] Famously, the evangelical leader John Wesley, who believed his family home in Lincolnshire had been haunted by an evil spirit, penned a "solemn protest" against "giving up witchcraft," which he considered "in effect giving up the Bible." This was written, however, in May 1768, as part of a journal not meant for publication. Moreover, the circumstances of the entry, which are described in the next chapter, had to do with apparitions, not witchcraft.[57] Most critics of the Witchcraft Act were probably more concerned about the effect it might have on spiritual beliefs than they were about prosecuting witches. They might even have concurred with Defoe's statement that the age of witches was long since past. The Act of 1736 simply acknowledged that reality. It was no turning point.

Mystics and Magia

Throughout the eighteenth century, popular magical beliefs remained in contact with an occult tradition that seems to have been almost defunct among the learned. In some cases, ordinary people reinvented the occult in terms that might have shocked seventeenth-century alchemists or astrologers. The mystical movement known as the French Prophets, for example, maintained that possession by spirits fulfilled divine intentions and was not always diabolical. The peculiar supernatural quality of their visionary experiences attracted the attention of alchemists as well as devotees of Jacob Boehme, and would influence the early Methodists. Spirit possession later became a feature of occult societies, eventually spinning off into the nineteenth-century Spiritualist movement, although its most unexpected impact was on the development of psychology. The French Prophets and their allies illustrate the reformulation of an occult tradition by men and women who were far outside the intellectual establishment.

Mysticism was a pan-European phenomenon of the period. It may seem incongruous to think of the first half of the eighteenth century as an era of mystical flowering, but in many parts of Europe it was. In France and the Low Countries, the disciples of Antoinette Bourignon (who died in 1680) and Jeanne Guyon (who lived until 1717) practised devotions shaped by the visions and personalities of these two remarkable female religious leaders. Societies of ecstatic visionaries or *convulsionnaires* sprang up in Paris during the 1730s. In Germany, mysticism flourished as an offshoot of Pietism, an introspective and disciplined form of Lutheranism. The most celebrated Pietist mystic was Count Zinzendorf, who drew on the example of the English Philadelphians as he set about reviving the sect of the Moravian Brethren.[58] Mystics, however, were not necessarily advocates of occult thinking. The desire for union with the godhead usually had more to do with negation of the self than with claiming supernatural wisdom or power. It was usually far removed from the philosophies of nature that were associated with the occult. Nonetheless, some varieties of mysticism, particularly those that relied on spontaneous experience, converged with occult thinking on a central point: namely, that human beings could become vessels for benevolent spirits. This allowed direct conversation with God as well as with the angels—a supernatural exchange that resulted in divine knowledge.

The largest British mystical movement in the early eighteenth century was the French Prophets, who generated a brief sensation and left a long, tangled legacy. Prophets declaring the imminent end of the world had arisen among the beleaguered French Protestants of the mountainous Cévennes region in the 1670s. Inspired by millenarian hopes and driven to desperate opposition by the revocation of the Edict of Nantes, these southern, rural Protestants finally rose up in a doomed rebellion in 1702. After its suppression, so-called "Camisards" emigrated to London, where they made many English converts among the middling sort. Between 1706 and 1708, the French Prophets, as both the immigrants and their English followers were known, gained notoriety by asserting that the Holy Spirit was announcing the Apocalypse through their voices. Like the radical sectarians of the Civil War period, they called on the rich to divest themselves of wealth, allowed women to preach and excoriated the clergy of the established Church.[59] They also staged shocking stunts, such as when a female Prophetess ran naked to the altar of the Sardinian chapel in Duke Street and declaimed for fifteen minutes. The movement began to falter after March 1708, when the planned resurrection from the dead of a follower failed to materialize.[60]

To raise a man from the grave was a supernatural act that pulled mysticism into the realm of the occult. The failure of Dr Thomas Emes to renounce eternal rest, however, moved the Prophets towards more settled practices. Already, by the end of 1707, they had organized congregations in private houses in London and other towns, where they carried out "Prophetic Blessings" by the laying-on of hands. They began to engage in silent prayer, called "waiting on God," to keep regular records of their assemblies and even to accept a system of grades marking spiritual progress.[61] The language of the Prophets, however, remained passionate and frequently violent. It was centred on the Holy Spirit, who entered physically into their bodies. Even in such states of mystic rapture, they did not surrender their identities and continued to speak as themselves. Their human consciousness was suddenly elevated to a divine level, as in a magical ritual.

Parallels between the mysticism of the French Prophets and occult thinking may explain why the movement was so attractive to alchemists. Among the latter was Sir Isaac Newton's former assistant in alchemy the Swiss Nicolas Fatio de Duillier, who was one of three Prophets pilloried in 1707 for blasphemy. Fatio retained his fascination with alchemy until his death in 1753, when he bequeathed in his will a "Vegetable Menstruum" for the benefit of his friend and fellow French Prophet the apothecary Francis Moult. An enthusiastic scientist, Moult and his cousin George, a Fellow of the Royal Society, became the first marketers of Epsom salts. In 1721, Francis Moult had a vision of the alchemical "Powder of Projection," which he described in a poem addressed to his friend Charles Portales, another French Prophet who had become an admirer of Jacob Boehme's works.[62] The unfortunate Dr Emes, "Chirurgo-Medicus" as he called himself, was also an alchemist. Before refusing to rise from the dead, he authored two pamphlets on alkalis, a treatise attacking deism and a philosophical work in which, contrary to the materialists or "Spinozists," he equated God with "meer Mind."[63] Perhaps the most extraordinary alchemist among the French Prophets, however, was Timothy Byfield, a tireless self-promoter who marketed a universal medicine, the *Sal volatile oleosum*. In the same cheerful, helpful tone that characterized his commercial publications, Byfield expounded his views on the reunion of the individual spirit with that of God. "In Man is a peculiar, vivifying innate Spirit," he wrote, "which contributes both Light and Life to the Body."[64] Apparently, that spirit could be animated either by visionary preaching or by Byfield's miraculous elixir.

The teachings of Jacob Boehme, widely regarded as a portal to the occult, infiltrated the ranks of the French Prophets through two other mystical groups, the Scots Quietists and the Philadelphians. The Quietists arose within the Episcopal Church of Scotland, which had been disestablished at the Glorious Revolution and whose clergy had become Nonjurors.[65] Their spiritual leader was George Garden, a professor at King's College, Aberdeen, who was deprived of his position in 1692. He became an admirer first of Antoinette Bourignon, and later of Madame Guyon.[66] Eschewing emotional experience, Guyon's mysticism was based on a total renunciation of the outside world and immersion in quiet, inner prayer—an utterly different method from that of the French Prophets. The Scottish Quietists included Garden's brother James, who had corresponded with John Aubrey about second sight. In England, the movement was represented by two notable medical men, James Keith in London and George Cheyne in fashionable Bath. Another celebrated Scottish Quietist was Andrew Michael Ramsay, the son of a Presbyterian baker from Ayr who would later migrate to France, where he befriended Madame Guyon herself.[67]

Socially well connected and orthodox in their theology, the Scots Quietists regarded the occult as diabolic. Recounting in his Life of Madame Bourignon how she had discovered a nest of young witches at an orphanage in Lille, George Garden opined with horror that "when ever any of them [witches] are discovered and tried, if strict Enquiry be made about them, their number appears incredible."[68] A more unsettling (and amusing) episode of demonic spirits was recorded in 1718 by James Keith, based on the testimony of his friend Simon Ockley, professor of Arabic at Cambridge University, who had been briefly imprisoned for debt in Cambridge Castle. While incarcerated, Ockley was tormented by "a Cacodæmon" who moved under his bed, banged on the door, tapped, thumped and even attacked the venerable academic in "the House of Office": that is, the privy. Keith was inclined to think it "a Ludicrous Spirit," but Ockley insisted it was "a malignant evil Genius."[69] Keith knew that his friend and patient was under stress, but he did not question the veracity of his account.

The improbable link between the Scots Quietists and the French Prophets was provided by an impressionable gentleman of Barns in Fife, James Cunningham. He had encountered a group of Prophets in Edinburgh during the spring of 1709. Excited by the spiritual possibilities, he wrote to George Garden to ask his opinion, quoting Jacob Boehme to the effect that union with God must be through "the Increated superessential Light" of Jesus Christ. In a later letter, Cunningham asked Garden about "the characteristicks, fallible rules and marks laid down in Scripture for discerning betwixt good and bad spirits," which suggests a Neoplatonic approach to the unseen world. The learned Garden was quick to discern the sources of his correspondent's confusion. He recommended "the prayer of silence," that is, internal meditation without agitation, and he reminded him that "[w]e are call'd to be the followers of our Lord J. Christ," not of Jacob Boehme. As for "the Platonists," Garden recognized their insights but condemned their intellectual pride.[70] His cautionary words had an effect on Cunningham, who encouraged the Prophets to settle into regular meetings and to question some of their own predictions. Still, he shared in their public "warnings," announcing on one occasion, as if in answer to Garden, that Scripture gave "Abundance of Characters, and distinguishing Marks, whereby to know a good, from a bad Spirit." Journeying to London in 1712, Cunningham was almost drowned by a mob—like a witch—when he cried out, "Repent, Repent," during evensong in St Paul's Cathedral. Three years later, he showed the strength of his political convictions by joining the rebellion in favour of the Stuart claimant to the throne. Captured by the Hanoverian army at the Battle of Preston, he died a prisoner.[71]

Cunningham's Behmenism may have been derived from the Philadelphians. They were more open-minded than the Quietists regarding spirits, but they did not all embrace spirit possession. Although they had officially disbanded by the time of Jane Lead's death in 1704, members of the group remained prominent in mystical and prophetic circles. London Philadelphians continued to meet at a congregation in Bow Street, where their chief spokesman was a German-speaking immigrant from Nuremberg, Andreas Dionysius Freher. A letter that he apparently wrote to Jane Lead from Utrecht in 1701 introduces Freher as a confident, dynamic personality, steeped in occult thought. Addressing Lead as "Blessed Virago, most endeared and remarkable Soul," the letter praises "the highly illuminated Jac. Behme" and points to astrological predictions of dominion by the "fiery trigon," a group of three zodiacal signs.[72] The mixture of Theosophy and occult science was typical of Freher. His voluminous writings, none of them published, were carefully copied out by his followers Allen Leppington, a London hop merchant, and the artist Jeremias Daniel Leuchter. They exceed even Boehme in their lavish use of astrological and alchemical language. In one manuscript treatise, redemption is described as a "Process," and the individual believer is referred to as "the Artist or Magus." Union with the divine here takes the form of a chemical reaction:

> in the Philosophical Work, a Breaking forth of the Solarish Power in a Golden Lustre, from the Fire's Center, and Tincturing this white Lunarish Appearance of Venus, is all in Vain expected: Because the Pure Union, and Universal Tincture cannot be made manifest, except first all the dark Wrath and Poison of Saturn, Mercury and Mars, be wholly drowned and swallowed up in Blood and Death.[73]

Freher's overwrought imagery is far removed from Jane Lead's intimate style, even if it follows the same Behmenist pattern. As so many of the French Prophets were alchemists, however, it might have held a special appeal for them.

Freher's colourful language lent itself to visualization. His friend Leuchter obligingly devised a series of "Hieroglyphica Sacra, or Divine Emblems," showing the religious principles of the Philadelphians in graphic form, no doubt as an instructional tool. Perhaps the most enduring invention of their partnership was the so-called "Three Tables," which depicted the progress of humanity from "Primeval Man" to "Fallen Man" to "Angelical Man," with surrounding zodiacal symbols of "his Exterior Astral & Elementary Life."[74] The baroque effect of these illustrations, which were made into prints and accompanied by extensive notes, contrasts with the simplicity and spontaneity of the "warnings" issued by the French Prophets. While the latter strove to articulate the words of a single informing spirit, Freher and Leuchter sought to illuminate a universe of diverse spiritual entities, accessible through occult knowledge.

Freher did not lead a unified Philadelphian group, such as had briefly existed in the 1690s. The mastermind of that earlier movement, Francis Lee, was not a member of the Bow Street church, and he was drifting away from prophecy. In 1709, he published an anonymous attack on Montanism, an early Christian heresy that emphasized ecstatic visions, which he believed to be demonic. So that nobody could miss the contemporary point, the treatise was bound together with two attacks on the French Prophets.[75] Soon after, Lee began a study of the apocryphal Second Book of Esdras (also confusingly known as 4 Ezra), an apocalyptic work frequently cited by visionaries as foretelling future events.[76] When it finally appeared in 1722, three years after the author's death, it constituted not a vindication, but a final renunciation of visionary religion. Although he admired some of the beautiful passages in 2 Esdras, Lee also found in it "such a multitude of Things to shock me, so that it was hard for me not to throw it presently away with the utmost Contempt and Indignation." He felt as if the Church of England, by including it among scriptural texts, might just as well have given authority to Mother Shipton's prophecy or John Partridge's astrological predictions.[77]

Lee's growing aversion to prophecy was in part a horrified response to the French Prophets. By contrast, his Philadelphian colleague the Reverend Richard Roach embraced them. Roach persisted in using the language of John Pordage and Jane Lead, at least in his diary, where he enthused about "[t]he Magick Sight, the Magick Will," and scrawled down alchemical recipes.[78] On 1 June 1710, "Mr. Richd. Roach belonging to the People call'd Philadelphians" appeared at a meeting of the French Prophets in London, where Mary Keimer was giving out blessings (her brother and fellow Prophet, Samuel, a printer, later moved to Philadelphia, where he took Benjamin Franklin as an apprentice). Roach proceeded to read out "w[ha]t. he calld an Inspiration" spoken by Sarah Wiltshire. Wiltshire was a former Quaker who seems to have succeeded Jane Lead in Roach's estimation as a female fount of prophecy. Roach and Wiltshire had allies among the French Prophets. At least three of them—the wool-comber Abraham Whitrow, the watchmaker John Cuff and the lawyer Thomas Dutton—were said to be "sometime Philadelphians." Three days after proclaiming the "Inspiration," Roach and Wiltshire founded the "Polemica Sacro-Prophetica," which called for a redirection of the message of the French Prophets towards love and peace rather than imminent destruction. Not surprisingly, some of the Prophets reacted badly to the proposal, denouncing Roach as a "Ranter" and even punching Wiltshire. Roach continued to attend their meetings, but was unable to steer them in a more pacific direction.[79]

He was not discouraged. Indeed, Roach's sojourn with the Prophets seems to have further unshackled his visionary powers. Why should he despair when he had access to angels? Visits from the Archangel Raphael continued throughout his life. On St John's Eve in 1726, he noted a "Change of Angel" that caused him to begin a new diary.[80] Around the same time, Roach began to commit his mystical and prophetic thoughts to print. In the anonymously published *Great Crisis* (1727), he postulated that battles seen in the air, meteors, blood-red rainbows, fires in the sky and monstrous births in Scotland constituted "God's *Speaking* to mankind." The divine message, however, was still one of love and peace, symbolized by the harmony of Solomon's rulership. Roach praised the "many Famous Inlighten'd Virgins" who had carried that message, from Teresa of Avila to Madame Bourignon and Jane Lead.[81] In a sequel, *The Imperial Standard of Messiah Triumphant*, Roach openly revealed his vision of "the Imperial Standard," which had appeared to him in February 1723. This foretold "the blessed *Millenium*, or *Solomonitical* Kingdom," which would expire with the Second Coming of Christ. Most of "the Perfected Ones" would then reascend with Christ, but some would remain to witness a general decline of religion on earth, and the forming of Satan's army, "instructed in Witchcraft and in the dark *Magia* . . . Against these the Blessed Inhabitants, the *Divine Magi* fight in Spirit." The result was the consummation of the world and a new creation.[82] Like earlier radicals, Roach envisaged rule by the saints before the coming of Christ, but the evocation of a final confrontation between two types of magic, good and evil, was entirely his own.

Roach devoted special attention to "the Divine Sophia or Wisdom," explaining it as "the Bridal or *Virgin* Nature in God," a kind of female version of the godhead, such as was postulated in Kabbalism.[83] The exaltation of female spirituality in Roach's published writings goes beyond the Behmenist theory of androgyny and reveals a remarkable sensitivity to female visionary experience. Perhaps the most unusual feature of *The Imperial Standard*, however, was the index, in which Roach defined the terms of Philadelphian philosophy. They included many alchemical expressions such as "Grand Arcanum" and "The Great Secret of the Chymical Philosopher for Transmutation or changing of grosser Metals into Gold, and for Universal Medicine." Jacob Boehme's Theosophy was discussed as relating "to the First Cause of all Things and its Act upon . . . both the Invisible and Visible Creation." One of the longest discussions was reserved for "*Magia*" in its natural, diabolical and divine forms. "*Natural Magic* . . . perform'd by the Agency of Middle Spirits residing in, or Regent of the Air or Elements," was no more lawful than the "Operation of Wicked and Infernal Spirits," or "*Diabolical Magic*," according to Roach. On the other hand, he fully endorsed "Divine Magia . . . the Operation of God Himself by the agency of his Holy Spirit."[84] The message of the French Prophets blares forth in this last statement.

When Richard Roach died in August 1730, the Prophets were still active. Their last Prophetess, Hannah Wharton, made tours of London in 1730 and of Birmingham and Worcester in 1732, where she spoke in the voice of the Holy Spirit to audiences that included Nicolas Fatio and Francis Moult. The endless torrent of inspired words that fell from her mouth comprised, as she put it, "the Privileges of Wisdom to manifest the Liberty which is a Liberty from the Word, for the Word is in it and so the Liberty of the Word is the Liberty the Chosen are in."[85] It was a public exultation of the self as divine. This may be why it so disturbed John Wesley. At London in 1739, he visited a French Prophetess, a young woman of about twenty-five, who spoke for about ten minutes "as in the person of God, and mostly in Scripture words," while her whole body went into "convulsive motion." Wesley thought she must be "either hysterical or artificial." Later in the same year, he condemned the French Prophets in a sermon.[86] Some of Wesley's own Methodist listeners, of course, would undergo similar convulsions while hearing him preach. He never fully approved of this, but its persistence illustrates a significant consequence of the emotionally expressive, spontaneous mystical effusions of the early eighteenth century. Because the Prophets had led the way, the evangelical revival would be marked by a popular belief in spirits, and would never be fully under the control of the preachers.

Among the educated elite, it was not Wesley and his associates who most eagerly upheld the spiritual inheritance of the French Prophets: rather, it was a medical man. The celebrated Dr George Cheyne was sympathetic to mysticism in all its forms, and strove to reconcile its spiritual attractions with a contemporary understanding of physiology. The result was a powerful if not always coherent combination of Newtonian science, Lockean philosophy and occult thought, a "natural supernaturalism." Cheyne grew up among the Aberdonian mystics, and remained in close contact with them after moving to England, but he was less staid or traditional than they were. James Cunningham, the ill-fated Scottish prophet, confided spiritual secrets to him.[87] Cheyne was educated in medicine at Edinburgh University under the Newtonian Archibald Pitcairne, a man described as a Jacobite, deist and believer in apparitions, who claimed to have been informed in a vision of the time of his own death.[88] Given this background, Cheyne's interest in spirits is hardly surprising.

Cheyne's *Philosophical Principles of Religion: Natural and Revealed* was first published in 1705. After the rise and fall of the French Prophets, it was substantially revised and reissued. Virtually ignored by the intellectual establishment, the book was popular enough to go through a number of different editions. Its purpose was to apply Newtonian principles to the operations of the mind, including religious sentiments. Cheyne pompously organized the treatise into *Lemmatas*, Propositions, Corollaries and *Scholia*, just like Newton's *Principia Mathematica*. In the first part, which dealt with the body, Cheyne equated the term "Spirit" with "the nervous Juice," carried along through the arteries with the blood and into the muscles. The mind acts on these "Animal Spirits" to bring about voluntary motion, while involuntary motion is created by "Mechanical Necessity."[89] While he did not discuss the French Prophets directly, Cheyne's theory might be used to explain their agitated convulsions as the action of a stronger spirit on a lesser one. In the second part, Cheyne defines "Spirit" as "an extended, penetrable, active, indivisible, intelligent Substance," sharing nothing with Body, or matter, except extension. "The *Principle* of Action in Spiritual Subsistences," Cheyne continues, "is, or ought to be, that essential one of REUNION with the *Origin* of their Being, impress'd on ev'ry Individual of this Rank of Creatures."[90] All Spirits, in other words, are aspects of the Supreme Spirit, towards which they move continually, hindered only by the existence of Body. Thus, the mystic's goal of union with God is inherent in the Newtonian law of attraction, by which the whole universe moves.

Cheyne's *magnum opus* was reviled by the Newtonians, casting him into depression and overeating. The immense reputation that he enjoyed among the British public in the 1720s and 1730s rested, not on his philosophy, but on his writings about his dietary regime, by which he succeeded in reducing his own gargantuan bulk to manageable size. These works were informed by his theory of spirits, although of course one did not have to be a mystic to appreciate them. What was not generally recognized was the extent to which the famous diet-doctor justified mystical union as a force of nature. Cheyne provided mystics with physiological arguments that few of them had been willing to think through for themselves. He linked religious experience with nervous impulses, unfocused sentiments and unconscious desires—in short, with what would later become the science of psychology.

Rediscovering Boehme: Byrom and Law

Ensconced in fashionable Bath, Dr Cheyne knew everybody who was anybody, or so it seemed. Late in 1741, he wrote a letter to a poet and master of shorthand, John Byrom of Manchester, whose character had been praised by his friend Selina, Countess of Huntingdon. Cheyne wanted to ask Byrom's opinion concerning a recent work by a French follower of Madame Guyon and Jacob Boehme, Charles Hector de St George Marsay. The diet-doctor also attempted, without success, to solicit a further opinion on Marsay from Byrom's close friend the Reverend William Law. Cheyne admitted that Marsay's "discoveries about the states and glory of the invisible world and the future purification of lapsed intelligences, human and angelical," caused him some intellectual difficulties. Nevertheless, he continued to praise "this wonderful author," whose works he had recommended to his close friend Dr David Hartley, the bearer of Cheyne's second letter to Byrom.[91]

In this correspondence we catch a glimpse of the nerve centre of English mysticism in the mid-eighteenth century. All the main players are here: the celebrated Dr Cheyne, promoter of mental health and vegetarian diets; the brilliant David Hartley, whose later writings on mind and sensation would surpass in fame Cheyne's own work; and the two Nonjurors John Byrom and William Law, the first of them a spiritual seeker, the second already known as the caustic opponent of dry religious rationalism. Add to them the energetic countess of Huntingdon, not a mystic herself but friendly towards them, and later to give her name to a denomination of Methodists. All of these men and women appeared to be well connected, prosperous and influential members of the social elite. We have come a long way from the French Prophets.

Yet the marginality of the mystics persisted into the mid-eighteenth century. Cheyne was famous but worried that his spiritual cravings were not quite respectable. The Methodist countess was an outsider in aristocratic circles. Hartley, who had reservations about the Thirty-Nine Articles, took up medicine because he could not become a clergyman.[92] Byrom and Law refused to recognize the Hanoverians as lawful monarchs, which made them ineligible for any office in Church or State. Byrom was actually removed from the governing body of the Royal Society in 1727 when he opposed an address to George II.[93] Law lost a fellowship at Cambridge in 1713 for making a public speech that was interpreted as rank Jacobitism—at that point, even Byrom thought him "a vain, conceited fellow."[94] These men and women were not among the favoured few of Whig society, which may be why they were less reluctant to delve into the occult philosophies of the past.

The learned mystics were forerunners of a major cultural shift, away from the scientific rationalism of the Newtonians, towards a revaluation of feeling, sentiment and emotion. Among its other precursors was John Hutchinson, a former estate steward, fossil collector and self-educated "natural philosopher," who began publishing attacks on Newtonianism in the 1720s. In *Moses's Principia*, Hutchinson used the favourite alchemical trope of the spirit of God moving on the waters to explain the origin of "an invisible, penetrating, powerful, created Agent, which he [God] stiles Spirit." According to Hutchinson, the natural world was sustained by Spirit, not by gravity. Moreover, the original Hebrew language was informed by Spirit, "and so conveyed perfect Ideas of the Things by the Words."[95] In the 1730s, Hutchinson began to identify the Hebrew letters with angels or cherubim, who actually inhabited the original, unaccented script. Modern Jews, however, were "Apostates" who had polluted their religion with concepts of natural magic, and their language with accent marks (which served as vowels). Hutchinson's own writings are so poorly composed as to be almost indecipherable. Both Stukeley and Warburton, who detested his rambling notions, called them "Cabalistic."[96] Nonetheless, "Hutchinsonianism" eventually came to describe critics of rationalism in the Church of England, who subscribed to Hutchinson's elevation of Spirit, even if they rarely noticed the angels staring out at them from the pages of the Hebrew Bible.

Hutchinson viewed nature through an occult lens that recognized spirits as active in the physical world. The separation between natural and supernatural virtually disappears. This became a distinctive feature of English mystical thought in the mid-eighteenth century. While ordinary people, like the French Prophets, might experience a sudden, inexplicable possession by spirits, the clergymen and doctors who kept mysticism alive in the mid-eighteenth century sought to promote spiritual regeneration by examining the operations of spirit in nature. Like the Newtonians, they appropriated aspects of occult thinking, although they did not openly recommend occult practices. John Byrom and William Law were the most important figures in this learned mysticism. Law was never at ease with the role. He criticized Madame Bourignon as "peevish" and "fretful," opined that Madame Guyon was "more prudent than Mrs. Bourignon, yet [got] carried away," and complained "that the Philadelphians, Dr. Lee, &c., were strange people."[97] On the other hand, his friend Byrom, who was not ordained, was seldom able to restrain himself from embracing "the wonderful." He had a boundless appetite for spiritual experience of all varieties, as well as for occult philosophy.

Byrom's taste for the occult can be judged by the catalogue of books in his library. Even if we do not know exactly *how* he read them, they present a clear picture of his interests. As might be expected, he had many works by Madame Bourignon, Madame Guyon and Jacob Boehme, as well as Pordage's *Theologia Mystica* and Roach's *Imperial Standard*. He was an equally voracious reader of magical works. Chetham's Library in Manchester contains a sixteenth-century *Tractatus de Nigromatia* or treatise on necromancy that once belonged to him. It includes pentacles, Chaldean scripts and invocations to the "Queen of the Pharies." Byrom owned works both by and belonging to John Dee, which betokens an extraordinary interest in the Elizabethan magus. On the other hand, he purchased Balthasar Bekker's *The World Bewitched* as early as 1722, so he would have been aware of the objections to occult thinking, even if he disagreed with them.[98] Perhaps the most striking aspect of his collection from an occult point of view is the considerable number of works relating to alchemy, among them the *Divine Pimander*, Ashmole's *Way to Bliss*, the works of Roger Bacon and Paracelsus, a tract by Sendivogius and a number of German works on the Hermetic art. Alongside *Magia Adamica* and the *Man-Mouse*, the catalogue lists two copies of Thomas Vaughan's edition of the *Fama et Confessio* of the Rosicrucians. Some of the books are annotated, and Byrom's copy of Artephius's *Secret Booke of the Blessed Stone*, in the testy words of the catalogue editor, is "crowded with cabalistic figures and observations in the numeric writing of some devotee of the Rosy Cross."[99]

Byrom's journals, which he wrote in a shorthand of his own devising, mainly during his regular sojourns in London, give us further clues to his attitudes. They frequently refer to meetings of the "Cabala Club," a group that Byrom attended from 1723, the year before his election to the Royal Society, until around 1730. It met at the Sun tavern in St Paul's Churchyard, and later at the King's Head in Holborn. The members included Martin Ffolkes, who introduced Byrom to the club, Sir Hans Sloane, George Graham, clockmaker and inventor of the mercury pendulum, and Benjamin Hoadly, physician, playwright and son to a Whig bishop. All were Fellows of the Royal Society, which Sloane and Ffolkes served as successive presidents. Aside from topics of the day like education or the unlawfulness of the theatre (on which Law had written a pamphlet), the Cabala Club discussed "the art of memory," "petrified towns in Muscovy," and "the miracles which Moses wrought in Egypt, and how the magicians could do the like," suggesting that this illustrious assembly was a forum for subjects not usually discussed in the Royal Society, some of them having occult significance.[100] Ffolkes, a close friend of Stukeley, was grand master of a lodge of Freemasons that met upstairs at the Sun tavern. When Sloane offered to take Byrom to it, the latter-replied, "I said I would, and come

1 The aspiring young alchemical adept accepts a book of secrets from his aged master in this engraving from Elias Ashmole's *Theatrum Chemicum Britannicum*. Above them, angels rejoice and the Holy Spirit sends out celestial rays. The two columns and the lions suggest that the location is Solomon's Temple, while the borders are filled with the abundance of Nature. The alchemist's quest is at the center of the divine and natural universes.

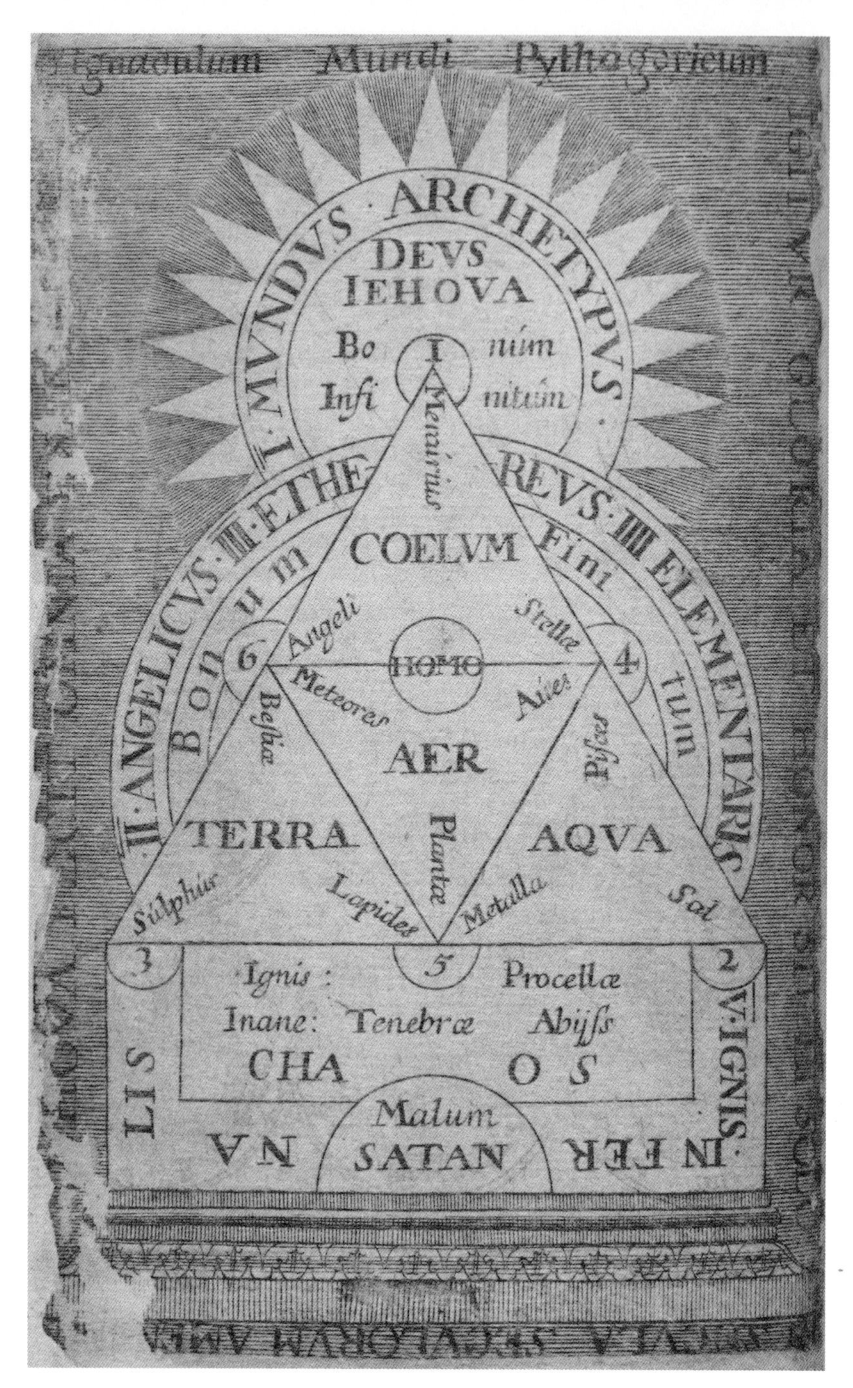

2 Inspired by the illustrations to early editions of Jacob Boehme's works, this alchemical diagram from *The Philosophical Epitaph of W.C. Esq*. represents a "Pythagorean" or rather Copernican universe, in which Man, located between the celestial and elemental spheres, revolves around a solar God. The rudiments of alchemy—sulphur, stones, plants, metals, salt—stand above the primeval chaos and the infernal fire in which Satan resides. They are elevated by mercury, which points directly towards the divine. This is evidently a spiritual as well as a natural quest.

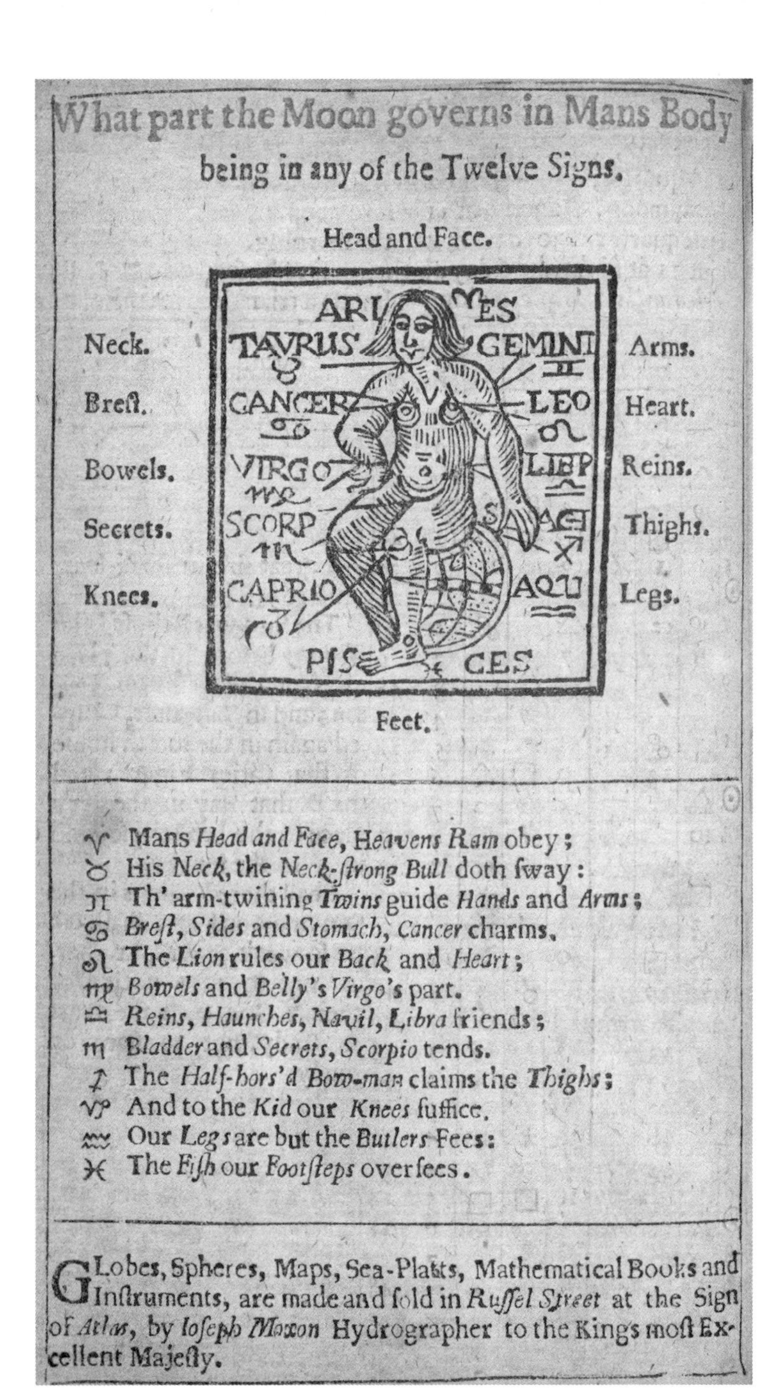

What part the Moon governs in Mans Body
being in any of the Twelve Signs.

Head and Face.

Neck. | ARIES TAURUS GEMINI | Arms.
Breſt. | CANCER LEO | Heart.
Bowels. | VIRGO LIBR | Reins.
Secrets. | SCORP SAGI | Thighs.
Knees. | CAPRIO AQU | Legs.
PISCES

Feet.

♈ Mans *Head and Face*, *Heavens Ram* obey;
♉ His *Neck*, the *Neck-ſtrong Bull* doth ſway:
♊ Th' arm-twining *Twins* guide *Hands* and *Arms*;
♋ *Breſt*, *Sides* and *Stomach*, *Cancer* charms,
♌ The *Lion* rules our *Back* and *Heart*;
♍ *Bowels* and *Belly's Virgo's* part.
♎ *Reins*, *Haunches*, *Navil*, *Libra* friends;
♏ *Bladder* and *Secrets*, *Scorpio* tends.
♐ The *Half-hors'd Bow-man* claims the *Thighs*;
♑ And to the *Kid* our *Knees* ſuffice.
♒ Our *Legs* are but the *Butlers* Fees:
♓ The *Fiſh* our *Footſteps* overſees.

GLobes, Spheres, Maps, Sea-Platts, Mathematical Books and Inſtruments, are made and ſold in *Ruſſel Street* at the Sign of *Atlas*, by *Ioſeph Moxon* Hydrographer to the Kings moſt Excellent Majeſty.

3 The astrological man from John Gadbury's almanac *ΕΦΗΜΕΡΙΣ* for 1668. The moon as it passes through each zodiacal sign governs a different body part. At the bottom of the page is an advertisement for a mathematical instrument maker. The facing page, not shown here, contains a table of "dignities," or the celestial mansions and houses in which the planets were located, along with advertisements: for a bookseller who marketed both ink and toothpaste, and for a table of astrological houses designed for "the ingenious Arti[st]s in Astrologie."

4 A portrait of John Heydon, from his book *Theomagia: Or, The Temple of Wisdom* (1664). Richly attired and surrounded by his own books, he basks in celestial rays. Below the portrait is a coat of arms that marks him as an Esquire. The planetary signs that surround him form a kind of nativity chart. At the bottom left, an obedient dog labeled "Lilly" bows towards the "Astromagus."

5 The frontispiece to the second part of Joseph Glanvill's *Saducismus Triumphatus* shows the Devil carrying out various types of mischief, including levitation. The drummer of Tedworth is at the upper left, and at the lower right, an angel appears to a disabled girl in Amsterdam, who is cured of her affliction. Evidently, some spirits can be benign, but human beings cannot enter into voluntary contact with them.

6 A ray of celestial light directly illuminates the sight of a young woman as she enters the Palace of Secrets, which resembles a mausoleum or perhaps the outer gate to Solomon's Temple. Running through parted waters, she carries both the Old and the New Testaments as well as a set of keys and a fading torch. To entice alchemists further, all four elements are represented in this frontispiece to *Kabbala Denudata*. The ocean rolls back to reveal the earth just as the cloudy skies break up to reveal the fiery sun.

7 Gold and silver, personified in the gods Apollo (the sun) and Diana (the moon), stand knee-deep in a watery solution beneath the Tree of Life in the frontispiece to the alchemical aphorisms of Baro Urbigerus. Above them are a serpent and a winged dragon, symbols of mercury in the alchemical process. At the right, the two divine beings have been combined into a single, hermaphroditic figure.

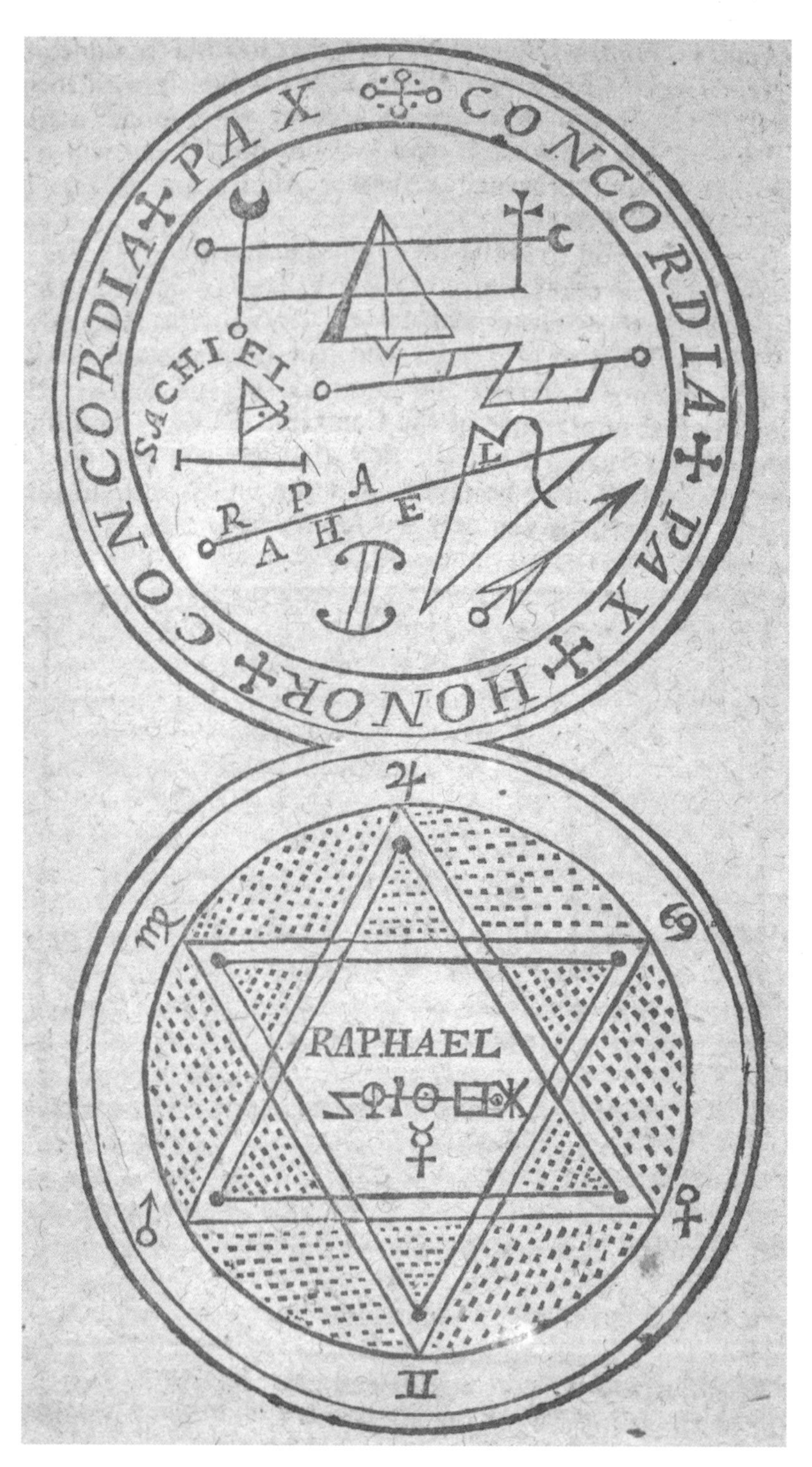

8 The sigil whose sale by the astrologer Henry Coley in 1698 was so vehemently denounced by John Partridge in his almanac. The Cherubim Sachiel or Zadkiel is mentioned in the Kabbala and was associated with the planet Jupiter, while Raphael appears in the Biblical Book of Tobit and is linked, as here, with the planet Mercury.

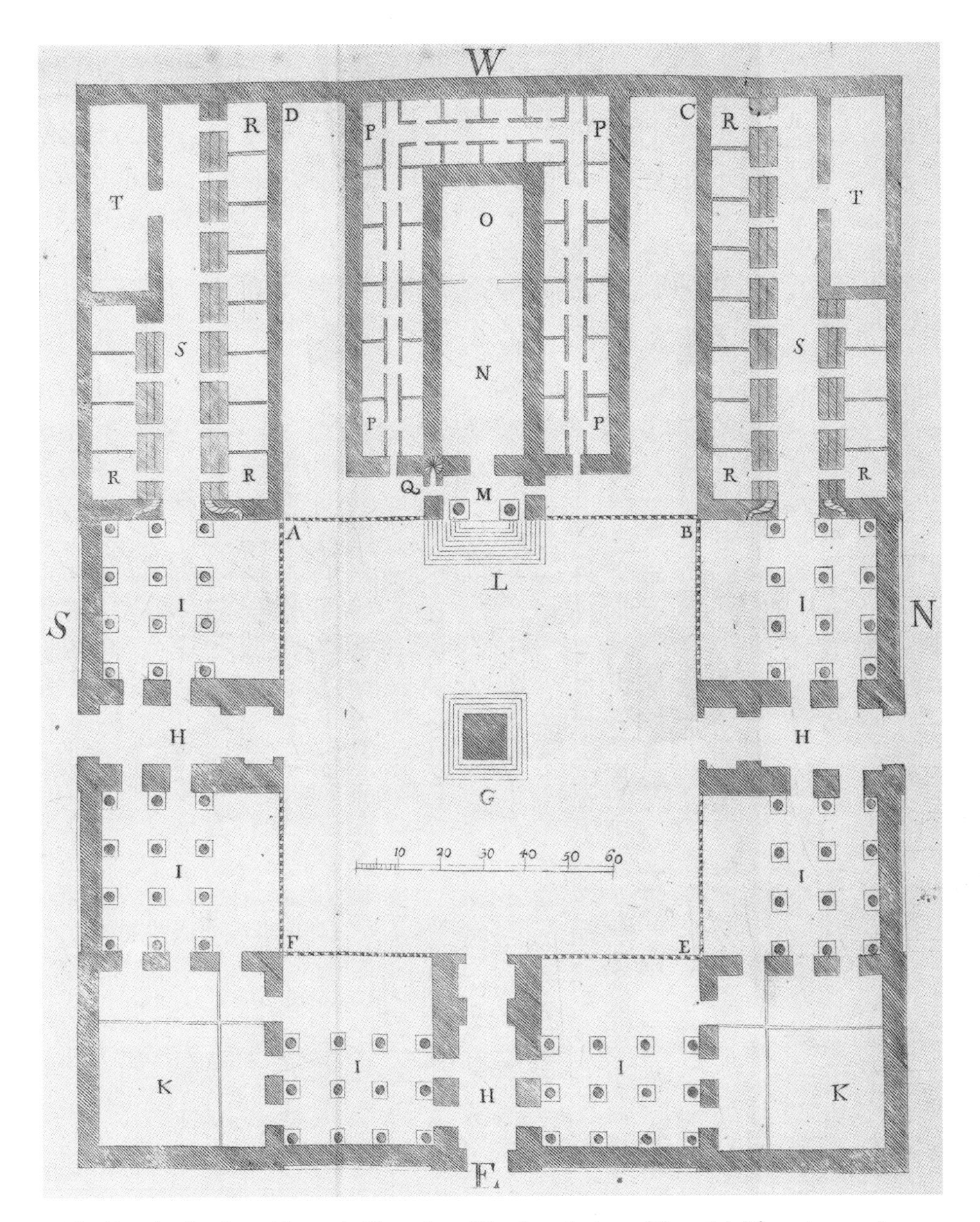

9 The Temple plan from Newton's *Chronology*. West is at the top of the print. The outer court or Court of the People surrounds an inner wall, containing the Court of the Priests and the Temple proper. The altar, marked "G," is at the centre of the Court of the Priests, in front of the Temple porch, which is supported by the two legendary pillars named Jachin and Boaz. The letter "O" marks the Holy of Holies, surrounded by the Treasure Chambers—filled, perhaps, with the fruits of Solomon's alchemy.

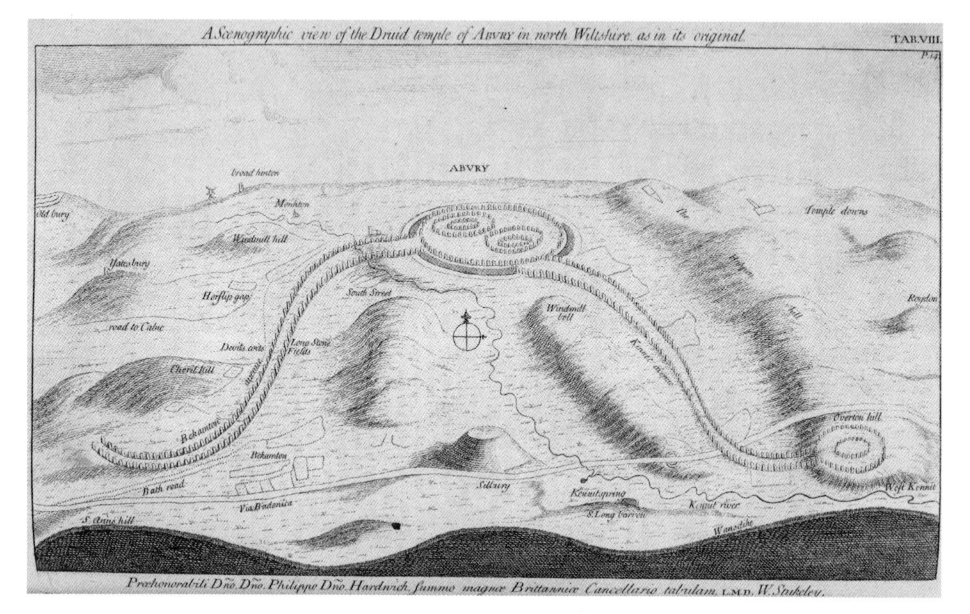

10 William Stukeley's conception of Avebury as a winged serpent is clearly represented in this engraving from *Abury, A Temple of the British Druids* (1743). The head of the snake is at lower right, while the concentric circles at the centre are the (not very convincing) wings. Compare this image to the serpent and winged dragon in Plate 7, which are alchemical symbols for mercury.

11 Duncan Campbel's portrait, from his *Secret Memoirs*, sports a magnificent wig that emphasizes his respectability. The absence of occult symbols is notable, but emphasis is placed on Campbel's eyes, which served as his conduit to predicting the future. He is a polite prophet, not a magician.

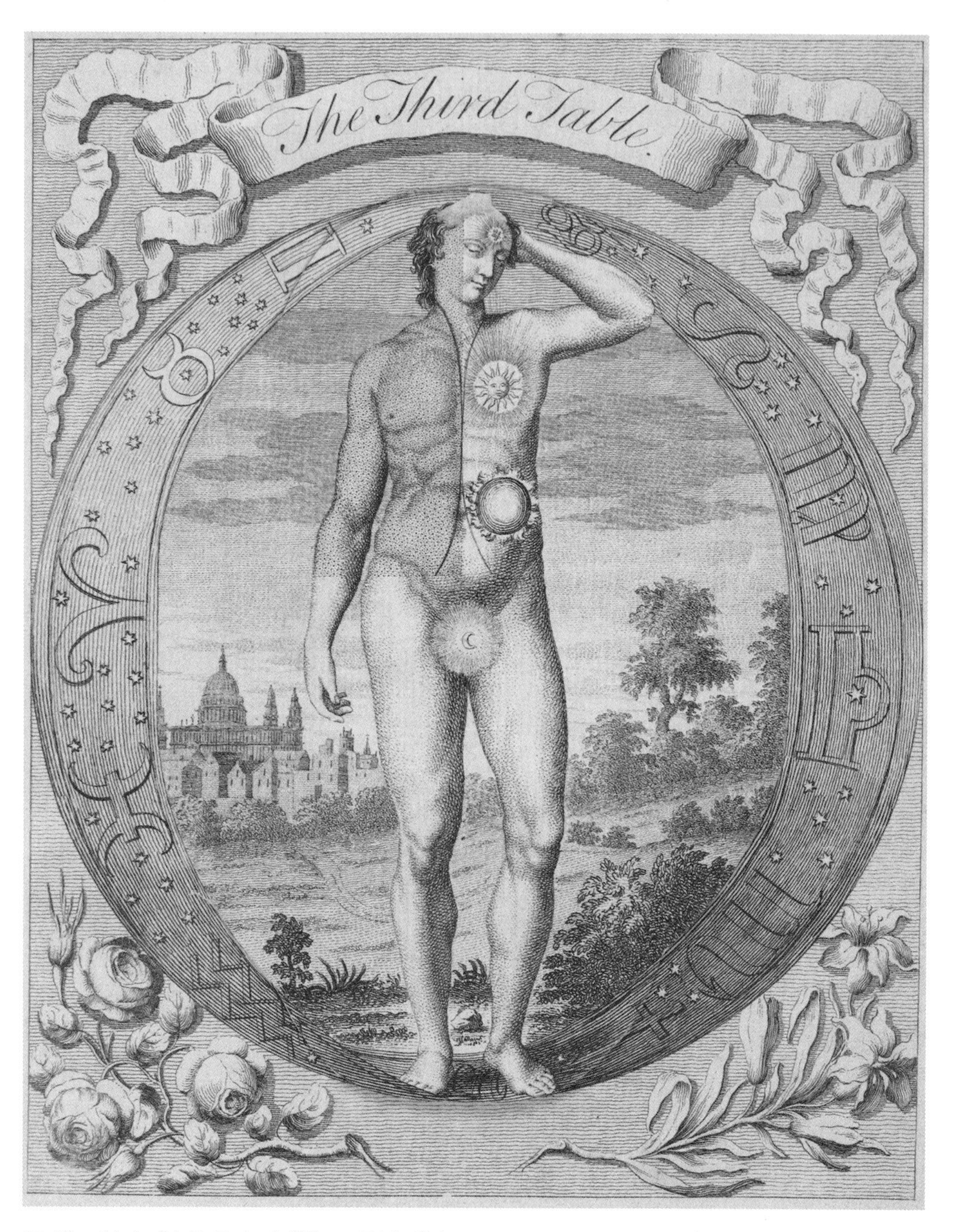

12 The third of A.D. Freher's "Three Tables," showing Man moving towards a spiritual or regenerated state, as illustrated in the third volume of *The Works of Jacob Behmen* (1772). These elaborate cutout engravings were arranged in multiple folded layers that could be lifted up to reveal changes to the body and the spirit. As each layer was raised, the appearance and spiritual organs of the earthly Man progressively degenerated and then were gradually restored. In keeping with Freher's original designs, the figures are surrounded by astrological signs and the stages in their transformations are represented by celestial or alchemical symbols.

13 The beaming countenance of Ebenezer Sibly, from his *Medical Mirror* (1794), displays the confidence of a Member of the Royal College of Physicians, Aberdeen. The initials "F. R. H. S." probably refer to a branch of the Harmonic Society, which was dedicated to magnetic healing; the "R" may stand for Rosicrucian rather than Royal. No doubt Sibly was a founding Fellow. The only other occult reference here is to Mercury, who bears alchemical symbols on his shield. The vignette at the bottom of the page depicts the Biblical story of the Good Samaritan, and at right is the Nehushtan, the serpent wound around a staff that appeared to Moses—obviously, a Scriptural counterpart to Mercury's staff or caduceus.

14 The immediate source of light in Joseph Wright of Derby's remarkable painting, "The Alchymist," may be the glowing retort containing phosphorus that radiates at the centre of the alchemist's laboratory, but the vessel merely reflects the divine light dimly viewed through the window at the top of the scene. The picture is heavily laden with references to Freemasonry that would have been obvious to any initiate.

15 Ebenezer Sibly's famous astrological chart of the birth of the United States on July 4, 1776, is carried aloft by a winged figure of Victory. Below, George Washington gestures towards Justice and a young Federal Union, while a rather ludicrous looking Indian, derived from tobacco advertisements, toasts him and points to symbols of trade. A military camp and a prosperous port town are seen in the background. This is a rare example of a strongly pro-American print, engraved in England only 12 years after American Independence.

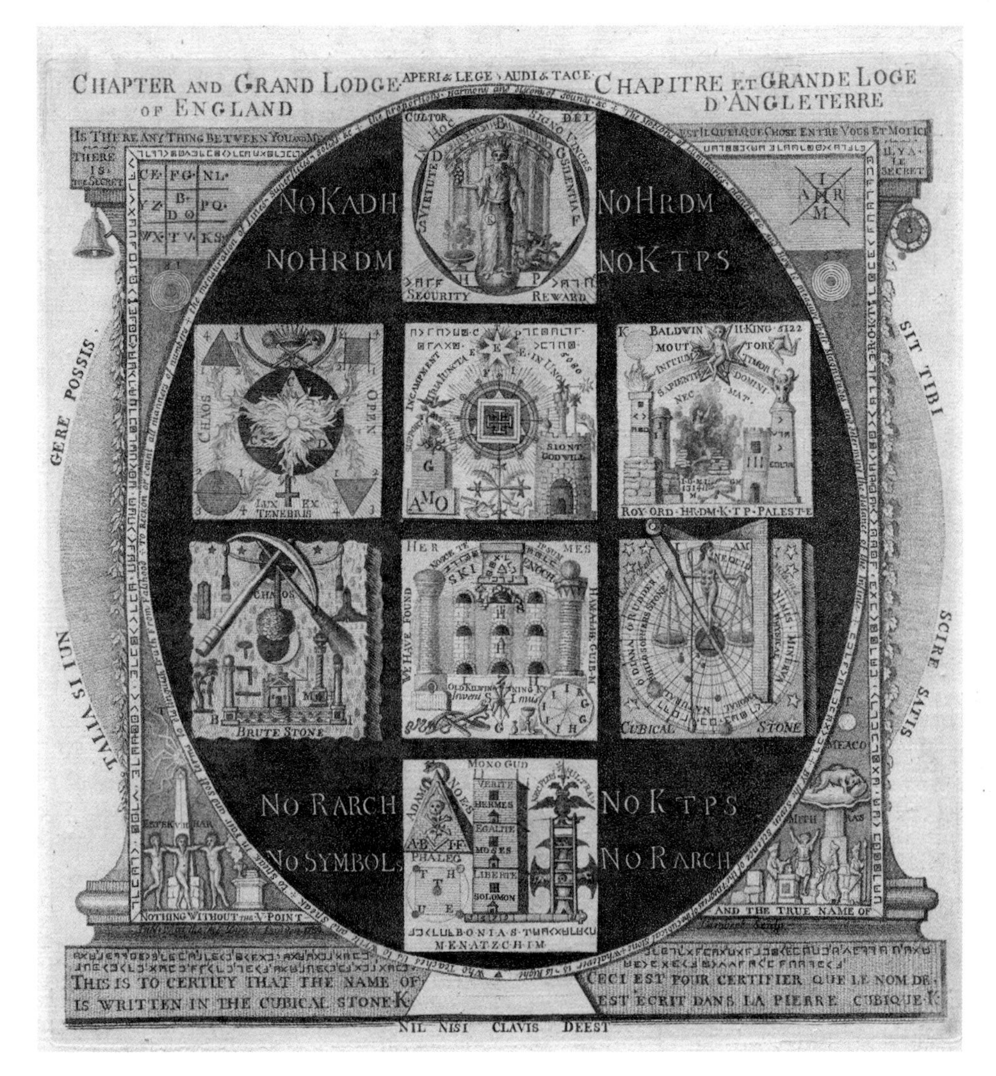

16 The most imaginative and detailed of Peter Lambert de Lintot's Masonic engravings, dating from 1789, displays the symbols of the different degrees granted by the breakaway Grand Lodge of England. The use of alchemical imagery and language ("Chaos," "Hermes," etc.) is striking, as are the multiple representations of Solomon's Temple. The arrangement of the seven degrees might be compared to Newton's plan of the Temple. The inscriptions around the edges are written in English, French and an indecipherable quasi-Hebraic script (perhaps the language of Adam) for the benefit of the multi-cultural members of the Grand Lodge.

17 The famous depiction of animal magnetism from Ebenezer Sibly's *Key to Physic, and the Occult Sciences* (1795) shows a male magnetizer operating on a female patient. He stands at a discrete distance from her, his hands radiating magnetic energy at her face and breast. She sits passively and registers no visible signs of a "Crisis". This was a tame representation of the controversial therapy, engraved at a point when it was no longer widely acceptable among the English elite.

18 The morose and misguided Urizen calmly measuring out the universe with a compass at the opening of William Blake's *Europe: A Prophecy*. The instrument is an unmistakable reference to Freemasonry, and to the Masonic concept of God as the architect of the universe. Urizen's uncomfortable crouch also resembles the bending pose of Isaac Newton in a print issued by Blake in 1795, where the great scientist uses a compass to measure out a conical section. The compositional structure of the Urizen painting, with its combination of a circle and a triangle, can be compared to the alchemical diagram in *The Philosophical Epitaph of W.C. Esq.*, which was in turn derived from the illustrations to Jacob Boehme's works. In the end, however, Blake's personal vision trumps Masonry, Newton, alchemy and even Boehme.

back if there was anything I did not like, and then he bid me sit down." By 1730, however, the name of "Mr. John Byram" appears in a list of members of the Swan tavern lodge in Long Acre.[101]

Byrom first encountered William Law in March 1729, when the two men met at an inn in Putney. The learned clergyman had just published *A Serious Call to a Devout and Holy Life*, a classic of moral rigourism. While Byrom admired it, his relationship with Law was not initially close. He was at this time seeking out all sorts of religious teachers, including Edward Elwall, an eccentric ironmonger of Wolverhampton who lived according to his own interpretation of Jewish law. Byrom was gradually settling on a mystic path, however, and was pleased when Law, in a rare moment of humility, said of Madame Bourignon that "he wished he could think like her."[102] Byrom did not introduce Law to Jacob Boehme, but his transition towards "mystic divinity" definitely preceded that of the man often seen as his mentor. The journal's first reference to the Teutonic Theosopher comes in January 1731, when Byrom bought "two pieces of Jacob Behmen" at a book auction in London. He mentioned Boehme to Law in April 1737, at which point his friend responded "that it was by force that he had writ, that he had desired that all his books had been in one [set of volumes]." Clearly, Law had read at least some of Boehme's works by this time. By Law's own account, given to Byrom in 1743, "Dr. Cheyne was the providential occasion of his meeting or knowing of Jacob Behmen, by a book which the Dr. mentioned to him in a letter, which book mentioned Behmen." This book, as is known through later testimony, was *Faith and Reason Compared* by a German Philadelphian named Baron Metternich.[103]

Faith and Reason Compared actually owed more to John Pordage and Jane Lead than to Boehme. Metternich refers to God as the "Magic Eye," which was one of Pordage's favourite images.[104] He argues in favour of a religion based on direct revelation by God, working either through the imagination or the intellect. Metternich aimed to confute "Modern Rationalists," who judge revelation, scriptural or personal, according to "Right Reason." Far from providing a basis for judgment, in Metternich's view, "Reason darkens our pure Understanding, and hinders it from perceiving the subtile Influences of divine Light."[105] Law's research into Boehme, therefore, began with a Philadelphian, and it continued to be deeply affected by that movement. The remaining Philadelphians gave him open access to their archives, and Law became a busy copyist. He cited a manuscript work by Andreas Dionysius Freher to Byrom in April 1737, shortly *before* his first recorded remark concerning Boehme. He painstakingly copied Freher's "Serial Elucidations," that is, his thoughts on Jacob Boehme, along with three versions of the "Three Tables." Byrom participated in this rediscovery of the Philadelphians; he kept his own manuscript version of Freher's "Three Tables" and owned a large collection of mystical diagrams that resemble the illustrations of Boehme made by Freher's disciple J.D. Leuchter.[106]

The Philadelphians held to unconventional beliefs concerning alchemy, astrology, "Magia" and angelic visions. Law never endorsed these things in print. When he took up the struggle against "Modern Rationalists," he fashioned it as a defence of Christian orthodoxy rather than of immediate revelation. Law was not actively seeking personal union with God, and he remained deeply suspicious of spirit possession. Yet he threw himself into the study of Boehme, on whom he lavished extraordinary praise—"as a *chosen Servant* of God, he may be placed among those who had received the highest Measures of Light, Wisdom and Knowledge from *Above*."[107] What Boehme added to the fight against rationalism, in Law's view, was a mystical synthesis of theology and the material world. According to Law, Boehme "has made all that is found in the kingdom of grace and the kingdom of nature, to be one continual demonstration, that *dying* to self to be *born again* of Christ is the one only possible salvation of the sons of fallen *Adam*." In Law's estimation, Boehme spoke not just to religious matters: he also provided insight into the structure of nature.

In investigating this aspect of the Theosopher's writings, Law finally crossed the line separating mystic divinity and occult philosophy, proposing that the Newtonian cosmos should be turned on its head. The bold idea, no doubt derived from the Philadelphians, was germinating in Law's mind by 1742, when he published his first extended defence of Boehme. There he suggested: "The illustrious Sir *Isaac Newton* when he wrote his *Principia* . . . could have told the world, that the *true and infallible* Ground of what he there advanced, was to be found in the *teutonick Philosopher*, in his *three first Properties of Eternal Nature*."[108] The Newtonian theory of gravity, in other words, had been plagiarized from Boehme. Soon after, in a letter to Dr Cheyne, Law explained the evidence for this outrageous claim. "Dr. Newton," an unidentified relative of the great man, had informed Law that he and Sir Isaac had set up furnaces to find the Philosopher's Stone after reading the works of Boehme. They failed, but Law opined that Newton had learned from the experience. He noted that attraction was a universal property in Boehme as well as "the grand foundation of the Newtonian Philosophy." This could not be a coincidence. No one could try to learn the secret of the tincture from Boehme "without knowing and believing as B— does, the ground of Universal attraction, and therefore Sir Isaac's silence, and ignorance of this ground must have been affected & for certain reasons which can now only be guess'd at." Law repeated this astonishing story to Byrom in May 1743.[109]

Its veracity is highly dubious. No extensive transcripts by Newton from Boehme's works have survived, and the two men had very different understandings of alchemy as well as of gravity. Furthermore, the notion of extracting an alchemical recipe from Boehme's writings is absurd—unless one follows Freher's handwritten treatise on redemption as a spagyric process, which Law must have read. In fact, the story of the Behmenist origins of gravity tells us more about Law than it does about Newton. Law wanted to give it credit because he believed in Boehme as well as in alchemy. He confessed to Byrom that he had confidence in certain claims of the discovery of the Philosopher's Stone, and the two men "agreed that it could not possibly be forgery." Law had evidently heard about Newton's spagyric experiments, and was eager to count the great scientist in the Behmenist camp.[110]

Law convinced himself that Newton had been misled—in fact, the man of science had reversed the true order of nature. In a 1752 tract entitled *The Spirit of Love*, Law maintained that "all the *Matter* of this World is from *spiritual Properties*, since all its Workings and Effects are according to them." Regarding the laws of matter and motion, "the illustrious Sir *Isaac* ploughed with *Behmen*'s Heifer": that is, he concocted worldly theories out of principles that pertained to spirits.[111] Did Law weigh the philosophical implications of this argument? If matter *consisted* of spirit, and all spirit was part of God, then the deity was present in everything—an arrangement not far removed from that set forth in *Kabbala Denudata*, or the pantheist philosophy that was usually called "Spinozism." Boehme's heifer, in other words, was ploughing a spiritual version of Spinoza's "Substance." No wonder Bishop Warburton, who detested Law, accused Boehme of "rank Spinozism." Byrom, whose piety and benevolence Warburton actually admired, denied the charge, which he considered tantamount to an accusation of atheism, in a polite exchange of letters with the bishop in 1752.[112] It remains unclear, however, whether Law would have justified a Neoplatonic universe of differentiated spirits, or a Kabbalistic one in which all spirits were essentially versions of the same divine being.

In any case, we should not assume, as their critics did, that Law and Byrom were simply credulous men who were willing to stomach things that defied rational judgment. Byrom, for example, took a non-committal position regarding Mary Toft, who supposedly gave birth to rabbits: "I neither believe nor disbelieve, because I do not suppose the matter has as yet been thoroughly examined on both sides." As to witches, he had "no notion of those things," although he was inclined to believe Madame Bourignon's story of the "witches' school."[113] For his part, Law mocked rationalists for their obsession with wanting to know the unknowable, like "the inward Structure of Solomon's

Temple, and all of its Services," an unsubtle jab at the preoccupations of Newton, Stukeley and the Freemasons.[114] We should also be wary of linking mystical religious attitudes too closely with a Jacobite mindset, as there were considerable differences among the adherents of the exiled Stuart claimant to the throne. Jacobitism did not induce heightened spirituality or acceptance of the supernatural, even if many Jacobites believed that the exiled Pretender had the ability to cure scrofula by the laying-on of hands.[115] Jacobites did not often write in favour of the royal healing power, and it is difficult to say what Law or Byrom thought of it.

As he aged, Law wrote less and less about worldly affairs. Ensconced in his native village of King's Cliffe, Northamptonshire, he spent his last years occupied with charitable works and reverential reading of the Teutonic Theosopher. "Next to the *scriptures* my only book is the *illuminated Behmen*," he admitted in 1759.[116] His last great project was to encourage a new edition of Boehme's writings. As will be seen, that editorial enterprise would have momentous consequences for the history of occult thinking in Britain. It would preserve the Behmenist magic of the Philadelphians, which Law had absorbed, into the last decades of the century, and would produce spiritual manifestations beyond anything John Byrom could imagine.

Magical Architecture: John Wood of Bath

The learned mystics tried to separate certain strands of occult thinking from popular beliefs. Others moved in the opposite direction, by popularizing learned arguments that borrowed from the occult. This can be observed in the literature of Freemasonry. By the mid-eighteenth century, offshoots or rivals of the Grand Lodge of England were using promises of occult knowledge to gain adherents. The Antient Grand Lodge, which officially separated from the mainstream of English Masonry in 1751, wanted a return to the "Old Constitutions," meaning a greater concentration on the Temple of Solomon as the source of "the secret Mysteries of the Craft." The chief publicist for the Antients, Laurence Dermott, claimed to have been visited in a dream by the four head porters of Solomon's Temple, who assured him that the Masons who built that structure "were the greatest Cabalists then in the World." Dermott defined the Kabbala as "their secret Science of expounding divine Mysteries."[117] Initiates into Antient Masonry would presumably learn those same mysteries.

The renewed focus on the secrets of Solomon's Temple is also found in the writings of the remarkable architect and historian John Wood the elder of Bath. He was the designer of many prominent buildings in the spa town, including the Royal Circus and Queen's Square. His chief patron was Ralph Allen, the mastermind of the English Post Office system, who owned the quarry that provided Wood with stone, and whose house at Prior Park Wood designed. The architect died in 1754, three years after the founding of the Antient Grand Lodge, but there is no record of his being a member. His writings, however, are almost incomprehensible without the assumption of Freemasonry behind them. Their confident pronouncements about the hidden meanings of buildings show that the changing landscapes of eighteenth-century Britain, both rural and urban, could still be seen as loaded with ancient mysteries.

Wood was one of a number of British architects of the first half of the eighteenth century whose work displays the influence of Freemasonry.[118] The most important among them was Nicholas Hawksmoor, member of a Masonic lodge in Ludgate Street whose master was the antiquarian Richard Rawlinson, a Nonjuror and friend of Richard Roach. Hawksmoor made notes on Ezekiel's vision of the Temple, and he incorporated into his buildings aspects of Solomonic architecture, such as the twisted columns and cube design at St Mary Woolnoth in London. His plans for colleges at Oxford resemble Villalpando's Temple reconstructions. The fabled tomb of Mausoleus at Halicarnassus provided a model for the tower of St George's, Bloomsbury, and Hawksmoor constructed another classical mausoleum for the earl of Carlisle at Castle Howard. To Freemasons, the original mausoleum to which all later examples referred was the grave of Hiram Abiff. Hawksmoor's buildings, therefore, embody a symbolism of death and regeneration that reflected the ritual of the lodges.[119] Hawskmoor's admirer the architect Batty Langley was a tireless publicist for the Freemasons as well as for a "Gothic" or eclectic style, in opposition to classical Palladianism. Langley's *magnum opus*, the gigantic *Ancient Masonry* (1732–6), was dedicated to the grand masters of the Craft.[120]

In contrast to Hawksmoor, John Wood the elder was one of the leading architects of the Palladian style, which may show that Masonic affiliations did not dictate stylistic choices. Wood's *Origin of Building: or, The Plagiarism of the Heathens Detected* (1746) can be read as an attempt to reconcile Palladianism, which looked to Roman architecture for models, with the Solomonic roots of Masonry. Wood's account is loaded with Masonic lore, such as the story of the two pillars on which all human knowledge was inscribed and which survived the Flood. He also included many of his own interpretations, such as his reading of biblical names, which "discover to us the source of the Art Magick."[121] Wood wandered quite willingly into the occult, without any of the hesitations that restrained more learned authors. He paid considerable attention to magical questions, such as how Joktan son of Heber learned the "Trick, of animating inanimate Things," which must have been quite a party turn. According to

Wood, the magic of the Chaldeans was bequeathed to the Druids, while that of the Egyptians was learned by Moses, providing a foundation for the art of building. The skilled architect, Wood opined, had to be a good magician, as he needed to know all "the Wisdom of the Egyptians," including "Astrology, Geometry, Optics, Arithmetic, History, Philosophy, Music, Physic."[122]

Like Newton, whose *Chronology* he frequently cited, Wood perceived the construction of the Temple of Jerusalem as a turning point in human history, not so much because of its prophetic significance, but because it "represented the Universe." Wood agreed with Newton that the Temple was destroyed by "King Bacchus" or Sesostris, whose "sacred Scribe," Hermes Trismegistus, was "the Inventor of all the Arts and Sciences."[123] What part Hermes played in disseminating the architecture of the Temple to the Greeks and Romans is not clear, but Wood had no doubt that the Temple of Diana at Ephesus was based on Solomon's Temple. As for the buildings of the Druids, Stonehenge "answers the very Description of the Temple of *Jerusalem*, as it was directed to be built by *Cyrus*."[124] Wood proudly assures us that his own renovations at the cathedral of Llandaff in Wales adopted the same model. We may find all this to be a fantastic mishmash, but we should remember that it differs mainly in tone, not in method, from the more learned but equally questionable works of Newton or Stukeley. It also provides us with an unparalleled insight into how a major working architect perceived his own craft.

Encouraged by the Tory collector and antiquarian Edward Harley, 2nd earl of Oxford, Wood made a careful description of Stonehenge in 1740. He even claimed to know its original name, *Choir Gaure*. The dimensions of Stonehenge's megaliths, which Wood measured precisely, were in his view derived from Pythagorean number symbolism related to the lunar year. In determining its origins and purpose, Wood fell back on the Druidic theory that had already been established by Stukeley, but added his own odd perspective. Druidism was for Wood a global phenomenon that had apparently spread from Britain to India and China, where it inspired Confucius. The Druidic courts met, or so Wood maintained, yearly on the feast of John the Baptist, which happened to be the chief Masonic commemoration day.[125] Wood suggested that the Druids practised in their great Temple forms of necromancy in honour of Proserpine:

> Can there now, my Lord [Oxford], remain any doubt but that the Ceremony of Conjuration was one of the uses which the Druids, so eminent for their Magick, as well as for their Skill in playing upon the Harp, put those parts of our Antient Works . . .? And where could this Magical Ceremony be better performed here, than in the Temple of her that was supposed to preside over the Dead as Queen of the Infernal Regions?[126]

This weird passage evokes the classical underworld, central to the learned pretensions of Masonic ritual, but it relates Druidic beliefs to popular magic rather than to ancient mysteries.

Stukeley blew up at this—eventually. Warburton, who knew Wood through his friend Ralph Allen, first alerted Stukeley in November 1747 that "the Bath architect was printing a book on Stonehenge ag^{t}. me," which was incorrect as Wood's treatise did not target Stukeley's work.[127] Apparently, Stukeley did not bother to read the book for sixteen years, by which time Wood had been dead for almost a decade. In August 1763, Stukeley recorded: "I read over *Wood* the architects acc^{t}. of Stonehenge, written to contradict me. Tis such a heap, a ruin of trifling, nonsensical, impertinent, & needless measuring of the Stones, designd to be rude, as if they were the most nice & curious Grecian pillars." This was just the beginning: "the whole performance," Stukeley fumed, "he stuffs with fabulous whimsys of his own crackt imagination, wild extravagancys, concerning Druids, without the least true foundation." In the end, Stukeley labelled it "a diabolical work, quite needless . . . a hodgpoch [*sic*] of conceit, & ignorance, & impudent malice." Wood's naming of Stonehenge as "rocking stone" (*Choir Gaure* in Welsh) "may have amused the vulgar, fond of giving into a magical notion in every thing, belonging to the Druids," but, to the learned antiquarian, Wood's "entrance into the sacred inclosure, seems . . . like *Satan* breaking over the hallowed mound of *Paradise*." Warburton confirmed that Wood "was a great Fool, & not less a knave," whose book on architecture was "ridiculous."[128]

Stukeley's rage at Wood's theories may seem disingenuous, as they closely resembled those of the learned antiquarian himself. His ranting at Wood's measurements is particularly curious. These were perhaps the Bath architect's most original contribution to the history of Stonehenge, and Wood would use them as a basis for the design of the famous Circus at Bath. Of course, what Stukeley really resented was that an unlearned provincial of the middling sort would dare to propose an interpretation of the great English monument. Worse still, Wood's treatment of Stonehenge was littered with "vulgar" notions, many of them having to do with magic. He might have been even more incensed had he read Wood's final publication, *A Description of Bath*.

This amazing, bizarre and hugely successful guidebook, first published in 1742 and reissued in an expanded, two-volume version in 1749, was designed as publicity for the taste and civility of Bath, the booming spa town that was the site of most of Wood's important building projects. Bath was at the forefront of the "urban renaissance," the expansion of public and private spaces in English towns that reflected the new commercial prosperity as well as the desires of a growing body of consumers.[129] Wood's *Description* was in part a compendium of fantasies about his native town, which he grandiosely compared with

Alexandria, Babel, Ezekiel's vision of the Temple and Babylon. According to Wood, Bath was founded by King Bladud, whom he described "not only as a Magician; but, by the Magical Art, [as] making the Hot Waters of the City boil out of the Ground in three different Places." Wood proposed the hypothesis that Bladud had studied with Pythagoras, making him a sort of Masonic precursor. His city at Bath was built in the form of a "T," which "forms the Hieroglyphical Figure of the Antients that represented the Principle of all Evil, and their Deliverance from it." "T" stood for Typhon, a monster of Greek mythology who also appears in alchemical literature.[130]

Wood went on to praise the British Druids as "the most religious People in the World; they never grew weary of Life till they had seen a thousand Years compleat; and therefore . . . could not be without the Belief of the Immortality of the Soul." These long-living Druids (had Wood been reading Robert Samber?) were worshippers of Apollo and Diana, who knew mathematics as well as necromancy and built a "great School of Learning" at Bath. In short, they were not so different from some of the enterprising eighteenth-century inhabitants of the town, including Wood himself. The architect's plans for improving Bath through paving, lighting and the construction of a "Grand Place of Assembly," along with a "Grand Circus," were meant to restore the metropolis to its former Druidic glory as "the very *Elysian Fields* of the Antients."[131] To give a further flavour of mystery to the place, Wood ended his long description with several ghost stories, including one that involved a young woman who hanged herself after reading a passage about betrayal in *Orlando Furioso*, and another concerning the phantom of "a *Black Moor*" who somehow failed to materialize during a "Ceremony" at a wealthy Quaker's house.[132]

We should not take Wood's book too seriously. As in all his writings, he was trying to entertain as well as educate his readers. But though they might tremble at ghosts and gasp at the monstrous Typhon, they also longed to turn Bath into a hub of commerce and civilization. In his general outlook, Wood was not very far removed from John Cannon, who lived only a few miles away and who knew Ralph Allen's family.[133] Cannon was less bombastic, but he shared with Wood a fascination with magic, omens and apparitions, which he did not perceive as contradictory to modern learning. Stukeley, Warburton and the defenders of Newtonian orthodoxy might fume, but ordinary Britons continued to graft "vulgar" notions of occult philosophy to the latest cultural trends. While the West Country temperament doubtless has to be taken into account, it is not unlikely that the mentality of people like Wood and Cannon could be found in many other parts of Britain. Neither backward nor unsophisticated, it preserved the occult thinking of the seventeenth century well into the age of "urban renaissance" and Enlightenment.

By the last decades of the eighteenth century, however, the occult mentality was changing. Formerly, its main concern had been the defence of long-held beliefs, including the reality of spirits, the persistence of magic or the significance of alchemy. After 1760, due in part to the efforts of mystics like Law, new beliefs were created out of the old, ranging from a refashioned Behmenism to a revamped astrology. A revival of occult thinking was set in motion throughout Britain, from which the modern concept of "the occult" would arise. John Wood would have felt at home in such an intellectual environment. Its character was brash, commercial, cosmopolitan and urban-centred. It focused on educated members of the middling ranks of society. It would shake up the settled cultural universe of the Newtonians beyond recognition.

PART THREE
GLAD DAY, 1760–1815

CHAPTER SEVEN

The Occult Revival

BETWEEN 1760 and 1800, England witnessed a remarkable revival of occult thinking.[1] The same phenomenon does not appear to have happened in Scotland. The English revival was more a reinvention than a simple revamping of traditional ideas. The established practices of alchemy, astrology and ritual magic, which had been declining among educated people for some time, were reconfigured—pulled apart, jumbled together and combined with different elements. New conceptions of occult philosophy and science emerged that would last into the modern age. Their main characteristics were: first, a high degree of commercialization; second, a greater insistence on the interconnectedness of occult thought, whether magical or mystical, learned or popular; and, third, a relative indifference to empirical or scientific "proof" of occult claims. "The occult," a term that was coming into fashion by the early nineteenth century, was increasingly imagined as an underlying or alternative reality that operated by its own rules and might not be susceptible to rational verification. The existence of such a sphere was upheld by the authority of time-honoured traditions, as well as by experience. This was a leap into heterodoxy, both from a religious and a scientific point of view. For some, it marked a final rejection of the intellectual respectability craved by Elias Ashmole and Isaac Newton alike. It would disgust many scientific or philosophical minds, but it attracted creative writers and artists, who began to perceive the occult as a territory of boundless imaginative liberty.

That liberty was never really complete. Occult thinking continued to look back to older models of explanation, which were often constricting, and it never fully separated itself from prevailing standards of aesthetic or even scientific judgment. Most occult thinkers continued to crave acceptance, and they were acutely sensitive to changes in the cultural climate that might leave them looking backward or out of touch. For this reason, they regularly attempted to accommodate those trends that were associated with the Enlightenment, although they brought to the task a high degree of hostility (often misplaced) to some of the main figures of that intellectual movement, among them Newton, Locke and David Hume. At the same time, by claiming imaginative freedom, they could put themselves at odds with prevailing political trends. By the 1790s, occult philosophy had established a strong link with reformist and even radical thought, which would engender suspicion and hostility from those in power.

What were the causes of the occult revival? This chapter will consider the most important of them. Without the increasing commercialization of the press, occult writings would not have rediscovered an audience. That audience, however, no longer consisted of educated, professional people and would-be gentlemen; it had moved deeper into the ranks of the middling sort, to encompass tradesmen, shopkeepers, skilled craftsmen and artisans who were often less interested in reading philosophy than in gaining practical knowledge, or simply being entertained. An appeal to the feelings or sentiments became essential to the success of many occult projects. Literature that was associated with sentimentality often drew on occult themes, and the popular literary style known as the "Gothic" was virtually constructed from them. As in previous centuries, however, religious change was probably the most significant stimulus for occult thinking. Evangelicalism, the upsurge of Behmenism and the influence of the followers of Emanuel Swedenborg provided considerable boosts to esoteric speculation. At the same time, occult strains of Freemasonry were emerging in Germany and France, due in part to the creation of higher degrees in England and Scotland. Taken together, these factors created a multitude of active cells of occult thinking, rather than a unified movement. Within those cells and their successors, the occult would be preserved for the next century, and longer.

Marketing the Occult

Ultimately, magic depended on money. The commercial prosperity of late eighteenth-century England was indispensable to the occult revival. Much of that prosperity was generated in London, the financial and trading capital of a growing empire. The leading figures of the occult revival were able to exploit this commercial growth, earning a living from the occult in various ways: by publishing books, marketing medicines, giving astrological consultations or selling their ideas to patrons. Gradually, new economic opportunities arose for those who practised astrology, alchemy and magic.

To witness the occult rising again, we have only to examine the booksellers' catalogues. Bookselling in the late eighteenth century was big business, encompassing publishing, retailing of original works, dealing in second-hand works and auctioneering. Since the days of William Cooper in the late seventeenth century, auctions had provided access to second-hand books. By the late 1760s, however, some booksellers were keeping second-hand titles in stock and advertising them. The largest booksellers in London operated out of extensive emporia or warehouses, issuing annual, biannual or quarterly catalogues that publicized their wares to a national audience, including bookshops.[2] Sections on occult subjects appeared regularly in the catalogues of these big booksellers from the late 1760s onwards. For example, George Wagstaffe's "Matchless Collection of Scarce Books" listed works on "Astrology, Magic, Chiromancy," as well as on "Magic, Witchcraft."[3] Occult books were often lumped together with those on scientific or medical subjects, under headings like "Alchemy, Astrology, Occult Philosophy, Mines, Witches and Witchcraft, Mathematicks, Natural History, Physick, &c." Richard Dymott, the bookseller who came up with this all-encompassing title, clearly valued the trade in alchemical tracts, as he mentioned it on the front page of his 1770 and 1772 catalogues. His shop was in the Strand, opposite Somerset House, a central location for anyone who was seeking this kind of reading material.[4]

The book trade was booming in the 1780s, when its reigning monarch was James Lackington. Born in the West Country, Lackington had converted to Methodism as a young man, but after establishing himself as a bookseller in London, he drifted away from his evangelical faith. His first catalogue was issued in 1779, and by the mid-1780s he was selling 100,000 books a year, most of them remaindered or second-hand. Lackington seems an unlikely person to have been a retailer of occult items. In his celebrated *Memoirs*, which appeared in 1791, he heaped scorn on apparitions, devils and those "who suffer themselves to be made miserable by vain fears of preternatural occurrences." Yet the prosperous bookseller hinted that he had once held such beliefs himself. Moreover, he continued to esteem someone who had held them throughout his life, his former business partner John Denis, whom he remembered fondly as "an HONEST man." According to Lackington, Denis was a convinced devotee of Jacob Boehme and a follower of the vegetarian regime of Thomas Tryon. He also owned "the best collection of scarce, valuable, mystical and alchymical books, that ever was collected by one person."[5]

The son of an oilman, John Denis was partner to Lackington for only two years before they broke up in 1780. Thereafter, Denis ran his own bookselling businesses in Fleet Street. As Lackington said, he was an avid collector of occult items. At a sale in Islington that took place in 1782, Denis purchased a number of manuscripts belonging to the Philadelphians, including a copy of Andreas Dionysius Freher's "Three Tables" drawn by his disciple J.D. Leuchter, a unique portrait of Freher by Leuchter and some extracts from Boehme's writings in Freher's hand. He bequeathed these rare finds to his son, John Denis the younger, who inherited the business after his father died in 1785 and later operated a bookstore in Middle Row, Holborn. He continued to publish catalogues into the early 1790s. They contained "several very curious Articles, particularly in the *Occult Sciences*," according to the literary historian John Nichols.[6]

The elder Denis was doubtless responsible for including an occult book section in the first catalogue issued by his partner, Lackington, in 1779. It was never subsequently removed, in spite of the termination of their business relationship. We need not assume that Lackington retained any admiration for the occult, however. Commercial considerations, rather than personal beliefs, provide a sufficient explanation for the stock of occult books—between a hundred and 150 volumes—that he regularly advertised in his catalogues, under the catch-all title "Astrology, Alchemy, Palmistry, Magic, Witchcraft, Apparitions, Devils, &c." The number of occult volumes listed in the catalogue increased to about 250 in the years just before Lackington's retirement in 1798, when his immense domed bookshop in Finsbury Square, called the Temple of the Muses, was taken over by his cousin George. In its 1800 catalogue, the new firm of Lackington and Allen listed no fewer than 260 items under a heading that included "magnetism" and "metals" as well as astrology, alchemy, palmistry, magic, witchcraft and apparitions.[7]

The marketing of occult books has to be kept in perspective. They represented only 0.5 per cent of Lackington's thirty thousand-volume catalogue of 1784; by the early nineteenth century, moreover, the firm was advertising over 800,000 volumes, so the percentage of occult books actually declined, although the number increased. Works on occult subjects were usually rare and not available in multiple copies. In addition, the Lackingtons, like their competitors, listed under the general heading of "Astrology, Alchemy, Etc." items that were not, strictly speaking, occult, such as Robert Burton's *Anatomy of Melancholy* or Vannoccio Biringuccio's *Pyrotechnia*, a treatise on metals in which alchemy was mocked. The significance of such listings had little to do with the proportion of the items that actually dealt positively with the subject, however. The chief effect of giving separate space in a catalogue to occult books was the same in 1780 as it would be today: namely, it conferred intellectual authority on the discipline. To list works on astrology, alchemy, etc under their own, distinct heading was to suggest that they deserved the same status as works on law or religion or history. Whether sceptics were inclined to accept this inference is irrelevant; it counted in the minds of those who bought such books, which is all that mattered. Moreover, in typical Enlightenment fashion, the creation of a category altered the definition of what should be included in that category. By lumping works on occult philosophy, science and magical practice together, Lackington and his bookselling colleagues were suggesting that they could all be understood as part of the same thing: namely, "the occult."

Because the sale of used books was normally anonymous, it is difficult to trace those who purchased them. Library auction catalogues, however, can provide some information on the biggest collectors. One of them was Richard Cosway, a fashionable painter of miniatures whose occult fixations will be mentioned in subsequent chapters. After suffering a series of strokes, Cosway sold his extensive library by auction in 1821, shortly before his death. The third day of the auction was devoted to "Books on Magic, Witchcraft, &c.," and comprised 366 separate printed volumes (not including almanacs) along with manuscripts and engravings. Cosway's collection included a wide array of tracts on alchemy, astrology and ritual magic, from Agrippa and the *Notory Art of Solomon* to more recent German publications. Among the occult manuscripts were eight folio volumes by Freher, bound in green vellum.[8] Some items had cost the extravagant Cosway a good deal of money. In 1781, he purchased for £26.5s. 0d. a manuscript concerning the "Cabalistic Principles" of the human figure, ascribed to the painter Piers Paul Rubens. In fact, it was a commentary on Freher's "Three Tables." Cosway must have liked it, as he kept it until his death, after which it was auctioned off at a sale in Paris.[9] Even more costly was a manuscript showing sixty-seven emblems from a seventeenth-century work, *Coronatio Naturae*. It was advertised for 200 guineas in the *Morning Herald* newspaper in November 1797, and no prospective buyer was to see it without first laying down 10s. 6d. Alexander Tilloch, the wealthy alchemist who ultimately purchased it, called the work "very sound Hermetical Philosophy," but added sadly that "no light can be obtained from it for Practice."[10]

There was certainly money to be made from the occult, and not just in the second-hand book or manuscript trade. Its commercial potential was also seen in the publication of new books, which were often actually reissues of older works, like the 1784 edition of John Aubrey's *Miscellanies on Fatality, Omens, Dreams, Apparitions, Voices, Impulses, Knockings, Invisible Blows, Magic, Transportation in the Air, Visions in a Beril, Etc.*, or the 1786 edition of John Whalley's *Ptolemy Quadripartite*, an astrological treatise first published in 1701. *Nocturnal Revels, or Universal Interpreter of Dreams and Visions* (1789) gave no indication of being a version of a treatise that had originally appeared in 1706–7. New works also appealed to the public, especially those that gave access to practical aspects of the occult, such as *Dreams and Moles* (c. 1780), whose title speaks for its bizarre content. This handy guide to interpreting dreams as well as the shapes of pesky skin blemishes was published by Thomas

Sabine of Shoe Lane, Holborn, who seems to have specialized in short, instructive works on subjects like fortune-telling.[11] Ebenezer Sibly, a celebrated astrologer and medical writer whose impact on the occult revival will be discussed in the next chapter, was the author of numerous works that appeared in the Lackingtons catalogues.

By 1801, the firm of Lackington and Allen felt confident enough about the commercial prospects of the occult to advertise its own compendium under the provocative title *The Magus, or Celestial Intelligencer*. Its author was Francis Barrett, "F.R.C." [i.e. "Frater Rosae Crucis," or Rosicrucian Brother], "Professor of Chemistry, natural and occult Philosophy, the Cabala, &c., &c." Barrett would subsequently gain celebrity as a balloonist, although the failure of one of his early efforts led *The Times* to comment that "he does not seem to possess a sufficient knowledge of chemistry to inflate his balloon properly." He later made a short ascent before an estimated ten thousand people at Swansea. Unfortunately, he was less intrepid as a writer than as an aeronaut. *The Magus* was almost wholly unoriginal, except in the inclusion of absurd pictures of the faces of demons. Sections of it were plagiarized from Cornelius Agrippa. Nonetheless, its uncritical descriptions of alchemy, astrology and "Cabalistical" or ceremonial magic had a considerable influence on nineteenth-century occult movements, and the book doubtless proved a good investment for Lackington and Allen.[12] Sibly and Barrett were, quite literally, names to conjure with in the late Georgian period.

Sibly, who specialized in the serial publication of massive encyclopaedic tomes, was an assiduous marketer of his own wares. For sixpence, readers could purchase a weekly instalment of one of his medical compendia, such as *Culpeper's English Physician; and Complete Herbal*, a reworking of the seventeenth-century medical classic. The complete volume, an expensive item that cost £1.11s. 6d. in boards (that is, unbound), had gone through fourteen editions by 1813. Sibly's shorter gynaecological tract, entitled *The Medical Mirror or Treatise on the Impregnation of the Human Female*, reached six editions by 1814. Before he died in 1799 at the age of forty-seven, Sibly wrote two further big quasi-scientific books: *A Key to Physic, and the Occult Sciences* (five editions by 1814) and *An Universal System of Natural History*, which classified and described the plants and animals of the world with the exuberance (or, perhaps, the aggressive cultural imperialism) typical of the Enlightenment. In his marketing strategies, Sibly targeted a family audience that regarded such works as a sound investment because they could be used for practical medical purposes as well as for edification and entertainment. He advertised *Culpeper's English Physician* as "WHAT NO FAMILY SHOULD BE WITHOUT," and tried to establish its significance by maintaining that "all attempts to cry down this interesting Book, have been defeated. The Act of Parliament, by which the Work was at first suppressed, under an idea that it discovered secrets dangerous to be known, has been since repealed."[13] Who could resist a book that might reveal "secrets dangerous to be known"? (The Act cannot be traced.) Equally impressive was the medical degree that Sibly fixed to his name, from the "Royal College of Physicians," Aberdeen (which is to say that it was purchased from King's College, Aberdeen, before 1787 when an actual medical exam was instituted).[14]

Like so many astrologers and alchemists before him, Sibly sold his own patent medicines, but his advertising leaflets carried the commercialization of the occult to new levels. The hype that he issued to publicize his "Solar and Lunar Tinctures" showed a keen sense of how to exploit the intellectual pretensions and insecurities of his readers. The Solar Tincture, which could even be taken "for the RESTORATION of LIFE, in CASES OF SUDDEN DEATH," was explained in the following quasi-scientific fashion:

> The researches made by Dr. SIBLY, into philosophical and chemical enquiries; his long and laborious application to the study of second causes, which are the hidden result, or spiritual operations of nature in all her works; the chymical analysation of medical plants, herbs and minerals; a contemplation of the human structure, with the principles of life and death; a minute investigation of the ancient and modern practice of physic; of hereditary, accidental, and acquired, diseases; and the dreadful consequences of a mistaken or misguided treatment of them; are the sources from whence this medicine is recommended to the notice of a candid and discerning public.[15]

Such passages remind us that the widening sphere of eighteenth-century discourse was not inherently rational, however much emphasis it may have placed on making subjects sound reasonable.[16] Sibly presents himself here as an empiricist, because he values "experience" over "abstract reasoning." After all, he had analysed the chemicals and seen their effects in practical trials. His endorsement of magic was apparently upheld by strict methods of inquiry. What more did members of the public need to convince them that his Solar Tincture could conquer death?

Sibly certainly belonged among those marketers of ineffective remedies whom Roy Porter has labelled "quacks," but he was not necessarily a charlatan.[17] To read his books alongside his advertising claims can only lead one to conclude that he believed in what he was doing, and that his stupendous assertions were based on real conviction. The same might not be said of other patent-medicine pedlars, most of whom were neither astrologers nor spagyrists, even if their potions and pills sounded alchemical. John Ching was an apothecary of Cheapside and maker of "Worm-destroying LOZENGES, for Fits, Pains in the stomach, Pains in the Head or Side, and for Pale, Languid and Emaciated Appearances in young Persons." Like many iatrochemical remedies, Ching's Lozenges contained mercury and were poisonous. After they killed one young man at Hull in 1803, the victim's grieving father, a printer by trade, published a pamphlet denouncing them.[18] Attacks on quackery were not uncommon, but in spite of them the late eighteenth century saw a dramatic rise in the number of patent medicines, which were heavily marketed through advertising. Dr Samuel Solomon of Liverpool claimed to have spent £5,000 a year on publicizing his highly successful "Balm of Gilead," a large bottle of which cost as much as a guinea. His tireless self-promotion rested on claims that he had solved age-old mysteries. The "Balm of Gilead," designed to cure nervous disorders and "Female complaints," was "extracted from the SEED of GOLD, which our alchymists and philosophers have so long sought after in vain."[19] Solomon presented himself as a scientist, but the appeal of his advertising undoubtedly rested on the notion that he had found the Philosopher's Stone.

The use of advertising for specifically occult purposes was also widespread, a point underlined by the editor of a collection of London handbills from the 1770s and 1780s. "That the occult science called white magic, and the study of astrology, flourishes among us, is evident," observed the anonymous compiler. The collection included an advertisement for W. Lacy of Bartlett Buildings, Holborn, who offered "ASTRONOMICAL and ASTROLOGICAL Demonstrations" for ladies and gentlemen, including the drawing-up of nativities. Lacy would show "how and at what time any animal or plant is under the celestial rays, which is sufficient to convince unbelievers that astrology is not a vain opinion (as some think)." An inventor as well as a seer, Lacy had already announced his "new invented astronomical machines" in the *St. James's Chronicle*, a newspaper for the elite. More traditional in her approach was "Mrs. Corbyn from Germany," who "undertakes to answer all lawful questions in Astrology, in a very particular manner." From nine in the morning to nine at night, she was available at her home in Stanhope Street, Clare Market, where she would "give an account of absent persons either by sea or land." Clearly, her customers included the wives and sweethearts of military and naval personnel. Far more impressive international credentials were presented by Mrs Edwards, who "in Hungary, Russia, China, and Tartary, has studied the abstruse and occult sciences, under the most learned SAGES, AUGURS, ASTRONOMERS and SOOTHSAYERS." She was willing to advise ladies on "all ADMISSIBLE QUESTIONS IN ASTROLOGY" from 10 a.m. to 9 p.m., at 22 Crown Court, Russell Street, near the seedy but popular Covent Garden market.[20]

The use of advertising demonstrates that these astrologers did not simply depend on neighbourhood connections or verbal recommendations in order to raise business. None of them was linked to an almanac or had been apprenticed to a famous astrologer. Two of them were women. These facts provide a contrast with the previous century, when the astrologers whose names appeared in print advertisements were almost without exception men, and most were almanac compilers. No self-respecting English astrologer of the seventeenth century, moreover, would have claimed to have studied abroad (especially in Catholic lands), and they were more likely to design talismans than machines. The celestial science was becoming more cosmopolitan as well as more competitive and up to date in its publicity.

A sign of this trend was the successful breach of the Stationers' Company's monopoly on astrological publishing. Until 1775, the almanac trade remained firmly in the hands of the Company, which continued to exploit it in the old-fashioned way, by strictly controlling the compilation, printing, distribution and sales of its most lucrative wares. The annual profits from almanac sales had risen from a few hundred pounds in the early eighteenth century to around £2,000 in the last decades of the century. In 1775, the Company was stunned when the Court of Common Pleas ruled that it did not have an exclusive right over the printing of almanacs. Following this legal setback, it failed in its attempt to persuade Parliament to limit the damage by allowing no further almanac publishers, although it managed to raise the stamp tax on paper so as to discourage further competition.[21]

The Company also responded to the loss of its privileges in more positive ways. Almost at once, it increased the level of advertising for its almanacs in newspapers. After 1786, the Company paid Charles Hutton, a respected professor of mathematics at the Royal Military Academy, Woolwich, to compile the astronomical information for its almanacs, at a handsome annual salary of 130 guineas.[22] The same almanac titles, however, remained in circulation throughout the late eighteenth century, although some of them were not particularly popular. Among the dozen or so book almanacs published by the Company in this period, only one was extending its sales and making a healthy profit: *Vox Stellarum*, first compiled by Francis Moore and later famous as *Old Moore's Almanac*. Since at least 1768, *Vox Stellarum* had been selling far more copies than all the other book almanacs combined. In 1800, for example, it reached sales of almost 340,000, compared to 71,000 for its competitors. The steady rise of *Vox Stellarum* occurred in spite of inflation which drove up the cost of a copy from 9 pence in 1781 to 16 pence in 1798.

Why was *Vox Stellarum* a runaway bestseller among late eighteenth-century almanacs? While its rivals had been largely purged of astrological or occult material, and filled instead with puzzles, poetry or general information, *Vox Stellarum* remained a traditional source of predictions and was "profound in occult science," as William Hone later wrote, disparagingly.[23] Every issue contained planetary directions, short prognostications, a table showing "The Dominion of the Moon in Man's Body," essays on the main events of the upcoming year (often supported by quotations from Nostradamus) and "An Hieroglyphic, alluding to these present Times," offering what amounted to a graphic prophecy. The 1777 volume, for example, contained a depiction of "a City in Flames" and the advice "that Perjury, Rebellion, Treachery, &c. make Nations to mourn, as surely as they do Families or private Persons."[24] Britain was already fighting a rebellion in the American colonies, so this was hardly a revelation, but the promise to divulge secrets through a "Hieroglyphic" doubtless added to the mysterious allure of the almanac.

Vox Stellarum was compiled by a genuine astrologer, Henry Andrews, who was paid a measly £20 for his work in 1800, and according to his son never received more than £25. A pirated version of his famous almanac appeared for a few years after 1789, which further testifies to its success. The Stationers' Company was not eager to create competition for Andrews, and when Thomas Jackson of Newcastle, Staffordshire, who styled himself "Student and practticer [*sic*] in Astrology," proposed to them a new almanac containing "Astrological Observations" in 1773, he apparently received no encouragement.[25] *Vox Stellarum* would remain the leading source of astrological predictions until well into the nineteenth century, eliciting scandalized comments from respectable printers and publishers, who denounced the Stationers as "the only Company that gives bread to conjurors."[26]

Who read almanacs in the late eighteenth century? The Stationers' Company itself provided a clue in presenting its complaint against competitors, arguing that their criminal actions would endanger simple rural souls: "as most of the Almanacks are Sold in the Country, Sedition and Scandal will hereafter inflame the Minds of many Persons who now seldom see a News Paper or a Magazine."[27] The snobbish inference is reminiscent of the prosecuting counsel's question at the *Lady Chatterley's Lover* obscenity trial in 1960: "Is it a book that you would even wish your wife or your servants to read?" It reveals, however, a fundamental point. The rural market was crucial to almanac sales, as is suggested by the number of provincial newspapers in which the Company advertised its wares after 1774. Country folk may indeed have been the main audience for *Vox Stellarum*, although there is no reason to think that it sold poorly in London or other large towns, as it was also advertised in Manchester, Bristol and Leeds. The Scottish market, however, had been largely abandoned, and advertising space was purchased in only one Aberdeen newspaper.[28] Through almanacs, the commercialized London book trade of the late eighteenth century was reaching into the far corners of the English, if not of the Scottish, realm.

Sentimentality and Terror

Commercialism was not the only force that transformed the occult. The last forty years of the eighteenth century witnessed a cultural trend towards the expression of sentiment in literature and the visual arts. This had its roots in the evangelical revival, as well as in the enlightened validation of natural rather than artificial feelings. The notion that everyone shared the same "sensibility" was built on George Cheyne's studies of the nervous system and David Hartley's theories of human nature. To be sure, one was not supposed to give way to vulgar passions: sensibility was governed by inherent goodness and benevolence. The acceptable sentimental repertoire limited itself to what was noble and uplifting: love of God, family, country, humanity. "*Sentiment*," wrote an anonymous novelist in 1785, "is a refinement of moral feeling, which animates us in performing the dictates of Reason, and introduces many graces and decorums to the great duties of Morality."[29]

Sentimental writing had a connection with mysticism from its inception. Samuel Richardson, author of the novels *Pamela* and *Clarissa*, was a friend of Dr Cheyne and printed works by both William Law and John Byrom. *Clarissa* has even been interpreted as an illustration of Philadelphian principles, with the heroine corresponding to Divine Wisdom, or what Jane Lead called the Virgin Sophia.[30] Pious and sentimental readers could also find much to admire in Henry Brooke's novel of 1766, *The Fool of Quality*. The complicated—indeed, interminable—plot concerns the son of an aristocrat who is separated from his family and raised virtuously in a poor farming household. The rambling storyline is punctuated with uplifting incidents of benevolence, as well as with philosophical, moral and political disquisitions, which reflect Brooke's attachment to the theology of William Law and Jacob Boehme. In one exchange, "the Author" is asked, "Do you think there is any such thing in nature as spirit?" His reply, which would have delighted Law, is: "I know not that there is any such thing in nature as matter." He then elaborates a spiritual version of pantheism: "If one infinite spirit, as is said, fills the universe, all other existence must be but as the space where he essentially abides or exists." The divine spirit alone preserves the continuity of the universe.[31] In spite of his distrust of Boehme, the evangelist John Wesley was so entranced by this novel that he edited a second edition with the assistance of the novelist's nephew, an artist also named Henry Brooke. Wesley omitted "great part of the Mystic Divinity, as it is more philosophical than Scriptural," but he praised the novel because "it continually strikes at the heart."[32]

The characters in sentimental novels are ordinary human beings, but by the 1760s, critics were calling for more otherworldly stuff. William Duff, who when he was not writing about culture served as a Scottish Presbyterian minister, suggested that the creation of "supernatural characters" like witches and fairies comprised "the highest efforts and the most pregnant proofs of truly ORIGINAL GENIUS."[33] It was precisely because they could not be accepted as real that they were so difficult to make convincing. Duff became a great advocate for the poems of Ossian, supposedly written by a Celtic bard but actually composed by the Scottish writer James Macpherson from ancient fragments. Although the poems are full of omens, ghosts and spirits of nature, the central figures in them are human heroes. Macpherson actually took a sceptical view of their occult content, even condemning "the ridiculous notion of second sight."[34]

Reticence about the occult began to change in the 1760s. The sentimental novel was succeeded by the genre known as the Gothic, in which supernatural events were frequent and the reader was induced by them to feel apprehension, fear and even terror rather than doubt or revulsion. The Gothic novel owed its genesis in part to a strange incident of 1762, that of the so-called "Cock Lane Ghost." Elizabeth Parsons, a twelve-year-old girl living in a house in West Smithfield, London, claimed that her room was haunted by the spirit of a former lodger, who communicated through various tappings and scrapings the message that she had been poisoned by her lover. The episode contained several of the main elements of later Gothic fiction, including a young female protagonist whose body became a testing ground for the supernatural as she suffered fits and participated in seances in her bedroom. Methodists, eager for signs of spiritual intervention in human affairs, upheld the girl's testimony, while the general public flocked to the house, seeking edification or simply amusement. More surprisingly, the London literary community became entranced by the goings-on. Samuel Johnson conducted an investigation that produced no sign of the supernatural. His friend the poet, dramatist and sentimental novelist Oliver Goldsmith wrote an account of the affair, debunking the girl's story. Goldsmith acknowledged "the credulity of the vulgar," but claimed that the public had known all along that it was a trick. In the end, Parsons's father, mother and aunt were imprisoned for the imposture, with her father suffering the further indignity of being pilloried.[35]

A century earlier, this would probably have been treated as a case of demonic possession, but by 1762, in London at least, witches were no longer convincing sources of supernatural power. The situation was clearly different in Bristol, where in the same year a case of fits and visions among the three daughters of a local innkeeper led to rumours of witchcraft among the local Methodist community.[36] Popular rather than learned phenomena, ghosts were dramatically interesting to a London public that was used to theatrical representations of wonderful events. The "miraculous" British victories in the Seven Years' War, which was just coming to an end, may have increased the general sensitivity of Londoners to omens and portents. Some, however, were sceptical from the first, including Horace Walpole, son of the former prime minister, who on a visit to Cock Lane was acutely aware of the extent to which the experience resembled a theatre performance. He described it as "not an apparition, but an audition." He half-expected to see "rope dancing between the acts," and he commented wittily that "they told us, as they would at a puppet show, that it [the ghost] would not come that night till seven in the morning."[37]

Two years later, Walpole published *The Castle of Otranto*, the first Gothic novel. In the preface, the author (who initially maintained anonymity) apologized for the occult elements in his medieval Italian tale:

> Miracles, visions, necromancy, dreams, and other preternatural events, are exploded now even from romances. That was not the case when our author wrote; much less when the story itself is supposed to have happened. Belief in every kind of prodigy was so established in those dark ages, that an author would not be faithful to the *manners* of the times, who should omit all mention of them. He is not bound to believe them himself, but he must represent his actors as believing them.[38]

As he claimed to have translated the story from an Italian book found among the papers of a Catholic family, these excuses may have been designed to avert accusations of "popish superstition." The book did so well, however, that Walpole claimed the second edition as his own work. A new preface compared the plot to the work of Shakespeare, a national icon and safely Protestant author, describing the novel as "an attempt to blend two types of romance, the ancient and the modern."[39] Walpole had accomplished a remarkable literary feat: he had made the occult acceptable by "modernizing" it.

Yet the supernatural events of *The Castle of Otranto*—including an enormous helmet that falls from the sky, a walking, talking ancestral portrait and a gigantic foot—are silly enough, even by eighteenth-century standards, to make the reader wonder whether the author took them any more seriously than he did the Cock Lane ghost. They are essentially stage effects, designed to cause wonderment, but not belief, on the part of readers. They remind us of how magic had been kept alive on the English stage, even when it was disappearing from print. The witches and ghosts in Shakespeare's *Macbeth* had been made more striking, although perhaps not any scarier, by William

Davenant's 1664 revisions to the play, which added dialogue, dances and songs.[40] Witches and magicians were also frequently seen in the operas written by George Frideric Handel.[41] These supernatural elements added to the unreal or fairytale quality of the operas; in spite of the complicated machinery of smoke, trap doors and hidden wires deployed to make them astonishing as spectacles, they were not meant to be believed. The occult happenings in *The Castle of Otranto* operate in the same way.

The idea that fear could be a pleasurable emotion was typical of the late eighteenth century; it would not have made any sense to an audience of the mid-seventeenth century. Perhaps this was because the late eighteenth-century public had fewer things to be genuinely afraid of, although that explanation seems dubious. While plague and famine were less threatening, war, disease, infant mortality and sudden death would have seemed just as familiar in 1760 as in 1660. More likely, the public had developed the cultural ability to discern between different types of fear, by separating those that arose from the prospect of actual harm from those that involved no bodily danger. This capacity may have been more pronounced among urban audiences, who were more exposed to the theatre and to novels, than among labouring folk in the countryside. The sense of control over fear was analysed by Anna Laetitia Barbauld in an essay of 1773, "On the Pleasure Derived from Objects of Terror":

> This is the pleasure constantly attached to the excitement of surprise from new and wonderful objects. A strange and unexpected event awakens the mind, and keeps it on the stretch; and where the agency of invisible beings is introduced, of "forms unseen, and mightier far than we," our imagination, darting forth, explores with rapture the new world which is laid open to its view, and rejoices in the expansion of its powers. Passion and fancy co-operating elevate the soul to its highest pitch; and the pain of terror is lost in amazement.[42]

Although Barbauld suggests that these reactions are innate, her examples imply that they have been learned through exposure to "strange and unexpected events."

The pleasure derived from terror may have been particularly acute among women readers. The rising level of female literacy in the eighteenth century spurred the growth of types of publications that were designed, at least in part, to suit the tastes of women, among them Gothic novels.[43] The fear experienced by female characters in these works is often connected with the possibility of rape and the loss of an honourable reputation—a real enough scenario, but one that could create horrified excitement in readers of both sexes, who trusted that deliverance would arrive for the beleaguered heroine in the end. Moreover, by recounting tales that transgressed moral as well as rational boundaries, Gothic novels could be subversive of contemporary gender values, even if they usually returned to stable social and personal relations in the final pages.

Women were prominent among Gothic novelists. The best known of them, Ann Radcliffe, author of the celebrated *Mysteries of Udolpho*, was known for employing the device of "the explained supernatural," where an apparently occult event is ultimately revealed as having natural causes. Her religious background as a rational Unitarian may account for this approach.[44] Nevertheless, Radcliffe acknowledged a spiritual aim in her use of occult themes, even if she almost always debunked them. They stirred up terror, which for her was a sublime emotion, and quite distinct from horror—the former "expands the soul, and awakens the faculties to a high degree of life," while the latter "contracts, freezes and nearly annihilates them."[45] The distinction was shared by other writers, and its existence complicates attempts to interpret, not just Gothic novels, but all writings of the late eighteenth century that refer to supernatural events. Were they meant to be taken as possible, or as ways of "expanding the soul" through exercising the imagination?

The two Gothic writers whose works are most confusing in this respect are William Beckford and Matthew "Monk" Lewis. Younger and wilder than either Walpole or Radcliffe, they treated occult phenomena with an awed reverence that does not allow an easy assessment of how they should be judged. Both were the offspring of Jamaican planter families, whose fortunes were based on the real horror of slavery. One of the richest men in England, Beckford seems never to have regretted the human misery from which his vast wealth was derived. The son of a prominent Tory politician who died when he was ten years old, Beckford was dominated by his mother, whose authority he apparently resented. He was thought to be obsessed with the supernatural from a young age, although the extent of his real interest in magic is questionable.[46] He spent much time in Switzerland and Italy, and is supposed to have been initiated into a Masonic lodge in France. Beckford became known for extravagance, especially after holding a lavish coming-of-age party in 1781 at his estate in Wiltshire, followed by an equally splendid Christmas party for which his country house was decorated by the well-known theatrical designer Philippe Jacques de Loutherbourg. Three years later, he caused a public scandal when he either horsewhipped or sodomized (or both) an aristocratic young man with whom he was enamoured. Forced to go abroad, where his first wife died in childbirth, Beckford was shocked when, against his wishes, the literary scholar Samuel Henley published an English translation of *Vathek*, an "Eastern tale" that Beckford had written in French.

This short novel is an extraordinary performance. Purporting to be a true story from the Abbasid Caliphate, its central character is a young, self-indulgent caliph under the influence of a powerful mother. The latter is an adept in astrology and necromancy, although her spells are parodies of witchcraft and bear little relationship to ritual magic. After renouncing religion and devoting himself to a horrible Giaour or evil spirit, who demands the sacrifice of young boys, Vathek is promised "the diadem of Gian Ben Gian; the talismans of Solomon; and the treasures of the pre-adamite sultans." After various encounters with lustful ghouls and talking fish, as well as a final warning from a good spirit, Vathek enters the palace of Eblis or Satan, where he is shown the talismans, kept within "cabalistic depositaries," and beholds the "pre-adamite" Sultan Soliman himself, tortured for his impiety by a perpetually burning heart. Vathek's mother suffers a similar ghastly fate, while the caliph is merely condemned to an eternity without hope.[47] Shaped by Beckford's own fantasies as well as by travellers' accounts of the Middle East, *Vathek* does not obviously reflect any contemporary strain of occult thinking—indeed, the author would later regret that he knew nothing of actual astrology.[48] Distancing itself from the charge of "superstition" by its Arabian setting, the text is careful to avoid heterodoxy: for example, by pointing out that Soliman is not the same as the biblical king. It answers charges of immorality with a final condemnation of excessive "curiosity." Nonetheless, the novel plays with the notion that magic, or unlimited power, is both unlawful and temptingly real.

For Beckford, the occult represents a full-fledged freedom of the imagination, for which the author himself may long, but which he cannot openly endorse, because it is so dangerous to conventional morality. As already mentioned, the shocking details were the author's own invention, as he was apparently not well informed about occult thinking of any variety. The library at Fonthill Abbey, the vast Gothic pile that he designed to house his fantasies, contained only three alchemical works among the twenty thousand volumes sold at an auction in 1823.[49] Beckford's contemporary Matthew "Monk" Lewis, on the other hand, knew much more about occult practices, and went further in his fiction towards a kind of magical realism. Lewis's mother absconded with a music master when he was a child. By the time he inherited his father's Jamaican plantations in 1812, Lewis had become a critic of slavery, determined to improve the lives of slaves, although not necessarily to free them. His previous life had been marked by privilege as well as by rebelliousness. Lewis first embarked on a diplomatic career, journeying to the German court of Saxe-Weimar-Eisenach in 1792, where he met Goethe.[50] If he was exposed to occult Freemasonry there or in Berlin, it could account for some of the themes in his first novel, *The Monk*, which he published in 1795, at the age of only nineteen.

Rambling and sometimes incoherent, *The Monk* remains a compelling read, combining passionate emotion with diabolism and soft-core pornography.

Lewis had clearly read manuals of ritual magic, like the *Little Key of Solomon*, on which he relied for an extraordinary scene in the novel, where the monk of the title, hoping to violate a lovely young woman, solicits the help of a nun in summoning up Satan:

> She led him through various narrow passages; and on every side as they past along, the beams of the Lamp displayed none but the most revolting objects; Skulls, Bones, Graves, and Images whose eyes seemed to glare on them with horror and surprize. At length they reached a spacious Cavern, whose lofty roof the eye sought in vain to discover . . . She motioned that Ambrosio should be silent, and began the mysterious rites. She drew a circle round him, another round herself, and then taking a small Phial from the Basket, poured a few drops upon the ground before her. She bent over the place, muttered some indistinct sentences, and immediately a pale sulphurous flame arose from the ground.

Eventually, the Devil appears, in the unexpected form of a beautiful young man: "He was perfectly naked: A bright Star sparkled upon his fore-head: Two crimson wings extended themselves from his shoulders; and his silken locks were confined by a band of many-coloured fires, which played around his head."[51] Did the youthful Lewis identify with the handsome Lucifer? Was this winsome Satan the object of demonic, homoerotic desire? Did Lewis mean his readers to sympathize with the lecherous, magic-mad monk? The novel leaves these questions open to interpretation.

Unlike Walpole or Radcliffe or even Beckford, Lewis did not try to distance himself from "superstition." The supernatural is neither written off as a sign of the times nor explained in natural terms, and the objects of magic are not so fantastical as to be unreal, as in *Vathek*. Only the assumed fictitiousness of the narrative separates it from the occult stories found in Ebenezer Sibly's works. At the same time, *The Monk* lacks a redeeming religious vision of any sort. One searches in vain even for the sketchy warning against excessive curiosity that can be found in *Vathek*. Part of the sublime terror evoked by *The Monk* consists of guessing whether the author will himself fall into the pit of occult belief, dragging the unwitting reader along with him. Even at the end of the novel, we cannot be quite sure that he has avoided it. The cautious reader is still expected to arrive at moral judgments about the scenes laid out before him or her, but the text does not provide much assistance. We have begun to move here from the uncertain, self-conscious moral subversion of the Gothic novel to the

Romantic exaltation in freedom from moral constraint, which flourished after 1800. The contrast with the earnestly pious occult literature of previous generations could not be more starkly displayed. It was the heterodoxy and intellectual daring of occult sources, not their longing for respectability, that would most impress the Romantics, from Samuel Taylor Coleridge to Lord Byron and Mary Shelley. The wicked antics of Lewis's Devil-worshipping monk pointed towards the appropriation of occult thinking by a generation of Romantic writers who would employ it to serve their own literary agendas.

Supernatural Spectacles

Lewis was not always so brave in depicting the occult. He followed up the success of *The Monk* by writing a popular play, *The Castle Spectre* (1798), which revolves around a ghost. In a postscript to the printed version of the play, Lewis defended himself against objections that the apparition "ought not to appear, because the belief in Ghosts no longer exists! In my opinion, this is the very reason why she *may* be produced without danger; for there is now no fear of increasing the influence of superstition, or strengthening the prejudices of the weak-minded." Apparitions in a tragedy were as permissible as fairies in a pantomime, or gods and goddesses in a grand ballet.[52] Theatricality became the last line of defence against the accusation that a writer was defying reason—after all, it was just a play, and the ghost a mere trick.

This contention had long provided the basis for fairground conjuring, which did not claim to be actual magic. When Isaac Fawkes, who practised conjuring at the annual London fair known as Bartholomew Fair until his death in 1731, raised up an apple tree that bore ripe apples in less than a minute, it might be a wonderful trick, but it was not designed to evoke belief in magic. Conjurors of the mid-eighteenth century often mixed traditional occult terms with a "modern" scientific vocabulary so as to distinguish what they were doing from necromancy. The French conjuror "Comus," for example, who made periodic visits to London in the 1760s and 1770s, exhibited a "Learned Mermaid," an "Educated Clock" and the principle of "Perpetual Magnetic Motion," all of them impossible but sounding very up to date.[53] The most popular conjuring act of the last quarter of the century was that of the German Philip Breslaw, who obligingly spelled out how his tricks were performed in a pamphlet first printed in 1784. Entitled *Breslaw's Last Legacy; or, The Magical Companion*, it went through twelve editions by 1794, proving that the conjuror's legacy was both enduring and popular. Breslaw denied that his magic had anything to do with "the Black Art," asserting, "Every thing in this book has its rise in nature, consequently is by no means criminal." He was not being entirely truthful. The little book included instructions on how to make an air balloon, examples of legerdemain and "Strange Tricks performed by Electricity," with a bow to "[t]he great Doctor Franklin," but it also contained chapters on the interpretation of dreams (perfectly scriptural, according to Breslaw) and on fortune-telling—presented as an "innocent" diversion, but of dubious legality under the 1736 Witchcraft Act. Equally questionable was Breslaw's claim to use second sight in his performances.[54]

In some conjuring books of this period, the distinction between deception and reality is deliberately obfuscated for commercial purposes. Perhaps the most astonishing example is *The Key of Knowledge, or Universal Conjuror* (1800) by Malcolm Macleod, who was apparently a Doctor of Divinity. The introduction to his work presents a diatribe against "superstitious curiosity," which had led to widespread deception by "sharpers." "By a careful acquaintance with the following treatise," Macleod promises, "the reader will be enabled to develop the arts and methods used in deception by the sons of the occult science, and not only be guarded against their tricks, but may also, by dint of industry, become an adept himself in all the amusements here delineated."[55] Hence one could use Macleod's book not only to discover tricksters, but also to become one. Among the "amusements" he delineated were occult philosophy, consisting mostly of herbal remedies, and astrology. Not surprisingly, Macleod was also the author of a treatise on witchcraft and apparitions, which pretended to doubt their existence but affirmed that in fact spirits walked freely in the material world. Evidently a Scot by origin, Macleod cited numerous supernatural events from Scottish history, including a prophecy of the Apocalypse that he claimed had been found in a Hebridean cave by Samuel Johnson.[56]

The showman who best personifies the confusion of theatrical spectacle with reality in the period is Dr Gustavus Katterfelto. Reportedly the son of a Prussian hussar officer, he appeared around Gloucester in 1777, became a sensation in London in the early 1780s and made several provincial tours, dying at Bedale, Yorkshire, in 1799. Although he specialized in the demonstration of scientific marvels, such as a solar microscope or phosphorus matches, which he falsely claimed to have invented, Katterfelto cultivated the appearance of a magician. He wore a long black cloak and cap, carried a wand and used a black cat to generate electrical sparks. He also did card tricks and sold a patent medicine to cure influenza, which he claimed arose from "insects" in drinking water. His shows were advertised as "WONDERS! WONDERS! WONDERS! And WONDERS!" and he puffed himself up as "the greatest philosopher in this kingdom since Sir Isaac Newton." Audiences were promised that he would "shew his Occult Secrets" along with his famous solar microscope.[57]

The distinction between theatricality and reality was more seriously explored by the artist Philippe Jacques de Loutherbourg, who had turned William Beckford's house into an enchanted Arabian palace at Christmas 1781. Born in Strasbourg and trained as a painter in Paris, Loutherbourg became a highly successful theatrical designer in London during the 1770s. Working for David Garrick at the Drury Lane Theatre, he was known for his striking and often spectacular scenic effects. In *A Christmas Tale* (1773), which dealt, unexpectedly enough, with magicians, Loutherbourg depicted spirits, demons and a rock that split apart to reveal a castle set in a fiery lake. A year later, he designed an ancient Egyptian set for *Sethona*, including a temple of Osiris and mysterious catacombs. The *St. James' Magazine* complained of "the supernatural aid of unnecessary peals of thunder" used in this production.[58] All of this could be dismissed as mere stagecraft, except that Loutherbourg believed in it as a reflection of real magic. As will be seen, he was one of the most ardent devotees of the occult in late eighteenth-century Britain.

When, in February 1781, he opened a spectacle called the *Eidophusikon* at his house in Leicester Square, he did not mean it as an idle amusement. Described as "Moving Pictures" representing "Phoenomena of Nature," it was in fact an animated diorama with stunning sound effects and lighting, showing five land and seascapes. By January 1782, Loutherbourg had added a final extravaganza: "SATAN arraying his TROOPS on the Banks of the FIERY LAKE, with the RAISING of the PALACE of PANDEMONIUM, from MILTON." A harpsichord sonata was provided by Charles Burney, with vocal accompaniment. All this was to be experienced for the handsome price of five shillings. Perhaps "Pandemonium," which involved Beelzebub, Moloch and thousands of demons, proved too frightening: Loutherbourg replaced it in March with a storm and shipwreck, along with four "Transparent Pictures," including one entitled "An Incantation." Nonetheless, when the show reopened in the Strand four years later, "Pandemonium" was back, and it may have remained part of the spectacle until 1800, when the dioramas were destroyed in a fire.[59]

The *Eidophusikon* was one of a number of popular entertainments in the late eighteenth century that astonished audiences through their use of apparently occult effects. These shows not only employed the premise of the Gothic novel, that terror might be pleasurable, they also required a partial suspension of critical inquiry or disbelief. To appreciate the *Eidophusikon*, one had to *imagine* that the scene was real, rather than a picture in a box. This would become the premise for magic-lantern shows that depicted frightening illustrations of ghosts and demons. The first of them, the *Phantoscopia*, opened at the Lyceum, Westminster, in 1795. It was probably a copy of the

Phantasmagoria, a show that was then terrifying Parisian audiences through the back-projection of images of the dead, including some that were cast onto smoke. Towards the end of 1801, an English version of the *Phantasmagoria* opened in London, under the direction of the mysterious Paul de Philipsthal. Having made a reputation for himself in central Europe among audiences that included occult Freemasons, Philipsthal was not reluctant to introduce ritual magic into his shows, including circles, candles, books and talking spirits.[60] The *Phantasmagoria* represented the height of "artificial terror." On the one hand, it could be described as nothing but images painted on glass, projected through a system of lenses onto screens, or perhaps onto smoke, installed in a theatre where the next day one might see jugglers or trained monkeys. On the other hand, it offered a horrifying glimpse into the hidden recesses of the supernatural. Wonders, indeed!

It did not take long for the theatrical suspension of disbelief about the supernatural to become a vehicle for patriotism and imperialism. In 1785, Loutherbourg designed a celestial "Apotheosis of Captain Cook" for the pantomime *Omai*. This popular piece centred on the true story of a Polynesian "prince" who had been brought to England by Cook's second expedition and who became London's favourite "noble savage." Loutherbourg excelled himself in concocting stage effects for Tahitian sorcerers, ghosts and, best of all, a guardian spirit who appeared in a "blazing and liquid fire." The climax of the play witnessed Captain Cook's elevation into heaven by Britannia, a spectacularly patriotic scene that may have been informed by conceptions of symbolic rebirth that Loutherbourg had assimilated from Freemasonry. The "martyred" captain was holding a sextant resembling a Masonic compass.[61] In Loutherbourg's theatrical imagination, and perhaps in that of some members of his audience, Britannia had become a celestial figure, and her global imperial abode an earthly Temple of Solomon.

Spiritual Persons: Behmenists and Swedenborgians

Religion was a vital element in many of the cultural trends that gave rise to the occult revival. Late eighteenth-century England and Scotland were not secular societies, although many religious people were afraid that they were becoming so. As evidence of growing irreligion, the pious often referred to the horrendous argument of the Reverend Conyers Middleton that miracles had ceased with Christ's Apostles, or to the unholy views of David Hume, which denied any instance of the miraculous that could not be proven to violate the laws of nature.[62] These were shockingly rationalist assertions that fed into widespread contemporary anxieties. The evangelical revival of the late eighteenth century, however, was sustained by more varied and complicated emotions than mere anxiety: it also sought to exalt individual spiritual experience. This allowed evangelicals to strike out in unexpected intellectual directions. In some cases, they adopted occult ways of thinking that arose from the tradition of Jacob Boehme or the new teachings of the Swedish baron Emanuel Swedenborg.

The evangelical awakening, of which Methodism was the most significant product, was made possible by a decline in the authority of mainstream Anglicanism. Under the broad toleration of the eighteenth century, religion became more than ever a voluntary activity, an individual choice based on personal commitment, rather than a social or state obligation.[63] Religious fragmentation provided fertile ground for evangelical efforts, but also for occult speculation, which was sustained by the evangelical insistence on supernatural intervention. Methodists emphasized human perfectionism, a concept drawn from seventeenth-century mystical thought and favourable to occult interpretations, especially Behmenism. For his own part, John Wesley firmly insisted that the early Methodists "could never swallow . . . Jacob Behmen, although they often advised with one that did [i.e. William Law]."[64] It would be a mistake, however, to consider Methodism, even in its initial phases, as a unified movement under Wesley's direction. In fact, as David Hempton has stressed, it was from the first "a religion of the people," based on local communities of believers, who might follow diverse spiritual directions.[65]

Wesley was himself accused of every manner of credulous belief. The bookseller James Lackington, an apostate from Methodism, vilified him as "a dupe and a rank enthusiast . . . [a] believer in dreams, visions, immediate revelations, miraculous cures, witchcraft, and many other ridiculous absurdities."[66] Lackington contemptuously compared Wesley's *Primitive Physic*, a collection of mostly harmless homeopathic remedies, with the rather disgusting cures used by the Franciscan monks of Uruguay, according to an account by the French occult writer the Abbé Antoine-Joseph Pernety. This was a multiple insult, implying that Wesley was as "superstitious" as a Catholic monk and as credulous as a notorious occultist.[67] However it was intended, the accusation was overblown. Wesley believed in many supernatural things, but he was not gullible, and he usually demanded evidence for wondrous claims.

Like Joseph Glanvill, for example, he was convinced that empirical verification of the reality of apparitions would provide an impregnable bulwark for Christian faith against sceptics: "they know . . . that if but one account of the intercourse of men with separate spirits be admitted, their whole castle in the air (Deism, Atheism, Materialism), falls to the ground." Searching for such proof, Wesley copied into his journal for 1768 a long account by a young

Methodist woman of Gateshead, Northumberland, Elizabeth Hobson, who claimed to have been able to see ghosts from an early age. Wesley must have been pleased by her affirmation that the dead displayed their own fate in the form of the illumination they carried about them: "I observed all little children, and many grown persons, had a bright, glorious light round them; but many had a gloomy, dismal light, and a dusky cloud over them." The Methodist acceptance of the innocence of children is balanced in Hobson's testimony by harsh judgments reserved for adults. Later, she would have premonitions of the deaths of a wicked lodger and a beloved uncle, and would be visited by a drowned neighbour as well as by a brother lost at sea. Most of Hobson's stories, however, concerned nocturnal appearances by the ghost of her grandfather, who urged her to pursue the inheritance of his house in Durham. She describes him as "an exceeding wicked man," and his spirit frequently pulled the bedclothes off her, allowing the interpretation that she feared being sexually molested by him. Wesley did not believe she could have invented it all. Samuel Johnson, who discussed the tale in London ten years later, was not so convinced, although he felt the question of ghosts remained "undecided."[68]

Methodists around England followed Wesley's lead in championing those who reported supernatural occurrences, such as the Cock Lane ghost, the Lamb Inn bewitchment or the Yatton demoniac. The last of these cases involved George Lukins, a resident of Yatton in Somerset, who after collapsing during a drunken revel at Christmas 1769 began to experience hysterical fits. Believing himself to be bewitched, Lukins received treatment from several cunning folk, which did little good. Eventually, the fits subsided, but they returned in 1787, at which point he claimed to be possessed by seven devils. Only the prayers of seven ministers could cast them out. An Anglican vicar, Joseph Easterbrook, along with six local Methodist ministers, took up the challenge, and the devils duly fled from Lukins.[69] A report in the *Bristol Gazette*, however, brought the matter to public attention, and Lukins was denounced as an impostor, first in a letter to the newspapers, then in a pamphlet authored by a local surgeon.

Although the Yatton demoniac would later be cited as evidence of Methodist credulity concerning supernatural happenings, the circumstances were complicated. No evidence was produced to show that Lukins was pretending; rather, he seems genuinely to have suffered from a disorder that made him speak and sing in the Devil's voice. A writer to the *Bristol Gazette* called it a "most singular case of perverted reason and bodily suffering," which sounds accurate. Reverend Easterbrook, who was not a Methodist, defended Lukins from the charge of imposture, stating that his own "desire ha[d] been to investigate the Truth."[70] His sceptical antagonist the local surgeon, on the other hand, reached a high pitch of Nonconformist religious fervour in denouncing "this disgraceful ignorance," imploring his readers to "[p]ull down the Hierarchy, suffer the heavenly Doctrines of the Gospel, as a burning and shining light, to illumine the inhabitants of this Isle!"[71] One may wonder who the real enthusiast was in this debate.

Belief in spirits was widespread among the English populace, so the Methodist openness to instances of apparitions or bewitchment may reflect nothing more than the broad popular basis of the movement. Like the French Prophets, moreover, some evangelicals accepted spirit possession that was non-demonic. The most shocking examples of this were the followers of Ann Lee, the prophetess from Manchester whose visions gave rise to the Shaker movement. While it is hard to find any trace of traditional occult thinking among her admirers, they certainly saw benevolent spirits as operating within the world.[72] Other evangelicals derived a similar conviction from more established occult sources. For them, it was not ghost stories or demoniacs that led towards "Mystical Divinity"—it was reading Jacob Boehme.

Reading the Theosopher had become much easier due to the publication in 1764 of a two-volume edition of his writings initiated by William Law. This work firmly established Boehme's reputation as an occult philosopher. The first volume contained an anonymous address "to the Earnest Lovers of Wisdom" that underlined Boehme's relationship, not to Christianity, but to ancient pagan wisdom. It was actually written by the lawyer John Sparrow for his 1661 translation of Boehme's *Forty Questions of the Soul*, and it placed the Teutonic Theosopher in the company of alchemists, magicians, Hermeticists and Neoplatonists. Boehme's writings, according to Sparrow, "reach into the deepest Mysteries of Nature, and lead to the attaining of the highest powerful natural Wisdom, such as was among the Philosophers *Hermes Trismegistus, Zoroaster, Pythagoras, Plato* and other deep Men, both ancient and modern, conversant in the Mysteries of Nature." They brought together the astrological, alchemical and magical wisdom of the past:

> These Principles lead to the attaining such Wisdom as was taught in *Egypt*, in all which Learning *Moses* had Skill, to the Wisdom which was taught in *Babylon* among the Caldeans, *Astrologians*, and Wisemen or *Magi*, among whom *Daniel* was educated ... The Ground and Principles in his Writings lead to the attaining the Wisdom of the East, which *Solomon* had ... Such Wisdom as this sees and knows all Mysteries, speaks all Tongues of Men and Angels, that Tongue which *Adam* named all the Creatures by in Paradise, it can also do all Miracles ... That which seems different in the Writings of the profound *magical, mystical, chemic Philosophers*, from that which we find in others, may be reconciled, by considering what this Author teaches.[73]

Any late eighteenth-century reader who was new to these works would have been introduced to them as the pure essence of occult philosophy.

When a third volume appeared in 1772, it added a new dimension to Behmenist thought by reproducing the graphic figures that Law had copied from Freher and J.D. Leuchtner. These included the "Three Tables" with multiple folding parts, "The True Principles of All Things," "The Tree of the Soul" and more than a dozen others.[74] They would become the most recognizable summations of Behmenist doctrine, and were frequently reproduced. Because several of the diagrams resembled celestial charts and contained zodiacal signs, they gave the impression that Boehme was a kind of spiritual astrologer. In fact, while he occasionally used astrological terms, they occurred far less commonly in his works than references to alchemy.

The effects of reading this highly occult edition of Boehme were in some souls immediate and electric. One of those most excited by it was a Lancashire Methodist named Ralph Mather, who sometimes accompanied John Wesley on his travels. In February 1774, a worried Wesley recorded in his journal that "I had much conversation with Ralph Mather, a devoted young man, but almost driven out of his senses by Mystic Divinity. If he escapes out of this specious snare of the devil he will be an instrument of much good." Two weeks later, however, Wesley declared himself "grieved to find that Ralph Mather's falling into Mysticism and Quakerism."[75] Soon after, Mather became a correspondent of the artist Henry Brooke, to whom he sent in November 1775 a remarkable account of "Spiritual Persons" whom he had met around England and Northern Ireland. Under the entry for his home town of Leigh in Lancashire, Mather noted the following: "Near this town Wm. Crompton, farmer; and in it, R. Darwell and young Geo. Darwell, and J. Marsh, poor people, love J. Behmen and W. Law." No doubt his own activities had something to do with the remarkable appeal of Theosophy among the common folk of Leigh. Boehme and Law were also "favorite authors" of an unnamed person in Birmingham. Mather further mentioned on his list the Reverend John Fletcher of Madeley, Shropshire, the Swiss-born cleric whom Wesley regarded as his successor; Francis Okely, Moravian minister of Northampton, who published a life of Boehme in 1780; Thomas Mills, printer of Bristol; and the Owen sisters, schoolteachers at Publow near Bristol. Mills was Ebenezer Sibly's first publisher and later owned a collection of Freher's manuscripts.[76]

Within a few years, Mather had moved far beyond the views of a "tender Methodist." Like Behmenists before him, he lost his belief in hell and thought that God was in all things—the same spiritual pantheism that Warburton had denounced in William Law. Mather's friend Henry Brooke was scandalized by such heterodoxy.[77] By this time, Mather had more worldly concerns as well. He had become the advocate in London for the spinners and weavers of Bolton, which lies about nine miles from his home town. In 1780, he co-authored his first known published work, an appeal to Parliament to alleviate the plight of the cotton-spinners of Lancashire, whose living conditions had worsened as a result of the introduction of machine-spinning during the American War of Independence. The pamphlet proposed a tax on machinery that would allow hand-spinners to compete with the big manufacturers.[78] Mather's social conscience did not mean that he had given up on spirituality—he was already contemplating emigration to the American colonies "on some search of religious Souls among the Dunkards": that is, the German Baptists of western Virginia.[79]

In the mid-1780s, Mather became a follower of the doctrines of Emanuel Swedenborg. With his friend Joseph Whittingham Salmon, a former Methodist preacher, he went on missionary expeditions to London, Salisbury, Liverpool, Manchester and Norwich, preaching the new dispensation. He clearly encountered much criticism of his behaviour, which inspired him to publish a short tract on "*backbiting* and *detraction*" in 1786. Mather became one of the founding members of the New Jerusalem Church, a formal Swedenborgian denomination, which declared its separate status in December 1788. He later served the Church as an ordained minister in Liverpool.[80] He moved to the United States in 1792, settling at Germantown near Philadelphia, where he founded a Swedenborgian congregation. Mather played a role in encouraging Robert Carter, one of the wealthiest tobacco planters in Virginia and a convert to Swedenborgianism, to free 452 of his slaves—the largest voluntary manumission in North American history. After 1799, Mather was pastor of the Baltimore congregation where Carter worshipped.[81]

Because he never wrote down anything about them, the role of the occult in Mather's religious opinions is hard to judge. Nevertheless, the two biggest influences on him seem to have been the recent edition of Boehme and the writings of Swedenborg. The first was presented as a collection of occult texts; the second particularly attracted those already familiar with occult thinking. Mather's passage from Methodism to Swedenborgianism via Behmenism was not unique. James Lackington noted after Wesley's death in 1791 that "the *Swedenborgians*, or *New Jerusalemists*, are gaining ground very fast: many of the methodists are already gone over to their party; many more will now, undoubtedly, follow."[82] He was not entirely wrong about this, although he overstated the case. Swedenborg's doctrines would attract many of those who have already been named in this chapter, including Ebenezer Sibly, Philippe Jacques de Loutherbourg and the irrepressible occult Freemason Antoine-Joseph Pernety. For those obsessed with "Mystic Divinity," Swedenborg was indeed a godsend.

The Swedish baron, born in the year of the Glorious Revolution, lived much of his life in England, and experienced his "vocational visions" in London in 1744–5. Prior to that time, he had been known as a geologist, a physiologist and a pioneer of atomic theory: in short, a paragon of the Enlightenment. His scientific writings, however, rejected mechanistic explanations and identified primal energy as the motivating force of an organic universe. He also longed for an intuitive knowledge that would provide insight into the connection between the physical and spiritual worlds. By the 1740s, he was recording dreams in which he conversed with angels. Sadly, the charming story that he was dining at a London inn when an angel sitting in the corner of the room told him not to think so much about food is apocryphal, but he did begin to experience daytime visions in the mid-1740s, which led him to formulate new religious ideas. He upheld an absolute human freedom maintained by divine love, the existence of multiple heavens and hells, conjugal relations among the souls of the departed and the presence of alien beings on other planets, who were kind enough to visit him in order to explain themselves. Although he drew freely on Neoplatonism, observing a material world infused by benign spirits, Swedenborg claimed never to have read Boehme. Remaining a member of the Lutheran Church until he died in London in 1772, Swedenborg had no intention of founding a separate denomination to uphold his doctrines.[83]

Swedenborg's writings, which only gradually appeared in print, are best regarded as a collection of visionary insights from which his early supporters, most of them fixated on their own spiritual journeys, drew messages that suited their personal objectives. Only after the foundation of the New Jerusalem Church did this spiritual liberty begin to diminish, although the tendency for followers to make their own interpretations was never fully extinguished. Early Swedenborgians might therefore differ fundamentally from "the Assessor," as he was called, on specific matters. A good example is the issue of magic, which Swedenborg associated with Satanic devices or the false religion of the Egyptians, and whose practices he absolutely rejected as "profane abuses of the divine order."[84] His followers, however, were often drawn to magic, both natural and supernatural, because they tended to mix extraneous elements, like Behmenism, with Swedenborg's teachings. In their minds at least, there was no essential contradiction between the baron's scientific inclinations and astrology, alchemy or even necromancy.

Swedenborgian principles had a powerful impact on the development of European Freemasonry. In 1800, Ralph Mather travelled from Philadelphia to Paris, where he met Benedict Chastanier, a French-speaking Swedenborgian and long-time resident of London. Chastanier advocated the creation of a specifically Swedenborgian type of Masonry that would include the study of occult science. What the two men discussed in Paris is unknown.[85] Mather may not have shared Chastanier's enthusiasms, but few Swedenborgians would have been ignorant of recent occult developments in Masonry, which should be considered as another of the underlying causes of the English occult revival.

Occult Freemasonry

In 1771, the artist Joseph Wright of Derby painted an alchemist kneeling in pious supplication before a glowing retort. The figure gestures under a vaulted ceiling, amid the collected paraphernalia of a laboratory, with two admiring assistants behind him and a glowing moon shining through a window. The laborious title Wright gave to this painting was "The Alchymist, in Search of the Philosopher's Stone, Discovers Phosphorus, and Prays For the Successful Conclusion of his Operation, As Was the Custom of the Ancient Chymical Astrologers." It is one of the few positive depictions of an alchemist in European art. A tradition of painting alchemists as hopeless dreamers, bent on a ruinous quest, had begun in the southern Netherlands in the sixteenth century, and was carried on by Dutch painters like Adrian van Ostade, David Teniers and Jan Steen. Other than illustrations to spagyric texts, no precedent existed for a triumphant portrayal of the search for the Philosopher's Stone. Yet Wright's painting was executed at a time when English alchemy was considered to be moribund, which explains the reference to "Ancient Chymical Astrologers" in its title. Besides, the painter is more generally associated with works—"The Air Pump," "The Orrery"—that illustrate the spread of Newtonian science. Why on earth would he want to glorify an alchemist?

Interest in alchemy had certainly waned in mid-eighteenth-century England, but it never entirely disappeared. The 1740s, a decade marked by war and political upheavals, produced a brief flurry of fresh interest in it. A recent German anthology of alchemical texts was translated and published in 1744 under the title *Hermippus Redivivus*. It was reprinted five times in three separate editions, the last version appearing in the same year as Wright's painting.[86] The republication of another German work on alchemy, *An Apology for the Hermetic Sciences*, prompted a review in a fashionable magazine, *The Museum*, in 1747. The reviewer—probably the sentimental poet and physician Mark Akenside—admitted that the book was "very well calculated to possess the minds of young students with a high opinion of this Art, and to soften if not obliterate the Prejudices which Men of riper Years and more mature Judgment, have unwarily entertained against the Hermetic science."[87] Evidently, Newtonianism had not killed off alchemy entirely, although its occasional infusions of life came mainly from Germany.

Joseph Wright's papers point to the involvement of his friend the surveyor and artist Peter Perez Burdett in the creation of "The Alchymist." An ink-and-wash study for the painting exists on the back of a letter from Burdett. While he confessed himself "a stranger" to the subject matter, Wright's friend was clearly interested in the painting.[88] Burdett is the figure shown taking notes in Wright's famous "Orrery" painting. The older man standing next to him is Washington Shirley, Earl Ferrers, a Freemason who served as grand master of the Grand Lodge in 1762–4. Burdett lived with the earl and was doubtless also a Freemason. His interest in an image of alchemy may therefore be seen as part of a long tradition within the Craft. It may have had a more commercial motivation as well. A clue to this aspect of the painting's origins is provided by a trip made in 1771 by the celebrated Chevalier d'Eon, an eccentric French nobleman who habitually dressed as a woman and who also resided with Earl Ferrers. He accompanied the mentally unstable Ludwig IX, landgrave of Hesse-Darmstadt, on a visit to Burdett and Wright's home town of Derby, but they left the next day for Liverpool, where the two Englishmen had recently moved.[89] These eccentric foreigners, both Freemasons, may have been seeking Wright's painting. Was the landgrave, famously besotted by alchemy, the intended purchaser? If so, he did not actually buy it, as it remained in Wright's studio until the painter's death.

Burdett's possible connections with German Freemasonry do not end there. Three years later, he travelled to Karlsruhe to become surveyor to the margrave, Karl Friedrich of Baden-Durlach, an enlightened ruler and dedicated Freemason who was brother-in-law to the landgrave of Hesse-Darmstadt.[90] Burdett described Baden in a letter to his friend Benjamin Franklin as "this delicious philosophical retreat," inviting the American scientist to join him there. In 1777, despite his reservations about American independence, Burdett recommended to Franklin the services of Baron Friedrich Wilhelm von Steuben, a Prussian officer who would reform the drill and tactics of the fledgling American patriot army. The baron was an enthusiastic Freemason, who later joined two New York lodges and had a third named after him. Franklin, of course, was one of the most prominent Masons in the colonies.[91]

These are circumstantial links, but they suggest that "The Alchymist" may have had Masonic origins. Such an interpretation would make sense of the three figures in the picture, who are of different ages and may represent the degrees of Entered Apprentice, Fellow Craft and Master Mason. The arched ceiling overhead would stand for the fourth or Royal Arch degree, while within the paned windows can be recognized the outline of Masonic tools, a compass and plumb line. The alchemist's discovery may illuminate even higher degrees.[92] Wright had already painted a canvas entitled "The Philosopher by Lamp Light" that contains three figures, including two searching youths and an older philosopher contemplating human remains (the telltale signs of Hiram's murder). This strange work may have served as an early version of "The Alchymist." Another painting, showing "Miravan, a Young Nobleman of Ingria [*sic*: Izra], Breaking Open the Tomb of his Ancestors," was executed by Wright in 1772. Based on an obscure Orientalist tale, it depicts a scene reminiscent of the discovery of Hiram's tomb. Wright called it "a favourite picture," and although he never sold it, he was confident enough of its success to have an engraving made of it.[93]

The purpose of this detailed investigation is not to uncover the secrets of Wright's paintings, fascinating though they may be, but to point out that links between English and continental Freemasonry were more active than has often been supposed. The tendency to divide late eighteenth-century Masonry into "rational" English or Scottish varieties and "occult" continental strains is misleading, because the two intermingled more often, and with fewer constraints, than is usually realized.[94] Contacts with France, Germany, the Dutch Republic and Sweden brought English and Scottish Freemasons into close relationships with representatives of continental European Masonry. Some British Masons became members of foreign lodges, and brought the ideas of French or German Masonry back to England and Scotland. Conversely, the continental movements were deeply indebted to British influence, and some esoteric strains of Masonry may have begun in Britain. It was a Scot, Andrew Michael Ramsay, called Chevalier Ramsay after his induction into the Order of St Lazare of Jerusalem, who set off the whole chain of inventive fantasy that would lead to Strict Observance, the Avignon Rite and other manifestations of occult Freemasonry. Although esoteric degrees may have existed before his famous "Discours," any discussion of the subject must begin with this remarkable Scotsman.

Ramsay should be regarded as a mystic who opened the door to the occult, but did not walk through it himself. An adherent of Scottish Quietism, he was unconventional enough to write to a friend in 1709 that "I shall embrace you at meeting with all the freedom of a Philadelphian." After his conversion to Roman Catholicism, Ramsay briefly served as tutor to Prince Charles Edward Stuart at Rome, but the Pretender James III thought him "a madd man," and he soon left again for Paris.[95] Among his forms of madness was a conviction that "the great Men of all Times, and of all Places, have the same Ideas of the Divinity, and of Morality."[96] This was the enlightened lesson taught to a young Persian prince in Ramsay's masterpiece, *The Travels of Cyrus*, which appeared in French and English in 1727. Prince Cyrus voyages around the ancient world in search of wisdom, meeting great men of his time, including Pythagoras and the prophet Daniel, both of whom turn out to be mystics. At the work's culmination, Cyrus frees the Jews from bondage and sponsors the rebuilding of Solomon's Temple. The liberation of the Jews by Cyrus became the central myth in the Royal Arch degree of Masonry. The book was an instant sensation, in spite of critics denouncing it as deist, a charge Ramsay vehemently denied. As a result of his fame, Ramsay was invited to England in 1729, where he was initiated into the Grand Lodge and elected a Fellow of the Royal Society.[97]

Ramsay's biggest impact on European Freemasonry came through his "Discourse," written in 1736 and published, in an altered version, the following year. In it, Ramsay calls the world "a great Republic" in which the Masons attempt "to revive and spread those ancient maxims, fixed in the nature of man." They form "a spiritual nation" that will bind those of diverse backgrounds into a new people, cemented "by the bonds of virtue and of science."[98] What more enlightened sentiments could be imagined? Ramsay affirmed the origins of Freemasonry in the ancient mysteries, "the famous celebrations of Ceres at Eleusis . . . as well as those of Isis in Egypt, of Minerva at Athens, of Urania among the Phoenicians and of Diana in Scythia."[99] It was his references to "our ancestors, the Crusaders," however, that drew the most attention. During the Crusades, he maintained, "several Princes, Lords and Citizens . . . engaged themselves by oath to use their talents and their goods to bring architecture back to its primitive institution." This led to a union of the Masonic order with the Knights of St John of Jerusalem. Kings and nobles returning from the Crusades duly set up Masonic lodges in their own countries, starting with the Kilwinning lodge of Scotland, founded in 1286.[100]

Ramsay's "Discours" was designed to welcome men of all social ranks into Freemasonry, but it had the effect of enticing French and German noblemen to join what was now seen as a distinguished fraternity with the pedigree of a knightly order. Although Ramsay had said nothing about adding further degrees or rituals, aristocratic European Masons were eager to distinguish themselves from the common herd by adding to Freemasonry a dazzling variety of new grades. This was already happening in England and Scotland, in circles that were not necessarily aristocratic. The shadowy existence in London of a Masonic order of "Scotch H[ere]d[o]m, or Ancient and Honorable Order of K[ilwin]n[in]g" can be traced through newspaper advertisements dating back as far as 1743. William Mitchell, a Scot living in the Dutch Republic, received a patent from an English grand master in 1750 allowing him to form a lodge of Heredom in The Hague. The original five Heredom lodges, located in and around London, were probably Jacobite associations, within which the exiled Stuarts were regarded as hereditary grand masters. They initiated Masons into mysterious "higher" degrees that conferred priestly or knightly status—the term “Heredom” or “Harodim” may refer to a Temple priest, and masters of the order claimed the title “Sir.”[101] A Scottish version of the rite, known as the “Royal Order” and including both a Heredom and a “Rosy Cross” degree, is known from the 1750s, although it may well have preceded the English lodges.

English and Scottish Masonry, in other words, was moving towards Ramsay’s vision of Christian and hierarchical knighthood just as surely as was French or German Masonry—and, apparently, more rapidly. To be sure, the most astonishing system of Masonic novelty was created outside Britain. This was Strict Observance, concocted around 1754 by the Lusatian nobleman Karl, Baron Hund, a counsellor to the king of Poland. His initiation into a French Jacobite lodge in the early 1740s led Hund to conclude that the Stuart Pretender was the hidden grand master of the whole Masonic Brotherhood. He also reckoned that the Freemasons were descended from the Knights Templar, suppressed by the papacy and the French crown for heresy and necromancy in the early fourteenth century, rather than from the Knights of St John, as Ramsay had suggested. The connection of the Templars with ritual magic was particularly exciting to many German Masons. Hund managed to convince a 1767 Convent of German Masons to adopt Strict Observance, and it remained dominant among lodges in German-speaking lands until it was debunked at the Convent of Wilhelmsbad in 1782. Even after that debacle, the system retained supporters. Throughout its existence, however, Strict Observance had to compete with a number of other rites, including a priestly system that was supported by the ruling family of Sweden and the Order of the Golden or Rosy Cross, which flourished at the Prussian court. The fervent preoccupation with alchemy that accompanied all of these rites was endemic to German Masonry and probably owed little to the inventions of Baron Hund.[102]

In France as well, new versions of Freemasonry appeared that were resolutely Christian and aristocratic. They included the Chapter of Clermont, a Jacobite organization founded in 1754, which had higher “Temple” grades, and the Ordre des Chevaliers Maçons Elus-Coëns de l’Univers, founded around 1760 by the mysterious Martinez de Pasqually, who became known for his fixation with the supernatural. Several of these movements came from southern France, where the authority of the official Grand Orient lodge seems to have been weak. The most innovative of them, from an occult point of view, was the Scots Philosophic Rite of Avignon, initiated by the Abbé Pernety, a runaway Benedictine monk who had served as librarian to Frederick II of Prussia.[103] Pernety was best known for compiling a dictionary of mythic and Hermetic terms, which was essentially a guide to alchemy.[104] Not surprisingly, his lodge would become known for its occult practices. In 1784, Benedict

Chastanier presented a plan for an occult Swedenborgian rite to a Parisian convent of Freemasons. Although it was not adopted, the assembled Brothers declared that the occult sciences "had a striking relationship with Masonic usages, documents, ceremonies, rites and other materials."[105]

None of these movements or trends established itself securely in England or Scotland, but they did have an influence on prominent British Masonic figures. Among them was the printer William Preston, perhaps the most important historian of English Masonry of the late eighteenth century. Born in Edinburgh, Preston had been apprenticed to Thomas Ruddiman, the Jacobite grammarian and printer. He had later been employed in London by another Scot, William Strahan, the king's printer, whose presses he superintended. Preston was initiated in 1763 into a Scots lodge of Antients in the English capital, but he soon joined the Moderns of the Grand Lodge of England.[106] He became famous among Freemasons for an address that he gave at a Grand Gala in 1772, published as *Illustrations of Masonry*. In a second edition three years later, he added considerable amounts of material pertaining to Masonic history. Preston claimed that Masonry was a "progressive science" based on the study of the liberal arts. At the same time, the rites of the Craft corresponded with those of the ancient Egyptians and Druids, as well as with the philosophy of Pythagoras. He affirmed that the grand master of the Knights Templar had supervised the Masons under Henry II, and that they continued under the patronage of the Templars until the end of the twelfth century.[107] The combination of Newtonianism with ideas derived from occult Masonry was typical of Preston's eclectic viewpoint.

Preston rose within English Masonry to the position of assistant secretary to the grand master, but he was apparently dissatisfied with the direction being taken by the Modern Grand Lodge, especially its attempts to impose rules on member lodges. A dispute over whether Masons needed the permission of the Grand Lodge to wear regalia in public led the Lodge of Antiquity, of which Preston was a member, into open secession.[108] It reaffiliated in 1779 with the independent Grand Lodge of York, an archaic institution that had recently been revived, to establish a branch "South of the River Trent." Preston became a leading figure in this breakaway organization, which quickly opened itself to the influence of European Masonry. The first lodge chartered by the "Grand Lodge South of the River Trent" took the title "Perfect Observance." Its members were mostly foreign, and its grand master was the dynamic French engraver Peter Lambert de Lintot. In 1782, Lambert de Lintot successfully petitioned the Scottish Grand Lodge for permission to create a "Rite of Seven Degrees," probably modelled on that of the Chapter of Clermont. It included the stages of Heredom, Knight Templar and "Rose Croix" within the sixth degree, which required alchemical knowledge. Lambert de Lintot was also responsible for designing the symbol of the Perfect Observance Lodge, inspired by Leuchter's illustrations of Boehme—it included magic circles and astrological signs as well as various Masonic emblems.[109]

William Preston must have been aware of the growing occult influence within the new Grand Lodge. His own attitude towards higher degrees may be judged by his service, first as "Scribe Nehemiah" and then as "Joshua" or high priest, in the Supreme Grand Chapter of Royal Arch Masons in 1781–3. He resigned from the latter position, possibly under pressure from the Grand Lodge of England.[110] His apostasy from that organization, however, lasted only a decade, when he decided to return to official Masonry. He brought back with him the concept of a priestly Masonic order, to be titled "the Chapter of Harodim."

Some foreign observers did not think the English would easily adopt the occult predilections of the German Freemasons. The Prussian officer and Freemason Johann Wilhelm von Archenholz, who lived in England in the 1760s and 1770s, was of this opinion. "Magic, contented with exercising its despotism over the ten circles of High Germany," he wrote contemptuously, "has not as yet, by a bold flight, attempted to cross the ocean." If it did, he argued, the results would be "very uncommon," as in England "every thing is in extremes." Nonetheless, he admitted that "the English have a high opinion of the German alchymists," which allows foreign projectors to "dupe them of their guineas." Archenholz also observed that among the Jews of London, who he thought were rightly hated by the English for "roguery," was a man "called Cain Chenul Falk, but better known by the name of Doctor Falkon, who for thirty years has been famous for his cabalistical discoveries." Falk lived in a large house and, according to Archenholz, gave a great deal to the poor—a comment that complicates his otherwise anti-Semitic tone. "It is most probable that he is a very great chymist," proposed the curious traveller, "and that he has, in that occult science, made some extraordinary discoveries, which he does not choose to communicate."[111] Samuel Falk, a German immigrant known as a "Ba'al Shem" or spiritual healer, resided in England for forty years after 1742. He spoke with angels, discovered hidden treasure and treated a number of illustrious non-Jewish patients, including Baron Theodore de Neuhoff, an adventurer who for a few months in 1736 had reigned as elected king of Corsica. Falk is supposed to have had extensive Masonic connections throughout Europe. Archenholz should perhaps have asked himself: in a diverse, commercial society that could maintain Samuel Falk in wealth and security, was it so unlikely that occult Freemasonry would find an audience?

In concluding this chapter, however, we should turn Archenholz's scepticism northwards, and ask why an occult revival was developing in London, Bristol and other English towns, but not, apparently, in Edinburgh or Glasgow. The commercial prospects for publishing works of occult thinking were more limited in Scotland than in England, due in part to competition with the London press. While the sentimental novel made a considerable splash north of the Tweed—the success of Henry Mackenzie, author of *The Man of Feeling*, provides evidence of this—the Gothic genre does not seem to have been as popular, perhaps because Scots still took the Devil seriously. Evangelical religion certainly made inroads in the north, especially through mass revival meetings like the celebrated Cambuslang Rant in 1742, but not on the same scale or with the same intensity as in England. Swedenborgianism gained converts very slowly there. Finally, and most significantly, the dominance of the Moderate Presbyterian connection from the 1740s until the 1780s, within both the universities and the Kirk, meant that any attempt at occult thinking would meet with formidable opposition from a relatively united intellectual establishment, which condemned such wrong-headedness as "superstition" or diabolism.[112] Outside Freemasonry, Scots with an interest in occult matters were likely to feel isolated, so they tended to migrate south or to publish their works in London.

This point should remind us that there was no single British Enlightenment. The English variety had roots in the empirical philosophy of the late seventeenth century, which was established as orthodoxy after 1715. Those who continued to "think for themselves" were often placed in a position of antagonism to what resembled a semi-official English culture. Newton and Locke were firmly rooted national icons, so it was difficult to re-examine their premises without seeming to question the whole basis of post-revolutionary English society. The speculative discussions of science, moral judgment and "common sense" that marked the Scottish Enlightenment were more difficult to initiate in England without inviting the accusation of scepticism or enthusiasm. At the same time, English culture in the late eighteenth century allowed enormous scope to thinking that was on the margins of respectability—so long as it posed no immediate threat to conventional ideas. In part, this reflected an absence of effective means of internal suppression or censorship. England also lacked the structural coherence among academic and clerical institutions that gave unity and direction to Scottish intellectual life. As a result, the Enlightenment that emerged in England during the late eighteenth century was more oppositional, more splintered, more varied and, in some ways, weaker than its Scottish counterpart. On the one hand, it did not generate radical philosophies that supplanted old suppositions; on the other, it permitted the flourishing of a multiplicity of different critical viewpoints, including occult ones. Tolerance of marginal ideas was less likely to happen in the smaller, more homogeneous world of Scottish culture. Yet, as will be seen, no matter how marginal they were, the denizens of the English occult revival showed little intention of actually *opposing* the Enlightenment. On the contrary, they would do their best to *accommodate* it. The next chapter will consider how successful their efforts were.

CHAPTER EIGHT

An Occult Enlightenment?

How did the occult revival relate to the Europe-wide phenomenon known as the Enlightenment? The question is far from a simple one. In some contexts, occult thinking was antipathetic to a movement associated with rationalist or sceptical ideas. In other ways, however, occult thinkers consciously and deliberately attached themselves to the concept of enlightenment, by lavishing praise on scientific advancement and the improvement of modern life. From one perspective, the occult might be seen as an alternative to the Enlightenment, because it was founded on sentiment and personal revelation rather than the application of pure reason. Thus, Joscelyn Goodwin has written of a "Theosophical Enlightenment" that extended from the late eighteenth century to the founding of the Theosophical Society in 1875. On the other hand, the occult could be imagined as part of a "Super-Enlightenment" that elevated human potential and wisdom beyond the limits of rational understanding.[1] While the occult revival encompassed all of these possibilities, its major figures rarely took positions of opposition to the Enlightenment, which they tended to see positively, in terms of continuing intellectual growth. They rejected the complacent notion that England had been enlightened since Newton and had no further need of new ideas, least of all foreign ones. Insofar as we can identify an English Enlightenment in cultural terms, focused on human perfectibility, the occult revival fell in line with it.

Yet how compatible was the occult with science? In England, the late eighteenth century was an age of continuing scientific popularization, but apart from the private researches of Henry Cavendish, published as articles in the *Philosophical Transactions*, it did not produce many dazzling discoveries.[2] It was a period when Joseph Priestley, noted scientist, Unitarian minister and admirer of the writings of David Hartley, could accept the existence of an unseen substance, first postulated by the alchemist J.J. Becher, that was released through combustion: namely, phlogiston. Priestley called phlogiston the "*unknown cause* of certain well-known events," which made it an occult quality. He imagined its importance as equal to that of gravity. Phlogiston might be seen as a spiritual essence—alchemists had long held to the notion that spirits were gaseous—except that Priestley believed matter and spirit to be inseparable, which strengthened his certainty that phlogiston could be measured.[3] Behind Priestley's scientific ideas lay the conviction that a benevolent God produced inexhaustible variety in nature through simple causes. The distance between such an outlook and alchemy was hardly immense.

In Scotland, to be sure, more radical scientific ideas were fermenting, particularly the geologist James Hutton's theory of the age of the earth, which envisioned "no vestige of a beginning,—no prospect of an end."[4] Occult philosophy, dependent on interpretations of the biblical story of creation, was impossible to reconcile with this view. Hutton's friend the great Scottish chemist Joseph Black stated unequivocally that alchemy was no longer part of science. In the lectures that he gave at the University of Glasgow in the 1780s, Black condemned the "Extravagances" of what he called "this Visionary pursuit . . . the Golden Dreams of the Alchymists." He mocked "the Dupes to Alchymy" who "Were quite intoxicated With the prospect of that power, riches, & Grandeur, Which they were at the point of enjoying," but he added: "What is Still more remarkable is that an infatuation so strange & ridiculous Should have prevailed in this enlightened Age." He pointed particularly to the case of Dr James Price, "a Physician of reputation, learning & Worth, in England," who in 1782 had published a pamphlet "in Which he informs us, that in some Experiments he made, he converted Mercury into Gold & Silver." Black regretted that this work "may engage men of Genius & learning into the illusive researches of the Philosophers Stone." While he gave alchemists credit for developing processes that were of benefit to medicine, Black was contemptuous of their practices, pouring special scorn on the "arrogance, Absurdity & profligacy" of Paracelsus.[5]

Hutton was a deist and Joseph Black a Moderate Presbyterian. Neither was likely to be tempted by occult thinking, although Black clearly feared its appeal to others. South of the Tweed, in fact, the scientific commitment to rationalism was at times less rigid. The affair of James Price illustrates a continuing fascination with alchemy among the English scientific establishment. Price was a promising young chemist in 1782. Only twenty-five years old, he had a degree from Magdalen Hall, Oxford, a Fellowship of the Royal Society, the patronage of the noted chemist Richard Kirwan—who supported phlogiston and considered Hutton an atheist—as well as an inheritance from a relative, which had required him to change his name from Higginbotham.[6] In May 1782, at

Stoke near Guildford in Surrey, Price performed a series of experiments with mercury. Using "a certain powder of a deep red colour," he was able to produce small amounts of pure gold, and with a white powder he made silver. Price carried out his first experiments in the presence of a small number of local gentlemen, but his last attempts were made under the scrutiny of three peers (Lords Onslow, Palmerston and King) as well as William Man Godschall, a Fellow of the Royal Society. Price published the results of his work in a pamphlet printed by Oxford University Press, and within a short time received a medical degree from that university, which he publicly attributed to his previous labours in chemistry, rather than to his spagyric discoveries.[7]

By then, Price had become worried by the reaction to his experiments. His former patron Kirwan and other Fellows of the Royal Society were shocked by Price's "charlatanism," as the Society's president, Joseph Banks, reported to his close friend Charles Blagden. A medical doctor, Blagden was at first open-minded, although he reported that Price "must be the highest of chemists or a lunatic." Nonetheless, he blasted the conferral of the Oxford degree as a "disgrace," and soon decided that the experiments were "an imposture." Banks himself remained more equivocal, as he entered into direct communication with Price in the late summer of 1782. The young chemist declared to the president that he had deduced the idea of extracting gold from the experiments of an unnamed friend, who had discovered how to make silver by a similar process. Price refused to reveal the name of his friend or the nature of the two powders. His secrecy concerning these remarkable additives, as well as his inability to reproduce them, aroused the suspicions of reviewers in the press, although they were careful not to reject his claims entirely. By December, Godschall was advising Price either to repeat his experiment in a laboratory that was not his own, or to reveal the secret of the powders. Cornered, Price saw no way out other than to take his life by drinking laurel-water, which he did on 31 July 1783. His unconscious body was discovered two hours later by a fellow physician. Godschall judged him insane, reporting to Banks that his father had suffered from the same malady.[8]

The sad affair of James Price happened at the historical moment when the British colonies in America were being lost and the nation faced defeat at the hands of France. The sense of apprehension at being overtaken by the French in scientific as well as military terms is evident in the correspondence of Joseph Banks. Price had capitalized on it. The noblemen who had observed his experiments were all Whigs and reluctant supporters of peace; they may have seen his processes as a way of salvaging the reputation of Britain through a single remarkable scientific coup. As for Banks, he was a beleaguered president, and in 1782 was marshalling his forces for a fight against the Royal Society's foreign secretary—none other than Charles Hutton, the compiler of almanacs. To win the struggle, Banks had to play his cards carefully. He remained duly cautious about Price, giving the young man ample opportunity to prove himself.

Young though he was, Price knew the game he was playing. By including an account of an experiment by Robert Boyle in the first edition of his pamphlet, he established a direct link with the only member of the Royal Society who had ever had the temerity to publish a paper on alchemy in the *Philosophical Transactions*. Price vaguely acknowledged the resemblance of his work to "passages in ancient chemical writers," without acknowledging that the red and white powders were celebrated among students of the spagyric art.[9] He was also aware that no alchemist had ever fully described the powders, which were usually ascribed to a mysterious friend or benefactor. In short, Price exploited an understanding of alchemy that was already in the minds of his audience. Few of his critics explicitly denied that alchemy was possible; they merely doubted Price's results. It was only in the aftermath of the affair that Joseph Black could look back on it as a final repudiation of alchemy.

Price's story can be compared to the claims of the electrochemists Marvin Fleischmann and Stanley Pons in 1989 to have discovered "cold fission." In both cases, the announcement of experimental success commanded broad media attention, in part because it addressed current anxieties—the failure of the Chernobyl reactor in 1986 had caused public disillusionment with nuclear science. The scientific community demanded further proof, but did not rule out the validity of the claims until it proved impossible to replicate the experiments. That this would be the case with nuclear fission may not be surprising. That it applied in 1782–3 to work on alchemy suggests that the attitude of scientists towards the occult philosophies of the past may have been more ambivalent than is usually recognized. Ambivalence particularly characterized the behaviour of Banks, who will appear repeatedly in this chapter, not as a symbol of enlightened science, but as a colleague and patron of some of the most remarkable occult thinkers in late eighteenth-century England.[10]

The following sections deal with a number of these individuals. We will begin with a comparison of two men with very different occult inclinations: the Swedenborgian clergyman John Clowes and the Neoplatonist Thomas Taylor. They represent not just the diversity of approaches to occult traditions, but also the wide scope of responses to the Enlightenment. Subsequent sections deal with the astrologer Ebenezer Sibly, the alchemist Sigismund Bacstrom and the occult Freemasons, concluding with the career of the great international charlatan Count Cagliostro. The activities of these individuals illustrate a tangled and shifting relationship between enlightened discourse and occult thinking. The result may not have been a steroid-driven "Super-Enlightenment," but it was certainly a dynamic exchange. Shockingly, the occult even began to seem respectable, although insufficiently so to save James Price from exposure and suicide, or Count Cagliostro from humiliation and exile.

The Mystic and the Pagan

The occult revival was not a unified phenomenon. It encompassed too many different points of view for that to be the case. Even within a relatively well-defined group like the Swedenborgians, deep divisions existed on the most fundamental issues, such as eternal punishment. As occult thinking in this period was often personal and individualistic, it might be wondered whether its revival had any intellectual coherence at all. On closer inspection, however, it can be seen that the same issues that had perplexed occult thinkers in the past gave their successors a certain unity of direction in the late eighteenth century. One of those issues was the role of spirits in the natural world.

Two contrasting figures serve as examples of occult thinking on spirits. John Clowes, born in 1743, was the rector of St John's Church in Manchester, which had been founded by John Byrom's son, Edward. Clowes was among a tiny number of Anglican clergymen who adopted the doctrines of Emanuel Swedenborg. He refused to support the move towards an independent Swedenborgian Church, however, and remained a practising minister of the Church of England. Famed for his piety, Clowes was deeply conservative in politics.[11] Living in a part of England that was marked by profound economic, social and religious changes, by the dramatic growth of the cotton industry and a sudden rise in population, Clowes rejected the path taken by Ralph Mather, who preached the doctrines of Swedenborg to labouring folk in the open air and supported the rights of textile-workers.[12] Instead, Clowes cultivated the life of a reclusive mystic. Thomas de Quincey, the future essayist and opium-eater, as a boy knew Clowes well and called him "holy, visionary, apostolic, he could not be treated disrespectfully . . . Assuredly, Mr. Clowes was no trifler, but lived habitually a life of power, though in a world of religious mysticism and apocalyptic visions."[13] Never married, Clowes was petrified of attractive women, and kept around his house images of St John the Baptist, whose saintly features he apparently resembled.

He was no occult enthusiast. He probably never read a line of Paracelsus and would have considered Agrippa diabolical. In fact, he took a dim view of non-religious literature in general. In his manuscript autobiography, Clowes draws attention to his early education at the Salford school directed by the

Reverend John Clayton, an ardent Jacobite. There, he notes with approval, "the young Mind, being instructed in the *Doctrines of the Gospel*, was less exposed to the Danger resulting from the perusal of *Heathen Literature*, & from the *perplexities & Impurities of Heathen Mythology*."[14] Could a less enlightened statement be imagined? The young Clowes's reading list was indeed very religious, although hardly orthodox. It included the mystics William Law, Madame Guyon and Pierre Poiret, the Neoplatonists Henry More and Ralph Cudworth, Jacob Boehme and, most surprisingly, Jane Lead. No wonder Clowes gravitated towards Swedenborg. One morning, he awoke to a feeling of "most delightful Harmony in the Interior of his Mind," which he interpreted as an awareness of "a *Divine Glory*, surpassing all Description . . . in close Connection with that *Divinum Humanum*, or *Divine Humanity*" that he had recognized in Swedenborg's works.[15] This amounts to a Behmenist reading of the baron, who saw himself as specially gifted with insight into the spiritual world but was not always generous in dispensing the visionary benefits of "Divine Humanity" to all.

In several expository pamphlets, Clowes confronted head-on the question of direct contact with spirits, which for many was the most problematic aspect of Swedenborgian theology. He stuck to the idea that everyone had access to the unseen world. In a 1788 tract, Clowes put the following words into the mouth of a supporter of the baron:

> Know, then, Sir, and understand, that according to the Testimony of the sacred Writings, as opened by Baron Swedenborg, every Man hath Communication and Association with the invisible World of Spirits, whether he knows it or not, according to the Nature, Quality, and Measure of his Love, and the Nature, Quality, and Extent of his Wisdom, as grounded in that Love.[16]

This did not mean that every human being was on the same spiritual level. Clowes shared Swedenborg's belief that spirits were differentiated by the degree of love that they manifested in their worldly lives. The afterlife simply eternalized the earthly condition of the human spirit—it was a continuation of the essential state of a spirit, rather than a simple punishment. Clowes preached to his flock at Manchester that "your immortal spirits and their INTERNAL FORMS are in a continual state of change, either to a greater and more infernal deformity, or to a higher and more angelic state of BEAUTY and loveliness."[17] Although the term "INTERNAL FORMS" suggests Neoplatonism, for Clowes not even the forms of spirits were fixed; they matured or became degraded over time. Nonetheless, everyone had constant access to them. In a letter of 1799 to the Swedenborgian printer Robert Hindmarsh, Clowes expressed a belief that many of his sermons were "dictated throughout by spirits, when I have chanced to awake in the course of the night."[18] This went far beyond the cautious theories of More and Cudworth.

Clowes's thinking was certainly mystical, but what made it occult? The answer lies in his approach, not to spiritual experience, but to nature. Mystical thinking focused on the individual's relationship to God; occult thinking sought to bring supernatural power or understanding to bear on nature. In this sense, occult thinking was always a counterpart to natural philosophy or science, even among mystics in the age of the Enlightenment. For all his disdain for "Heathen" literature and secular philosophies, Clowes never turned his back on the natural world. He particularly praised Swedenborg for giving a spiritual account of nature:

> He did not think it the Province of Science to darken the sublime Truths of Theology; and you will therefore always find him referring natural Phænomena to spiritual Agency. He never loses Sight of the close Connection between the two Worlds of Matter and of Spirit; and thus his System opens to the Mind the most edifying Speculations, by teaching it to consider all the visible Universe, with every thing that it contains, as a Theatre and Representation of that invisible World from which it first derived it's [*sic*] Existence, and by Connection with which it continually subsists.[19]

Clowes referred to Swedenborg's theology as "heavenly Science."[20] He was delighted to meet, among the Swedenborgians in London, the mathematical instrument-maker George Adams junior, author of a series of lectures on experimental philosophy that were intended to counter the "destructive ideas of the atheists of France" by vindicating "a DIVINE MIND or WISDOM that hath wrought with a view to certain *ends*."[21] Clowes wanted to grasp that divine wisdom. He actually wrote a book on natural science, supposedly dictated to him by spirits. According to his own account, while riding between York and Hull, "a Book appeared to be presented to his mental eye for perusal entitled *a Work on Science* ... During his Ride, he had an Opportunity of reading the Book attentively through, from Beginning to End." Happily, he was able to write down the chapter titles, and the contents came back to him over the next few years.[22]

Thomas Taylor the Platonist seems the diametrical opposite of Clowes in a number of ways. Born into a Dissenting family in 1758, he was at first intended for the ministry, but his fondness for mathematics, Latin and Greek led him in different directions. He eloped at a young age, causing his wife's family virtually to disinherit her. Taylor was obliged to seek employment, first as a school usher, then as a bank clerk. Keen to make a mark on the world, he designed a "perpetual lamp," supposedly based on ancient designs, which he demonstrated at the Freemason's Tavern. The whole scenario was a cliché of the Enlightenment—an eternal light revealed to the public in a house of Masonic brotherhood—but, unfortunately, the lamp exploded. The incident brought Taylor to public attention nonetheless, and he soon found a patron, the businessman William Meredith, who was willing to support his scholarly endeavours. These included translations of the Platonist philosophers Plotinus and Porphyry, a version of the "Hymns of Orpheus" with a preliminary discourse on Orphic philosophy, and an essay on the mystery cults.[23] Few contemporary writers could be more distant from the mystic Clowes than Taylor, who became known as "the Pagan." While it may not be true that he sacrificed a bull to Zeus in his suburban home, Taylor did come to despise Christian priests, whose characters he described as "consummate arrogance united with a profound ignorance of antient wisdom and blended with matchless hypocrisy and fraud."[24] Clowes would have been horrified.

Taylor was not writing for saints. His audience consisted of sophisticated lovers of antiquity, which they appreciated for its distinctly non-Christian side. The fascination of the English elite with classical art had never been greater than in the 1780s. The Grand Tour to Europe had become a standard element in the education of the well-born and wealthy, and Rome was no longer out of bounds for young Protestant tourists. Ample supplies of money allowed them to buy heaps of classical statuary, cameos, gems, vases—often faked or restored by Roman dealers, but highly desirable nonetheless as status symbols and indicators of educated taste. The Society of Dilettanti, formed in 1732, became the leading club for aristocratic collectors, admirers and promoters of classical art. Connected from the first with Freemasonry and tinged with libertinism, the Dilettanti were drawn towards interpretations of antique art that emphasized the Eleusinian mysteries, symbolic representations of myth and, above all, sex. They were guided by the works of Pierre François Hugues, who called himself the baron d'Hancarville, and who edited a series of lavishly illustrated volumes on Greek vase painting.[25] In a lengthy treatise on Greek art published in 1785, Hancarville argued for a universal system of symbolic representation, diffused through Egypt, Persia, India and Japan as well as the Greco-Roman world. The basic message of this symbolic system, as preserved in the rites of the mystery cults, was the generative power of the supreme deity: in short, divine sex.[26]

Hancarville's confusing symbolic notions were rendered more coherent by Richard Payne Knight in his 1786 study of the ancient worship of Priapus. For Knight, the penis in classical art stood for "the generative or creative powers" and was the basis for interpreting the worldwide system of divine symbols. Like Hancarville, Knight did not hesitate to make comparisons with Hindu or Japanese art, although he regarded Christianity as an enemy to Priapic religion. By maintaining that ancient forms of representation ultimately rested on sex, Knight was launching a thinly veiled attack on the Christian beliefs of his own day. His work was disseminated chiefly among the Dilettanti, who included Sir Joseph Banks. It would have a profound impact on several important connoisseurs of ancient art, among them Charles Townley, whose collection of marble statuary can still be admired at the British Museum.[27]

Thomas Taylor shared Knight's pagan and anti-Christian proclivities, but none of his enthusiasm for "generation." His avowed intention was to revive ancient Platonism, a more respectable intellectual tradition than the worship of Priapus. Like Hancarville, however, Taylor felt that nobody prior to him had succeeded in understanding the ancients. In discussing the meaning of the Eleusinian mysteries, for example, Taylor dismissed Warburton's "malevolent and ignorant aspersions" regarding "this sublime institution."[28] For him, the central point of the mysteries was not the immortality of the soul, but its purification through a separation from the dirt and deadness of matter. Here he parted company with Hancarville and Knight. Far from seeing sex as its foundation, Taylor recognized in Greek religion a celebration of a self-motivated soul "more ancient than body . . . all corporeal motion must be the progeny of soul, and of her inherent energy."[29] This unworldly and ascetic message may have been too esoteric for Freemasons or Dilettanti, but it was sure to attract their attention. Taylor was trying to make ancient religion more philosophically acceptable, by removing its offensive part: the divine phallus. Clowes would surely have approved.

At the same time, Taylor did not confine himself to theory. He concocted an alternative form of religious belief, including a new definition of the occult. In a short work of 1805, entitled "The Platonic Philosopher's Creed," he summed up his belief in a universe that depended on a "divine intellect," within which reside ideas that "are the paradigms or models of every thing which has a perpetual subsistence according to nature." This universe, however, was not one of dead matter; rather, it was a living entity, "a divine animal," containing beings that were themselves little worlds, with a divine intellect, a divine soul and, ultimately, a deified body. Humans had a "gnostic" capacity to unite themselves with the divine intellect, but this was possible only through purification "from the defilements of a mortal nature" and elevation "to the vision of true being." After death, the human soul would pass into other bodies, including those of animals, until eventually it "would be conjoined with the gods."[30]

Taylor's use of language was tortuous. He avoided the word "spirit," which was not part of the Platonic vocabulary that he affected to imitate, but he freely employed the term "soul." He coined the adverb "occultly" to mean "symbolically" or "non-materially." In the story of Proserpine's rape, for example, "the soul's descent, viz. her desertion of a life wholly according to intellect . . . is occultly signified by the separation of Proserpine from Ceres."[31] In his "Creed," Taylor coined the term "the occult" to refer to the non-material causality by which qualities are produced within the divine intellect. He expressed this in a woefully constructed sentence: "number may be considered as subsisting occultly in the monad, and the circle in the centre; this *occult* being the same in each with *causal* subsistence."[32] His understanding of the occult included the process by which the ritually purified soul merged with the godhead, elevating itself above nature.

Although he longed to escape from Christianity into a pagan Neverland, Taylor's principles were strongly marked by Christian influences. His revulsion against materiality seems closer to Christian mysticism than to paganism or even Gnosticism, in which the world is not quite so easy to shake off, and immateriality is more a destiny than a choice. Notions of the essential goodness of "divine intellect," the moral badness of unbridled sexuality and the ultimate happiness of the afterlife keep creeping into his argument, in spite of the ambiguity of his ancient sources. Taylor's Platonic forms or paradigms resemble the angelic spirits invoked by Swedenborg, because they are perfect, and because human souls, weighed down by material deformities, are constantly striving towards them. It would be wrong to call Taylor a Christian, and his absolute rejection of the material universe goes much further than Swedenborg's view of matter as debased spirit. Nonetheless, the distance between Taylor the pagan and the mystic Clowes was not unbridgeable.

In fact, Taylor and Clowes were connected through the sculptor John Flaxman. Taylor gave lectures at Flaxman's house, and the artist's line illustrations of Greek myths were informed by the Platonist's researches. Flaxman, however, was an ardent Swedenborgian, whose attitude towards the baron's writings closely reflected that of his good friend Clowes.[33] In 1814, the sculptor received a letter from the venerable rector of St John's, praising him and his family for "the heavenly Affection with which all of you cherish the Truth of that new & blessed Dispensation, which . . . I have been called upon to patronize & defend."[34] Five years later, Flaxman presented a tablet to the Manchester church commemorating his friend's fifty years of ministry. In it, Clowes is seen pointing the way to heaven for the benefit of a little crowd of well-behaved children. Austere and classical, the tablet depicts a Platonic world of perfect forms.

Flaxman perceived the beliefs of Taylor and Clowes as operative descriptions of the universe. He provided his own judgment on them in the lectures that he delivered at the Royal Academy after 1810. "Beauty," he maintained, "is to be considered as pertaining to two orders of creation—the supernatural and the natural. In the Pagan mythology, the supernatural order consists of superior and inferior divinities, beatified heroes, and purified spirits." According to Flaxman, however, pagan artists could not approach Christian supernaturalism. "The gradations of celestial power and beauty in the orders of angels and archangels, the grandeur and inspiration of prophets . . . and the sanctity of apostles, have produced examples of grace, beauty, and grandeur of character, original in themselves, and not to be found in such variety among the remains of antiquity."[35] For Flaxman, supernatural beauty is the ultimate aim of art.

If Clowes was part of a mystical tradition that drew on older occult ideas, Taylor looked forward to the New Age philosophies of the twentieth century, which seek to revive the spiritual and supernatural wisdom of ancient religions. Some critics recognized the link between Taylor and religious enthusiasm. Horace Walpole offered a scathing, catty assessment of the Platonist's writings in a letter of 1789 to Lady Ossory:

> Taylor's book [*The Philosophical and Mathematical Commentaries of Proclus . . . on the First Book of Euclid's Elements*] was shown to me this summer by one of those wiseacres that call themselves learned men, and who told me it was tremendous. I was neither alarmed nor curious . . . I guess however that the religion this new apostle recommends is, not belief in the pantheon of pagan divinities, but the creed of the philosophers, who really did not believe in their idols, but whose metaphysics were frequently as absurd; and yet this half-witted Taylor prefers them to Bacon and Locke . . . Taylor will have no success, not because nonsense is not suited to making proselytes, witness the Methodists, Moravians, Baron Swetenberg [*sic*] and Louterbourg the painter, but it should not be learned nonsense.[36]

Walpole was correct in predicting that Taylor's works would not attract many readers. He gained only a tiny number of devotees. One of them was the eccentric society painter Richard Cosway, a Swedenborgian who attended Taylor's lectures at Flaxman's house. He was reputed by the satirist "Anthony Pasquin" to have become "an adept in the Orphean Art," which involved the use of magic to control both living and inanimate objects.[37] Whether or not magical power had been Taylor's intention is beside the point; by invoking the supernatural features of ancient paganism, he allowed his audience to make what they wanted of it, even if they violated the austere principles that he endeavoured to inculcate. Like his "perpetual lamp," it seems, Taylor's Platonic philosophy was always dangerously close to blowing up in his face.

The Astrologer: Ebenezer Sibly

Unlike those of Thomas Taylor, the writings of Ebenezer Sibly, which Walpole might have labelled "plain nonsense," sold huge numbers of copies. Sibly was the most successful writer of the English occult revival, and if we wish to understand its relationship to the Enlightenment, he has to be given serious attention.[38] The occult philosophy that is scattered throughout his works was not particularly original or profound. Nonetheless, Sibly was an important intellectual figure for "lowbrow" readers of the middling ranks, whose appetite for his enormous multi-part encyclopaedias seems to have been almost limitless, and who cannot have read far into them without discovering that they were informed by an occult point of view almost as strongly entrenched as those of Clowes and Taylor.

Sibly's career took place amid an upsurge of interest in the principles of astrology, after more than sixty years of comparative neglect. Defeat in the American War of Independence, which shook the confidence of Britons in their own providential destiny, may have had something to do with this. Suddenly, the public wanted to know more about an uncertain future. In 1785, George Mensforth made a pitch to younger audiences in *The Young Student's Guide in Astrology*, a cheaply priced how-to book for beginners that described astrology as "a natural science." Addressing readers who were more familiar with the Bible than with Newton, Mensforth argued that the Copernican system was "more agreeable to nature," and that scriptural descriptions of the sun rising had been designed for "vulgar understandings."[39] Mensforth's pupil Richard Phillips made a brief defence of the art in *The Celestial Science of Astrology Vindicated*. Only eighteen years old at the time, Phillips went on to become an almanac-maker, a wealthy bookseller and a radical London politician, as well as a vegetarian and a denier of the theory of gravity.[40] The rebirth of astrology was further celebrated in *The Astrologer's Magazine*, which appeared in monthly instalments in 1793–4. This extraordinary periodical allowed devotees to compare observations and even to quarrel with each other's interpretations. Ebenezer Sibly was often criticized in its pages.[41]

Like other astrologers of the period, Sibly was a largely self-taught man of humble origins. Born in London in 1751, his father, described as a "mechanic," was a carpenter by trade and a Baptist in religion. Ebenezer's early education was never considered worth mentioning. He moved in the final years of the American War of Independence to the naval town of Portsmouth, where he practised as an astrologer and medical healer among naval officers and local merchants, some of whose portraits adorn his work. In 1784, he left Portsmouth for Bristol. As Ralph Mather had noted, however, Bristol was home to some who held to an "inward" Methodism, inspired by the teachings of William Law and Jacob Boehme. Ebenezer Sibly was associated with one of them, the bookseller Thomas Mills, who published his earliest known work. It was a tribute to a fellow Bristolian and practitioner of astrological medicine, the Quaker doctor John Till Adams, who was apparently Sibly's mentor.[42] Sibly's first major astrological publication, *A Complete Illustration of the Celestial Science of Astrology*, was issued between 1784 and 1788. The initial three parts of the work dealt with astrology, the fourth with apparitions, witchcraft, divination and necromancy. The massive tome contained an unusual astrological exercise that would ensure Sibly's undying fame: the nativity or birth chart of the United States of America, dated 4 July 1776. An online search reveals just how widely this chart is still used today.[43] Sibly was bold enough to publish it right after the end of the war.

He could be daring in part because he did not have to conform to the expectations of patrons. Sibly's works were always published for a broad public, without the support of subscribers. They were written in a chatty, matter-of-fact style that was easy to follow, and they were full of anecdotes. In spite of his breezy literary voice and obvious commercial aspirations, Sibly was a serious student of occult philosophy. He had read widely in alchemy and ritual magic as well as astrology. In the fourth part of his *Celestial Science*, he even ventured to offer a theory of the occult. Employing a distinction that was common among earlier astrologers, he separated astrology, which he called "natural," from magic, which he labelled as diabolical. Both types of occult science operated through spiritual powers that defied human reason, but the former was benign whereas the latter could result in damnation. By the end of the treatise, however, Sibly had confused his categories, and was arguing "that there are two distinct species of magic; one whereof, being inherent in the occult properties of nature, is called *natural magic*; and the other, being obnoxious and contrary to nature, is termed *infernal magic*, because it is accomplished by infernal agency or compact with the devil."[44] Both types of magic depended on the work of spirits. This definition was evidently borrowed from the writings of Agrippa, who exerted a strong influence on the astrologer's imagination.

Sibly's conceptions of the spirit world were derived from Jacob Boehme as well as from "the noble and learned Swedenbourg," whose nativity chart was included in his first major compilation. To this mixture he added dashes of Hermeticism and Neoplatonism (especially the idea of a universal soul), along with thinly disguised bits of the notory or divinatory arts, mostly pinched from

Agrippa. Like Swedenborg, Sibly perceived man as a spirit, moving from worldly constraints towards an angelic state; like Boehme, he saw palpable signs of human divinity in the body as well as in the stars. He divided non-human spirits into three groups, a classification he seems to have invented himself. The first was "*astral spirits*, which belong to this outward world, and are compounded of the elemental quality, having their source from stars." They transmitted astrological influence, offered up the treasures of the earth to alchemical adepts, and facilitated herbal, electrical or magnetic healing. This was an admission of a belief rarely discussed by astrologers: that the stars were inhabited by angels. The second group of spirits was infernal or diabolical, the source of black magic. The third group consisted of the ghosts or apparitions of dead people, which did not seem to have any innate moral qualities at all.[45] By making room for ghosts among the three classes of spirits, Sibly was taking account of the widespread popular acceptance of apparitions, and gesturing towards the preconceptions of his readers. He did not try to make his views on ghosts consistent with Neoplatonic or Swedenborgian concepts of spirits; rather, he addressed the fears and somewhat muddled perceptions of ordinary Anglicans or Methodists of the middling sort.

Seeking an even larger audience for his work, Sibly moved to London soon after the publication of his *Celestial Science*. There he joined his younger brother, Manoah, who had set up in the capital during the late 1770s as an astrological publisher, teacher of Greek and Hebrew, and transcriber of legal proceedings. Manoah Sibly's astrological publications were reprints of classic works, including a collection of nativities by Placidus de Titus, the seventeenth-century Italian astrologer whose claim that the stars foretold the time of a person's death had been revived by John Partridge. For Manoah, these grim forecasts demonstrated "the infallibility of that science."[46] Manoah Sibly would later become a Swedenborgian minister and, curiously enough, head of the Chancery Office at the Bank of England. As a preacher, he seems to have avoided occult matters, unlike so many other Swedenborgians. His didactic and rather boring sermons, delivered before regular New Jerusalem congregations, did not so much as mention astrology.[47] Whether the topic ever came up at the Bank of England is a matter of pure speculation.

Ebenezer followed in his brother's enterprising footsteps by setting up the British Directory Office, a publishing firm, in the printers' quarter near St Paul's. From these premises, and from his house in Upper Titchfield Street, Sibly marketed his "Solar Tincture," a universal medicine based on alchemical and astrological principles. Sibly was determined to connect his work with an expanding consumer market among the middling sort. To do this, he had to reject the assumption that the occult should be kept *secret*. As a result, almost everything in Sibly's writings is open, transparent, simplified, easy to grasp. For example, he put into print the supposedly terrifying (or, to sceptical readers, quite ridiculous) names of demons, derived from handwritten necromantic texts.[48] Agrippa had done the same, but his audience consisted exclusively of learned readers. Sibly was writing for a broader, less erudite public that was ignorant of Latin and unfamiliar with previous occult writings. His big books also came out in instalments, a marketing ploy that appealed to readers of limited means who sought inexpensive sources of encyclopaedic knowledge.

Sibly's endorsement of natural magic and spiritual cures was supposedly upheld by strictly empirical methods. His commercial bravado, therefore, did not undercut his embrace of science. He argued that astrology itself was "a Science which treats of the natural body of Heaven, after the same manner as Geology describes that of the Earth." While his new science of "Uranology" rested on spiritual influence, sympathies and antipathies, we should not underestimate the extent to which Sibly's approach appeared scientific. His *Medical Mirror* contains numerous anatomical diagrams and discussions of the human reproductive system that are surprisingly accurate. Although he subscribed to the opinion that "the vegetative or procreative faculties of women are universally governed by the lunations of the moon," most of his advice on childbirth was straightforward and sensible.[49] He rejected "superstitious" notions, like the idea that a mother's imagination could confer physical characteristics on her unborn child.[50] Sibly's edition of *Culpeper's Herbal* was enlivened by detailed descriptions of the symptoms of illness, including a section on venereal disease that is unjudgmental and unusually sympathetic to sufferers. Sibly was keen to flaunt his medical qualifications, and to cite current scientific writers like Joseph Priestley, Benjamin Franklin or even Joseph Black, whose burning hostility to the occult has already been mentioned here. In *The Key to Physic*, Sibly even takes up controversial scientific positions, espousing a kind of atomism and criticizing the French naturalist Buffon for dismissing the idea of "sensitive plants."[51]

The Natural History was Sibly's primary scientific contribution. It relies heavily on the classifications of the Swedish botanist Linnaeus, which are extended into the domain of animals and human beings. Here, Sibly adopts degrading ethnic aspects of scientific categorization. Africans are described as "crafty, indolent, and careless," American Indians as "obstinate," "Asiatics" as "grave, haughty and covetous," while Europeans are "of gentle manners, acute in judgment, of quick invention, and governed by fixed laws." By linking racial with moral characteristics, Sibly foreshadows later "scientific racism," although he balances this with a Behmenist emphasis on the essential divinity of all humans.[52] In racial matters, Sibly's science was apparently less humane than his mysticism.

Sibly linked himself to the project of enlightenment in other ways as well. His *Celestial Science* was dedicated to the Brotherhood of Freemasons. Sibly had been a Freemason since his days in Portsmouth, and he helped to found a lodge in London in 1789. In dedicating his edition of *Culpeper's Herbal* to a well-known provincial grand master, Thomas Dunckerley, Sibly linked himself with one of the most influential men in the Brotherhood. He did not hesitate to use the language of enlightenment that was so much associated with the Freemasons in an international context. He hoped that "my Masonic Brethren" would find in his work "an ample store of Precepts, whereby the blessings of Health might be universally dispensed, and the happiness of Mankind more permanently secured; to promote which is the leading Feature of masonic Principles." It is startling to note that, only a few pages after this eulogy to the rational improvement of humanity, Sibly opined "that there is indisputably an innate and occult virtue infused into all sublunary things, animal, vegetable, and mineral, by the action of the heavenly bodies."[53] Whether occult virtue promoted or stood in the way of human happiness was not explained. Clearly, however, the good doctor saw no clash between enlightened principles and occult explanations of nature.

When he explained them directly, as opposed to hinting at them in passages that might well be paraphrases of the work of others, Sibly's social views tended to be reformist. His Swedenborgian religious beliefs, for example, led him to oppose slavery, no matter what he wrote elsewhere about race. "Since, then, that we are all derived from one common parent," he wrote, "is it not barbarous and inhuman, to make perpetual slaves of our fellow-creatures, merely because they differ from us in colour, and are less informed in the arts and subtilties of life?"[54] While this statement is doubtless ambiguous (was temporary slavery acceptable?) and somewhat condescending, it would have put him at odds with many of his former neighbours in Bristol, where the slave trade provided a large part of mercantile profits. Sibly could also be broad-minded on issues of gender. Although he presents gender differences as absolute, based on astrology (men were "solar," women "lunar") as well as physiology, this did not prevent him from arguing, like Jacob Boehme, that Adam was both male and female, a concept that had implications for gender equality. Sibly praised the "admirable structure" of the female body, and condemned "the confinement of females," recommending exercise and outdoor activities for women. Unlike other members of the all-male medical profession, he embraced the experiential knowledge of midwives and herbalists.[55]

Ebenezer Sibly's writings brought the secret world of the magical adept before the public gaze, where it took on the sheen of empirical or scientific validity. A key to his success was, paradoxically enough, his appearance of honesty. Sibly may have been an enthusiastic self-promoter who made unbelievable claims, but he was not a con man. His tone was earnest and direct, devoid of allegory or allusion. In his transparency, his preoccupation with science and his desire to classify the whole world in easily understood categories, Sibly was a typical writer of the Enlightenment. Still, we should not place his encyclopaedias of the occult alongside the writings of Edward Gibbon, Adam Smith or Jeremy Bentham. What differentiated Sibly from them was his reinvention of older traditions of magical and mystical thought, and his rejection of whatever challenged them, which he referred to as "abstract reason." Even as he sought to make occult forces visible, he insisted that their operations were hidden, and that even their natural effects "were infinitely beyond our knowledge and comprehension."[56] "Secondary causes" in nature were spiritual phenomena that could not be analysed or even classified. Transparency, in other words, had its limits within the science of Uranology.

Sibly was unusual in attempting to reconcile the astrologer's art with enlightened science, and to separate it from ritual magic. Most of his colleagues were unembarrassed by magical practices. An unidentified astrologer living in the Midlands in the 1760s and 1770s kept a notebook entitled "Theomagia" (shades of John Heydon) that contained not only the nativities of his customers, but also various spells for practical purposes, such as one "to secure a House from theft" by writing talismanic signs and numbers on a piece of paper and burying it. The notebook also includes ritual incantations for summoning spirits. Similarly, the self-styled "Magus" Francis Barrett would later endorse the use of images, seals and talismans that "derive Virtue from the Celestial Bodies."[57] Even Sibly's best-known pupil, John Parkins, who may also have studied with Barrett, relied on selling magical charms. Parkins, a cunning-man from Lincolnshire, marketed "*holy consecrated philosophical lamens, pentacles, papers, writings, amulets, telesmes*, &c.," which he advertised in a series of publications that appeared in the early nineteenth century.[58] The anti-magical reforms of John Gadbury and John Partridge had obviously not touched all those who aspired to read the heavens. What might have earned a powerful rebuke from those long-dead masters of the celestial art passed without much notice in the popularized, frenetically commercial astrology of a later age. In a sense, enlightened tolerance had made the public sphere safer for the magical talismans of Barrett or Parkins.

Some astrologers avoided magic because they were religiously orthodox. After Sibly, the most influential astrological writer of the time was John Worsdale, author of *Genethliacal Astrology* (1798). A devout Protestant, Worsdale equated Hermes Trismegistus with the biblical Joseph, thought Moses had learned astrology from the Egyptians and argued that the celestial science was no more diabolical than studying "the occult principles of the magnet."[59] Worsdale categorically asserted that there was "no such thing as *Chance* in Nature." He shared none of Sibly's confidence in the innate divinity of human beings, or his fascination with the spirit world.[60] Worsdale's piously Christian theory of astrology, based on Ptolemaic rather than Copernican principles, was summed up in a poetic preface to his main work:

> With strong and occult Force, the Pow'rs above,
> Subject the wandering Stars, which always move
> By HIS Decree; from whom they all receive
> Those immense Virtues which they daily give.

This could have been written a century earlier. On the other hand, Worsdale viewed astrology as a progressive science, as the final lines of his poem attest:

> In Spite of Censure, SCIENCE will *advance*;
> Tho' ART has no such FOE as IGNORANCE.[61]

He even used the common Enlightenment comparison of the universe to "a Watch made up of small Wheels, one within another."[62] While his interpretation of occult philosophy was constrained by conventional piety and never as scientifically inclined as that of Sibly, Worsdale was not entirely at odds with the enlightened spirit of his times.

Who read these works on astrology and occult science? And what did they make of them? Lacking much direct evidence, we have to rely on internal clues. Sibly, Barrett, Parkins and Worsdale may have appealed to two types of readers, one general, the other more exclusive. The first type was a Protestant of the middling or labouring ranks, male or female, probably influenced by evangelicalism, who accepted that the supernatural really operated in this world. Literate, but outside the orthodox influence of academic learning, such a person might already be familiar with Culpeper's *Herbal* or with astrological almanacs, and might buy one of Sibly's works for its medical information, or *Genethliacal Astrology* for its handy guidance on reading the stars. Readers of this type were numerous enough to keep Sibly's compendia in print for decades. In industrial Lancashire as late as the 1860s, his medical-astrological books outsold "all other works on the same subjects put together."[63] The second, more exclusive type of reader was a person genuinely intrigued by the occult, perhaps a Swedenborgian or a member of one of the occult intellectual circles that sprang up in late eighteenth-century England. The painter Richard Cosway, for example, owned at least two of Sibly's works.[64] Although these individuals were far fewer in number than the first type of reader, they were enthusiastic consumers of publications like those of Barrett. Through their own activities and writings, they sent further shock waves of renewed life into the hitherto-moribund body of occult philosophy. The galvanizing effect of the occult revival was even successful in reviving alchemy, a subject that, like Uranology, deserves to be drawn out of the shadows and into a critical historical light.

The Alchemist: Sigismund Bacstrom

There can be little debate about the most important alchemist operating in England in the late eighteenth century. His handwritten notes and copies of older alchemical works are strewn throughout great library collections in the English-speaking world, from Glasgow to Los Angeles. Yet we are not certain in what country he was born. His name was Sigismund Bacstrom, which sounds Swedish. So thought the Prussian publicist J.W. von Archenholz, who edited a German version of Bacstrom's only published article in 1802, calling him "an Englishman of Swedish origin."[65] Beyond the name, however, no evidence can be found of a Swedish connection—he wrote in English, German and Dutch, and he used the Dutch digraph "ij" for "y." Bacstrom described his father as the possessor of "great medicinal Arcana" relating to "the quintEssences of Metalls, Minerals, Vegetable and Animal Substances," which suggests that he was both a physician and an alchemist.[66] Born in 1743, young Sigismund studied medicine and chemistry at the University of Strasbourg. This unusual institution had both a Lutheran and a Jesuit college, and it is not clear which one Bacstrom attended, although he seems to have been a Protestant later in life.[67] He made three sea voyages as a surgeon on Dutch ships between 1763 and 1770. Between these journeys, he resided at Amsterdam.

By the time he came to London in 1771, Bacstrom was apparently fluent in English. Hoping to take part in James Cook's second expedition to the Pacific, he addressed a letter to the naturalist Joseph Banks, who had accompanied Cook's first voyage in 1768–71. Pleading his impoverished state, Bacstrom assured Banks of his sailing experience and his ability to trap live birds. In a separate letter, probably written to Banks's associate the Swedish botanist Daniel Solander, Bacstrom suggested that participation in the expedition might "intitle me to more Respect and Encouragement, either here or in Germanij, than any merit of mine own may deserve!"[68] Impressed by his eagerness, Banks engaged him at a generous salary of £100 per year. Soon after, however, Banks withdrew in anger from the Cook expedition, due to disputes over his accommodation, and decided to make a trip with Solander to Iceland and the Faeroe Islands instead. Bacstrom served as secretary to the two celebrated naturalists on this excursion. He later made copies of the notes Solander had taken on the plants of New Zealand, illustrating them with his own watercolours. As Solander was a leading disciple of Carl Linnaeus, whose system of taxonomy he adopted, this would have introduced Bacstrom to the latest methods in botany.[69]

Bacstrom was not commercially minded. A skilled copyist, translator and illustrator, he always depended on wealthy patrons for support. After leaving the service of Banks and Solander in 1775, he attached himself for four years to Captain William Kent, a collector of plant specimens. Between 1780 and 1786, Bacstrom took to the sea again, making four northern voyages to the whale fisheries as a surgeon on merchant ships. Although he found that his captains had "little or no education" and complained about his treatment at their hands, he made use of his experience to write an account of a voyage to the Arctic island of Spitzbergen.[70] Exasperated by the living conditions on whaling ships, Bacstrom turned to the slave trade. He made two personally disastrous expeditions, first to the West African coast and then to Jamaica. On the second voyage, he suffered an attack of blindness, as a result of "an epidemical Distemper, which was among our Slaves." Bacstrom never stated any moral opposition to slavery, but he admitted that he had no wish to engage in further slaving expeditions.[71]

Following his return to England, he wrote again to Banks, offering "to assist a Gentleman to do chemical Experiments . . . I do not mean the Lapis Philosophorum seu potius Insanorum [Stone of the Philosophers or rather of the insane]." This may have been a private joke; it certainly did not signify a distaste for alchemy. Having tried in vain to obtain patronage from Hugh Percy, 2nd duke of Northumberland, "a Lover of Chemical Philosophy," Bacstrom suggested an introduction to Count Cagliostro, the "Egyptian Mason" and alchemist who was visiting England. Banks apparently made some efforts on his behalf, but none proved successful, and Bacstrom considered engaging himself on an expedition to New Holland (Australia), to seek specimens for botanical collectors as well as to search for gold, diamonds and precious stones. He promised Banks that he would keep his discoveries "sub Sigillo Harpocratis [under the seal of Harpocrates, Egyptian god of silence], for my Employers only."[72]

At this low point in his career, Bacstrom was fortunate enough to find a protector—Edward Shute, another "Lover of Chymical Experiments," who gave him an allowance of £150 a year and set him up in a laboratory in the appropriately named Paradise Row, Marylebone, where he was to make medicines. Shute lived in the Inner Temple (although he was not a barrister) and apparently had an interest in Dr Norris's Antinomial Drops, a patent medicine, as a letter of endorsement from him appeared in printed advertisements for that nostrum.[73] By 1789, however, Bacstrom's patron was dead. He and his wife were now reduced to selling their own clothes, and he again begged Banks for support. General Charles Rainsford, a dedicated alchemist who happened to be a distant cousin of Banks, had proposed that a subscription might be raised for Bacstrom among "his chemical friends." Banks contributed five guineas, while the instrument designer and alchemist Peter Woulfe sent another two, but Rainsford did not keep his promise to gather more money.[74]

Happily, Bacstrom was soon after engaged to serve on an expedition to the Pacific, to discover "valuable druggs or natural products." It was funded by the shipowner Theophilus Pritzler, who had visited Bacstrom's laboratory, and William Curtis, a banker, Member of Parliament for the City of London and supporter of the government of William Pitt the younger. The expedition may have had the unstated goal of challenging Spanish territorial claims to the fur-trading area around Nootka Sound on the northwest coast of North America. A naval expedition had been sent out in spring 1791 under the command of Captain George Vancouver, with the intention of settling the Nootka question in favour of British interests. The flotilla of three merchant ships sent out by Curtis and his associates later that year may have been designed to bolster Vancouver's bargaining position with the Spanish, although it was certainly also planned as a scientific voyage. Banks offered to pay Bacstrom for specimens, "sixpence for each species of which there is either flowers or fruits & a shilling when there are both."[75]

The expedition took a bad turn when it reached Nootka Sound, where its commander, Captain William Brown, allowed his men to rob and kill Haida Indians. Bacstrom became disgusted with the captain's violent conduct. Watercolour sketches that he made of Haida chiefs and their families testify to his sympathetic attitude towards them. He opted to jump ship, seeking shelter at the Spanish military settlement. Bacstrom's ultimate intention, however, was to return to Britain, which he attempted first on a Newcastle brig, then on an American ship with French owners that was impounded at Macao by the British, and finally on an ex-East Indiaman with an English captain and a mixed foreign crew. A mutiny on the last of these ships led to Bacstrom's confinement for six months on the French island of Mauritius in 1794.[76]

It was here, in the "Pineapple Canton," that he met the comte de Chazal, who initiated him into the "Société de la R[ose]. Croix," an occult Masonic fraternity that was probably an offshoot of the Chapter of Clermont. Formed around 1740 (although its members claimed that it had originated in 1490), these Rosy Crucians had some remarkable rules according to the various admission certificates found in Bacstrom's papers. Dedicated to "the great work"—namely, alchemy—membership in the Society was to be kept secret. Each initiate was to instruct "one or two persons at most in our Secret Knowledge." Amazingly, "as there is no distinction of Sexes in the Spiritual world . . . our Society does not exclude a worthy woman from being initiated." Although the Society was avowedly Christian and recommended charity to the poor, the initiate who found the secret to making gold was not to donate any money towards the building of churches, chapels or hospitals, "as there are already a sufficient number of such public buildings and institutions." Nor was he or she to "aid or assist or Support with Gold or Silver any Government King or Sovereign (except by paying taxes)," instead leaving public affairs "to the Government of God."[77] The disillusionment of a French aristocrat who had just witnessed the revolution in his own country might be read into these words, although it is possible of course that Bacstrom himself composed them.

Bacstrom finally left Mauritius on an American ship, but an attempt to reach Britain failed when the vessel in which he was travelling was blown by gales to the Virgin Islands. There a kindly British governor befriended him, and paid for his passage back to London, which he reached in July 1795. Having had plenty of time on board various ships to think about occult matters, he came home with his head full of ideas, which he set down in a treatise. This included, among other things, "the curious Scientific Allegories in the Old Testament," and Bacstrom hoped to publish it by subscription. He solicited Banks once again, found thirteen other supporters for the scheme and was even received at the Masonic Lodge of Antients no. 10, "with a View to get Subscribers at the Lodges."[78] In spite of this brief burst of salesmanship, however, it does not seem that the book was ever published.

By 1797, Bacstrom was employed again as an alchemist, but his new patron was more interested in old-fashioned gold-making than in occult philosophy. He was Alexander Tilloch, a Scottish printer resident for the past decade in London. Having invented a process for stereotyping or printing by letterpress plates rather than moveable type, Tilloch had become a very wealthy man. He spent his money on the purchase of a newspaper, *The Star*, as well as on a scientific journal, *The Philosophical Magazine*, which he founded in 1798 "to diffuse Philosophical Knowledge among every Class of Society."[79] Bacstrom's only published article appeared in this periodical. Tilloch was the perfect model of a practical, enlightened businessman of the late eighteenth century, but two details set him apart. First, he was a member of a small Calvinist Church, the Sandemanians, who held to a narrow interpretation of faith that depended on correct judgment; second, he was a committed devotee of the occult sciences.

Both points were duly noted in an obituary that appeared soon after Tilloch's death in 1826. After praising a study of the Apocalypse on which Tilloch had laboured for forty years, the author described his religious views as "what in general estimation would be deemed somewhat singular." With evident embarrassment, the obituarist admitted of his subject that "the occult sciences, in early life, at one time attracted much of his attention," but claimed that "it was not long that he wandered in those visionary regions." Still, "judicial astrology he was never disposed to treat with sovereign contempt."[80] In fact, Tilloch's interest in alchemy lasted until at least 1808, when he was almost fifty years old. Bacstrom initiated him into the Rosy Cross Society, and copied out for him a stunning variety of alchemical tracts.[81] Tilloch was an attentive reader and did not hesitate to make cutting comments on the errors and enthusiastic expressions of other alchemists, including Bacstrom. "These remarks are more fanciful than solid," he noted drily on one recipe, painstakingly reconstructed from a private conversation and transcribed by the assiduous doctor (a title Bacstrom now freely used, although he may not have had an M.D.). Regarding another process, the hard-nosed Tilloch writes: "In the work before us there is no small share of sophistry."[82] As might be imagined, Tilloch was more concerned with how to achieve the goal of alchemy and less fascinated than Bacstrom with obscure philosophical points.

Tilloch did not maintain his partner in luxury. By 1804, Bacstrom was living in Albion Street, a new development south of Commercial Road in the East End of London. He complained to Tilloch that the location of his "hut" was "excessively dirty" and "inaccessible without boots." One experiment "filled our 3 rooms with poisonous vapours, so that we had nearly been all 3—Mrs. B, myself and Alexsen [his assistant]—been suffocated if I had not quickly thrown open all the Windows."[83] As this shows, he did not labour alone, however. While in Tilloch's employ, he had at least three assistants—S.M. Belisario, Mr Hawkins and the unfortunate Captain Alexsen, who almost asphyxiated him. He also records numerous conversations with other local adepts, including Mr R. Ford, Mr Lentz who had lived in New York, Mr Hands and his friend Mr Clerck.[84] Bacstrom knew Ebenezer Sibly, who provided him with transcriptions of alchemical manuscripts and letters between 1789 and 1792. He did not think much of the astrologer's scholarship, as he pointed out a "blunder" in dating one manuscript and a "barbarous translation" in another. Bacstrom also owned three handwritten astrological treatises by Sibly, dating from 1795, which may have been given to him by Tilloch.[85] Unlike his patron, however, he never showed much interest in astrology.

Bacstrom's work depended heavily on processes that had been relayed to him verbally by others. He spent enormous time and effort trying to interpret the recipe confided by John Yardley, a glover and silversmith in Worcester, in a letter of 1716 to Mr Garden, silversmith of London. In 1787–9, Bacstrom made several visits to the Goldsmiths Almshouses in Hackney, where Garden's septuagenarian son lived—having "spent foolishly and without judgment 40,000£ upon the great Secret." The younger Garden insisted that his father had been able to make gold, but Bacstrom still had a number of questions about Yardley's process, which were apparently never resolved.[86] Even more elusive was the recipe of Dr Dippelius, conveyed to Bacstrom by his friend Abraham Gommée, supposedly an alderman of Amsterdam, whose father (allegedly *burgemeester* of the city) had often seen Dippelius transmute mercury into gold. Bacstrom mislaid the paper on which he wrote the recipe, and did not find it again for twenty years.[87] He also exchanged notes on alchemy with his "good friend Baron von Rosenheim," a Viennese aristocrat. For years, Bacstrom laboured in vain to reconstruct the lead-based process of Frederic Lafontaine of Chelsea. This well-connected individual was the son of George I's court painter at Hanover, brother to the court painter at Brunswick (a Freemason, who depicted himself in a series of portraits of members of the local lodge) and uncle of the popular novelist August Lafontaine. As late as 1804, Bacstrom interviewed Mrs Van Hest, a widow living in the Dutch Almshouses near Finsbury Square, whose father, a minister at Ziericksee, had been questioned many years before on suspicion of witchcraft after making various experiments with plants.[88]

The impression given by Bacstrom's manuscripts, therefore, is not that of a recluse working in isolation, but of a sociable man who toiled away at alchemy with the help of many acquaintances and associates. His relationship with written sources was similarly engaged and interactive. He read medieval and early-modern alchemical texts with reverence, awe and excitement, but he never ceased trying to understand them in the context of his philosophical ideas. He did not simply follow recipes: he interpreted them. Bacstrom's own theories were expressed in a set of "Aphorisms" that he wrote down in 1797. They amounted to a Neoplatonic vision of the universe, in which all souls and spirits are part of an *anima mundi* created by God. The omnipresent Soul of the World takes visible form only in fire, but it can become material in "the Stone, or Medicine of the Philosophers." The "Magnet" used to attract the stone is man or, more specifically, "the Dust or *red earth* of Man," which seems to mean either urine or semen, "that precious fluid, wherein dwells the Universal Spirit." From this point, Bacstrom turned to the practical methods of multiplying medicines, including electricity, which will "introduce the Electrical Universal principle, or the Universal Spirit of Nature into the subject by motion."[89] The influence of Dr Franz Anton Mesmer's theory of magnetic healing is evident here.

Bacstrom maintained an interest in contemporary science, even if he did not think much of it. He was concerned, for example, to hear from Miss Ford in November 1808 about a recent newspaper article referring to a lecture at the Royal Society given by Humphry Davy, the greatest public experimenter. It related to the isolation of elements, including metals, from alkaline earth samples through electrolysis. The article suggested that this experiment made possible the *creation* of metals and might give new heart to alchemists, although, as Bacstrom disapprovingly observed, "Modern Chemists exclude themselves for ever by their unbelief and Mockery, and their Experiments will never cause them to discover *that Truth*, which was better known 2000 Years ago, than at present."[90] Was there a note of resentment against Alexander Tilloch in this peevish comment? Bacstrom did not mention that Davy's presentation—the Royal Society's Bakerian Lecture for 1808—had been printed in Tilloch's *Philosophical Magazine*, with the effusive praise of the editor. Within two years, Davy had taken on a youthful assistant in his experiments at the Royal Institution, Michael Faraday, future discoverer of electromagnetism. Like Tilloch, Faraday was a Sandemanian who had worked in the printing trade. As members of the same tiny London congregation, the two men must have known one another.[91] Perhaps Tilloch was moving away from Bacstrom's old-fashioned alchemy, towards the new promise of Davy's modern chemistry, with young Faraday going before him. Whatever the case, nothing more is known about Tilloch's alchemical pursuits after 1808.

As for Bacstrom, to the very end he looked to the past, even if he remained aware of a threatening present. Considering his wide experience of the world and his encounters with imperialism, slavery, the mistreatment of native peoples and global conflict, one might have imagined that his alchemy would be shaped by contemporary political and social problems. In fact, it was almost completely detached from them. This does not mean that alchemy was for him mere escapism, because it required a lot of hard work and provided him with a living. Still, his alchemical quest was unquestionably a romance, a beautiful dream of knowledge, riches and power that remained eternally unfulfilled. He separated this dream from the harsh realities of poverty and exploitation that surrounded him, although of course it was at least in part a reaction to them too. While Bacstrom saw the "great work" as eternal and unchanging, his passionate, uncompromising, wholly transparent and largely self-directed approach to it could only have thrived in the late eighteenth century. The Enlightenment made Sigismund Bacstrom possible, even if he never acknowledged its impact on him.

The last dated entry in Bacstrom's manuscripts is for 8 November 1808. It concerns a conversation with Mr Ford, who believed Humphry Davy's experiments showed the way forward for alchemy. Bacstrom remained unconvinced, asserting that, "against all the Barkers and Deriders, the Truth of the blessed Stone of the earliest Antiquity will stand firm like a Rock, as long as the Earth will endure."[92] To the end, he asserted an intellectual freedom to look back towards verities that were immutable. For the aged voyager, the rock still stood firm.

The Occult Freemasons

Sigismond Bacstrom had little regard for regular Freemasons. "I have found them a set of Trifflers [*sic*]," he complained in the late 1790s, "not a hair better than any other men, perfectly ignorant of Natural Knowledge, for which reason I do not intend to visit their Lodges any more during the remainder of my Life."[93] Above all, they were ignorant of "the Allegory of *King Solomon's Navigation to Ophir* and *King Hiram's Ships*," which according to Bacstrom paralleled the Greek myth of Jason and the Golden Fleece. Both voyages revealed the secret of the Philosopher's Stone. Through his knowledge of alchemy, King Hermes (or Chiram) of the Phoenicians, mistakenly identified as Hiram the architect by the Freemasons, provided the gold that built the Temple of Solomon. Here was the hidden message of Newton's *Chronology*; but the secret was revealed only to the mysterious Rosy Crucians, not to their benighted brethren in the Masonic lodges.[94]

Every occult branch of Freemasonry in the late eighteenth century claimed to have secrets similar to those bestowed upon Bacstrom by the Rosy Crucians. They were passed on by initiation into the higher degrees devised after 1740. Masonic secrets might be expressed in the language of alchemy, but they tended towards spiritual enlightenment rather than gold-making. The nature of that enlightenment was often a combination of Behmenist, Neoplatonic and Hermetic ideas, labelled as "Swedenborgianism." The history of international Freemasonry in the last two decades of the eighteenth century therefore offers a fascinating Europe-wide perspective on the relationship between occult thinking and the Enlightenment. Among the "higher-grade" Freemasons, occult philosophy and science reached a level of respectability that they had never before enjoyed in Britain. This would soon prove problematic, however, because it opened the door to all sorts of impostures and social dangers.

The Knight Templar degrees that were thriving in German, French and other European lodges in the 1770s and 1780s had English and Scottish counterparts as early as the 1740s. In 1783, the successful attempt of Peter Lambert de Lintot, master of the London Lodge of Perfect Observance, to obtain a charter from the Grand Lodge of Scotland for a Rite of Seven Degrees, including Templar grades, marked a new phase in the development of occult Freemasonry in Britain. The Rite comprised three "Lights" or groups of secrets:

the first ("the Law of Moses") was connected with the building of the Temple of Solomon; the second ("the Law of Christ") had to do with the Templar Order and the Crusades; the third ("Nature") focused on the suppression of the Templars by the papacy and on "the Natural Religion," which largely consisted of alchemy. The initiate was to learn about the four elements, "the fluid of the sun that gives life to any thing in being" and the place of the soul in nature. He would then proceed to "Physic, Metaphysiq, Philosophy and Moral," as well as to "the knowledge of the salts of Hermess [i.e. Hermes]," before reaching "the real Philosophical Stone by mathematics, astrology and all the Sciences that proves the real existence of the Eternal being."[95] That the Scottish Grand Lodge did not blink at endorsing this scheme for Hermetic instruction suggests that the existing Heredom rites may not have been far removed from it. The Scots Masons may also have been impressed by the inclusion among the members of Lambert de Lintot's lodge of the duke of Brunswick and the landgrave of Hesse-Cassel, both admitted *in absentia*. It was not until 1788 that the Perfect Observance lodge began initiating English and Irish Brothers. They were mostly men of the middling sort, including a sergeant-major in the Coldstream Guards, an attorney, a button-maker, a victualler and a medical doctor, although the Irish earl of Antrim, protector of the Grand Lodge of Antients, was also initiated.[96]

Lambert de Lintot represented his interpretation of Templar Masonry in six engravings. The simplest two, "Free Masons at Work" and "Free-Masonry Crown'd," show winged cherubs using the tools of the Craft on a symbolic diagram of the heavens and admiring an elaborate tracing board. The diagram, loaded with triangles and numbers, resembles the illustrations to Jacob Boehme's *Works*. The tracing board, representing the Rite of Seven Degrees, displays traditional Masonic symbols as well as alchemical signs. A print of 1787, entitled "Grand Elect," was dedicated to the duke of Cumberland, George III's wayward brother, who was patron of the Grand Chapter of Royal Arch Masons and master of the Grand Lodge. A fourth print, "Night," shows "A Bonfire before the Ruins of H.R.D.M. [HARODIM] Castle," and commemorates the foundation of the Royal Cumberland Freemasons' School in 1788, a charitable institution for the daughters of indigent members of the Craft. The two last prints, dating from 1789, are the most complicated. In "Foundation of the Royal Order of the Free Masons in Palestine A.M. 4037," Lambert de Lintot depicted the murder of Hiram by three apprentices and the scattering of his other apprentices, who brought the message of Masonry to the world. The final engraving was a stunningly elaborate symbolic chart, depicting the grades of the Rite of Seven Degrees on "cubical stones." King Baldwin of Jerusalem appears as the founder of the Order of Harodim (a myth that persists in the so-called Baldwin Rite); next to him are the symbols of the Rose Croix degree. The alchemical aspects of the third "Light" are depicted in a square showing "CHAOS OPEN," along with geometrical shapes, numbers and the inscription "LUX EX TENEBRAS." At the top of the chart appears a bearded King Solomon, who resembles the royal personification of gold in many alchemical texts—this became the floor-cloth design for the Knights of the East and West.[97]

Lambert de Lintot died in the 1790s, leaving an impressive collection of Masonic manuscripts, drawings and jewels. An inventory of these materials is found among the papers of General Charles Rainsford, the commander-in-chief of occult Masonry in late eighteenth-century England.[98] A professional soldier who had witnessed the battles of Fontenoy and Culloden, Rainsford became equerry to George III's brother the duke of Gloucester, with whose patronage he gained a seat in the House of Commons. His friendship with Hugh Percy, 2nd duke of Northumberland, a fellow military officer, led to further Parliamentary service, although the general was not an active politician. The height of Rainsford's military career came in 1776–8, when he was the commissary responsible for moving German troops through the Dutch Republic to the Americas to serve in the War of Independence. The German prince on whom he most relied during this process, Frederick II of Hesse-Cassel, was later initiated into Lambert de Lintot's Perfect Observance lodge, as was the son and heir of Charles, duke of Brunswick, who had also provided soldiers for the expedition. This may not have been a coincidence, since Rainsford clearly knew the lodge's master. After 1778, promotions fell rapidly on Rainsford's head: he became governor of Chester Castle, aide-de-camp to King George III, organizer of the military camps established during the Gordon Riots and commander of the garrison of Gibraltar. He served for decades as deputy lieutenant of the Tower of London, and was buried there after his death in 1809.[99]

Towards the end of his career, Rainsford proudly recorded his progress through the ranks of the army, his Fellowship in the Royal Society, and his membership of the Society of Antiquaries, the Society for Making Discoveries in Africa and the Society for Helping the Poor, along with a bewildering number of Masonic societies: the Rosy Crucians, the Grand Orient at Paris, Pernety's Order of Illuminati of Avignon and the Grand Lodge of England, among others. He was inspector of Masonic lodges "universally" and "Member of 32 Elevations to 7th Degree exclusive," meaning he had been initiated into Lambert de Lintot's Rite.[100] Rainsford also noted his membership of the Exegetical Society of Stockholm, a quasi-Masonic organization founded for the propagation of Swedenborgian doctrines. Its most prominent member was Charles, duke of Södermania, brother of King Gustav III, grand master of the

Strict Observance Rite and later himself to become monarch of Sweden.[101] Rainsford did not record some of the more curious stages in this triumphant progress to enlightenment: how in 1756, for example, he had copied out manuscripts supposedly belonging to John Dee on the conjuration of spirits and the names of angels, then added thirty years later anecdotes about the astrological healer Dr Richard Napier that showed how he was assisted by spirits. Rainsford had encountered more conventional sources of wisdom as well. While travelling through Germany with the duke of Gloucester in 1770, the unmarried Rainsford became enamoured of a woman he called "charming lovable Jeanette," a Jewish Berliner. He asked her to recommend him to "the great Mendelssohn the Philosopher so celebrated and enlightened . . . of whom I would very much like to be the Pupil."[102] He meant Moses Mendelssohn, the renowned scholar of the Haskalah or Jewish Enlightenment. What if Rainsford had become his devotee? Would astrology and magic have figured so largely in his mental framework?

Although Rainsford's correspondence and papers have not survived in their entirety, what is left of them shows that he was in touch with Freemasons throughout Europe. He answered questions about the antiquity of the Craft from the "Écharpes Blanches" (White Sashes) of Paris (probably a branch of the Élus Coens), received Count Grabianka, grand master of the Avignon Masons, when he visited England in 1786, and kept himself informed about the "*Society of Illuminés*," headed by King Frederick William II of Prussia, who "pretend to supernatural Powers, and of bringing Those that are Dead or Alive to whatever Place they chuse to call them."[103] He was equally involved with international Swedenborgianism, receiving reports of the spread of the baron's works in White Russia and reading bitter complaints from Benedict Chastanier about a New Jerusalem Church minister who was "rather a Minister of Belial than a Servant of J.C."[104] Rainsford combined these pursuits with a passion for occult philosophy. A correspondent at Harwich sent him news of his investigations at Algiers into "Cabalistic Magic" and Rosicrucianism. Another forwarded a prophecy received from Hanover, whose author had "intended to write and to publish something about Hyeroglyphics, but was prevented by his death.[105] Ebenezer Sibly gave him a copy of "The Tables of Rotalo," a series of compass-like wheels by which the future could be foretold according to the "Science" of "Cabala." The user was assured that "[f]rom this work Cagliostro learnt his surprising feats." Sibly claimed that he had paid 300 guineas to copy the work, which sounds dubious. "My Brother the Minister"—that is, Manoah Sibly—carried the strange treatise over to Rainsford's house. Like the general, Ebenezer Sibly was a member of the Order of Harodim. An invitation to a 1796 chapter meeting addressed to the astrologer can be found among Rainsford's papers.[106]

Rainsford clearly regarded occult thinking as perfectly compatible with his religious beliefs. Like other Swedenborgians, he accepted the authority of visions, but he recorded only one of his own, which he experienced at London on the morning of 8 May 1786. Before waking, "I had an Information as it were given to me" concerning a Hebrew book. Although he interpreted the vision as relating to the New Testament, his mind was fixed at the time on the Book of Enoch, a "lost book" of the Bible that pertains to wicked angels who mated with human women and sired giants. According to Rainsford, these angels taught "*Magick* & *Incantations*, or, the Art of *Divination*," and became evil spirits.[107] At some point in the late 1780s, he wrote a long letter to Count Grabianka, praising "the doctrine of that great Man, Swedenborg," but adding a further list of spiritual worthies:

> I have employed myself for some time, in studying the Cabala of Fludd . . . who according to my Ideas was the most profound of his time in the true doctrines as well as in the Holy Bible . . . I have also searched in the Mysteries of Masonry . . . I will say nothing of the Science of Cagliostro; because I know nothing either of his Principles, or of his Aim. But I would strongly wish to establish here among the true searchers and Advocates of the sacred Science a Regime that might be able to do Honor to Man and sustain the Cult and Adoration of the Lord.[108]

Rainsford went on to send compliments to Grabianka on the *Fables Egyptiennes* and *Dictionnaire Hermetique*, works written by Antoine-Joseph Pernety. He asked for his own ideas to be passed on to the famous Abbé.

Alchemy remained the general's passion. He was, of course, fascinated by James Price's experiments with "red and white powders" in 1782–3, as were the Écharpes Blanches and the mysterious writer from Harwich.[109] He wondered in a 1785 letter to a Masonic friend whether his etymology of the word "Alchemy" "agrees with any Ideas of your Friend Behmen." Four years later, he received a reply. "I am disposed to believe Jacob Behmen when he says that a Man must be purified into a divine Magus, before he can have such a command over nature as to effect the Philosophical Change," maintained his correspondent.[110] Unfortunately, this learned Freemason did not explain where he had read such an extraordinary passage in Boehme, who generally denied that physical alchemy was possible. Rainsford's own approach to alchemy was summed up in the notebooks that he kept in 1786–7 and that record a series of experiments. Clearly, he was searching for an actual gold-making process, but he also wrote down philosophical quotations from Boehme and Georg von Welling, a Bavarian alchemist of the early eighteenth century.[111] Welling's chief work, *Opus Mago-Cabalisticum et Theosophicum*, was hugely popular in late eighteenth-century Germany—even Goethe used it as the basis for his forays into alchemy. Rainsford eventually had Ebenezer Sibly transcribe an English copy for him.[112]

The general's Behmenist interpretation of alchemy is reflected in a heavily corrected manuscript of 1799 that was put in the same binding as his experimental papers. The work, which does not seem to be in Rainsford's handwriting, describes the divine and androgynous origins of Adam, "the perfect red, passive and Spiritual Earth or vessel." Adam "fell into deep magical Sleep, became thickened in his inward astral elements," which led to his splitting into two genders. Eve, unfortunately, was an "inferior astral and paradysical vessel," who dragged poor Adam down with her. When Adam and Eve admitted "the gross and unharmonized inferior nature and Spiritual fiery Tincture of the Serpent, they were both Tinctured and subdued thereby." To achieve "reunion with God" would require "ascending by the True Jacobs Ladder . . . by the ordained degrees of purifications, to the inmost and uppermost steep [*sic*] where God is." Christ, the Second Adam, came to transmute "this boddy of Earth . . . by the overruling Energy of the Divine omnipotent Tincture of Love."[113] The philosophy and language of the treatise are Behmenist, but, unlike the original Theosopher, the author leaves open a path to practical alchemy (through Christ's "transmuting" of Adam's "red earth"). The references to Jacob's Ladder and to degrees of purification are essentially Masonic. Rainsford may have thought of this philosophy as Swedenborgian, but it bears none of the baron's emphasis on correspondences or visions.

Rainsford's alchemy was supported and assisted by two close friends who were also Freemasons. The first was the Irishman Peter Woulfe, a noted maker of chemical apparatus. Rainsford called him "one of the most able Chemists of the Century, as well as a profound Philosopher." Woulfe was, like his friend, a Fellow of the Royal Society. He gave the Society's prestigious Bakerian Lecture three times and was sent to investigate James Price's alchemical claims in 1783. He was a long-time friend of Sir Joseph Banks, whom he supplied with perfumes, chemicals and bottles for use on the second Cook expedition. Woulfe remained a highly respected figure in chemical circles throughout the late eighteenth century.[114] Rainsford's other alchemical friend was Hugh Percy, who became the 2nd duke of Northumberland in 1786, and whose activities resembled those of his Tudor ancestor, the "Wizard Earl." Percy was a professional soldier, who served in the Seven Years' War and the American War of Independence. During the latter conflict, he gradually came to sympathize with the American patriots. Percy was an amiable, albeit unconventional and extravagant person. Giacomo Casanova met him in Turin in 1762, when young

Baron Warkworth, as Percy then was, tempted the Italian lover's mistress away from him with a promise of 2,000 guineas. Casanova was posing as a "Kabbalist" or magician who could predict the outcome of lotteries through a mathematical system (perhaps he had read the "Tables of Rotalo"), and was contemplating a trip to London. Percy cheerfully gave him a miniature portrait of himself by way of introduction to his mother, the duchess.[115]

In 1785, Percy sent his friend Rainsford an amusing letter, inquiring about his alchemical experiments and sending him the compliments of three house guests at his ancestral home of Alnwick Castle, who were themselves engaged in the purging of lead ore. "I heartily wish you was here to enjoy our Experiments & our Fun," wrote Percy merrily. The group included Louis Dutens, a Huguenot clergyman whom Percy had met in Turin and who became historiographer to King George III, as well as "Mr. Morse," who might be the military engineer Robert Morse. The most unexpected guest was the "venerable Secretary of the Learned Society of Antiquaries," who "promises on this Condition not to trouble you on your first Entrance into that most ancient Society [of alchemists], till [Rainsford answers] any Questions either ordinary or Extraordinary respecting the Runick Medal in his Possession."[116] This can only refer to the Reverend John Brand, recently appointed secretary of the Society of Antiquaries, whose parish was in the gift of the dukes of Northumberland. He later became Percy's secretary and librarian. Brand was best known for reissuing Henry Bourne's *Antiquitates Vulgares*, to which he added his own observations. Although he was no less scathing than his predecessor in condemning "the superstitious Notions and Ceremonies of the People," Brand showed more interest than Bourne in the meticulous chronicling of their details. His participation in Percy's alchemical ventures casts a new light on a sentence that appears in the preface to his reissue of *Popular Antiquites*: "By the chemical Process of Philosophy, even Wisdom may be extracted from the Follies and Superstitions of our Forefathers."[117] Was Brand implying that knowledge of alchemical processes might be enhanced by the investigation of witch beliefs, second sight or "Vulgar Superstitions Concerning the Moon"?

How seriously the alchemical activities of Percy and his guests should be taken is a moot point. The irrepressible Percy once added a cheeky P.S. to a letter to his friend Rainsford, asking, "but where is the gold?"[118] For his own part, Rainsford was wholly dedicated to the spagyric science, as was Peter Woulfe. From all indications, they made little attempt to disguise their passion for it. Unlike the Newtonians of the first half of the century, they did not fear the consequences of being perceived as occult thinkers. Neither of them can be described as marginal. Remarkably, by the 1780s, the occult sciences were beginning to seem respectable, at least as a private pursuit. For a learned person to publish works on alchemy or astrology or ritual magic was to run a risk, as the affair of James Price demonstrated, but to study them privately was no longer something of which to be ashamed.

This shift may be linked to the diffuse, unfocused and broadly tolerant nature of the English Enlightenment. If the effects of a dominant strain of enlightened thought had been felt more strongly in England, perhaps Rainsford, Woulfe, Lambert de Lintot and Sibly would have been held to stricter account. Perhaps an English version of Immanuel Kant would have arisen, a philosopher who took Swedenborg's writings seriously but condemned them as the dreams of a "spirit-seer."[119] Instead, English critics like Horace Walpole may have scoffed at the baron, but they did not bother to read his works. We should not suggest, of course, that the English case was entirely unique. A dismissive tolerance towards occult thinking might be traced almost anywhere in Europe. If England was more open to practitioners of the occult than Scotland, it was arguably less so than France or Germany, which were the seedbeds of occult thinking in the late eighteenth century. England produced no occult prose writer as original as Louis Claude de Saint-Martin, "the Unknown Philosopher," who refracted Jacob Boehme's Theosophy through a strange prism composed of Freemasonry, mystical number theory and Jean-Jacques Rousseau.[120] In other parts of Europe, however, occult philosophy was hotly contested, while in England it was simply ignored by those who did not agree with it—up to a point. When that point was crossed and the occult began to seem threatening to the social and political order, the situation might change. The first sign of such trouble was in the treatment of that magnificent charlatan, Count Cagliostro.

Cagliostro in London

Hugh Percy's 1785 letter to General Rainsford ends on a hopeful note:

> By the bye I hope you know that the famous Count Caliostro [*sic*] is at Paris & that the manner in which he lives & the stories told of him are so wonderful, that I long much to know whether there is any truth in them. I will only tell you that he is said to be 300 Years old, & lives, without any visible means of acquiring such Wealth, at a greater Expence, then the first of all the Nobility at Paris.[121]

The implication was clear: this remarkable Italian must have knowledge of the Philosopher's Stone. In fact, Giuseppe Balsamo, the self-styled Count Cagliostro, claimed to have much more wisdom than that. He was perhaps the most successful in a string of wandering Italians who made a sensation in late eighteenth-century European society by being thought to know secrets. They included the seedy Casanova, as well as the so-called count de St.-Germain, a talented composer who lived in London in the mid-1740s. The latter's real name was probably Giovannini, but it was for his fabled wealth and longevity (he was said to be thousands of years old), not for his music, that he became legendary. St.-Germain was seen as an alchemical adept, although scholars now doubt whether he actively courted this reputation. He was also said to have studied "Freemasonry and other dark sciences" with the landgrave of Hesse-Kassel, at whose court he died in 1784.[122] Cagliostro, however, made a bigger splash than any of them, before suffering a quick and devastating fall from grace.

Giuseppe Balsamo was born in Palermo in 1743, although in his "Confession" he claimed to have grown up in Medina, the orphaned child of Christian parents. His tale of living as a Muslim, but with "true religion" in his heart, before at last being recognized by the Knights of Malta, is a sentimental Orientalist fantasy.[123] Together with his redoubtable wife, Seraphina, "the Great Copt," as he called himself, travelled across Europe, from St Petersburg to Portugal, pursuing various schemes of self-enrichment. He made three trips to London: first, in 1771–2, as a would-be painter; second, in 1776, as the possessor of a system to win at lotteries (he may have derived the idea from that wily "Kabbalist" Casanova); and third, in 1786–7, as the grand master of "Egyptian Rite" Freemasonry. By the time of the third visit, Seraphina was heading a female branch of the order. The big secret of the Egyptian Rite was communication with the dead, usually through a young boy or girl who acted as a medium. The promise of hidden treasure was frequently hinted at, and the seances themselves were accompanied by all the symbolic paraphernalia of ritual magic—candles, circles, incantations. Cagliostro was essentially marketing an old product under an exciting new label, with the addition of dramatic stage effects, and he found a large number of willing customers. Unfortunately, his lechery, thievery and pomposity kept getting in the way of a successful sales pitch, and he usually ended up absconding from the stage only one step ahead of the authorities. His greatest blunder was to involve himself in the turgid French affair of Queen Marie Antoinette's diamond necklace. One of Cagliostro's child oracles helped to persuade the cardinal de Rohan to borrow the dazzling 2,840-carat necklace on credit from a jeweller. The cardinal thought he was delivering it to the queen, whom he imagined to be in love with him, but in fact the recipient was the countess de la Motte, a close associate of the Cagliostros. Discovered, "the Great Copt" and Seraphina rapidly made off for London.[124]

Cagliostro started out well there, meeting the prince of Wales, prince Edward later duke of Kent and the duke of Clarence, all Freemasons. He moved into a house in Sloane Square, next door to Samuel Swinton, proprietor of the *Courier de l'Europe*, an international newspaper that had supported the American cause in the War of Independence. A retired naval officer, Swinton belonged to a well-known landowning family from the Scottish Borders. In spite of the sympathies proclaimed by his newspaper, and his friendship with the French spy and dramatist Pierre de Beaumarchais, he had run a network of British agents at Boulogne during the war. He was as determined a huckster as the count. By 1785, he was encountering financial difficulties, which led him to invite Cagliostro to go into business with him, manufacturing "Egyptian pills" for 36 shillings a box.[125] He also introduced "the Great Copt" to two men who would cause him a great deal of harm: Lord George Gordon, who gave his name to the famous riots of 1780 and whose admiration for Cagliostro incited him to make vicious attacks on Marie Antoinette; and the journalist Théveneau de Morande, a blackmailer and French agent. Gordon was considered mad, which did the count's image no good, while Morande would work tirelessly to destroy him.[126]

While disaster was brewing, Cagliostro was seeking out the Freemasons. On 1 November 1786, he made an appearance at the Lodge of Antiquity—the same lodge that had spurred the defection of 1779 and the formation of the Grand Lodge South of the River Trent. He must have been aware that this new Grand Lodge had sponsored Lambert de Lintot's Rite of Seven Degrees, and was no doubt hoping that it would adopt his "Egyptian Rite" as well. At the lodge meeting, however, the count was reportedly mocked by a certain Brother Marsh, an optician, who called him "a *travelling Doctor*" and imitated his voice in praising the efficacy of his "*balsamo*" (a barbed reference to his real name). Nevertheless, the following day, an advertisement appeared in the *Morning Herald*, calling for Freemasons and Swedenborgians to come together in forming "the new Temple of New Jerusalem" at O'Reilly's tavern in Great Queen Street. This daring move by Cagliostro had little effect, because the *Courier de l'Europe* had already published a withering account of the 1 November lodge meeting. Smelling blood, the London press followed up with finishing blows. James Gillray issued a print showing the intrepid Brother Marsh using "Satire's laugh" to "strip the vile Imposter of his Mask." On 29 November, the *General Advertiser* ran its own account of the Lodge of Antiquity affair, lambasting Cagliostro's "ridiculous" costume, "not unlike that of a Drum Major." When he reappeared at the lodge on 6 December, Brother Black asserted that he was "unworthy to be received." All was not yet lost—Brother Cooper, who had defended Cagliostro in a letter to the *General*

Advertiser, maintained that the newspaper report was "a misrepresentation," an opinion upheld by a unanimous vote of the lodge.[127]

Cagliostro tried to defend himself publicly in a rambling, tendentious "Letter to the English People," written in French, which mostly consists of a detailed defence of his behaviour in London on his second visit of 1776–7—Morande had accused him of fleeing from creditors.[128] Never a good writer, the count was now trapped in a thicket of his own inventions. Lord George Gordon did not help him by suddenly converting to Judaism. Cagliostro's most faithful supporter at this low point in his career was Philippe Jacques de Loutherbourg, whom he had first met at a lodge of occult Freemasons in Strasbourg. Among Loutherbourg's pastimes was alchemy, although his wife Lucy's tolerance for it was limited—when she caught her husband conducting nocturnal experiments, she reportedly smashed his crucible and "broke his head with a urinal."[129] Together with the Loutherbourgs, Cagliostro and Seraphina fled London in the spring of 1787, eventually settling at Bienne near Basel. It took less than a year for the artist to become thoroughly disgusted with the count, who had borrowed a good deal of money from him. In the end, he satirized "the Great Copt" as a medical quack and spiritual impostor.[130] Even in these biting attacks on his former friend, however, Loutherbourg recognized the count as a splendid showman—which indeed he was, up to the time of his arrest in Rome, which led to his imprisonment and a wretched death in 1795.

It would be wrong to conclude, as Masonic historians often have, that Cagliostro's absurd pretensions were rejected by the clear-headed English Brothers. On the contrary, the Lodge of Antiquity did not expel him, although it did not adopt his "Egyptian Rite" system either. In fact, one has to question whether he had even bothered to devise such a system. The only surviving evidence of its existence is a series of watercolours executed by Loutherbourg. Their most surprising elements are a female initiate (perhaps Seraphina herself), the presence of howling witches and the appearance of the glorious figure of Cagliostro, who dispels Time and slays Mercury (doubtless an alchemical reference) before ushering the initiate into the Temple of Arcane Mysteries. Cagliostro was apparently more familiar with the symbolism of alchemy and magic than with that of the higher grades of Masonry. In the end, however, it was the newspapers, not the Knights Templar or the Harodim, who turned against him.

The count's fundamental crime was an inability to explain his identity, in an age when the arbiters of English culture were increasingly insistent on proper social identification. Anyone whose nationality, parentage, status, race and religious beliefs were unfixed, as Cagliostro's undoubtedly were, could prove dangerous to the good order of society.[131] In part, this attitude was generated by the requirements of commerce, which depended on trust and openness on the part of those who engaged in it. In part, it was a reaction to the destabilizing effects of social mobility, which made it harder to determine who was and who was not a gentleman. Finally, it may have been a response to the loss of the American colonies, which put British national honour in question and encouraged assertions of patriotic belligerence against mysterious foreigners. In such an atmosphere, the question of whether Cagliostro was really Giuseppe Balsamo became central—in fact, it determined the truth of all his other claims. In the 1790s, as will be seen in the next chapter, attacks on occult thinkers were extended even further. Were they insane, or masking subversive purposes? Their existence, it was felt, only increased the menaces facing a governing elite and a national ideology already under threat from the French Revolution.

CHAPTER NINE

Prophets and Revolutions

IN THE 1790s, the occult revival faltered, slowed and in some respects came to a grinding halt. The intellectual energy that it had projected since the 1760s suddenly diminished, and the respectability that it had begun to enjoy was severely curtailed. This does not mean that occult thinking disappeared or that fewer people were attracted to it. New editions of Ebenezer Sibly's encyclopaedias continued to appear into the new century, while Sigismond Bacstrom kept working at his experiments in the dingy "hut" in Albion Street. After war broke out with the French republic in 1793, however, the cultural climate changed. Unconventionality was suspect. Predictions or prophecies came to be regarded as potentially dangerous. In the late 1790s, a devastating attack on occult Freemasonry was launched by the Abbé Barruel, a French émigré, who saw it as the cause of the French Revolution. By then, anything new in the realm of occult thought was likely to be derided or censured by the press. The sole significant exception—Francis Barrett's *The Magus* of 1801—was published by Lackington and Allen during the short-lived Peace of Amiens between Britain and France.

As the war continued, even the rushing stream of Gothic fantasy dried up. A last, provocative example of the genre was the radical William Godwin's 1799 novel *St. Leon*, dealing with a French aristocrat who learns the secret of alchemy but whose efforts to improve the world are thwarted by fear, ignorance and suspicion.[1] The literary sensations of the war years would be Walter Scott's historical romances, in which supernatural elements are virtually absent.[2] When Lackington and Allen ventured again into the realm of occult publishing in 1814, with a volume on apparitions, the compiler was careful to note his own scepticism concerning most such tales. While God might allow some instances of hauntings, "by no means do I believe they are suffered to appear half so frequently as our modern ghost-mongers manufacture them."[3] Only after the war was over in 1815 did Lackington and Allen follow up with a sequel to *The Magus* in the form of a collection of biographies of noted alchemists.[4]

The reversal of occult fortunes after 1793 was due not to government repression, but to a shift in public opinion. It is difficult to measure the extent of such a shift, but its impact was palpable. The press was vital in encouraging and shaping it. Newspapers that supported the government like *The Times* became increasingly hostile to the occult in all of its forms. Anyone who held sectarian religious views might come under scrutiny from the press, because they were perceived as potential fifth columnists, working against the established constitution in Church and State. Swedenborgians were bound to be included among potential subversives, even though the New Jerusalem Church leaders made heartfelt protestations of patriotism and loyalty. Like them, the astrologer John Parkins was careful to proclaim himself "*a most dutiful subject to the best of Monarchs*."[5]

Many devotees of the occult genuinely abhorred the French Revolution. Some, however, invited public retribution by espousing reform at a time when Britain was threatened by republican France. Consider, for example, the extraordinary Swedenborgian effort to settle poor black people living in England, mostly freed slaves and former sailors, on the west coast of Africa. Combining social benevolence with imperial ambitions, the scheme did not seem very seditious.[6] The baron had argued that Africans "think more interiorly and spiritually than others" and that a new revelation was beginning in the African interior.[7] Inspired by these teachings, two Swedish followers, Carl Bernhard Wadström and August Nordenskjöld, became passionate proponents of African settlement schemes. Their heads were full of occult projects: Wadström, director of the Swedish Royal Assay Office, dreamed of a Swedenborgian Freemasonry, while Nordenskjöld, a physician and mineralogist, was captivated by alchemy. He wrote a treatise on the subject, translated into English in 1779 by Mordechai Gumpel Schnaber Levison, the first Jew to be awarded a medical degree in the British Isles (like Sibly, he simply purchased the honour, in his case, from Marischal College, Aberdeen).[8] Ten years later, Nordenskjöld sent an address to the New Jerusalem Church in London, in which he maintained that Swedenborg had discovered "*the Spiritual Stone*," but that the "*natural Philosopher's Stone*," which would abolish "the Tyranny of Money," could only be found through "the Manifestation of *Urim* and *Thummim*," whatever that meant.[9] He was no doubt well aware that Africa was a major source of gold.

In 1787, Wadström was asked by King Gustavus III to look into the foundation of a Swedish colony in West Africa. He embarked on a voyage to the Guinea coast that led to the publication of *Observations on the Slave Trade*, a work frequently cited by English abolitionists.[10] Settling in London, he and

Nordenkjöld became founding members of the New Jerusalem Church and editors of the *New Jerusalem Magazine*. They also wrote up a proposal for the spiritual liberation of humanity, published in 1789 as a *Plan for a Free Community upon the Coast of Africa*. "Man is born to Liberty," proclaimed the authors, adopting the tone of Jean-Jacques Rousseau's *Social Contract*, "and according to his ability and industry, he is intitled to all the prerogatives that the Community can afford him; but Liberty is restrained, and all true access to every thing agreeable in life is shut up." This was blamed on economic exploitation, as well as on "Anti-conjugal" tendencies that had restricted sexual freedom. The only way to cure people of the resulting "*Lust of Dominion*" was to form a new community, governed by boards that would regulate health, education, economic life, justice and foreign affairs.[11] Towards the end of the pamphlet, "the vile Traffic in human Flesh carried on with Africa" was condemned. The authors' solution to it was the creation of European colonies among the Africans, "not for the base purpose of transplanting our vices . . . but with a view to their Civilization." Instead of enslavement, "a gentle Servitude is to be instantly adopted." Former slaves would serve an "Apprenticeship" before being granted freedom.[12]

In pursuit of this Swedenborgian utopia, Nordenskjöld and Wadström travelled to Sierra Leone, where the former died in 1792. Returning to England, Wadström published *An Essay on Colonization*, to which the abolitionists Thomas Clarkson, Granville Sharpe and William Wilberforce, along with Wadström's friend General Rainsford, were subscribers.[13] Within a year, however, Wadström had lost a considerable sum of money on a Manchester cotton-spinning venture, and decided to relocate to France. There, in a democratic republic that had recently ended slavery, he joined the leading abolitionist society, the Amis des Noirs, and lobbied the Directory government to oppose slave trading around the world. Having become a French citizen and director of an agricultural credit society, he died in 1799.

Wadström's defection to the side of Britain's mortal enemy can only have increased the suspicions of the authorities regarding West African colonization. Their attention focused on Olaudah Equiano (or Gustavus Vasa), former commissary of the Sierra Leone Company, a freed slave and anti-slavery advocate who had published a popular autobiography in 1789. He had a lot of supporters in occult circles: Wadström, Rainsford, Hugh Percy and Richard Cosway subscribed to his book, which began with a letter from Alexander Tilloch defending the author's veracity.[14] Equiano's account of growing up in West Africa, which may not have been based on his own experience (evidence suggests that he was born in South Carolina), affirms Swedenborg's opinion of the Africans as a particularly spiritual people. Equiano even calls them descendants of the Jews.[15] Government attention was drawn to Equiano when it was discovered that he lodged with Thomas Hardy, secretary of the London Corresponding Society, a radical democratic group sympathetic to the French Revolution. After Hardy was arrested and charged with sedition in 1794, a letter from Equiano was found among his papers, which showed that the famous African was an early member of the Corresponding Society.[16] Another link between the colonization scheme and radicalism was the printer, engraver and poet William Blake. In his early Swedenborgian phase, he knew Wadström and Nordenskjöld, and even wrote an odd poem about the spirituality of Africans, "The Little Black Boy." An opponent of slavery, Blake clearly sympathized with radical causes as well as with the French Revolution.[17] Blake was the quintessential sectarian radical the government was continually searching for in the revolutionary period, but they did not catch up with him until after 1800.

Admittedly, the chain of connections that has been drawn here is circumstantial and mostly trivial: it does not demonstrate the existence of a Swedenborgian conspiracy in favour of French republicanism. What it does show, though, is that anybody who wanted to believe in such a conspiracy did not have to look very far for evidence. Moreover, while, the suspicions of loyalists concerning sectarian movements were exaggerated, the billowing smoke of sedition that they claimed to see did exist—albeit given off by small fires. The jump from occult thinking to radical politics was easy enough to make. In contrast to the anti-democratic impulses of some occult movements in the nineteenth and twentieth centuries, the occult revival of the late eighteenth century espoused many of the ideals of human improvement lauded by revolutionaries.

Arguably, the boldest radical voice in the occult circles of the 1790s was that of the *Astrologer's Magazine*. Amid articles on witches and demons, ghosts, magic circles and the moon's effects on madmen, readers of the journal might have noticed in September 1793—eight months after Louis XVI's execution and the subsequent French declaration of war on Britain—an article by "Astrologus," answering a friend's request for predictions concerning the progress of military operations on the continent. "Astrologus's" reading of the stars was prefaced with the following astonishing words:

> My friend, like myself, laments those detestable extremes to which many measures have been pushed in France . . . yet . . . the late king of France ungratefully and treacherously endeavoured to sap the foundation of that constitution which he had repeatedly, and voluntarily, sworn to maintain; a constitution which had for its object, the first end and aim of all legitimate

> government—the happiness of the people ... Monarchy, therefore, being abolished in France, the querent is anxious, as many other friends to the peace and happiness of mankind appear to be, that the French Republic may be indivisible, incorruptible, and immortal, and that by proving a salutary lesson to tyrants in every clime, and of every description, that revolution may preclude the necessity of others.[18]

This was strong stuff, justifying the fate of King Louis and suggesting that every monarch might learn a salutary lesson from it. In retaliation for similar statements, Joseph Priestley's house had been ransacked by a mob, while effigies of Tom Paine had been hanged, shot and burned by loyalists throughout England.[19] Other professors of the celestial arts, however, shared the views of "Astrologus." Henry Andrews wrote a sympathetic account of Napoleon Bonaparte in the *Vox Stellarum* for 1799, and as late as 1805 a dispute broke out between Thomas Orger and John Worsdale as to whether Napoleon's nativity marked him as a great lawgiver or a tyrant.[20]

It was not wrong-headed, therefore, for the loyalist public to suspect practitioners of the occult. This chapter explores how that fear emerged: first, through the chequered history of magnetic healing; second, through hardening attitudes towards visionary prophets; third, through the theory that a conspiracy of occult Freemasons had set off the French Revolution. Two individuals who resisted contemporary trends towards loyalism are also considered: Mary Pratt and William Blake. The letters of Pratt, the last Behmenist of the eighteenth century, reveal a remarkable mind, steeped in a feminized version of occult thinking and hostile to every form of power. Blake, the mournful bard of the occult breakdown, left voluminous writings and graphic works in which he criticized occult thinking for being too conformist. He was not a lone visionary cursing at the governing systems of the day, since others experienced the same sense of impending defeat for spiritual forces at the hands of material authority. While Blake's genius may have been more expansive than theirs, other minds were thinking similarly gloomy thoughts amid the maelstrom of the French Revolution.

Magnetic Healing

"The rapid manner in which Magnetists have multiplied upon us, may seem to you [the public], incredible," wrote John Martin, an entrenched critic of the phenomenon, in 1790.[21] At that time, there were about a dozen major practitioners of medical cures by animal magnetism in London, and at least one in Bristol. John Bell, perhaps the most popular proponent of animal magnetism in England, lectured in London, Bristol, Gloucester, Worcester, Birmingham, Wolverhampton, Shrewsbury, Chester, Liverpool and Manchester, as well as Dublin. Between them, the magnetists had many hundreds of students, who paid up to 50 guineas for extended instruction—in fact, lessons in the healing technique, not actual cures, were the main sources of income for most magnetists. Within a few years, however, animal magnetism was virtually defunct in England. Why was its rise so rapid and its fall so sudden?

The researches of Patricia Fara have cast considerable light on the English version of animal magnetism, but its significance remains shrouded in mystery.[22] We should begin by noting that animal magnetism in England was different from its French, German and Italian counterparts. It had relatively little to do with Dr Anton Mesmer, the famous German promoter of a system of cures that depended on magnetism, baths, a form of hypnosis and a complex theory of "universal fluid," sensible only to the magnetist. Mesmer's methods created a sensation at the courts of Vienna and Paris, and were widely imitated. While his fame definitely set off the phenomenon of animal magnetism in England, the latter did not follow Mesmer's teachings very closely.[23] Only one prominent English magnetist, the former male midwife John Bonniot de Mainauduc, had studied magnetism in France. By the time Mainauduc arrived back in London in 1785, a committee of academicians appointed by the French king, including Benjamin Franklin, had issued a condemnation of Mesmer's treatments, arguing that their effects were imaginary. As a result, Mainauduc was compelled to concede that Mesmerism had been "laid aside by those who have gone further," and was "fallacious."[24] Mesmer's name was thus seldom mentioned by English devotees of animal magnetism.

Instead, the English magnetists offered in their published writings a simplified version of Mesmerism that emphasized the power of the mind to effect physical changes at a distance. "The *thought*, or soul," John Bell wrote, "goes to any distance; no obstacles can resist it. It arrives and unites itself, by a sympathetic power, to any object it wishes."[25] The equivalence of *thought* and *soul* is vital, because it indicates how heavily English magnetism was influenced by religion. Bell, a minister as well as a healer, claimed to be a member of the Philosophical Harmonic Society of Paris, which was dedicated to the preservation of Mesmer's principles, and he announced that his lectures "were entirely grounded on the Mesmerian Principles," but as the title page of another pamphlet suggested, the "SECRETS and PRACTICE" were Bell's own. He emphasized religious justifications for animal magnetism. "Nothing proves more peremptorily the existence of a Supreme Being, who governs all things," Bell exulted.[26] Mesmer had famously argued that religious cures, like the exorcisms performed by the priest J.J. Gassner in Bavaria, were forms of magnetism; in England, conversely, magnetism was often turned into an aspect of religious healing.[27] The anonymous author of *Wonders and Mysteries of Animal Magnetism Displayed* went so far as to maintain that animal magnetism was known to King Solomon and was a gift from God.[28] Mary Pratt, who wrote a pamphlet praising the "Manuductions" or magnetic cures carried out by Philippe Jacques de Loutherbourg and his wife, Lucy, described them as "made by the Almighty power of the Lord Jehovah." She also compared them to the miraculous healings of the French Prophets.[29]

The English magnetists, however, were not simply faith healers. They employed a scientific language, borrowed in part from Mesmer, which set them apart from previous marketers of magnetic healing such as Gustavus Katterfelto. They imagined the whole body as a loadstone or magnet, with the nerves following a certain polarity. By means of an invisible attraction similar to gravity, the magnetist could penetrate the universal fluid that surrounded a patient's body and induce a reaction in the internal electric fluid, producing a "Crisis."[30] Satirists delighted in mocking the "Crisis" as sexual, especially as so many patients of the magnetists were female. Even among practitioners, the "Crisis" was highly controversial. John Holloway accused his rival John Cue of inducing a convulsive state that was "both hysterical and dangerous."[31] Both men were Dissenting ministers, and the charge is reminiscent of those made against French Prophets or Methodist preachers in earlier decades. In his published lectures, Mainauduc barely mentioned the term "Crisis," which clearly embarrassed him. He alleged that Mesmer had derived the technique from Athanasius Kircher and Robert Fludd, and that it was often confused with "supernatural exaltations," especially by "impostors" who would "disgrace the Science."[32] The particular features of a "Crisis" differed according to the individual. Bell admitted that a general hysteria could result from inducing a "Crisis" in one person. "This phenomenon is often seen in manufactories, schools, and other public places," Bell observed, and he did not hesitate to compare it to the fits experienced by "the *Trembleurs*" or Shakers in the United States. He argued that patients could be treated without a "Crisis" and, drawing on the hypnotherapy of Mesmer's follower the marquis de Puységur, he recommended somnambulism as an alternative.[33]

The details of this scientific theory may have been of less importance to English magnetists than the basic concept of curing through the *sympathy* of mind and body. On this subject, English medicine had long depended on the writings of George Cheyne and David Hartley, which did not rule out the possibility of carrying out sympathetic cures. Cheyne had even theorized, like Mesmer, that the nervous system was a conduit for the movement of fluid spirits. In addition, the idea of controlling another body through mental action by a qualified guide was already deeply rooted in contemporary treatments of mental illness.[34] What chiefly distinguished the magnetists was their willingness to extend that type of treatment to physical illness. They did not rely on blood-letting, pills, potions or any of the standard practices of contemporary doctoring. The patient was induced to cure herself (less frequently, himself). A remarkably optimistic view of human physiology underpinned animal magnetism—anyone was capable of physical self-restoration. To be sure, animal magnetism also depended on the almost total power of the (normally male) magnetist over another (usually female) human being, which could be unsettling. Betsy Sheridan reported that when her sister-in-law Elizabeth, wife of the playwright Richard Brinsley Sheridan, was magnetized by Mainauduc in 1788, she was "thrown into a state which She describes as very distressing. It was a kind of fainting without absolute insensibility. She could hear and feel but had no power to speak or move."[35] In earlier generations, her "state" might have been equated with demonic possession; by the late eighteenth century, it was emblematic of the power of the enlightened male over women and the ignorant.

The second distinguishing feature of English animal magnetism was its high degree of commercialization, which reflected the social diversity of its clients. This had not been the intention of Mainauduc. He proposed the formation of "an Hygiæn Society," consisting of "Ladies," meaning upper class women, who would take charge of the diffusion of magnetic teachings in London. His early cures were entirely aimed at the elite and court circles. The duchess of Devonshire, leading hostess of her day, accompanied Elizabeth Sheridan on her second visit to Mainauduc. This time, Mrs Sheridan "found herself attack'd as before but in a more violent degree, her limbs being now convuls'd." The duchess herself "was thrown into Hysterics, Lady Salisbury put to sleep the same morning—And the Prince of Wales so near fainting that he turned quite pale and was forced to be supported."[36] Here was a truly blue-blooded roomful of convulsionaries! A list of Mainauduc's patients includes the duke of Gloucester, Lords Milford and Rivers, the Marchioness Townshend, the countess of Hopetown, Lady Archer, Lady Luttrell and two Ladies Beauclerk, General Rainsford, Richard Cosway and his wife, Maria. The sceptical George Winter, who attended Mainauduc's lectures in 1788, wrote that his fellow students included 3 male lay peers, 6 peeresses, a bishop, 5 Right Honourable gentlemen and ladies, two baronets, 7 Members of Parliament, a clergyman, two physicians, 7 surgeons and ninety-two other people "of respectability." The 1798 subscription list to Mainauduc's published lectures comprised persons no less well-born: viscount Chetwynd, the marquess and marchioness of Hertford, Lady Clive, Lady Charlotte Campbell (future novelist and friend of "Monk" Lewis) and assorted colonels.[37] This was the sort of high-society crowd that

Mesmer himself had cultivated in Vienna and Paris; but it was not big enough to sustain more than one successful magnetist.

Mainauduc's chief rivals aimed at a less exalted clientele, attracting them with lower fees for instruction. They relied heavily on public advertising, in a variety of forms. John Bell introduced his lectures through an advertising pamphlet, while Loutherbourg, John Holloway, Benedict Chastanier and the mysterious Dr Yeldall advertised in newspapers. Chastanier and Holloway also issued broadsheets.[38] Holloway offered lectures on animal magnetism six days a week, either at his house in Hoxton or at another site in Pall Mall. A course of three afternoon lectures normally cost £1.5s.0d. per person, although it could rise as high as 5 guineas, and Winter huffed that Holloway had realized £2,000 in fees. "A Gentleman and his Wife will be admitted as one person," Holloway added, liberally. Those living at a distance from London could engage his services, provided they could gather a sufficient number of pupils. Holloway would travel anywhere in England or Scotland to speak to a class of thirty people, and claimed to have educated almost two hundred.[39] Perhaps the most successful advertising technique of all, however, proved to be word of mouth. Loutherbourg and his wife offered free treatments to paupers at their house in Hammermith, and were soon overwhelmed by customers. Mary Pratt claimed that they cured two thousand people between Christmas 1788 and July 1789, adding that crowds of three thousand had lined up for tickets. These charitable efforts forced the exhausted Loutherbourgs to retire to the country.[40]

The burgeoning sphere of public discourse in London provided further advertising for the magnetists through debating clubs and the theatre. In September 1789, the Coach Makers' Hall Society of Cheapside debated the question of whether it was "consistent with reason or religion to believe, that Mr. Loutherbourg has performed any cures by a divine power without any medical application?" The artist was defended by at least three gentlemen, and the debate was adjourned to the following week, when it was finally decided against him. In the same month, Dr Yeldall was called upon to defend his methods before an audience at the weekly forum known as the City Debates. Yeldall's oration upholding the validity of animal magnetism "impressed that Conviction on a numerous and brilliant Audience, which caused them almost unanimously to declare, that his Practice of Animal Magnetism was founded on the sound Principles of Philosophy."[41] The dramatist Elizabeth Inchbald added to the public debate through her farce *Animal Magnetism*; it debuted at Covent Garden in 1788 and remains very funny. The story revolves around a valet who pretends to be "Doctor Mystery, author, and first discoverer of that healing and sublime art, *Animal Magnetism*."[42] Although *The Times* wished the play to be as successful against magnetism as Ben Jonson's *The Alchemist* was against gold-making, it did not present a straightforward condemnation of the practice. One of the actresses was reportedly magnetized during rehearsals and thrown into convulsive fits of laughter![43]

It is difficult to estimate the size of the audience stirred up by this publicity, but it was undoubtedly substantial, and must have extended into the middling and even lower ranks of society. Hoxton was not a fashionable destination for the upper classes (it was full of Nonconformists), so the customers at Holloway's house were probably of the middling sort. John Cue, who also lived in Hoxton, taught and practised healing free of charge, although Martin sneered that he accepted money from "suitable patients."[44] The Loutherbourgs' clients included a teenage apprentice, the daughter of a chairman, a news-carrier and several women who seem to have been servants. As already suggested, women were always prominent among the magnetized, although practising female magnetists were rare.[45] Lucy de Loutherbourg cured patients alongside her husband, and Mainauduc had at least one female assistant, Ann Prescott. A disgruntled student of John Holloway, "Maria," published a short pamphlet entitled *The Secret Revealed: or Animal Magnetism Displayed.*[46] George Winter asserted that Mary Pratt performed magnetic cures, although there is no other evidence for this.[47]

The third point to be made about animal magnetism in England is that it depended heavily on the occult. The same might be said of the phenomenon in Strasbourg, where it was dominated by Swedenborgians, or in Lyons, where it was practised by the occult Masons of the Élus-Coens.[48] The impact of occult philosophy was noted with disapproval by the English opponents of magnetic healing. John Martin accused the magnetists of reading nothing but "*arcana*" or occult writings, such as Agrippa, Fludd, J.B. van Helmont, the seventeenth-century Scottish physician William Maxwell and Paracelsus—precisely the books recommended for study by the author of *Wonders of Animal Magnetism Displayed*, although he added Sir Kenelm Digby, a few astrologers (Culpeper, Lilly, Coley, Saunders), Henry More and others.[49] John Bell referred to Paracelsus as one of the precursors of animal magnetism, suggesting that he, "as well as many other anatomists, have admitted poles in man."[50] Writers who were sympathetic to animal magnetism compared it to Sir Kenelm Digby's weapon salve and to the methods of the seventeenth-century Irish "Toucher" Valentine Greatrakes. Like the Royal Touch in earlier times, animal magnetism was advertised as an effective treatment for the King's Evil, or scrofula.[51]

The relationship of animal magnetism to occult science was explained by the astrologer Ebenezer Sibly, who included a long discussion of the practice in his *Key to Physic, and the Occult Sciences* (1795). He perceived it as proof of the traditional theory of sympathies and antipathies in nature. As he put it in his somewhat tortured prose, "the atmospherical particle to each individual receives from the general fluid the proper attraction and repulsion." Sibly equated the universal fluid to a "vital force" that was subject to celestial as well as earthly forces.[52] This was one of the most original readings of animal magnetism to be published in England, and it reached a large audience, as the work was reprinted in 1800, 1802, 1806 and 1814. It was accompanied by an engraving of "The Operator putting his Patient into the Crisis" that has since become a standard illustration of the technique. Sibly may have also had something to do with the republication in 1793 of a treatise that had first appeared fifty years before on "Magnetical Cures," falsely attributed to the Dutch chemist Herman Boerhaave. It made the same argument as Sibly about sympathies and antipathies, but it recommended healing by "True Magick, grounded upon natural Causes," and even endorsed figures, sigils and talismanic images, "because their Operation is natural, and perform'd by the wonderful Influence of the celestial Bodies agreeing with our Bodies."[53] Sibly did not market sigils or talismans, but the occult theory behind this work was very similar to his. Francis Barrett, who *did* endorse talismans, included chapters on magnetic healing in *The Magus*, where he presented a typically confusing pastiche of natural magic with what he called "the spirit of the blood." Much of Barrett's discussion was derived from Sibly.[54]

Some were willing to extend the occult foundations of animal magnetism beyond Europe. According to a scandalized John Martin, the magnetist John Holloway announced in one of his lectures that animal magnetism "is exactly similar to the *Heathen priestesses*, when they gave out their answers in pagan Temples." Holloway then recounted a story about two European ships voyaging to India that were separated near the coast. "To give them satisfaction, one of the Indians being worked upon [i.e. subjected to animal magnetism], became insensible, and had all the symptoms of a crisis." After his recovery, "he assured the sailors, he had seen their companions, that they were safe, and would ere long arrive at the same place: which came to pass." Holloway followed this up with another "extravagant" tale about an Indian "who possessed great powers of magnetism," and was allowed to heal people, although he had to commit a murder once a year. Martin thought the anecdote revealed that magnetism was "from Satan and not from God."[55] Holloway's Indian analogies signify the beginnings of a cross-cultural interchange on the subject of visions that would influence British ideas of magnetic healing into the mid-nineteenth century.[56]

Occult Freemasons, alchemists and Swedenborgians were thrilled by animal magnetism. While serving as governor of Gibraltar, General Rainsford translated and wrote a preface to a French account of a young woman who experienced visions while under magnetic treatment. The testimony of "Mlle

N–" suggested that "the *Will* of the *Spirit* & of the *Soul* shew themselves most sensibly in the *Solar Plexus*." Rainsford also translated a letter on somnambulism addressed to the Swedenborgians at Strasbourg. Animal magnetism, the author concluded, was a kind of divine spiritual healing.[57] The Loutherbourgs, who cured simply by touch, held the same opinion. "Anthony Pasquin" relates how Loutherbourg's successful career as a magnetist ended when a crowd of invalids broke into his house at Hammersmith and destroyed "his most valued medicaments," which probably means his alchemical work. Loutherbourg's friend Richard Cosway attempted his own extravagant magnetic therapies. He believed he had the ability to look inside people's bodies, and once diagnosed a friend as suffering from "a *hole* in your *liver*."[58] In animal magnetism as in other occult matters, Cosway was an incorrigible dilettante.

After an initial burst of enthusiasm, some Swedenborgians had second thoughts about magnetic healing, among them Benedict Chastanier. He served as assistant to Mainauduc for ten months, then began to offer lessons on animal magnetism himself. By 1786, however, Chastanier had moved away from conventional Mesmerist notions, endorsing the view that they were "not only vicious as to morality, but also very dangerous as to physic."[59] According to a Swedenborgian critic of animal magnetism, Dr William Spence, Chastanier "at last found out its evil tendency, and like an honest man first abandoned the practice and next exposed it." In a 1787 work on the spirit world, Chastanier denounced animal magnetism as "modern quackery, which is a true branch of magic."[60] He meant diabolical magic, as he was not opposed to occult science; apparently, Chastanier practised alchemy "to distract himself."[61] Chastanier always followed his own lights, but his initial fascination with animal magnetism may be connected with a deeper religious issue: namely, universal salvation. He was well known in Swedenborgian circles as the possessor of certain original manuscripts by Swedenborg, passed on to him by Auguste Nordenskjöld. He insisted that they gave him an insight into "the Assessor's" mind to which no other follower could aspire. In 1791, in *The New Magazine of Knowledge Concerning Heaven and Hell*, he defended "universal restitution" as being part of Swedenborg's teachings.[62] In short, the punishment of the wicked was not eternal.

It seems odd that "universal restitution" should have become a divisive question for animal magnetists, but it did. Both John Holloway and John Cue attacked the doctrine, although neither was a Swedenborgian.[63] Universal salvation, of course, provided a justification for human freedom and the perfectibility of society. It was conducive to radical political views. When the English Dissenters, on three separate occasions between 1787 and 1790, asked Parliament for the suspension of the Test and Corporation Acts, which kept them from holding political office, the spread of the doctrine of universal salvation among them—especially among Unitarians like Joseph Priestley—was a factor in the rejection of their demands.[64] Animal magnetism could be seen as promising an earthly form of universal salvation, by which any ailment could be healed by an occult power. Critics perceived that this would distribute divine blessings indiscriminately. "Magnetic attraction," one of them fumed, "seems to have levelled all distinctions; so that believers, and unbelievers, Turks, Jews, and Schismaticks, may be found mingled together in the number of its disciples." In his own condemnation of animal magnetism, George Winter compared its alleged cures to tales of people being suddenly struck dead by the hand of God. "Can man perform such acts as the above?" he asked, answering sternly, "No."[65] Only divine power could decide who was fit to receive supernatural assistance.

An association with controversial religious doctrines did animal magnetism no good in the eyes of loyalist commentators at a time when a supposedly "atheist" and utopian revolution was raging in France. Added to this, most of those in the upper ranks of society who had received treatment or lessons from magnetists were supporters of the Whig Party, some of whose leaders were accused of sympathy with the French. The practice of magnetizing was already declining by 1793, when the outbreak of war heightened the atmosphere of suspicion and mistrust. At this point, animal magnetism almost disappeared. Evidence of classes and healing sessions virtually vanishes. The planned second volume of Mainauduc's *Lectures* never appeared, probably due to a lack of subscribers. The accounts by Sibly and Barrett were the only significant descriptions of the therapy published between 1795 and 1815. Magnetic healing did not revive again until after the conflict with France was over. In England, animal magnetism was effectively a casualty of war.

If it depended so much on the occult, should animal magnetism be interpreted as exemplifying what Robert Darnton has called "the end of the Enlightenment"? No magnetist wrote of bringing the Enlightenment to an end, and none was dismissive of science. English animal magnetism mixed an older rhetoric of spiritual healing with the more recent, quasi-scientific language of Mesmer and his followers. No contradiction between the two was admitted. After all, the mutual attraction of invisible forces was compatible with various ways of interpreting the universe. It was the basis of Newtonian gravity, but also of Behmenist spirituality and of what Swedenborg had called "correspondences" between the spiritual and physical worlds. Recognizing this, the English magnetists tried to combine the languages of spirituality and science. They stressed the powers of the mind, which they equated with the spirit or soul, and sometimes even accepted that they were working through the imaginations of their patients. Yet they had no doubt that real physiological changes would result from their treatments. In a sense, they were stretching the Enlightenment concept of rationality to include things that might be regarded as irrational, just as Sigmund Freud and Carl Jung would later attempt to do.

The critics of magnetism also mixed reason and religion, and were quick to deny that they were rationalist sceptics. Some saw magnetists as falling into diabolic practices—if their claims to healing were true, then Satan must be at the bottom of it. Others believed that only God could carry out the cures to which animal magnetism aspired. As for opposition to magnetism from the scientific establishment, it was sporadic and uncoordinated, as one might expect in a nation that lacked a powerful source of intellectual authority. No leading scientist chose to write extensively on the subject, and no commission of the Royal Society was appointed to investigate it. In the end, it was political events, not science, that ended the convulsive rise of animal magnetism in England.

Nephew of the Almighty

Animal magnetism could generate prophetic visions. This became a source of fascination for Swedenborgians, who regarded the "Crisis" as an "exstatic state" that "can not be reconciled with all the psychological experiences that are known to us."[66] Prophecy that arose from a sensory link to the supernatural, rather than from reading Scripture, had always fascinated devotees of the occult. By the late eighteenth century, the Swedenborgians were actively looking for prophets, and they were not the only ones. The American and French revolutions seem to have revived the almost defunct spirit of prophecy in England, and given it a new edge. Those who now dared to predict the will of God, almost all of them ordinary people of the lower social ranks, tended to take an anti-establishment stance, criticizing the government and the Church while calling for immediate moral change so as to avert divine wrath. This tendency towards subversive prophecy had been seen before, of course, in the mid-seventeenth century. What was new was the extent to which prophets were listened to and even sponsored by learned people with occult interests. The most famous of these relationships involved Richard Brothers, "Nephew of the Almighty," whose prophecies made a sensation in the mid-1790s. His case convinced the government that prophecy was potentially dangerous, and dragged members of occult circles into the glare of an unwelcome publicity.

A pro-Brothers pamphlet of 1795 detailed other recent examples of prophetic powers. They included John Lambert of Leeds, who in 1770 told a visiting American minister that "a great man shall arise in your country, and you shall have a king and no king." A few years later, Lord George Gordon read and took to heart the words of Martha Ery of Suffolk, who lived by spinning and was thought to be a lunatic. In 1764, she had written down a prophecy concerning "a young man of noble blood" who "shall come out of the North . . . and he shall trouble the money-changers, and he shall fall by the hands of the Queen . . . Kings shall die, and more kings yet!" Although this probably foretold an unlikely Jacobite restoration, Gordon believed that it referred to himself. A third prophet, Hannah Green of Leeds, a.k.a. Ling Bob, foretold in 1785 that kings and queens would lose their lives, and that "a distant nation, who have been dragged from their country, will rise, as one man, and deliver themselves from their oppressors." Green's words were interpreted as a reference to the Haitian slave uprising. Two better-known prophets were also mentioned in this pamphlet: Ebenezer Sibly, who had predicted a revolution in France as early as 1784, and Joseph Priestley, who had announced that the wars in Europe presaged the end of the world.[67] Without doubt, local prophets like Lambert, Ery and Green had been casting forth similar predictions throughout the eighteenth century, but the American and French revolutions suddenly brought attention to these obscure figures.

Brothers was not the only one to pick up the signal that many people in England were waiting for a prophet. In 1792, Henry Hardy published an account of waking on a Sabbath morning to the sight of "thousands and thousands and tens of thousands of angels, sitting down in regular ranks." As he was carried up to heaven, the angels began to sing, asking God to protect him. He became infused with divine knowledge. The Lord told him that Britain was to become a special domain: "The kingdom of heaven was taken for the Jews, and is now given to this nation." In order for this to be achieved, God had raised up a man "to put an end to the power of the Pope." Who was that man? Hardy made it plain enough by assuring his readers that "I shall come forward when I am called for," adding that he could be contacted through Mr James Ridgway, bookseller of St James's Square. This prophecy may seem patriotic rather than subversive, but Hardy condemned the Anglican bishops for ignoring him and warned that God would punish his enemies.[68] He does not seem to have enjoyed much of a following, and he was mocked in one magazine as "either an inspired vessel, or a lunatic: for the sake of his humility, we should be glad to think him the latter."[69] By this time, however, Richard Brothers was already experiencing similar visions, which, when published in 1795, would make a far bigger impact. The difference was the outbreak of war with France.

Meanwhile, the devotees of the occult continued their hunt for prophets. Whether they were trying to find a visionary successor to Swedenborg, or were simply interested in what the future might portend, is not clear. In 1788, the Reverend Richard Clarke, an Independent minister, sent General Rainsford an account that he had received from a colleague in West Auckland, Durham, regarding his maid, a young woman from Darlington named Margaret. She had experienced visions of an angel "who has told her the Lord was shortly about to destroy the Wicked from the face of the Earth." More surprisingly, her employer, accompanied by another preacher, saw the angel appear in a wood near his house. Clarke was certain that this vision foretold "a wonderful Event to fall out this Year."[70] Then, in 1790, Suzette Labrousse, the Prophetess of Périgord, emerged in France. Piously Catholic and extraordinarily self-effacing, her inspired utterances favoured the French Revolution. Already a practitioner of magnetic healing by the time she became famous, Labrousse was adopted by occult enthusiasts and Mesmerists in Paris, who published her statements in the *Journal Prophétique*. Unfortunately, in 1792, Labrousse went on an ill-advised journey to Rome, to convert the pope to revolutionary principles, which resulted in six years of imprisonment.[71]

The career of Suzette Labrousse provided a model for that of Richard Brothers. He first appeared on the public stage in 1794, in the midst of government prosecutions against the leaders of the London Corresponding Society and other radical clubs. These legal tactics failed, and in 1795 the London radicals began to organize mass meetings to demand universal manhood suffrage and peace with France. A growing dearth of foodstuffs increased the appeal of their message. When an attack was made on the king's coach, William Pitt the younger's government took the opportunity to propose both a Bill extending the definition of treason and a Seditious Meetings Bill, allowing magistrates to disperse public meetings. When these "Two Acts" became law, they effectively crushed the organizing activities of the radicals.[72] Brothers had no personal connection with the democratic clubs, so far as is known, but he did favour peace with France. As the policy of the French government changed in 1794–5 from the furious patriotism of the Jacobins to the milder republicanism of the Directory, peace became thinkable for Britain's government; but the pressure of alliances, combined with French military successes, made negotiations difficult.[73] As a result, Pitt's ministry desperately wanted to stifle any popular peace movement before it gathered momentum.

Richard Brothers seems an unlikely man to have led such a movement. Born in Placentia, Newfoundland, he became a sailor in the Royal Navy and rose to the rank of lieutenant before being discharged at the end of the American War of Independence. He travelled through Europe, settling in London in 1787, where he worshipped as a Baptist, although Quaker influences may have induced him to become a vegetarian and refuse to swear oaths. Unable to draw his naval pension because he objected to taking the required oath, Brothers became destitute and was confined first to a workhouse, then to Newgate prison on a charge of non-payment of debts. He was finally released after accepting his pension, which he agreed to do only after striking King George's "blasphemous" titles from the document. He began receiving visions from God in 1791, and within two years became convinced that certain people in Britain were descendants of the ancient Jews, including himself. Only he could recognize these people, because he was the divinely designated "Prince of the Hebrews," descended from James, brother of Jesus, and therefore "Nephew to the Almighty."[74] Two volumes of his prophecies were published in the summer of 1794 by George Riebau, a Swedenborgian who styled himself "Printer to the Nephew of the Almighty." In the first volume, Brothers revealed that God had told him to "shew an example of precision to the Learned," as well as to "give instruction to the Poor." London, "the SPIRITUAL BABYLON," marked by commerce and luxury, was to be destroyed, but the descendants of the Jews were to be saved. They must acknowledge, however, that "I am the Prophet that will be revealed to the Jews to order their departure from all Nations to go to the Land of Israel, their own country."[75]

The second volume was more politically explosive. Brothers identified the winged lion in the vision of Daniel with George III, and the plucking of his wings with "taking away the Power of the King." He added that "the Revolution in France, and its consequences, proceeded entirely from the Judgement of God to fulfill this Prophecy of Daniel." He predicted the destruction of Prussia, Spain and Sardinia, as well as a Dutch defection to the French side. He foresaw a new war with the United States. To bolster his credibility, Brothers recounted a vision foretelling the 1792 assassination of King Gustavus III of Sweden. A pointing finger had revealed to him "the speedy End of the present King of England and his Empire, like Belshazzar and Babylon." His work culminated with an amazing statement: "The Lord God commands me to say to you, George the Third, King of England, that immediately upon my being revealed in London to the Hebrews as their Prince, and to all nations as their Governor, your Crown must be delivered up to me, that all your power and authority may instantly cease."[76] The government might have ignored even this, if Brothers's prophecies had not become so popular. In 1795, the year of corn shortages and mass meetings, four editions of his visions were published in London. Stirred to action, the Pitt administration had him questioned by a committee of the Privy Council, which decided to declare Brothers insane and have him confined to a madhouse. They did not, however, prevent him from publishing further works, or from keeping in touch with his supporters.[77]

Scriptural prophecy, of course, is an established feature of Christianity, and while it may test the limits of conventional religion, it usually has nothing to do with occult ways of thinking. What connected Brothers to the occult? First, he claimed supernatural power, by representing himself, not just as the interpreter, but as the enforcer of the divine will. His belief in the "invisible Hebrews" related to hidden signs only Brothers could interpret. It was also reminiscent of the theory that the Druids were descendants of ancient Jews. Brothers may have been aware of the recent revival of interest in the Druids, spearheaded by the Welsh ex-stonemason and poet Iolo Morganwg (Edward Williams), which led to meetings of the "Bardic Order" at Primrose Hill, north of London, in the early 1790s. Iolo was an admirer of the French Revolution and a believer in the transmigration of souls. He concocted elaborate Druidic myths and designed fantastical costumes for initiates of his Order. Like William Stukeley, he envisioned the Druids as the inheritors of true patriarchal religion. He saw their descendants as the modern Welsh, however, and he did not claim to know them by visionary insight.[78]

A second link between Brothers and the occult was revealed in later editions of his prophecies. In a peroration, which was twice repeated, the prophet addressed the noted chemist, alchemist and Fellow of the Royal Society Peter Woulfe: "And you PETER WOULFE—one of the Avignon Society, whom the Lord my God commands me to mention here as a testimony of his great regard—your Property confiscated in France will all be restored with interest, and much kindness shewn to you by the Members of its government."[79] Woulfe had already returned the compliment. In July 1794, he sent General Rainsford copies of the first edition of Brothers's work. Woulfe maintained that "they contain very wonderful things, and I fear we shall find all he says to be true. The Lord Allmighty prepare us to receive with patience & submission to his holy will, the afflictions which he is about to send us." Woulfe was no radical—in fact, he finished his letter by exhorting God to protect the king and his family, for "would not he be in danger, if our vile english Jacobins were in Power?"[80] Woulfe read the prophecies of Brothers not as promises of liberation from monarchical tyranny, but as a forecast of "afflictions." It is impossible to say how many other readers interpreted them similarly.

The "Avignon Society" was the Masonic lodge of Illuminés, founded by Pernety and later headed by Count Grabianka. Rainsford was an initiate, and it has to be assumed that Woulfe was too. So were the two "Hebrews" identified by Richard Brothers in his later writings: John Wright and William Bryan. In a pamphlet of 1796, written in the madhouse, Brothers described these men as his "two particular witnesses."[81] They had certainly witnessed remarkable things. John Wright was a carpenter from Leeds who in 1788 was told by the Holy Spirit that he must leave his large family and go to London. There he became involved with the Swedenborgians, and met a like-minded copper-plate engraver named William Bryan. In January 1789, the Holy Spirit instructed the two men to go to Avignon, which was heart-wrenching for Bryan as his wife was recovering from a still birth. After many adventures, they reached the papal city, where they were welcomed by the lodge. Wright describes how the Illuminés met every evening to share bread and wine in commemoration of the death of Christ, which makes them sound like part-time monks. The two Englishmen were able to consult the lodge's mysterious oracle (who may have been a young woman) and were eventually initiated. The oracle spoke a language, informed by occult philosophy, that diverged from that used to express the popular Christian beliefs of Wright, although Bryan, who read more widely, may have been familiar with it. She made predictions about the downfall of the Ottoman Empire and how Palestine "shall be the *centre* of that faith, *of which* it was the *cradle*." She told them that "we are continually surrounded with spirits, good and bad, and they are almost continually in conversation with men." She told Wright that his spiritual guide was named "RAPHAEL." The two men eagerly accepted what was told them. After six months of spiritual discoveries, they went back to England.[82]

Wright first met Richard Brothers on 14 July 1794, the anniversary of the fall of the Bastille, after hearing about his books of prophecy. Bryan, who encountered Brothers's writings when they were "read in a party of my friends at Bath," was not at first convinced that the retired sailor really was the "Prince of the Hebrews," but he soon changed his mind.[83] Before the end of the year, a grateful Brothers had included both men in the second edition of his prophecies. Peter Woulfe, on the other hand, had already decided that "Bryant" was dangerous, writing to Rainsford: "You cannot now doubt, but there was good foundation for what I wrote to you about Bryant last September when you were at Southamton [*sic*]; had you attended to it, the wicked designs of our republican societies would have been then known. Bryant is gone to settle at Bath."[84] Bryan's connections with "republican societies" cannot be traced, but he trained in copper-plate printing with William Sharp, a member of the London Corresponding Society. Sharp had been examined by the Privy Council in connection with the treason trials of 1794, but was released. Like Bryan, he practised animal magnetism and became a supporter of Brothers. Another link between Bryan and radical circles was the publisher George Riebau, a Swedenborgian who was also a member of the London Corresponding Society.[85]

His attachment to the Avignon Society brought fierce opprobrium on Brothers's head. Sarah Flaxmer, a self-proclaimed prophetess, asserted that Satan had established "a synagogue at Avignon," whose members "are his angels; some of these are dispersed into all nations, and go about as angels of light, to deceive the elect of God." They had duped Brothers, but if *she* were in that synagogue, "and Satan their High Priest at the head, and all his Angels around me, the Lord would send his Angels to deliver me from their power." Evoking the Apocalyptic vision of the woman clothed with the sun (Revelation 12:1–2), Flaxmer called for a female leader to restore Jerusalem—and, of course, she offered herself.[86] Brothers made no reply to her. In fact, he only alluded to the Avignon Society once in his later writings. In a passage in which he named John Wright as "chief of the priesthood" and promised to provide for Bryan, he assured them that their trip to Avignon was "for the purpose of receiving a testimony of me."[87] He said nothing at all about the occult philosophy of the lodge.

Brothers was generally indifferent to the views of his supporters. One of the latter was Nathaniel Brassey Halhed, the only Member of Parliament who spoke up for the "Prince of the Hebrews." An Orientalist, Halhed had served in the East India Company and was known as the translator of a set of Brahmin lawcodes from Persian. Curiously, he established no connection between Hindu sacred writings and Brothers's visions. While he admitted himself to have been "fortunate enough to discover the true meaning couched under the Hindu triad of Energies or Powers," he made no attempt to apply this to Brothers's critical view of the Trinity. Halhed simply believed Brothers to be neither an impostor nor a madman, which meant that he had a good claim to being a second Moses.[88]

The prophet's own lack of an opinion on most theological subjects may have been an attractive feature in the minds of his adherents. We do not know how many of the latter existed, but they were certainly numerous, as fear of Brothers's popularity became intense in 1795. One critic alleged that "the whole herd of Jacobins, and some under the name of Patriots," were defending him, and that "an army of *Brotherites*" would "rise and erect their Prophet."[89] This was a fantasy, but it was widely accepted. Throughout 1795, Brothers's pretensions were furiously denounced in print, and just as ardently upheld.[90] Only one work published in this controversy, however, contained occult material, and it was a spoof. "Moses Gomez Pereira," allegedly a Jewish supporter of Brothers, presented the "supernatural" prophecies of the "Prince of the Hebrews" as a key to the signs of the zodiac. He also implied that Brothers was a Freemason.[91]

Brothers's moment of fame passed with the end of the year. The imposition of the Two Acts and the gradual easing of the corn shortage stabilized the government and weakened the opposition. Eventually, many of Brothers's followers drifted away to a new leader, a prophetess who claimed, like Sarah Flaxmer, to be the woman clothed in the sun. She was Joanna Southcott, a farm servant from Devon, who began publishing her revelations in 1801. Her communications with the Spirit and with angels were direct, highly emotional and at times charged sexually. She believed in witches, but thought astrology to be wrong because it distracted people from Scripture. She expressed no interest in occult philosophy or science, and was dismayed by the Swedenborgian view of a world full of spirits, which she found unscriptural.[92] Southcott deliberately cultivated an anti-intellectual stance on issues about which she was better informed than she cared to admit. Occult thinking was hardly unknown in the lower ranks of society, especially in the West Country, and the Methodists among whom she grew up were not immune to its appeal. Her rejection of learned aspects of the occult seems to have been a conscious choice, made in the wake of the Brothers affair. She had no desire to be reviled as a tool of occult Freemasonry or locked up as a madwoman.

Brothers remained in the madhouse until after the death of William Pitt the younger in 1806. By that time, he had adopted an almost fawning stance towards the British government, and he no longer demanded that George III stand aside for him. He attacked Joanna Southcott, condescendingly, in a pamphlet that associated women with the weakness of Eve.[93] His most interesting later work, however, and the only one of his writings that can be considered an effort at occult philosophy, was a description of Jerusalem based on Ezekiel's vision. This far-ranging treatise begins with a utopian description of the rebuilt city as it would appear under its new prince, with regular streets, parks, colleges and other public buildings. Every house was to have a garden, "where the poorest families may walk and enjoy themselves—where their children may play in safety, to acquire daily fresh health and strength." The land of Palestine was to be improved through the communal labour of all men and women. Brothers proceeded to pronounce on the measurements of the Temple, and to offer a theory of biblical architecture. He went even further, attacking the "sophistical delusion" of the Trinity, along with the Pythagorean theory of the transmigration of souls (which he traced to the Brahmins), Newton's theory of gravity and the heliocentric universe of Copernicus.[94] Although he relied on Scripture and what he thought of as common sense in making these claims, Brothers was evidently trying to address issues that had obsessed occult thinkers, from Solomon's Temple to the cosmos. As was typical of him, his responses showed little awareness of previous writings.

Today, Brothers is sometimes seen as a precursor of British colonialism and Zionism, because he advocated a resettlement of Palestine without much regard for the existing inhabitants.[95] This may put too conventional a gloss on his writings. He was an embarrassment to later colonizers, not a heroic forerunner. Palestine was never more than a blank slate on which his vast dreams were to be realized, just as Wright and Bryan and the Avignon Society were just supporting elements in his magnificent fantasy of princedom. By involving them in his world-shaking schemes, however, he tainted them as subversive, dangerous and perhaps insane. We may have sympathy for Brothers as a man wrongly imprisoned, who seems genuinely to have cared about the plight of the poor; but, ultimately, everybody and everything around him was sacrificed without compunction to his consuming prophetic vision.

Barruel and the Occult Lodges

By now, the pattern of the occult breakdown of the 1790s has become clear: first, the members of an occult circle become involved in a wider cause or movement—anti-slavery, animal magnetism, the prophetic ambitions of Richard Brothers. Second, negative publicity links that cause and its supporters with social levelling, subversive ideas and revolutionary radicalism. The effects of such publicity were often paralysing to occult groups, because they tended to shun open debate and anxiously feared any loss of respectability. The result might be a purge or reorganization by the wider group to which the circle was affiliated. Those whose adherence to occult ideas was strongest would have to keep quiet and accept a reshaped public image that was more in keeping with conventional opinion. This helps us to understand the 1791 petition to Parliament of the Swedenborgian New Jerusalem Church, asserting that its members were "loyally and affectionately attached to his Majesty's Royal Person," and requesting religious toleration in exchange for taking the oaths of allegiance and supremacy.[96] Another example of setting aside occult thinking in order to conform to political realities can be found in the assertion of Grand Lodge control over the higher and occult degrees of Freemasonry.

For English Freemasons, the backlash that resulted from the Cagliostro affair was minimal, but worse problems were brewing for the Brotherhood. In 1784–5, the Bavarian government suppressed an allegedly subversive Masonic organization known as the Illuminati. Led by Adam Weishaupt, a professor at the University of Ingolstadt, the Illuminati actually represented a rationalist reaction *against* occult Masonry. Although they retained some exotic elements—a sense of identification with Zoroastrianism led them to label one higher grade "Magus"—the Illuminati rejected the Templar myth, Swedenborgianism and the whole system of occult higher degrees. They concocted various utopian social and political schemes, but had no concrete plans for realizing them. As the Illuminati consisted of professors, writers, artists, diplomats and members of the German nobility, it is difficult to see them as potential revolutionaries, although the same might be said of many French associations that ended up supporting the 1789 revolution.[97] Yet the fearful fantasy that the Bavarian Illuminati were (and still are) an international fraternity of subversive agitators, addicted to various occult beliefs, has been widespread since the late eighteenth century. No Englishman or Scot was a member of the Illuminati, although General Rainsford was affiliated with them through the lodge of Amis Réunis at Paris, which corresponded with the Bavarian Masons.

Whether the Illuminati affair had a role in the history of the Order of Knights Templar in England is difficult to determine, but by 1791 the latter had decided to end their quasi-separate status and put themselves under the direction of a leading figure within the Grand Lodge. This was Thomas Dunckerley, the provincial grand master to whom Ebenezer Sibly had dedicated his edition of *Culpeper's Herbal.* A former gunner in the Royal Navy, Dunckerley was an entirely self-made man, but claimed the curious distinction of being an illegitimate son of King George I, which he based on the deathbed confession of his mother. How his illustrious parentage may have aided him in attaining high office within the Grand Lodge is unknown, but patriotic zeal and indefatigable energy surely assisted his efforts, so that by the 1780s he was second only to the grand master in authority. Evidently a man with a taste for the occult (Sibly would not otherwise have selected him as a dedicatee), Dunckerley was also attracted to the higher degrees, having served on the Grand Chapter of the Royal Arch Masons as early as 1766. He did not join the schism of the Grand Lodge South of the River Trent, however, opting instead to rise to further distinction as grand master of several English provinces. In 1791, the previously self-governing Knights Templar of York chose Dunckerley as "Head and Chief" of their Order, which effectively meant putting themselves under the protection of the Grand Lodge.[98] This was a smart move at a time when the higher degrees were coming under increasing suspicion as a result of the convulsions in France. Despite his plebeian background, Dunckerley had come to embody Masonic respectability and loyalism in an age of upheaval.

The French Revolution shook Freemasonry to its foundations. As in America, the loyalties of Masons were divided according to politics and self-interest. Collectively, they neither supported nor opposed the events of 1789 and after in France. Individually, some took prominent roles in those events, but many more ultimately suffered as a result of them. The changing relationship of Masons to the revolutionary government can be observed in the case of the Avignon Society, which had effectively ceased to exist by 1795, just at the moment when, ironically, it became so notorious in England. The papal authorities at Avignon, convinced that all Masons were dangerous, had begun to clamp down on the lodge in 1791. At the end of that year, however, the territory of Avignon was annexed by the French Republic. Initially, the Brothers welcomed the revolutionary government, but in the dark days of the Terror several of them were arrested, including Pernety and Grabianka. Others fled the city. The lodge became inoperative.[99] Richard Brothers's blessing did them no good.

To the conspiracy theorists proliferating in the aftermath of the shock of 1789, the divisions among Masons did not matter. These critics were aware that revolutionary demands had first arisen within clubs and associations that promoted enlightened values and the free exchange of ideas.[100] Having little understanding of the diversity of beliefs and lack of political focus typical of Freemasonry, they imagined that the occult lodges had to be responsible for bringing down the French government. Such was the thesis famously proposed by the former Jesuit Augustin Barruel in his three-volume history of Jacobinism (1797–8), a work almost immediately translated into English. The Abbé Barruel entered into a detailed description of the Templar and higher-degree lodges in France, in order to demonstrate that they were committed to a single world government, which made them bitter opponents of national monarchies. "All classes, therefore, every code of [occult] Masonry," he concluded, "Hermetic, Cabalistic or Martinists, and Eclectic [i.e. the Bavarian Illuminati], all and each forwarded the Revolution; and it little imported to the sect which struck the blow, provided ruin ensued."[101] Barruel was careful to separate the "occult Lodges" (or "*Arrières Loges*," as he wrote in French), from the "common" lodges, and he advised his readers "not to confound English Masonry with the occult Lodges, which they have prudently rejected."[102] Living in exile in England, he was too tactful to pick a fight with the Grand Lodge, although he knew that the English also worked the higher and Templar degrees. His scandalized condemnation of Masonic ritual, however, amounted to a blanket condemnation of the myths and rituals of the Brotherhood. No Mason could read his treatise without taking some offence.

Barruel's work was published at almost the same time as *Proofs of a Conspiracy* by John Robison, professor of natural philosophy at Edinburgh, secretary of the Royal Society there and a close friend of Joseph Black. Robison argued for the existence of a conspiracy against religion and government led by the Freemasons, who longed to be "Citizens of the World." The original benevolence of the English and Scottish Masons, he argued, had been perverted among the French and Germans by the infiltration of Jesuits and Jacobites, as well as by the "spirit of innovation."[103] The dreadful result was the Order of Illuminati. "Nothing is more clear than that the design of the Illuminati was to abolish Christianity," Robison maintained, adding that they had an even more insidious sexual goal, since "we now see how effectual this would be for the corruption of the fair sex, a purpose which they eagerly wished to gain, that they might corrupt the men." Of course, he believed that the Illuminati had actually grown stronger after their suppression in Bavaria, which led him to the same conclusion as Barruel: "That the Illuminati and other hidden Cosmo-political Societies had some influence in bringing about the French Revolution, or at least in accelerating it, can hardly be doubted."[104] Robison ended his almost five-hundred-page demonstration with strident flourishes of British patriotism.

Robison's book went into five editions within a year. Having eventually read Barruel, he appended a postscript to the second edition, noting with satisfaction of the Jesuit writer that "he confirms all that I have said of the *Enlighteners*."[105] Robison went on to echo Barruel in exempting British Masons from his attacks (which he had not done in the original text), although he argued that they did not really understand the subversive meaning of their own rituals. They owed this happy naivety, Robison claimed, to the British character: "As the good sense and sound judgment of Britons have preserved them from the absurd follies of Transmutation, of Ghost-raising, and of Magic, so their honest hearts and innate good dispositions have made them detest and reject the mad projects and impious doctrines of Cosmopolites, Epicurists, and Atheists."[106] Whether or not Robison realized the incorrectness of the first part of this statement is irrelevant. He was arguing here more as a Scotsman than as a Briton. By equating Britishness with an anti-occult viewpoint, Robison vindicated not only the scientific basis but also the religious and political reasoning of the Scottish Enlightenment.

Such attacks were not ignored by occult Freemasons in Britain. Hugh Percy, the duke of Northumberland, who only recently had been poring over a tablet containing "some of the highest & most secret Mysteries of the Order," sent to him by "one of the Magi," was duly alarmed by Barruel's book.[107] In January 1799, he complained to General Rainsford that "the Abbé Barruel is too severe," although he recognized that the "three Degrees of Old Masonry, are exempt from the severest Charges," and were "only a kind of Ground Work to all the Wickedness & Blasphemy of the other higher Degrees," by which "Atheism, & Rebellion, & every other smaller Crime is taught & practised." If Barruel had "unjustly accused the Fraternity," it was in targeting these higher degrees. "As far as I have gone," Percy added, with admirable equanimity, "I confess I see no Grounds for his Assertions, but apparent Injustice, but as the Portuguese say, *veremos* [we will see]."[108] Evidently, Percy was unsure about the public reaction to Barruel's attacks—or the government reaction for that matter. The last page of his letter is missing, and Rainsford may have destroyed it for fear that its contents could bring unwanted attention from the authorities. After all, a war was raging and everybody knew that the government was opening correspondence and searching for evidence of subversion. It is difficult to say whether Rainsford had anything to worry about, but in any case the outcome of Barruel's onslaught among English Masons was fairly clear. The influence of the occult lodges waned in the early nineteenth century, to the point of their being labelled "un-English" by some Masonic historians. The higher degrees, as has been seen, were already being brought under control. In 1813, when the Grand Lodge of England and the Grand Lodge of Antients were finally reunited, the degree system became uniform throughout England, and an era of ritual experimentation was closed.[109]

The Masonic writer William Preston responded to Barruel and Robison by denying any connection between English Masonry and the Illuminati, but few dared to defend the occult lodges.[110] One lonely champion was the Irish lawyer, patriot and Parliamentarian Francis Dobbs, a vocal opponent (on Scriptural grounds) of the Act of Union with Great Britain. In 1800, he published at Dublin and London a book of prophecy that bears some resemblance to the outpourings of Richard Brothers. Dobbs regarded the Avignon Society as having "an intercourse with good spirits," although he condemned the Illuminati for being influenced by evil spirits and "preparing the way for the Antichrist." He recalled a meeting in London with thirty members of the Avignon Society, probably in 1786 when Grabianka was visiting the British capital. Sharing a prophetic dream with them, he found that three of those present had experienced the same vision, which could only have happened "by supernatural means."[111] Dobbs's attempt to separate the benign, occult Masons of Avignon from the diabolical, rationalist Masons of Bavaria may not have been very convincing to educated British or Irish readers, who had been led by Barruel and Robison to view all foreign Freemasons with equal horror.

Barruel had not spared the Swedenborgians from complicity in the French Revolution, since so many occult lodges (including that of Avignon) had looked to Swedenborg as a spiritual guide. This prompted the Reverend John Clowes—working, as he assured the publisher Robert Hindmarsh, under direct angelic inspiration—to take up his pen in an attempt to refute the Abbé's unfair aspersions. Clowes indignantly countered Barruel by maintaining that Swedenborg was a convinced monarchist, and "by shewing that his ideas of *liberty, equality, reason and the rights of man* were not such as were propagated by the *occult lodges*."[112] On the contrary, if Swedenborg occasionally mentioned such concepts, they referred to spiritual rather than political states of being. Of course, it is difficult to grasp how they could fail to have political implications too, since the spiritual and material worlds were so closely intertwined in Swedenborg's mind. Clowes was offering a narrow and restrictive interpretation of the baron's highly adaptable ways of thinking. It was an interpretation that would delight the founders of the New Jerusalem Church, who were seeking to escape from the glare of public disapproval.

Clowes's conservative rewriting of Swedenborg would not play so well among other admirers of the baron, notably William Blake. Unlike those former advocates of occult thinking who were moving worriedly towards loyalism in the 1790s, Blake stuck stubbornly to more dangerous visionary opinions. His visions reflected the survival of a politically engaged reading of occult sources. As an artist, Blake was unique. In his combination of the radical and the occult, however, he was not alone.

Against Pharaoh: Mary Pratt

The private views of those who were interested in the occult are difficult to penetrate, but we have been granted extraordinary insight into the mind of one female Behmenist who shared many things with William Blake. Her name was Mary Pratt, and she was hardly an influential figure in late eighteenth century society. She left to posterity only a short pamphlet on magnetic healing, referred to above, and a few rapturous letters on mystical union with God. Her other writings and drawings were destroyed after her death.[113] She was nonetheless important, and not only because she drew from many of the same sources as Blake. Pratt's mysticism arose from a particularly trying set of female experiences. Her hardships, while hardly typical, were common among women who aspired to break out of a contemporary mould of femininity. This did not make Pratt a proto-feminist, like Mary Wollstonecraft. Rather, she espoused a feminized path to mysticism that depended on the occult. It was more subjective than ideological, but its implications were shocking to those who knew her.

Mary Pratt's social milieu was very different from the artisanal world of William Blake. Her family lived in comfortable circumstances in a fashionable district of London. Born Mary Moule around 1740, she was married in June 1760 to Jonathan Pratt at St Mary's Church, Marylebone Road. Her husband was a distant relative of chief justice Sir Charles Pratt, who later became Lord Camden. A son, named for his father, was born to the Pratts in November 1763, and christened at St Mary's. Two daughters would follow. Mary's husband was a liveryman or fully enroled member of the Haberdasher's Company, but in a tradesman's directory for 1790 his occupation was listed as "bricklayer, plaisterer and slater," and his wife described him as a builder. By 1776, the family was living at 41 Great Portland Street, near where the Adam brothers would soon lay out the very grand Portland Place. As the area gentrified, the Pratts acquired a famous neighbour, James Boswell, who purchased number 47 in 1790 and died there five years later. Boswell's literary friend William Seward resided next door to the Pratts at number 40, and another friend, the Irish poet John Courtenay, rented "a neat little house" around the corner. Jonathan Pratt was a man of enough property to be chosen as a juror for the Middlesex sessions in 1790.[114]

If Mary Pratt enjoyed a privileged social standing, she was still far enough below the position of a gentleman's wife to have to devote more time to housewifery than to leisure.[115] As she put it, her husband's business "calls for my attendance at home, where my domestic avocations occupy me wholly." It was not a happy household. Mrs Pratt complained that she had "a persecuting husband and an ungodly infamous son, who is allowed plenty of money, while I am dealt with like Hagar the Ismaelite—kept without a shilling."[116] On account of her religious visions, she had been imprisoned by her relatives in a private madhouse for six weeks: "I have been in prison, for the cause, and have been stript of all things for the Lord's sake . . . from thence My Beloved the Lord Jehovah set me free: and I adore him for it."[117] In retelling the story, she fashioned it to reflect tales of Christian martyrdom, rather than to protest the victimization of her gender, but it can only remind modern readers of the legal powerlessness of married women in the face of their husbands' authority.

Jonathan Pratt was a Swedenborgian and a member of the New Jerusalem Church. He was also a contributor to the *New Magazine of Knowledge Concerning Heaven and Hell*, a monthly Swedenborgian publication that appeared in 1790–1. Several letters were addressed to the *New Magazine* by an anonymous writer titling himself "Ignoramus." A marginal notation in a copy owned by the British historian E.P. Thompson identified "Ignoramus" as none other than Jonathan Pratt.[118] His contributions began with two letters arguing that astrology should be taken seriously, as an example of the influence of spirits on matter. The moon, in particular, might affect the brain, "as to modify the rational influx of the soul, into the disordered ideas of a madman's ravings."[119] Was he thinking of his wife, Mary? "Ignoramus's" letters then shifted to the deeper topic of the nature of evil, which he interpreted as the loss of man's original divinity. He confirmed that Jacob Boehme "is no despicable author on that head, although I must freely acknowledge that I do not fully comprehend him."[120] In August 1791, "Ignoramus" entered into a controversy with Benedict Chastanier regarding universal restitution or salvation for all. Sticking to the more conventional view, "Ignoramus" concluded that "till the will is changed from evil to good, misery must be the consequence."[121] If he rejected universalism, "Ignoramus" nonetheless believed that Christ was not God, although he contained the divine within his humanity. He opined that, just as Christ inherited divine nature from his Father and corporeal nature from his mother, so too "the form of a man's soul being from the father, remains to eternity, but the form induced from the mother may be put off, and is put off as to gross corporeity by all."[122] This disparaging comment on mothers was "Ignoramus's" last major contribution to the journal.

E.P. Thompson associated "Ignoramus" with a conservative, denominational strain of Swedenborgianism that was rejected by William Blake.[123] Yet in many respects Jonathan Pratt was not very far removed from Blake. Pratt was a founding member of the New Jerusalem Church at its inception in April 1792.

Blake had attended the meeting three years before at which the idea of a new denomination was suggested; he and his wife signed the proposal. As late as 1797, his friend John Flaxman thought that Blake could be brought into the fold of the New Jerusalem Church.[124] Blake's alienation from Swedenborgianism, which was never total, seems to have originated in his beliefs that humans possessed an innate divinity and no soul was destined to damnation, views he may have derived from Boehme. Pratt also lauded Boehme; for him, damnation was not predestined, but was equivalent to the human choice of evil. Blake's views on gender, at least in this period, were similar to those of Pratt.[125] Both men can be considered as free interpreters of Swedenborg.

By contrast, Mary Pratt really despised "the deluded Swedenborg," as she called him in her letters. "My partner in life," she wrote in 1792, "is an adherent to these wild doctrines who call themselves the New Jerusalem Church . . . poor hoodwinked mortals, blindfolded by the seducer, to their own destruction."[126] Blake never expressed himself so strongly against "the Assessor" or his followers. By the time she wrote these words, moreover, Mary Pratt was already a public figure, whose pamphlet on spiritual healing had gone through two editions. She was probably better known as a writer than Blake, whose poems had appeared in tiny editions, or her own husband, who wrote anonymously.

A sign of her independence from her husband's religious views may be found in a 1778 collection of religious poems, addressed to members of the Congregational Church in Redcross Street. Mary subscribed to the volume; her husband did not.[127] Her marital status was not mentioned in the pamphlet on magnetic cures, which she printed at her own expense in 1789. Her name appeared as "M.P." on the title page, where she was also identified as "a Lover of the Lamb of God"; but she signed the dedication to the archbishop of Canterbury as "Mary Pratt [no Mrs], 41 Portland Street, Mary-le-Bone."[128] While the work is hardly a feminist tract, its point of view is distinctly female. Lucy de Loutherbourg is given credit for the cure of "a woman possessed with Evil Spirits" who happened to be a near-neighbour of Mary Pratt and whose condition ("she was like a Lunatic") paralleled her own alleged madness.[129] Mary Pratt may have seen aspects of herself in these female figures, both sufferers and healers.

She was totally disinterested in the scientific aspects of magnetic healing. For her, the cures were divine, and suggested parallels with the miracles of the Apostles. She called for public prayers to be offered up "for such an astonishing proof of God's love to this favoured Land." The last comment was not a statement of national pride; in fact, Mary Pratt had little confidence in God's continuing favour to Britain. The public prayers, she wrote, were necessary now, as at the time of King George's recovery from madness, "that we as a People may avert and deprecate those judgments, which at this awful hour have fallen on other

Nations."[130] The pamphlet was dedicated on 21 July, one week after the fall of the Bastille. Thus, Pratt linked the miraculous cures of the Loutherbourgs with the political situation of the nation, just as her own recovery from supposed madness might be linked with the recovery of King George.

By 1791, Mary Pratt had become "the most intimate friend" of an Anglican minister of mystical inclinations, the Reverend Richard Clarke. Like Blake, Clarke believed in universal salvation and continuing revelation, or "the Everlasting Gospel." He also had faith in alchemy, but not in Swedenborg.[131] It was Clarke who brought Mary Pratt into contact with his friend Henry Brooke, an Irish painter and nephew of the celebrated novelist of the same name. A disciple of Boehme, Brooke sought out like-minded mystics throughout the British Isles. In a correspondence that lasted from December 1791 to October 1792, Pratt instructed Brooke in a supremely confident tone that frequently verged on the ecstatic. "I (truly) live in Paradise," she wrote, "having passed by the Angel that stands at the Gate to guard the Tree of Life . . . Jehovah has clothed me and I see and rejoice in my own beauty: not by my attainments; not by my sufferings—tho' grievous and terrible . . . No—it was by the Lords free gift . . . He espoused vile me!" She did not mean this in a figurative sense: she really believed that she was living in heaven, as the bride of Jehovah. She made the amazing claim: "I am the first, who ever had the honor to have the seventh seal opened to them: the time was not come, till it came to me."[132]

This was not simply madness. It was a mystical conviction based on experience as well as on extensive reading. Pratt eagerly shared with Brooke the list of her favourite authors, an eclectic and international bunch. She recommended Boehme, of course, but also the Spanish Catholic mystic Miguel de Molinos and the French Quietists, Madame Guyon and Madame Bourignon. Among English mystics, Pratt had been inspired by the puritan Peter Sterry and the Philadelphians Richard Roach and William Bromley, although she noted that none of them had entered paradise while alive, as she had. She mentioned her "delight" in the writings of the radical Civil War preacher William Erbery, but we should not readily assume, as E.P. Thompson did, that she identified with his politics, because she said nothing about them. She omitted Jane Lead, the spiritual leader of the Philadelphians, although Brooke noted in a letter to Clarke the similarities between Pratt's mystical assertions and those of the late seventeenth-century prophetess, who also had a vision of the breaking of the seventh seal. Mary Pratt further asserted that she had read "many (almost all) Hermetic books," and had "sought Earth, Sea and Air, speaking in a figure," meaning that she had studied alchemy and ritual magic.[133]

Mary Pratt was not a passive reader: she brought to these mystical and occult tracts a highly gendered sensibility that focused on the travails of the female body as the starting point for spiritual exaltation. Like other mystics, she condemned "[t]his foul body" as "like a beast; its appetites, its passions, its gratifications are vile." Yet at the same time, her body provided a way to the divine. Heaven had opened up to her through the pain of childbirth: "I felt, when the Man child was born in me,—you would hardly credit it—the pain was the pain of hell, intolerable; neither could the humanity have sustained it: but Love tried the crucible, in a sevenfold fire." The "Man child" was both her "ungodly infamous son," Jonathan, and Jesus Christ, whose divinity is nowhere acknowledged by her. This contrasts sharply with her husband's view of Christ's divine maleness, paired in him with a degraded human femaleness.[134]

Mary Pratt preferred Jehovah to Jonathan, and she often evoked images of marriage and union to describe her relationship with the Almighty. It may be impossible today to read her description of "the ecstatic rapture of a Union with him Jehovah, the Lord," without thinking of sexual abandonment: "You feel dissolved, annihilated, melted, dignified, swallowed up in him." Her vision of heaven, however, was rooted not in sexuality but in a chaste matrimonial harmony, centred on the sharing of food: "for in equality as between man and wife, the connubial endearments are in Union, they taste reciprocal delights, for my beloved is mine, and I am his, he feedeth among the lilies; or he feedeth with me in spotless purity.—Come walk in the garden of Love, and taste pure delight and ineffable pleasure . . . It is extatic! It is glorious! it is divine!"[135] Pratt frequently used images of eating and drinking, of "mannah" and "celestial food," to convey the pleasures of union with God. Medieval female mystics drew the same connection between the maternal body as a source of food and the nourishing power of Christ's body.[136] Pratt had clearly absorbed this tradition, although it is not clear where she had encountered it.

It was only in her last communication with Brooke that she veered into national affairs. "The times wear a most favorable aspect viz. French Republic," she predicted. "The time is approaching very fast, when every man shall feed under his own vine and fig tree, and none shall make them afraid." Again, self-sufficiency in food, this time for men, was equated with spiritual bliss. She went on to make her predictions more subjective. "I have not time to print my letters, Pharoah will in this life be obeyed. He is the Prince of the power of the air, and we who are witnesses of the resurrection, he persecutes more than any others; but the man child is out of his reach, it dwells with God; and all his floods cannot drown it."[137] By "Pharoah," did she mean her husband or George III? Whatever the case, in this passage she foreshadowed the two most popular millenarian prophets of the period: Richard Brothers, who called for peace with France, and Joanna Southcott, who claimed to be pregnant with the new Messiah, the "man-child" Shiloh.

It was all too much for Henry Brooke, who broke off the correspondence after this letter. He chided Pratt for being so resentful towards those who had wronged her, and urged that, "instead of being inflamed at opposition," she should "pray for, a mistaken friend, a persecuting Pharoah, or an infamous relation." Brooke later told Richard Clarke that, although he admired her piety, he feared that tapping into her "rich vein of enthusiasm" might "aggravate her malady."[138] He did not mention her political views or attitude towards her family. If Brooke was condescending towards Mary Pratt's feminine mysticism, he was not lacking in sympathy for her. For nine months he had encouraged her to open up her inner world to him, and it was only when she threatened his own equanimity that he broke off from her.

Mary Pratt may not have been a female Blake, but she has to be placed in the same intellectual milieu of heterodoxy, religious subjectivity and occult philosophy. Like him, she was a self-taught visionary, who drew on radical religious traditions as well as quasi-magical knowledge to shape her own approach to God. In her temperament and language, she looks forward to the Romantic age, and beyond it to the Spiritualists and Theosophers of the Victorian era.[139] As a woman mystic, however, she incorporated (the term is apt) a point of view that Blake did not share, based on concepts of physical union with the deity and of the maternal body as the source of life. By laying claim to a physical superiority over men, rather than a moral equality to them, Mary Pratt was reformulating an old argument about female spirituality. To be sure, it was more effective in establishing the exalted character of women than in winning rights for them. She never argued in terms of earthly equality. On the other hand, neither did she subscribe to a belief in essential or natural gender differences. Her Swedenborgian husband may have been an essentialist in gender matters, but she simply ignored any discussion of the self that was premised on natural hierarchies. All that counted was her own supernatural yet physical link to God. Ultimately, that may have been all that mattered to Blake too. In that respect at least, we might call him a male Mary Pratt.

Urizen Wept: William Blake

Yet Blake differed in many essential respects from Mary Pratt, as he did from every other occult thinker of the late eighteenth century. For one thing, the God that mattered to him was part of himself. Did this qualify him as a mystic? Perhaps not; but then, categorizing Blake in any way is difficult. His relationship to the occult remains murky, in spite of the painstaking research carried out by Kathleen Raine and others into the Neoplatonic and Hermetic references that run through his poetry.[140] Some scholars, eschewing Raine's approach, have chosen to read Blake's visionary writings in strictly political terms, emphasizing his radical opposition to monarchy and organized religion.[141] They have drawn out the contemporary relevance of his works, but fail to explain why he chose to compose mythic fantasies rather than political allegories. His imagination was bounded neither by current events, which he bent to his own purposes, nor by occult traditions. This might lead us to disregard him as a madman or self-absorbed loner with almost no audience. In an occult as well as a poetic context, however, Blake was a pivotal figure. A relentless opponent of rationalism, he foreshadowed the modern occult mentality, in which reason is not the instrument but the enemy of vision. Like William Law, Blake resented the constrictions imposed by modern philosophies. He went much further than Law in condemning them. Scorning respectability, Blake regarded occult thinking itself as utterly corrupted by an insidious collaboration with science and materialism.

Blake's religious roots and artisanal background figured in the formation of his ideas, although their significance is hard to decipher. His mother was apparently a Moravian, at least for part of her life. The joyful impulse in Blake's early poetry, as well as his exaltation of Jesus as a full-fledged God, may owe something to her beliefs.[142] By the late 1780s, Blake and his wife, Catherine, were involved with the Swedenborgian New Jerusalem Church, of which his friend John Flaxman was a strong supporter. Soon, however, Blake became critical of Swedenborgianism, and he never joined any other religious group. Despite E.P. Thompson's suggestion, no evidence exists to link him with the Muggletonians, the descendants of a radical Civil War sect.[143] As for Blake's politics, they were highly personal. Working as a printer and engraver, Blake rubbed shoulders with radicals like William Sharp, and he was employed by the Unitarian bookseller Joseph Johnson, who published radical pamphlets. Yet Blake was never a member of any political organization, and he was not involved with any seditious publications. Expression of his strong anti-monarchical and anticlerical views was confined to self-published writings that circulated among a tiny number of friends.[144]

Access to works of occult philosophy may have been provided by his early mentor the miniature painter Richard Cosway, who praised Blake's engravings as "works of extraordinary genius and imagination." Through him, Blake may have encountered Boehme, Freher, spiritual healing and ritual magic.[145] Whether or not Blake was introduced to animal magnetism or the prophecies of Richard Brothers by William Sharp, as has been mooted, is an unanswerable question. The two men were not close friends. Lacking evidence, we can no more infer that Blake shared the attitudes of Cosway or Sharp than we can assume that his passing acquaintance with Alexander Tilloch, whose invention of a device to prevent banknote forgeries Blake endorsed in 1797, had its basis in a shared love of alchemy.[146]

Blake applauded the American and French revolutions as blows against tyranny and slavery. Like the "Nephew of the Almighty," however, he understood these momentous events in a prophetic sense entirely detached from the conventional rhetoric of rights and liberties. In fact, Blake's poetry displays a marked ambivalence towards the goals and methods of revolutionaries. His verses on the American War of Independence begin with a sexual assault by the rebellious Orc, who is chained to a rock like Prometheus, on his unnamed sister, who recognizes him as "the image of God who dwells in darkness of Africa" (a reference to the Swedenborgian dream of finding an African source of revelation). Orc then stirs up a cosmic conflict between the thirteen angels of the American colonies (who sit in "magic seats") and the angels of Albion. While the American angels seem to be carrying out a judgment on the British monarchy, the plagues that they shoot back at Britain do not present much of a case for republicanism.[147] Blake's unfinished poem on the French Revolution is even more insistent on representing that upheaval as a curse, as well as a liberation. When "Fayette" marches his army out of Paris, he is surrounded by "pestilential vapours" on which "flow frequent spectres of religious men weeping," driven from their abbeys "by the fiery cloud of Voltaire, and thund'rous rocks of Rousseau."[148] For once, Blake seems to feel sorry for the clerics. Revolution is a disease spread by "deists" (Voltaire, Rousseau and later Edward Gibbon), whom Blake pilloried as the destructive, warmongering advocates of natural religion. They may be instrumental in the overthrow of kings, priests and aristocrats, who are far worse than they are, but nobody really seems to benefit much from their efforts.[149] Revolution, in short, was a necessary evil in an imperfect moral universe.

Blake's own philosophical views were first expressed in his 1790 pamphlet, *The Marriage of Heaven and Hell*, whose title is derived from a work by Swedenborg. Blake took the opportunity to scorn his former spiritual teacher. "Any man of mechanical talents," he wrote, "may from the writings of Paracelsus or Jacob Behmen, produce ten thousand volumes of equal value with Swedenborg: and from those of Dante or Shakespeare, an infinite number."[150] We may assume that Blake himself was that prolific mechanic, but we cannot know what volumes of Boehme or Paracelsus he had read. In philosophical terms, at this stage, not much separates Blake from Swedenborg. Blake maintains that there is no division between body and soul, that all living things are holy and that they are infused by the essential life force of energy—all propositions with which the baron would have agreed.[151] What distinguishes Blake is his insistence that reason (which encompasses conventional religion) puts a cloying damper on energy, whose negative effects can only be overcome by demonic power. Although Swedenborg did occasionally converse with demons, Blake's sympathy for the Devil is a novel feature of his theology. It owes more to John Milton's *Paradise Lost*, in which

Satan takes on heroic characteristics and foreshadows Christ, than to any occult work. Blake's identification of the life force with sexuality was perhaps less original—the concept was not foreign to Swedenborg. It contrasts nonetheless with the strait-laced moralism of the Platonist Thomas Taylor, whose lectures Blake attended at the house of their mutual friend John Flaxman.

The Marriage of Heaven and Hell, therefore, is a bold, albeit not entirely convincing, declaration of independence from the visions and philosophies of others. Already, Blake was using the names of mythological characters to express his alienation from the material world. While these "Eternals," as he called them, are infused with the characteristics of classical gods (they have female "Emanations" who often behave as headstrong or lascivious goddesses), they do not correspond precisely to any ancient pantheon. Blake evoked them with a portentous seriousness reminiscent of James Macpherson's Ossian poems. Swedenborg claimed to have encountered spirits from other planets, but he never constructed mythic stories out of their lives as Blake did.[152]

The "Eternals" appear to stand for aspects of the human mind, which may link them to various psychological theories, from Plato to Hartley. In the early "Lambeth Books" composed in that London suburb from 1790 to 1795, however, they are more active than acted upon, and can be identified more easily by what they do rather than by any correspondence to ideal mental states. Generally speaking, the "Eternals" spread despair and misery, without offering much hope of eventual transcendence. The mythic characters who will eventually confer divinity on human beings—Jesus and Albion, the original man—do not have a strong presence in the "Lambeth Books." Eventually, readers will learn that Albion's fall into materiality resulted in the separation of the Four Zoas—Urizen, Urthona-Los, Luvah and Tharmas, who stand for reason, intuition or imagination, emotion and bodily sensation. The division of Albion's spirit may reflect the fragmentation of Adam Kadmon, which Blake could have read about in an English-language synopsis of *Kabbala Denudata*.[153] In his earlier books, however, the name Albion appears chiefly as the title of a rather sinister angel whose voice issues the "thunderous command" to bring plagues on the rebellious Americans, "as a storm to cut them off / As a blight cuts the tender corn when it begins to appear."[154]

If the "Lambeth Books" do not contain much spiritual optimism, neither are they very positive about occult philosophy. The subject is mentioned specifically only once, in *The Song of Los* (1795), where we read that "To Trismegistus. Palamabron gave an abstract Law: To Pythagoras Socrates & Plato."[155] As Palamabron was the offspring of the "Eternal" Los, who represents (more or less) the creative or imaginative faculties, this might be regarded as a benevolent gift, but it actually comes from Urizen or reason, whose lawgiving always has a negative connotation in Blake's poetry. Furthermore, Palamabron's description as a "horned priest" in *Europe: A Prophecy* (1794) hardly seems encouraging.[156] His gift of "abstract Law," therefore, cannot be interpreted as an endorsement of Hermeticism, Pythagoreanism or Platonism, which are apparently no better than any other established system of belief. Blake does not spare Hinduism either, as he describes Palamabron's brother Rintrah giving "Abstract Philosophy to Brama in the East." A few lines later, modern philosophy will be lumped into the same overall condemnation. Urizen weeps piteously as he delivers "a Philosophy of Five Senses . . . into the hands of Newton & Locke." Meanwhile, in another sign of reason's dulling power, "Clouds roll heavy upon the Alps around Rousseau and Voltaire."[157] Evidently, the constraints imposed by Urizen's laws on the senses (Blake accepted many more than five) and the imagination are embedded in empirical science and natural religion as well as in occult philosophy. All are actually concerned with the material rather than the spiritual world. Boehme had signalled in a similar direction by urging "*Seekers* of the Metallic *Tincture*" to "apply yourselves to the *New Birth* in Christ," but Blake booms in a different register.[158] No writer of the eighteenth century had gone so far as to reject the whole tradition of Western and Eastern thought as misguided.

The attack on occult philosophy underpins *The Book of Urizen* (1793). Urizen, the "Eternal" associated with reason, worldliness and sensory knowledge, is depicted in a colour plate, measuring the universe with a compass that radiates out from his fingers.[159] Anyone familiar with the symbols of Freemasonry could have identified him as the Divine Architect, planning out the cosmos. The egomaniacal Urizen goes on to behave like a god of the alchemists, forming an earthly world by controlling the three other seething elements, then writing down his secrets in "books formed of metals":

First I fought with the fire; consum'd
Inwards, into a deep world within:
A void immense, wild dark & deep,
Where nothing was: Natures wide womb
And self balanc'd, stretch'd o'er the void
I alone, even I! the winds merciless
Bound; but condensing, in torrents
They fall & fall; strong I repell'd
The vast waves, & arose on the waters
A wide world of solid obstruction
Here alone I in books formd of metals
Have written the secrets of wisdom
The secrets of dark contemplation.[160]

These images may be inspired by the engravings showing the creation of the universe in Robert Fludd's *Utriusque Cosmi*, but there is a big difference: for Blake, they mark the beginning of a cursed world of misery and subjection operating under the slogan "One King, One God, One Law."[161] Apparently, the fulfilment of alchemy does not entail the liberation of the spirit, but the enslavement of nature to a unitary code of material science.

The fatal association of the occult with materialism and science is emphasized again in *Vala: or The Four Zoas* (1797–1804), a confusing, unfinished poem that provides a link between the "Lambeth Books" and the later epics, *Milton* and *Jerusalem*. Here, Urizen's rationalizing efforts serve to pervert both the Temple of Solomon and the ancient mysteries. On the seventh night of the poem, Urizen "& all his myriads / Builded a Temple in the image of the human heart." Blake may have had in mind the roughly circular stone "temples" ascribed by William Stukeley to the Druids, and regarded by him as versions of the Temple of Jerusalem. On the last page of his poem *Jerusalem* (1804–20), Blake would copy Stukeley's engraving of the "serpent-temple" at Avebury, behind a scene of writhing "Eternals."[162] As with all his borrowings, however, Blake complicates the original image. The serpent signifies for him the materialism of an earth-bound creature. Urizen's heart-like structure turns out to be a weird parody of Solomon's Temple. Like the pagan temples of Babylon, Jerusalem's opposite, it is served by priestesses as well as priests, "clothd in disguises beastial." Urizen goes on to imprison the sun in the centre of his temple, where it takes the place of the Ark of the Covenant:

> they put the Sun
> Into the temple of Urizen to give light to the Abyss
> To light the War by day to hide his secret beams by Night.[163]

Light is held in darkness so as to conceal secrets—a swipe, perhaps, at the promise of Freemasonry to reveal what is hidden.

Above the temple rises the Tree of Mystery, which Kathleen Raine has compared to the Tree of the Soul, one of Leuchtner's illustrations to Boehme's works.[164] Blake's Tree, however, is a site of anger, despair and mourning—"in fierce pain shooting its writhing buds"—not a path to paradise. The Lamb of God is eventually nailed to it, but he will return to "rent the Veil of Mystery." When the "Synagogue of Satan" rises up against Urizen, the tree is burned, so that "Mysterys tyrants are cut off & not one left on earth." Soon, however, a successor forms in its place:

> The Ashes of Mystery began to animate they calld it Deism
> And Natural Religion as of old so now anew began.[165]

By using the term "Mystery" as if it were the proper name of the tree, Blake suggests that its grisly power lies in fear of the hidden or unknown. This may seem contradictory, as natural religion was supposed to *reveal* the hand of God in the universe, but, for Blake, the material world actually *disguises* that which is obvious to the inner imagination. Thus, deism becomes the offspring of mystery, or the occult. Through the image of a tree, Blake may also have intended to target the adaptation of ancient mystery cults by Freemasons.[166] Aeneas found the entrance to Hades beside an elm, and Warburton, among others, had argued that the hero's descent into the underworld (Urizen's domain) mirrored the Eleusinian mysteries. In Masonic myth, the remains of Hiram were discovered under a blossoming acanthus tree. Blake was not celebrating these stories in *The Four Zoas*: rather, he was identifying them as sources of mental slavery.

Blake's attitude towards traditional occult philosophy remains unflaggingly hostile throughout his early writings. Above all, he seems to vilify its attempt to explain nature, which links it to the material world and sensory experience. Of course, he also imagined a more benign magical world, existing entirely in his own fantasy, full of talkative fairies straight out of Shakespeare, a radiant Zodiac, transmuting angels and divinely blessed lily flowers, but these were not associated with any particular philosophical approach.[167] At least they served to lighten the gloom of the "Lambeth Books." On the whole, Blake's mental universe, with its abundant spirits, four elements and Ptolemaic geocentrism, is perfectly compatible with that of Thomas Vaughan, Elias Ashmole and William Lilly. What the poet rejects is any systematic analysis of that universe, which only serves to impose boundaries on thought, leading to subjection and misery. *The Four Zoas* finally points towards a solution for the pain of the world, in the restoration of "the Eternal Man" to full divinity—a concept straight out of Boehme. Even here, however, Blake's creative powers labour mightily to make the concept his own.

No other writer of the period combined Blake's knowledge of occult thinking with his critical viewpoint and radical politics. The closest parallel may be Samuel Taylor Coleridge, who was similarly steeped in the writings of Boehme, Swedenborg and Neoplatonism. The son of a schoolmaster, Coleridge did not grow up among the privileged, although he later attended Cambridge and fell in with an ambitious young literary set. He became famous for a visionary poem, "The Rime of the Ancient Mariner" (1798), that contains occult elements of the author's own devising, as well as an unsettling moral message. The despairing tone of this work as well as other writings of the period by Coleridge—"The Wanderings of Cain," "Fire, Famine and Slaughter"—is not unlike that of Blake's "Lambeth Books." An abolitionist and framer of utopian schemes, Coleridge was an early supporter of the French Revolution, although he soon became disillusioned by it. Two factors, however, set Coleridge clearly apart from Blake. First, he admired Joseph Priestley and was attracted to Unitarianism. Second, in 1798–9, Coleridge made a trip to Germany, where he encountered the writings of Kant. From that point on, he would move towards an increasingly conservative philosophical idealism.[168] Blake was never so enamoured of any way of thinking as he was of his own.

The poetry of William Blake pointed towards a rejection of what would become known as "the occult tradition." For him, the idea of a "tradition" was too much linked to conventional scholarship and respectability. Later proponents of "inner vision," from the Spiritualists, the Theosophists and the Hermetic Order of the Golden Dawn to the New Age movements of the mid-twentieth century, would follow Blake in picking and choosing the elements of occult thinking they found most appealing, combining Western and Eastern sources without committing themselves to any particular philosophy.[169] In this sense at least, Blake accurately prophesied the future. The period in which occult thinking tried to attach itself to mainstream science and philosophy was effectively over. After Blake—or, more precisely, after the traumas of the French Revolution and the stigmatization of magnetic healing, visionary prophecy and occult Freemasonry—the denizens of the occult would tend to look inwards, positioning themselves as the mortal enemies of the rational Enlightenment.

CONCLUSION

THE OCCULT may always have been with us, but it has not always been the same. Within England and Scotland during the period 1650–1815, it can be understood in two principal ways, neither of them fixed or static. First, it related to a philosophical tradition constructed during the fifteenth and sixteenth centuries from Neoplatonic and Hermetic thought, which informed the theory and practice of alchemy, astrology and ritual magic. By the late eighteenth century, the coherence of this Renaissance tradition of occult thinking was in tatters. The re-examination of ancient art and philosophy by Stukeley, Hancarville, Payne Knight and Taylor added entirely new dimensions to the interpretation of classical culture. An awareness of other religious and spiritual traditions, especially Hinduism and Buddhism, had begun to penetrate the British intellectual elite by the late eighteenth century. These could not easily be assimilated within Western occult philosophy. At the same time, astrology and ritual magic had been largely relegated to the cultural sphere of the less educated. While the occult philosophical tradition retained some importance in the minds of early nineteenth-century Romantic writers, it had begun to fragment into its component parts, which might be combined in startlingly unconventional ways. In the late nineteenth century, Theosophy would attempt to meld elements of Western occult thinking with (Westernized) versions of other global traditions. Since that point, the Renaissance occult tradition has been primarily a focus of scholarly interest rather than a starting point for new intellectual or religious movements.

A second way of understanding the occult is in more practical terms, as a way of harnessing supernatural power or divine knowledge for human objectives. Again, this approach did not remain the same over time. For a start, the dividing line between the supernatural and the natural became increasingly rigid. In an earlier age of wonders, signs and providences, supernatural events seemed to be everywhere, but they were defined in rather imprecise ways. Their immediate causes might be entirely natural, so that only their incidence or the way in which they were interpreted placed them in a category beyond nature. Agrippa's vague explanation of magic as the use of *natural* means for wondrous effects made sense to those who perceived the supernatural in everyday occurrences. Hobbes's insistence that miracles had to defy natural laws, however, marked the beginning of an intellectual change that would eventually alter the stance of most educated people. Simply put, wonders became rarer because natural causes were no longer seen as acceptable contributors to them. This suited not just scientists, but also clerics who wanted to restrict miracles to explicit interventions by God, happening mostly in the past, so that they could not be claimed by present-day "enthusiasts" as indications of divine favour towards them.

The clergy had other reasons to resist a loose understanding of the supernatural: it smacked of "superstition," against which they were increasingly vigilant, and it might lead to diabolism. The desire to suppress "superstitious" beliefs did not expire with the Glorious Revolution of 1688. It was a primary factor in the decline of the occult as a practical aspiration, especially in Scotland where the Presbyterian clergy were obsessed with "Popery." Opposition to "superstition" often went hand in hand with a deep-seated fear of diabolism. Many of the clergy were convinced that alchemy, astrology and ritual magic represented works of the Devil. They lacked the judicial means of enforcing this view, but that did not prevent them from disseminating it, and in the course of the seventeenth century it gained a wider, more receptive audience. In Scotland, the Presbyterian campaign to demonize practical aspects of the occult was so successful that they were virtually wiped out among the educated elite by the mid-eighteenth century.

The supernatural might be activated through contact with spirits. This method was usually hidden within occult ways of thinking, because it was so controversial. Ritual magic was most open in seeking control over spirits, but alchemists and astrologers were sometimes willing to admit that they were aiming at a similar goal by different means. Alchemists dreamed that the divine wisdom found in the Philosopher's Stone would give them the ability to converse with angelic beings. Astrologers viewed the planets as inhabited by spirits or angels, whose influence on humans was exerted through invisible, long-distance forces. On a more sophisticated level, Neoplatonists described the world as inhabited by an infinite number of spirits, although only the most daring thinkers suggested that human beings could consciously interact with them. By contrast, Jacob Boehme's English followers, the Philadelphians, who were open to the influence of occult thinking as well as popular magic, pursued endless spiritual interactions. While John Wesley remained wary of spirits, many Methodists were eager to know more about them, which helps to explain the attraction of Emanuel Swedenborg. He adopted the Philadelphian view that spirits were ready and eager to talk with humans. In the eyes of the established Churches, however, the spirits with which Behmenists and Swedenborgians communicated were simply devils or illusions. This attitude did not alter much over the entire period, and it served to marginalize anybody who testified openly to such experiences.

In spite of these challenges, the history of the occult between 1650 and 1815 does not follow a simple pattern. The assumption of many historians, that occult thinking was debunked by experimental science in the late seventeenth century, is essentially wrong. Scientific writing in this period almost never set out to undermine or attack occult assumptions. On the other hand, many scientists, including Newton, Boyle and Whiston, embraced aspects of occult thinking, especially alchemy and astrology. The wider enterprise of science, however, which developed mainly within the Royal Society and the Scottish universities, simply did not have much use for the occult. In Scotland, where science was to become almost an ideology among the educated elite, anything connected with the occult was likely to be vilified as diabolical or "superstitious." As a result, in both England and Scotland, occult thinking became less respectable among scientists, although, conversely, those who adhered to it were eager to assimilate scientific findings and even to set up a dialogue with science. At times, their attempt at conversation seemed to work, at least temporarily. This can be noted as late as 1782–3, when James Price's experiments caught the attention of both Oxford University and the Royal Society. In most circumstances, however, the dialogue was notably one-sided.

The issue of respectability and social acceptance was far more significant in the history of occult thinking than the question of whether one could prove particular occult claims to be true or false. All of the major intellectual objections to the veracity of the occult were known long before 1650—alchemy was denounced as a waste of time, astrology as improbable, ritual magic as delusional or diabolical. Nothing much was added to this arsenal of negative arguments in the age of scientific revolution and the Enlightenment. No major scientific figure of the period chose to publish a work against the occult (Flamsteed's unpublished attack on astrology is the nearest we come to an exception), although sharp criticisms of occult thinking do appear in the lectures and writings of Scottish and English scientists after 1760. For their part, adherents of the occult were surprisingly quick to adapt to new ideas. With a few notable exceptions, astrologers had accepted Copernicanism by 1700. Ebenezer Sibly was an avid reader of Linnaeus, Buffon and other scientific writers in the 1780s and 1790s. Even the highly traditional Sigismund Bacstrom was aware of what Humphry Davy was up to in the first decade of the nineteenth century. Empirical science was almost never perceived as the enemy of the occult. Instead, its leading foe, according to occult thinkers, was "abstract reason," often associated with Hobbes. One wonders whether this may have been little more than a straw man, similar to the ubiquitous "atheism" that was denounced by religious writers. William Blake, for whom "abstract reason" was equivalent to "deism," identified only one English representative of that terrible, imagination-killing doctrine: Edward Gibbon. Perhaps he really did see "deists" all around him, but he was not very precise in naming them.

The long-term nemesis of occult thinking, as Blake well knew, was organized religion. Throughout the whole period, the position of the established Churches regarding occult philosophy, attempts to harness divine power, contact with spirits, ritual magic and popular "superstition" of all sorts was abundantly clear: it was all inspired by the Devil. While individual clergymen might be lenient towards neighbours who practised alchemy or read astrological almanacs, or even towards popular magical practices, clerical writers generally had no doubt that these things were either diabolical or could lead in that direction. The witch craze bolstered the presumed link between the occult and the Devil, but the mentality of diabolism survived without witch prosecutions. Even those who did not see the Devil as having active power in the everyday world, like Richard Baxter, could nonetheless accept that diabolism was rife. After all, Satan remained the great tempter, the spiritual source of evil, the seducer and deluder of those who aimed at knowledge or power too great for human beings to exercise. No wonder, then, that William Blake, whose version of occult philosophy was deliberately formulated to spite the defenders of organized religion, made the Devil his champion.

Surprisingly, the Anglican and Scottish Episcopal Churches did not move in the aftermath of the Restoration to suppress occult practices, even though they were often associated with religious ideas that could be stigmatized as heterodox or heretical. The clergy had bigger problems on their minds, particularly what to do about the organized followers of Protestant Dissent. As a result, alchemy, protected by important establishment figures like Sir Robert Moray and even King Charles II himself, became more public than ever. Elias Ashmole sought to raise the spagyric art to a level of intellectual respectability that it had never previously known. Thomas Vaughan gave it an infusion of imaginative speculation, while "Eirenaeus Philalethes" provided a practical underpinning for its experiments. As for astrology, while it did not reach the same intellectual levels as alchemy, its popular appeal remained as powerful in Restoration England as it had been before 1660.

The loud alarm bells sounded by clerical writers like Meric Casaubon and Joseph Glanvill against witchcraft, however, served to remind the orthodox that all occult thinking, especially alchemy and ritual magic, was diabolic. By the 1680s, political and professional rivalries among the best-known astrologers were beginning to put a definite strain on the celestial art as well. The appearance of *Kabbala Denudata*, which some hoped would give a new direction to occult philosophy, resulted instead in renewed concerns about heterodoxy. The rejection of occult thinking by mainstream Neoplatonist scholars like Henry More was particularly damaging. The occult was under increasing intellectual pressure in the last years of the Restoration Period, which the Glorious Revolution did nothing to alleviate.

The latter resulted in heightened competition between the two new political parties, Whig and Tory, with further dire consequences for occult thinking. It would be misleading, however, to suggest that one party was sceptical about the occult, while the other was more credulous or accepting. Alchemists who espoused heterodox religious ideas were more favourable towards the Whigs, because the party stood up for Dissenters. Astrologers were divided between the two camps, although the Whig John Partridge would eventually emerge as the most influential almanac writer of the early eighteenth century. Because they upheld the views of the Anglican clergy, the Tories were more likely to defend belief in witches, and to extend accusations of diabolism to others aspects of the occult, while Whig writers increasingly doubted the plausibility of witchcraft and disdained "vulgar" magical practices. In this polarized context, occult thinking began to retreat into the private sphere. New alchemical works became scarcer in the 1690s and eventually stopped appearing. Partridge went so far as to assert that astrology was a natural science, without any connection to supernatural forces. Ritual magic dwindled away almost entirely, at least among the educated elite.

The Hanoverian Succession of 1715 and the subsequent triumph of the Whig Party meant that the intellectual establishment would henceforth be dominated by followers of Newton. The great man himself had largely abandoned alchemy, but he retained a fascination with other aspects of occult thinking, which found their way into his last writings. His followers, like William Stukeley and William Whiston, were open to the influence of occult philosophy, but were careful not to speculate openly about such matters in their published works. Thus, the hidden past of Newtonianism endured, at least in a shadowy form, but it did not have much impact on the direction of science. At the same time, Freemasonry was attracting a growing number of initiates. While never a predominantly occult movement, Masonry harboured publicists like Robert Samber who sought to enhance the rituals and myths of the Brotherhood through alchemical and even magical allusions. The most significant result of these efforts was the theory that Freemasonry originated in the mystery cults of the ancient world, a conclusion that could easily be deduced from a reading of William Warburton's *Divine Legation of Moses*.

While it was struggling among the educated elite, occult thought flourished in the first half of the eighteenth century among less educated members of the population, in both England and Scotland. At this social level, it intersected with popular magical beliefs, but it remained the domain of the literate, who had access to occult books. When it came to the occult, no clear separation existed between folk culture and print culture. The diary of John Cannon illustrates the survival of ritual magic in the west of England, partly through folk customs, partly through published texts. Fairy belief in Scotland was less reliant on literacy and remained more of a popular survival. Second sight became an object of fascination for observers of Highland life, although they tended to downplay its cultural significance. During the same period, examples can be found of learned men, compelled to live on the margins of respectability because of their religious or political disaffection with the Whig establishment, who preserved a strong attachment to occult thinking, which they were often shy to publicize. While they were wary of possession by spirits as promulgated by the French Prophets, they perceived the occult as a support to mystical religion. The most influential of them were John Byrom and William Law, both Nonjurors and Jacobites. Law would become central to the revival of the occult in the late eighteenth century, because he encouraged the republication of Jacob Boehme's writings.

The four fat volumes of that work fell on newly fertile soil. By the 1760s and 1770s, Methodism had begun to spread a religion of the heart to wide audiences. Sentimental poetry and Gothic novels reintroduced readers to the strange and wonderful. Terror became a sentiment to be relished rather than avoided. Occult forms of Freemasonry flourished not only in France and Germany, but within English lodges as well. The groundwork for a revival of the occult was being laid. It is hard to avoid the conclusion that this revival depended mainly on the middling ranks of society rather than the elite, although it attracted some well-connected figures like General Rainsford and was even tolerated by the celebrated Joseph Banks. For the most part, however, the occult revival was a phenomenon of urban middling culture. The booksellers of London noticed its commercial potential and did everything they could to exploit it, by reselling old works and publishing new ones. Conjuring shows and magic acts captivated a broad public. The occult revival produced a burst of publications in astrology, notably those of Ebenezer Sibly, as well as a renewal of alchemical experiments. A theological underpinning to these developments was provided by the writings of Swedenborg, who disdained magic but whose visionary theology proved particularly appealing to those who fervently read Boehme or who practised alchemy. By the early 1790s, it looked as if occult thinking might become a respected feature of middling culture in England—although not in Scotland, where it was effectively resisted by the Moderate Presbyterian establishment and never took root.

The occult revival was eventually undermined by political developments that branded it as radical, treasonable and (again) heterodox. The short-lived fad of magnetic healing, which mixed occult methods with quasi-scientific theory, began to subside when war with France broke out in 1793. The prophet Richard Brothers brought further suspicion on occult movements through his connection with the Freemasons of Avignon. By 1798, the occult lodges had been denounced as the fomenters of the French Revolution, an accusation that spread to include the whole Masonic fraternity. In these dire circumstances, William Blake began to write his prophetic poems, as a protest against the rule of "abstract reason" and a vindication of his own poetic conception of the occult. The long-standing, albeit awkward, relationship between occult thinking, on the one hand, and science and the Enlightenment, on the other, was rejected outright by Blake. In this respect, he stands at the beginning of an era of Romantic detachment from enlightened thought that would continue well into the nineteenth century.

War with France delayed the next stage of development for occult thinking. After 1815, a younger generation of Romantic writers would emphasize novel and imaginative occult themes, often centred on acts of creation, as epitomized in Mary Shelley's *Frankenstein*. The occult movements of the nineteenth century, especially Spiritualism and Theosophy, would build on this Romantic heritage. A conception of the occult as inimical to the rationalist project of Enlightenment would endure into the twentieth century. At the same time, the occult would experience ups and downs in commercial popularity, as older forms of publicity like astrological almanacs fell out of favour, to be replaced by new ones like newspaper horoscopes. The yearning among practitioners of the occult to achieve respectability would never fully be realized, although it would be given a different twist after the advent of personal computers and the Internet. Today, thanks to the profusion of online sources and the changing relationship of public and private spaces which has created "virtual communities" that only exist through electronic communication, the occult is more widespread than ever, and probably more accepted as a feature of contemporary culture than it has been since the mid-seventeenth century. Whether that means more people believe in it today than did 350 years ago, however, remains dubious. Many are willing to dabble in various aspects of occult thinking without becoming intellectually attached to it as a system of belief.

Perhaps the single most important point to be derived from this discussion is that the occult was not killed off by science or the Enlightenment. On the contrary, it coexisted with them, borrowed from them and was rarely the object of attacks from scientific or enlightened writers. In turn, this suggests something about what can be called modernity—an ideologically charged concept, to be sure, but one that forces itself into any discussion of change over the past four centuries. Modernity is a prescriptive concept, not a descriptive one: it tells us what we should be, not necessarily what we are, or even what we have been in the past. To be modern has come to mean embracing the scientific revolution and the Enlightenment, while casting aside magic and "superstition." Yet this is not what many people did in late seventeenth- and eighteenth-century England or Scotland—on the contrary, they were able to retain both points of view, scientific and occult, at least in some measure. In Scotland, to be sure, the Enlightenment did eventually shake off the occult, but that did not happen in England, or in Germany or France, for that matter. The Scottish case was exceptional, and can be ascribed to a century of determined Presbyterian denunciation of anything occult as diabolical.

Throughout the emerging industrial countries today—China, India, Indonesia, Brazil—can be found occult practices and beliefs that owe their origins to very different traditions from those of western Europe. Modernity—or globalization, if one wishes to use an even more aggressively reductionist term—seems to demand that they disappear so the nation can progress into a prosperous future. In most of western Europe, however, the occult did not vanish. It remained an intellectual force of some importance until the early eighteenth century, and has since then experienced periodic revivals. It particularly appealed to those in the middling ranks of society, who have often been the engines of social and economic change. It did not retard or undermine intellectual development, and may have enhanced it, through liberating the imagination. While its survival is not assured, the occult cannot be interpreted as a sign of tragic backwardness. Of course, that should not be taken as an argument to put our trust in it, because it has always suffered from deep weaknesses as an explanatory system, as well as from an inability to sustain critical inquiry. On the other hand, we should be encouraged to lay to rest a conception of the occult as the eternal bogeyman of modernity, bent on the undoing of reason and progress. That bogeyman never really existed, except in the overheated imaginations of those who feared him. As with other devils in history, when we look beyond what frightens us, we may recognize a diminished evil. We may even notice a trace of the gleaming features of a former angel of light.

MANUSCRIPT SOURCES

1. Archives

Great Britain

British Library (B.L.), London.

Additional Mss. 5767–93: D.A. Freher papers.
Additional Ms. 15,911: letters to Simon Ockley.
Additional Mss. 23,667–70, 23,675–6: Charles Rainsford papers.
Additional Ms. 27,986: John Gadbury notebook.
Additional Ms. 39,781: John Flaxman letters.
Egerton Ms. 2378: John Partridge casebook.
Harley Mss. 6481–4, 6486–7: "Dr Rudd" papers.
Lansdowne Ms. 841: letters of James Keith.
Sloane Ms. 696: catalogues of books on magic.
Sloane Mss. 630, 1321, 2577A: alchemical collections.
Sloane Mss. 3632, 3646, 3697: Robert Kellum alchemical papers.

Bodleian Library (Bodl. Lib.), Oxford.

Mss. Ashmole 180, 183, 240, 421, 423, 426–8, 430: astrological papers of William Lilly and John Booker.
Mss. Ashmole 2, 243, 339, 1446: astrological and alchemical papers of Elias Ashmole.
Ms. Aubrey 24: "Zecorbeni" by John Aubrey.
Ms. Ballard 66: conjuring manual.
Mss. Rawlinson C.136, D.1067: Masonic records.
Ms. Rawlinson A.404–5: papers of John Pordage.
Mss. Rawlinson D.832–3, 1152–7, 1341: papers and diaries of Richard Roach.
Mss. Rawlinson Poet 11, 133–4b: Robert Samber papers.
Mss. Rylands d.2–4, 8–10: Masonic records.
Mss. English. Misc. c.533, d.455–6, d.719/1–22, e.127–40, e.196, 650: diaries and papers of William Stukeley.

Glasgow University Library (GUL), Glasgow.

Ferguson Collection.
Mss. 5, 9, 28, 43, 85, 155–6, 204, 210, 253, 260, 274, 281–2: alchemical manuscripts.
Mss. 22, 25, 46, 93, 311, 314, 322: Sigismund Bacstrom papers.
Mss. 36, 40, 51, 62: notes on chemistry courses.
Ms. 86: Samuel Hieron astrological casebook.
Ms. 125: D.A. Freher's three tables.
Ms. 128: astrological notebook.
Mss. 99, 305, 310: Ebenezer Sibly transcripts.

Wellcome Institute (Wellcome), London.
Mss. 957: Tables of Rotalo.
Mss. 1027, 1030–1, 3657: Sigismund Bacstrom papers.
Mss. 1854: treatise on astrology, 1665.
Mss. 2946: astrological notebook 1794–1814.
Mss. 4021: Norris Purslow astrological diary, 1673–1737.
Mss. 4032–9: alchemical notes by Charles Rainsford.
Mss. 4594: alchemical works transcribed by Ebenezer Sibly.
Mss. 4729: astrology tracts belonging to William Stukeley.
Dr Williams's Library (DWL), London.
The Walton Theosophic Library.
Mss. I.1.4, 11, 23–4, 31–4, 39, 49, 54, 68, 70, 79: D.A. Freher papers.
Ms. I.1.43: Henry Brooke letter book.
Swedenborg House, London.
Manuscripts A/26–9: papers of Benedict Chastanier.
Manuscript A/187: commonplace book of J.W. Salmon.
Library of Freemasonry, Grand Lodge of England (GLE), London.
Ms. 1130 STU, vols 1–3: tracts by William Stukeley.
Kew Botanical Gardens (KBG), Kew, London.
Banks Papers 1–2: letters to Sigismund Bacstrom.
East Sussex Record Office (ESRO), Lewes, East Sussex.
Frewen Mss. 5421–5634: letters of the Reverend John Allin to Phillip Firth and Samuel Jeake the younger of Rye.
Rye Museum, Rye, East Sussex.
Jeake Ms. 4/1: library catalogue of Samuel Jeake the elder.
Selmes Mss. 32, 34: astrological papers of Samuel Jeake the younger.
Chetham's Library, Manchester.
Mss. A.2.82, A.7.64, A.4.33: records of French Prophets.
Ms. A.3.51–2: autobiography of John Clowes.
Ms. A.4.98: *Tractatus de Nigromatia.*
Ms. A.6.61–4: copies of Paracelsus.
Alnwick Castle Archives, Alnwick, Northumberland.
Mss. 573A–B, 581, 588, 595, 599, 603, 626, 629, 624: Charles Rainsford papers.

United States

Beinecke Rare Book Library (Beinecke Lib.), Yale University, New Haven, Conn.
Mellon Alchemical Manuscripts.
Mss. 62–3, 69, 89, 93, 124, 128, 140: alchemical works.
Mss. 70, 78, 80: Isaac Newton papers.
Mss. 134, 141: Sigismund Bacstrom notebooks.
Getty Research Institute (GRI), Los Angeles, Cal.
Manly Palmer Hall Collection (MHC).
Box 18, vols 1–19: Bacstrom Alechemical Collections.
Box 43: collection of drawings by J.D. Leuchter.
William Andrews Clark Memorial Library (Clark Library), Los Angeles, Cal.
Ms. J43M3/A859: Samuel Jeake, junior, "Astrological Experiments Exemplified."

2. Microfilm, Digital and Online Resources

Records of the Stationers' Company (RSC), 1554–1920, Ann Arbor, Mich., ProQuest, 1990.
Stationers' Company Archives.

State Library of New South Wales (SL, NSW), Australia, http://www2.sl.nsw.gov.au/banks/.
Papers of Sir Joseph Banks.

Royal College of Physicians, Edinburgh, http://www.rcpe.ac.uk/library/read/collection/ripley/ripley.php.
Ms. BE.D.: The Ripley Scroll, ed. R.I. McCallum.

Royal Society Archives, London, http://ttp.royalsociety.org.
Ms. LXIX.a.2, William Stukeley, "Memoirs of Sr. Isaac Newton's Life 1752."
EC/1766/ 20; EC/1781/08; EC/1789/02: election certificates of Peter Woulfe, James Price and Robert Morse.

The Hartlib Papers Project (Hartlib Papers), Ann Arbor, Mich., University Microfilms, 1996.
CD-ROM collection of Samuel Hartlib's Papers.

The Manuscripts and Papers of Sir Isaac Newton (*M&P*), Cambridge, Chadwyck-Healey, 1991.
Microfilm collection of Newton's papers.

The Newton Project, http://www.newtonproject.sussex.ac.uk.
Papers of Sir Isaac Newton.

NOTES

Introduction: What Was the Occult?

1. This has been recognized in the works of Ronald Hutton, the pre-eminent historian of British pagan beliefs and their modern, occult versions. See his *The Pagan Religions of the Ancient British Isles: Their Nature and Legacy* (Oxford, 1991); *Stations of the Sun: A History of the Ritual Year in Britain* (Oxford, 1996); *The Triumph of the Moon: A History of Modern Pagan Witchcraft* (Oxford, 2001); *The Druids* (Ronceverte, 2007); *Blood and Mistletoe: The History of the Druids in Britain* (New Haven, Conn., 2009).
2. Carl Jung, *Psychology and Alchemy*, trans. R.F.C. Hull (2nd ed., Princeton, 1968), and *Alchemical Studies*, trans. R.F.C. Hull (Princeton, 1967), in *Collected Works of C.G. Jung*, vols 12 and 13.
3. The differences between ancient and modern concepts of the occult are discussed in Erik Hornung, *The Secret Lore of Egypt: Its Impact on the West*, trans. David Lorton (Ithaca, N.Y., 2001).
4. Eric Hobsbawm, "Introduction: Inventing Traditions," in Eric Hobsbawm and Terence Ranger, eds, *The Invention of Tradition* (Cambridge, 1983), pp. 1–14.
5. Samuel Johnson, *A Dictionary of the English Language* (2 vols, London, 1755: 1-volume reprint, London, [1965]).
6. A full-text search for the word "occult" at Early English Books Online, which contains 100,000 works printed in the seventeenth century, yielded 1,898 matches in 584 documents. A similar search at Eighteenth-Century Online, which includes about 150,000 works printed in the eighteenth century, resulted in 5,997 results (many of them different editions of the same work). Less than half of the uses of "occult" in the seventeenth century referred to occult philosophy or science. The percentage was lower among a sampling of works that used the word "occult" in the eighteenth century.
7. Henry Home, Lord Kames, *Sketches of the History of Man* (2 vols, Edinburgh, 1774), vol. 1, p. 355.
8. Walter Charleton, *Physiologia Epicuro-Gassendo-Charltoniana: or, A Fabrick of Science Natural, upon the Hypothesis of Atoms* (London, 1654), book 3, ch. 15, p. 343. See also Keith Hutchison, "What Happened to Occult Qualities in the Scientific Revolution?" *Isis*, 73, 2 (1982), pp. 233–53.
9. John Baptist Porta [Giambattista della Porta], *Natural Magick* (London, 1658), book 1, ch. 2, pp. 1–2.
10. Thomas Browne, *Miracles, Works above and Contrary to Nature* (London, 1683), p. 42 (*sic*: should be 61). The author is not the celebrated Sir Thomas Browne.
11. See Stuart Clark, *Thinking with Demons: The Idea of Witchcraft in Early Modern Europe* (Oxford, 1997), chs 11, 14.

12. John Henry, "The Fragmentation of Renaissance Occultism and the Decline of Magic," *History of Science*, 46 (2008), pp. 1–48.
13. This division between practice and theory has not been imitated by historians who work on other parts of Europe: for example, Pamela H. Smith, *The Business of Alchemy: Science and Culture in the Holy Roman Empire* (Princeton, 1994); Anthony Grafton, *Cardano's Cosmos: The Worlds and Work of a Renaissance Astrologer* (Cambridge, Mass., 2001); Tara Nummedal, *Alchemy and Authority in the Holy Roman Empire* (Chicago, 2007).
14. Keith Thomas, *Religion and the Decline of Magic* (New York, 1971).
15. This was forcefully expressed in the debate between Thomas and Hildred Geertz: "An Anthropology of Religion and Magic: Two Views," *Journal of Interdisciplinary History*, 6 (1975), pp. 71–109.
16. Learned magic is directly discussed on pp. 222–31, 273, 437–8 and 643–4 of *Religion and the Decline of Magic*, a total of twelve out of 688 pages.
17. Annabel Gregory, "Witchcraft, Politics and 'Good Neighbourhood' in Early 17th-Century Rye," *Past and Present*, 133 (1991), pp. 31–66; James Sharpe, *Instruments of Darkness: Witchcraft in England, 1550–1750* (Philadelphia, 1995); Deborah Willis, *Malevolent Nurture: Witch-Hunting and Maternal Power in Early Modern England* (Ithaca, N.Y., 1995); Jonathan Barry, M. Hester and G. Roberts, eds, *Witchcraft in Early Modern Europe: Studies in Culture and Belief* (Cambridge, 1996).
18. Ian Bostridge, *Witchcraft and its Transformations, c. 1650–c. 1750* (Oxford, 1997); Owen Davies, *Witchcraft, Magic and Culture, 1736–1951* (Manchester, 1999). Davies's other publications include *Popular Magic: Cunning-Folk in English History* (Hambledon, 2007) and *Grimoires: A History of Magic Books* (Oxford, 2009). With Willem de Blécourt, Davies has edited *Witchcraft Continued* (Manchester, 2004). For witch beliefs and magic outside Britain, see Steven Wilson, *The Magical Universe: Everyday Ritual and Magic in Pre-Modern Europe* (Hambledon and London, 2000); Owen Davies and Willem de Blecourt, eds, *Beyond the Witch Trials: Witchcraft and Magic in Enlightenment Europe* (Manchester and New York, 2004); Marijke Gijswit-Hofstra, Brian P. Levack and Roy Porter, eds, *Witchcraft and Magic in Europe: The Eighteenth and Nineteenth Centuries* (London, 1999).
19. Bernard Capp, *Astrology and the Popular Press: English Almanacs 1500–1800* (London, 1979); Patrick Curry, *Prophecy and Power: Astrology in Early Modern England* (Princeton, 1989); Louise Hill Curth, *English Almanacs: Astrology and Popular Medicine, 1500–1700* (Manchester, 2008).
20. Alan Macfarlane, "Civility and the Decline of Magic," in Peter Burke, Brian Harrison and Paul Slack, eds, *Civil Histories: Essays in Honour of Sir Keith Thomas* (Oxford, 2000), pp. 145–60.
21. The classic work on the subject is Christina Larner, *Enemies of God: The Witch-Hunt in Scotland* (Baltimore, 1981). More recent assessments are found in P.G. Maxwell-Stuart, *Satan's Conspiracy: Magic and Witchcraft in Sixteenth-Century Scotland* (East Linton, 2001); Julian Goodare, ed., *The Scottish Witch-Hunt in Context* (Manchester, 2001), which contains an article by James Sharpe, "Witch-Hunting and Witch Historiography: Some Anglo-Scottish Comparisons," on pp. 182–97; Julian Goodare, Lauren Martin and Joyce Miller, eds, *Witchcraft and Belief in Early Modern Scotland* (Basingstoke, 2008).
22. Lizanne Henderson and Edward J. Cowan, *Scottish Fairy Belief: A History* (East Linton, 2001); Lizanne Henderson and Edward J. Cowan, "The Last of the Witches: The Survival of Scottish Witch Belief," in Goodare, ed., *The Scottish Witch-Hunt*, pp. 198–217.
23. Recently, William R. Newman and Lawrence M. Principe have argued that alchemy should be considered primarily as an experimental rather than as an occult pursuit. While it serves as an important corrective, this view does not fully explain the motivations of the majority of alchemists. See William R. Newman, *Gehennical Fire: The Lives of George Starkey, an American Alchemist in the Scientific Revolution* (Cambridge, Mass., 1994); Lawrence M. Principe and William R. Newman, "Some Problems with the Historiography of Alchemy," in William R. Newman and Anthony Grafton, eds, *Secrets of Nature: Astrology and Alchemy in Early Modern Europe* (Cambridge, Mass., 2001),

pp. 385–431; William R. Newman and Lawrence M. Principe, *Alchemy Tried in the Fire: Starkey, Boyle and the Fate of Helmontian Chymistry* (Chicago, 2002); William R. Newman, *Promethean Ambitions: Alchemy and the Quest to Perfect Nature* (Chicago, 2005); William R. Newman, *Atoms and Alchemy: Chymistry and the Experimental Origins of the Scientific Revolution* (Chicago, 2006).

24. William Fleetwood, *An Essay upon Miracles* (London, 1701), p. 10. Apart from Keith Thomas, few historians of magic have considered "church magic": prophecies and prayer. The boundary between magic and religion, however, has been a central concern for cultural anthropologists: Stanley Tambiah, *Magic, Religion and the Scope of Rationality* (Cambridge, 1990).
25. Richard Kieckhefer, *Magic in the Middle Ages* (Cambridge, 1990), pp. 1, 9, 14. For more on the definition of magic, see the essays collected in Brian P. Levack, ed., *Articles on Witchcraft, Magic and Demonology* (12 vols, New York and London, 1992), vol. 1.
26. A good introduction is Antoine Faivre, *Access to Western Esotericism* (New York, 1994). See also the immense bibliography in Richard Caron, Joscelyn Godwin, Wouter J. Hanegraaff and Jean-Louis Vieillard Baron, eds, *Ésotérisme, Gnoses et Imaginaires Symboliques: Mélanges Offertes à Antoine Faivre* (Leuven, 2001), pp. 875–918. The subject can be further explored through Arthur Versluis, *Magic and Mysticism: An Introduction to Western Esotericism* (Lanham, 2007) and Nicholas Goodrick-Clark, *The Western Esoteric Traditions: A Historical Introduction* (Oxford, 2008). For a definition of the field, see Wouter Hanegraaff, "Some Remarks on the Study of Western Esotericism," *Esoterica*, 1 (1999), pp. 3–19.
27. General works on the development of occult philosophy include Lynn Thorndike, *A History of Magic and Experimental Science* (8 vols, New York, 1923–58); D.P. Walker, *Spiritual and Demonic Magic: From Ficino to Campanella* (London, 1958); Désirée Hirst, *Hidden Riches: Traditional Symbolism from the Renaissance to Blake* (London, 1964), chs 1–4; Wayne Shumaker, *The Occult Sciences in the Renaissance: A Study in Intellectual Patterns* (Berkeley, Cal., 1972); D.P. Walker, *The Ancient Theology: Studies in Christian Platonism from the Fifteenth to the Eighteenth Centuries* (London, 1972); Brian Vickers, ed., *Occult and Scientific Mentalities in the Renaissance* (Cambridge, 1984, 2005); Brian P. Copenhaver, "Astrology and Magic," in Charles B. Schmitt, ed., *The Cambridge History of Renaissance Philosophy* (Cambridge, 1988), pp.; P.G. Maxwell-Stuart, ed., *The Occult in Early Modern Europe: A Documentary History* (New York, 1999); Mark Morrisson, *Modern Alchemy: Occultism and the Emergence of Atomic Theory* (Oxford, 2007). For Hermes Trismegistus, see Garth Fowden, *The Egyptian Hermes: A Historical Approach to the Late Pagan Mind* (Cambridge, 1986); Brian Copenhaver, ed. and trans., *Hermetica: The Greek Corpus Hermeticum and the Latin Asclepius in a New English Translation with Notes and Introduction* (Cambridge, 1992); Florian Ebeling, *The Secret History of Hermes Trismegistus: Hermeticism from Ancient to Modern Times*, trans. David Lorton (Ithaca, N.Y., 2007).
28. Jolande Jacobi, ed., *Paracelsus: Selected Writings*, trans. Norbert Guterman (New York, 1951), p. 119.
29. "Superstition" is discussed in various historical contexts in S.A. Smith and Alan Knight, eds, *The Religion of Fools? Superstition Past and Present* (Oxford, 2008).
30. For the interpretation of printed texts, see Elizabeth Eisenstein, "An Unacknowledged Revolution Revisited," *American Historical Review*, 107, 1 (2002), pp. 87–105; Adrian Johns, "How to Acknowledge a Revolution," *ibid.*, pp. 106–25; and Eisenstein's reply, *ibid.*, pp. 126–8; also, William H. Sherman, *John Dee: The Politics of Reading and Writing in the English Renaissance* (Amherst, Mass., 1995); Adrian Johns, *The Nature of the Book: Print and Knowledge in the Making* (Chicago, 1998).
31. Herbert Butterfield, *The Origins of Modern Science, 1300–1800* (London, 1949); I. Bernard Cohen, *Revolution in Science* (Cambridge, Mass., 1985); David C. Lindberg, "Conceptions of the Scientific Revolution from Bacon to Butterfield: A Preliminary Sketch," in David C. Lindberg and Robert S. Westman, eds, *Reappraisals of the Scientific Revolution* (Cambridge, 1990), pp. 1–26.

32. See Peter Dear, *Revolutionizing the Sciences: European Knowledge and its Ambitions* (2nd ed., Princeton, 2009); Steven Shapin, *The Scientific Revolution* (Chicago, 1998); Margaret C. Jacob, *The Cultural Meaning of the Scientific Revolution* (New York, 1987); Brian Vickers, ed., *Occult and Scientific Mentalities in the Renaissance* (Cambridge, 1984); M.L. Righini Bonelli and William R. Shea, eds, *Reason, Experiment and Mysticism in the Scientific Revolution* (New York, 1971).
33. The paradigm theory derives from Thomas S. Kuhn, *The Structure of Scientific Revolutions* (3rd ed., Chicago, 1996). For respectability and trust, see Simon Schapin, *A Social History of Truth: Civility and Science in Seventeenth-Century England* (Chicago, 1994); Adrian Johns, "Identity, Practice and Trust in Early Modern Natural Philosophy," *Historical Journal*, 42, 4 (1999), pp. 1125–45.
34. Frances Yates, *The Rosicrucian Enlightenment* (London, 1972); Robert S. Westman and J.E. McGuire, *Hermeticism and the Scientific Revolution* (Los Angeles, 1977); Brian P. Copenhaver, "Natural Magic, Hermeticism, and Occultism in Early Modern Science," in Lindberg and Westman, eds, *Reappraisals*, pp. 261–301; Christopher McIntosh, *The Rosicrucians: The History, Mythology and Rituals of an Esoteric Order* (3rd ed., York Beach, Maine, 1997), which traces the later history of Rosicrucian organizations; Carlos Gilly and Cis van Heertum, eds, *Magic, Alchemy and Science: The Influence of Hermes Trismegistus* (Florence, 2002); Didier Kahn, "The Rosicrucian Hoax in France," in William R. Newman and Anthony Grafton, eds, *Secrets of Nature: Astrology and Alchemy in Early Modern Europe* (Cambridge, Mass., 2001), pp. 235–344.
35. Richard S. Westfall, *Never at Rest: A Biography of Isaac Newton* (Cambridge, 1980), esp. ch. 8; Betty Jo Teeter Dobbs, *The Foundations of Newton's Alchemy: or, The Hunting of the Greene Lyon* (Cambridge, 1975); Betty Jo Teeter Dobbs, *The Janus Faces of Genius: The Role of Alchemy in Newton's Thought* (Cambridge, 2002); Michael Hunter, "Alchemy, Magic and Moralism in the Thought of Robert Boyle," *British Journal of the History of Science*, 23 (1990), pp. 387–410; Larry Principe, *The Aspiring Adept: Robert Boyle and his Alchemical Quest* (Princeton, 1998).
36. David Stevenson, *The Origins of Freemasonry* (Cambridge, 1988), and Margaret Jacob, *The Origins of Freemasonry: Facts and Fictions* (Philadelphia, 2006).
37. Immanuel Kant, "An Answer to the Question, 'What is Enlightenment?' " in H.S. Reiss, ed., *Kant: Political Writings* (Cambridge, 1991), pp. 54–60.
38. Auguste Viatte, *Les Source Occultes du Romantisme* (2 vols, Paris, 1927); Ernst Benz, *The Mystical Sources of German Romantic Philosophy*, trans. Blair R. Reynolds and Eunice M. Paul (Allison Park, Pa., and Paris, 1968); René Le Forestier, *La Franc-Maçonnerie Templière et Occultiste aux XVIIIe et XIXe Siècles* (Paris and Louvain, 1970); Robert Darnton, *Mesmerism and the End of Enlightenment in France* (Cambridge, Mass., 1968); Glenn Alexander Magee, *Hegel and the Hermetic Tradition* (Ithaca, N.Y., 2001); Antoine Faivre, *Philosophie de la Nature: Physique Sacrée et Théosophie, XVIIIe–XIXe Siècles* (Paris, 1996).
39. An excellent introduction is Alexander Broadie, *The Scottish Enlightenment: The Historical Age of the Historical Nation* (Edinburgh, 2001).
40. Roy Porter, *The Creation of the Modern World: The Untold Story of the British Enlightenment* (New York, 2000).
41. Roy Porter, *Quacks: Fakers and Charlatans in Medicine* (Stroud, Gloucs, 2003); Patricia Fara, *An Entertainment for Angels: Electricity in the Enlightenment* (Duxford, Cambs, 2002), and her *Fatal Attraction: Magnetic Mysteries of the Enlightenment* (New York, 2005).

Chapter One: The Alchemical Heyday

1. Dee has been the subject of television shows as well as several biographies, including Peter French, *John Dee: The World of the Elizabeth Magus* (2nd ed., London, 1987); Nicholas Clulee, *John Dee's Natural Philosophy: Between Science and Religion* (London, 1988); Benjamin Woolley, *The Queen's Conjurer: The Science and Magic of Dr. John Dee,*

Adviser to Queen Elizabeth I (New York, 2001): Glyn Parry, *The Arch Conjuror: John Dee* (New Haven, 2012). Recent studies of his writings include William H. Sherman, *John Dee: The Politics of Reading and Writing in the English Renaissance* (Amherst, Mass., 1995); Deborah Harkness, *John Dee's Conversations with Angels: Cabala, Alchemy and the End of Nature* (Cambridge, 1999); György E. Szóny, *John Dee's Occultism: Magical Exaltation through Powerful Signs* (Albany, 2004).

2. This conclusion is based on the research of the modern alchemist Adam Maclean, who has made a graph of the printing dates of 432 alchemical works published in English between 1500 and 1800. He noticed a "sudden explosion" of publications in the late seventeenth century. The graph can be found on Maclean's alchemical website at http://www.levity.com/alchemy/eng_bks.html. The bibliographies of "Chymical Works" compiled by William Cooper in 1673, 1675 and 1688, which are described below, reinforce the same point: see Lauren Kassell, "Secrets Revealed: Alchemical Books in Early-Modern England," *History of Science*, 49, 162 (2011), pp. 61–87. John Ferguson, the Scottish collector, calculated that more alchemical works appeared in English between 1650 and 1675 or 1680 "than in all the time before or after those dates." Quoted in Ronald Sterne Wilkinson, "The Hartlib Papers and Seventeenth-Century Chemistry, Part I," *Ambix*, 15, 1 (Feb. 1968), p. 56.
3. C.H. Josten, ed., *Elias Ashmole (1617–1692): His Autobiographical and Historical Notes, his Correspondence and Other Contemporary Sources Relating to his Life and Work* (5 vols, Oxford, 1966), vol. 1, pp. 57, 391, vol. 4, p. 1891 n. 1.
4. Frederick Talbot, "The Life of John Heydon," in John Heydon, *The Wise-Mans Crown: or, The Glory of the Rosie-Cross* (London, 1664), pp. [i–xvi]; William R. Newman, *Gehennical Fire: The Lives of George Starkey, An American Alchemist in the Scientific Revolution* (Boston, 1994; Chicago, 2003).
5. For Hartlib and his circle, see George H. Turnbull, *Hartlib, Dury and Comenius* (London, 1953); Charles Webster, *The Great Instauration: Science, Medicine and Reform 1626–1660* (London, 1975); Mark Greengrass, M.P. Leslie and T.J. Raylor, eds, *The Advancement of Learning in the 17th Century: Samuel Hartlib and his World* (Cambridge, 1994).
6. For the mystery of his identity, see Karin Figala and Ulrich Petzold, "Alchemy in the Newtonian Circle: Personal Acquaintances and the Problem of the Late Phase of Newton's Alchemy," in J.V. Field and F.A.J.L. James, eds, *Renaissance and Revolution: Humanists, Scholars, Craftsmen and Natural Philosophers in Early Modern Europe* (Cambridge, 1993), pp. 173–92. For Shadwell, see Daniel Lysons, *The Environs of London, Volume 3: County of Middlesex* (London, 1795), pp. 383–90.
7. "Christian Rosencreutz" [Johann Valentin Andraea], *The Hermetick Romance; or The Chymical Wedding*, trans. E. Foxcroft (London, 1690). Foxcroft is referred to frequently in the correspondence of his relative Lady Conway with the philosopher Henry More: see Marjorie Hope Nicolson and Sarah Hutton, eds, *The Conway Letters: The Correspondence of Anne, Viscountess Conway, Henry More, and their Friends, 1642–1684* (Oxford, 1992), *passim*. The identification of Foxcroft as the "Mr. F." of Newton's manuscripts, especially King's College Library (KCL), Cambridge, Keynes Ms. 33, accessed through *Sir Isaac Newton: Manuscripts and Papers* (forty-three-reel microfilm collection, 1991: hereafter *M&P*), reel 19, has been challenged by Karin Figala, "Newton as Alchemist," *History of Science*, 15 (1977), p. 103; but he appears again in a document edited by Karin Figala, John Harrison and Ulrich Petzold, "*De Scriptoribus Chemicus*: Sources for the Establishment of Isaac Newton's (Al)chemical Library," in Peter Harman and Alan Shapiro, eds, *The Investigation of Difficult Things: Essays on Newton and the History of the Exact Sciences* (Cambridge, 1992), pp. 146–7.
8. Beinecke Library, Mellon Ms. 62, f. 143.
9. Newman, *Gehennical Fire*, p. 173. The quotation is from Samuel Hartlib.
10. East Sussex Record Office (ESRO), FRE 5465; also FRE 5700–3 for Starkey's letters; Newman, *Gehennical Fire*, pp. 46–8.

11. John Matson to Robert Boyle, 18 May 1676, in Michael Hunter, Antonio Clericuzio and Lawrence M. Principe, eds, *The Correspondence of Robert Boyle* (6 vols, London, 2001), vol. 4, p. 409.
12. Peter Elmer, "The Library of John Webster," *Medical History*, Supplement, 6 (1986), p. 19; *The Last Will and Testament of Basil Valentine, Monk of the Order of St. Bennet* (London, 1671), with note to the reader by J.W. For Webster as a member of the "Antinomian underground" in the 1630s, see David Como, *Blown by the Spirit: Puritanism and the Emergence of an Antinomian Underground in Pre-Revolution England* (Stanford, 2004), pp. 314–15.
13. Wellcome Library, Ms. 3657, ff. [13–24], quotation on f. [15].
14. Ronald Sterne Wilkinson, "The Hartlib Papers and Seventeenth-Century Chemistry, Part II," *Ambix*, 17, 2 (July 1970), p. 105.
15. John Heydon, *A New Method of Rosie Crucian Physick* (London, 1658), p. 38.
16. F.E. Hutchinson, *Henry Vaughan: A Life and Interpretation* (Oxford, 1947), esp. ch. 11; Alan Rudrum, "Bibliographical Introduction," in Alan Rudrum and Jennifer Drake-Brockman, eds, *The Works of Thomas Vaughan* (Oxford, 1984), pp. 1–31.
17. John Aubrey, *Brief Lives*, ed. Oliver Lawson Dick (Harmondsworth, Middlesex, 1982), p. 282; Rudrum, "Bibliographical Introduction," p. 23.
18. David Stevenson, ed., *Letters of Sir Robert Moray to the Earl of Kincardine, 1657–73* (Aldershot and Burlington, 2007), p. 128, and references in the index to chemists, Glauber and Paracelsus. Moray's Freemasonry is discussed below, in Chapter four.
19. Newman, *Gehennical Fire*, pp. 3–9; Wilkinson, "Hartlib Papers, Part I," pp. 64–5.
20. Royal College of Physicians, Edinburgh, Ms. BE.D. (Ripley Scroll), accessed at http://www.rcpe.ac.uk/library/read/collection/ripley/ripley.php. See also R.I. McCallum, "The Ripley Scroll of the Royal College of Physicians of Edinburgh," *Vesalius*, 2, 1 (1996), pp. 39–49; Stanton J. Linden, "Reading the Ripley Scrolls: Iconographic Patterns in Renaissance Alchemy," in György Szónyi, ed., *European Iconography, East and West* (Leiden, 1996), pp. 236–49. Sixteen Ripley Scrolls exist in the UK, and four in the US. They date from the late sixteenth to the early eighteenth century. Copies were owned by John Dee (Wellcome Lib., Ms. 692), the astrologer Simon Norton (Bodl. Lib., Ashmole Roll 53) and William Sancroft, archbishop of Canterbury (Fitzwilliam Museum, Cambridge, Ms. 276).
21. Dickinson and Twysden are noted in *ODNB*; for Twysden and Faber, see KCL, Keynes Ms. 50, *M&P*, reel 19.
22. Newman published a translation of Basil Valentine's *Triumphant Chariot of Antimony* (London, 1678), with notes by the physician Theodor Kirkringius.
23. William Salmon, *Medicina Practica, or Practical Physick* (London, 1692), pp. 163–696.
24. Glasgow University Library (GUL), Ferguson Ms. 322.
25. See Allen Debus, *The English Paracelsians* (New York, 1965) and *The Chemical Philosophy: Paracelsian Science and Medicine in the Sixteenth and Seventeenth Centuries* (2nd ed., New York, 2002).
26. P.M. Rattansi, "The Helmontian-Galenist Controversy in Restoration England," *Ambix*, 12 (1964), pp. 1–23; Charles Webster, "English Medical Reformers of the Puritan Revolution: A Background to the 'Society of Chymical Physicians,'" *Ambix*, 14 (1967), pp. 16–41; Harold J. Cook, "The Society of Chemical Physicians, the New Philosophy, and the Restoration Court," *Bulletin of the History of Medicine*, 61, 1 (1987), pp. 61–77.
27. Meric Casaubon, *Of Credulity and Incredulity in Things Natural, Civil and Divine* (London, 1668), pp. 16–17; Harold J. Cook, *The Decline of the Old Medical Regime in Stuart London* (Ithaca, N.Y., 1986).
28. Figala and Petzold, "Alchemy in the Newtonian Circle," p. 182.
29. This appears in the Getty Library copy of Elias Ashmole, *The Way to Bliss* (London, 1658), p. 26.
30. Rudrum, "Biographical Introduction," p. 12; Stephen Clucas, "The Correspondence of a XVII-Century 'Chymicall Gentleman': Sir Cheney Culpeper and the Chemical Interests

of the Hartlib Circle," *Ambix*, 40, 3 (Nov. 1993), p. 149. "Mistress Ogelby" may have been the wife of John Ogilby, Charles II's cosmographer; her death in 1677 was noted by Ashmole: Josten, ed., *Ashmole*, vol. iv, p. 1507.

31. Newman, *Gehennical Fire*, pp. 82–3.
32. J. Kent Clark, *Goodwin Wharton* (Oxford, 1984), pp. 7–9, ch. 4. No mention of alchemy is found in Maurice Ashley, *Major John Wildman, Plotter and Postmaster: A Study of the English Republican Movement in the Seventeenth Century* (London, 1947).
33. Josten, ed., *Ashmole*, vol. 1, *passim*; also, Michael Hunter, "Elias Ashmole, 1617–1692: The Founder of the Ashmolean Museum and his World," in his *Science and the Shape of Orthodoxy: Intellectual Change in Late Seventeenth-Century Britain* (Woodbridge, Suffolk, 1995), pp. 21–42.
34. Robert Latham, ed., *The Shorter Pepys* (Berkeley and Los Angeles, 1985), pp. 89, 136.
35. Josten, ed., *Ashmole*, vol. 2, p. 505.
36. Jason Peacey, *Politicians and Pamphleteers: Propaganda during the English Civil Wars and Interregnum* (Aldershot, 2004), ch. 4.
37. Lois Schwoerer, "Liberty of the Press and Public Opinion, 1660–1695," in J.R. Jones, ed., *Liberty Secured? Britain before and after 1688* (Stanford, 1982), pp. 199–230. The best overall account of censorship in the early-modern period remains Frederick Seaton Siebert, *Freedom of the Press in England, 1476–1776* (Urbana, Ill., 1965), pp. 219–33.
38. Simon Thurley, *Whitehall Palace: An Architectural History of the Royal Apartments, 1240–1690* (New Haven, 1999), p. 114; M.L. Wolbarscht and D.S. Sax, "Charles II: A Royal Martyr?" *Notes and Records of the Royal Society of London*, 16, 2 (1961), pp. 154–7; Antonia Fraser, *Royal Charles: Charles II and the Restoration* (New York, 1979), p. 450.
39. "James Hasolle" [Elias Ashmole], "Prolegomena," in Arthur Dee, *Fasciculus Chemicus: or Chymical Collections* (London, 1650), pp. [viii–ix].
40. George Thor, *An Easie Introduction to the Philosophers Magical Gold: To Which Is Added Zorasters Cave; As Also John Pontanus Epistle upon the Mineral Fire; Otherwise Called, The Philosophers Stone* (London, 1667), p. [i].
41. J[ohn] W[ilkins], *Mathematicall Magick* (London, 1648), p. 226.
42. This is not the view of William R. Newman and Lawrence M. Principe, who have argued that alchemy was primarily a practical pursuit. While they acknowledge a separate strain of alchemy, which they call "mystical," they do not give it much attention. This chapter takes a different approach, but Newman and Principe deserve enormous credit for reviving interest in seventeenth-century alchemy.
43. Keith Thomas, *Religion and the Decline of Magic* (New York, 1970), pp. 270–1; Christopher Hill, *The World Turned Upside Down: Radical Ideas during the English Revolution* (Harmondsworth, Middlesex, 1991), p. 185; Nicolson and Hutton, eds, *Conway Letters*, p. 42.
44. Hermes Trismegistus, *The Divine Pymander*, trans. John Everard (London, 1650). A 1657 reissue of this work added the short tract known as the *Asclepius*, which had been known in a Latin version throughout the Middle Ages.
45. Heinrich Cornelius Agrippa, *Three Books of Occult Philosophy*, trans. J. F[reake] (London, 1651), sigs A^{v}_{1}-A_{2}, b_{1}-b_{2}. For Child, see Newman, *Gehennical Fire*, pp. 41–2, and Wilkinson, "Hartlib Papers, Part II," pp. 99–100.
46. Agrippa, *Three Books*, book 1, ch. 2, pp. 2–3.
47. D.P. Walker, *Spiritual and Demonic Magic from Ficino to Campanella* (London, 1958), pp. 90–6; also, Wayne Shumaker, *Occult Sciences in the Renaissance: A Study in Intellectual Patterns* (Berkeley and Los Angeles, 1972), pp. 134–56; John S. Mebane, *Renaissance Magic and the Return of the Golden Age: The Occult Traditions of Marlowe, Jonson and Shakespeare* (Lincoln, Nebraska, 1989), ch. 4.
48. The best overall treatment of the phenomenon is Brian Levack, *The Witch-Hunt in Early Modern Europe* (3rd ed., London, 2006). For England, see James Sharp, *Instruments of Darkness: Wichcraft in Early Modern England* (Philadelphia, 1997).

49. *ODNB*; Robert Turner, *Ars Notoria: The Notory Art of Solomon* (London, 1657), p. 136. See also S. Liddell MacGregor Mathers, ed., *The Key of Solomon the King (Clavicula Salomonis)* (London, 1888, repr. 1972).
50. Heinrich Cornelius Agrippa, *His Fourth Book of Occult Philosophy*, trans. Robert Turner (London, 1664).
51. Elias Ashmole, *Theatrum Chemicum Britannicum* (London, 1652), sig. A_2, p. 436. The comparison between England and ancient nations was first made by Ashmole in the preface to *Fasciculus Chemicus*.
52. Josten, ed., *Ashmole*, vol. 1, pp. 76–8, vol. 2, pp. 567–9, 588–9, 643. A detailed discussion of Ashmole's alchemy can be found in Bruce Janacek, *Alchemical Belief: Occultism in the Religious Culture of Early Modern England* (University Park, Pa., 2012), ch. 5.
53. Robert Turner, trans., *Paracelsus: Of the Chymical Transmutation, Genealogy and Generation of Metals and Minerals* (London, 1657), sig. A_2. Turner also translated *Paracelsus: Of the Supreme Mysteries of Nature. Of the Spirits of the Planets. Of Occult Philosophy* (London, 1655), which shows that he was not just interested in iatrochemical medicines.
54. Josten, ed., *Ashmole*, vol. 2, pp. 733–4, citing an allusion to Everard in the preface to Elias Ashmole, ed., *The Way to Bliss* (London, 1658), that is clarified in Bodl. Lib., Ashmole Ms. 537.
55. Lauren Kassell, "Reading for the Philosopher's Stone," in Marina Frasca-Spada and Nick Jardine, eds, *Books and the Sciences in History* (Cambridge, 2000), pp. 135–42. Ashmole's copy of this manuscript is in Bodl. Lib., Ashmole Ms. 1419, ff. 57–82. Isaac Newton also had a copy, which is in KCL, Keynes Ms 22, *M&P*, reel 18.
56. Ashmole, *Theatrum Chemicum Britannicum*, sigs A^{v}_{3}-B_1.
57. Ashmole, *Theatrum Chemicum Britannicum*, p. 444; Josten, ed., *Ashmole*, vol. 1, pp. 72, 226–7, and references in index under "Sigils," "Talismans" and "Telesmes."
58. Arthur Dee, *Fasciculus Chemicus: or Chymical Collections*, ed. James Hasolle [Elias Ashmole] (London, 1650), pp. x–xi.
59. Ashmole, *Theatrum Chemicum Britannicum*, pp. 444–7.
60. "Eirenaeus Philalethes" [George Starkey], *Ripley Reviv'd; or, An Exposition upon Sir George Ripley's Hermetico-Poetical Works* (London, 1678), Advertisement.
61. This is the central premise of Lawrence M. Principe and William R. Newman, "Some Problems with the Historiography of Alchemy," in William R. Newman and Anthony Grafton, eds, *Secrets of Nature: Astrology and Alchemy in Early Modern Europe* (Cambridge, Mass., 2001), pp. 385–431.
62. KCL, Keynes Ms 22, *M&P*, reel 18; Principe, *The Aspiring Adept*, pp. 191–200, 310–16.
63. [George Starkey], *Ripley Reviv'd*, pp. 4, 7, 46, 107. "*Chalybs*" denotes iron or steel.
64. For his advice to doctors, see George Starkey, *Nature's Explication and Helmont's Vindication* (London, 1658). Newman's treatment of Starkey's life in *Gehennical Fire* is exhaustive, but he tends to discount the cryptic language of Starkey's alchemy as a mere convention.
65. All of these tracts are superbly edited, with copious annotations, in the 1984 edition of Vaughan's *Works* by Alan Rudrum, which supersedes the previous editions by A.E. Waite.
66. Wilkinson, "Hartlib Papers, Part I," p. 63; Rudrum, "Biographical Introduction," pp. 11–13. Henshaw hinted at his clandestine activities during the Commonwealth period, and expressed his passionate hatred of Cromwell, in his *Vindication of Thomas Henshaw, Esquire* (The Spaw, 1654).
67. Recent works on the early Rosicrucians include Carlos Gilly. *Cimelia Rhodostaurotica: Die Rosenkreuzer im Spiegel der zwischen 1610 und 1660 entstandenen Handschriften und Drucke* (Amsterdam, 1995), an exhibition catalogue from the Ritman Library; Friedrich Niewöhner and Carlos Gilly, eds, *Rosenkreuz als europäisches Phänomen im 17. Jahrhundert* (Amsterdam, 2001); Didier Kahn, "The Rosicrucian Hoax in France," in Newman and Grafton, eds, *Secrets of Nature*, pp. 235–344.

68. Theophilus Schweighardt, *Speculum Sophium Rhodo-Stauraticum Das ist: Weitläuffige Entdeckung des Collegii und axiomatum von der sondern erleuchen Fraternitat Christ-RosenCreutz* (1618), p. 3.
69. "Eugenius Philalethes" [Thomas Vaughan], "Preface," *The Fame and Confession of the Fraternity of R: C: Commonly, of the Rosie Cross* (London, 1653), in Rudrum, *Works*, pp. 479–510. For Rosenkreuz on alchemy, see *Fama Fraternitatis oder Entdeckung der Bruderschafft des löblichen Ordens des Rosenkreuzes* (Danzig, 1615), pp. 47–9. Rosenkreuz's opposition to gold-making may be a joke, as his name suggests the "rosebud-on-cross" symbol that is associated with mercury, the alchemist's favourite substance.
70. Frances Yates, *The Rosicrucian Enlightenment* (London, 1972); Hutchinson, *Henry Vaughan*, pp. 148–9.
71. "Eugenius Philalethes" [Thomas Vaughan], *Magia Adamica: or, The Antiquitie of Magic, and The Descent Thereof from Adam Downwards, Proved* (London, 1650), in Rudrum, ed., *Works*, p. 150.
72. [Vaughan], *Magia Adamica*, p. 215, and note on p. 652 (an unclear reference in the text seems to imply that Vaughan saw Boehme as a fellow Rosicrucian); see also the note on p. 677 to a possible reference to Boehme in "Eugenius Philalethes" [Thomas Vaughan], *Lumen de Lumine* (London, 1651), p. 313. Blunden's publications are discussed in Philip West, *Henry Vaughan's "Silex Scintillans": Scripture Uses* (Oxford, 2001), p. 63. For Vaughan and Boehme, see Serge Hutin, *Les Disciples Anglais de Jacob Boehme au XVII et XVIII Siècles* (Paris, 1960), p. 77, and B.J. Gibbons, *Gender in Mystical and Occult Thought: Behmenism and its Development in England* (Cambridge, 1996), ch. 3.
73. "Eugenius Philalethes" [Thomas Vaughan], *Anthroposophia Theomagica* (London, 1650), p. 53; Jacob Boehme, *The Epistles of Jacob Behmen, aliter, Teutonicus Philosophus* (London, 1649), pp. 1–17.
74. These ideas appear in *Anthroposophia Theomagica*, pp. 66–8, 78, and throughout *Magia Adamica*.
75. Heinrich Khunrath, *Ampitheatrum Sapientiae Aeternae* ([Vienna], 1602), p. 147. For Hartlib and Khunrath, see Clucas, "Correspondence of a 'Chymical Gentleman,'" p. 149.
76. Boehme's "Sophia" appears in ch. 52 of his *Mysterium Magnum*. Humphrey Blunden published parts of this work, but not this particular chapter, in a 1649 English compilation entitled *Mercurius Teutonicus*. A full translation of *Mysterium Magnum* was published by Blunden in 1654. It is possible that Vaughan did not read Boehme's whole work until after his own discussion of the passage from Genesis was published in *Anthroposophia Theomagica*, pp. 58–63. Fludd's version of the scene is graphically depicted in the "First Treatise" of *Utriusque Cosmi Maioris* (2 vols, Oppenheim, 1617), vol. i, p. 49.
77. [Vaughan], *Magia Adamica*, pp. 180–1. See also Wolf-Dieter Müller-Jahncke, "Agrippa von Nettelsheim et la Kabbale," in Antoine Faivre and Frédérick Tristan, eds, *Kabbalistes Chrétiens* (Paris, 1979), pp. 197–209.
78. As with almost every aspect of the history of this period, there is disagreement about how to interpret the divisions within the Church of England. For conflicting views, see Nicholas Tyacke, *Anti-Calvinists: The Rise of English Arminianism, c. 1590–1640* (Oxford, 1987), and Julian Davies, *The Caroline Captivity of the Church: Charles I and the Remoulding of Anglicanism, 1625–1641* (Oxford, 1992).
79. Henry More, *Enthusiasmus Triumphantus* (London, 1655). More saw Jacob Boehme as a naive enthusiast, and he may have put Vaughan in the same category: see Sarah Hutton, "Henry More and Jacob Boehme," in Sarah Hutton, ed., *Henry More (1614–1687): Tercentenary Essays* (Dordrecht, 1990), pp. 157–68. Vaughan admitted that his "*Revelations*" might be counted among those of "*Ranters* and *Anabaptists*" in *Euphrates, or The Waters of the East* (London, 1655), p. 515. An interpretation of Vaughan's debate with More that emphasizes its importance for empirical science is found in Frederic B. Burnham, "The More-Vaughan Controversy: The Revolt against Philosophical Enthusiasm," *Journal of the History of Ideas*, 35, 1 (1974), pp. 33–49.

80. [Vaughan], *Anthroposophia Theomagica*, p. 54.
81. Michael Sendivogius, *A New Light of Alchemy* (London, 1650); Newman, *Gehennical Fire*, pp. 215–27.
82. West, *Henry Vaughan's "Silex Scintillans"*, ch. 2; E.C. Pettet, *Of Paradise and Light: A Study of Vaughan's "Silex Scintillans"* (Cambridge, 1960), ch. 4; Elizabeth Holmes, *Henry Vaughan and the Hermetic Philosophy* (New York, 1932, 1967).
83. Rudrum, "Biographical Introduction," pp. 18–21; "Eugenius Philalethes" [Thomas Vaughan], *The Second Wash: or The Moore Scour'd Once More* (London, 1651), in Rudrum, ed., *Works*, pp. 429–31.
84. "Alazonomastix Philalethes" [Henry More], *Observations upon "Antroposophia Theomagica" and "Anima Magica Abscondita"* ("Parrhesia" [London], 1650), pp. 26, 88–90. For More and Descartes, see A. Rupert Hall, *Henry More and the Scientific Revolution* (Cambridge, 1990), ch. 8.
85. "Eugenius Philalethes" [Thomas Vaughan], *The Man-Mouse Taken in a Trap, and Tortur'd to Death* (London, 1650), p. 243.
86. [Henry More], *The Second Lash of Alazonomastix, Laid On in Mercy against that Stubborn Youth Eugenius Philalethes* (Cambridge, 1651), pp. 4, 72, 109, 179.
87. *Ibid.*, p. 193.
88. [More], *Enthusiasmus Triumphatus*, pp. 1, 5.
89. The British Library contains copies of eighteen auction catalogues issued by Cooper between 1676 and 1688. The quotation is from his first catalogue, *Catalogus Variorum et Insignium Librorum Instructissimae Bibliothecae Clarissimi Doctissimiq; Viri Lazari Seaman, S.T.D.* (London, 1676), "To the Reader." A satirical Latin dialogue, evidently aimed at a scholarly audience, was written on the last of his sales, held at Oxford: [George Smalridge?], *Auctio Davisiana Oxonii Habita* (London, 1689). For auctions in England during this period, see Iain Pears, *The Discovery of Painting: The Growth of Interest in the Arts in England, 1680–1768* (New Haven, Conn., 1988), pp. 57–67.
90. [William Cooper, ed.], *Collectanea Chymica: A Collection of Ten Several Treatises in Chymistry Concerning the Liquor Alkahest, the Mercury of Philosophers, and Other Curiosities Worthy the Perusal* (London, 1684), "To the Reader," p. [i]. This preface is signed "W.C.B." for William Cooper, *Bibliopolam*, and was therefore written by Cooper himself.
91. Newman, *Gehennical Fire*, pp. 262–70; B.J.T. Dobbs, "Newton's Copy of *Secrets Reveal'd*," *Ambix*, 26, 3 (1979), pp. 145–69.
92. The identity of "W.C., Esq." as "William Chamberlain" was discovered by P.J. Ash and published in Josten, ed., *Ashmole*, vol. 3, p. 1289, Addendum. Unfortunately, the information was not noticed by the compilers of the *ODNB* articles on William Cooper and William Chamberlayne. Josten did not connect the author of the *Philosophicall Epitaph* with the poet, but it is very likely that they were the same man, as no other person of that name was actively publishing during the period. William Chamberlayne of Shaftesbury was chiefly known for the heroic epic *Pharonnida* (London, 1659), in which a wonder-working alchemist appears in book 5, canto 3. Lauren Kassel, however, is cautious about the identity of William Chamberlayne in "Secrets Revealed," p. 65.
93. "Eirenaeus Philalethes" [George Starkey], *Secrets Reveal'd: or, An Open Entrance to the Shut-Palace of the King*, ed. W[illiam] C[hamberlayne] (London, 1669), Dedication, p. [ii]; W[illiam] C[hamberlayne], *A Philosophicall Epitaph in Hieroglyphicall Figures with Explanation* (London, 1673), Dedication to Elias Ashmole.
94. William Jenkyn, *Exodus . . . A Sermon Preach't Sept. 12 1675 by Reason of the Much Lamented Death of that Learned and Reverend Minister of Christ, Dr. Lazarus Seaman* (London, 1675).
95. Both Jenkyn and Manton are noted in *ODNB*. For Pinners' Hall, see Michael R. Watts, *The Dissenters: From the Reformation to the French Revolution* (Oxford, 1978), pp. 294, 296.
96. *Defensio Legis, or, The Whole State of England Inquisited and Defended for General Satisfaction* (London, 1674), p. 313.

97. Frederick Helvetius, *A Brief of the Golden Calf, or The Worlds Idol*, ed. and trans. W[illiam] C[hamberlayne] (n.p., n.d.), "To the Reader," p. [iv], printed in C[hamberlayne]., *Philosophicall Epitaph.*
98. For illustrations of the pelican in alchemical works, see Alexander Roob, *The Hermetic Museum: Alchemy and Mysticism* (Cologne, 2001), pp. 138, 180, 415, 439. For its Christian significance, see Peter and Linda Murray, *The Oxford Companion to Christian Art and Architecture* (Oxford, 1996), p. 58.
99. C[hamberlayne]., *Philosophicall Epitaph*, frontispiece and p. [11]. For the *anima mundi*, see Shumaker, *Occult Sciences*, ch. 3; Walker, *Spiritual and Demonic Magic.*
100. C[hamberlayne]., *Philosophicall Epitaph*, p. [21].
101. Shumaker, *Occult Sciences*, p. 127.
102. The original is Paul Felgenhauer, *Das Buchlein Jehi Or, oder Morgenröhte der Weißheit* (Amsterdam, 1640). For Felgenhauer, see Alastair Hamilton, *The Apocryphal Apocalypse: The Reception of the 2nd Book of Esdras (4 Ezra) from the Renaissance to the Enlightenment* (Oxford, 1999), pp. 178–83, 222–3.
103. [Paul Felgenhauer], *Jehior or The Day Dawning; or Morning Light of Wisdom*, pp. 22, 36–7, 55–7, printed with C[hamberlayne]., *Philosophicall Epitaph.*
104. *Ibid.*, pp. 43–5, 58, 71–2.
105. Pordage is discussed below in Chapter Four; for Erbery, see Hill, *The World Turned Upside Down*, pp. 92–7; Christopher Hill, *The Experience of Defeat: Milton and Some Contemporaries* (New York, 1984), pp. 84–97.
106. See William R. Newman and Lawrence Principe, *Alchemy Tried in the Fire: Starkey, Boyle, and the Fate of Van Helmontian Chymistry* (Chicago, 2001). Cooper published Sir Kenelm Digby, *A Choice Collection of Rare Secrets and Experiments in Philosophy*, ed. George Hartman (London, 1682); J.B. van Helmont, *Praecipiolum: or The Immature-Mineral-Electrum the First Metal: Which Is the Minera of Mercury* (London, 1683); and *The Works of Geber* (London, 1686).
107. William Cooper, ed., *A Catalogue of Chymicall Books* (London, 1675). The first edition was published along with the *Philosophicall Epitaph* in 1673, and a third edition appeared in 1688. See Kassell, "Secrets Revealed," pp. 70–8. A list of magical books, possibly by Cooper, is in BL, Sloane 696.

Chapter Two: The Silver Age of the Astrologers

1. Patrick Curry's classic work, *Prophecy and Power: Astrology in Early Modern England* (Princeton, 1989), ch. 2, places the heyday of astrology in the period 1640 to 1660. Keith Thomas suggests a similar chronology in *Religion and the Decline of Magic* (New York, 1971), chs 10–12.
2. Booker, Culpeper and Tanner were republicans; Wharton and Saunders were royalists; Wing accepted any regime in power. Lilly's complicated politics in this period, and the impact of astrological language on the times, are the subjects of Ann Geneva, *Astrology and the Seventeenth-Century Mind: William Lilly and the Language of the Stars* (Manchester, 1995).
3. Curry, *Prophecy and Power*, pp. 21, 40–3. The Astrologers' Feast was revived by Elias Ashmole in 1682–3, in the wake of the Exclusion Crisis. By that point, most leading astrologers were Tories, which suggests that the renewed Feast may have had a political connotation.
4. For astrology and medicine, see Louise Hill Curth, *English Almanacs, Astrology and Popular Medicine, 1550–1700* (Manchester, 2008).
5. Lauren Kassell, *Medicine and Magic in Elizabethan London: Simon Forman, Astrologer, Alchemist and Physician* (Oxford, 2007), pp. 75–99; Michael Macdonald, *Mystical Bedlam: Madness, Anxiety and Healing in 17th-Century England* (Chicago, 1983); Mordechai Feingold, "The Occult Tradition in the English Universities of the Renaissance: A Reassessment," in Brian Vickers, ed., *Occult and Scientific Mentalities in the Renaissance* (Cambridge, 1986), pp. 73–94.

6. Joshua Childrey, *Indago Astrologica: or, A Brief and Modest Enquiry into Some Principal Points of Astrology, As It Was Delivered by the Fathers of It, and Is Now Generally Received by the Sons of It* (London, 1653), p. 9.
7. Henry Coley, *Nuncius Sydereus: or, The Starry Messenger for the Year of our Redemption 1687* (London, 1687), sig. C_7v. The title of Coley's almanac was also that of a celebrated tract by Galileo. Not all astrologers accepted Copernicus. For an anti-Copernican argument, see James Bowker, *Bowker, 1680: An Almanack for the Year of our Lord God 1680* (London, 1680), sigs C_3v–C_8. See Noriss S. Hetherington, "Almanacs and the Extent of Knowledge of the New Astronomy in Seventeenth-Century England," *Proceedings of the American Philosophical Society*, 119, 4 (1975), pp. 275–9.
8. One of the endearing peculiarities of the original *Dictionary of National Biography* was that virtually every major astrologer was noticed in it. They are also included in the new *ODNB*.
9. Lilly was imprisoned in 1653 by Parliament, in 1661 by the royalist government. He complained in 1644 that his almanacs were censored by the Parliamentary licenser of the press, John Booker, a fellow astrologer. He was more quiescent in the 1660s and 1670s, when his almanacs were censored by the king's infamous licenser, Sir Roger L'Estrange. Booker himself complained of "obliterations" made in his predictions for 1665–6 concerning the Anglo-Dutch War: John Booker, *Telescopium Uranicum Repurgatum et Limatum: or, Physical, Astrological and Meteorological Observations for the Year of Christ's Incarnation MDCLXVII* (London, 1667), sig.C_2. Astrological books could also be suppressed for their political content: for example, *The Book of the Prodigies, or Book of Wonders* in 1662. See Curry, *Prophecy and Power*, pp. 46–8, where a different interpretation is placed on this evidence.
10. Joseph Blagrave, *Blagrave's Introduction to Astrology* (London, 1682). The copy in the Huntington Library (shelfmark 325764) belonged to John Evelyn.
11. John Goad, *Astro-Meteorologica, or Aphorisms and Discourses of the Bodies Celestial, their Natures and Influences* (London, 1686); John Goad, *Astro-meteorologia Sana: Sive Principia Physico-Mathematica* (London, 1690).
12. Goad, *Astro-Meteorologica*, pp. 12, 530.
13. John Flamsteed, "Hecker," in Michael Hunter, "Science and Astrology in Seventeenth-Century England: An Unpublished Polemic by John Flamsteed," in his *Science and the Shape of Orthodoxy: Intellectual Change in Late Seventeenth-Century Britain* (Woodbridge, Suffolk, 1995), pp. 245–85, quotation on p. 281; John Gadbury, *Cardines Coeli: or, An Appeal to the Learned and Experienced Observers of Sublunars and their Vicissitudes, Whether the Cardinal Signs of Heaven Are Not Most Influential upon Men and Things?* (London, 1685), sig. A_2v, p. 5.
14. Flamsteed, "Hecker," in Hunter, "Science and Astrology," p. 273; and for Flamsteed and Goad, *ibid.*, pp. 249–50, 251.
15. A good starting place for understanding the practice of astrology is J.C. Eade, *The Forgotten Sky: A Guide to Astrology in English Literature* (Oxford, 1984).
16. Alice Culpeper, "To the Reader," in [Nicholas Culpeper], *Mr. Culpepper's Treatise of Aurum Potabile . . . To Which Is Added: Mr. Culpepper's Ghost* (London, 1656), sig. A_5v.
17. Lancelot Coelson, *Uranicum: or, An Almanack for the Year of our Redemption 1687* (London, 1687), sig. C_3v.
18. [William Drage], *Daimonomageia: A Small Treatise of Sicknesses and Disease from Witchcraft, and Supernatural Causes* (London, 1665), p. 39.
19. Josten, ed., *Ashmole*, vol. 2, p. 538; vol. 4, pp. 1608–32, and notes in the index under "Sigils." According to Keith Thomas, *Religion and the Decline of Magic*, p. 635, Lilly sent Ashmole "a trunkload" of sigils in January 1667. Lilly describes them only as "the greatest Arcana's any privat person in Euroap hath," which could denote a variety of occult objects or even texts. As they belonged to Sir Robert Holborne, a devotee of astrology, Thomas is probably right in assuming that they included sigils. Josten, ed., *Ashmole*, vol. 3, p. 1076, citing B.L., Sloane Ms. 3822, f. 48. Henry Coley,

Lilly's successor, was accused of making sigils in the 1690s, as will be seen below, in Chapter five.

20. Bodl. Lib., Ashmole Ms. 180 (Booker), 183 (Booker), 339, ff. 176–9 (Booker), 426 (Booker), 427 (Lilly); 428 (Booker), 430 (Lilly); Thomas, *Religion and the Decline of Magic*, pp. 305–22. It is not clear how Thomas derived social information from these casebooks. Curiously, nobody since Thomas seems to have made a systematic study of them, and nobody has yet broken Booker's shorthand.
21. Bodl. Lib., Ashmole Ms. 427 (Lilly), ff. 200, 260.
22. Wellcome Lib., Ms. 4279; Robert Latham and William Matthews, eds, *The Diary of Samuel Pepys* (11 vols, Berkeley and Los Angeles, 2000), vol. 9: 1668–9, pp. 100–1; Historical Manuscripts Commission, *12th Report, Appendix, Part 7: The Manuscripts of S.H. Le Fleming, Esq., of Rydal Hall* (London, 1890), p. 55 n. 956.
23. Thomas, *Religion and the Decline of Magic*, pp. 319, 330.
24. The most important work on almanacs is Bernard Capp, *English Almanacs, 1500–1800: Astrology and the Popular Press* (Ithaca, N.Y., 1979).
25. Cyprian Blagden, "The Distribution of Almanacks in the Second Half of the Seventeenth Century," *Studies in Bibliography*, 11 (1958), pp. 108–17, Table 1. The treasurer's Warehouse Book on which Blagden relied is now available on microfilm as *Records of the Stationers' Company* (RSC), reel 84. The collection is described in Robin Myers, ed., *The Stationers' Company Archive: An Account of the Records, 1554–1984* (Winchelsea and Detroit, 1990).
26. Blagden, "Distribution of Almanacks," p. 114.
27. William and Robert Chambers, *Chambers' Encyclopaedia: A Dictionary of Universal Knowledge for the People* (London and Edinburgh, 1874), vol. 1, p. 162; [John Forbes], *An Almanack or, New Prognostication* (Aberdeen, 1666), sig. C_5, for his response to a triennial almanac originating at Edinburgh. Forbes later wrote and printed *The Mariner's Everlasting Almanack* (2nd ed., Aberdeen, 1683).
28. James Paterson, *Edinburgh's True Almanack; or A New Prognostication for the Year of Our Lord 1685* (Edinburgh, 1685), sig. A_2.
29. A pamphlet that sold twenty thousand copies in the seventeenth century would have been considered a runaway bestseller. Several almanacs regularly reached that number, and a few surpassed it. No reliable figures for overall newspaper circulations exist before 1710, but it is likely they outsold almanacs on a yearly basis, even before the repeal of the Licensing Act in 1694. A bi-weekly journal with a circulation of 2,500 would sell 260,000 copies annually, which compares well with *total* almanac sales. On the other hand, even using a multiplier of three readers per newspaper, this would mean only 7,500 people were exposed to each issue. A successful almanac could reach twice as many people as that.
30. The best recent treatment of the period is in Tim Harris, *Restoration: Charles II and his Kingdoms, 1660–1685* (London, 2005), chs 3–4, 6.
31. Henry Coley, *Nuncius Coelestis: or, Urania's Messenger, Exhibiting a Brief Description and Survey of the Year of Humane Redemption 1680* (London, 1679), sig. C_5.
32. Capp, *English Almanacs*, pp. 92–3; Gadbury, *Cardines Coeli*, p. 35. The information behind the "Meal Tub Plot" was discredited in court, which led to Gadbury's release: see *The Case of Tho. Dangerfield* (London, 1680), pp. 5–9, for Gadbury's testimony; Thomas Dangerfield, *Animadversions upon Mr. John Gadbury's Almanack, or Diary for the Year of Our Lord 1682* (London, 1682), for the chief informer's response. Gadbury always denied being a Roman Catholic convert.
33. Partridge changed the name of his almanac from the obscure ΕΚΚΛΗΣΙΑΛΟΓΙΑ to *Mercurius Coelestis* in 1681 and *Mercurius Redivivus* in 1684. He also published *Prodromus: or, An Astrological Essay upon Those Configurarions of the Celestial Bodies, Whose Effects Will Appear in 1680 and 1681 in Some Kingdoms of Europe* (London, 1680), which contained reflections on the Popish Plot.
34. John Tanner, *Angelus Britannicus: An Ephemeris for the Year of our Redemption 1683* (London, 1683), sig. C_4v.

35. Capp, *English Almanacs*, p. 50.
36. Coley, *Nuncius Coelestis . . . 1680*, sig. C_6v.
37. Goad, *Astro-Meteorologica*, p. 39.
38. Partridge, *Prodromus*, p. 5.
39. Willliam Lilly, *Christian Astrology* (2nd ed., London, 1659), Dedication, sigs A_4-A_4v.
40. Henry Coley, *Astrologiae Elimata: or, A Key to the Whole Art of Astrology New Filed and Polished* (2nd ed., London, 1676), sigs A_3-A_3v. This work was dedicated to Elias Ashmole, whose copy is in Bodl. Lib., Ashmole Ms. 150.
41. William Lilly, *Mr. Willliam Lilly's History of his Life and Times* (London, 1715), pp. 11–12, 21–2, 31–2, 74, 115–16. The original is in Bodl. Lib., Ashmole Ms. 421, ff. 178–222^{v}. The presentment at Middlesex sessions is found at *ibid.*, f. 229.
42. Lilly, *History of his Life*, pp. 98–103; Bodl. Lib., Ashmole Ms. 421, ff. 220–1.
43. The most notable female astrologer was Sarah Jinner, who compiled an almanac full of radical social views in 1658–9: see Capp, *English Almanacs*, p. 87. Henry Coley wrote contemptuously of "many ignorant and illiterate Professors of both Sex". Coley, *Clavis Astrologia*, sig. A_4v.
44. Bodl. Lib., Ashmole Ms. 240, ff. 284–303. For angels in astrology and ritual magic, see Owen Davies, "Angels in Elite and Popular Magic, 1650–1790," in Peter Marshall and Alexandra Walsham, eds, *Angels in the Early Modern World* (Cambridge, 2006), pp. 297–319.
45. Cornelius Agrippa, *Three Books of Occult Philosophy* (London, 1650), book 3, ch. 12, p. 379.
46. Robert Fludd, *Mosaicall Philosophy, Grounded upon the Essentiall Truth, or Eternal Sapience* (London, 1659), section 1, book 4, ch: 2, pp. 59–60.
47. Sir Thomas Browne, *Religio Medici*, in Geoffrey Keynes, ed., *The Works of Sir Thomas Browne*, vol. 1 (Chicago, 1964), p. 41.
48. George Wharton, "A Brief Discourse of the Soul of the World, and the Universal Spirit Thereof," in John Gadbury, ed., *The Works of the Late Most Excellent Philosopher and Astrologer Sir George Wharton Bar[onet]*., (London, 1683), pp. 645, 659.
49. Booker, *Telescopium Uranicum . . . MDCLXVII*, Dedication, sig. A_1v.
50. Josten, ed., *Ashmole*, vol. 2, p. 537, n. 3.
51. Lilly, *Christian Astrology*, pp. 465–6.
52. Blagrave, *Astrological Practice of Physick*, "To all my Loving Country-Men." Needless to say, the book was dedicated to Elias Ashmole. On p. 28, Blagrave states that "the stars are God's Messengers."
53. *Ibid.*, p. 36.
54. *Ibid.*, p. 140.
55. John Booker, *Telescopium Uranicum: or, An Almanack and Prognostication, Physical, Astrological, & Meteorological, for the Year of CHRIST's Incarnation MDCLXIV* (London, 1664), sig. C_7.
56. Gadbury, ed., *Works of Wharton*, Preface, sig. a_2.
57. John Gadbury, ΕΦΗΜΕΡΙΣ*: or, A Diary Astronomical and Astrological for the Year of Grace 1664* (London, 1664), sig. C_5v. For the accusation that Gadbury had once been a follower of Abiezer Coppe, the Ranter, see [John Partridge], *Mene Tekel: Being an Astrological Judgment on the Great and Wonderful Year 1688* (London, [1689]), p. 2. The political implications of Gadbury and Partridge's new approaches to astrology are considered in Patrick Curry, "Saving Astrology in Restoration England: 'Whig' and 'Tory' Reforms," in Patrick Curry, ed., *Astrology, Science and Society: Historical Essays* (Woodbridge, Suffolk, 1987), pp. 245–60.
58. John Gadbury, ΕΦΗΜΕΡΙΣ*: or, A Diary Astronomical and Astrological for the Year of Grace 1679* (London, 1679), sig. C_8v.
59. John Gadbury, *Thesaurus Astrologiae: or, An Astrological Treasury* (London, 1674), sig. A_5v.
60. Gadbury, *Cardines Coeli*, p. 15.
61. Goad, *Astro-Meteorologica*, sig. a_1v.

62. Robert Moray, "Some Experiments Propos'd in Relation to Mr. Newton's Theory of Light," in *Philosophical Transactions*, no. 80, 20 May 1672, pp. 4059–62. The full debate can be followed at the website of the Newton Project, beginning with Newton's letter to the Royal Society expounding his new theory, at http://www.newtonproject.sussex.ac.uk/view/texts/normalized/NATP00006.
63. Goad, *Astro-Meteorologica*, p. 34.
64. *Ibid.*, pp. 390–43, 122, 151–4, 301, 321, 355 [*sic*: actually 362].
65. *Ibid.*, p. 156.
66. Josiah Childrey, *Britannia Baconica: or, The Natural Rarities of England, Scotland, & Wales* (London, 1661), sigs B_5–B_5v.
67. John Partridge, ΜΙΚΡΟΠΑΝΑΣΤΡΩΝ*: or An Astrological VADE MECUM* (London, 1693), p. 1.
68. Bodl. Lib., Ashmole Ms. 2, f. 3; *The Ladies Champion Confounding the Author of the Wandering Whore* (London, 1660), title page. The latter was a furious response to Heydon's *Advice to a Daughter* (London, 1658), which in turn was a critique of Francis Osborne, *Advice to a Son* (Oxford, 1658). Osborne's witty and popular book was condemned by Heydon (or "Eugenius Theodidactus" as he styled himself) for misogyny, although much of *Advice to a Daughter* consists of self-promoting references to Heydon's other works. When the poet and lawyer Thomas Pecke blasted Heydon's lack of learning in *Advice to Balam's Ass* (London, 1658), the undaunted astrologer issued a second edition of *Advice to a Daughter*. It was apparently his most controversial work.
69. [Heydon], *Advice to a Daughter*, p. 192. He repeated this statement in the second edition, p. 177.
70. Robert Latham, ed., *The Shorter Pepys* (Berkeley and Los Angeles, 1985), p. 736. Heydon had also been arrested for sedition in 1663.
71. The biographical details in this paragraph are derived from *ODNB* and from the Life by Frederick Talbot inserted in John Heydon, *Elhavareuna or The English Physitians Tutor* (London, 1665). Heydon's notes on his own birth are found in Bodl. Lib., Ashmole Ms. 339, f. 97. Ashmole also possessed the nativity of an illegitimate son of Heydon's father: Bodl. Lib., Ashmole Ms. 243, f. 169.
72. John Heydon, *Eugenius Theodidacticus, the Propheticall Trumpeter Sounding an Allarum to England* (London, 1655).
73. John Heydon, *A New Method of Rosie Crucian Physick* (London, 1658), sig. A_3; Carlo Ginzburg, *The Night Battles* (Baltimore, 1999).
74. Heydon, *Rosie Crucian Physick*, pp. 38, 52.
75. John Heydon, *The Rosie Crucian Infallible Axiomata, or Generall Rules to Know All Things Past, Present, and to Come* (London, 1660), pp. 2, 34, 122.
76. Heydon claimed to have been imprisoned with John Hewit, the Anglican divine who was executed in 1658 on a charge, which he denied, of giving shelter to the duke of Ormonde: Heydon, *Rosie Crucian Infallible Axiomata*, sig. A_3v. After the Restoration, Ormonde made inquiries about the circumstances of Heydon's arrest (*ODNB*, "Heydon, John"). Buckingham supposedly met Heydon at an astrological gathering at the home of John Digby, who may have been the son of Sir Kenelm Digby (*ODNB*, "Villiers, George, Second Duke of Buckingham"). According to the "Astromagus," one of his books saved the duke from an assassination attempt: John Heydon, *Theomagia, or The Temple of Wisdom* (London, 1664), Dedication, sigs A_3v–A_4.
77. Heydon, *Theomagia*, Preface, sigs A_2v–B_4. The dietary laws of Heydon's Rosicrucians were motivated by principles quite different from those of contemporary vegetarians, like the Behmenist Thomas Tryon, who abstained from eating meat out of sympathy with other creatures. See Keith Thomas, *Man and the Natural World: A History of the Modern Sensibility* (New York, 1983), p. 291.
78. John Heydon, *Psonthonphancia: Being a Word in Season to the Enemies of Christians and An Appeal to the Natural Faculties of the Mind of Man, Whether There Be Not a God* (London, 1664), pp. 39–66.

79. John Heydon, *The Wise-Man's Crown: or, The Glory of the Rosie-Cross* (London, 1664), sig. B_1v.
80. Heydon, *Rosie Crucian Infallible Axiomata*, p. xvii.
81. John Heydon, *The Harmony of the World* (London, 1662), p. 99. The last piece of information must have been derived from the Genius himself, as it does not appear in Scripture. Heydon accepted the Copernican system (*ibid.*, pp. 49–50), although it may not have made much difference to his astrological projections, which were based as much on numerology as on charting the planets.
82. Ashmole, ed., *Way to Bliss*, pp. ii–iii. The offending volume by Heydon was entitled *The Wise-Man's Crown*, but I have not been able to discover an edition of this work that predates 1664.
83. Heydon, *Harmony of the World*, sig. C_3.
84. Heydon, *A New Method of Rosie Crucian Physick*, p. 38.
85. Bodl. Lib., Ashmole Ms. 423, f. 232.
86. Heydon, *Harmony of the World*, Postscript.
87. Heydon, *A New Method of Rosie Crucian Physick*, p. 38; John Heydon, ΨΟΝ΄ΟΟΝΦΑΝΧΓΑ*: or, A Quintuple Rosie-Crucian Scourge for the Due Correction of That Pseudochymist and Scurrilous Emperick, Geo. Thomson* (London, 1665); George Thomson, *Loimologia: A Consolatory Advice, and Some Brief Observations Concerning the Present Pest* (London, 1665).
88. Heydon, *ELHAVAREVNA*, p. 59.
89. Heydon, *Wise-Man's Crown*, Dedication.
90. Heydon, *Theomagia*, p. 314, B.L. 8632.b.49.
91. "The First Journal of J. Roche," in Bruce Stirling Ingram, ed., *Three Sea Journals of Stuart Times* (London, 1936), p. 75.
92. Josten, ed., *Elias Ashmole*, vol. 2, p. 318.
93. The best account of his life remains T.W.W. Smart, "A Biographical Sketch of Samuel Jeake, Senior, of Rye," *Sussex Archaeological Collections*, 13 (1861), pp. 57–79. A list of the elder Jeake's works is found in Rye Museum, Jeake Ms. 4/4. After his death in 1690, his son undertook the publication of ΛΟΓΙΣΤΙΚΗΛΟΓΙΑ, *or Arithmetick Surveighed and Reviewed* (London, 1696), and drew up a nativity of the author that was attached to the dedication. The publication of Jeake senior's other book, *Charters of the Cinque Ports, Two Ancient Towns, and their Members* (Lonodn, 1728), was supervised by his grandson, Samuel Jeake III.
94. Rye Museum, Selmes Ms. 16, sermon of 16 July 1665. Under the Five-Mile Act of that year, Jeake had to remove his congregation to a village near Rye.
95. Michael Hunter, Giles Mandelbrote, Richard Ovenden and Michael Smith, eds, *A Radical's Books: The Library Catalogue of Samuel Jeake of Rye, 1623–90* (Cambridge and Woodbridge, 1999), which is based on Rye Museum, Jeake Ms. 4/1.
96. ESRO, FRE 4636, 4638, Blagrave to Jeake, 4 and 18 Oct. 1672. Blagrave refers in these letters, not to astrological works, but to a copy of the sermons of the Independent minister Matthew Meade, probably ΕΝ ΟΛΙΓΩ ΧΡΙΖΤΙΑΝΟΣ*: The Almost Christian Discovered: or, The False Professor, Tryed and Cast* (London, 1671).
97. Michael Hunter and Annabel Gregory, eds, *An Astrological Diary of the Seventeenth Century: Samuel Jeake of Rye, 1652–1699* (Oxford, 1988), p. 87.
98. Rye Museum, Selmes Ms. 25, a notebook of 1666 entitled "Miscelanea."
99. Hunter and Gregory, eds, *Astrological Diary*, p. 117.
100. *Ibid.*, p. 92.
101. Rye Museum, Selmes Ms. 32. Most of the individuals whose nativities appear in this folio volume were religious Dissenters, and it may be wondered whether Jeake was searching for a common thread in their charts that would allow him some insight into the duration of their sufferings.
102. Rye Museum, Selmes Ms. 34, and Hunter and Gregory, eds, *Astrological Diary*, p. 106.

103. Accounts of Rye in the Exclusion Crisis can be found in Paul Halliwell, *Dismembering the Body Politic: Partisan Politics in England's Towns, 1650–1730* (Cambridge, 1998), pp. 132–5, 268–76; Paul Monod, *The Murder of Mr. Grebell: Madness and Civility in an English Town* (New Haven, Conn., 2003), ch. 2.
104. Hunter and Gregory, eds, *Astrological Diary*, pp. 143–5.
105. *Ibid.*, pp. 98, 132, 153–4, 193, 259.
106. Samuel Jeake, junior, "Astrological Experiments Exemplified. In a Complete Systeme of Solar Revolutional Directions: Attended On by their Respectively Proporticable [*sic*] Effects. During the Space of One Whole Year," Clark Library, Los Angeles, Ms. J43M3/A859, pp. 1–2.
107. *Ibid.*, pp. 7, 15–19.
108. *Ibid.*, pp. 3–4.
109. *Ibid.*, pp. 90–147.
110. Hunter and Gregory, eds, *Astrological Diary*, pp. 206–8.
111. *Ibid.*, pp. 47–8, 51; Hunter, "Science and Astrology," p. 251.

Chapter Three: The Occult Contested

1. Samuel Butler, *Hudibras*, ed. John Wilders (Oxford, 1967), first part, canto I, pp. 16–17, ll. 519–40; see also second part, canto III, pp. 168–81, ll. 575–1002, for the debate between Hudibras and Sidrophel.
2. [William Cooper, ed.], "To the Reader," *Collectanea Chymica: A Collection of Ten Several Treatises in Chymistry Concerning the Liquor Alkahest, the Mercury of Philosophers, and Other Curiosities Worthy the Perusal* (London, 1684), p. [i].
3. Compare R.F. Jones, *Ancients and Moderns: A Study of the Rise of the Scientific Movement in Seventeenth Century England* (2nd ed., Saint Louis, Mo., 1961), with Charles Webster, *From Paracelsus to Newton: Magic and the Making of Modern Science* (Cambridge, 1982). The idea of progress towards modernity, however, remains central to the concept of a seventeenth-century scientific revolution, which is championed by I. Bernard Cohen in *The Newtonian Revolution* (Cambridge, 1985).
4. For this subject, see Jerome Friedman, *The Battle of the Frogs and Fairford's Flies: Miracles and the Pulp Press during the English Revolution* (New York, 1993), and William E. Burns, *An Age of Wonders: Prodigies, Politics and Providence in England 1657–1727* (Manchester, 2002).
5. [Thomas Totney alias Tany], *TheaurauJohn his Aurora in Transfogorum in Salem Gloria. Or, The Discussive of the Law and the Gospel betwixt the Jew and the Gentile in Salem Resurrectionem* (London, 1651), preface.
6. Ariel Hessayon, *"Gold Tried in the Fire:" The Prophet TheorauJohn Tany and the English Revolution* (Aldershot, Hants, and Burlington, Vt., 2007); also Hessayon's biography of Tany in *ODNB*.
7. John Pordage, *Innocencie Appearing, through the Dark Mists of Pretended Guilt. Or, A Full and True Narration of the Unjust and Illegal Proceedings of the Commissioners of Berks (for Ejecting Scandalous and Insufficient Ministers) against John Pordage of Bradfield in the Same County* (London, 1655), pp. 66–71, for testimony concerning spirits; C.H. Josten, ed., *Elias Ashmole (1617–1692)* (5 vols, Oxford, 1966), vol. 2, pp. 518, 522, 554, 667–8; Christopher Hill, *The Experience of Defeat: Milton and Some Contemporaries* (New York, 1984), pp. 220–42. Two volumes of Pordage's papers are in Bodl. Lib., Ms. Rawlinson A.404–5.
8. J.P. [John Pordage], *Theologia Mystica, or, The Mystic Divinitie of the Aeternal Invisibles* (London, 1683), pp. 65, 98.
9. S.P. [Samuel Pordage], *Mundorum Explicatio, or, The Explanation of an Hieroglyphical Figure: Wherein Are Couched the Mysteries of the External, Internal and Eternal Worlds, Shewing the True Progress of a Soul from the Court of Babylon to the City of Jerusalem; from the Adamical Fallen State to the Regenerate and Angelical* (London, 1661), p. 35.
10. *Ibid.*, p. 181.

11. For her life and writings, see Serge Hutin, *Les Disciples Anglais de Jacob Boehme au XVIIe et XVIIIe Siècles* (Paris, 1960), ch. 4; D.P. Walker, *The Decline of Hell: Seventeenth-Century Discussions of Eternal Torment* (London, 1964), ch. 13; B.J. Gibbons, *Gender in Mystical and Occult Thought: Behmenism and its Development in England* (Cambridge, 1996), ch. 7; Paula McDowell, *The Women of Grub Street: Press, Politics and Gender in the London Literary Marketplace, 1678–1730* (Cambridge, 1998), pp. 168–79; Paula McDowell, "Enlightenment Enthusiasms and the Spectacular Failure of the Philadelphian Society," *Eighteenth-Century Studies*, 35, 4 (2002), pp. 515–33; Julie Hirst, *Jane Leade: Biography of a Seventeenth-Century Mystic* (Aldershot, Hants, and Burlington, Vt., 2005); Sarah Apetrei, *Women, Feminism and Religion in Early Enlightenment England* (Cambridge, 2010), pp. 187–98.
12. Jane Lead, *The Revelation of Revelations Particularly as an Essay Towards the Unsealing, Opening and Discovering the Seven Seals, the Seven Thunders, and the New-Jerusalem State* (London, 1683), pp. 38, 40, 51. Lead's first published work, *The Heavenly Cloud Now Breaking* (London, 1681), is a more conventional statement of Behmenist spirituality.
13. *Some Memoirs of the Life of Mr. Thomas Tryon, Late of London, Merchant: Written by Himself* (London, 1725), pp. 26–7; Tryon's biography in *ODNB*; Gibbons, *Gender in Mystical and Occult Thought*, pp. 115–16; Keith Thomas, *Man and the Natural World: A History of the Modern Sensibility* (New York, 1983), pp. 291–2.
14. Thomas Tryon, *A Treatise of Dreams and Visions* (London, 1689); Thomas Tryon, *Pythagoras his Mystick Philosophy Reviv'd; or, The Mystery of Dreams Unfolded* (London, 1691).
15. "Philotheus Phileologus" [Thomas Tryon], *Friendly Advice to the Gentlemen-Planters of the East and West Indies* (London, 1684).
16. Thomas Hobbes, *Leviathan*, ed. Richard Tuck (Cambridge, 1996), book 1, ch. 2, pp. 15, 18–19. The best treatment of Hobbes's views on the supernatural is in Ian Bostridge, *Witchcraft and its Transformations, c. 1650–c. 1750* (Oxford, 1997), ch. 2.
17. Hobbes, *Leviathan*, book 3, ch. 37, p. 300.
18. *Ibid.*, book 3, ch. 37, p. 303.
19. *Ibid.*, book 4, ch. 45, p. 443.
20. [John Wagstaffe], *The Question of Witchcraft Debated; or A Discourse against their Opinion That Affirm Witches* (London, 1669), p. 75. A second edition, with Wagstaffe's name on the title page, appeared in 1671. The pamphlet was reprinted at least twice in the early eighteenth century. See also Michael Hunter, "The Witchcraft Controversy and the Nature of Free-Thought in Restoration England: John Wagstaffe's *The Question of Witchcraft Debated* (1669)," in his *Science and the Shape of Orthodoxy: Intellectual Change in Late Seventeenth-Century Britain* (Woodbridge, Suffolk, 1995), pp. 286–307.
21. Anthony Grafton, "Protestant versus Prophet: Isaac Casaubon on Hermes Trismegistus," in *Defenders of the Text: The Traditions of Scholarship in an Age of Science, 1450–1800* (Cambridge, Mass., 1991), pp. 145–61. See also Anthony Grafton, Joanna Weinberg and Alastair Hamilton, *"I Have Always Loved the Holy Tongue": Isaac Casaubon, the Jews and a Forgotten Chapter in Renaissance Scholarship* (Cambridge, Mass., 2011).
22. Meric Casaubon, *A True and Faithfull Relation of What Passed for Many Yeers between Dr. John Dee (a Mathematician of Great Fame in Q. Eliz. and King James their Reignes) and Some Spirits* (London, 1659), Preface, sigs E_4–E_4v; also Bostridge, *Witchcraft and its Transformations*, pp. 56–65. Mentioned by various early Church Fathers, the Book of Enoch was supposedly written by Adam's son, who had "walked with God" and knew the language of angels.
23. Meric Casaubon, *Of Credulity and Incredulity; In Things Divine and Spiritual* (London, 1670), pp. 15–17.
24. *Ibid.*, pp. 171–91.
25. John Webster, *Academiarum Examen: or, The Examination of Academies* (London, 1653), pp. 51, 106–7. The pamphlets are reprinted in Allen Debus, ed., *Science and Education in the Seventeenth Century: The Webster-Ward Debate* (New York, 1970).

26. John Webster, *Metallographia: or, An History of Metals* (London, 1671), pp. 7, 33–5.
27. *Ibid.*, pp. 11–15.
28. John Webster, *The Displaying of Supposed Witchcraft* (London, 1677), p. 7.
29. *Ibid.*, p. 266.
30. *Ibid.*, chs 16–17.
31. The first of Glanvill's witchcraft collections was *A Philosophical Endeavour towards the Defense of the Being of Witches and Apparitions* (1666), which was reissued, with additional material, in two subsequent editions. Material from this work later appeared in *Saducismus Triumphatus*. For a discussion of Glanvill's works, see Bostridge, *Witchcraft and its Transformations*, pp. 73–7; Ferris Greenslet, *Joseph Glanvill: A Study of English Thought and Letters of the Seventeenth Century* (New York, 1900), ch. 6; Jackson I. Cope, *Joseph Glanvill, Anglican Apologist* (St. Louis, 1956), ch. 4.
32. In a fascinating article, Michael Hunter has shown that, in his various accounts of the Tedworth drummer story, Glanvill changed his tone from ironic humour to moral seriousness in order to strengthen his message: "New Light on 'the Drummer of Tedworth': Conflicting Narratives of Witchcraft in Restoration England," *Historical Research*, 78, 201 (2005), pp. 312–53.
33. Joseph Glanvill, *Saducismus Triumphatus: or, Full and Plain Evidence Concerning Witches and Apparitions* (London, 1681), p. 40.
34. *Ibid.*, pp. 43, 45.
35. [Henry More], "The Easie, True, and Genuine Notion and Consistent Explication Of the Nature of a Spirit," in Glanvill, *Saducismus Triumphatus*, p. 174. A Latin version of this essay had previously appeared in More's *Enchiridion Metaphysicum* (London, 1671).
36. Hartlib Papers, 18/1/9A.
37. [Henry More], "Dr. H.M. his Letter with the Postscript to Mr. J.G.," in Glanvill, *Saducismus Triumphatus*, pp. 13–14. For a different and more sympathetic view of More's position, see Allison Coudert, "Henry More and Witchcraft," in Sarah Hutton, ed., *Henry More (1614–1687): Tercentenary Essays* (Dordrecht, 1990), pp. 115–36.
38. Marjorie Hope Nicolson and Sarah Hutton, eds, *The Conway Letters: The Correspondence of Anne, Viscountess Conway, Henry More, and their Friends, 1642–1684* (Oxford, 1992), p. 294.
39. Margaret Cavendish, duchess of Newcastle, *Philosophical Letters: or, Modest Reflections, upon Some Opinions in Natural Philosophy* (London, 1664), pp. 298–303; for fairies, see p. 227. Cavendish's response to Glanvill is discussed in Jacqueline Broad, "Margaret Cavendish and Joseph Glanvill: Science, Religion and Witchcraft," *Studies in History and Philosophy of Science*, 38, 3 (2007), pp. 493–505.
40. For the decline of English witchcraft, see Keith Thomas, *Religion and the Decline of Magic* (New York, 1971), ch. 18; James Sharpe, *Instruments of Darkness: Witchcraft in Early Modern England* (Philadelphia, 1996), chs 9–11; James Sharpe, *Witchcraft in Early Modern England* (London, 2001), pp. 73–88.
41. Brian Levack, "The End of the Scottish Witch-Hunt," in Julian Goodare, ed., *The Scottish Witch-Hunt in Context* (Manchester, 2002), pp. 166–81.
42. George Sinclair, *Satan's Invisible World Discovered* (Edinburgh, 1685), preface, sigs A_4v–A_5. For biographical details, see *ODNB* and the prefatory notice to the 1871 edition of the work, edited by Thomas George Stevenson and published by him at Edinburgh.
43. For the book's long-lasting appeal, see James Sharpe, "Witch-Hunting and Witch Historiography: Some Anglo-Scottish Comparisons," in Goodare, ed., *Scottish Witch-Hunt in Context*, p. 195, citing the preface to the Stevenson edition, p. l.
44. Steven Shapin and Simon Shaffer, *Leviathan and the Air Pump: Hobbes, Boyle and the Experimental Life* (Princeton, 1985).
45. For example, Hartlib Papers 7/126A-B; 8/28/1A-6B; 16/6/7; 16/9/9–17; 26/57A–B; 26/63A–B; 26/65/1A–B; 55/16/1A–14B.
46. William Newman and Lawrence Principe, *Alchemy Tried in the Fire: Starkey, Boyle and the Fate of Helmontian Chymistry* (Chicago, 2002), chs 3–5.

47. Hartlib Papers, 31/1/56B: John Beale to Samuel Hartlib, 15 Sept. 1657.
48. Hartlib Papers, 25/5/1A, 6A, Beale to Hartlib, 28 May 1657; also, 25/5/22B, Beale to Hartlib, 21 June 1657.
49. Hartlib Papers, 25/5/18A, 19B, Beale to Hartlib, 8 June 1657. For more on the subject of visions, see Hartlib Papers, 60/1/1A–4B, a scribal copy of a letter from Beale to an unnamed correspondent, 28 Nov. 1659.
50. Hartlib Papers, 16/9/3A.
51. He was involved in the Blackloist Conspiracy, an attempt to obtain toleration for Catholics from Cromwell's government in exchange for their acceptance of an Independent church settlement. The conspirators had close links with Hobbes. See Jeffrey Collins, "Thomas Hobbes and the Blackloist Conspiracy of 1649," *Historical Journal*, 45, 2 (2002), pp. 305–31.
52. Sir Kenelm Digby, *A Late Discourse Made in a Solemne Assembly of Nobles and Learned Men at Montpellier in France . . . Touching the Cure of Wounds by the Powder of Sympathy* (London, 1658), p. 3.
53. For the older view, see Allen Debus, *The Chemical Philosophy: Paracelsian Science and Medicine in the Sixteenth and Seventeenth Centuries* (2nd ed., New York, 2002), pp. 205–93, and the three articles by Betty Jo Dobbs, "Studies in the Natural Philosophy of Sir Kenelm Digby, Parts I–III," *Ambix* 18 (1971), pp. 1–25; 20 (1973), pp. 143–63; 21 (1974), pp. 1–28. Newer interpretations are found in Elizabeth Hedrick, "Romancing the Salve: Sir Kenelm Digby and the Powder of Sympathy," *British Journal of the History of Science*, 41 (2008), pp. 161–85; Mark A. Waddell, "The Perversion of Nature: Johannes Baptista van Helmont, the Society of Jesus and the Cure of Wounds," *Canadian Journal of History*, 38 (2003), pp. 180–97; Bruce Janacek, *Alchemical Belief: Occultism in the Religious Culture of Early Modern England* (University Park, Pa., 2011), ch. 4.
54. Digby, *Discourse*, pp. 23, 43.
55. The dependence of the following paragraphs on Michael Hunter, *Boyle: Between God and Science* (New Haven, Cohn., 2009), esp. ch. 11, and Lawrence Principe, *The Aspiring Adept: Robert Boyle and his Alchemical Quest* (Princeton, 1998), will be obvious to those who have read these two splendid studies.
56. Robert Boyle, "Of the Study of the Booke of Nature," in Michael Hunter and Edward B. Davis, eds, *The Works of Robert Boyle* (14 vols, London, 1999), vol. 13, p. 156.
57. R[obert] B[oyle], *Some Motives and Incentives to the Love of God* (Known as *Seraphic Love*), in Hunter and Davis, eds, *Works of Robert Boyle*, vol. 1, p. 66.
58. *Ibid.*, pp. 78, 132.
59. Robert Boyle, "An Hydrostatical Discourse Occasioned by the Objections of the Learned Dr. Henry More, against Some Explications of New Experiments Made by Mr. Boyle," in Hunter and Davis, eds, *Works of Boyle*, vol. 7, p. 183.
60. *The Devill of Mascon*, trans. Peter Du Moulin, in Hunter and Davis, eds, *Works of Boyle*, vol. 1, pp. 13–39.
61. "Robert Boyle's Dialogue on the Converse with Angels Aided by the Philosopher's Stone," in Principe, *Aspiring Adept*, pp. 312, 315. The original is in Royal Society, Boyle Papers, vol. 7, ff. 134v–150. Unfortunately, this volume is not yet available at Boyle Papers Online, which can be viewed at http://www.bbk.ac.uk/boyle/boyle_papers/boylepapers_index.htm.
62. Glanvill to Boyle, 7 Oct. 1677, in Michael Hunter, Antonio Clericuzio and Lawrence Principe, eds, *The Correspondence of Robert Boyle* (6 vols, London, 2001), vol. 4, pp. 460–1.
63. "B.R." [Robert Boyle], "Of the Incalescence of Quicksilver with Gold," in Hunter and Davies, eds, *Works of Boyle*, vol. 8, p. 561; H.W. Turnbull. ed., *The Correspondence of Isaac Newton* (6 vols, Cambridge, 1958–65), vol. 2, p. 2: Newton to Oldenbourg, 26 April 1676.
64. Michael Hunter shows how the Society "sidestepped" occult matters in "The Royal Society and the Decline of Magic," *Notes and Records of the Royal Society*, 65, 2 (2011), pp. 103–19.

65. Thomas Sprat, *The History of the Royal Society of London, for the Improving of Natural Knowledge* (4th ed., London, 1734), pp. 37–8.
66. Bodl. Lib., Ms. Aubrey 24. The diverse individuals cited in this manuscript would comprise a study in themselves. They include "Mr Wyld Clarke (who was a factor at Santa Cruce in Barberie 16 years)," Mr Lancelot Morehead, "a Divine & very learned man," "Mr Hitchcock a Clerke in Chancery Lane, at the Rolls office he has been under sheriffe of Bucks" and "Dr. Ezekiel Tongue," i.e. Israel Tonge, one of the original informers in the Popish Plot: *ibid.*, ff. 56b[v], 57, 92[v], 101.
67. *Ibid.*, f. 92.
68. John Aubrey, *Miscellanies* (London, 1696), Dedication.
69. The classic treatment of the royal healing power is Marc Bloch, *The Royal Touch*, trans. J.E. Anderson (New York, 1990); for magical healing in general, see Keith Thomas, *Religion and the Decline of Magic* (New York, 1971), ch. 7.
70. Hunter, *Boyle*, p. 149–51; *Conway Letters*, pp. 244–52, 261–74; Valentine Greatrakes, *A Brief Account of Mr. Valentine Greatraks, and Divers of the Strange Cures, by Him Lately Performed. Written by Himself in a Letter, Addressed to the Honourable Robert Boyle* (London, 1666), pp. 3, 43–9; *Correspondence of Boyle*, vol. 3, pp. 82–90, 93–107, quotation on p. 93.
71. "Robert Boyle's Notes on his Interview with Lord Tarbat," reprinted in Michael Hunter, ed., *The Occult Laboratory: Magic, Science and Second Sight in Late 17th-Century Scotland* (Woodbridge, Suffolk, 2001), pp. 51–3. The original is in Royal Society, Boyle Papers 39, fols 216–17. See also Lizanne Henderson and Edward J. Cowan, *Scottish Fairy Belief* (Edinburgh, 2001), pp. 174–6.
72. The best overall guide to Newton's alchemical manuscripts can be found at the Newton Project website, http://www.newtonproject.sussex.ac.uk, but see also Peter Jones, ed., *Sir Isaac Newton: A Catalogue of Manuscripts and Papers Collected and Published on Microfilm by Chadwyck-Healey* (Cambridge, 1991).
73. KCL, Keynes Ms. 49, f. 1, *M&P*, reel 19.
74. *Correspondence of Newton*, vol. 2, p. 2: Newton to Oldenbourg, 26 April 1676.
75. Betty Jo Teeter Dobbs, *The Foundations of Newton's Alchemy; or, "The Hunting of the Green Lion"* (Cambridge, 1975); Richard S. Westfall, "The Role of Alchemy in Newton's Career," in M.L. Righini Bonelli and William R. Shea, eds, *Reason, Experiment and Mysticism in the Scientific Revolution* (New York, 1975), pp. 189–232; Richard S. Westfall, *Never at Rest: A Biography of Isaac Newton* (Cambridge, 1980), esp. ch. 8; Betty Jo Teeter Dobbs, *The Janus Faces of Genius: The Role of Alchemy in Newton's Thought* (Cambridge, 1991). Among other works on the subject, see Karin Figala, "Newton as Alchemist," *History of Science*, 15 (1977), pp. 102–37.
76. See both his notes on the Hermetic creation myth in KCL, Keynes Ms. 28, *M&P*, reel 19, which are translated in Dobbs, *Janus Faces of Genius*, pp. 271–7, and his letter of Jan. 1681 on the biblical story of Creation, written to Thomas Burnet, in *Corrrespondence of Newton*, vol. 2, pp. 329–35.
77. Isaac Newton, *Mathematical Principles of Natural Philosophy and his System of the World*, trans. Florian Cajori (Berkeley and Los Angeles, 1962), p. 547.
78. Cited in Dobbs, *Janus Faces of Genius*, p. 230; the original "MS on Miracles" is in Lehigh University Libraries, Bethlehem, Pennsylvania, and was printed by A. Rupert and Mary Boas Hall, *Isis*, 52, 4 (1961), pp. 583–5, but is not in *M&P*. Newton was responding to Leibniz's argument that gravity was either an occult force or a miracle, made in an exchange of papers with Samuel Clarke: see H.G. Alexander, *The Leibniz-Clarke Correspondence* (Manchester, 1956), pp. 66, 92, 94–5, 115, 118, 170, 177, 184, 186–8.
79. On radical plotting, the best sources are the three books by Richard L. Greaves, *Deliver Us from Evil: The Radical Underground in Britain, 1660–1663* (New York, 1986), *Enemies under his Feet: Radicals and Nonconformists in Britain, 1664–1677* (Stanford, 1990), and *Secrets of the Kingdom: British Radicals from the Popish Plot to 1688* (Stanford, 1992).

For suspected Catholic plots, see John Miller, *Popery and Politics in England, 1660–1688* (Cambridge, 1973).

80. For earlier printed literature on secrets, see William Eamon, *Science and the Secrets of Nature: Books of Secrets in Medieval and Early Modern Culture* (Princeton, 1994), which concentrates on Italian publishers, and Allison Kavey, *Books of Secrets: Natural Philosophy in England, 1550–1600* (Urbana and Chicago, 2007), esp. ch. 1.
81. William Salmon, *Polygraphice* (5th ed., London, 1685). Boyle noticed the plagiarism in the first edition and commented on it in a tract of 1675–6, "Experiments, Notes, &c. about the Mechanical Origine or Production of Divers Particular Qualities," *Works of Boyle*, vol. 8, p. 317.
82. Salmon, *Polygraphice*, pp. 478–509.
83. Cited in Allison Coudert, *The Impact of the Kabbalah in the Seventeenth Century: The Life and Thought of Francis Mercury van Helmont (1614–16)* (Leiden, 1998), p. 101 and ch. 6 for an excellent account of *Kabbalah Denudata*. See also Gershom Sholem, *Kabbalah* (New York, 1974); Enrst Benz, "La Kabbala Chrétienne en Allemagne du XVIe au XVIIIe Siècle," in Antoine Faivre and Frédérick Tristan, eds, *Kabbalistes Chrétiens* (Paris, 1979), pp. 91–148; Joseph Dan, ed., *The Christian Kabbalah: Jewish Mystical Books and their Christian Interpreters* (Cambridge, Mass., 1997).
84. The work was originally issued in two parts, published in 1677 and 1678, to which a third was added in 1684. Both the original and expanded editions, however, were usually bound in two volumes. In both versions, the title page of the first volume bears the date 1677. The important section entitled "*Adumbratio*" was appended to some but not all copies of the full work. I have used two copies found in the British Library: [Christian Knorr von Rosenroth et al], *Kabbala Denudata Seu Doctrina Hebraeorum Transcendentalis et Metaphysica Atque Theologica* (1 vol. in 2 parts, Sulzbach, 1677–8); *Kabbala Denudata Tomus Secundus: Id est Liber Sohar Restitutus* (2 vols, Frankfurt, 1684), which contains part 3 of the work. I have also consulted an online version available at http://www.billheidrick.com/Orpd/KRKD/index.htm, which includes digitized photographs derived from both the original and the expanded editions. For a list of the contents, see Don Karr, "The Study of Christian Kabbala in English: Addenda," pp. 99–108, which is available at http://www.digital-brilliance.com/kab/karr/ccineb.pdf.
85. *Kabbalah Denudata* (1684), vol. 1, "*Adumbratio Kabbalae Christianae*," p. 6. Scholem assumed that this was written by Van Helmont, and Coudert has followed his lead, but on the evidence of John Locke's papers, Victor Nuovo has argued that this section should be ascribed to Rosenroth.
86. Henry More, "Fundamenta Philosophiae sive Kabbalae Aeto-Paedo-Melissææ Ejustdem," *Kabbala Denudata* (1677–8), vol. 2, pp. 293–307; Allison Coudert, "A Cambridge Platonist's Kabbalist Nightmare," *Journal of the History of Ideas*, 36, 4 (1975), pp. 633–52; Stuart Brown, "Liebniz and More's Cabalistical Circle," in Hutton, ed., *Henry More*, pp. 77–96; David Katz, "Henry More and the Jews," in *ibid.*, pp. 173–9.
87. [Francis Mercury van Helmont], "Ad Fundamenta Kabbalae Aeto-Paedo-Melissææ Dialogus," *Kabbala Denudata* (1677–8), vol. 2, pp. 308–12. This was translated as *A Kabbalistical Dialogue in Answer to a Learned Doctor in Philosophy and Theology, That the World Was Made of Nothing* (London, 1682).
88. More had written in favour of the pre-existence of souls, and his friend Joseph Glanvill had anonymously authored *Lux Orientalis, or The Opinion of the Eastern Sages, Concerning the Praeexistence of Souls* (London, 1662). For a recent discussion and a letter by Glanvill on the subject, see Rhodri Lewis, "Of 'Origenian Platonism': Joseph Glanvill on the Pre-Existence of Souls," *Huntington Library Quarterly*, 69, 2 (2006), pp. 267–300.
89. Francis Mercury van Helmont, *The Paradoxal Discourses of F.M. van Helmont, Concerning the Macrocosm and Microcosm* (London, 1685), pp. 105, 137.

90. "A Lover of Philalethes," *A Short Enquiry Concerning the Hermetick Art . . . To Which Is Annexed a Collection from Kabbala Denudata, and Translation of the Chymical-Kabbalistical Treatise, Intituled Aesch Mezereph* (London, 1714).
91. *Kabbalah Denudata* (1677–8), vol. 2, p. 183.
92. [Anne Conway], *The Principles of the Most Ancient and Modern Philosophy* (London, 1692). A Latin version was printed at Amsterdam in 1690. The best treatment of Conway's life and work is Sarah Hutton, *Anne Conway: A Woman Philosopher* (Cambridge, 2004).
93. Bodl. Lib., Ms. Locke c.27, ff. 75–7. I am grateful to Victor Nuovo for giving me a transcription of this manuscript, and for allowing me to read chapter 6 of his book *Christianity, Antiquity and Enlightenment: Interpretations of Locke* (Dordrecht, 2011) prior to its publication. See also Allison Coudert, "Leibniz, Locke, Newton and the Kabbalah," in Dan, ed., *Christian Kabbalah*, pp. 149–79.
94. A debate arose in the 1980s over the possible influence of the Kabbala on Newton's concepts of time and space, but the most reliable summary of his stated views on the subject remains Frank Manuel, *The Religion of Isaac Newton* (Oxford, 1974), pp. 68–71.
95. [Francis Mercury van Helmont], *One Hundred Fifty Three Chymical Aphorisms Briefly Containing Whatsoever Belongs to the Chymical Science* (London, 1688), pp. 3–4.
96. [Nicolas de Montfaucon, Abbé de Villars], *The Count of Gabalis, or, The Extravagant Mysteries of the Cabalists Exposed*, trans. "P.A." [Philip Ayres] (London, 1680). Another version, published in the same year but translated by "A.L." (A. Lovell), was more ambiguously subtitled *Conferences about Secret Sciences*, which may have deceived the curious into thinking it was a genuine Kabbalist text.
97. Pierre's first letter to Boyle, dated 13/23 Dec. 1677, is in *Correspondence of Boyle*, vol. 4, pp. 470–4. Nineteen other letters followed, with the last on 10/20 Aug. 1678, which is in *Correspondence of Boyle*, vol. 5, pp. 112–14. See Principe, *Aspiring Adept*, pp. 115–32; Hunter, *Boyle*, pp. 183–5.
98. The first letter from the "Patriarch of Antioch," Georges du Mesnillet, is dated 14/24 Dec. 1677 and is in *Correspondence of Boyle*, vol. 4, pp. 475–6; a further letter of 28 Jan./8 Feb. 1678 is found in *ibid.*, vol. 5, pp. 17–19. The letter of appointment from "the Asterism" is in *ibid.*, vol. 5, pp. 38–42, and one from the monk "Sephrozimez" (a play on *Sephiroth*?) is in *ibid.*, vol. 5, pp. 59–61.
99. *Ibid.*, vol. 5, pp. 121–6. As late as 1680, Boyle was still interested in Pierre's experiments and his movements, and mentioned him again in 1682: *ibid.*, vol. 5, pp. 186, 194, 295–6.
100. *Ibid.*, vol. 5, pp. 1, 131. Boyle's copy was sent from Amsterdam by the Quaker Benjamin Furly, an associate of Van Helmont.
101. D. Knoop and G.P. Jones, *The Genesis of Freemasonry* (Manchester, 1947); David Stevenson, *The Origins of Freemasonry* (Cambridge, 1988), chs 3, 5; Frances Yates, *The Art of Memory* (London, 1966).
102. Stevenson, *Origins of Freemasonry*, ch. 7; David Stevenson, ed., *Letters of Sir Robert Moray to the Earl of Kincardine, 1657–73* (Aldershot, Hants, and Burlington, Vt., 2007), pp. 62, 63, 66, 67, 80, 125, 128, 140, 263, 280. In explaining the pentacle mark, Moray referred to Egyptian and Greek sources, but he cannot have been unaware of its use in ritual magic.
103. Josten, ed., *Elias Ashmole*, vol. 2, pp. 395–6; also Norman Rogers, "The Lodge of Elias Ashmole, 1646," in *Ars Quatuor Coronatorum*, 45 (1953), pp. 35–53.
104. Reprinted in Douglas Knoop, G.P. Jones and Douglas Hamer, eds, *Early Masonic Pamphlets* (Manchester, 1945), pp. 30–1. The short-lived *Poor Robin's Intelligencer* may have been the work of William Winstanley. A royalist in politics, he made fun of occult philosophy in *Poor Robin's Almanac*.
105. J.R. Jones, "The Green-Ribbon Club," *Durham University Journal*, 49, 1 (1956), pp. 17–20; David Allen, "Political Clubs in Restoration London," *Historical Journal*, 19, 3 (1976), pp. 561–80.

106. For coffee-houses and politics, see Brian Cowan, *The Social Life of Coffee: The Emergence of the British Coffeehouse* (New Haven, Conn., 2007), ch. 7; Steven Pincus, "'Coffee Politicians Does Create': Coffeehouses and Restoration Political Culture," *Journal of Modern History*, 67 (1995), pp. 807–34.
107. Andrew Wear, *Knowledge and Practice in English Medicine, 1550–1680* (Cambridge, 2000), chs 8–9. Wear writes of the failure of a "Helmontian Revolution" after 1660, referring to the writings of J.B. van Helmont, whose anti-Galenic theories relied heavily on Paracelsus.

Chapter Four: A Fading Flame

1. These generalizations are based on the charts of alchemy books made by Adam MacLean, which can be accessed at http://www.alchemywebsite.com/statists.html.
2. Because figures for the total number of almanacs sold are lacking, this has to be judged from the total yearly receipts, which remained at about the same level, about £3,000, until 1712, when they went up to £3,700. In subsequent years, they exceeded £4,000, due to the effects of the Stamp Act, which raised the price of each almanac. RSC, reel 84, Books in the Treasurers' Warehouse, accounts for 1688–1715.
3. When the medical doctor and astrologer John Case, a devotee of Thomas Tryon, published a study of astrology as "Divine Magick" in 1697, he may not have realized how old-fashioned his approach seemed. John Case, *The Angelical Guide Shewing Men or Women their Lott or Chance in This Elementary Life* (London, 1697).
4. Patrick Curry, *Prophecy and Power: Astrology in Early Modern England* (Princeton, 1989), pp. 78–91; Patrick Curry, "Saving Astrology in Restoration England: 'Whig' and 'Tory' Reforms," in Patrick Curry, ed., *Astrology, Science and Society: Historical Essays* (Woodbridge, Suffolk, 1987), pp. 245–60.
5. Michael Hunter, "'Aikenhead the Atheist': The Context and Consequences of Articulate Irreligion in the Late Seventeenth Century," in his *Science and the Shape of Orthodoxy: Intellectual Change in Late Seventeenth-Century Britain* (Woodbridge, Suffolk, 1995), pp. 308–32; Ian Bostridge, *Witchcraft and its Transformations, c. 1650–c. 1750* (Oxford, 1997), pp. 24–8, 30–2. For the Second Book of Esdras, see Alastair Hamilton, *The Apocryphal Apocalypse: The Reception of the Second Book of Esdras (4 Ezra) from the Renaissance to the Enlightenment* (Oxford, 1999). Aikenhead's father was an apothecary who sold love potions (Hunter, "Aikenhead," p. 309), so a taste for alchemy may have run in the family.
6. See Michael Hunter, "The Crown, the Public and the New Science, 1689–1702," in his *Science and the Shape of Orthodoxy*, pp. 151–66.
7. *The Athenian Mercury*, vol. 16, no. 24, 9 March 1695. For a discussion of the social views of the periodical, see Helen Berry, *Gender, Society and Print Culture in Late Stuart England: The Cultural World of the Athenian Mercury* (Aldershot, Hants, and Burlington, Vt., 2003).
8. *Athenian Mercury*, vol. 10, no. 11, 2 May 1693; Michael Hunter and Annabel Gregory, eds., *An Astrological Diary of the Seventeenth Century: Samuel Jeake of Rye, 1652–1699* (Oxford, 1988), pp. 49–50, 221.
9. *Athenian Mercury*, vol. 3, no. 13, 8 Sept. 1691.
10. *Athenian Mercury*, vol. 4, no. 7, 20 Oct. 1691; vol. 4, no. 10, 31 Oct. 1691 (Halloween issue). See also Peter Marshall, *Mother Leakey and the Bishop: A Ghost Story* (Oxford, 2007), pp. 182–5; Sasha Handley, *Visions of an Unseen World: Ghost Beliefs and Ghost Stories in Eighteenth-Century England* (London, 2007), pp. 41–3.
11. *Athenian Mercury*, vol. 7, no. 11, 3 May 1692.
12. Richard Baxter, *The Certainty of the World of Spirits, Fully Evinced by Unquestionable Histories of Apparitions and Witchcrafts, Operations, Voices &c.* (London, 1691), p. 236. For Baxter, see William Lamont, *Richard Baxter and the Millennium: Protestant Imperialism and the English Revolution* (London, 1979).

13. J.R. Glauber, *The Works of the Highly Experienced and Famous Chymist, John Rudolph Glauber*, trans. Christopher Packe (London, 1689), sig. A_2. Packe was the author of the *Chymical Aphorisms*, also published by William Cooper.
14. Michael Hunter, Antonio Clericuzio and Lawrence M. Principe, eds, *The Correspondence of Robert Boyle* (6 vols, London, 2001), vol. 6, pp. 288–9.
15. Michael Hunter, *Boyle: Between God and Science* (New Haven, 2009), p. 234; Michael Hunter, *Robert Boyle (1627–91): Scrupulosity and Science* (Woodridge, Suffolk, 2000), pp. 111–12.
16. Owen Ruffhead, ed., *The Statutes at Large* (8 vols, London, 1763), vol. 3, pp. 436.
17. H.W. Turnbull et al, eds, *The Correspondence of Isaac Newton* (Cambidge, 1959–77), vol. 3, p. 218.
18. Richard S. Westfall, *Never at Rest: A Biography of Isaac Newton* (Cambridge, 1980), pp. 524–31; Betty Jo Teeter Dobbs, *The Janus Faces of Genius: The Role of Alchemy in Newton's Thought* (Cambridge, 1991), pp. 171–2, 293–305 (a printed edition of "Praxis"). The original is now in the Grace K. Babson Collection at the Huntington Library, Babson Ms. 420, *M&P*, reel 42; the quotation is from p. 18a.
19. For his career at the Mint, see Westfall, *Never at Rest*, ch. 12; also, Ming-Hsun Li, *The Great Recoinage of 1696 to 1699* (London, 1963).
20. "Baro Urbigerus," *Aphorismi Urbigerani, or Certain Rules, Clearly Demonstrating the Three Infallible Ways of Preparing the Great Elixir or Circulatum Majus of the Philosophers* (London, 1690), pp. 5–6, 84.
21. "Eirenaeus Philiponos Philalethes," *A True Light of Alchemy* (London, 1709); "A Lover of Philalethes," *A Short Enquiry Concerning the Hermetick Art . . . To Which Is Annexed a Collection from Kabbala Denudata, and Translation of the Chymical-Cabbalistical Treatise, Intituled Aesch Mezereph* (London, 1714).
22. W. Yworth, *Chymica Rationalis: or, The Fundamental Grounds of the Chymical Art, Rationally Stated and Demonstrated* (London, 1692), illustration facing p. 10; W.Y. [William Yworth], *The Britannia Magazine: or A New Art of Making above Twenty Sorts of English Wines* (London, 1694), "To the Reader"; *ODNB*; Karin Figala and Ulrich Petzold, "Alchemy in the Newtonian Circle: Personal Acquaintances and the Problem of the Late Phase of Newton's Alchemy," in J.V. Field and F.A.J.L. James, eds, *Renaissance and Revolution: Humanists, Scholars, Craftsmen and Natural Philosophers in Early Modern Europe* (Cambridge, 1993), pp. 173–92. Yworth's career makes an interesting contrast with that of another Dutch immigrant, the medical doctor Joannes Groenevelt, as related in Harold J. Cook, *Trials of an Ordinary Doctor: Joannes Groenevelt in Seventeenth-Century London* (Baltimore and London, 1994).
23. Westfall, *Never at Rest*, pp. 526, 531 n. 215. Newton owned three manuscript copies of Yworth's testament to his children, which includes an alchemical process: KCL, Keynes Ms. 65, *M&P*, reel 18; Hampshire Record Office, NC 17, *M&P*, reel 32; Beinecke Library, Mellon Ms. 80 (not in *M&P*).
24. "Cleidophorus Mystagogus" [William Yworth], *Mercury's Caducean Rod: or, The Great and Wonderful Office of the Universal Mercury, or God's Vicegerent, Display'd* (2nd ed., London, 1704), pp. 72–6, "Philosophical Epistle," p. 2.
25. *Ibid.*, pp. 63–4.
26. "Cleidophorus Mystagogus" [William Yworth], *Trifertes Sagani, or Immortal Dissolvent* (London, 1705), pp. 27–8.
27. *Ibid.*, pp. 43–4.
28. "The Methods and Materials Pointed At, Composing the Sophick Mercury, and Transmuting Elixir," in *True Light of Alchemy*, p. 97.
29. Raymond Astbury, "The Renewal of the Licensing Act in 1693 and its Suspension in 1695," *The Library*, 23, 4 (1978), pp. 296–322; R.B. Walker, "Advertising in London Newspapers, 1650–1750," *Business History*, 15, 1 (1973), p. 117.
30. J.C. [Anne Conway], *The Principles of the Most Ancient and Modern Philosophy* (Amsterdam, 1690; London, 1692), inside cover. Conway might have approved of the

advertisement, as her husband, Edward, viscount Conway, had defended unlicensed medical practitioners against the wrath of the Royal College of Physicians in the early 1680s: see Cook, *Trials of an Ordinary Doctor*, p. 129.

31. Elizabeth Lane Furdell, *Publishing and Medicine in Early Modern England* (Rochester, N.Y., 2000), p. 133.
32. William R. Newman, *Gehennical Fire: The Lives of George Starkey, an American Alchemist in the Scientific Revolution* (Chicago, 1994), pp. 196–200; A.S. Hargreaves, "Lionel Lockyer and his *Pillula Radiis Solis Extracta*," *Pharmaceutical Historian*, 29, 4 (1999), pp. 55–63; [Lionel Lockyer], *An Advertisement, Concerning Those Most Excellent Pills, Call'd Pillula Radiis Solis Extracta* (London, 1664), pp. 15–17; George Starkey, *A Smart Scourge for a Silly, Sawcy Fool* (London, 1664), pp. 1–2.
33. "Philo-Chemicus," *Aut Helmont, Aut Asinus: or, St. George Untrust, Being a Full Answer to his Smart Scourge* (London, 1665), p. 8.
34. David Boyd Haycock and Patrick Wallis, "Quackery and Commerce in 17th-Century London: The Proprietary Medicine Business of Anthony Daffy," *Medical History Supplement*, 25 (2005), pp. 1–37.
35. "Philalethes," *True Light of Alchemy*, p. 98.
36. William Salmon, *The London Almanack for the Year of Our Lord, 1692* (London, 1692), sig. A_2v.
37. Samuel Garth, *The Dispensary: A Poem* (London, 1699), p. 25, canto III, ll. 6–7, where an apothecary lays "S— Works" under his head in order to lull himself to sleep. The identification of "S—" as William Salmon was made in *A Compleat Key to the Seventh Edition of the Dispensary* (London, 1716), p. 11. Salmon, who died in 1713, is there described as "a late Quack Doctor, and indefatigable Scribbler."
38. G.N. Clark, *A History of the Royal College of Phyisicians* (2 vols, Oxford, 1964–6), vol. 2, chs 1–5; William Salmon, *Rebuke to the Authors of a Blew-Book, Call'd the State of Physick in London* (London, 1698), pp. 5, 7; Cook, *Trials of an Ordinary Doctor*, ch. 7, esp. pp. 180–3.
39. "Eyrenaeus Philoctetes," *Philadelphia, or Brotherly Love to the Studious in the Hermetick Art* (London, 1694), pp. vi–vii.
40. "Philadept," *An Essay Concerning Adepts* (London, 1698), pp. 5, 8.
41. *Ibid.*, p. 39.
42. *Ibid.*, pp. 45–6.
43. *Ibid.*, p. 50.
44. [Anon.], *Annus Sophiae Jubilaeus. The Sophick Constitution: or, the Evil Customs of the World Reform'd* (London, 1700), p. 22.
45. *Ibid.*, pp. 50, 59, 65.
46. Daniel Defoe, *An Essay upon Projects* (London, 1697), pp. 20, 28. Defoe associates the rise of projects with Prince Rupert, a promoter of the Royal Society as well as an alchemist, and Bishop John Wilkins, author of *Mathematical Magick*; *ibid.*, p. 25.
47. Rae Blanchard, ed., *The Correspondence of Sir Richard Steele* (London, 1941), pp. 11, 21, 429–30, 433–4, quotations on p. 435.
48. Delarivier Manley, *The New Atalantis*, ed. Ros Ballaster (London, 1992), pp. 102–4, quotation on p. 102.
49. Jonathan Swift, *A Tale of a Tub*, in Herbert Davis, ed., *The Prose Works of Jonathan Swift, Vol. 1: A Tale of a Tub with Other Early Works, 1696–1707* (Oxford, 1939), pp. 79, 95, 96, 104–5, 118–19; and for Paracelsus again, Jonathan Swift, *The Battle of the Books*, in Davis, ed., *Prose Works of Swift*, vol. 1, pp. 152, 156.
50. "J.D.," *A Letter to Dr. John Freind, on the Bill Now Depending, for the Inspection of Drugs and Medicinal Compositions in Apothecaries, Chymists, and Druggists Shops* (London, 1724). Freind, a doctor and Member of Parliament, had written a noted textbook on chemistry.
51. B.L., Sloane 3646, f. 130. Kellum's papers are in B.L., Sloane 3632–6, 3657, 3686–9, 3697–9, 3715.

52. Paul Hopkins, "Sham Plots and Real Plots in the 1690s," in Eveline Cruickshanks, ed., *Ideology and Conspiracy: Aspects of Jacobitism, 1689–1759* (Edinburgh, 1982), pp. 89–110.
53. [Joseph Addison, Richard Steele and others], *The Spectator* (8 vols, London, 1713–14), vol. 3, no. 225, 17 Nov 1711, pp. 317–18; Lawrence Klein, "Liberty, Manners and Politeness in Early Eighteenth-Century England," *Historical Journal*, 32, 3 (1989), pp. 583–605.
54. Thomas Tryon, *The Way to Health, Long Life and Happiness: or, A Discourse of Temperance* (3rd ed., London, 1697), pp. 18, 19, 21.
55. See, for example, the course of chemistry offered by J.F. Vigani of Verona at Cambridge University in 1705: GUL, Ferguson Mss. 62, 165.
56. An excellent study of the role of the Company in this period is Timothy Feist, *The Stationers' Voice: The English Almanac Trade in the Early Eighteenth Century* (Philadelphia, 2005).
57. Bernard Capp, *English Almanacs, 1500–1800: Astrology and the Popular Press* (Ithaca, N.Y., 1979), p. 238.
58. [John Partridge], *Mene Tekel: Being an Astrological Judgment on the Great and Wonderful Year 1688* (London, [1689]).
59. [John Gadbury], *Merlini Liberati Errata: or, The Prophecies and Predictions of John Partridge, for the Year of Our Lord 1690* (London, 1692), p. 20.
60. John Partridge, *Merlinus Liberatus . . . 1692* (London, 1692), sig. C_8v; John Gadbury, ΕΘΗΜΕΡΙΣ . . . *1692* (London, 1692), sig. A_2.
61. John Gadbury, ΕΘΗΜΕΡΙΣ . . . *1693* (London, 1693), part 2, pp. 1–15.
62. *The Athenian Mercury*, vol. 9, no. 8, Saturday, 7 Jan. 1692 [i.e. 1693]. Gadbury was defended by "A Student of Astrology" in *Athenian Mercury*, vol. 10, no. 23, 13 June 1693.
63. John Partridge, *Opus Reformatus: or, A Treatise of Astrology, in Which the Common Errors of That Art Are Modestly Exposed and Rejected* (London, 1693), p. ii.
64. *Ibid.*, pp. 15–16.
65. *Ibid.*, pp. x–xi.
66. John Gadbury, ΕΘΗΜΕΡΙΣ . . . *1695* (London, 1695), sigs C_1–C_6v.
67. John Partridge, *Defectio Geniturarum: Being an Essay towards the Reviving and Proving the True Old Principles of Astrology, Hitherto Neglected, or At Leastwise, Not Observed or Understood* (London, 1697), sig. b_2.
68. *Ibid.*, p. 91.
69. Lynn Thorndike, *A History of Magic and Experimental Science* (8 vols, New York, 1923–58), vol. 8, pp. 302–4.
70. John Gadbury, ΕΘΗΜΕΡΙΣ . . . *1698* (London, 1698), pp. 3–15.
71. John Partridge, *Flagitiosus Mercurius Flagellatus: or The Whipper Whipped: Being an Answer to a Scurrilous Invective Written by George Parker in his Almanack for MDCXCVII* ([London, 1697]), pp. 3, 8, 15. This pamphlet was appended to *Defectio Geniturarum* but is separately paginated. Partridge continued to pummel Parker in *Merlinus Liberatus . . . 1699* (London, 1699), sigs C_7v–C_8.
72. George Parker, *Mercurius Anglicus . . . 1698* (London, 1698), sigs A_1v–C_8v. Parker had declared his admiration for Halley, Kepler, Galileo and Tycho Brahe as early as 1692: *Mercurius Anglicus . . . 1692* (London, 1692), sigs A_3–A_6.
73. John Partridge, *Merlinus Liberatus . . . 1698* (London, 1698), sigs C_6–C_7v.
74. Henry Coley, *Merlinus Anglicus Junior . . . 1698* (London, 1698), sig. C_2v.
75. John Partridge, *Merlinus Liberatus . . . 1708* (London, 1708), sigs C_7v–C_8.
76. *Ibid.*, sigs C_1v–C_2v.
77. B.L., Add. Ms. 27986, ff. 4v, 59, 61v, 65, 72, 78v. The long quotation is on f. 57v. Gadbury can be identified as the author of the notebook from internal evidence relating to members of his family.
78. B.L., Add. Ms. 27986, f. 25v.
79. John Gadbury, ΕΦΗΜΕΡΙΣ*: or, A Diary Astronomical and Astrological for the Year of Grace 1679* (London, 1679), sigs C_7v–C_8v.

80. B.L., Egerton 2378, ff. 2v, 25v, 34v. By "the War," Partridge meant the Great Northern War, which lasted beyond the end of the War of the Spanish Succession.
81. *Ibid.*, ff. 9v, 20v, 35v, 37v, long quotation from f. 31v.
82. *Ibid.*, f. 21v.
83. *Ibid.*, ff. 3v, 33v.
84. William A. Eddy, "Tom Brown and Partridge the Astrologer," *Modern Philology*, 28, 2 (1930), pp. 163–8; William A. Eddy, "The Wits versus John Partridge, Astrologer," *Studies in Philology*, 29, 1 (1932), pp. 29–40. Eddy's references to Partridge's early life are not reliable, and are corrected in George Mayhew, "The Early Life of John Partridge," *Studies in English Literature, 1500–1900*, 1, 3 (1961), 31–42.
85. "Isaac Bickerstaff" [Jonathan Swift], *Predictions for the Year 1708* (London, 1708), in Davis, ed., *The Prose Works of Jonathan Swift, Vol. 2: Bickerstaff Papers and Pamphlets on the Church* (Oxford, 1940), pp. 141–3.
86. *Ibid.*, p. 145.
87. John Partridge, *Mr. Partridge's Answer to Esquire Bickerstaff's Strange and Wonderful Predictions for the Year 1708* (London, 1708), in Davis, ed, *Prose Works of Swift*, vol. 2, pp. 203–7.
88. "Isaac Bickerstaff" [Jonathan Swift], *A Vindication of Isaac Bickerstaff Esq; Against What Is Objected to Him by Mr. Partridge, in his Almanack for the Present Year 1709* (London, 1709), in Davis, ed., *Prose Works of Swift*, vol. 2, pp. 159, 161, 162.
89. "Isaac Bickerstaff" [Richard Steele and others], *The Tatler*, ed. George A. Aitken (2 vols, London, 1899), vol. 1, no. 1, 12 April 1709, p. 42; no. 7, 26 April 1709, p. 88; no. 11, 5 May 1709, p. 124; no. 14, 12 May 1709, p. 147; no. 36, 12 July 1709, p. 312; no. 44, 21 July 1709, p. 265; vol. 2, no. 56, 18 Aug. 1709, p. 54; no. 59, 25 Aug. 1709, p. 72; no. 73, 27 Sept. p. 177; no. 76, 4 Oct. 1709, p. 200; no. 96, 19 Nov. pp. 319, 323; no. 99, 26 Nov. 1709, p. 339.
90. John Partridge, *A Letter to a Member of Parliament from Mr. John Partridge, Touching his Almanack for the Year 1710* (London, 1709), in Records of the Stationers' Company, Reel 98, B4/i. Patrick Curry's biography of Partridge in *ODNB* contains details of the dispute.
91. *The Wills and Testaments of J. Partridge, Student in Physick and Astrology, and Dr. Burnett, Master of Charter-House* (London, 1716).
92. Wellcome Lib., Ms. 4021.
93. Edmund Calamy, *The Nonconformist's Memorial: Being an Account of the Ministers, Who Were Ejected or Silenced after the Restoration*, ed. Samuel Palmer (2 vols, London, 1777), vol. 1, pp. 370–1.
94. GUL, Ferguson Ms. 86, p. 18.
95. *Ibid.*, p. 100.
96. Swift, *A Tale of a Tub*, pp. 104–5.
97. John Locke, *An Essay Concerning Human Understanding*, book 3, ch. 6, sect. 11, p. 325.
98. *Ibid.*, book 4, ch. 12, sect. 12.
99. "Copy of a Letter Sent to the Bishop of Glocester, by the Rev. Mr. Arthur Bedford, Late Vicar of Temple, in the City of Bristol," in Henry Durbin, *A Narrative of Some Extraordinary Things That Happened to Mr. Richard Giles's Children, at the Lamb, without Lawford's Gates, Bristol; Supposed to Be the Effect of Witchcraft* (Bristol, 1800), pp. 56–60; GUL, Ferguson Ms. 125, following p. 546; Jonathan Barry, "Piety and the Patient: Medicine and Religion in Eighteenth-Century Bristol," in Roy Porter, ed., *Patients and Practitioners: Lay Perceptions of Medicine in Pre-industrial Society* (Cambridge, 1985), pp. 157, 160–1.
100. Bodl. Lib., Ms. Ballard 66; Bodl. Lib., Ms. Rawl. D.1067. The invocations in the latter manuscript are based on the *Little Key of Solomon*.
101. B.L., Harley 6481–7.
102. A careful reconstruction of the sources of these manuscripts is found in Arthur Edward Waite, *The Brotherhood of the Rosy Cross* (London, 1924), pp. 397–401.

103. B.L., Harley 6483, f. 1. This work has appeared in print: Stephen Skinner and David Rankine, eds, *The Goetia of Dr. Rudd* (Singapore, 2007). The editors equate "Dr. Rudd" with the military engineer Thomas Rudd (d. 1656), which seems unlikely. The identification was first suggested by Frances Yates, *The Rosicrucian Enlightenment* (London, 1972), pp. 258–9.
104. B.L., Harley 6483, f. 414[v].
105. B.J. Gibbons, *Gender in Mystical and Occult Thought: Behmenism and its Development in England* (Cambridge, 1996), chs 7–8; D.P. Walker, *The Decline of Hell: Seventeenth-Century Discussions of Eternal Torment* (London, 1964), ch. 13; Paula McDowell, "Enlightenment Enthusiasms and the Spectacular Failure of the Philadelphian Society," *Eighteenth-Century Studies*, 35, 4 (2002), pp. 515–33; Julie Hirst, *Jane Leade: Biography of a Seventeenth-Century Mystic* (Aldershot, Hants, and Burlington, Vt., 2005); [Francis Lee], *The State of the Philadelphian Society: or, The Grounds of their Proceedings Consider'd* (London, 1697); Bodl. Lib., Ms Rawl. D. 832, ff. 82–8.
106. [Christopher Walton], *Notes and Materials for an Adequate Biography of the Celebrated Divine and Theosopher, William Law* (London, 1854), pp. 192, 199–205. The copy in the Bodleian Library, call mark 210.a238, is a presentation copy with Walton's original notes.
107. Jane Lead, *A Fountain of Gardens* (2 vols, London, 1697–8), vol. 1, pp. 17–18.
108. [Francis Lee], "A Letter of Resolution," in Lead, *Fountain of Gardens*, vol. 1, p. 504.
109. Bodl. Lib., Ms. Rawl. D.832, ff. 62–7.
110. Bodl. Lib., Ms Rawl. D.833, ff. 27–8, 92.
111. Bodl. Lib., Ms. Rawl. D.1152, f. 5.
112. "Letters from Dr. Ja. Garden . . . to Mr. J. Aubrey," in Michael Hunter, ed., *The Occult Laboratory: Magic, Science and Second Sight in Late 17th-Century Scotland* (Woodbridge, Suffolk, 2001), p. 143; G.D. Henderson, ed., *Mystics of the North-East* (Aberdeen, 1934), pp. 59, 61–5. Lee's link to the Aberdeen mystics was through the London physician James Keith.
113. Robert Kirk, "The Secret Commonwealth" (1692), in Hunter, ed., *The Occult Laboratory*, p. 106; also, Lizanne Henderson and Edward J. Cowan, *Scottish Fairy Belief: A History* (Edinburgh, 2001), ch. 6. A more conventional treatment of second sight can be found in a pamphlet by the Episcopal minister John Frazer, entitled ΔΕΥΤΕΡΟΣΚΟΠΙΑ *[Deutoroskipia] or, A Brief Discourse Concerning the Second Sight, Commonly So Called* (Edinburgh, 1707), which appears in Hunter, ed., *The Occult Laboratory*, pp. 187–204.
114. Kirk, "Secret Commonwealth," in Hunter, ed., *Occult Laboratory*, pp. 79, 82.
115. J. Kent Clark, *Goodwin Wharton* (Oxford, 1984), pp. 30–1, 218–326.
116. Kirk, "Secret Commonwealth," in Hunter, ed., *Occult Laboratory*, p. 86; "Letters from Garden to Aubrey," in *ibid.*, p. 143.
117. See Carlo Ginzburg, *The Night Battles* (Baltimore, 1995).
118. *The Athenian Mercury*, vol. 3, no. 10, 29 Aug. 1691.
119. Alexander Pope, "The Rape of the Lock," in Aubrey Williams, ed., *Poetry and Prose of Alexander Pope* (Boston, 1969), p. 79.
120. *Ibid.*, canto 1, ll. 37, 71; canto 3, ll. 35–6, 152.
121. The best general explanation of the decline of witch beliefs is James Sharpe, *Instruments of Darkness: Witchcraft in Early Modern England* (Philadelphia, 1996), chs 9–11; but see also Bostridge, *Witchcraft and its Transformations*, ch. 6, to which the following discussion is heavily indebted.
122. *A Relation of the Diabolical Practices of the Witches of the Sheriffdom of Renfrew* (London, 1697); Michael Wasser, "The Western Witch-Hunt of 1697–1700: The Last Major Witch-Hunt in Scotland," in Julian Goodare, ed., *The Scottish Witch-Hunt in Context* (Manchester, 2002), pp. 146–65. For Dumfries and Galloway, see Lizanne Henderson, "The Survival of Witch Prosecutions and Witch-Beliefs in South-West Scotland," *Scottish Historical Review*, 85, 1 (2006), pp. 52–74.

123. *A Full and True Relation of the Witches at Pittenweem* (Edinburgh, 1704). One pamphlet writer decried the "horrible Murder committed in *Pittenweem*" and denounced the chief witness as "a Cheat": *An Answer of a Letter from a Gentleman in Fife, to a Nobleman, Containing a Brief Account of the Barbarous and Illegal Treatment, These Poor Women Accused of Witchcraft, Met With from the Baillies of Pittenweem and Others, with Some Few Observations Thereon* ([Edinburgh?], 1705). He was answered in *A Just Reproof, to the False Reports, Bold, & Unjust Calumnies, Dropt in Two Late Pamphlets* (Edinburgh, 1705), a pamphlet that defended the magistrates and blamed the murder (p. 13) on the presence of "a great many Strangers, some *Englishmen*, some from *Orkney*." See also Stuart Macdonald, "In Search of the Devil in Fife Witchcraft cases, 1560–1705," in Goodare, ed., *Scottish Witch-Hunt*, p. 44.
124. "A Lover of the Truth," *Witch-Craft Proven, Arreign'd and Condemn'd in its Professors, Professions and Marks, by Diverse Pungent, and Convincing Arguments* (Glasgow, 1697); [John Bell], *Tryal of Witchcraft, or, Witchcraft Arraign'd and Condemn'd* (Glasgow, 1705). Only one copy of the second pamphlet now exists, in the Scottish National Library. It is summarized in Christina Larner, "Two Late Scottish Witchcraft Tracts: *Witch-craft Proven* and *The Tryal of Witchcraft*," in Sidney Anglo, ed., *The Damned Art: Essays in the Literature of Witchcraft* (London, 1977), pp. 227–45.
125. Ralph Davis, *An Account of the Tryals, Examination and Condemnation of Elinor Shaw, and Mary Philip's (Two Notorious Witches), at Northampton Assizes, on Wednesday the 7th of March 1705 for Bewitching a Woman, and Two Children, Tormenting them in a Sad and Lamentable Manner till they Dyed* (London, 1705); Ralph Davis, *The Northamptonshire Witches* (London, 1705); *A Full and True Account of the Tryal, Examination and Condemnation of Mary Johnson a Witch* (London, 1706); *The Whole Trial and Examination of Mrs. Mary Hicks and her Daughter Elizabeth, But of Nine Years of Age, Who Were Condemn'd the Last Assizes Held at Huntington for Witchcraft; and there Executed on Saturday the 28th of July 1716* (London, [1716]). That the first two pamphlets and the last were written by the same author, and that they did not refer to real incidents, were demonstrated in Wallace Notestein, *A History of Witchcraft in England from 1558 to 1718* (Washington, 1911), pp. 375–83. Notestein also pointed out their similarities to an earlier pamphlet describing a fictitious witchcraft case at Worcester in 1645.
126. Balthasar Bekker, *The World Bewitch'd; or, An Examination of the Common Opinions Concerning Spirits . . . Vol. 1* (London, 1695). See also Andrew Fix, *Fallen Angels: Balthasar Bekker, Spirit Belief and Confessionalism in the Seventeenth Century Dutch Republic* (Dordrecht, 1999).
127. John Beaumont, *An Historical, Physiological and Theological Treatise of Spirits, Apparitions, Witchcrafts and Other Magical Practices* (London, 1705), p. 347.
128. *Ibid.*, p. 328.
129. See Margaret C. Jacobs, *The Newtonians and the English Revolution, 1689–1720* (Ithaca, N.Y., 1978).
130. A reiteration of this view can be found in *The Black Art Detected and Expos'd: or, A Demonstration of the Hellish Impiety, of Being, or Desiring to Be a Wizzard, Conjurer or Witch* (London, 1707).
131. [Joseph Addison], *The Spectator*, vol. 2, no. 117, 14 July 1711, p. 186.
132. Arthur Wellesley Secord, ed., *Defoe's Review, Reproduced from the Original Editions* (9 vols in 22 books, New York, 1965), vol. 8 (book 20), no. 90, 20 Oct. 1711, pp. 361–4.
133. [Addison], *Spectator*, no. 117, vol. 2, p. 189.
134. Phyllis J. Guskin, "The Context of Witchcraft," *Eighteenth-Century Studies*, 15, 1 (1981), pp. 48–71; Victoria County History, *A History of the County of Hertford: Volume 3* (London, 1912), pp. 151–8.
135. For this interpretation of witchcraft, see Deborah Willis, *Malevolent Nurture: Witch-Hunting and Maternal Power in Early Modern England* (Ithaca, N.Y., 1995), as well as Lyndal Roper, *The Witch-Craze* (New Haven, Conn., 2008).

136. [Francis Bragge, junior], *A Full and Impartial Account of the Discovery of Sorcery and Witchcraft, Practis'd by Jane Wenham of Walkerne in Hertfordshire* (2nd ed., London, 1712), preface, [p. iii].
137. For Curll, see Paul Baines and Pat Rogers, *Edmund Curll, Bookseller* (Oxford, 2007). The second (anonymous) pamphlet by Bragge was *Witchcraft Farther Display'd* (London, 1712).
138. *The Impossibility of Witchcraft, Plainly Proving, from Scripture and Reason, That There Never Was a Witch, and That it Is Both Irrational and Impious to Believe There Ever Was* (London, 1712). For the *Protestant Post-Boy*, see Phyllis J. Guskin, "The 'Protestant Post-Boy' and 'An Elegy on the Death of Pamphlets,'" *Notes and Queries*, 223 (Feb. 1978), pp. 40–1.
139. *The Impossibility of Witchcraft, Further Demonstrated* (London, 1712); Francis Bragge [junior], *A Defense of the Proceedings against Jane Wenham* (London, 1712); G.R., *The Belief of Witchcraft Vindicated* (London, 1712).
140. "A Physician in Hertfordshire," *A Full Confutation of Witchcraft: More Particularly of the Depositions against Jane Wenham, Lately Condemned for a Witch; at Hertford* (London, 1712), pp. 3, 45, 48.
141. [Henry Stebbing], *The Case of the Hertfordshire Witchcraft, Consider'd* (London, 1715), p. 12.
142. On the politics of this period, see Geoffrey Holmes, *The Trial of Dr. Sacheverell* (London, 1973); Daniel Szechi, *Jacobitism and Tory Politics, 1710–14* (Edinburgh, 1984).
143. His biography can be found in *ODNB*, and his role in the medical controversies of the late 1690s is discussed in Cook, *Trials of an Ordinary Doctor*, pp. 183–4.
144. [Richard Boulton], *A Compleat History of Magick, Sorcery, and Witchcraft* (2 vols, London, 1715–16), vol. 1, preface, sig. A_3.
145. *Ibid.*, pp. 5–6.
146. *Ibid.*, pp. 18–23.
147. Bostridge, *Witchcraft and its Transformations*, pp. 143–4.
148. Francis Hutchinson, *An Historical Essay Concerning Witchcraft* (London, 1718), pp. vi, xiv.
149. *Ibid.*, p. 133.
150. Richard Boulton, *The Possibility and Reality of Magick, Sorcery, and Witchcraft, Demonstrated. Or, a Vindication of a Compleat History of Magick, Sorcery, and Witchcraft* (London, 1722), pp. xii–xiii.

Chapter Five: The Newtonian Magi

1. The best discussion of Newton's followers is found in Larry Stewart, *The Rise of Public Science: Rhetoric, Technology and Natural Philosophy in Newtonian Britain, 1660–1750* (Cambridge, 1992). For the impact of science on religion, see Margaret Jacob, *The Newtonians and the English Revolution, 1689–1720* (Ithaca, N.Y., 1976). Stewart and Jacob have cowritten a general examination of Newton's cultural significance entitled *Practical Matter: Newton's Science in the Service of Technology and Empire, 1687–1851* (Cambridge, Mass., 2004).
2. For the criticism of "wonders" by the Newtonians Edmond Halley and William Whiston, see William E. Burns, *An Age of Wonders: Prodigies, Politics and Providence in England 1657–1727* (Manchester, 2002), pp. 160–3, 166–70. Whiston later reversed his views, as will be seen. John Flamsteed, a reluctant collaborator of Newton, disliked astrology but was open-minded on the subject of ghosts: Sasha Handley, *Visions of an Unseen World: Ghost Beliefs and Ghost Stories in Eighteenth-Century England* (London, 2007), ch. 3.
3. Jean-Théophile Desaguliers, *The Newtonian System of the World, the Best Model of Government*, in Pierre Boutin, *Jean-Théophile Desaguliers: Un Huguenot, Philosophe et Juriste, en Politique* (Paris, 1999), pp. 229–33, ll. 121, 123, 153–5, 175.

4. New College, Oxford, Ms. 361(2), f. 133, *M&P*, reel 24, cited in Frank E. Manuel, *Isaac Newton, Historian* (Harvard, 1963), p. 149.
5. Royal Society, Ms. LXIX.a.2, William Stukeley, "Memoirs of Sr. Isaac Newton's Life 1752," p. 131, f. 57 (accessed at http://ttp.royalsociety.org).
6. *Ibid.*, p. 151, f. 67.
7. Newton to Locke, 14 Nov. 1690, in H.W. Turnbull et al, eds, *The Correspondence of Isaac Newton* (7 vols, Cambridge, 1959–77), vol. 3, pp. 82–129. These letters were not published until 1754. The issue of heresy was by no means buried in Hanoverian England, although the charge against heretics that was usually brought in ecclesiastical courts was changed to "blasphemy."
8. Desaguliers, "Newtonian System," in Boutin, pp. 221–2, 229, ll. 7, 19–20, 33, 127.
9. Newton is called a "Pythagorean Magus" in Penelope Gouk, *Music, Science and Natural Magic in Seventeenth-Century England* (New Haven, 1999), ch. 7.
10. Freemasons Hall Library (hereafter FHL), 1130 STU, Stukeley Mss., vol. 1, pp. 51–67.
11. For sociability, see Peter Clark, *British Clubs and Societies, 1580–1800* (Oxford, 2000); for Freemasons, Margaret C. Jacob, *The Origins of Freemasonry: Facts and Fictions* (Philadelphia, 2006), and David Stevenson, *The Origins of Freemasonry* (Cambridge, 1988).
12. Jonathan Swift, *Gulliver's Travels*, ed. Paul Turner (Oxford, 1971), pp. 149, 154–5, 158–9.
13. *Ibid.*, p. 169.
14. *Ibid.*, p. 190.
15. *Ibid.*, p. 206.
16. The assertion that Swift was himself a Freemason rests mainly on the publication in 1724 of an anonymous pamphlet entitled *A Letter from the Grand Mistress of Free-Masons, to Mr. George Faulkner, Printer*. It is peppered with insider jokes aimed at other Masons. Swift is now acknowledged to have been the author.
17. The indebtedness of this section to Richard S. Westfall, *Never at Rest: A Biography of Isaac Newton* (Cambridge, 1980), chs 12–17, as well as to Manuel, *Newton, Historian* and Frank Manuel, *The Religion of Isaac Newton* (Oxford, 1974), will be obvious to anyone who has read those works. Also of importance are the essays in James E. Force and Richard H. Popkin, eds, *Newton and Religion: Context, Nature and Influence* (Dordrecht, 1999).
18. Much of that history is laid out in Helen Rosenau, *Visions of the Temple: The Image of the Temple of Jerusalem in Judaism and Christianity* (London, 1979), but see also Jim Bennett and Scott Mandelbrote, *The Garden, the Ark, the Tower, the Temple: Biblical Metaphors of Knowledge in Early Modern Europe* (Oxford, 1998), pp. 134–55.
19. Hieronimo Prado and Juan Bautista Villalpando, *In Ezechiel Explanationes et Apparatus Urbis, ac Templi Hierosolymitani Y* (3 vols, Rome, 1596–1605). Prado worked only on the first volume, which deals with Ezekiel's prophecy; the description of the Temple, with lavish illustrations, appears in the second and third volumes, which were authored by Villalpando alone. For discussions of Villalpando's work, see René Taylor, "Villalpando's Mystical Temple," in Juan Antonio Ramírez et al, *Dios Arquitecto: J.B. Villalpando y el Templo de Salomón* (Madrid, 1991), pp. 153–211; René Taylor, "Architecture and Magic: Considerations on the Idea of the Escorial," in D. Fraser, M. Hibbard and H.J. Lewine, eds, *Essays Presented to Rudolf Wittkower* (2 vols, London, 1967), vol. 1, pp. 81–109.
20. Samuel Lee, *Orbis Miraculum, or The Temple of Solomon Pourtrayed by Scripture-Light* (London, 1659), p. 189.
21. *Ibid.*, p. 168; also, John Bunyan, *Solomon's Temple Spiritualiz'd*, ed. Graham Midgley, *Miscellaneous Works of John Bunyan*, vol. 7 (Oxford, 1989), pp. 1–115.
22. Johann Valentin Andreæ, *Christianopolis*, trans. Edward H. Thompson (Dordrecht, 1999), pp. 84–90, 161–2, 209–40, 257–8. See also Donald Dickson, *The Tessera of Antilia: Utopian Brotherhoods and Secret Societies in the Early Seventeenth Century* (Leiden, 1998), chs 2–3.

23. Francis Bacon, *The New Atlantis*, in James Spedding, R.L. Ellis and D.D. Heath, eds, *The Works of Francis Bacon*, vol. 3 (London, 1876), pp. 129–65; J.C. Davis, *Utopia and the Ideal Society: A Study of English Utopian Writing, 1516–1700* (Cambridge, 1981), ch. 5.
24. For Hartlib and Villalpando, see Bennett and Mandelbrote, *The Garden, the Ark*, pp. 141–2; for Hartlib and Andreæ, see Dickson, *Tessera of Antilia*, ch. 5; for Macaria, see Charles Webster, *Utopian Planning and the Puritan Revolution: Gabriel Plattes, Samuel Hartlib and Macaria* (Oxford, 1979).
25. Christopher Wren, "Tracts on Architecture," in Christopher Wren and Stephen Wren, eds, *Parentalia: or, Memoirs of the Family of the Wrens* (London, 1750), pp. 356, 359–60.
26. Bennett and Mandelbrote, *The Garden, the Ark*, pp. 150–1; A.K. Offenberg, "Jacob Jehudah Leon (1602–1675) and his Model of the Temple," in Johannes van den Berg and Ernestine G.E. van der Wall, eds, *Jewish-Christian Relations in the Seventeenth Century* (Dordrecht, 1988), pp. 95–115; "Traditional Reconstructions," in Ramírez et al, *Dios Arquitecto*, pp. 100–4.
27. For Wren's grand mastership, see James Anderson, *The Constitutions of the Freemasons* (London, 1723), pp. 41, 43, 46; [Anonymous], *The Pocket Companion and History of Free-Masons* (London, 1754), pp. 85–7, 91. His friendship with Robert Moray and his regard for stonemasons are confirmed in Wren and Wren, eds, *Parentalia*, pp. 210–11, 293, 306–7. For the importance to Freemasonry of the Temple, as well as the Tower of Babel, see Alex Horne, *King Solomon's Temple in the Masonic Tradition* (London, 1971).
28. Hannah Smith, *Georgian Monarchy: Politics and Culture, 1714–1760* (Cambridge, 2006), pp. 39–40.
29. George Renolds, *The State of the Greatest King, Set Forth in the Greatness of Solomon, and the Glory of his Reign* (Bristol, 1721), pp. 72–3.
30. [Anonymous], *The Temple of Solomon, with All its Porches, Walls, Gates, Halls, Chambers, Holy Vessels, the Altar of Burnt-Offering, the Molten-Sea, Golden-Candlesticks, Shew-Bread, Tables, Altar of Incense, the Ark of the Covenant, with the Mercy-Seat, the Cherubim, &c. As Also the Tabernacle of Moses, with All its Appurtenances According to the Several Parts Thereof; Contained in the Following Description and Annexed Copper Cuts. Erected in a Proper Model and Material Representation* (London, 1724), quotation on sig. A_2, p. 1; also, Home, *King Solomon's Temple*, pp. 54–5; W.H. Rylands, "Schott's Model of Solomon's Temple," *Ars Quatuor Coronatorum*, 13 (1900), pp. 24–5; Barthold Feind, "Dramaturgy of Opera," in Lorenzo Bianconi, *Music in the Seventeenth Century* (Cambridge, 1987), p. 325.
31. Newton's reading of Villalpando is recorded in two documents, Yahuda Ms. 14 and 28, both now held in the National Library of Israel, Tel Aviv; *M&P*, reels 38, 39. A transcript of part of Yahuda Ms. 28 is found at the Newton Project, http://www.newtonproject.sussex.ac.uk/view/texts/normalized/THEM00274.
32. Newton's computation of the "sacred cubit," written in Latin, was translated into English and published as "A Dissertation upon the *Sacred Cubit* of the *Jews* and the *Cubits* of the Several Nations; in Which, from the Dimensions of the Greatest *Egyptian* Pyramid, as Taken by Mr. *John Greaves*, the Antient Cubit of *Memphis* Is Determined," in John Greaves, *Miscellaneous Works* (2 vols, Oxford, 1737), vol. 2, pp. 405–53. A transcript is available online at the Newton Project, http://www.newtonproject.sussex.ac.uk/view/texts/normalized/THEM00276.
33. Isaac Newton, "A Treatise or Remarks on Solomon's Temple . . . Prolegomena ad Lexici Prophetici partem secundam, in quibus agitur de forma Sanctuarij Judaici," Huntington Library, Babson Ms. 434, *M&P*, reel 42, reproduced in Isaac Newton, *El Templo de Salomón: edición crítica, traducción española y estudio filológico*, ed. Ciriaco Morano (Madrid, 1996), pp. 1–69, quotation on p. 1; also available online at the Newton Project, http://www.newtonproject.sussex.ac.uk/view/texts/normalized/THEM00079.
34. Isaac Newton, *The Chronology of Ancient Kingdoms Amended. To Which Is Prefix'd, A Short Chronicle from the First Memory of Things in Europe, to the Conquest of Persia by Alexander the Great* (London, 1728), pp. 71–95.

35. *Ibid.*, pp. 188–90.
36. *Ibid.*, pp. 223–46.
37. *Ibid.*, p. 328. Newton was less harsh in his criticism of pagan religion than many of his sources, including Richard Cumberland, bishop of Peterborough, whose work *Sanchoniatho's Phoenician History* (London, 1720) deplored the idolatry of "Heathenism."
38. Newton, *Chronology of Ancient Kingdoms*, pp. 12, 25. According to Manuel, Newton reduced the voyage of the Argo to "a practical diplomatic mission," but this undervalues the transmission of the arts and science to the whole world: Manuel, *Newton, Historian*, p. 80.
39. Antoine Faivre, *The Golden Fleece and Alchemy* (Albany, 1994), pp. 24–9; Betty Jo Teeter Dobbs, *The Foundations of Newton's Alchemy; or "The Hunting of the Greene Lyon"* (Cambridge, 1975), pp. 112, 130–1; Smithsonian Institution, Dibner Library, NMAHRB Ms. 1028B, NMAHRB Ms. 1032B (notes on Maier), *M&P*, reel 43; John T. Young, *Faith, Medical Alchemy and Natural Philosophy: Johann Moriaen, Reformed Intelligencer, and the Hartlib Circle* (Aldershot, Hants, 1998), pp. 234–7 (Nuysement and the Hartlib Circle).
40. Newton, *Chronology of Ancient Kingdoms*, pp. 15, 17.
41. *Ibid.*, p 25; Angela Voss, "The Musical Magic of Marsilio Ficino," in Michael J.B. Allen, Valery Rees and Martin Davies, eds, *Marsilio Ficino: His Theology, his Philosophy, his Legacy* (Leiden, 2001), pp. 227–42; Peter Branscombe, *Die Zauberflöte* (Cambridge, 1991), pp. 12, 54.
42. Stuart Pigott, *William Stukeley, an Eighteenth-Century Antiquary* (rev. ed., London, 1985); Peter J. Ucko, Michael Hunter, Alan J. Clark and Andrew David, *Avebury Reconsidered: From the 1660s to the 1990s* (London, 1991), pp. 53–7, 74–98; David Boyd Haycock, *William Stukeley: Science, Religion and Archaeology in Eighteenth-Century England* (Woodbridge, Suffolk, 2002); Aubrey Burl and Neil Mortimer, eds, *Stukeley's Stonehenge: An Unpublished Manuscript, 1721–1724* (New Haven, Conn., 2005), pp. 1–21, for criticism of Haycock. The antiquarian context is described in Rosemary Sweet, *Antiquaries: The Discovery of the Past in Eighteenth-Century Britain* (London, 2004).
43. W.C. Lukis, ed., *The Family Memoirs of the Reverend William Stukeley, M.D., and the Antiquarian and Other Correspondence of William Stukeley, Roger and Samuel Gale, Etc.*, Surtees Society 73, 76, 80 (3 vols, Durham, 1882–7), vol. 1, p. 51; Bodleian Library, Ms. Engl. Misc. c.553, ff. 34v, 35–7.
44. The trend away from astrology in almanacs is documented in Bernard Capp, *English Almanacs, 1500–1800: Astrology and the Popular Press* (Ithaca, N.Y., 1979), pp. 245–7.
45. Edmund Weaver, *The British Telescope . . . 1731* (London, 1731), p. 36.
46. Bodl. Lib., Ms. Engl. Misc. d.719/1, f. 28; Ms. Engl. Misc. d.719/3, f. 8; Ms. Engl. Misc. e.132, ff. 53v–4.
47. Capp, *English Almanacs*, p. 242.
48. Bodl. Lib., Ms. Engl. Misc. d.719/2, f. 28; Ms. Engl. Misc. d.719/3, ff. 15, 28.
49. Wellcome Library, Ms. 4729. The manuscript originally belonged to Richard Edlyn, a noted astrologer of the reign of Charles II.
50. Bodl. Lib., Ms. Engl. Misc. d.719/6, ff. 20v, 24.
51. Bodl. Lib., Ms. Engl. Misc. d.719/7, f. 23; Ilsetraut Hadot, *Studies on the Neoplatonist Hierocles*, trans. Michael Chase, Transactions of the American Philosophical Society, 94 (Philadelphia, 2004), pp. 99–124, quotation on p. 113. For the Cambridge Neoplatonist influence on Stukeley, see Haydon, *Stukeley*, pp. 149–50.
52. Bodl. Lib., Ms. Engl. Misc. d.719/8, f. 5.
53. Stukeley's conversations with Newton about the ancient world, dating from April 1726, are found in Bodl. Lib., Ms. Engl. Misc. c.533, p. 41. In the fourth edition of his *New Science of the Earth, from its Original to the Consummation of All Things* (London, 1725), p. 169, and in later editions of the same work, Stukeley's friend William Whiston proposed that the zodiac was divided into twelve parts before the Deluge, but he mentioned nothing about the zodiacal symbols.

54. Athanasius Kircher, *Oedipus Aegyptiacus* (3 vols, Rome, 1652–5), vol. 2, part 1, pp. 160–2. For Kircher, see Paula Findlen, ed., *Athanasius Kircher: The Last Man Who Knew Everything* (New York, 2004), and Joscelyn Godwin, *Athanasius Kircher: A Renaissance Man and the Quest for Lost Wisdom* (London, 1979); also Haydon, *Stukeley*, pp. 140–1.
55. Bodl. Lib., Ms. Eng. Misc. d.719/10, ff. 4–5; William Stukeley, *Palæographia Britannica: or Discourses on Antiquities That Relate to the History of Britain. Number III. Oriuna Wife of Carausius, Emperor of Britain* (London, 1752), pp. 33–4. The Bible does not mention Adam sacrificing two pigeons, although Noah sacrifices two doves after the Ark reaches land. Doves and pigeons were the only birds that could lawfully be sacrificed by the Israelites, according to Leviticus 12:6–8.
56. "Eirenaeus Philalethes" [George Starkey], *Secrets Reveal'd* (London, 1669); Dobbs, *Foundations of Newton's Alchemy*, pp. 176, 181–3; *A Short Enquiry Concerning the Hermetick Art . . . By a Lover of Philalethes* (London, 1714).
57. Bodl. Lib., Ms. Engl. Misc. c.533, ff. 22, 27; Ms. Engl. Misc. d.719/18, f. 11[v]; Ms. Engl. Misc. d.456, f. 167; for Diana, Ms. Engl. Misc. c.533, f. 37; FHL, 1130 STU, vol. 3, ff. 33–4, 41–4.
58. Bodl. Lib., Ms. Engl. Misc. d.719/19, f. 9; Ms. Engl. Misc. e.196, ff. 39–40, 52; Ms. Engl. Misc. e.129, f. 2.
59. Bodl. Lib., Ms. Engl. Misc. c.533, f. 37; FHL, Stukeley Mss., vol. 3, no. 4, ff. 1, 4, 33–4, 41–4; FHL, Stukeley Mss., vol. 3, no. 9B, "Bezaleel." The dedication of the second part of "Bezaleel" to Martin Ffolkes has been crossed out, suggesting that it was written around the time of Ffolkes's death in 1754.
60. Bodl. Lib., Ms. Engl. Misc. e.128, f. 96; Ms. Engl. Misc. e.131, ff. 19, 30–1; Ms. Engl. Misc. e.132, ff. 5[v]–12, 53[v]–58, 61, 75, 77.
61. Bodl. Lib., Ms. Engl. Misc. e.139, ff. 72, 74.
62. William Stukeley, "Cosmogonia, or Spring, Asserted to Be the Time of Creation," in *Palæographia Sacra. Or Discourses on Sacred Subjects* (London, 1763), p. 65.
63. The significance of the Druids in British culture has been underlined by several important works, including A.L. Owen, *The Famous Druids: A Survey of Three Centuries of English Literature on the Druids* (Oxford, 1962); Stuart Piggott, *The Druids* (Harmondsworth, 1975), ch. 4; Ronald Hutton, *The Druids: A History* (Hambledon, 2007); Ronald Hutton, *Blood and Mistletoe: The History of the Druids in Britain* (New Haven, Conn., 2009), esp. chs 2–4. See also Alexandra Walsham, *The Reformation of the Landscape: Religion, Identity and Memory in Early Modern Britain and Ireland* (Oxford, 2011), pp. 296–326.
64. Bodl. Lib., Ms. Engl Misc. e.135, f. 15; Piggott, *Stukeley*, ch. 4; Haycock, *William Stukeley*, ch. 7; Hutton, *Blood and Mistletoe*, pp. 86–102.
65. Bodl. Lib., Ms. Engl. Misc. e.135, f. 19. For British national sentiment in this period, see Linda Colley, *Britons: Forging the Nation, 1707–1837* (New Haven, 1982), and Colin Kidd, *British Identities before Nationalism: Ethnicity and Nationhood in the Atlantic World, 1600–1800* (Cambridge, 1999), ch. 3.
66. Paul-Yves Pezron, *The Antiquities of Nations: More Particularly of the Celtae or Gauls, Taken Originally to Be the Same People as our Ancient Britons*, trans. D. Jones (London, 1706).
67. Henry Rowlands, *Mona Antiqua Restaurata: An Archaeological Discourse on the Antiquities, Natural and Historical, of the Isle of Anglesey, the Antient Seat of the British Druids* (Dublin, 1723), pp. 55, 62–3, 71. The Druidic doctrine of transmigration had also been emphasized by Thomas Brown in his "Short Dissertation about the Mona of Caesar and Tacitus, the Several Names of Man, Whether Io Was the Principal Seat of the Ancient Druids, &c.," printed in William Sacheverell, *An Account of the Isle of Man* (London, 1702), pp. 145–75.
68. Rowlands, *Mona Antiqua Restaurata*, p. 62.
69. John Toland, "A Specimen of the Critical History of the Celtic Religion and Learning: Containing an Account of the Druids," in *A Collection of Several Pieces of Mr. John*

Toland (2 vols, London, 1726), vol. 1, p. 8; Justin Champion, *Republican Learning: John Toland and the Crisis of Christian Culture, 1696–1722* (Manchester, 2003), pp. 213–35.
70. Toland, "A Specimen," pp. 161–3.
71. William Stukeley, *Stonehenge: A Temple Restor'd to the British Druids* (London, 1740), p. 2; William Stukeley, *Abury: A Temple of the British Druids* (London, 1743), pp. 96–7.
72. Stukeley, *Abury*, p. 54.
73. Stukeley, *Abury*, p. 54; Kircher, *Oedipus Aegyptiacus*, vol. 2, part 1, pp. 160, 506–10, quotation on p. 508.
74. Athanasius Kircher, *Mundus Subterraneus* (2 vols, Amsterdam, 1678), vol. 2, pp. 96–101.
75. Kircher, *Oedipus Aegyptiacus*, vol. 2, part 1, pp. 387–434, esp. p. 405.
76. The figure of a king wrapped in the embrace of a dragon appears occasionally in alchemical literature; for example, on the title page of a 1610 novel by the French writer Béroalde de Verville, *L'Histoire Véritable ou Les Voyages du Prince Fortuné* (Albi, 2005), where the dire situation is described on pp. 57–60. The interpretation of the constellation Engonasis as a Christian allegory had been specifically condemned as a heresy by the early Church Father Hippolytus, whose writings on the Druids were read by Stukeley, but this part of Hippolytus's text was not known until 1851. Hippolytus, "The Refutation of All Heresies," trans. J.H. MacMahon, in Alexander Roberts, James Donaldson and A. Cleveland Coxe, eds, *The Ante-Nicene Fathers, Vol. v: Hippolytus, Cyprian, Caius, Novatian* (Buffalo, 1888), book IV, chs 47–8, pp. 43–5; book V, ch. 11, p. 65.
77. Bodl. Lib., Ms. Engl. Misc. e.133, f. 56; Stukeley, *Stonehenge*, pp. 51–4. Stukeley later named Midian as the grandfather of the wife of Hercules, which made Abraham the physical forebear of the Druids. William Stukeley, "A Sunday's Meditation. June 24, 1759. Hescol, sive Origines Brittanicæ," in *Palæographia Sacra*, pp. 121–33.
78. George Wither, *A Collection of Emblemes, Ancient and Moderne* (4 vols, London, 1635), vol. 1, nos 45, 47. Wither's emblems were widely copied throughout the seventeenth and eighteenth centuries.
79. "Lambsprinck," *De Lapide Philosophico* (Frankfurt, 1577), reprinted in *Musæum Hermeticum Reformatum et Amplificatum* (Frankfurt, 1625), p. 353; Michael Maier, *Atalanta Fugiens* (Oppenheim, 1618), *Emblema* 14.
80. "Eirenæus Orandus," ed., *Nicolas Flammel, his Exposition of the Hieroglyphicall Figures Which he Caused to Bee Painted upon an Arch on St. Innocents Church-yard in Paris. Together with the Secret Booke of Artephius, and the Epistle of John Pontanus: Concerning Both the Theoricke and the Practicke of the Philosopher's Stone* (London, 1624), pp. 7–8. For an eighteenth-century illustrated version of Flamel, see "Abraham Eleazar," *Uraltes Chymisches Werck* (Erfurt, 1735), whose emblems can be admired at http://www.alchemywebsite.com/britlib1.html.
81. Dobbs, *Foundations of Newton's Alchemy*, pp. 130–2.
82. Stukeley, *Abury*, p. 38.
83. Bodl. Lib., Ms. Engl. Misc. e.133, f. 53v.
84. Bodl. Lib., Ms. Engl. Misc. e.133, f. 14; Ms. Engl. Misc. e.134, ff. 11–12; Ms. Engl. Misc. e.138, f. 14.
85. FHL, Stukeley Mss., vol. 1, pp. 125–90, quotation on p. 153.
86. Bodl. Lib., Ms. Engl. Misc. e.133, f. 23.
87. Bodl. Lib., Ms. Engl. Misc. e.129, ff. 12–18; Ms. Engl. e.134, ff. 56–9; Ms. Engl. Misc. d.719/13, f. 32v.
88. Bodl. Lib., Ms. Engl. 719/13, ff. 28v–52v, numbered backwards.
89. Stukeley, *Abury*, p. 56.
90. Arthur Macgregor, *Sir Hans Sloane: Collector, Scientist, Antiquary, Founding Father of the British Museum* (London, 1994), pp. 213, 271; Bodl. Lib., Ms. Engl. Misc. e.132, f. 27v. Sloane's alchemical manuscripts have been listed by Adam Maclean at http://www.alchemywebsite.com/britlib1.html.

91. William Whiston, *A New Theory of the Earth, from its Original to the Consummation of All Things* (6th ed., London, 1755), pp. 3, 34. Whiston was responding to the theories of Thomas Burnet, *The Sacred History of the Earth* (2 vols, London, 1681–2), according to which the universe was created from nothing and the earth was originally a smooth, round egg, broken apart by the Deluge. Burnet's evolutionary approach left little room for an alchemical rediscovery of primal matter. For the controversy, see James T. Force, *William Whiston, Honest Newtonian* (Cambridge, 1985), pp. 32–62; Paolo Rossi, *The Dark Abyss of Time: The History of the Earth and the History of Nations from Hooke to Vico*, trans. Lydia Cochrane (Chicago, 1984), pp. 66–9.
92. His Arianism and subsequent religious struggles are discussed in Stewart, *Rise of Public Science*, ch. 3, and his prophetic views in Force, *William Whiston*, pp. 63–89.
93. William Whiston, *An Account of a Surprizing Meteor, Seen in the Air, March the 6th, 1715, at Night* (London, 1716), p. 88.
94. Bodl. Lib., Ms. Engl. Misc. 719/7, f. 40. In *Memoirs of the Life and Writings of Mr. William Whiston* (2 vols, London, 1753), vol. 1, p. 132, Whiston also reversed his opinion on whether comets and meteors were signs of the Apocalypse. For his changing view of "wonders," see Burns, *Age of Wonders*, pp. 170–4.
95. William Whiston, *A Vindication of the Sibylline Oracles* (London, 1715). Christians had long accepted the oracles relating to the birth of Christ, but Whiston went further in arguing that all of these arcane pronouncements were prophetic utterances. For Whiston's fixation with the prophetic biblical book 2nd Esdras, see Alastair Hamilton, *The Apocryphal Apocalypse: The Reception of the Second Book of Esdras (4 Ezra) from the Renaissance to the Enlightenment* (Oxford, 1999), pp. 267–79.
96. William Whiston, *Astronomical Principles of Religion, Natural and Reveal'd* (London, 1717), p. 127; William Whiston, *An Account of the Dæmoniacks* (London, 1737), pp. 49–75; William Whiston, *Mr. Whiston's Account of the Exact Time When Miraculous Gifts Ceas'd in the Church* (London, 1749), p. 25.
97. William Whiston, *Memoirs of the Life and Writings of Mr. William Whiston* (2nd ed., 2 vols, London, 1753), vol. 2, pp. 108–10. The best account of Whiston's role in the Toft affair is is Dennis Todd, *Imagining Monsters: Miscreations of the Self in Eighteenth-Century England* (Chicago, 1995), pp. 38–44.
98. William Whiston, *Memoirs of the Life and Writings of Mr. William Whiston* (London, 1749), pp. 333–4, 602–10.
99. Stukeley, *Stonehenge*, p. 39. Avebury, in Stukeley's view, was twice as old as Stonehenge, and built without tools.
100. Bodl. Lib., Ms. Engl. Misc. d.719/8, f. 17^{v}.
101. For various aspects of Freemasonry in this period, see Margaret C. Jacob, *Living the Enlightenment: Freemasonry and Politics in Eighteenth-Century Europe* (Oxford, 1991); John Money, "Freemasonry and the Fabric of Loyalism in Hanoverian England" in Eckhart Hellmuth, ed., *The Transformation of Political Culture: England and Germany in the Late Eighteenth Century* (Oxford, 1990), pp. 235–74, as well as a work on colonial and republican America that has resonance for Britain, Steven C. Bullock, *Revolutionary Brotherhood: Freemasonry and the Transformation of the American Social Order, 1730–1840* (Chapel Hill, N.C., 1996).
102. Toland's reading of Bruno has been examined in numerous works, including Jacob, *Living the Enlightenment*, pp. 228–45; Champion, *Pillars of Priestcraft Shaken*, pp. 150–4; Champion, *Republican Learning*, pp. 31–2, 172; Robert Rees Evans, *Pantheisticon: The Career of John Toland* (New York, 1991), pp. 95–9.
103. John Toland, "De Genere, Loco, et Tempore Mortis Jordani Bruni Nolani," in *A Collection of Several Pieces of Mr. John Toland*, vol. 1, p. 312.
104. John Toland, *Pantheisticon. Sive Formula Celebrandæ Sodalitatis Socraticæ* ("Cosmopoli," i.e. Amsterdam, 1720), pp. A_2, 5, 9. An English translation is found in John Toland, *Pantheisticon: or, The Form of Celebrating the Socratic-Society* (London, 1751), but it is often more difficult to follow than the original.

105. The original sentence is awkwardly constructed: "*Hinc, Spagyricis, proh dolor! spes ulla Chrysopoeia non relinquitur.*" The English translation of 1751 is more blunt: "Hence, Chymists, alas! may despond of ever finding the Philosopher's Stone." Toland, *Pantheisticon* (Latin ed.), p. 40; Toland, *Pantheisticon* (English ed.), pp. 55–6.
106. Toland, *Pantheisticon* (Latin ed.), p. 77; Toland, *Pantheisticon* (English ed.), pp. 95–6.
107. J.M. Blom, "The Life and Works of Robert Samber (1682–circa 1745)," *English Studies*, 70, 6 (1989), pp. 507–50; also, the article on Samber by J.M. and F. Blom in *ODNB*.
108. Robert Samber, *Roma Illustrata: or A Description of the Most Beautiful Pieces of Painting, Sculpture and Architecture, Antique and Modern, at or near Rome* (London, 1723), Dedication. For Burlington's role as a patron, see James Lees-Milne, *Earls of Creation* (London, 1962), ch. 3; Jacques Carré, *Lord Burlington (1694–1753): Le connoisseur, le Mécène, l'Architecte* (Clermont-Ferrand, 1993); John Harris, *The Palladian Revival: Lord Burlington, his Villa and Garden at Chiswick* (New Haven, Conn., 1994).
109. [James Anderson], *The Constitutions of the Free-Masons* (London, 1723), p. 48; Carré, *Burlington*, pp. 66–72.
110. Bodl. Lib., Ms. Rawl. Poet. 134b, f. 82. For Wharton, see Lewis Melville, *The Life and Writings of Philip, Duke of Wharton* (London, 1913); Mark Blackett-Ord, *Hell-Fire Duke: The Life of the Duke of Wharton* (Windsor, 1982). Burlington has also been labelled a Jacobite, on more slender and questionable grounds, by Jane Clark in "The Mysterious Mr. Buck: Patronage and Politics, 1688–1745," *Apollo*, May 1989, pp. 317–22, "'Lord Burlington Is Here,'" in Toby Barnard and Jane Clark, eds, *Lord Burlington: Architecture, Art and Life* (London, 1995), pp. 251–310, and "'His Zeal Is Too Furious': Lord Burlington's Agents," in Edward Corp, ed., *Lord Burlington: The Man and his Politics Questions of Loyalty* (Lewiston, N.Y., 1998), pp. 181–98.
111. "Eugenius Philalethes" [Robert Samber], *Long Livers: A Curious History of Such Persons of Both Sexes Who Have Liv'd Several Ages and Grown Young Again* (London, 1722). The preface was republished with an introduction by the Masonic historian Edward Gould in 1892. The work is further discussed in Edward Armitage, "Robert Samber," *Ars Quatuor Coronatorum*, 11 (1896), pp. 103–32. See also "Eugenius Philalethes" [Robert Samber], *A Treatise of the Plague* (London, 1721).
112. [Samber], *Long Livers*, pp. v, vi, xxii–iii, xlix, li–ii. The "book M" is introduced in "Christian Rosenkreuz" [J. V. Andræa], *Fama Fraternitatis, or, A Discovery of the Fraternity of the Most Laudable Order of the Rosy Cross*, p. 5, which was included in "Eugenius Philalethes" [Thomas Vaughan], *The Fame and Confession of the Fraternity of R:C: Commonly, of the Rosie Cross* (London, 1652). As Samber adopted Vaughan's pseudonym, it is probable that he used this translation of Rosenkreuz's work.
113. Bodl. Lib., Ms. Rawl. Poet 11, ff. 74–5.
114. Bodl. Lib., Ms. Rawl. Poet 133, ff. 79–160^{v}, quotation on f. 91^{v}. For Cuper and Jurieu, see Gerald Cerny, ed., *Theology, Politics and Letters at the Crossroads of European Civilization: Jacques Basnage and the Baylean Huguenot Refugees in the Dutch Republic* (Dordrecht, 1987), pp. 99, 167. An explanation of Teraphim is found in *The Jewish Encyclopedia* (12 vols, New York, 1901–6), vol. 12, pp. 108–9. Their connection with astrology is not of course biblical, but is derived from rabbinical literature.
115. Bodl. Lib., Ms. Rawl. Poet 133, No. III, ff. 162^{b}–168.
116. Steele supported a proposal by Samber to publish a translation of Ovid's *Metamporphoses*: Bodl. Lib., Ms. Rawl. Poet. 134^{b}, f. 152^{v}.
117. R.F. Gould, "Martin Clare," *Ars Quatuor Coronatorum*, 4 (1891), pp. 33–41; Martin Clare, *Youth's Introduction to Trade and Business* (5th ed., London, 1740), title page; [Martin Clare], *Rules and Orders for the Government of the Academy in Soho-Square, London* ([London], [c. 1740]).
118. Martin Clare, *The Movement of Fluids, Natural and Artificial* (2nd ed., London, 1746), sigs A_2, A_4.
119. "A Defence of Masonry, Publish'd *A.D. 1730*. Occasion'd by a *Pamphlet* Entitl'd *Masonry Dissected*," in James Anderson, *The New Book of Constitutions of the Ancient and*

Honorable Fraternity of Free and Acceped Masons (London, 1738), pp. 219–22. As Anderson's name appeared on this edition of the *Constitutions*, there was no need to disguise his authorship of the "Defence." Samuel Prichard's anti-Masonic pamphlet, *Masonry Dissected*, appeared in 1730 and was frequently reprinted.

120. "Defence of Masonry," pp. 224–5.
121. That the Eleusinian mysteries were well known to a broad audience is illustrated by their description in standard works of reference like *A Dictionary of All Religions, Ancient and Modern* (London, 1723).
122. Lewis Theobald to Warburton, 24 Feb. 1730, in John Nichols, ed., *Illustrations of the Literary History of the Eighteenth Century* (8 vols, London, 1817–58), vol. 2, p. 517, a reference to Masonry in Shakespeare. This comment may be directed at Alexander Pope, who was a Freemason. Warburton, of course, later befriended the poet and became his literary executor. For *The Divine Legation*, see also B.W. Young, *Religion and Enlightenment in Eighteenth-Century England: Theological Debate from Locke to Burke* (Oxford, 1998), ch. 5.
123. William Warburton, *The Divine Legation of Moses* (3 vols in 2 parts, London, 1738–41), vol. 1, pp. 133–4.
124. *Ibid.*, vol. 1, p. 182. Warburton devoted fifty pages of the first volume to Aeneas's journey into Hades.
125. *Ibid.*, pp. 332–3, 403–9, quotation on p. 408. For more against "the infamous Spinoza," see part 2, vol. 2, part 1, pp. 310–11.
126. *Ibid.*, vol. 2, part 1, pp. 113, 153.
127. *Ibid.*, vol. 2, part 1, pp. 201, 206.
128. *Ibid.*, vol. 2, part 2, p. 639. Unlike Stukeley, Warburton concentrates on the formal characteristics of ritual or writing and is not much concerned with the origins of the sacred ideas behind them.
129. Still poorly understood, the difficulties of British Freemasonry in the mid-eighteenth century were first indicated by R.F. Gould in *The History of Freemasonry: Its Antiquities, Symbols, Constitutions, Customs, Etc.* (6 vols, London, 1882–7), vol. 3, chs 17–19.

Chapter Six: The Occult on the Margins

1. This question has been asked more often by historians of other parts of Europe, beginning with Peter Burke, *Popular Culture in Early Modern Europe* (New York, 1978) and including F. Steven Wilson, *The Magical Universe: Everyday Ritual and Magic in Pre-Modern Europe* (Hambledon and London, 2000).
2. Alexandra Walsham, "Recording Superstition in Early Modern Britain: The Origins of Folklore," in S.A. Smith and Alan Knight, eds, *The Religion of Fools? Superstition Past and Present*, Past and Present Supplement 3 (Oxford, 2008), pp. 178–206.
3. Henry Bourne, *Antiquitates Vulgares: or, The Antiquities of the Common People* (Newcastle, 1725), pp. x–xi. For Bourne, see Walsham, "Recoding Superstition," pp. 193–9; Sash Handley, *Visions of an Unseen World: Ghost Beliefs and Ghost Stories in Eighteenth-Century England* (London, 2007), pp. 181–3. The campaign to reform popular customs is considered in David Underdown, *Revel, Riot and Rebellion: Popular Politics and Culture in England, 1603–1660* (Oxford, 1985), and Ronald Hutton, *The Rise and Fall of Merry England: The Ritual Year, 1400–1700* (Oxford, 1994).
4. Bourne, *Antiquitates Vulgares*, p. 63.
5. *Ibid.*, pp. 77, 84.
6. *Ibid.*, pp. 114, 224.
7. Handley, *Visions of an Unseen World*, ch. 2, gives a thorough analysis of these.
8. John Frazer, ΔΕΥΤΕΡΟΣΚΟΠΙΑ *[Deutoroskopia] or, A Brief Discourse Concerning the Second Sight, Commonly So Called* (Edinburgh, 1707), p. 25, reprinted in Michael Hunter, ed., *The Occult Laboratory: Magic, Science and Second Sight in Late 17th-Century Scotland* (Woodbridge, Suffolk, 2001), p. 200.

9. *Ibid.*, pp. 11–12. For more on second sight, see "Theophilus Insulanus" [Donald Macleod], *A Treatise on the Second Sight, Dreams and Apparitions* (Edinburgh, 1763); Martin Rackwitz, *Travels to Terra Incognita: The Scottish Highlands and Hebrides in Early Modern Traveller's Accounts, c. 1600–1800* (Münster, 2007), pp. 505–12.
10. Discussions of these three works can be found in Rodney Baine, *Daniel Defoe and the Supernatural* (Athens, Georgia, 1969), and Katherine Clark, *Daniel Defoe: The Whole Frame of Nature, Time and Providence* (Basingstoke, 2007). See also Ian Bostridge, *Witchcraft and its Transformations, c. 1650–c. 1750* (Oxford, 1997), pp. 136–8; Paula R. Backscheider, *Daniel Defoe: His Life* (Baltimore, 1989), pp. 522–6; John J. Richetti, *The Life of Daniel Defoe* (Oxford, 2005), pp. 169–73.
11. [Daniel Defoe], *The Political History of the Devil* (London,1726), pp. 2, 226.
12. *Ibid.*, pp. 341, 343–4.
13. [Daniel Defoe], *An Essay on the History and Reality of Apparitions* (London, 1727), p. 341.
14. *Ibid.*, p. 21.
15. [Daniel Defoe], *A System of Magick; or, A History of the Black Art* (London, 1727), sig. A_3, pp. 1–2.
16. *Ibid.*, pp. 65, 102–3, 226.
17. *Ibid.*, pp. 285–316. The profession in general is discussed in Owen Davies, *Cunning-Folk: Popular Magic in English History* (London, 2003). A certain Dr Borman was assessed for eight hearths in the parish of Bexley, Kent in 1664: Duncan Harrington, ed., "Kent Hearth Tax Assessment, Lady Day, 1664: CKS Q/RTh," accessed at http://www.hearthtax.org.uk/communities/kent/kent_1664L_transcript.pdf. Bexley is not near Maidstone, but it is on the main road to it from London. Daniel Borman was town chamberlain of Maidstone in 1685–6, and William Borman a common councilman, or town officer, in 1745: http://www.kent-opc.org/Parishes/Court/MaidstoneChamberlains.html; http://www.kent-opc.org/Parishes/Court/MaidstoneJuratsetal.html.
18. [Defoe], *System of Magick*, pp. 316, 318, 320.
19. *Ibid.*, pp. 321–35.
20. *Ibid.*, pp. 397–403, quotation on p. 397.
21. *Ibid.*, p. 378.
22. William Bond, *The History of the Life and Adventures of Mr. Duncan Campbell* (2nd ed., London, 1720), pp. 281–2; [Duncan Campbel], *Secret Memoirs of the Late Mr. Duncan Campbel, the Famous Deaf and Dumb Gentleman* (London, 1732), pp. 39–40. The judge who took Coates's affidavit was Robert Raymond, later lord chief justice. See also *Eliza Haywood, a Spy on the Conjuror: or, A Collection of Surprising and Diverting Stories . . . By Way of Memoirs of the Famous Mr. Duncan Campbell* (London, 1724); Baine, *Defoe and the Supernatural*, ch. 7, and Owen Davies, "Decriminalizing the Witch: The Origin of and Response to the 1736 Witchcraft Act," in John Newton and Jo Bath, eds, *Witchcraft and the Act of 1604* (Leiden, 2008), pp. 214–18. Haywood was a well-known playwright and a friend of Richard Steele.
23. [Campbel], *Secret Memoirs*, p. 7.
24. [Duncan Campbel], *The Friendly Dæmon, or The Generous Apparition* (London, 1725), pp. 9, 14. This account was also included in his *Secret Memoirs*, pp. 166–95.
25. [Campbel], *Secret Memoirs*, sigs [A_1-A_1v], pp. 12, 196 ff. The Scots lords were the duke of Argyle, the earl of Marchmont and viscount Stair, while the Tories included Sir Nathaniel Curzon and Sir Richard Grosvenor. Davies, "Decriminalizing the Witch," also mentions William Wyndham, the future earl of Egremont, as a customer.
26. W. Harbutt Dawson, "An Old Yorkshire Astrologer and Magician, 1694–1760," *The Reliquary*, 23 (1882–3), pp. 197–202.
27. John Money, ed., *The Chronicles of John Cannon, Excise Officer and Writing Master* (2 vols, Oxford, 2010), vol. 1, p. 21.
28. *Ibid.*, vol. 1, pp. 42–4. John Read also taught Cannon how to predict the weather from the phases of the moon: *ibid.*, vol. 2, p. 400.

29. *Ibid.*, vol. 2, pp. 116, 149–50, 171, 277–8, 319, 346–7, 351, 390–1, 399–400, 450, 461, 548, for examples.
30. *Ibid.*, vol. 2, pp. 353, 458. "Sky battles" and other celestial phenomena caused widespread consternation in the early years of George I: see Vladimir Jankovic, "The Politics of Sky Battles in Early Hanoverian Britain," *Journal of British Studies*, 41, 4 (2002), pp. 403–28; Elisha Smith, *The Superstition of Omens and Prodigies; with the Proper Reception, and Profitable Improvement. A Divinity Lecture upon the Surprising Phænomenon of Light, March 6, 1715. On the Sunday After* (London, 1716).
31. Money, ed., *Chronicles of Cannon*, vol. 2, p. 458; Geoffrey of Monmouth, *The British History*, trans. Aaron Thompson (London, 1718), pp. v, 203 ff.; Davies, *Witchcraft, Magic and Culture*, pp. 142–7.
32. *Nixon's Cheshire Prophecy at Large* (5th ed., London, 1718), p. 18. The edition of Mother Shipton's prophecies used by Cannon may have been J. Tyrrel, *Past, Present, and to Come, or Mother Shipton's Yorkshire Prophecy* (London, 1740), although he could also have read the chapbook *The History of Mother Shipton* (London, 1750[?]). Apparently, the predictions of Shipton and Nixon were published together for the first time only in 1797.
33. Money, ed., *Chronicles of Cannon*, vol. 2, pp. 450, 559–60; John Partridge, *Merlinus Liberatus . . . 1743* (London, 1742), sigs C_7–C_{10}. I have not been able to trace a copy of *Vox Stellarum* for 1740.
34. Money, ed., *Chronicles of Cannon*, vol. 2, p. 303; *Gentleman's Magazine*, 7 (March 1737), p. 157. Smith's fascination with eclipses was further evidenced in a short pamphlet, George Smith, *A Dissertation on the General Properties of Eclipses; and Particularly the Ensuing Eclipse of 1748, Considered thro' All its Periods* (London, 1748), as well as in the projection he made to show the path of the 1737 eclipse around the globe: B.L., Maps *23.(10), accessed at http://www.mapforum.com/07/bleclip.htm#8.
35. Money, ed., *Chronicles of Cannon*, vol. 2, p. 400; John Middleton, *Practical Astrology* (London, 1679); Richard Saunders, *The Astrological Judgment and Practice of Physick* (London, 1677). Woodward was the compiler of an almanac, *Vox Uraniae*, that ran through the 1680s, and of an ephemeris that appeared in the early 1690s.
36. Money, ed., *Chronicles of Cannon*, vol. 2, p. 516; William Whiston, *The Cause of the Deluge Demonstrated* (London, 1717); Richard S. Westfall, *Never at Rest: A Biography of Isaac Newton* (Cambridge, 1980), pp. 391–7.
37. Money, ed., *Chronicles of Cannon*, vol. 2, p. 400.
38. *Ibid.*, vol. 2, p. 529.
39. *Ibid.*, vol. 2, pp. 314, 488.
40. *Ibid.*, vol. 2, p. 285.
41. *Ibid.*, vol. 2, pp. 457–8.
42. *The Statutes at Large* (7 vols, London, 1742), vol. 7, p. 52, 9 G. II, c. 5. The best accounts of the Witchcraft Act are in Bostridge, *Witchcraft and its Transformations*, ch. 8, and Owen Davies, *Witchcraft, Magic and Culture, 1736–1951* (Manchester, 1999), ch. 1. Much of Bostridge's chapter also appears in his article "Witchcraft Repealed," in Jonathan Barry, Marianne Hesther and Gareth Roberts, eds, *Witchcraft in Early Modern Europe: Studies in Culture and Belief* (Cambridge, 1996), pp. 309–34.
43. *London Journal*, no. 974, 8 April 1738, cited in *The London Magazine, and Monthly Chronologer* (London, 1738), pp. 178–9. For coffee-houses, see Brian Cowan, *The Social Life of Coffee: The Emergence of the Coffehouse* (New Haven and London, 2005).
44. T.J.F. Kendrick, "Sir Robert Walpole, the Old Whigs and the Bishops, 1733–36: A Study in Eighteenth-Century Parliamentary Politics," *Historical Journal*, 11, 3 (1968), pp. 421–45; Stephen Taylor, "Sir Robert Walpole, the Church of England, and the Quaker Tithes Bill of 1736," *Historical Journal*, 28, 1 (1985), pp. 51–77; Peter Clark, "The Mother Gin Controversy in the Early Eighteenth Century," *Transactions of the Royal Historical Society*, 5th series, 38 (1988), pp. 63–84; Jonathan White, "The 'Slow But Sure Poison:' The Representation of Gin and its Drinkers, 1736–1751," *Journal of British Studies*, 42, 1 (2003), pp. 35–64.

45. Alexander Carlyle, *Autobiography of the Reverend Alexander Carlyle, Minister of Inveresk, Containing Memorials of the Men and Events of his Time* (3rd ed., Edinburgh, 1861), pp. 9, 61; Romney Sedgwick, ed., *The History of Parliament: The House of Commons, 1715–54* (2 vols, London, 1970), vol. 1, pp. 569–70, 595, vol. 2, pp. 14–17, 121–2. As a judge of the Court of Session, Erskine was given the title "Lord Grange" when in Scotland.
46. Carlyle, *Autobiography*, p. 10. The leader of the Secessionists, Ebenezer Erskine, gave a sermon on "The sovereignty of Zion's King," in which he condemned "laws countenancing witchcraft." D. Fraser, ed., *The Whole Works of the Reverend Ebenezer Erskine* (3 vols, Philadelphia, 1836), vol. 2, p 194.
47. The best treatments of Scottish witch beliefs in this period are Edward J. Cowan and Lizanne Henderson, "The Last of the Witches? The Survival of Scottish Witch Belief," in Julian Goodare, ed., *The Scottish Witch-Hunt in Context* (Manchester, 2003), pp. 198–217; Peter Maxwell-Stuart, "Witchcraft and Magic in Eighteenth-Century Scotland," in Owen Davies and Willem de Blécourt, eds, *Beyond the Witch Trials: Witchcraft and Magic in Enlightened Europe* (Manchester, 2004), pp. 81–99; Lizanne Henderson, "The Survival of Witch Prosecutions and Witch Beliefs in South-West Scotland," *Scottish Historical Review*, 85, 1 (2006), pp. 52–74.
48. Alan Ramsay, *The Gentle Shepherd: A Scots Pastoral Comedy* (7th ed., Glasgow, 1743), act II, scene 2, p. 19. Scotland is not included in Davies, *Cunning-Folk*.
49. Edward Burt, *Letters from a Gentleman in the North of Scotland to his Friend in London* (2 vols, London, 1754), vol. 1, pp. 278–9, 280–1, 285–6.
50. *Ibid.*, vol. 1, p. 341.
51. Witches were sometimes targeted in Highland feuds, as in an incident along the coast of Ross and Cromarty in 1750, when several members of the Munro clan, armed with swords, broke into the houses of their enemies and terrorized their wives and daughters, "calling them Witches and Divils." Maxwell-Stuart, "Witchcraft and Magic," p. 89.
52. Davies, *Witchcraft, Magic and Culture*, pp. 94–7; W.B. Carnochan, "Witch-Hunting and Belief in 1751: The Case of Thomas Colley and Ruth Osborne," *Journal of Social History*, 4 (1970–1), pp. 389–403. Davies mentions three more cases that occurred before 1800: in 1773 at Seend, Wiltshire; in 1774 at Rochford, Essex; and in 1776 at Aston, Leicestershire. For the Rochford incident, see Eric Maples, *The Dark World of the Witches* (New York, 1964), p. 123. To these may be added cases in 1776 at Farnham, Suffolk; in 1785 in Northamptonshire; and in 1792 at Stanningfield, Suffolk. The list is certainly not complete.
53. Joseph Juxon, *A Sermon upon Witchcraft, Occasion'd by a Late Illegal Attempt to Discover Witches by Swimming. Preached at Twyford, in the County of Leicester, July 11, 1736* (London, 1736), p. 19.
54. [Titus Oates], *The Witch of Endor: or, A Plea for the Divine Administration by the Agency of Good and Evil Spirits* (London, 1736), p. xl.
55. [John Webster], *A Discourse on Witchcraft. Occasioned by a Bill Now Depending in Parliament* (London, 1736), p. iv.
56. Davies, *Witchcraft, Magic and Culture*, pp. 16–17.
57. Nehemiah Curnock, ed., *The Journals of the Rev. John Wesley, A.M.* (8 vols, London, 1909–16), vol. 5, p. 265.
58. Jean-Robert Armogathe, *Le Quiétisme* (Paris, 1973); George Balsama, "Madame Guyon, Heterodox . . .," *Church History*, 42, 3 (1973), pp. 350–65; Joyce Irwin, "Anna Maria von Schurman and Antoinette Bourignon: Contrasting Examples of Seventeenth-Century Pietism," *Church History*, 60, 3 (1991), pp. 302–15; B. Robert Kreiser, *Miracles, Convulsions and Ecclesiastical Politics in Early Eighteenth-Century Paris* (Princeton, 1978); W.R. Ward, *The Protestant Evangelical Awakening* (Cambridge, 1992); Hans Schneider, "'Philadelphische Brüder mit einem lutherischen Maul und mährischen Rock': Zum Zinzendorfs Kirchenverständnis," in Martin Brecht and Paul Paucker, eds, *Neue Aspekte der Zinzendorf-Forschung* (Göttingen, 2006), pp. 11–36.

59. These aspects of the prophetic movement were emphasized by the Nonjuring minister Nathaniel Spinckes in his blistering attack on them, *The New Pretenders to Prophecy Re-Examined: And their Pretences Shewn Again to Be Groundless and False* (London, 1710).
60. Hillel Schwartz, *The French Prophets: The History of a Millenarian Group in Eighteenth-Century England* (Berkeley and Los Angeles), p. 108; John Lacy, *The Prophetical Warnings of John Lacy, Esq; Pronounced under the Operation of the Spirit* (London, 1707); John Lacy, *Warnings of the Eternal Spirit, by the Mouth of his Servant John, Sirnam'd Lacy. The Second Part* (London, [1707]); *Predictions Concerning the Raising the Dead Body of Mr. Thomas Emes, Commonly Call'd Doctor Emes* ([London?], [1708?]).
61. Chetham's Library, Ms. A.4.33 (this collection of blessings originally belonged to John Lacy); Schwartz, *French Prophets*, pp. 148–9, 165–6.
62. Schwartz, *French Prophets*, pp. 233–51.
63. Thomas Emes, *The Atheist Turned Deist, and the Deist Turn'd Christian* (London, 1698); T[homas]. E[mes]., *A Dialogue between Alkali and Acid* (London, 1698); Thomas Emes, *A Letter to a Gentleman Concerning Alkali and Acid* (London, 1700); T[homas]. E[mes]., *Vindiciæ Mentis: An Essay of the Being and Nature of Mind* (London, 1702).
64. Timothy Byfield, *A Short Description and Vindication of the True Sal Volatile Oleosum of the Ancients: Wherein 'tis Proved the Great Medicine of the Spirits; and Consequently, An Universal Remedy* (London, 1699), p. 8; see also Timothy Byfield, *Directions Tending to Health and Long-Life, &c.* (London, 1717); Timothy Byfield, *Some Long-Vacation Hours Redeem'd. The Christian Examiner, Part 1* (2nd ed., London, 1720); Timothy Byfield, *A Closet Piece. The Experimental Knowledge of the Ever-Blessed God* (London, 1721).
65. The mystical tendency among Scots Episcopalians can be traced to the publication of [Henry Scougall], *The Life of God in the Soul of Man* (London, 1677).
66. [George Garden], *An Apology for M. Antonia Bourignon* (London, 1699); Charles Leslie, *The Snake in the Grass: or, Satan Transform'd into an Angel of Light* (2nd ed., London, 1698), pp. ii–xxx. Leslie, an English Nonjuror, directed this pamphlet against Quakers, but added a preface to the second edition denouncing Bourignon.
67. G.D. Henderson, ed., *Mystics of the North-East, Including I. Letters of James Keith, M.D., and Others to Lord Deskford; II. Correspondence between Dr. George Garden and James Cunningham* (Aberdeen, 1934), pp. 11–74.
68. [Garden], *Apology for M. Bourignon*, pp. 283–95, quotation on pp. 284, 292; Leslie, *Snake in the Grass*, p. xxviii, accused Bourignon's own teachings of being "*Witch-craft*."
69. B.L., Lansdowne 841, ff. 90–4v.
70. Henderson, ed., *Mystics of the North-East*, pp. 205–6, 236, 220, 254; B.J. Gibbons, *Gender in Mystical and Occult Thought: Behmenism and its Development in England* (Cambridge, 1996), pp. 181–4.
71. Chetham Library, Ms. A.2.82, p. 397; *Warnings of the Eternal Spirit, to the City of Edenburgh, Pronounc'd by the Mouths of Margaret Mackenzie, and James Cunninghame* (London, 1710), p. 20; Schwartz, *French Prophets*, pp. 157–62, 165–7.
72. Bodl. Lib., Ms. Rawl. D.832, f. 47. The letter is unsigned but inscribed "L.F." For more on Freher, see Charles A. Muses, *Illumination on Jacob Boehme: The Work of Dionysius Andreas Freher* (New York, 1951).
73. Dr Williams's Library (DWL), Ms. Walton I.1.11; for the German Philadelphians, see D.P. Walker, *The Decline of Hell: Seventeenth-Century Discussions of Eternal Torment* (London, 1964), ch. 14; and for Freher's circle, Arthur Versluis, *Wisdom's Children: A Christian Esoteric Tradition* (Albany, N.Y., 1999), pp. 79–83, as well as Serge Hutin, *Les Disciples Anglais de Jacob Boehme aux XVIIe et XVIIIe Siècles* (Paris, 1960), ch. 5. Allen Leppington's father, Lemuel, was a member of the Salters' Company, but he and his brother became hop merchants in Bread Street, Cheapside: *The Poll of the Livery-Men of the City of London* (London, 1710), p. 137; *A Compleat Guide to All Persons Who Have any Trade or Concern with the City of London and Parts Adjacent* (London, 1740), p. 135; *Kent's Directory for the Year 1759* (London, 1759), p. 71; London Metropolitan Archives, Watney Combe Reid and Co. Brewers, ACC/1399/027, a–b, "lease taken by Allen

Leppington of Bread St., hop merchant, on two mills in Isleworth for grinding Brazil wood into red dye, Oct. 1746."

74. DWL, Ms. Walton I.1.39, f. 11v; also, Ms. Walton I.1.31, 32, 70, 79, Walton Bundle XXXVII; B.L., Add. Ms. 5786–8 (*Three Tables*), 5789 (*Paradoxa Emblemata*), 5790 (*Hieroglyphica Sacra, or Divine Emblems*).
75. [Francis Lee], "An Historical Account of Montanism," in George Hickes, *The Spirit of Enthusiasm Exorcised* (4th ed., London, 1709), pp. 73–352; Nathaniel Spinckes, "The New Pretenders to Prophecy, Examined," in *ibid.*, pp. 353–530.
76. See Alastair Hamilton, *The Apocryphal Apocalypse: The Reception of the Second Book of Esdras (4 Ezra) from the Renaissance to the Enlightenment* (Oxford, 1999), pp. 261–6; B.L., Add. Ms. 15,911, nos 3, 5, 10; B.L. Add. Ms. 23,204, ff. 14, 26. Apocryphal books of the Old Testament do not appear in the Jewish Bible and do not have canonical authority as sources of doctrinal evidence.
77. Francis Lee, *An Epistolary Discourse, Concerning the Books of Ezra, Genuine and Spurious* (London, 1722), pp. 2, 5.
78. Bodl. Lib., Ms. Rawl. D.1152, ff. 4, 295v.
79. Chetham Library, Ms. A.4.33, "A Collection of Blessings By the Eternal Spirit . . . 1712," pp. 336–8, 346; *ODNB*, Keimer, Samuel; Bodl. Lib., Ms. Rawl. D.832, ff. 34–5; Schwartz, *French Prophets*, pp. 142–3; [Richard Kingston], *Enthusiastick Impostors No Divinely Inspir'd Prophets* (London, 1707), p. 73; Walker, *Decline of Hell*, ch. 15; Gibbons, *Gender in Mystical and Occult Thought*, pp. 152–8.
80. Bodl. Lib., Rawl. Ms. D.1154, f. 51v; D.1155, f. 1; D.1157, 8 June 1729.
81. [Richard Roach], *The Great Crisis: or, The Mystery of the Times and Seasons Unfolded* (London, marked 1725, but actually 1727), pp. 5–14, 96–112, 165–71, quotations on pp. 49, 165.
82. Richard Roach, *The Imperial Standard of Messiah Triumphant* (London, [1727]), pp. 56–71, quotation on pp. 69–70.
83. *Ibid.*, pp. 187–8.
84. *Ibid.*, pp. 300–1.
85. Hannah Wharton, *Divine Inspiration: or, A Collection of Manifestations* (London, 1732), p. 48; for Fatio, see p. 84. The London inspirations are collected in Hannah Wharton, *Some Manifestations and Communications of the Spirit, in a Forty Days Ministration in That Place London* (London, 1730).
86. Curnock, ed., *Journal of Wesley*, vol. 1, p. 436; vol. 2, pp. 136–7, 226.
87. Henderson, ed., *Mystics of the North-East*, p. 203. For Cheyne and Boehme, see Gibbons, *Gender in Mystical and Occult Thought*, pp. 184–7. Cheyne's medical theories are considered in Anita Guerrini, *Obesity and Depression in the Enlightenment: The Life and Times of George Cheyne* (Norman, Oklahoma, 2000), while G.S. Rousseau discusses the relationship between his mysticism and medicine in *Enlightenment Borders: Pre- and Post-Modern Discourses, Medical, Scientific* (Manchester, 1991), pp. 78–117.
88. Robert Wodrow, *Analecta: or, Materials for a History of Remarkable Providences* (3 vols, Edinburgh, 1842–3), vol. 2, pp. 47–8, 255, 379; Thomas M'Crie, ed., *The Correspondence of the Reverend Robert Wodrow* (3 vols, Edinburgh, 1842–3), vol. 1, p. 437. For Cheyne's training, see Anita Guerini, "James Keill, George Cheyne and Newtonian Physiology, 1690–1740," *Journal of the History of Biology*, 18, 2 (1985), pp. 247–66.
89. George Cheyne, *Philosophical Principles of Religion: Natural and Revealed* (2 parts, London, 1715), part 1, pp. 135, 137–8, 341.
90. *Ibid.*, part 2, p. 4.
91. Richard Parkinson, ed., *The Private Journals and Literary Remains of John Byrom*, Chetham Society, vols 23, 24, 40, 44 (2 vols in 4 parts, Manchester, 1854–7), vol. 2, part 1, pp. 308–10; vol. 2, part 2, pp. 330–2, quotation on p. 331; and for Marsay, Hans Schneider, *German Radical Pietism*, trans. Gerald T. Macdonald (Plymouth, 2007), pp. 95–7.
92. For Hartley, see Richard C. Allen, *David Hartley on Human Nature* (Albany, N.Y., 1999).
93. Parkinson, ed., *Remains of Byrom*, vol. 1, part 1, pp. 252 ff.

94. *Ibid.*, vol. 1, part 1, pp. 20–1; Andrew Starkie, "William Law and Cambridge Jacobitism, 1713–16," *Historical Research*, 75, 190 (2002), pp. 448–67. The best accounts of Law are the short biography in *ODNB* by Isabel Rivers and the study by the pacifist Stephen Hobhouse, *William Law and Eighteenth-Century Quakerism* (London, 1927: reissued New York, 1971); see also Stephen Hobhouse, ed., *Selected Mystical Writings of William Law* (2nd ed., Rockcliff, Md., 1948), appendix 1, and B.W. Young, *Religion and Enlightenment in Eighteenth-Century England: Theological Debate from Locke to Burke* (Oxford, 1998), ch. 4.
95. J[ohn] H[utchinson], *Moses's Principia* (2 vols, London, 1724, 1727), vol. 1, p. 10; vol. 2, p. xxix.
96. J[ohn] H[utchinson], *The Covenant in the Cherubim: So the Hebrew Writings Perfect. Alterations by Rabbies Forged* (London, 1734), pp. 30–2, 64–5, 219–46, 450–76; William Stukeley, "Memoirs of Sr. Isaac Newton's Life, (1752)," Royal Society Ms. LXIX.a.2., p. 161, f. 72 (accessed at http://ttp.royalsociety.org); [William Warburton], *Letters from a Late Eminent Prelate, to One of his Friends* (2nd ed., London, 1809), pp. 58–9; John C. English, "John Hutchinson's Critique of Newtonian Heterodoxy," *Church History*, 68, 3 (1999), pp. 581–97, with information on Hutchinson's followers; David S. Katz, "The Hutchinsonians and Hebraic Fundamentalism in Eighteenth-Century England," in David S. Katz and Jonathan Israel, eds, *Skeptics, Millenarians and Jews* (Leiden, 2007), pp. 237–55.
97. Parkinson, ed., *Remains of Byrom*, vol. 2, part 1, pp. 105, 106; vol. 2, part 2, p. 365.
98. Chetham's Library, A.4.98; Thomas Rodd, ed., *A Catalogue of the Library of the Late John Byrom, Esq., M.A., F.R.S.* (London, 1848), pp. 41, 66, 168, 176, 181, 244, 245; Parkinson, *Remains of Byrom*, vol. 1, part 1, pp. 44–5; vol. 1, part 2, p. 348.
99. Rodd, ed., *Library of Byrom*, pp. 10, 11, 15, 106, 199, 204, 222. Byrom and some friends "talked much about Rosicrucian" at a tavern in 1725; Parkinson, ed., *Remains of Byrom*, vol. 1, part 1, p. 130.
100. Parkinson, ed., *Remains of Byrom*, vol. 1, part 1, pp. 51, 83, 181, 188, 194; vol. 1, part 2, pp. 328, 338.
101. *Ibid.*, vol. 1, part 1, p. 109; Bodl. Lib., Ms. Rylands d.9, p. 166. Byrom discussed Masonry with the Cabala Club and with the duke of Richmond, a prominent Brother: Parkinson, *Remains of Byrom*, vol. 1, part 1, pp. 92, 121.
102. *Ibid.*, vol. 1, part 2, pp. 337, 321–4, 337, 507.
103. *Ibid.*, vol. 1, part 2, p. 452; vol. 2, part 1, p. 113; vol. 2, part 2, p. 363; Francis Okely, ed. and trans., *Memoirs of the Life, Death, Burial, and Wonderful Writings of Jacob Behmen* (Northampton, 1780), pp. 105–6.
104. [Wolf, Freiherr von Metternich], *Faith and Reason Compared* (London, 1713), p. 42; J[ohn] P[ordage], *Theologia Mystica, or, The Mystic Divinity of the Æternal Invisibles* (London, 1683), pp. 10–11, 16–86 (illustration on p. 28), 114–15, 118–19. Boehme had referred to "an Eye of Eternity, an Abyssal Eye," but did not give the image as much attention as Pordage: Jacob Boehme, *Signatura Rerum, or The Signature of All Things*, trans. J. Ellistone (London, 1651), p. 13.
105. [Metternich], *Faith and Reason Compared*, p. 221.
106. DWL, Ms. Walton I.1.26–8 (Freher transcripts); Ms. Walton I.1.33–4 ("Three Tables," attested as being in Law's hand by Thomas Langcake in 1781); Ms. Walton I.1.35 (Lee transcripts); B.L., Add. Ms. 5785 ("Three Tables"); Rodd, ed., *Library of Byrom*, p. 240; Joy Hancock, *The Byrom Collection: Renaissance Thought, the Royal Society and the Building of the Globe Theatre* (London, 1992); Getty Research Institute (GRI), Manley Palmer Hall Collection, Ms. 43: collection of drawings and diagrams by J.D. Leuchter.
107. William Law, "Some Animadversions upon Dr. Trap's Late Reply," in *An Appeal to All That Doubt, or Disbelieve the Truths of the Gospel, Whether they Be Deists, Arians, Socinians, or Nominal Christians* (London, 1742), p. 322.
108. Law, "Some Animadversions upon Dr. Trap's Late Reply," p. 136.

109. DWL, Ms. Walton I.1.43, Letter Book of Henry Brooke, pp. 160–1, 164–6; Parkinson, *Remains of Byrom*, vol. 2, part 2, p. 364; Hobhouse, ed., *Selected Mystical Writings of Law*, pp. 397–422.
110. Parkinson, *Remains of Byrom*, vol. 2, part 1, p. 275.
111. William Law, *The Spirit of Love* (London, 1752), pp. 36–7.
112. Parkinson, *Remains of Byrom*, vol. 2, part 2, p. 538.
113. Parkinson, ed., *Remains of Byrom*, vol. 1, part 1, p. 233; vol. 2, part 1, p. 235.
114. Law, *Way to Divine Knowledge*, p. 126.
115. On Jacobites and the Royal Touch, see Paul Kléber Monod, *Jacobitism and the English People, 1688–1788* (Cambridge, 1989), pp. 127–32. For the Nonjuror Thomas Carte, who defended the Royal Touch in print, see Paul Kléber Monod, "Thomas Carte, the Druids and British National Identity," in Paul Monod, Murrray Pittock and Daniel Szechi, eds, *Loyalty and Identity: Jacobites at Home and Abroad* (Basingstoke, Hants, 2010), pp. 132–48, as well as Thomas Carte, *A General History of England* (4 vols, London, 1747–55), vol. 1, pp. 291–2 n. 4.
116. Law, "A Collection of Letters," Letter XXVII, p. 196.
117. Laurence Dermott, *Ahimon Rezon: or, A Help to a Brother; Shewing the Excellency of Secrecy, and the First Cause, or Motive, of the Institution of Free-Masonry* (London, 1756), pp. vi, x–xi, xiv, 19–20, 25–34, 43–5.
118. A general overview of the subject is found in James Stevens Curll, *The Art and Architecture of Freemasonry* (London, 1991); but for the peculiar myths of architecture that fed into Masonry, see J. Rykwert, *The First Moderns* (Cambridge, Mass., 1980).
119. Vaughan Hart, *Nicholas Hawskmoor: Rebuilding Ancient Wonders* (New Haven, Conn., 2002), esp. ch. 4; Bodl. Lib., Ms. Rawl. C.136, p. 125; also Bodl. Lib., Ms. Rylands. d.9, p. 218, printed in W.J. Songhurst, ed., *Quatuor Coronatorum Antigrapha: Masonic Reprints, Vol. 10: Minutes of the Grand Lode of Freemasons of England, 1723–1739* (London, 1913), pp. 191–2.
120. Eileen Harris, "Batty Langley: A Tutor to Freemasons (1696–1751)," *The Burlington Magazine*, 119, 890 (1977), pp. 327–35; Batty Langley, *Ancient Masonry, Both in the Theory and Practice* (London, 1736), Dedication.
121. John Wood, *The Origin of Building: or, The Plagiarism of the Heathens Detected* (Bath, 1746), pp. 4–11, 14, 20, quotation on p. 24. For Wood's career, see Tim Mowl and Brian Earnshaw, *John Wood: Architect of Obsession* (Taunton, 1988).
122. Wood, *Origin of Building*, pp. 29–30, 91–2.
123. *Ibid.*, pp. 124, 139.
124. *Ibid.*, pp. 169–74, 183–210, 221.
125. John Wood, *Choir Gaure, Vulgarly Called Stonehenge, on Salisbury Plain, Described, Restored, and Explained: in a Letter to the Right Honorable Edward Late Earl of Oxford, and Earl Mortimer* (Oxford, 1747), pp. 12, 18, 83–116.
126. *Ibid.*, p. 115.
127. Bodl. Lib., Ms. Eng. Misc. e.127, f. 68v.
128. Bodl. Lib., Ms. Eng. Misc. e.140, ff. 27–32. On Ralph Allen, Warburton and Wood, see Benjamin Boyce, *The Benevolent Man: A Life of Ralph Allen of Bath* (Cambridge, Mass., 1967).
129. Peter Borsay, *The English Urban Renaissance: Culture and Society in the Provincial Town, 1660–1770* (Oxford, 1989); R. Neale, *Bath: A Social History, 1680–1750* (London, 1981).
130. John Wood, *An Essay towards a Description of Bath* (2nd ed., 2 vols, London and Bath, 1749), vol. 1, pp. 1–6, 8, 83. For Typhon, see Michael Maier, *Atalanta Fugiens* (Oppenheim, 1618), Emblems XIX, XLIV, where he is identified with Set, the murderer of Osiris.
131. Wood, *Description of Bath*, vol. 1, pp. 180, 232; vol. 2, p. 440.
132. *Ibid.*, vol. 2, pp. 446–53.
133. Money, ed., *Chronicles of Cannon*, vol. 1, pp. lxxxi, 194; vol. 2, p. 573.

Chapter Seven: The Occult Revival

1. Aside from Joscelyn Goodwin, *The Theosophical Enlightenment* (Albany, N.Y., 1994), scholars have not previously noticed this revival, although a similar phenomenon in France and Germany has commanded attention: see Auguste Viatte, *Les Source Occultes du Romantisme* (Paris, 1927); Antoine Faivre, *Philosophie de la Nature: Physique Sacrée et Théosophie, XVIIIe–XIXe Siècles* (Paris, 1996).
2. For the book trade in this period, see John Feather, *A History of British Bookselling* (London, 1988), chs 7–10; James Raven, *Judging New Wealth: Popular Publishing and Responses to Commerce in England, 1750–1800* (Oxford, 1992), pp. 42–60; John Brewer, *The Pleasures of the Imagination: English Culture in the Eighteenth Century* (London, 1997), chs 3–4; Isabel Rivers, ed., *Books and their Readers in Eighteenth-Century England: New Essays* (London, 2001).
3. The following catalogues, all published at London in the year stated, contain sections on the occult: *Wagstaff's Catalogue for 1769; Wagstaff's Second Catalogue for 1769; Wagstaff's New Collection of Rare Old Books . . . to Be sold on Monday Next, Nov. 2, 1772; Wagstaff's Summer Catalogue of Rare Books for 1773; Wagstaff's Winter Catalogue of Rare Books for 1773; Wagstaff's Winter Catalogue of Rare Old Books for 1774; Wagstaff's Catalogue for 1776*. For Wagstaff, whose premises were in Brick Lane, Spitalfields, see Ian Maxted, "Exeter Working Papers in Book History," at http://bookhistory.blogspot.com/2007/01/london-1775-1800-w-z.html.
4. Richard Dymott, *A Catalogue of Several Thousand Books in Various Languages, Manuscripts . . . Books in Alchemy, &c.* (London, 1770), pp. 124–32; Richard Dymott, *A Catalogue for MDCCLXXII, of Several Libraries and Parcels of Books . . . Including . . . Alchemy* (London, 1772), pp. 58–64. Catalogues that list medical books with occult ones include Samuel Hayes, *A Catalogue of Books* (London, 1777), items 3328–98; Thomas Egerton, *A Catalogue of an Extensive Collection of Books* (London, 1796), pp. 260–70; Thomas Egerton, *A Catalogue of a General Collection of Books* (London, 1798), pp. 254–63.
5. James Lackington, *Memoirs of the First Forty-Five Years of the Life of James Lackington* (London, 1791), pp. 19–33 (quotation on p. 30), 205–8, 211. For John Denis's Behmenism, see DWL, Ms. Walton I.1.43, pp. 209–13, 238–44.
6. DWL, Ms. Walton I.1.31; Ms. Walton I.1.43, pp. 209–13, 238–44 (letters of John Denis, senior and junior, to Henry Brooke); B.L., Add. 5789, 5793; John Nichols, *Literary Anecdotes of the Eighteenth Century* (6 vols, London, 1812), vol. 3, p. 610; John Denis, *Denis's Catalogue of Ancient and Modern Books, for 1787* (London, 1787), pp. 160–78. For the fate of Freher's manuscripts, see Charles A. Muses, *Illuminations on Jacob Boehme: The Work of Dionysius Andreas Freher* (New York, 1951), ch. 2.
7. I have consulted the following editions of *Lackington's Catalogue*, all published at London: 1784; 1788 (2nd part); 1789; 1792 (2 vols, with occult listings in both); 1793; Sept. 1793–March 1794 (vol. 2). I have also consulted the following catalogues by Lackington, Allen and Co., entitled *A Catalogue of an Extensive Collection of Books*, and published at London: 1796–7; 1798–9; 1799–1800; Oct. 1800.
8. *A Catalogue of the Very Curious, Extensive, and Valuable Library of Richard Cosway, Esq. R. A.* ([London], [1821]), pp. 39–44.
9. GUL, Ferguson Ms. 125.
10. GUL, Ferguson Ms. 253.
11. Sabine sometimes published under the rubric "London and Middlesex Printing Office." His works include *The Universal Fortune-Teller; or, Mrs. Bridget's (Commonly Call'd the Norwood Gipsey) Golden Treasury Explained* (London, [1790?]), which contains a version of *Nocturnal Revels*.
12. Francis Barrett, *The Magus, or Celestial Intelligencer; Being a Complete System of Occult Philosophy* (London, 1801); *The Times*, 13 Aug. 1802, 22 Oct. 1802. The second report was contributed by Barrett himself. He is briefly noticed in *ODNB*.
13. B.L. call mark c.142.a.17, "Collection of Advertisements of Patent and Proprietary Medicines circa 1790–1810," no. 55, p. 8. For advertising in this period, see Neil

McKendrick, "George Packwood and the Commercialization of Shaving: The Art of Eighteenth-Century Advertising or 'The Way to Get Money and Be Happy,'" in Neil McKendrick, John Brewer and J.H. Plumb, *The Birth of a Commercial Society: The Commercialization of Eighteenth-Century England* (London, 1983), pp. 146–94.

14. Plans to establish a real medical school are found in *A Complete Collection of the Papers Relating to the Union of the King's and Marischal Colleges of Aberdeen* (Aberdeen, 1787), pp. 18, 117.
15. "Observations on the Virtues and Efficacy of Dr. Sibly's Reanimating Solar Tincture, or Pabulum of Life," bound in *Collection of Advertisements of Patent and Proprietary Medicines, circa 1790–1810*, BL., c.142.a.17.
16. The term "bourgeois public sphere" was coined in Jürgen Habermas, *The Structural Transformation of the Public Sphere: An Inquiry into a Category of Bourgeois Society*, trans. Thomas Burger (Oxford, 1989). See also James Van Horn Melton, *The Rise of the Public in Enlightenment Europe* (Cambridge, 2001).
17. Roy Porter, *Quacks: Fakers and Charlatans in Medicine* (Stroud, Gloucs, 2003), p. 154.
18. "Collection of Advertisements," no. 10; [Thomas Clayton], *Essay on Quackery* (Kingston-upon-Hull, 1805), pp. 14–25.
19. S. Solomon, *A Guide to Health: or Advice to Both Sexes* (2nd ed., London, 1796), p. 136; "Collection of Advertisements," nos 57–8; Porter, *Quacks*, pp. 254–7.
20. *A Guide to Health, Beauty, Riches, and Honor* (2nd ed., London, 1796), pp. iv, 34–6.
21. Cyprian Blagden, "Thomas Carnan and the Almanac Monopoly," *Studies in Bibliography*, 14 (1961), pp. 24–45; RSC, reel 99, box D, files 1–16. See also Ellic Howe, "The Stationers' Company Almanacks: A Late Eighteenth-Century Printing and Publishing Operation," in Giles Parker and Bernhard Fabian, eds, *Buch und Buchhandlung in Europa im achtzehnten Jahrhundert: The Book and the Book Trade in Eighteenth Century Europe* (Hamburg, 1981), pp. 195–209.
22. RSC, reel 85, Disbursements 1777–8; reel 98, box B, file 6.
23. William Hone, *The Year Book of Daily Recreation and Information* (London, 1832), col. 117; see also Maureen Perkins, *Visions of the Future: Almanacs, Time and Cultural Change, 1775–1870* (Oxford, 1996), ch. 3.
24. [Henry Andrews], *Vox Stellarum: or, A Loyal Almanack . . . 1777* (London, 1777), p. 9.
25. RSC, reel 98, box C, file 7/9. For Andrews, see RSC, reel 91, Almanac Statements 1800, as well as *ODNB*. For Thomas Wright, see [Henry Andrews], *Vox Stellarum, or, A Loyal Almanack . . . 1789* (London, 1789), p. 6; Perkins, *Visions of the Future*, p. 94; *Notes and Queries*, 7th series, vol. 3 (1887), pp. 164–5; Hone, *Year Book*, cols 1368–9.
26. Charles Knight, quoted in Blagden, "Thomas Carnan," p. 39.
27. RSC, reel 99, box D, file 7/1.
28. RSC, reel 85, Disbursements 1777–8.
29. *Matilda, or The Efforts of Virtue*, quoted in Markman Ellis, *The Politics of Sensibility: Race, Gender and Commerce in the Sentimental Novel* (Cambridge, 1996), p. 5. See also G.J. Barker-Benfield, *The Culture of Sensibility: Sex and Society in Eighteenth-Century Britain* (Chicago, 1992); Paul Goring, *The Rhetoric of Sensibility in Eighteenth-Century Culture* (Cambridge, 2005).
30. Margaret Anne Doody, "The Gnostic Clarissa," in David Blewett, ed., *Passion and Virtue: Essays on the Novels of Samuel Richardson* (Toronto, 2001), pp. 210–45.
31. Henry Brooke, *The Fool of Quality; or, The History of Henry, Earl of Moreland* (2nd ed., 4 vols, 1767), vol. 1, pp. 81–2; Ellis, *Politics of Sensibility*, ch. 4.
32. Henry Brooke, *The History of Henry Earl of Moreland*, [ed. John Wesley] (2 vols, London, 1781), vol. 1, pp. iv–vi; also, Nehemiah Curnock, *The Journals of John Wesley* (9 vols, 1909–16), vol. 6, p. 30 n. 2.
33. William Duff, *An Essay on Original Genius* (London, 1767), p. 143.
34. James Macpherson, *Fingal: An Ancient Epic Poem* (London, 1762), p. 68. For the impact of Ossian on Scottish identity, see William Ferguson, *The Identity of the Scottish Nation: An Historic Quest* (Edinburgh, 1999), ch. 11.

35. [Oliver Goldsmith], *The Mystery Revealed; Containing a Series of Transactions and Authentic Testimonials, Respecting the Supposed Cock-Lane Ghost; Which Have hitherto Been Concealed from the Public* (London, 1762), pp. 1, 3–4; E.J. Clery, *The Rise of Supernatural Fiction, 1762–1800* (Cambridge, 1995), ch. 1; Douglas Grant, *The Cock Lane Ghost* (London, 1965); Sasha Handley, *Visions of an Unseen World: Ghost Beliefs and Ghost Stories in Eighteenth-Century England* (London, 2007), pp. 141–8; *ODNB*, "Parsons, Elizabeth."
36. Jonathan Barry, "Public Infidelity and Private Belief? The Discourse of Spirits in Enlightenment Bristol," in Owen Davies and Willem de Blécourt, eds, *Beyond the Witch Trials: Witchcraft and Magic in Enlightenment Europe* (Manchester, 2004), pp. 117–43; Jonathan Barry, "Piety and the Patient: Medicine and Religion in Eighteenth Century Bristol," in Roy Porter, ed., *Patients and Practitioners: Lay Perceptions of Medicine in Pre-Industrial Society* (Cambridge, 1985), pp. 159–62; Henry Durbin, *A Narrative of Some Extraordinary Things That Happened to Mr. Richard Giles's Children, at the Lamb, without Lawford's Gate, Bristol; Supposed to Be the Effect of Witchcraft* (Bristol, 1800).
37. Walpole to George Montagu, 29 Jan. 1762, in W.S. Lewis, ed., *The Yale Edition of Horace Walpole's Correspondence* (48 vols, 1937–83), vol. 10, pp. 5–7.
38. Horace Walpole, *The Castle of Otranto: A Gothic Story*, ed. E.J. Clery (Oxford, 1996), p. 6.
39. *Ibid.*, p. 10.
40. Barbara A. Murray, *Restoration Shakespeare: Viewing the Voice* (Cranbury, N.J., 2001), pp. 50–63.
41. Winton Dean and John Merrill Knapp, eds, *Handel's Operas* (2 vols, Woodbridge, Suffolk, 2006); Reinhard Strom, *Essays on Handel and Italian Opera* (Cambridge, 1985), pp. 74, 263–4; David J. Buch, *Magic Flutes and Enchanted Forests: The Supernatural in Eighteenth-Century Musical Theatre* (Chicago, 2008), pp. 158–66.
42. "On the Pleasure Derived from Objects of Terror; with Sir Bertrand, A Fragment," in J. and A.L. Aikin, *Miscellaneous Pieces, in Prose* (London, 1773), p. 125.
43. Clery, *Rise of Supernatural Fiction*, ch. 6. Almost all English women in the sixteenth and seventeenth centuries were unable to sign their names. By 1750, women were about 20 percentage points behind men in literacy; by 1840, this had narrowed to 16 points: David Vincent, *Literacy and Popular Culture: England, 1750–1914* (Cambridge, 1989), p. 24. Men, however, remained the principal consumers of novels in the English provinces: see Jan S. Fergus, *Provincial Readers in Eighteenth-Century England* (Oxford, 2006).
44. On Ann Radcliffe, see Richard Miles, *Anne Radcliffe: The Great Enchantress* (Manchester, 1995); Rictor Norton, *Mistress of Udolpho: The Life of Ann Radcliffe* (London, 1999), esp. pp. 67–70; Terry Castle, "The Spectralization of the Other in Mysteries of Udolpho," in her *The Female Thermometer: 18th-Century Culture and the Invention of the Uncanny* (Oxford, 1999), pp. 120–39.
45. Quoted in Norton, *Mistress of Udolpho*, p. 198; see also Clery, *Rise of Supernatural Fiction*, ch. 7.
46. For a sceptical assessment of Beckford's interest in magic, see Boyd Alexander, *England's Wealthiest Son: A Study of William Beckford* (London, 1962), p. 82. The splendid exhibition catalogue edited by Derek E. Ostergard, *William Beckford, 1760–1844: An Eye for the Magnificent* (New Haven, 2001), more or less avoids the subject. The biographical details here are taken from these works as well as from Lewis Melville, *The Life and Letters of William Beckford of Fonthill* (London, 1910), and the biography in *ODNB*.
47. William Beckford, *Vathek*, ed. Roger Lonsdale (Oxford, 1983), pp. 36, 113.
48. Melville, *Life of Beckford*, p. 19.
49. *The Valuable Library of Books, in Fonthill Abbey. A Catalogue of the Magnificent, Rare, and Valuable Library (of 20,000 Volumes)* ([London], [1823]), lots 3557, 3609, 3640. No books on astrology or ritual magic were sold at the auction.

50. [Margaret Baron-Wilson], *The Life and Correspondence of M.G. Lewis* (2 vols, London, 1839), vol. 1, ch. 3; also, Elizabeth R. Napier, *The Failure of Gothic: Problems of Disjunction in an Eighteenth-Century Literary Form* (Cambridge, 1987); Michael Gamer, *Romanticism and the Gothic: Genre, Reception and Canon Formation* (Cambridge, 2000), pp. 73–89; David Lorne Macdonald, *Monk Lewis: A Critical Biography* (Toronto, 2000).
51. Matthew Lewis, *The Monk*, ed. Emma McEvoy (Oxford, 1995), pp. 275–7.
52. Matthew Lewis, *The Castle Spectre: A Drama* (London, 1798), "To the Reader," p. 102.
53. Henry Ridgely Evans, *History of Conjuring and Magic* (revised ed., Kenton, Ohio, 1930), pp. 42–4.
54. Philip Breslaw, *Breslaw's Last Legacy; or, The Magical Companion* (London, 1784), pp. x, 101.
55. Malcolm Macleod, *The Key to Knowledge; or Universal Conjuror* (London, 1800), p. iv.
56. Malcolm Macleod, *Macleod's History of Witches, &c. The Majesty of Darkness Discovered: in a Series of Tremendous Tales* (London, 1793), pp. 88–97.
57. Evans, *History of Conjuring*, pp. 53–6; Richard D. Altick, *The Shows of London* (Cambridge, Mass., 1978), pp. 84–5; *Guide to Health, Beauty, Riches and Honour*, pp. 59–61.
58. Ralph G. Allen, "The Stage Spectacles of Philip James de Loutherbourg," Yale School of Drama, D.F.A. thesis, 1960, pp. 67–79, 80–8; Christopher Baugh, *Garrick and Loutherbourg* (Cambridge and Alexandria, Va., 1990), pp. 97–115; David Worrall, *Theatrical Revolution: Drama, Censorship and Romantic Period Subcultures, 1773–1832* (Oxford, 2006), ch. 4.
59. "At the large house, fronting Leicester-Street, Leicester-Square, This present THURSDAY, January 31, 1782, will be Exhibited for the first time, EIDOPHUSIKON . . ." (handbill, London, 1782); "At the Large House, fronting Leicester-Street, Leicester-Square, On every MONDAY, WEDNESDAY, AND FRIDAY EVENINGS, will be exhibited ('till further Notice), EIDOPHUSIKON . . ." (handbill, London, 1782); Altick, *Shows of London*, pp. 117–27.
60. Clery, *Rise of Supernatural Fiction*, p. 146; Altick, *Shows of London*, pp. 217–18; Mervyn Heard, *Phantasmagoria: The Secret Life of the Magic Lantern* (Hastings, 2006), chs 3–7.
61. Allen, "Stage Spectacles," pp. 264–302; Kathleen Wilson, *The Island Race: Englishness, Empire and Gender in the Eighteenth Century* (London and New York, 2003), pp. 63–70; Harriet Guest, "Ornament and Use: Mai and Cook in London," in Kathleen Wilson, ed., *A New Imperial History: Culture, Identity and Modernity in Britain and the Empire, 1660–1840* (Cambridge, 2004), pp. 317–44; Daniel O'Quinn, *Staging Governance: Theatrical Imperialism in London, 1770–1800* (Baltimore, 2005), ch. 2.
62. Conyers Middleton, *A Free Inquiry into the Miraculous Powers, Which Are Supposed to Have Subsisted in the Christian Church, from the Earliest Ages through Several Successive Centuries* (London, 1749); David Hume, *Essays and Treatises on Several Subjects* (4 vols, London and Edinburgh, 1760), vol. 3: "An Enquiry Concerning Human Understanding," pp. 167–202. As Jane Shaw points out in *Miracles in Enlightenment England* (New Haven, 2006), pp. 160–1, 175, these were relatively late contributions to a long-running debate.
63. See David Hempton, *Methodism: Empire of the Spirit* (New Haven, Conn., 2005).
64. Jean Orcibal, "The Theological Originality of John Wesley and Continental Spirituality," in Rupert Davies and Gordon Rupp, eds, *A History of the Methodist Church in Great Britain* (4 vols, London, 1965–88), vol. 1, pp. 83–111; John Wesley, *A Second Letter to the Author of the Enthusiasm of Methodists and Papists Compar'd* (London, 1751), in Gerald R. Cragg, ed., *The Works of John Wesley: Volume 2: The Appeals to Men of Reason and Religion and Certain Related Open Letters* (Oxford, 1975), p. 416.
65. David Hempton, *The Religion of the People: Methodism and Popular Religion, c. 1750–1900* (London, 1996).

66. James Lackington, *Memoirs of the First Forty-Five Years of the Life of James Lackington* (rev. ed., London, 1794), p. 294. Earlier versions of Lackington's autobiography do not contain these remarks.
67. *Ibid.*, p. 305; John Wesley, *Primitive Physic: or, An Easy and Natural Method, of Curing Most Diseases* (20th ed., London, 1780); Antoine-Joseph Pernety, *The History of a Voyage to the Malouine (or Falklands) Islands, Made in 1763 and 1764, under the Command of M. de Bougainville* (London, 1771), pp. 153–62.
68. Curnock, ed., *Journals of John Wesley*, vol. 5, pp. 265–75; James Boswell, *Life of Johnson*, ed. George Birkbeck Hill (2 vols, London, 1904), vol. 2, pp. 224–5, 296; Handley, *Visions of an Unseen World*, pp. 148–53.
69. *A Narrative of the Extraordinary Case of Geo, Lukins, of Yatton, Somerset, Who Was Possessed of Evil Spirits, for Near Eighteen Years* (Bristol, 1788); Owen Davies, *Witchcraft, Magic and Culture, 1736–1951* (Manchester, 1999), pp. 20–2; and for the Methodist view of spirit possession, Clarke Garrett, *Spirit Possession and Popular Religion: From the Camisards to the Shakers* (Baltimore and London, 1987), ch. 4.
70. *Narrative of the Extraordinary Case*, p. 5; Joseph Easterbrook, *An Appeal to the Public Respecting George Lukins, (Called the Yatton Demoniac,) Containing an Account of his Affliction and Deliverance* (Bristol, 1788), p. 4.
71. Samuel Norman, *Authentic Anecdotes of George Lukins, the Yatton Demoniac; with a View of the Controversy, and a Full Refutation of the Imposture* (Bristol, 1788), p. 44.
72. For the history of Shakerism around Manchester between 1758 and 1774, see Garrett, *Spirit Possession*, chs 5–8. B.J. Gibbons, *Gender in Mystical and Occult Thought: Behmenism and its Development in England* (Cambridge, 1995), pp. 158–62, argues for the influence of "popular Behmenism" on the Shakers, which is not impossible given the location of their early community.
73. Jacob Boehme, *The Works of Jacob Behmen, the Teutonic Theosopher* (2 vols, London, 1764), vol. 1, pp. vii–ix; Jacob Boehme, *Forty Questions of the Soul*, trans. John Sparrow (London, 1661), sigs A_5–A_9. The phrase "from that which we find in others" replaced the original words "from that which we find in the Experimental *Physicians, Philosophers, Astronomers*." Clearly, the eighteenth-century editors of Boehme were less concerned than Sparrow to identify a scientific attitude that could be harmonized with magic through Theosophy.
74. Jacob Boehme, *The Works of Jacob Behmen, the Teutonic Theosopher, Vol. 3* (London, 1772), p. 12 ff. A fourth and final volume appeared in 1781; it contained Law's paraphrase of Boehme's *Way to Christ*.
75. Curnock, ed., *Journals of Wesley*, vol. 6, pp. 10–12; also, Garrett, *Spirit Possession*, pp. 145–6.
76. DWL, Ms. Walton I.1.43, pp. 104–19; Christopher Walton, *Notes and Materials for an Adequate Biography of . . . William Law* (London, 1854), pp. 595–7; Francis Okely, ed. and trans., *Memoirs of the Life, Death, Burial, and Wonderful Writings of Jacob Behmen* (Northampton, 1780), pp. 105–6; Muses, *Illumination on Jacob Boehme*, pp. 58–9; Barry, "Medicine and Religion," p. 155. Amazingly enough, Mills was the grandfather of Thomas Babington Macaulay, the Whig historian.
77. DWL, Ms. Walton I.1.43, pp. 67–74.
78. W.C. and R[alph] M[ather], *An Impartial Representation of the Case of the Poor Cotton Spinners in Lancashire, &c. With a Mode Proposed to the Legislature for their Relief* (London, 1780), reproduced in *Labour Disputes in the Early Days of the Industrial Revolution: Four Pamphlets, 1758–1780* (New York, 1970), p. 15.
79. DWL, Walton I.1.43, p. 74.
80. R.L. Tafel, ed., *Documents Concerning the Life and Character of Emanuel Swedenborg* (2 vols in 4 parts, London, 1875–7), vol. 2, part 2, p. 1253; F.J.F. Schreck, *History of the New Church in Birmingham* (London,1916), accessed at http://www.newchurchhistory.org/articles/ejs2007/ejs2007.php#footnotes; Ralph Mather, *Rational Reflections on Tale-Bearing and Detraction* (London, 1786). A commonplace book kept by J.W. Salmon in

1799, entitled "Fragments of Wisdom Collected by a Society of Gentlemen," is in Swedenborg House, London, Ms. A/187.

81. Carl Theophilus Odhner, *Annals of the New Church* (2 vols, Bryn Athyn, 1904), vol. 1, pp. 126, 128, 133, 147, 160, 166, 189–90, 191; Andrew Levy, *The First Emancipator: The Forgotten Story of Robert Carter, the Founding Father Who Freed his Slaves* (New York, 2005). A 1795 letter from Mather to Carter, mentioning the founding of the Philadelphia New Church, is in the Virginia Historical Society, Ms. C2468a 621. I owe this reference to my colleague Amy Morsman.
82. Lackington, *Memoirs*, p. 195.
83. An excellent introduction to Swedenborg's thought is Ernst Benz, *Emanuel Swedenborg: Visionary Savant in the Age of Reason*, trans. Nicholas Goodrich-Clarke (West Chester, Pa., 2002); but there is interesting biographical material in Signe Toksvig, *Emanuel Swedenborg: Scientist and Mystic* (New Haven, Conn., 1948); Inge Jonsson, *Emanuel Swedenborg*, trans. Catherine Djurklou (New York, 1971). See also Clarke Garrett, "Swedenborg and the Mystical Enlightenment in Late Eighteenth-Century England," *Journal of the History of Ideas*, 45 (1984), pp. 67–81, and for a conspiratorial approach, Keith Schuchard, "Jacobite and Visionary: The Masonic Journey of Emanuel Swedenborg (1688–1772)," *Ars Quatuor Coronatorum*, 115 (2002), pp. 33–72.
84. James Hindmarch, ed., *A New Dictionary of Correspondences, Representations, &c. Or the Spiritual Significations of Words, Sentences, &c. As Used in the Sacred Scriptures* (London, 1790), p. 227, which is derived from Emanuel Swedenborg, *Arcana Coelestia* (10 vols, New York, 1882), vol. 7, pp. 84–5, no. 6692. See also Emanuel Swedenborg, *Arcana Coelestia* (8 vols, London, 1749–56), vol. 6 (1753), p. 303; Emanuel Swedenborg, *True Christian Religion: Containing the Universal Theology of the New Church* (2 vols, London, 1781), vol. 2, p. 161; Emanuel Swedenborg, *The Wisdom of Angels Concerning the Divine Providence* (London, 1790), p. 423; Emanuel Swedenborg, *The Delights of Wisdom Concerning Conjugial Love* (London, 1794), pp. 235, 435.
85. Odhner, *Annals of the New Church*, vol. 1, pp. 195–6, 202.
86. Johann Heinrich Cohausen, *Hermippus Redivivus: or, The Sage's Triumph over Old Age and the Grave* (London, 1744). An expanded version of the work was printed in 1744, a second edition in 1749, a pirated Dublin edition in 1760 and a third edition in 1771.
87. *The Museum, or, The Literary and Historical Register*, vol. 3, no. 33, 20 June 1747, p. 256. Akenside was editor of *The Museum*, which was published by Robert Dodsley.
88. Elizabeth E. Barker and Alex Kidson, eds, *Joseph Wright of Derby in Liverpool* (New Haven, Conn., 2007), pp. 172–4; Judy Egerton, *Wright of Derby* (New York, 1990), pp. 84–91; also, Burdett's entry in *ODNB*.
89. The visit was mentioned by Stephen Glover in the gazetteer section of *The History of the County of Derby*, ed. Thomas Noble (2 vols, Derby, 1828), vol. 2, p. 616, and explained in a newspaper article by Maxwell Craven, "Why Did the Chevalier Who Liked to Dress as a Woman Visit Derby?" *Derby Evening Telegraph*, accessed at http://youandyesterday.com/articles. See also Maxwell Craven, *John Whitehurst of Derby, Clockmaker and Scientist, 1713–88* (Ashbourne, Derbyshire, 1996), p. 222. For Louis IX of Hesse-Darmstadt, see René Le Forestier, *La Franc-Maçonnerie Templière et Occultiste aux XVIIIe et XIXe Siècles* (Paris and Louvain, 1970), p. 628 n. 33. D'Eon's membership in the London Lodge of Immortality is chronicled in W.J. Chetwode Crawley, "The Chevalier d'Eon," *Ars Quatuor Coronatorum*, 16 (1903), pp. 231–51, and his long residence at the home of Earl Ferrers is mentioned in Gary Kates, *Monsieur d'Eon Is a Woman: A Tale of Political Intrigue and Sexual Masquerade* (Baltimore, Md., 1995), p. 189–90.
90. Johann Christian Gädicke, *Freimaurer-Lexicon* (Berlin, 1818), pp. 42, 102; *Allgemeines Handbuch der Freimaurerei* (3 vols, Leipzig, 1863), vol. 1, p. 61.
91. Leonard W. Labaree et al, eds, *The Papers of Benjamin Franklin* (39 vols, New Haven, Conn., 1959–2008), vol. 21, p. 386; vol. 24, p. 144. Burdett knew Franklin through the Lunar Society of Birmingham. For Steuben, see Albert J. Mackey and H.L. Haywood, eds, *Encyclopedia of Freemasonry* (2 vols, New York, 1920), vol. 2, p. 1084.

92. This interpretation has already been proposed by Janet Vertesi in "Light and Enlightenment in Joseph Wright's 'The Alchemist,'" accessed at http://www.reocities.com/jvertesi/wright/.
93. Egerton, *Wright of Derby*, pp. 91–4. The Miravan story is probably derived from [John Gilbert Cooper], *Letters Concerning Taste* (London, 1755), Letter X, pp. 69–70.
94. An early example of that view is found in Robert Freke Gould, *The History of Freemasonry* (6 vols, London, 1882–7), vol. 5, pp. 80–123.
95. G.D. Henderson, *Chevalier Ramsay* (London, 1952), pp. 20, 107.
96. Andrew Michael Ramsay, *The Travels of Cyrus* (2 vols, London, 1727), vol. 1, p. 86.
97. Bodl. Lib., Carte Ms. 246, f. 420; Henderson, *Ramsay*, chs 10–12. For Ramsay's relationship to scepticism, see Richard H. Popkin, "David Hume and the Pyrrhonian Controversy," in his *The High Road to Pyrrhonism*, ed. Richard A. Watson and James E. Force (Indianapolis, 1993), pp. 135–6; and for Ramsay's personal assessment of David Hume, *ibid.*, p. 142 n. 40.
98. Andrew Michael Ramsay, "Discours Prononcé à la Réception des Frée-Maçons [*sic*]," in *Lettre Philosophique, par M. de V***, avec Plusieurs Pièces Galantes et Nouvelles de Differens Auteurs* ([London?], 1775), pp. 44–5. Interestingly, this copy of the "Discours" is bound up with a selection of freethinking and erotic pieces. For the cancelled speech, see Bodl. Lib., Carte Ms. 246, f. 398. An English translation of the "Discours" was made by the Jacobite agent George Kelly. A scholarly discussion of the origins of the speech can be found in Alain Bernheim, "Ramsay and his Discours Revisited," a lecture delivered to the Grand Lodge of Ireland in 2003 and available at http://www.freemasons-freemasonry.com/bernheim_ramsay.html.
99. Ramsay, "Discours," pp. 51–4.
100. *Ibid.*, pp. 56–61.
101. The most reliable source for the early history of these lodges is Alain Bernheim, "Notes on the Order of Kilwinning or Scotch Heredom, the Present Royal Order of Scotland," available at http://www.freemasons-freemasonry.com/royal_order_scotland.html.
102. For Hund, see Le Forestier, *Franc-Maçonnerie Templière et Occultiste*, pp. 107–241, 610–78; Karl R. Frick, *Die Erleuchteten: Gnostisch-theosophische und alchemistisch-rosenkreuzerische Geheimgesellschaften bis zum Ende des 18. Jahrhunderts* (Graz, 1973), ch. 3; Antoine Faivre, *L'Esoterisme au XVIIIe Siècle en France et en Allemagne* (Paris, 1973); and for the Golden or Rosy Cross Masons, Christopher McIntosh, *The Rosicrucians: The History, Mythology and Rituals of an Esoteric Order* (York Beach, Maine, 1998), chs 7–8.
103. Le Forestier, *Franc-Maçonnerie Templière et Occultiste*, pp. 275–531; "Papus" [Gérard Encausse], *L'Illuminisme en France (1767–1774): Martinez Pasqually* (Paris, 1895); Arthur Edward Waite, *The Life of Louis Claude de St. Martin, the Unknown Philosopher* (London, 1901), pp. 22–86; Gould, *History of Freemasonry*, vol. 5, pp. 117–19.
104. Antoine-Joseph Pernety, *Dictionnaire Mytho-Hermétique* (Paris, 1758). For his life, see Joanny Bricaud, *Les Illuminés d'Avignon* (Paris, 1927), chs 1–3. Pernety was noticed in John Aikin, Thomas Morgan and William Johnson, *General Biography* (10 vols, London, 1799–1815), vol. 8, p. 54, the *ODNB* of its day.
105. Le Forestier, *Franc-Maçonnerie Templière et Occultiste*, pp. 784–5.
106. For Preston, see *ODNB* and his *Illustrations of Masonry* (reprint of 1804 ed., Wellingborough, Northants, 1986), introduction.
107. William Preston, *Illustrations of Masonry* (2nd rev. ed., London, 1775), pp. 6, 69, 156–7 n. 7, 186–8, 205–6. 210–11.
108. Preston's view of the dispute is found in the 1779 edition of *Illustrations of Masonry*, pp. 288–95. A summary of events is provided by Gilbert Y. Johnson, "The Grand Lodge South of the River Trent," in Harry Carr, ed., *The Collected Prestonian Lectures, Volume 1: 1925–60* (London, 1965), pp. 283–96.

109. William James Hughan, ed., *Masonic Sketches and Reprints: 1. History of Freemasonry in York. 2. Unpublished Records of the Craft* (London, 1871); Wilhelm Begemann, *Vorgeschichte und Anfänge der Freimaruerei in England* (2 vols, Berlin, 1909), vol. 2, pp. 417–42; W. Wonnacott, "The Rite of the Seven Degrees in London," *Ars Quatuor Coronatorum*, 39 (1926), pp. 63–98; George S. Draffen, "Some Further Notes on the Rite of Seven Degrees in England," *Ars Quatuor Coronatorum*, 68 (1955), pp. 94–110.
110. Bodl. Lib., Rylands Ms. D.8, pp. 6–7. The Royal Arch Supreme Grand Chapter was founded in 1765, probably in imitation of the Grand Lodge of Antients.
111. Johann Wilhelm von Archenholz, *A Picture of England* (2 vols, London, 1789), vol. 1, pp. 181–3. For Samuel Falk, see Cecil Roth, *Essays and Portraits in Anglo-Jewish History* (Philadelphia, 1962), pp. 139–64; Michal Oron, "Dr. Samuel Falk and the Eibeschuetz-Emden Controversy," in Karl Erich Grözinger and Joseph Dan, eds, *Mysticism, Magic and Kabbalah in Ashkenazi Judaism* (Berlin, 1995), pp. 243–56; Marsha Keith Schuchard, "Dr. Samuel Falk: A Sabbatian Adventurer in the Masonic Underground," in Matt Goldish and Richard Henry Popkin, eds, *Millenarianism and Messianism in Early Modern European Culture, Volume 1: Jewish Messianism in the Early Modern World* (Dordrecht, 2001), pp. 203–26. For his connections with Freemasons, see Gordon P.G. Hills, "Notes on Some Contemporary References to Dr. Falk, the Baal Shem of London, in the Rainsford Mss. at the British Museum," *The Jewish Historical Society of England: Transactions*, 8 (1915–17), pp. 122–8. Hills did not believe Falk himself was a Mason.
112. See Richard Sher, *The Enlightenment and the Book: Scottish Authors and their Publishers in Britain, Ireland and America* (Chicago, 2010); Richard B. Sher, *Church and University in the Scottish Enlightenment: The Moderate Literati of Edinburgh* (Edinburgh, 1990); Paul Wood, ed., *The Scottish Enlightenment: Essays in Reinterpretation* (Rochester, 2000); and for a comparison of the Enlightenment in Scotland and Naples, John Robertson, *The Case for the Enlightenment: Scotland and Naples, 1680–1760* (Cambridge, 2005).

Chapter Eight: An Occult Enlightenment

1. Joscelyn Goodwin, *The Theosophical Enlightenment* (Albany, NY, 1994); Dan Edelstein, ed., *The Super-Enlightenment: Daring to Know Too Much* (Oxford, 2010). The Super-Enlightenment can also be explored through the digital archive found at http://collections.stanford.edu/supere/.
2. Russell McCormack, *Speculative Truth: Henry Cavendish, Natural Philosophy and the Rise of Modern Theoretical Science* (Oxford, 2004); Bernadette Bensaude-Vincent and Christine Blondel, eds, *Science and Spectacle in the European Enlightenment* (Aldershot, Hants, and Burlington, Vt., 2008).
3. Quoted in Robert E. Schofield, *The Enlightened Joseph Priestley: A Study of his Life and Work from 1773 to 1804* (University Park, Pa., 2004), p. 99. See also John G. McEvoy, "Joseph Priestley, Scientist, Philosopher and Divine," *Proceedings of the American Philosophical Society*, 128, 3 (1984), pp. 193–8; W.H. Brock, "Joseph Priestley, Enlightened Experimentalist," in Isabel Rivers and David Wyckes, eds, *Joseph Priestley: Scientist, Philosopher and Theologian* (Oxford, 2008), pp. 49–79.
4. James Hutton, "Theory of the Earth: or An Investigation of the Laws Observable in the Composition, Dissolution, and Restoration of Land upon the Globe," *Transactions of the Royal Society of Edinburgh*, 1, part 2 (1788), p. 304.
5. GUL, Ferguson Ms. 40, Notes for lectures by Joseph Black, ff. 17–19.
6. Price's Royal Society election certificate, in Royal Society Archives (hereafter RSA), EC/1781/08, shows that he was sponsored by Kirwan. The name "Higginbotham" has been crossed out and replaced with "Price." Accessed at http://www2.royalsociety.org.

7. James Price, *An Account of Some Experiments on Mercury, Made at Guildford in May, 1782* (2nd ed., Oxford, 1782), pp. 1, 15. The first edition is entitled *An Account of Some Experiments on Mercury, Made at Guildford in May, 1782. To which Is Prefixed an Abridgement of Boyle's Account of a Degradation of Gold* (Oxford, 1782). It appeared in a German translation in 1783 under the title *Versuche mit Quecksilber, Silber und Gold. Nebst einem Auszuge aus Boyles "Erzählung"* (Dessau, 1783). Surprisingly, Price has a biography in *ODNB*, as well as in John Gorton, ed., *A General Biographical Dictionary* (3 vols, London, 1838), vol. 2.
8. Patrick O'Brian, *Joseph Banks; A Life* (London, 1988), pp. 206–7; Warren Dawson, ed., *The Banks Letters: A Calendar of the Manuscript Correspondence of Sir Joseph Banks* (London, 1958), pp. 54–5, 361; reviews are found in *Medical Commentaries for the Years 1781–2* (London, 1787), pp. 176–90, *The Critical Review, or, Annals of Literature*, 54 (1782), pp. 303–6, and *The British Magazine and Review* (3 vols, London, 1782–3), vol. 1, Oct. 1782, pp. 291–3. Gorton's *General Biographical Dictionary* gives the wrong date for Price's death, but states that Kirwan and the chemist Peter Woulfe were sent by the Royal Society to review his process.
9. Price, *Some Experiments*, p. i.
10. A different view of Banks can be found in John Gascoigne, *Joseph Banks and the English Enlightenment: Useful Knowledge and Polite Culture* (Cambridge, 2003).
11. The main contemporary printed source for his life is an autobiographical work, *A Memoir of the Late Rev. John Clowes, A.M., . . . Written by Himself* (Manchester, 1834). This is far less spiritually candid, however, than the two-volume manuscript entitled "A History of the Commencement & Progress in Great Britain of the Lord's New Church," which is found in Chetham's Library, Ms. A.3.51–2. The biography by Theodore Compton, *The Life and Correspondence of the Reverend John Clowes, M.A.* (London, 1874), virtually sanctifies him.
12. The changing religious situation in eighteenth-century Lancashire is discussed in Jan Albers, "Seeds of Contention: Society, Politics and the Church of England in Lancashire, 1688–1790," PhD dissertation, Yale University, 1988, and Mark Smith, *Religion in Industrial Society: Oldham and Saddleworth, 1740–1865* (Oxford, 1994). A gloomier picture is presented in Michael Snape, *The Church of England in Industrializing Society: The Lancashire Parish of Whalley in the Eighteenth Century* (Woodbridge, Suffolk, 2003).
13. Thomas de Quincey, *Autobiographical Sketches* (Boston, 1853), pp. 156, 158.
14. Chetham Library, Ms. A.3.51, ff. 14–15. For Clayton, see Richard Parkinson, ed., *The Private Journals and Literary Remains of John Byrom*, Chetham Society, vols 23, 24, 40, 44 (2 vols in 4 parts, Manchester, 1854–7), vol. 1, part 2, p. 509 n. 1.
15. Chetham's Library, Ms. A.3.51, ff. 49, 62–3.
16. [John Clowes], *Dialogues, on the Nature, Design, and Evidence of the Theological Writings of the Hon. Emmanuel Swedenborg, with a Brief Account of Some of his Philosophical Works* (London, 1788), p. 227. The publisher of this volume was John Denis, son of James Lackington's Behmenist partner.
17. John Clowes, *Sermons Preached at the Parish Church of St. John, Manchester* (London, 1790), Sermon 20, "Deformity," p. 228.
18. Compton, *Life and Correspondence of Clowes*, p. 62.
19. [Clowes], *Dialogues*, p. 7.
20. For examples, *ibid.*, p. 146; John Clowes, *The Caterpillars and the Mulberry Bush, or A True Picture of the Bad Passions and their Mischievious Effects* (Manchester, 1800), p. 10.
21. Chetham's Library, Ms. A.3.52, f. 106; George Adams, *Lectures on Natural and Experimental Philosophy* (5 vols, London, 1794), vol. 1, pp. 102, 281. In his *Essays on the Microscope* (London, 1787), p. xviii, a work printed by the Swedenborgian Robert Hindmarsh, Adams referred to two of Swedenborg's scientific tracts.

22. Chetham's Library, Ms. A.3.52, ff. 56–7. The book was *On Science: Its Divine Origin, Operation, Use and End; Together with its Various Interesting Properties, Qualities and Characters* (Manchester, 1809).
23. All of these materials, along with several biographical essays on Taylor, were published in Kathleen Raine and George Mills Harper, eds, *Thomas Taylor the Platonist: Selected Writings* (Princeton, 1969).
24. Thomas Taylor, "A Dissertation on the Eleusinian and Bacchic Mysteries," in Raine and Harper, eds, *Thomas Taylor*, p. 374.
25. Jason M. Kelly, *The Society of Dilettanti* (New Haven, Conn., 2009); Jonathan Scott, *The Pleasures of Antiquity: British Collections of Greece and Rome* (New Haven, Conn., 2003); Goodwin, *Theosophical Enlightenment*, ch. 1; Michael Vickers, "Value and Simplicity: Eighteenth-Century Taste and the Study of Greek Vases," *Past and Present*, 116 (1987), pp. 98–137, for Hancarville's influence on collecting; Peter Funnell, "The Symbolic Language of Antiquity," in Michael Clark and Nicholas Penny, eds, *The Arrogant Connoisseur: Richard Payne Knight, 1751–1824* (Manchester, 1982), pp. 50–64.
26. Pierre François Hugues, Baron d'Hancarville, *Recherches sur l'Origine, l'Esprit et les Progrès des Arts de la Grèce* (3 vols, London, 1785). Hancarville borrowed, without revealing it, some aspects of alchemical imagery, like "the philosophical egg," symbol of chaos, from which "the world issued by means of the Generative Being": *ibid.*, vol. 1, p. 176. Eager to establish his originality, he barely acknowledged a debt to previous theorists of the diffusion of symbols, like Athanasius Kircher or William Stukeley. Kircher is cited on minor matters in vol. 2, p. 300, and vol. 3, p. 154, while Stukeley appears in vol. 1, p. 458, in relation to the serpentine form of Avebury.
27. Richard Payne Knight, *An Account of the Remains of the Worship of Priapus* (London, 1786); B.F. Cook, *The Townley Marbles* (London, 1985).
28. Taylor, "Eleusinian and Bacchic Mysteries," p. 345.
29. Thomas Taylor, "The Hymns of Orpheus," in Raine and Harper, eds, *Thomas Taylor the Platonist*, p. 173.
30. Thomas Taylor, "The Platonic Philosopher's Creed," in Raine and Harper, eds, *Thomas Taylor the Platonist*, pp. 440–1, 442–3, 444–5.
31. Taylor, "Eleusinian and Bacchic Mysteries," p. 387.
32. Taylor, "Platonic Philosopher's Creed," p. 440.
33. Flaxman has been curiously neglected by biographers. See Margaret Whinney, "Flaxman and the Eighteenth Century," *Journal of the Warburg and Courtauld Institutes*, 19 (1956), pp. 269–82; Sarah Symmons, "The Spirit of Despair: Patronage, Primitivism and the Art of John Flaxman," *The Burlington Magazine*, 117, 871 (1975), pp. 644–51; David Bindman, ed., *John Flaxman* (London, 1979); David Irwin, *John Flaxman, 1755–1826: Sculptor, Illustrator, Designer* (New York, 1980); Scott, *Pleasures of Antiquity*, pp. 237–45.
34. B.L., Add. Ms. 39781, ff. 129–30.
35. John Flaxman, *Lectures on Sculpture* (London, 1829), pp. 331–2.
36. W.S. Lewis, A. Dayle Wallace and Edwine M. Martz, eds, *Horace Walpole's Correspondence with the Countess of Ossory* (3 vols, New Haven, Conn., 1965), vol. 3, pp. 82–3.
37. Goodwin, *Theosophical Enlightenment*, p. 133; "Anthony Pasquin" [John Williams], "Memoirs of the Royal Academicians," in his *An Authentic History of Painting in Ireland* (London, 1794: reprint, London, 1970), p. 120.
38. The only sustained study of Sibly's thought is Allen G. Debus, "Scientific Truth and Occult Tradition: The Medical World of Ebenezer Sibly (1751–1799)," *Medical History*, 26 (1982), pp. 259–78. Biographies of Ebenezer and Manoah Sibly are found in *ODNB*.
39. George Mensforth, *The Young Student's Guide in Astrology* (London, 1785), pp. v, 17–18.
40. Richard Phillips, *The Celestial Science of Astrology Vindicated* (London, 1785).
41. *The Astrologer's Magazine; and Philosophical Miscellany* (London, 1794). The successor to *The Conjuror's Magazine*, it ran for twelve monthly issues.
42. For details on Sibly's life, I am indebted to Susan Sommers of St Vincent's College. DWL, Ms. Walton I.1.43, pp. 112–17, printed in Christopher Walton, *Notes and Materials for an*

Adequate Biography of . . . William Law (London, 1854), pp. 595–6; Ebenezer Sibly, *An Elegy Sacred to the Memory of that Patron of Virtue, the Truly Admired and Pious John Till Adams, M.D. of Bristol* (Bristol, 1786); E. Ward, "Ebenezer Sibly," *Ars Quatuor Coronatorum*, 71 (1958), pp. 48–53; Jonathan Barry, "Piety and the Patient: Medicine and Religion in Eighteenth Century Bristol," in Roy Porter, ed., *Patients and Practitioners: Lay Perceptions of Medicine in Pre-Industrial Society* (Cambridge, 1985), pp. 155, 171.

43. Ebenezer Sibly, *A Complete Illustration of the Celestial Science of Astrology* (London, 1788), pp. 1051–55. A Google search for the term "Sibly Chart" produced about ten thousand matches in November 2011.
44. Sibly, *Celestial Science*, pp. 1059, 1117.
45. *Ibid.*, pp. 1060, 1082–3.
46. Placidus de Titus, *A Collection of Thirty Remarkable Nativities, to Illustrate the Canons, and Prove the True Principles of Elementary Philosophy*, ed. and trans. M.S. Sibly (London, 1789), preface, p. 5. The list of publishers of this work may identify a third Sibly brother, named Edmund, as well as a mysterious "J. Sibly," Manoah's partner, who was not his wife, Sarah. Manoah also published and added a preface to Claudius Ptolemy, *The Quadripartite; or, Four Books Concerning the Influences of the Stars*, ed. John Whalley and others (London, 1786).
47. Manoah Sibly, *Twelve Sermons* (London, 1796).
48. Sibly, *Celestial Science*, pp. 1093–5.
49. Ebenezer Sibly, *The Medical Mirror or Treatise on the Impregnation of the Human Female* (London, [1796]), p. 75.
50. Sibly, *Medical Mirror*, pp. 49–52.
51. Sibly, *Culpeper's English Physician*, pp. 202–11; Sibly, *Celestial Science*, pp. 59, 63, 66; Ebenezer Sibly, *A Key to Physic, and the Occult Sciences* (London, 1794), pp. 22–8, 51–2.
52. [Ebenezer Sibly], *An Universal System of Natural History* (London, [1794]), pp. 7–8. For racial thinking in this period, see Colin Kidd, *The Forging of Races: Race and Scripture in the Protestant Atlantic World, 1600–2000* (Cambridge, 2006), ch. 4.
53. Ebenezer Sibly, *Culpeper's English Physician; and Complete Herbal* (London, [1798]), pp. iii–iv, ix.
54. Sibly, *Universal System*, p. 312.
55. *Ibid.*, pp. 52–9; Sibly, *Medical Mirror*, p. iii; Sibly, *Culpeper's English Physician*, p. 215.
56. Sibly, *Culpeper's English Physician*, p. ix.
57. GUL, Ferguson Ms. 128, ff. 17–19, 27ᵛ–37, 50ᵛ–54; Francis Barrett, *The Magus, or Celestial Intelligencer; Being a Complete System of Occult Philosophy* (London, 1801), part 2, chs 34–46.
58. John Parkins, *The Cabinet of Wealth, or The Temple of Wisdom* (Grantham, 1812), p. 6. Parkins was also the author of *The Universal Fortune-Teller; or, An Infallible Guide to the Secret and Hidden Decrees of Fate* (London, 1810). For his biography, see Owen Davies, *Cunning-Folk: Popular Magic in English History* (London, 2007), pp. 73, 115–18, 140–3.
59. John Worsdale, *Genethliacal Astrology* (2nd ed., Newark, 1798), pp. xvii, 72–3. Worsdale also published *A Collection of Remarkable Nativities, Calculated According to the Rules and Precepts of Claudius Ptolemy* (Newark, 1799), which indicates that he rejected the Copernican system.
60. Worsdale, *Genethliacal Astrology*, p. 14.
61. *Ibid.*, pp. vii.
62. *Ibid.*, pp. 54–5.
63. J.F.C. Harrison, *The Second Coming: Popular Millenarianism 1780–1850* (New Brunswick, N.J., 1979), p. 49.
64. *A Catalogue of the Very Curious, Extensive, and Valuable Library of Richard Cosway, Esq., R.A.* ([London], [1821]), p. 43, lot 782.
65. S. Bacstrom, "Erzählung einer Reise nach Spitzbergen im Jahr 1780," in J.W. von Archenholz, ed., *Minerva*, 2, 6 (1802), pp. 406–29.
66. Kew Botanical Gardens (hereafter KBG), Banks Papers 1.222, 28 June 1786.

67. Wellcome Library, Ms. 1030, ff. 98–100. Bacstrom remembered hearing lectures at Strasbourg on "*the Spiritual Resuscitation of Plants*" by the Jesuit Father Erhard, but a student at the Lutheran college might have been able to attend lectures by a Catholic professor. I have calculated his birth year from a statement made in 1771 that he was then twenty-eight years old.
68. State Library, New South Wales (hereafter SL, NSW), Papers of Sir Joseph Banks, Series 06.140, dated March 1771; Series 06.141, Bacstrom to Banks, 8 March 1771, accessed through http://www2.sl.nsw.gov.au/banks/. The use of exclamation marks is typical. See also J.G. Beaglehole, ed., *The Endeavour Journals of Joseph Banks, 1768–71* (2 vols, Sydney, 1963), vol. 1, pp. 68, 73. Beaglehole calls Bacstrom a Dutchman, noting the occasional spelling of his name as "BacStrom." The bill for a hammock and two pillows for Bacstrom appears in SL, NSW, Papers of Sir Joseph Banks, Series 06.096, 4 May 1772.
69. Neil Chambers, ed., *The Letters of Joseph Banks: A Selection, 1768–1820* (London, 2000), pp. 35–6; H.E. Connor and E. Edgar, "History of the Taxonomy of the New Zealand Native Grass Flora," *Journal of the Royal Society of New Zealand*, 32, 1 (2002), p. 100. Bacstrom is not mentioned by name in the chief account of the northern expedition, Uno von Troil, *Letters on Iceland* (London, 1780), and he does not appear in Edward Duyker and Per Tingbrand, eds, *Daniel Solander: Collected Correspondence, 1753–1782* (Melbourne, 1995).
70. S. Bacstrom, "Account of a Voyage to Spitsbergen in the Year 1780," from *The Philosophical Magazine*, July 1799, reprinted in John Pinkerton, ed., *A General Collection of the Best and Most Interesting Voyages and Travels in All Parts of the World* (17 vols, London, 1808), vol. 1, pp. 614–20.
71. KBG, Banks Papers 1.222, 28 June 1786. These letters from Bacstrom to Banks, and Bacstrom's career down to 1801, are catalogued in Dawson, ed., *Banks Letters*, pp. 26–7, and are discussed in Douglas Cole, "Sigismund Bacstrom's Northwest Coast Drawings and an Account of his Curious Career," *BC Studies*, 46 (1980), pp. 61–86.
72. KBG, Banks Papers 1.222 (Northumberland); 1.240, 21 Aug. 1786 (Cagliostro); 1.245, 26 Sep. 1786 (New Holland). The planned colony for convicts in the latter was, of course, Botany Bay.
73. *A Short Essay on the Virtues of Dr. Norris's Antinomial Drops* (London, [1775?]), p. 31. The last edition of this pamphlet that contains Shute's letter was apparently printed in 1788. For admissions to the Inner Temple, see http://www.innertemple.org.uk/archive/itad/legal_profession.html.
74. KBG, Banks Papers 2.46, 15 June 1791; 2.49, no date. Unnamed in the letter, Shute is identified in GRL, MHC, Bacstrom Ms. 6, no. 2, p. [6]. For Paradise Row, see GRL, MHC, Bacstrom Ms. 2, no. 9. A drawing of a smelting furnace in Bacstrom's hand survives in the Rainsford papers at Alnwick Castle, Ms. 573A, pp. 191–2.
75. KBG, Banks Papers 2.50, 18 Aug. 1791; SL, NSW, Papers of Sir Joseph Banks, Series 73.035, Banks to Bacstrom, 21 Aug. 1791. The imperial dimensions of the Nootka Sound crisis are considered in John M. Norris, "The Politics of the British Cabinet in the Nootka Crisis," *English Historical Review*, 70, 277 (1955), pp. 562–80, while its local implications are treated in Daniel Wright Clayton, *Islands of Truth: The Imperial Fashioning of Vancouver Island* (Vancouver, 2000), ch. 7. See also George Vancouver, *A Voyage of Discovery to the North Pacific Ocean, and Round the World* (6 vols, London, 1801), and Janet R. Fireman, "The Seduction of George Vancouver: A Nootka Affair," *Pacific Historical Review*, 56, 3 (1987), pp. 427–43. A collection of sixty-three paintings by Bacstrom is in the Beinecke Library, WA MSS S-2405, under the title "Drawings and Sketches Made during a Voyage Around the World, 1791–1795." The paintings can be viewed online at http://beinecke.library.yale.edu/dl_crosscollex/SearchExecXC.asp?srchtype=CNO.
76. KBG, Banks Papers 2.153, 18 Nov. 1796.
77. Copies of this document can be found in Wellcome Library, Ms. 33657, ff. 1–7; GUL, Ferguson Ms. 22, ff. 6–12 (misdated 1797 for 1794); GRL, MHC, Bacstrom Ms. 19 (an ornate version, illuminated in colour).

78. KBG, Banks Papers 2.153. The Lodge of Antients no. 10 was constituted in 1751 at the Red Lyon, Cross Street, Long Acre, but in March 1792 was "granted and revived" to Lodge no. 159, which met at the Ship in the Strand. Bacstrom, who was living at East Street (now Lollard Street), Lambeth, may have been received by members of the old lodge. Robert Freke Gould, *The Atholl Lodges: Their Authentic History* (London, 1879), pp. 5, 31.
79. Alexander Tilloch, ed., *The Philosophical Magazine*, 1 (June 1798), sig. A_2.
80. *The Annual Biography and Obituary for the Year 1826*, vol. 10 (London, 1826), pp. 320–34, quotations on pp. 321–2, 331. Tilloch is also noticed in *ODNB*. His learned musings on the Apocalypse, dealing particularly with the date and structure of the book, were published as *Dissertations Introductory to the Study and Right Understanding of the Language, Structure and Contents of the Apocalypse* (London, 1823).
81. GUL, Ferguson Ms. 22, f. 19, where Tilloch's name is crudely scratched out of the initiation certificate; GRL, MHC, Bacstrom Mss. vols 1–19, of which vols 1, 9, 11, 15, 16 and 17 are mostly written out by Tilloch, and vol. 18 is in a third hand.
82. GRL, MHC, Bacstrom Ms. 2, no. 3, p. [i]; Bacstrom Ms. 5, no. 2, p. [ii].
83. GRL, MHC, Bacstrom Papers, vol. 14, letters of 29 Dec. 1805, 28 May 1808. Bacstrom must have been among the earliest inhabitants of Albion Street. It had disappeared by the early twentieth century.
84. GRL, MHC, Bacstrom Ms. 6, no. 8; Ms. 8, no. 3; Ms. 9, no. 7; Ms. 14, no. 13, letter of 29 Dec. 1805; Beinecke Library, Mellon Ms. 141, ff. 22^{v}–24. For a recipe communicated to Belisario by a rabbi, see GUL, Ferguson Ms. 311, no. 4.
85. GRL, MHC, Bacstrom Ms. 3, no. 5, and vol. 4; GUL, Ferguson Ms. 25 (same material as preceding), 99 (a collection of short texts transcribed by Sibly), 305 (astrology).
86. Wellcome Library, Ms. 3657, ff. 13–23; GRL, MHC, Bacstrom Ms. 14, no. 1; Beinecke Library, Mellon Ms. 141, f. 1. Bacstrom claimed that the younger Garden had founded the almshouses, which made his later residence there ironic. In fact, they were founded in 1703 by R. Morell, although Garden may well have given them a donation of £2,000, as Bacstrom asserts. Sampson Low, junior, *The Charities of London in 1861* (London, 1862), p. 185.
87. GRL, MHC, Bacstrom Ms. 14, no. 8. No *burgemeester* of Amsterdam had the name Gommée, which sounds like Gomes, a common surname among the Dutch city's Sephardic Jewish community.
88. GRL, MHC, Bacstrom Ms. 9, no. 3, Ms. 14, nos 6 (Rosenheim, Charas Stella), 7 (La Fountain); Wellcome Library, Ms. 1030, ff. 97^{v}, 98–100. For the Lafontaines, see Hans Vollmer, ed., *Allgemeines Lexicon der Bildenden Künstler*, vol. 22 (1928), pp. 208–9.
89. GUL, Ferguson Ms. 22, ff. 22–40^{v}.
90. GUL, Ferguson Ms. 1031, f. 31, 62–3.
91. Humphry Davy, "The Bakerian Lecture, on Some New Phænomena of Chemical Changes Produced by Electricity," in Alexander Tilloch, ed., *The Philosophical Magazine*, 32 (Oct.–Dec. 1808), pp. 3–18, 101–12, 146–54; Richard Knight, *Humphry Davy: Power and Science* (Cambridge, 1992), chs 5, 9; James Hamilton, *Michael Faraday* (London, 2002), ch. 1.
92. GUL, Ferguson Ms. 1031, ff. 31^{v}, 63.
93. GUL, Ferguson Ms. 314, no. 5.
94. GRL, MHC, Bacstrom Ms. 8, no. 1.
95. George S. Draffen, "Some Further Notes on the Rite of Seven Degrees in London," *Ars Quatuor Coronatorum*, 39 (1956), pp. 100–1.
96. W. Wonnacott, "The Rite of Seven Degrees in London," *Ars Quatuor Coronatorum*, 39 (1926), pp. 85, 86.
97. G.W. Speth, "A Symbolical Chart of 1789," *Ars Quatuor Coronatorum*, 3 (1890), pp. 36–7, and "Editor's Note," in *ibid.*, p. 109; "Masonic Charities," *The New Age Magazine*, 18, 2 (1913), p. 172; R.A. Gilbert, "Shaping the Cubic Stone: Masonic Symbolism in Lambert de Lintot's Engraving," *Hermetic Journal*, 39 (1988), pp. 23–8.

98. B.L., Add. Ms. 23,665, ff. 50–1.
99. *ODNB* remains the best source for his biography, but for his most important appointment, see "Commissary Rainsford's Journal of Transactions, etc., 1776–78," in *Collections of the New York Historical Society for the Year 1879* (New York, 1880), pp. 314–543. His letters on the posting of troops during the Gordon Riots are in B.L., Add. Ms. 23,669, ff. 63–6, 68–70.
100. B.L., Add. Ms. 23, 667, ff. 18v–19v. For the Avignon Masons, see Joanny Bricaud, *Les Illuminés d'Avignon* (Paris, 1927), chs 5–6; Clarke Garrett, *Respectable Folly: Millenarians and the French Revolution in France and England* (Baltimore and London, 1975), ch. 5.
101. L.F. Tafel, *Documents Concerning the Life and Character of Emanuel Swedenborg* (2 vols in 4 parts, London, 1877), vol. 2, part 2, p. 810; Lynne R. Wilkinson, *The Dream of an Absolute Language: Emanuel Swedenborg and French Literary Culture* (Albany, N.Y., 1996), p. 118; Samuel Beswick, *Swedenborg Rite and the Great Masonic Leaders of the Eighteenth Century* (New York, 1870), ch. 7. Beswick was the reviver of the "Swedenborg Rite of Masonry" in North America, and his treatment of its eighteenth-century origins is not always reliable, but his comments on the Exegetical Society are supported by other sources.
102. Alnwick Castle, Ms. 599, pp. 108. Mendelssohn had a daughter named Jeanette, who was six years old in 1770, but the intended recipient of this letter sounds older and there is no indication that Rainsford was praising her father. For Jewish women who led salons in Berlin, see Deborah Hertz, *Jewish High Society in Old Regime Berlin* (New Haven, Conn., 1988), ch. 6.
103. B.L., Add. Ms. 23, 675, ff. 11–16, 24, 33–4.
104. *Ibid.*, ff. 21–2; B.L., Add. Ms. 23, 669, f. 99.
105. B.L., Add. Ms. 23,669, ff. 85–6, 91.
106. B.L., Add. Ms. 23,670, f. 53; Add. Ms. 23,675, ff. 58–9; Wellcome Library, Ms. 957, "Extract from the Tables of Rotalo."
107. Alnwick Castle, Ms. 619, pp. 14, 16–17, 42.
108. B.L., Add. Ms. 23,669, ff. 123–4. For Grabianka, see M.L. Danilewicz, "The King of the New Israel: Thaddeus Grabianka (1740–1807)," *Oxford Slavonic Papers*, n.s. 1 (1968), pp. 49–73.
109. B.L., Add. Ms. 23,675, f. 15v; B.L., Add. Ms. 23,669, f. 86.
110. B.L., Add. Ms. 23,669, ff. 102–3, 129–30.
111. Wellcome Library, Mss. 4032–9.
112. Alnwick Castle, Ms. 624. For Goethe and Welling, see Nicholas Boyle, *Goethe: The Poet and the Age, Vol. 1* (Oxford, 1992), pp. 76, 88, 222.
113. Wellcome Library, Ms. 3078, ff. 2–27v.
114. B.L., Add. Ms. 23,675, f. 41; SL, NSW, Banks Papers 06.014; *Philosophical Transactions*, 57 (1768), pp. 410–12; Dawson, *Banks Letters*, pp. 158, 837; Gorton, ed., *General Biographical Dictionary*, vol. 2, under "Price, James" (information confirmed by biographical details available through RSA catalogue, accessed at http://www2.royalsociety.org). Woulfe's certificate of election as F.R.S., signed by the speech therapist Henry Baker, founder of the lectures, as well as by John Ellis and Daniel Solander, is in RSA, EC/1766/20, accessed at http://www2.royalsociety.org. Woulfe is noticed in *ODNB*.
115. Ian Kelly, *Casanova: Actor, Lover, Priest, Spy* (New York, 2011), p. 246. Percy is noticed in *ODNB*.
116. B.L., Add. Ms. 23,668, ff. 4–5. Dutens and Morse are noticed in *ODNB*. Rainsford was one of Morse's proposers for his Fellowship in the Royal Society in 1789: RSA, EC/1789/02, accessed at http://www2.royalsociety.org.
117. John Brand, *Observations on Popular Antiquities: Including the Whole of Mr. Bourne's Antiquitates Vulgares, with Addenda to Every Chapter of That Work: As Also an Appendix, Containing Such Articles on the Subject, As Have Been Omitted by That Author* (London, 1810; 1st ed. 1777), pp. iv, xi. Brand is noticed in *ODNB*.

118. B.L., Add. Ms. 23,668, f. 7v.
119. See Gregory R. Johnson, ed., *Kant on Swedenborg: Dreams of a Spirit-Seer and Other Writings* (Chicago, 2003).
120. The only English-language biography remains Arthur Edward Waite, *The Life of Louis Claude de Saint-Martin, the Unknown Philosopher, and the Substance of his Transcendental Doctrine* (London, 1901).
121. B.L., Add. Ms. 23,668, f. 5.
122. Isabel Cooper-Oakley, *The Comte de St. Germain: The Secret of Kings* (Milan, 1912: reissued on Google Books, 2008), p. 90. The words are those of the landgrave August von Hessen-Philipsthal. For a more critical but arguably rose-coloured view of St.-Germain as having nothing to do with the occult sciences, see J.H. Calmeyer, "The Count of St. Germain or Giovannini: A Case of Mistaken Identity," *Music and Letters*, 48, 1 (1967), pp. 4–16; David Hunter, "Monsieur le Comte de St.-Germain: The Great Pretender," *Musical Times*, 144, 1885 (2003), pp. 40–4. Many nonsensical stories have been built up around this interesting character.
123. "The Confession of Comte de Cagliostro," in Parkyns Macmahon, ed., *Memorial, or Brief, for the Count de Cagliostro, Defendant: against the King's Attorney General, Plaintiff: in the Cause of the Cardinal de Rohan, Madame de la Motte, and Others* (London, 1786), pp. 10–31.
124. Iain McCalman, *The Last Alchemist: Count Cagliostro, Master of Magic in the Age of Reason* (London, 2003), chs 1–5; W.R.H. Trowbridge, *Cagliostro* (New York, 1910), pp. 49–73, for details on the second London trip; Évelyne Lever, *L'Affaire du Collier* (Paris, 2004).
125. Hélène Maspéro-Clerc, "Samuel Swinton, Éditeur du *Courier de l'Europe* à Boulogne-sur-Mer (1778–1783) et Agent Secret du Gouvernement Britannique," *Annales Historiques de la Révolution Française*, 57 (1985), pp. 527–31; McCalman, *Last Alchemist*, ch. 6; "Lucia," *The Life of the Count Cagliostro* (London, 1787), pp. xxii–iii. "Lucia," hitherto unidentified, may in fact be Lucy de Loutherbourg, wife of Cagliostro's most ardent supporter in England.
126. For Gordon, see *ODBN* and Iain McCalman, "Mad Lord George and Madame La Motte: Riot and Sexuality in the Genesis of Burke's *Reflections on the Revolution in France*," *Journal of British Studies*, 35 (1996), pp. 343–67; for Morande, Simon Burrows, *A King's Ransom: The Life of Charles Théveneau de Morande, Blackmailer, Scandalmonger and Master-Spy* (London, 2010).
127. Copies of the Lodge minutes can be found in Bodl. Lib., Ms. Rylands d.2, pp. 138–40, with the *General Advertiser* article on pp. 151–7. For the *Morning Herald* advertisement and the Gillray print, see McCalman, *Last Alchemist*, pp. 169–72.
128. An English translation of the "Letter" is in P.A. Malpas, "Cagliostro: A Messenger Long Misunderstood," *The Theosophical Path*, 42, 1 (1932), pp. 101–20; an even longer version was worked into "Lucia," *Life of Cagliostro*, pp. 9–54.
129. "Anthony Pasquin" [John William], *Memoirs of the Royal Academicians* (London, 1796), pp. 80–1.
130. McCalman, *Last Alchemist*, ch. 6.
131. This is the main thesis of Dror Wahrman, *The Making of the Modern Self: Identity and Culture in Eigtheenth-Century England* (New Haven, Conn., 2004).

Chapter Nine: Prophets and Revolutions

1. William Godwin, *St. Leon*, ed. William Brewer (Peterborough, Ontario, 2006). Godwin's source of alchemical information was Johann Heinrich Cohausen, *Hermippus Redivivus: or, The Sage's Triumph over Old Age and the Grave*, ed. and trans. John Campbell (London, 1744). As his later *Lives of the Necromancers* (London, 1834) amply shows, Godwin was not an admirer of occult philosophy in general.

2. In 1832, Scott's close friend the scientist and inventor Sir David Brewster would address a work debunking magic to him: *Letters on Natural Magic, Addressed to Sir Walter Scott, Bart.* (London, 1852).
3. Joseph Taylor, *Apparitions; or, The Mystery of Ghosts, Hobgoblins, and Haunted Houses, Developed* (London, 1814), p. vii; Sasha Handley, *Visions of an Unseen World: Ghost Beliefs and Ghost Stories in Eighteenth-Century England* (London, 2007), pp. 212–13.
4. [Francis Barrett?], *The Lives of the Alchemystical Philosophers* (London, 1815). Whether Barrett actually wrote this work remains unclear.
5. John Parkins, *The Cabinet of Wealth, or The Temple of Wisdom* (Grantham, 1812), p. 5.
6. See Gretchen Gerzina, *Black London: Life before Emancipation* (New Brunswick, N.J., 1995), ch. 5; Christopher Leslie Brown, *Moral Capital: Foundations of British Abolitionism* (Chapel Hill, N.C., 2006), ch. 5.
7. Emanuel Swedenborg, *A Treatise Concerning the Last Judgment, and the Destruction of Babylon . . . Originally Published at London in Latin, in 1758* (Boston, 1828), p. 63.
8. Karl-Erik Sjödén, *Swedenborg en France* (Stockholm, 1985), ch. 1; H.M. Graupe, "Mordechai Schnaber-Levison: The Life, Works and Thought of a Haskalah Outsider," *Leo Baeck Institute Yearbook*, 41 (1996), pp. 1–20. Levison, who published several medical tracts under the name "George Levison" while working at the General Medical Asylum in Welbeck Street, is noticed in *ODNB*. I have not been able to trace a copy of *A Plain System of Alchemy*.
9. This very rare work, transcribed by Adam Maclean from a copy in the Helsinki University Library Rare Book Collection, is accessible at http://www.alchemywebsite.com/spiritual_stone.html.
10. C.B. Wadström, *Observations on the Slave Trade, and a Description of Some Part of the Coast of Guinea, during a Voyage, Made in 1787 and 1788, in Company with Doctor A. Sparrman and Captain Arrehenius* (London, 1789).
11. J.B. Wadström and Auguste Nordenskjöld, *Plan for a Free Community upon the West Coast of Africa, under the Protection of Great Britain; But Intirely Independent of All European Laws and Governments* (London, 1789), pp. iv, 31, 39–40. The best account of the Swedenborgian colonization plan is Deirdre Coleman, *Romantic Colonization and British Anti-Slavery* (Cambridge, 2005), ch. 2.
12. Wadström and Nordenskjöld, *Plan for a Free Community*, pp. 43–4, 50.
13. C.B. Wadström, *Plan for a Free Community at Sierra Leone, upon the Coast of Africa, under the Protection of Great Britain* (London, 1792); C.B. Wadström, *An Essay on Colonization, Particularly Applied to the West Coast of Africa* (2 parts, London, 1794–5).
14. Olaudah Equiano, *The Interesting Narrative and Other Writings*, ed. Vincent Carretta (Harmondsworth, Middlesex, 1995), pp. 5–6, 15–20, 183–4, 189–91; also, Vincent Carretta, *Equiano the African: Biography of a Self-Made Man* (Athens, Ga., 2005).
15. Equiano, *Interesting Narrative*, pp. 40, 43–4.
16. *Ibid.*, pp. 347–8; Carretta, *Equiano the African*, pp. 339–40, 345–50, 361–2. Hardy's trial was transcribed by Manoah Sibly in *The Genuine Trial of Thomas Hardy, for High Treason, at the Sessions House in the Old Bailey, from October 28 to November 5, 1794* (2 vols, London, 1795).
17. William Blake, "The Little Black Boy," *Songs of Innocence and of Experience*, in David V. Erdman, ed., *The Complete Poetry and Prose of William Blake* (rev. ed., New York, 1988), p. 9. Blake's ties to "international Swedenborgians," including Wadström, are noted in Robert Rix, *William Blake and the Cultures of Radical Christianity* (Aldershot, Hants, and Burlington, Vt., 2007), ch. 5.
18. *The Astrologer's Magazine; and Philosophical Miscellany*, Sept. 1793, p. 52. The printer, William Locke of Red Lion Street, Holborn, was known for issuing musical works. He was declared bankrupt in November 1793: Exeter Working Papers in Book Trade History: The London Book Trades, 1775–1800, accessed at http://bookhistory.blogspot.com/2007/01/london-1775-1800-l.html.

19. Frank O'Gorman, "The Paine Burnings of 1792–3," *Past and Present*, 193 (2006), pp. 111–55.
20. Stuart Semmel, *Napoleon and the British* (New Haven, Conn., 2004), pp. 101–4; and for an image of Napoleon as a benign conjuror, *ibid.*, pp. 48–9.
21. John Martin, *Animal Magnetism Examined: in a Letter to a Country Gentleman* (London, 1790), p. 9.
22. Patricia Fara, "An Attractive Therapy: Animal Magnetism in Eighteenth-Century England," *History of Science*, 33 (1995), pp. 127–77; Patricia Fara, *Sympathetic Attractions: Magnetic Practices, Beliefs, and Symbolism in Eighteenth-Century England* (Princeton, 1994). The term "magnetist" was used by practitioners of animal magnetism at the time, and I have employed it here, although "magnetizer" is more conventional English.
23. For Mesmerism in other parts of Europe, see Frank A. Pattie, *Mesmer and Animal Magnetism: A Chapter in the History of Medicine* (Hamilton, N.Y., 1994); Robert Darnton, *Mesmerism and the End of the Enlightenment in France* (Cambridge, Mass., 1968); Jessica Riskin, *Science in the Age of Sensibility: The Sentimental Empiricists of the French Enlightenment* (Chicago, 2002), ch. 6.
24. J.B. de Mainauduc, *Proposals to the Ladies, for Establishing an Hygiæn Society, in England, to Be Incorporated with That of Paris* (London, 1785), p. 11.
25. John Bell, *The General and Particular Principles of Animal Electricity and Magnetism, &c. in Which Are Found Dr. Bell's Secrets and Practice* (London, 1792), p. 23.
26. John Bell, *New System of the World, and the Laws of Motion* (London, 1788), pp. 6, 51.
27. For Gassner and Mesmer, see H.C. Erik Midelfort, *Exorcism and Enlightenment: Johann Joseph Gassner and the Demons of Eighteenth-Century Germany* (New Haven, Conn., 2005), pp. 18–31.
28. *Wonders and Mysteries of Animal Magnetism Displayed* (London, 1791), pp. 17–18, 28.
29. Mary Pratt, *A List of a Few Cures Performed by Mr. and Mrs. De Loutherbourg, of Hammersmith Terrace, without Medicine* (London, 1789), pp. 1, 10.
30. Contemporary exposés of the principles of magnetism include *A True and Genuine Discovery of Animal Electricity and Magnetism: Calculated to Detect and Overthrow All Counterfeit Descriptions of the Same* (London, 1790), which was reprinted in *A Practical Display of the Philosophical System called Animal Magnetism* (London, 1790). See also the article in *The Times*, no. 1879, 12 Jan. 1791, probably by "Maria" (see note 46 below), which does not mention the "Crisis."
31. Martin, *Animal Magnetism Examined*, pp. 30–1.
32. J.B. de Mainauduc, *The Lectures of J.B. de Mainauduc, M.D., Member of the Corporation of Surgeons in London* (London, 1798), vol. 1, p. 196. Only the first volume was published.
33. Bell, *General and Particular Principles*, pp. 19, 60–1, 67–76. For Puységur, see Pattie, *Mesmer*, pp. 216–27; Michel Pierssens, "Le Merveilleux Psychique au XIXe Siècle," *Ethnologie Française*, n.s. 23, 3 (1993), pp. 351–66; Henri F. Ellenberger, *The Discovery of the Unconscious: The History and Evolution of Dynamic Psychology* (New York, 1970), pp. 70–4. The comparison with Shakers was also made by the American Samuel Stearns in *The Mystery of Animal Magnetism Revealed to the World* (London, 1791), pp. 43–51.
34. See Roy Porter, *Mind-Forg'd Manacles: A History of Madness in England from the Restoration to the Regency* (Harmondsworth, Middlesex, 1987), ch. 4; Jonathan Andrews and Andrew Scull, *Undertaker of the Mind: John Monro and Mad-Doctoring in Eighteenth-Century England* (Berkeley and Los Angeles, 2001).
35. William LeFanu, ed., *Betsy Sheridan's Journal: Letters from Sheridan's Sister* (Oxford, 1986), pp. 123–4.
36. Mainauduc, *Plan for an Hygiæn Society*, p. 10; Lefanu, ed., *Betsy Sheridan's Journal*, p. 124.
37. Fara, "Attractive Therapy," pp. 142, 165 nn. 80–3, citing Royal College of Surgeons, Ms. 42. e.1; George Winter, *Animal Magnetism: History of; its Origin, Progress and Present State: its Principles and Secrets Displayed, As Delivered by the Late Dr. Demainauduc* (Bristol and London, 1801), pp. 14–15; Mainauduc, *Lectures*, pp. [xiii–xiv].

38. Fara, "Attractive Therapy," p. 163 n. 58, p. 166 nn. 85, 87, 91. Yeldall's first name is not known.
39. John Holloway, *Animal Magnetism*, broadsheet ([London], [1790?]), in B.L., shelfmark C.142.2.17; Martin, *Animal Magnetism*, p. 17; Winter, *Animal Magnetism*, pp. 17–18.
40. Pratt, *List of a Few Cures*, pp. 7–9.
41. *The Times*, nos 1253, 1259, 10, 17 Sept. 1789; Donna Andrews, "London Debates: 1789," *London Debating Societies 1776–1799*, London Record Society 30 (1994), nos 1528, 1529, 1531, 1533, accessed at http://www.british-history.ac.uk.
42. Elizabeth Inchbald, *Animal Magnetism* (Dublin, 1789), pp. 10, 34. The play was adapted from a French original.
43. *The Times*, no. 1059, 29 April 1788; LeFanu, ed., *Betsy Sheridan's Journal*, p. 124.
44. Martin, *Animal Magnetism*, p. 12; John Cue, *Goliath Slain with his Own Sword* (London, [1794]), p. 88.
45. Fara, "Attractive Therapy," p. 164 n. 67; [John Pearson], *A Plain and Rational Account of the Nature and Effects of Animal Magnetism* (London, 1790), p. 10, for Mainauduc being assisted by "several female pupils."
46. "Maria," *The Secret Revealed: or Animal Magnetism Displayed. A Letter from a Young Lady to the Rev. John Martin* (2nd ed., London, [1791?]), p. 5. She was probably also the author of an article in *The Times* of 12 Jan. 1791, for which see note 30 above.
47. Winter, *Animal Magnetism*, p. 18.
48. Darnton, *Mesmerism*, pp. 68–70; Sjödén, *Swedenborg en France*, ch. 4.
49. Martin, *Animal Magnetism*, p. 16; *Wonders of Animal Magnetism Displayed*, pp. 10–11.
50. Bell, *General and Particular Principles*, p. 30.
51. *Wonders of Animal Magnetism Displayed*, p. 14; Bell, *General and Particular Principles*, p. 45; Pratt, *A List of a Few Cures*, pp. 3–5.
52. Ebenezer Sibly, *A Key to Physic and the Occult Sciences* (5th ed., London, 1814), pp. 276, 281; Allen G. Debus, "Scientific Truth and Occult Tradition: The Medical World of Ebenezer Sibly (1751–1799)," *Medical History*, 26 (1982), pp. 274–77.
53. "Herman Boerhaave," *An Essay on the Virtue and Efficient Cause of Magnetical Cures* (London, 1793), pp. 24, 25. The original was published in London in 1743, five years after Boerhaave's death, supposedly translated by a relative from a Latin original.
54. Francis Barrett, *The Magus, or Celestial Intelligencer; Being a Complete System of Occult Philosophy* (London, 1801), book II, part 1, chs 1, 5.
55. Martin, *Animal Magnetism*, pp. 21–3.
56. Alison Winter, *Mesmerized: Powers of Mind in Victorian Britain* (Chicago, 1998), ch. 8. See also Kapil Raj, *Relocating Modern Science: Circulation and the Construction of Knowledge in South Asia and Europe, 1650–1900* (Basingstoke, Hants, 2007).
57. Alnwick Castle, Rainsford Ms. 616, vol. 1, p. 77; vol. 2, p. 76. See also B.L., Add. Ms. 23,675, ff. 35–6, for two cures by magnetism that were reported to Rainsford.
58. "Anthony Pasquin" [John William], *Memoirs of the Royal Academicians* (London, 1796), pp. 80–1; Pratt, *A List of a Few Cures*, p. 9; George C. Williamson, *Richard Cosway, R.A.* (London, 1905), pp. 57–9; Gerald Barnett, *Richard and Maria Cosway: A Biography* (Tiverton and Cambridge, 1995), pp. 177–8.
59. "Remarques de M. le Marquis de Thomé, sur une Assertion des Commissaires Nommé par le Roi pour l'Examen du Magnétisme-Animal," in Benedict Chastanier, *Tableau Analytique et Raisonnée de la Doctrine Celeste de l'Église de la Nouvelle Jérusalem* (London and The Hague, 1786), pp. 245–52, quotation on p. 250.
60. William Spence, *Essays in Divinity and Physic . . . with an Exposition of Animal Magnetism and Magic* (London, 1792), pp. 58–9. Spence was a surgeon, a member of the Exegetical Society of Stockholm and an orthodox Swedenborgian; his pamphlet was published by Robert Hindmarsh. I have not been able to find a copy of the work by Chastanier from which Spence quotes.
61. Sjödén, *Swedenborg en France*, p. 39. The source of this observation, Henry Servanté, was editor of the *New Jerusalem Magazine*.

62. *The New Magazine of Knowledge Concerning Heaven and Hell* (2 vols, London, 1790–1), vol. 2, June 1791, pp. 269–72; July 1791, pp. 293–6.
63. John Holloway, *Restoration Unscriptural: in a Letter to a Friend* (London, 1789); Cue, *Goliath Slain, passim.*
64. Albert Goodwin, *The Friends of Liberty: The English Democratic Movement in the Age of the French Revolution* (London, 1979), ch. 3; Robert E. Schofield, *The Enlightened Joseph Priestley: A Study of his Life and Work from 1773 to 1804* (University Park, Pa., 2004), pp. 268–76.
65. [Pearson], *Plain and Rational Account*, p. 44; Winter, *Animal Magnetism*, pp. 209–10.
66. B.L., Add. Ms. 23,675, f. 35.
67. *Wonderful Prophecies. Being a Dissertation on the Existence, Nature and Extent of the Prophetic Powers in the Human Mind* (London, 1795), pp. 56–8, 63–7, 74–81, 83–4. For prophecy in the late eighteenth century on both sides of the Atlantic, see Susan Juster, *Doomsayers: Anglo-American Prophecy in the Age of Revolution* (Philadelphia, 2003).
68. Henry Hardy, *A Vision from the Lord God Almighty, the Great and Mighty God of the Whole Earth* (London, 1792), pp. 7–8, 10, 13, 24, 26, 32. This was a cheaper version of an earlier work, *Mountain Engraved*, which I have not been able to find.
69. *The English Review, or, An Abstract of English and Foreign Literature*, 21 (1793), p. 154.
70. B.L., Add. Ms. 23,675, ff. 28–31.
71. Clarke Garrett, *Respectable Folly: Millenarians and the French Revolution in France and England* (Baltimore and London, 1975), chs 2–4. For the religious context, see Suzanne Desan, *Reclaiming the Sacred: Lay Religion and Popular Politics in Revolutionary France* (Ithaca, N.Y., 1990).
72. Goodwin, *Friends of Liberty*, ch. 10.
73. John Ehrman, *The Younger Pitt: The Reluctant Transition* (London, 1983), chs 13–15.
74. Garrett, *Respectable Folly*, ch. 8; J.F.C. Harrison, *The Second Coming: Popular Millenarianism, 1780–1850* (London, 1979), ch. 4; Juster, *Doomsayers*, pp. 179–96; and the biography of Brothers in *ODNB*.
75. Richard Brothers, *A Revealed Knowledge of the Prophecies and Times* (2nd ed., 2 vols, London, 1794), vol. 1, pp. 2, 39, 48.
76. *Ibid.*, vol. 2, pp. 7–8, 17–20, 25, 70, 106.
77. For the use of imagination in both the government response to Brothers and the radical appropriation of him, see John Barrell, "Imagining the King's Death: The Arrest of Richard Brothers," *History Workshop Journal*, 37 (1994), pp. 1–33.
78. Ronald Hutton, *Blood and Mistletoe: The History of the Druids in Britain* (New Haven, Conn., 2009), ch. 5; Prys Morgan, "From a Death to a View: The Hunt for the Welsh Past in the Romantic Period," in Eric Hobsbawm and Terence Ranger, eds, *The Invention of Tradition* (Cambridge, 1983), pp. 43–100; Geraint H. Evans, ed., *A Rattleskull Genius: The Many Faces of Iolo Morganwg* (Cardiff, 2009).
79. Brothers, *Revealed Knowledge*, vol. 2, pp. 76, 102 (wrongly numbered as 98).
80. B.L., Add. Ms. 23,670, f. 75.
81. Brothers, *Revealed Knowledge*, vol. 2, pp. 87, 91; Richard Brothers, *Notes on the Etymology of a Few Antique Words* (London, 1796), p. 36.
82. John Wright, *A Revealed Knowledge of Some Things That Will Speedily Be Fulfilled in the World* (London, 1794), pp. 20, 25–6, 27, 44, 62. William Bryan's account in *A Testimony of the Spirit of Truth, Concerning Richard Brothers* (London, 1795), pp. 9–29, is far less detailed.
83. Wright, *Revealed Knowledge*, pp. 22–4; Bryan, *Testimony*, pp. 2–5.
84. B.L., Add. Ms. 23,670, f. 75[v].
85. Garrett, *Respectable Folly*, pp. 161–2, 176–7; Mary Thale, ed., *Selections from the Papers of the London Corresponding Society, 1792–99* (Cambridge, 1983), pp. 132–3, 167, 252, 256, 351, 469.
86. Sarah Flaxmer, *Satan Revealed or The Dragon Overcome* (London, [1797?]), pp. 9, 12, 13–20.

87. Richard Brothers, *A Letter from Mr. Brothers to Miss Cott, the Recorded Daughter of King David, and Future Queen of the Hebrews* (Edinburgh, 1798), p. 94.
88. Nathaniel Brassey Halhed, *Testimony of the Authenticity of the Prophecies of Richard Brothers, and of his Mission to Recall the Jews* (2nd ed., London, 1795), p. 12. For Halhed's earlier work, see *A Code of Gentoo Laws, or Ordinations of the Pundits*, [trans. N.B. Halhed] (London, 1776). For Brothers on the Trinity, see "Wrote in Confinement. An Exposition of the Trinity: (18 April 1796)," which was attached to Brothers, *Notes on the Etymology*.
89. *A Word of Admonition to the Right Hon. William Pitt* (London, 1795), pp. 13, 16.
90. Anti-Brothers pamphlets include *The Age of Prophecy! Or, Further Testimony of the Mission of Richard Brothers* (London, 1795); *A Letter to Nathaniel Brassey Halhed, Esq. M.P. from an Old Woman* (London, 1795); *The Age of Credulity: A Letter to Nathaniel Brassey Halhed, Esq. M.P.* (London, 1795); George Horne, *Occasional Remarks: Addressed to Nathaniel Brassey Halhed, M.P.* (Oxford, n.d.); George Horne, *Sound Argument Dictated by Common Sense* (3rd ed., Oxford, n.d.). Those on the pro-Brothers side include J. Crease, *Prophecies Fulfilling: or, The Dawn of the Perfect Day* (London, 1795); [W. Sales], *Truth or Not Truth: or A Discourse on Prophets* (London, 1795); Samuel Whitchurch, *Another Witness! Or Further Testimony in Favor of Richard Brothers* (London, 1795); Nathaniel Brassey Halhed, *The Whole of the Testimonies to the Authenticity of the Prophecies and Mission of Richard Brothers, the Prophet* (London, 1794). Except for the last, all these pamphlets were printed by George Riebau and John Wright.
91. Moses Gomez Pereira, *The Jew's Appeal on the Divine Mission of Richard Brothers, and N.B. Halhed, Esq. to Restore Israel, and Rebuild Jerusalem* (London, 1795); Moses Gomez Pereira, *Circular Letter to the Corresponding Societies, in Great Britain* (London, 1796). As none of Pereira's occult references actually relates to Judaism, it is possible that he was a non-Jew writing under a pseudonym.
92. James K. Hopkins, *A Woman to Deliver her People: Joanna Southcott and English Millenarianism in an Era of Revolution* (Austin, Texas, 1982), pp. 24–33, 133–7.
93. Richard Brothers, *A Letter to His Majesty and One to Her Majesty . . . with A Dissertation; on the Fall of Eve* (London, 1802), pp. 49–64.
94. Richard Brothers, *A Description of Jerusalem* (London, 1801), quotations on pp. 34, 39, 75. George Riebau printed this work, but he was not as yet assisted by the Sandemanian Michael Faraday, who entered his employment in 1804: see James Hamilton, *Faraday* (London, 2003), p. 6.
95. Eitan Bar-Yosef, "'Green and Pleasant Lands': England and the Holy Land in Plebeian Millenarian Culture, c. 1790–1820," in Kathleen Wilson, ed., *A New Imperial History: Culture, Identity and Modernity in Britain and the Empire, 1660–1840* (Cambridge, 2004), pp. 155–75.
96. *The New Magazine of Knowledge Concerning Heaven and Hell, and the Universal World of Nature* (2 vols, London, 1790–1), vol. 1, pp. 392–6. The petition was presented by Lord Rawdon, a Whig military officer who was a close friend of the duke of York.
97. Leopold Engel, *Geschichte des Illuminaten-Ordens* (Berlin, 1906); René Le Forestier, *Les Illuminés de Bavière et la Franc-Maçonnerie Allemande* (Paris, 1915; reprint, Milan, 2001); René Le Forestier, *La Franc-Maçonnerie Templière et Occultiste aux XVIIIe et XIXe Siècles* (Paris and Louvain, 1970), pp. 642–8; J.M. Roberts, *The Mythology of the Secret Societies* (New York, 1972), ch. 5. Among the few websites on the Illuminati that contain reliable information is http://www.bavarian-illuminati.info/, where a number of original documents can be found.
98. Henry Sadler, *Thomas Dunckerley; His Life, Labours and Letters* (London, 1891), pp. 244–79, esp. pp. 260–1; Bodl. Lib., Ms. Rylands d.8, p. 1.
99. Garrett, *Respectable Folly*, pp. 116–18; Roberts, *Mythology of the Secret Societies*, pp. 146–88. For the mixed responses to revolution of Freemasons in another southern French city, see Kenneth Loiselle, "Living the Enlightenment in an Age of Revolution: Freemasonry in Bordeaux, 1788–1794," *French History*, 24, 1 (2010), pp. 60–81.

100. This conclusion was first proposed in non-conspiratorial form by the historian Augustin Cochin, whose writings can now be approached through Nancy Derr Polin, ed. and trans., *Organizing the French Revolution: Selections from Augustin Cochin* (Rockford, Il., 2007). Cochin's explanations were famously revived by François Furet in *Interpreting the French Revolution* (Cambridge, 1981).
101. Augustin Barruel, *Memoirs, Illustrating the History of Jacobinism* (3 vols, London, 1797–8), vol. 2, p. 358; Roberts, *Mythology of the Secret Societies*, pp. 188–202.
102. Barruel, *Memoirs*, vol. 2, pp. iv, 330. Barruel's translator, Robert Clifford, may have introduced the term "occult Lodges" into English. It is somewhat misleading: the original *Arrières Loges* suggests a system disguised from the public but not necessarily occult. Barruel was well informed enough to know that the Illuminati were not occult thinkers, but his translator may not been aware of it. Clifford went on to write his own treatise linking the United Irishmen and the British Corresponding Societies to the Illuminati: [Robert Clifford], *Application of Barruel's Memoirs of Jacobinism, to the Secret Societies of Ireland and Great Britain* (London, 1798).
103. John Robison, *Proofs of a Conspiracy against All the Religions and Governments of Europe, Carried On in the Secret Meetings of Freemasons, Illuminati and Reading Societies* (London, 1797), p. 99.
104. *Ibid.*, pp. 269, 358.
105. John Robison, *Postscript to the Second Edition of Mr. Robison's Proofs of a Conspiracy against All the Religions and Governments of Europe* (London, 1797), p. 23.
106. *Ibid.*, p. 27.
107. B.L., Add. Ms. 23,668, f. 78.
108. *Ibid.*, f. 82.
109. W.J. Hughan, *Memorials of the Masonic Union of A.D. 1813* (London, Truro and Philadelphia, 1874), pp. 15–34.
110. William Preston, "The Misrepresentations of Barruel and Robison Exposed," first published in 1799, reprinted in George Oliver, *The Golden Remains of the Early Masonic Writers* (5 vols, 1847–50), vol. 3, pp. 274–300.
111. Francis Dobbs, *A Concise View from History and Prophecy, of the Great Predictions in the Sacred Writings, That Have Been Fulfilled; Also of Those That Are Now Fulfilling, and That Remain to Be Accomplished* (Dublin, 1800), pp. 256–61; Garrett, *Respectable Folly*, pp. 118–19. Dobbs is noticed in *ODNB*.
112. John Clowes, *Letters to a Member of Parliament on the Character and Writings of Baron Swedenborg, Containing a Full and Compleat Refutation of All of the Abbé Barruel's Calumnies against the Honourable Author* (Manchester, 1799), p. 281; see also Theodore Compton, *The Life and Correspondence of the Reverend John Clowes, M.A.* (London, 1874), p. 62.
113. Mary Pratt's letters to Henry Brooke, copied out by Brooke's son-in-law F.H. Holcroft, are in DWL, Ms. Walton I.1.43. They are discussed in Désirée Hirst, *Hidden Riches: Traditional Symbolism from the Renaissance to Blake* (London, 1964), pp. 259–61, 276–80, and E.P. Thompson, *Witness against the Beast: William Blake and the Moral Law* (New York, 1993), pp. 43–4, 138–9.
114. Church of Latter-Day Saints, Genealogical Archive, source no. 942 B4HAV.47; source no. 0580904 (consulted online at www.familysearch.org); *A List of All the Liverymen of London* (London, 1776), p. 143; Marlies K. Danziger and Frank Brady, eds, *Boswell: The Great Biographer, 1789–1795* (New York, 1989), pp. 117–118, 239 (Courtenay), 250 (Seward); Roger Wakefield, *Wakefield's Merchant and Tradesman's General Directory for London . . . for the Year 1790* (London, [1790]), p. 266; *The Proceedings on the King's Commission of the Peace, Oyer and Terminer, and Gaol Delivery for the City of London* (London, 1790–1).
115. For middling and genteel households in the eighteenth century, see Margaret Hunt, *The Middling Sort: Commerce, Gender and the Family in England, 1680–1780* (Berkeley and Los Angeles, 1996), ch. 8; Amanda Vickery, *The Gentleman's Daughter: Women's Lives in Georgian England* (New Haven, Conn., 1998).

116. DWL, Ms. Walton I.1.43, pp. 326, 360. The "domestic dependence" of women in this period is discussed in Amanda Vickery, *Behind Closed Doors: At Home in Georgian England* (New Haven, Conn., 2010), ch. 7.
117. DWL, Ms. Walton I.1.43, p. 344. For nineteenth-century female imprisonment for madness, see Elaine Showalter, *The Female Malady: Women, Madness and English Culture, 1830–1980* (New York, 1985).
118. Thompson, *Witness against the Beast*, pp. 139, 148–9, 154, 170.
119. *The New Magazine*, vol. 1, pp. 229–31, 299–300. An article on the subject of madmen and the moon later appeared in the *Astrologer's Magazine*, vol. 1, Jan. 1794, p. 240.
120. *Ibid.*, vol. 2, pp. 51–3, 139–42 ("Behmen" quotation on p. 140), 191–3, 245–7, 352–3.
121. *Ibid.*, vol. 2, pp. 356–8.
122. *Ibid.*, vol. 2, pp. 387–90, quotation on p. 388.
123. Thompson, *Witness against the Beast*, chs 8–9.
124. *Minutes of a General Conference of the Members of the New Church* (London, 1792), p. 7; G.E. Bentley, Jr., *The Stranger from Paradise: A Biography of William Blake* (New Haven, Conn., 2001), pp. 126–9.
125. Thompson, *Witness against the Beast*, pp. 149–50; William Blake, "To Tirzah," *Songs of Innocence and of Experience*, in Erdman, ed., *Complete Poetry and Prose*, p. 30.
126. DWL, Ms. Walton I.1.43, pp. 337–8.
127. W.A. Clarke, *A Bed of Sweet Flowers; or, Jewels for Hephzi-bah* (London, 1778), p. xi.
128. Pratt, *A List of a Few Cures*, p. 2.
129. *Ibid.*, pp. 5–6.
130. *Ibid.*, pp. 2, 8.
131. DWL, Ms. Walton I.1.43, p. 320. For Clarke, see Hirst, *Hidden Riches*, pp. 246–63, 271–6.
132. DWL, Ms. Walton I.1.43, pp. 328–9, 341.
133. *Ibid.*, pp. 334–5, 358, 359–60, 361.
134. *Ibid.*, pp. 341, 360.
135. *Ibid.*, pp. 349, 364.
136. Caroline Walker Bynum, *Holy Feast and Holy Fast: The Religious Significance of Food to Medieval Women* (Berkeley and Los Angeles, 1987).
137. DWL, Ms. Walton I.1.43, pp. 367–8.
138. *Ibid.*, p. 368.
139. For these movements, see Alex Owen, *The Darkened Room: Women, Power and Spiritualism in Late Victorian England* (London, 1989); Alex Owen, *The Place of Enchantment: British Occultism and the Cult of the Modern* (Chicago, 2004).
140. Kathleen Raine, *Blake and Tradition* (2 vols, London, 1968); Kathleen Raine, *Golgonooza, City of Imagination: Last Studies in William Blake* (Hudson, N.Y., 1991); also, more recently, Marsha Keith Schuchard, *Why Mrs Blake Cried: William Blake and the Sexual Basis of Spiritual Vision* (London, 2006); Rix, *Blake and Radical Christianity*.
141. David V. Erdman, *Blake: Prophet against Empire* (Princeton, 1977); Thompson, *Witness against the Beast*. Jon Mee, *Dangerous Enthusiasm: William Blake and the Culture of Radicalism in the 1790s* (Oxford, 1992), places Blake's work in both a political and a prophetic context.
142. Keri Davies and Marsha Keith Schuchard, "Recovering the Lost Moravian History of William Blake's Family," *Blake: An Illustrated Quarterly*, 38, 1 (2004), pp. 36–43; Rix, *Blake and Radical Christianity*, pp. 7–13.
143. Thompson, *Witness against the Beast*, ch. 6. For the extraordinary history of the Muggletonians, see Christopher Hill, Barry Reay and William Lamont, *The World of the Muggletonians* (London, 1983). Although they held some unusual beliefs about the universe, their materialism and estrangement from traditional occult sources explain why Muggletonians have not been discussed in this book.

144. The biographical details here are taken from Bentley, *Stranger from Paradise*, chs 1–4.
145. *Ibid.*, pp. 118–19, 158. For animal magnetism, see Robert Rix, "Healing the Spirit: William Blake and Magnetic Religion," *Romanticism on the Net*, 25 (Feb. 2002), http://www.erudit.org/revue/ron/2002/v/n25/006011ar.html.
146. G.E. Bentley, *Blake Records* (2nd ed., New Haven, Conn., 2004), p. 78. Blake was one of nineteen engravers who testified that they were unable to copy Tilloch's notes.
147. William Blake, *America: A Prophecy*, in Erdman, ed., *Complete Poetry and Prose*, p. 52, plate 2, l. 8; p. 55, plate 10, l. 11.
148. William Blake, *The French Revolution*, in Erdman, ed., *Complete Poetry and Prose*, p. 298, lls. 274–6.
149. Erdman, *Blake*, ch. 23, for Blake's views of Voltaire and Rousseau. Although their disagreements were well known, he seems never to have distinguished between the two *philosophes*.
150. William Blake, *The Marriage of Heaven and Hell*, in Erdman, ed., *Complete Poetry and Prose*, p. 43, plate 22.
151. Ernst Benz, *Emanuel Swedenborg: Visionary Savant in the Age of Reason*, trans. Nicholas Goodrick-Clarke (West Chester, Pa., 2002), ch. 11. Admittedly, these ideas are mainly found in the baron's early scientific writings, with which Blake may not have been familiar, but they echo through his later thinking as well. Kathleen Raine makes the same point about *The Marriage of Heaven and Hell* in *Blake and Tradition*, vol. 2, ch. 15.
152. Emanuel Swedenborg, *The Earths in the Universe, and their Inhabitants; Also, their Spirits and Angels, from What Has Been Heard and Seen* (London, 1875). This work was first published as *De Telluribus in Mundo Nostro Solari, Quæ Vocantur Planetæ* (London, 1758), and does not appear to have been translated until the nineteenth century. Blake was probably not able to read the Latin original, but he could easily have known about it by reputation.
153. Only one such work has come to light: Jean Henri Samuel Formey, *A Concise History of Philosophy and Philosophers* (Glasgow, 1767), pp. 154–60.
154. William Blake, *America: A Prophecy*, in Erdman, ed., *Complete Poetry and Prose*, p. 56, plate 14, ll. 5–6.
155. William Blake, *The Song of Los*, in Erdman, ed., *Complete Poetry and Prose*, p. 67, plate 3, ll. 18–19.
156. William Blake, *Europe: A Prophecy*, in Erdman, *Complete Poetry and Prose*, p. 62, plate 8, l. 3.
157. Blake, *Song of Los*, p. 68, plate 5, ll. 15–17.
158. Jacob Boehme, "The Treatise of the Incarnation," in *The Works of Jacob Behmen, the Teutonic Theosopher* (4 vols, London, 1764–81), vol. 2, ch. 4, verse 35.
159. For Freemasonry in Blake's writings, see Stuart Peterfreund, *William Blake in a Newtonian World: Essays on Literature as Art and Science* (Norman, Oklahoma, 1998), ch. 3.
160. William Blake, *The [First] Book of Urizen*, in Erdman, ed., *Complete Poetry and Prose*, p. 14, ll 14–26.
161. The parallel with Fludd is noted in Raine, *Blake and Tradition*, vol. 2, pp. 74–80.
162. *Ibid.*, vol. 1, pp. 50–1; vol. 2, pp. 236–8.
163. William Blake, *The Four Zoas*, in Erdman, ed., *Complete Poetry and Prose*, p. 361 [95], ll. 32–3 [88], ll. 7, 14–16; and for an interpretation of the poem, Leopold Damrosch, Jr., *Symbol and Truth in Blake's Myth* (Princeton, 1980), ch. 4.
164. Raine, *Blake and Tradition*, vol. 2, ch. 3; *Works of Behmen*, vol. 3, fig. 2, and GRL, Manly Hall Ms. 43, for a full-colour, hand-painted copy.
165. Blake, *Four Zoas*, pp. 357 [82], l. 19; 379 [110], l. 2; 385 [114], l. 1; 388 [119], l. 13; 386 [115], ll. 22–3.
166. Raine, *Blake and Tradition*, vol. 1, pp. 134–5.

167. The fairy appears in *Europe: A Prophecy*, p. 60, plate 3, l. 7; the Zodiac pops up in *Four Zoas*, p. 385 [114], l. 17; an angel turns blue, then yellow, then pink, in *Marriage of Heaven and Hell*, p. 43, plate 23; the happy lily is in *The Book of Thel*, in Erdman, ed., *Complete Poetry and Prose*, p. 4, plate 2, ll. 15–25.
168. Richard Holmes, *Coleridge: Early Visions* (New York, 1990); John B. Beer, *Coleridge the Visionary* (London, 1970).
169. For the history of occult thinking in late nineteenth century Britain, see Victoria Butler, *Victorian Occultism and the Making of Modern Magic: Invoking Tradition* (Basingstoke, Hants, 2011).

INDEX